FRENCH STRUCTURALISM

GARLAND REFERENCE LIBRARY
OF THE HUMANITIES
(VOL. 160)

FRENCH STRUCTURALISM
A Multidisciplinary Bibliography
With a Checklist of Sources for
Louis Althusser, Roland Barthes,
Jacques Derrida, Michel Foucault,
Lucien Goldmann, Jacques Lacan
and an Update of Works on
Claude Lévi-Strauss

compiled by
Joan M. Miller

GARLAND PUBLISHING, INC. • NEW YORK & LONDON
1981

Library of Congress Cataloging in Publication Data

Miller, Joan M., 1941–
    French structuralism.

    (Garland reference library of the humanities ; v. 160)
    Includes indexes.
    1. Structuralism—Bibliography. 2. Philosophy,
French—20th century—Bibliography. I. Title.
II. Series.
Z7128.S7M54 [B841.4]   016.149′96′0944   78-68283
ISBN 0-8240-9780-7   AACR2

Printed on acid-free, 250-year-life paper   *BE*
Manufactured in the United States of America *4-30-82*

Because they have always cared,
this book is dedicated to my parents.

CONTENTS

III. Structuralism as Applied to Various Disciplines

INTRODUCTION

French Structuralism has been described as a movement, a method, and an ideology. As a movement, its origins date back to 1916 when Ferdinand de Saussure's students published their lecture notes under the title of *Cours de linguistique générale*. But it was Claude Lévi-Strauss who popularized the new intellectual fashion in the sixties by applying the linguistic model to anthropology and by offering conclusions of a philosophical nature. Structuralism as method soon spread to other disciplines. Structuralism as "ideology" or world view soon challenged other philosophies such as existentialism, Marxism, Christianity, and humanism. This three-part bibliography of more than 5650 items provides a comprehensive guide to the movement in both these aspects.

Description and purpose

Part I lists general and introductory works for those who wish to familiarize themselves with structuralism as a whole. With few exceptions, it covers the period from 1968 to 1978 and thus extends J.V. Harari's earlier bibliographical survey, *Structuralists and Structuralism. A Selected Bibliography of French Contemporary Thought (1960–1970)* (Ithaca, New York: *Diacritics*, 1971). While purposely reduced in size due to the number of subdivisions in the other two parts, Part I also includes items which do not easily fit the pre-selected categories.

Part II contains primary and secondary source bibliographies for Louis Althusser, Roland Barthes, Jacques Derrida, Michel Foucault, Lucien Goldmann, and Jacques Lacan. Structuralism's most notable exponent, Claude Lévi-Strauss, was to have received similar treatment, but this became unnecessary when François and Claire Lapointe published their *Claude Lévi-Strauss and His Critics: An International Bibliography (1950–1976)* (New York: Garland, 1977). Consequently, the items given in section G of Part II are meant to update, supplement, and/or correct those of the Lapointes. Althusser, Barthes, Derrida, Foucault, Goldmann, and Lacan were chosen for two main reasons. They are the names most often mentioned in the context of French Structuralism, and each relates to a different area of structuralist endeavor: Althusser—Marxism; Barthes—literary criticism; Derrida—philosophy and phenomenology; Foucault—the history of the human sciences, imprisonment, and sexuality; Goldmann—the sociology of literature and Marxism; Lacan—psychoanalysis. Since the bibliographies in Part II are intended to be reasonably complete through 1977, they should assist researchers studying these individuals either in their own right or in their relation to structuralism. For several, this is the first time such compilations are available.

Part III furnishes bibliographies on structuralism as applied or related to thirteen different disciplines. Once again, the period covered is from 1968 to 1978. Most items are examples of structural analysis at work, but general discussions of structuralist methodology are included in section H (philosophy), and the philosophical implications of structuralism are also treated in sections G (Marxism) and K (religion/scripture/theology).

While the scope of Part III is ambitious, the result is less satisfactory than intended, for several reasons. The interdisciplinary nature of the structuralist methodology makes clearcut divisions among the disciplines very difficult. Overlapping invariably occurs in such sections as D, E, F, I, and L. The indexes and cross-references between sections and parts sometimes alleviate the problem, sometimes complicate it. If specialists in each of the disciplines had compiled the bibliographies for their disciplines, each list would have been considerably longer and more detailed. As it is, the sections on philosophy and religion are the only ones nearly exhaustive since they are the compiler's own areas of specialization.

Organization and format

Every effort was expended to make this volume as useful a

research tool as possible. Many items are annotated. Detailed author and subject indexes are provided. To avoid unnecessary duplication, an extensive system of cross-referencing is used in all three parts.

The *primary sources* are *arranged chronologically* by year of publication. A further subdivision by language and form was considered and rejected in favor of the following. Within the same year of publication, books precede articles; items written earlier (e.g., prior to the date of publication) generally precede those written later; and items written in French precede those written in English or in the Romance and Germanic languages. The dates of subsequent editions are usually noted with the original edition, except in cases of substantial revision or changes in title, publisher, or number of volumes. Tables of contents or descriptive annotations are given for the original editions of most book-length primary sources. When available, the *collection* in which a volume appears is either indicated as such or enclosed in *parentheses* at the end of a reference. When available, the item numbers for *reviews and translations* are listed with the original; the languages of translations also appear there.

Secondary sources are *arranged alphabetically* by author. When no author is cited, such items are grouped together under *Anonymous*, then arranged alphabetically under the first major word of the title. *Journal names* are also incorporated into the author order.

The *reviews* in sections A–F of Part II are listed alphabetically by the original title, then alphabetically by reviewer. If a review appears untitled, that means the work being reviewed is the original; reviews of translated works are indicated as such. Reviews in Parts I and III and section G of Part II are not listed separately.

The *Author Index* contains the names of authors, editors, reviewers, and journals, with the Anonymous category heading the list. The *Subject Index* encompasses key words and names in each title and annotation as well as general topics and a Bibliography heading. Since some items are rather long, an item number is sometimes followed by a number or letter in parentheses to indicate that a chapter or part of the item is being indicated rather than the entire item. For example, 45(5) indicates chapter 5 of item 45, and 35(A.1) means number one of the Appendix of item 35. "+", as in 1726a+, is used to indicate the unnumbered item following item 1726a. *Annotations* are provided for many items. For the most part, an annotation is an indication of the importance of an item; however, in some instances, the presence or length of an annotation is more a measure of the item's availability or interest to the bibliographer. This situation occurs because the decision to include annotations was made after half of the items had already been compiled.

Asterisks are used throughout to indicate items with translations.

Sources

This bibliography was compiled and checked in Belgium, France, Canada, and the United States. Most of the compilation was done prior to the summer of 1979; however, over 300 items were added in the summer of 1980. All the standard references in English and French were consulted as well as a few in German. More than thirty were systematically used for the ten-year period, but three provided the greatest bulk of the material: the *Répertoire Bibliographique de la Philosophie*, 1949–1978; the *Bulletin Signalétique de la Philosophie*, 1968–1977; and *French VII: Bibliography of Critical and Biographical References for the Study of Contemporary French Literature*, which became *French XX*, no. 1 (1949) to no. 30 (1978). Special attention was also paid to the following bibliographies: John Leavey and David B. Allison's "A Derrida Bibliography" (*Research in Phenomenology*, 8 [1978], 145–160); François and Claire Lapointe's "Michel Foucault: A Bibliographic Essay" (*Diálogos*, 10, no. 26 [April 1974], 153–157) and their supplement to this bibliography which appeared in *Diálogos*, 11, no. 29–30 (November 1977), 245–254; Eduard Tell's "Bibliographie de Lucien Goldmann" (*Revue de l'Institut de Sociologie*, no. 3–4 [Belgium, 1973], pp. 787–806); and Michel de Wolf's "(Lacan:) Essai de bibliographie complète" (*Magazine Littéraire*, no. 121 [February 1977], pp. 28–36). While many items were personally inspected, sometimes it was impossible to check an apparent discrepancy or provide a complete reference because the item was no longer available to me. Such items were kept to a minimum but not eliminated, on the principle that it is better to have a partial reference than to have none at all.

Acknowledgments

The list of acknowledgments for this work must begin with those friends who introduced me to Structuralism in 1966 during my student days in Paris. Sincere thanks are also extended to Professor William A. Wallace who, in 1973, asked me to contribute an article on Structuralism to the *New Catholic Encyclopedia*, and to Professor Jacques Etienne, editor of the *Revue Philosophique de Louvain*, who encouraged me to expand my 1977 bibliographical survey into a book. For their help along the way, I would also like to thank Monique Lévy and the librarians of the University of Louvain, the Royal Library in Brussels, the Centre National de Recherche Scientifique in Paris, the University of Toronto, and the Hillman Library of the University of Pittsburgh. A final and special word of thanks is due to Michel Grimaud who reviewed the work before publication and offered numerous suggestions for its improvement.

Joan M. Miller
Associate Professor of Philosophy
Villa Maria College
Erie, Pennsylvania

I
GENERAL AND
INTRODUCTORY WORKS

1. Abel, Adeline. "Reviews." *Modern Language Journal*, 58, no. 1-2 (January-February 1974), 65-66.
   On Harari's bibliography (item 99).

2. Abril Castelló, V. "¿Qué es el estructuralismo?" *Arbor*, 84, no. 327 (1973), 15-22.

3. *Aletheia*, no. 4 (May 1966): issue entitled "Le Structuralisme. Claude Lévi-Strauss--Roland Barthes--Maurice Godelier." Paris: Aletheia (Honfleur, Impr. P.J. Oswald), 1966.

4. Anonymous. *Problemas do estruturalismo*. Rio de Janeiro: Zahar Ed., 1968. Trans. of the special issue no. 246 (1966) of *Les Temps Modernes* (item 197).

5. ————. *Structuralisme et symbolisme*. Geneva: M. Engelson, n.d., 151pp. *Cahiers Internationaux de Symbolisme*, 17-18.

6. ————. "Swipes at Structuralists." *The Times Literary Supplement*, no. 3633 (15 October 1971), p. 1269.
   On Lefèbvre's *Au-delà du structuralisme*, 1971.

7. ————. *Teoría y práctica del estructuralismo soviético*. Trans. Gloria Kue. Madrid: Alberto Corazón, 1972.

8. Apostel, Léo. "Structuralisme et théorie des systèmes." *Annales de l'Institut de Philosophie* (Brussels, 1970), pp. 163-173.

9. Arbeitskreis Philosophie-Naturwissenschaften. *Struktur--Strukturalismus: Material für eine wissenschaftliche Tagung des Arbeitskreises Philosophie-Naturwissenschaften der Universität Rostock*. Ed. Heinrich Vogel. Rostock: Universität Rostock, 1975. (Rostocker philosophische Manuskripte, Heft 14)

10. Archer, Luís J. "Estruturalismo biológico." *Revista Portuguesa de Filosofia*, 31 (July-September 1975), 253-267.

*11. Auzias, Jean-Marie. *Clefs pour le structuralisme*. Paris: Editions Seghers, 1967, 1968, 1971, 1975. (Clefs)

    Contains: (1) Le champ structuraliste; (2) Linguistique et structuralisme; (3) La grammaire même...; (4) Signes, signaux, sémantique; (5) L'histoire structurale; (6) Le structuralisme en personne [Claude Lévi-Strauss]; (7) Althusser, le marxisme et les structures; (8) L'homme est mort [Foucault]; (9) Jacques Lacan; (10) Pour (ne pas) conclure: critique et littérature.

12. ————. *La Chiave dello strutturalismo*. Trans. L. Banfi. Milan: U. Mursia, 1969.

4 General and Introductory Works

13. ——. *El Estructuralismo*. Trans. Santiago González Noriega.
2nd ed. Madrid: Alianza Ed., 1970.

14. ——. *Chaves do estruturalismo*. Trans. Natanael Caixeiro.
Rio de Janeiro: Civilização Brasiliera, 1972.

15. Babcock-Abrahams, Barbara. "Why Frogs are Good to Think and Dirt
is Good to Reflect on." *Soundings: An Interdisciplinary
Journal*, 58, no. 2 (Summer 1975), 167-181.

16. ——, ed. *The Reversible World: Essays on Symbolic Inversion*.
Ithaca, N.Y.: Cornell University Press, 1978.
On anti-structural processes and phenomena.

17. Bakker, Reinout. "Het Structuralisme." *Algemeen Nederlands
Tijdschrift voor Wijssbegeerte*, 65, no. 1 (1973), 32-43.

18. Bartnik, Czesław. "Nowe aspekty strukturalizmu." *Zeszyty Naukowe
Katolickiego Universytetu Lubelskiego*, 16, no. 2 (1973), 92-94.

19. Benavides Lucas, Manuel. *El Hombre estructural*. Madrid: Confedera-
ción Española de Cajas de Ahorros, 1974.

20. Benoist, Jean Marie. "Structuralism." *Cambridge Review*, 93, no.
2204 (22 October 1971).

21. ——. *La Révolution structurale*. Paris: Grasset, 1975, 350pp.

22. Bergonzi, Bernard. "A Grid of Codes. Views of Structuralism."
Encounter, 45, no. 1 (July 1975), 52, 54-58.

23. Black, Max, ed. *The Stubborn Structure*. Ithaca, N.Y.: Cornell
University Press, 1970.

24. Blackwell, Richard J. "A Structuralist Account of Scientific
Theories." *International Philosophical Quarterly*, 16 (December
1976), 263-274.

25. Blair, John G. "Structuralism, American Studies and the Humanities." *American Quarterly*, 30, no. 3 (1978), 261-281.

26. Blau, Herbert. "Seeming, Seeming: the Disappearing Act." *Drama
Review*, 20, no. 4 (December 1976), 7-24.

27. Botez, A. "The Concept of Structure in Mathematics" (in Rumanian).
Revista de Filozofie, 17, no. 5 (1970), 521-524.

28. Boudon, Raymond. *Structuralism*. Cambridge: Schenkman, 1977.

*29. Broekman, Jan M. *Strukturalismus. Moskau, Prag, Paris*. Munich-
Freiburg: Alber, 1971. Bibliography, pp. 160-169.

30. ——. *Structuralism: Moscow, Prague, Paris*. Trans. Jan F.
Beekman and Brunhilde Helm. Dordrecht, Holland-Boston, Mass.:
D. Reidl, 1974. Bibliography, pp. 108-113, not error-free.

31. ———. *Strukturalisme. Moskou-Praag-Parijs.* Amsterdam: Polak &
Van Gennep, 1973. Revised trans. of item 29. Bibliography,
pp. 153-160.

32. Bronk, A. "Structuralism: Mode, Method or Ideology" (in Polish).
Roczniki Filozoficzne, 20, no. 1 (1972), 101-118.

33. Brown, E.J. "Formalist Contribution." *Russian Review*, 33 (July
1974), 243-258.

34. *Cahiers Internationaux de Symbolisme*, no. 17-18 (1969).

35. Câmara, Joaquim Mattoso, et al. *Estruturalismo: grandes nomes
nacionais e estrangeiros.* Rio de Janeiro: Tempo Brasileiro,
1973. (Tempo Brasileiro, 15/16)

   Contains: (1) J. Mattoso Câmara, Jr.: O estruturalismo lingüístico; (2) L. Beider: Estrutura lingüística; (3) M. Lemle: O nôvo
   estruturalismo em lingüística: Chomsky; (4) C. Lévi-Strauss: A
   noção de estrutura em ethnologia; (5) R. Cardoso de Oliveira:
   Estruturalismo e estruturalistas na antropologia social; (6)
   R. Mangabeira Unger: O estruturalismo e o futuro das ciências
   culturals; (7) C.H. de Escobar: Resposta a Carpeaux: estruturalismo; (8) M. Godelier: Alguns aspectos do método do capital;
   (9) E. Portella: Crítica literária e estruturalismo; (10) M.
   Barata: Estruturalismo e história da obra de Rousseau a Lévi-Strauss; (12)
   Filosofia, mûsica e botânica de Rousseau a Lévi-Strauss; (12)
   A. Monomi: Implîcações filosóficas na obra de Claude Lévi-Strauss;
   (13) C.S. Katz: Nivels e dimensão do sistema filosófico: uma
   visão estrutural; Recenções: (1) B. Pottier: Além do estruturalismo em lingüística; (2) A. Ramos Trinta: Lingüística e ciências
   humanas; Apêndices: (1) C.S. Katz: Ciência, estruturalismo,
   psicanálise: dois problemas; (2) F.A. Doria: Ficção científica:
   a nova mitologia.

36. Caws, Peter James. "What is Structuralism?" *Partisan Review*, 35
(Winter 1968), 75-91.

37. ———. "Structuralism." In *Dictionary of the History of Ideas.
Studies of Selected Pivotal Ideas.* Ed. Philip P. Wiener. New
York: Charles Scribner's Sons, 1968, 1973, vol. 4, pp. 322-330.

38. ———. "What is Structuralism?" In *Claude Lévi-Strauss: The
Anthropologist as Hero.* Ed. Eugene Nelson Hayes and Tanya
Hayes. Cambridge, Mass.: M.I.T. Press, 1970, pp. 197-214.

39. ———. "The Recent Literature of Structuralism, 1965-1970."
*Philosophische Rundschau: Zeitschrift für philosophische
Kritik*, 18 (1971), 63-78.

   Eighteen works are reviewed in the light of their contribution
   to the understanding of structuralism. The movement is discussed
   under many of the headings used in this bibliography.

40. Cebik, L.B. "*Structuralism*, ed. by Jacques Ehrmann." *Georgia
Review*, 36, no. 2 (Summer 1972), 233-237.

6 General and Introductory Works

41. Châtelet, François. "Où en est le structuralisme?" *La Quinzaine Littéraire*, no. 31 (1-15 July 1967), 18-19.

42. ———. "Structuralisme." In *Grand Larousse Encyclopédique*, supplément. Paris: Librairie Larousse, 1968, pp. 814-815.

43. Chełstowski, Bogdan. "The Constructivistic Structuralism of J. Piaget." *Science and Society*, 35, no. 4 (Winter 1971), 481-489. A critical study of Piaget's *Le Structuralisme* translated from *Studia Filozoficzne*, 6 (1970), 128-134.

44. Chiaromonte, Nicola. "A proposito di strutturalismo." *Tempo Presente*, anno XI, no. 7 (July 1966), 6-8.

*45. Chvatík, Květoslav. *Strukturalismus a avantgarda*. Prague: Cs. spis., t. Stráž, Vimperk, 1970.

46. ———. *Strukturalismus und Avantgarde. Aufsätze zur Kunst und Literatur*. Trans. Hans Gaertner. Munich: Hanser, 1970.

47. Cohen, Robert. "Mizoguchi and Modernism: Structure, Culture, Point of View." *Sight and Sound*, 47 (Spring 1978), 110-118.

48. Corvez, Maurice. "Les Nouveaux structuralistes." *Revue Philosophique de Louvain*, tome 67, 3e série, no. 96 (November 1969), 582-605.

*49. ———. *Les Structuralistes: les linguistes, Michel Foucault, Claude Lévi-Strauss, Jacques Lacan, Louis Althusser, les critiques littéraires*. Paris: Aubier Montaigne, 1969. (Présence et pensée)

Contains: (1) Le structuralisme linguistique; (2) Le structuralisme anthropologique de Michel Foucault; (3) Le structuralisme ethnologique de Claude Lévi-Strauss; (4) Le structuralisme psychanalytique de Jacques Lacan; (5) Le structuralisme marxiste de Louis Althusser; (6) Le structuralisme en littérature, en critique artistique et littéraire, en histoire des religions; Conclusion générale.

50. ———. *Structuralisme*. Trans. F. Oomes. Utrecht-Antwerp: Het Spectrum, 1971, 171pp. (Aula 468)

51. ———. *Los Estructuralistas*. Trans. Leandro Wolfson. Buenos Aires: Amorrortu Ed., 1972.

52. Costabel, P. "La Physique de Pascal et son analyse structurale." *Revue d'Histoire des Sciences*, 29, no. 4 (1976), 309-324.

53. Coutinho, Carlos Nelson. *O Estruturalismo e a miséria da razão*. Rio de Janeiro: Paz e Terra, 1972. (Series Rumos da cultura moderna, v. 48)

54. Crémant, Roger. *Les Matinées structuralistes, suivies d'un Discours sur l'écriture et précédées d'une Introduction critique par Albert K***. Paris: Robert Laffont, 1969.

Culler, J. See item 4836.

55. Dadoun, Roger. "Qu'est-ce que le structuralisme?" *La Quinzaine Littéraire*, no. 67 (16-28 February 1969), pp. 22-23.

56. Daix, Pierre, and François Wahl. "Qu'est-ce que le structuralisme?" *Les Lettres Françaises*, no. 1268 (29 January-4 February 1969), pp. 4-6.

57. D'Amico, Robert. "The Contours and Coupures of Structuralist Theory." *Telos*, 17 (Fall 1973), 70-97.

58. De George, Richard T., and Fernande M. De George, eds. *The Structuralists: From Marx to Lévi-Strauss*. New York: Doubleday/ Anchor Books, 1972; Magnolia, Mass.: Peter Smith, 1976, 330pp.

59. Dehò, Giorgio. *Lo Strutturalismo dalla matematica alla critica letteraria*. Messina-Florence: G. D'Anna, 1975.

60. Deleuze, Gilles, and F. Guattari. *Rhizome: introduction*. Paris: Editions de Minuit, 1976.

61. *Delo*, 19, no. 12 (1973): Mesečni Književni Časopis.

62. De Vici, G.A. "Una Enciclopedia critica dell'attualità, ossia, Intorno allo strutturalismo." *Sophia*, 40, no. 1-2 (Padua, 1972), 121-125.

63. Diéguez, Manuel de. *Science et nescience*. Paris: Gallimard, 1970.

64. Domin, G., and H.-H. Lanfermann. "On the Essence and the Principal Limits of the Structural and Functional Conception in the Theory of Science." *Zagadnienia Naukoznawstiva*, special issue (Warsaw, 1972-1973), pp. 55-68.

65. Donato, E. "Structuralism: The Aftermath." *Sub-stance*, no. 7 (1973), pp. 9-26.

66. Donoghue, Denis. "Sovereign Ghost." *Sewanee Review*, 84 (Winter-Spring 1976), 98-118, 248-274.

67. Eco, Umberto, et al. *Introducción al estructuralismo*. Trans. Paloma Varela. Madrid: Alianza Ed., 1976.

68. Ehrmann, Jacques, ed. Special issue on "Structuralism." *Yale French Studies*, nos. 36-37 (1966), pp. 5-270. Contains: Introduction by J. Ehrmann plus items 4204, 4615, 3798, 3719, 3315, 3091, 3950, 3920, 4855, and bibliographies, pp. 252-270 (items 3778, 4088, 4343, 3372). Rpt. in item 69.

69. ——————, ed. *Structuralism*. Garden City, N.Y.: Doubleday/ Anchor Books, 1970. Rpts. item 68. Bibliographies, pp. 239-264.

*70. Erlich, Victor. *Russian Formalism: History and Doctrine*. The Hague: Mouton, 1955; *Il Formalismo russo*. Milan: Bompiani, 1966.

71. ———. "Russian Formalism." *Journal of the History of Ideas*,
     34 (October-December 1973), 627-638.

72. *Esprit*, 31e année, no. 322 (November 1963): issue entitled "*La
     Pensée Sauvage* et le structuralisme." Contains items 3758 and
     4724.

73. *Esprit*, 35e année, no. 360 (May 1967): issue entitled "Structur-
     alismes, idéologie et méthode." Contains items 2082, 2094,
     410, 3506, 2140, 4492, 4601, and 4727.

74. Ethier-Blais, Jean. "Le Structuralisme: mythe ou parodie?" *Les
     Nouvelles Littéraires*, no. 2366 (29 January-4 February 1973),
     pp. 1, 11.

*75. Fages, Jean-Baptiste. *Comprendre le structuralisme*. Toulouse:
     Edouard Privat, 1967.

76. ———. *Den Strukturalismus verstehen. Einführung in das
     strukturale Denken*. Trans. Michael Scotti-Rosin and Manfred
     Tietz. Giessen: Achenbach, 1974.

77. ———. *Le Structuralisme en procès*. Toulouse: Edouard Privat,
     1968.

     In this follow-up to item 75, Fages attempts to answer three
     questions: (1) Isn't a definition of structuralism based on the
     linguistic model too strict and limiting?; (2) Has structuralism
     thus defined been frozen into static and atemporal analyses?;
     (3) Isn't structuralism also a new vision of the world and man,
     a new ideology, a new trend in philosophy which will follow
     existentialism? Chapters 1 and 2 deal with transformational
     grammar and the analysis of ideologies as the most recent develop-
     ments of structuralism. Chapter 3 summarizes five major critiques
     of structuralism: scientific, socio-political, Marxist, existen-
     tialist and hermeneutical.

78. Fougeyrollas, Pierre. *Contre Lévi-Strauss, Lacan et Althusser.
     Trois essais sur l'obscurantisme contemporain*. Rome: Savelli;
     Paris: Editions de la Jonquière, 1976. See items 3530, 3253,
     and 434.

79. Francovich, Guillermo. *Ensayos sobre el estructuralismo*. La Paz,
     Bolivia: Universidad Mayor de San Andres, Facultad de Filosofía
     y Letras Centro de Estudiantes, 1970.

     Contains chapters on Lévi-Strauss, Foucault, Marxism, and
     Marcuse.

80. ———. *El Estructuralismo: Lévi-Strauss, Foucault, Marx, Sartre,
     Marcuse, McLuhan*. Buenos Aires: Editorial Plus Ultra, 1973.

81. Frenzel, Ivo. "Leitbilder des Strukturalismus." *Universitas*, 25
     (1970), 835-842.

82. Frye, Northrop. "The Road of Excess." In *The Stubborn Structure* (item 23).

83. Funt, David. "Piaget and Structuralism." *Diacritics*, 1 (Fall 1973), 15-20.

84. Furet, François. "Les Intellectuels français et le structuralisme." *Preuves*, no. 192 (February 1967), pp. 3-12.

85. G., P.-M. "De Nouvelles pièces au dossier du structuralisme." *Le Monde*, no. 6677 (2 July 1966), p. 11.

86. Galhardo, Miguel Angel Garrido. "El Estructuralismo genetico, cinco años después." *Cuadernos Hispanoamericanos*, no. 313 (July 1976), pp. 140-146.

87. Gallas, H., ed. "Strukturalismusdiskussion." *Alternative*, no. 54 (1967). See also item 3857.

*88. Gandillac, Maurice Patronnier de, Lucien Goldmann, and Jean Piaget, eds. *Entretiens sur les notions de "genèse" et de "structure."* (Congrès, Centre Culturel International de Cerisy-la-Salle, juillet-août 1959) Paris-The Hague: Mouton, 1965. See also items 2584, 2585, and 2660.

89. ———. *Las Acciones de estructura y génesis*. Buenos Aires: Proteo, 1969.

90. Gandy, Robin. "'Structure' in Mathematics." In *Structuralism: An Introduction* (item 176), pp. 138-153.

Gardner, H. See item 4527.

Gerber, R.J. See item 4536.

91. Gioanola, Elio. "Lo Strutturalismo." *Rivista di Studi Crociani*, 4 (January-March 1967), 64-74.

92. ———. "Lo Strutturalismo II." *Rivista di Studi Crociani*, 4 (April-June 1967), 141-152.

93. Głowinski, Michał. "Polish Structuralism." Trans. E.M. Thompson. *Books Abroad*, 49 (Spring 1975), 239-243.

94. Glucksmann, Miriam. "Structuralism." *British Journal of Sociology*, 22 (June 1971), 209-213.

95. Godden, Richard. "So That's What Frightens Them Under the Tree?" *Journal of American Studies*, 11 (December 1977), 371-377.

Gouthier, G. See item 5250.

96. Gritti, Jules, and Paul Toinet. *Le Structuralisme, science ou idéologie: dialogue entre Jules Gritti et Paul Toinet*. Paris: Beauchesne, 1968, 94pp. (Verse et controverse. Le Chrétien en dialogue avec le monde, 7)

97.   Grygar, Mojmír, comp. Pařížské rozhovory o strukturalismu. Prague:
      Svoboda, 1969.

98.   Guglielminetti, Marziano. "Le 'Nuove frontiere' dello struttural-
      ismo." Nuova Corrente, no. 49 (1969), pp. 195-199.

99.   Harari, Josué V. Structuralists and Structuralism. A Selected
      Bibliography of French Contemporary Thought (1960-1970). Ithaca,
      New York: Diacritics, 1971, 82pp.

100. Hayman, Ronald. "Holes and Corners." Encounter, 47 (July 1976),
      71-76.

101. Hermand, Jost. "French Structuralism from a German Point of
      View." Trans. E.T. Beck and J. Elliott. Books Abroad, 49 (Spring
      1975), 213-221.

102. Hina, H. "Eugenio d'Ors, precursor del estructuralismo." Cuadernos
      del Sur, 11 (Argentina, 1972), 194-209.

      Holenstein, E. See items 4562 and 4563.

103. Hullet, James. "Which Structure?" Educational Theory, 24 (Winter
      1974), 68-72.

104. Hyde, Gordon. "Structuralism: Tool or Totem?" Humanist, 86
      (September 1971), 265-266.

105. Hymes, D., and J.D. Fought. American Structuralism. Atlantic
      Highlands, N.J.: Humanities Press/Mouton, 1977.

106. Iglesias, Ignacio. "Carta de Paris: la moda del estructuralismo."
      Zona Franca, 111, no. 46 (June 1967), 42-45.

107. Izumi, Selichi. Közöshugi no seknai. Japan, 1969.

108. Jaeggi, Urs Josef Viktor. Ordnung und Chaos: der Strukturalismus
      als Methode und Mode. Frankfurt am Main: Suhrkamp, 1968, 169pp.

109. Jagrič, Janez, and Henrietta Beese. Russischer Strukturalismus
      1962-1972. Berlin: Ullstein-Taschenbuch-Verlag, 1978.

110. Jakobson, Roman. "A Few Remarks on Structuralism." MLN, 91
      (December 1976), 1534-1539.

      Jameson, F. See item 4172.

111. Jannone, Claudia. "Venus on the Half Shell as Structuralist
      Activity." Extrapolation, 17 (May 1976), 110-117.

112. Kahn, Jean-François. "La Minutieuse conquête du structuralisme."
      L'Express, no. 844 (21-27 August 1967), pp. 39-41.

113. Kirk, G.S. "Spicy Side of Structuralism." The Times Literary
      Supplement, no. 3985 (18 August 1978), pp. 922-923.

114. Kress, Gunther R. "Structuralism and Popular Culture." In *Approaches to Popular Culture*. Ed. Christopher W.E. Bigsby. Bowling Green, Ohio: Bowling Green University Popular Press, 1977, c. 1976, pp. 85-106.

115. Kurzweil, Edith. "Mythology of Structuralism." *Partisan Review*, 42, no. 3 (1975), 416-430.

116. L., R. "Le Structuralisme à l'université." *Magazine Littéraire*, no. 10 (September 1967), p. 35.

    On item 68.

117. Lamouche, André. "Mathématique et structuralisme." *Revue Générale des Sciences Pures et Appliquées*, 75 (1968), 133-139.

118. Land, Mary G. "Whatever Happened to the Ooze at the Bottom of the Mass Mind?" *Journal of Popular Culture*, 9 (Fall 1975), 423-432.

119. Lane, Michael, ed. *Structuralism: A Reader*. London: Jonathan Cape, 1970. Another edition of item 120.

120. ———. *Introduction to Structuralism*. New York: Basic Books, 1970, 1973. Another edition of item 119.

121. Lanteri, Laura. *Introducción al estructuralismo*. Buenos Aires: El Mangrullo Libros, 1969.

    Laughlin, C.D., et al. See item 5268.

122. Laurentin, René. "Le Structuralisme à l'Institut Catholique de Paris." *Le Figaro*, no. 7226 (21 November 1967), p. 12.

    On Ivan Simonis's defense of his thesis: *Claude Lévi-Strauss ou la passion de l'inceste*.

123. Lavers, Annette. "Long Live Structuralism." *The Times Literary Supplement*, no. 3888 (17 September 1976), pp. 1176-1177.

124. Leach, Edmund. "The Biology of Structuralism." *New Society*, 20 May 1971, pp. 873-874.

125. Lefèbvre, Henri. *Au-delà du structuralisme*. Paris: Editions Anthropos, 1971.

    A collection of texts taken from various journals and publications, 1957-1969. See also item 3583.

126. ———. *L'Idéologie structuraliste*. Paris: Editions du Seuil, 1975. A new abridged edition of item 125. (Points, 66)

127. Leiber, Justin. *Structuralism*. Boston: Twayne Publishers, 1973.

    Defends "universal" against "relative" structuralism in and outside linguistics.

128. Lenzen, Dieter, ed. *Die Struktur der Erziehung und des Unter-
      richts: Strukturalismus in den Erziehungswissenschaften.*
      Kronberg: Athenäum-Verlag, 1976.

129. Lepargneur, Hubert. *Introdução aos estruturalismos.* São Paulo:
      Editora Herder, 1972.

130. Levy, Zeev. *ha-Strukturalizm u-ma'amad ha-'arakhim.* Israel,
      1972.

      On structuralism and the status of values. The author's thesis
      "Structuralism--its Sources and Problems" at the Hebrew Univer-
      sity of Jerusalem. Table of contents and abstract in English.

131. ———. *Ṣṭruḳṭuralizm.* Israel, 1976.

132. Leymore, Varda Langholz. *Hidden Myth: Structure and Symbolism
      in Advertising.* London: Heinemann Educational, 1975.

      The applications of structuralism in advertising.

133. Leyvraz, Jean-Pierre. "Über den Strukturalismus." *Studia
      Philosophica,* no. 30-31 (1970-1971; appeared in 1972), pp.
      167-195. Rpt. in item 134.

      Reproduces the text of two lectures given in Zurich. The first
      part of the article deals with Lévi-Strauss, followed by a
      brief examination of the theories of Althusser and Foucault.
      In the second part the author tries to evaluate what the struc-
      turalists can tell us about our situation and our future.

134. ———. *Über den Strukturalismus.* Basel: Verlag für Recht und
      Gesellschaft, 1972, pp. 167-195. Rpt. of item 133.

135. Lupasco, S. *Qu'est-ce qu'une structure?* Paris: Christian Bour-
      gois, 1967.

      Macksey, R., et al. See items 4324-4326.

136. Madsen, Peter, ed. *Strukturalisme. En antologi.* Copenhagen:
      Rhodos, 1970.

137. Majer, Boris. *Strukturalizem.* Ljubljana: "Kommunist," 1971.
      (Poskus filozofske kritike)

138. Malagoli, Luigi. *Strutturalismo contemporaneo.* Bologna: Casa
      Editrice Prof. Riccardo Patròn, 1969, 279pp.

      Contains: (1) Il problema dello strutturalismo. Il concetto
      di struttura e la modernità; (2) Preliminari di uno struttu-
      ralismo integrale della poesia; (3) Strutturalismo e interpre-
      tazione marxista della letteratura: il carattere del concetto
      di struttura; (4) Strutturalismo critico e strutturalismo
      linguistico; (5) L'idealismo e la critica letteraria; (6) Del
      concetto di struttura e ancora dell'idealismo e della critica
      letteraria; (7) L'unità della storia e lo strutturalismo; (8)
      Forme e contenuto dello strutturalismo; (9) La validità dello

strutturalismo; (10) I problemi aperti dallo strutturalismo e
le questioni insolute: l'estetica del razionale; (11) Ancora
dei problemi aperti dallo strutturalismo: i fecondi fermenti;
(12) L'arte come vita totale; (13) La tecnica e il dinamismo
dell'arte; Conclusione; and a six-part section of Interpretazioni.

139. Marc-Lipiansky, Mireille. "Le Structuralisme en question."
     Archives de Philosophie, 38, no. 2 (January-March 1975),
     219-238.

140. Matte, Michel. *Le Structuralisme*. Tome 1. Le Langage de l'intel-
     lect: "pour un espéranto plastique du 21e siècle." Montreal:
     Editions Neuf, 1973.

141. McNicholl, Ambrose. "Structuralism." *Irish Theological Quarterly*,
     35 (1968), 233-267.

142. ———. "Structuralism II: The Latest from Paris." *Irish
     Theological Quarterly*, 35, no. 4 (1968), 343-383.

143. ———. "Lo Strutturalismo." Trans. U. Degl'Innocenti. *Aquinas*,
     13 (1970), 46-84, 262-305.

144. ———. *Structuralism*. Rome: Herder, 1975, 202pp.

145. Milicic, Vladimir, ed. *Symposium on Structuralism, Western
     Washington State College, 1973*. Bellingham?: n.p., 1973?

146. Miller, Joan M. "Structuralism." *New Catholic Encyclopedia*, vol.
     16 supplement 1967-1974, pp. 434-435. Washington, D.C.-New
     York: Publishers Guild Inc. with McGraw-Hill, 1967, 1974.

*147. Millet, Louis, and Madeleine Varin d'Aineville. *Le Structuralisme*.
     Paris: Editions Universitaires/Delarge, 1970, 1972. (Psycho-
     thèque, 5)

148. ———. *Lo Strutturalismo. Saussure, Lévi-Strauss, Lacan,
     Foucault, Althusser, Barthes*. Trans. A. Tombesi. Rome: Città
     Nuova, 1971.

149. ———. *El Estructuralismo como método*. Trans. Pere Vilanova.
     Madrid: Edicusa, 1972.

150. Mitchell, Bonner. "French Quarrel Over Structuralism and a
     Parallel of Sixty Years Ago." *Books Abroad*, 49 (Spring 1975),
     199-204.

151. Moravia, Sergio. *Lo Strutturalismo francese*. Florence: Sansoni,
     1975.

152. Nemoianu, Virgil. *Structuralismul. Cu o culegere de texte*. Trans.
     Gabriela Radulescu and Virgil Nemoianu. Bucarest: Editura
     pentru Literatura Universala, 1967, 204pp.

14   General and Introductory Works

153.   Nezel, Ivo. Strukturalistische Erziehungswissenschaft. Weinheim:
       Julius Beltz, 1976.

*154. Piaget, Jean. Le Structuralisme. Paris: Presses Universitaires
       de France, 1968 and subsequent editions. See item 161 for
       contents.

155.   ———. El Estructuralismo. Buenos Aires: Proteo, 1968.
       (Estudios y ensayos fundamentales, 3) Rev. ed. 1969.

156.   ———. Lo Strutturalismo. Trans. Andrea Bonomi. Milan: Il
       Saggiatore, 1968, 1969.

157.   ———. L'Estructuralisme. Trans. Jaume Costa and Gabriele
       Woith. Barcelona: Edicions 62, 1969.

158.   ———. "Le Structuralisme." Cahiers Internationaux de Symbol-
       isme, no. 17-18 (1969), pp. 73-85.

       On the positive and negative aspects of structuralism, seen
       essentially as a precise and general method (which should not
       be made into a philosophy) which only becomes truly explanatory
       in communication with other methods, and in particular with
       genetic constructivism.

159.   ———. Strukturalisme. Trans. Leo Rijkens. Meppel: J.A. Boom
       & Zoon, 1970.

160.   ———. O Estructuralismo. Trans. Moacir Renato de Amorim.
       São Paulo: Difusão Européia do Livro, 1970.

161.   ———. Structuralism. Trans. Chaninah Maschler. New York:
       Basic Books, 1970.

       Contains: (1) Introduction and Location of Problems, pp. 3-16;
       (2) Mathematical and Logical Structures, pp. 17-36; (3) Physical
       and Biological Structures, pp. 37-51; (4) Psychology Structures,
       pp. 52-73; (5) Linguistic Structuralism, pp. 74-96; (6) Struc-
       tural Analysis in the Social Sciences, pp. 97-119; (7) Struc-
       turalism and Philosophy, pp. 120-135; Conclusion, pp. 136-143;
       Selected Bibliography; Index.

162.   ———. Structuralism. Trans. Chaninah Maschler. New York:
       Harper and Row; London: Routledge & Kegan Paul, 1971.

163.   ———. Der Strukturalismus. Trans. Lorenz Häflinger. Freiburg:
       Walter-Verlag, 1973.

164.   ———. "Structuralism." Humanitas, 11, no. 3 (November 1975),
       313-327.

       Positive and negative aspects of structuralism. Definition
       and characteristics of a structure. Different types of structure.
       Structuralism vs. other theories and methods of research.
       Structuralism in the human sciences; the relation between struc-
       ture and function in Lévi-Strauss and Foucault. The notion of
       genesis, its history and evolution.

165. Poole, Roger. "Structuralism Side-Tracked." *New Blackfriars*, 50, no. 590 (July 1969), 533-544.

166. Presseisen, Barbara Z. "Piaget's Conception of Structure: Implications for Curriculum." *Dissertation Abstracts International*, 33, no. 1 (July 1972), 148A. Temple University, 1972.

167. Proverbio, Germanio, ed. *Studi sullo strutturalismo*. Vol. 1. Natura e problemi dello strutturalismo; Vol. 2. Proposte didattico-educative. Turin: SEI, 1976. (I Rubini, 25-26)

*168. Puglisi, Gianni. *Che cosa è lo strutturalismo*. Rome: Ubaldini, 1970.

169. ————. *Qué es verdaderamente el estructuralismo*. Trans. María Dolores Fonseca. Madrid: Edic. Doncel, 1972.

170. Rada García, E. "Notas sobre el estructuralismo." *Revista de Filosofia*, 28, no. 108-111 (Madrid, 1969; appeared in 1970), 95-101.

171. Redondi, Pietro. "Introductory Notes on Epistemology and the History of Science in France." *Scientia: An International Review of Scientific Synthesis*, 110 (1975), 171-196.

172. Reif, Adelbert, ed. *Antworten der Strukturalisten. Roland Barthes, Michel Foucault, François Jacob, Roman Jakobson, Claude Lévi-Strauss*. Trans. Britta Reif-Willenthal and Friedrich Griese. Hamburg: Hoffmann und Campe, 1973, 193pp. (Standpunkt) Includes items 312, 869-870, 1991-1993, and 3169.

173. Riegel, Klaus F., and George C. Rosenwald, eds. *Structure and Transformation: Developmental and Historical Aspects*. New York: Wiley, 1975. Includes items 3953, 4890, 4681, and 4744.

174. Robert, Jean-Dominique. "Analyse *structurale* et analyse *symbolique*. Quelques aperçus capitaux d'un livre récent sur la communication." *Revue Philosophique de Louvain*, 70 (1972), 465-479.

On item 194.

175. ————. Reviews of items 49 and 207. *Revue Philosophique de Louvain*, 72, no. 14 (May 1974), 429-431.

176. Robey, David, ed. *Structuralism: An Introduction*. Oxford: Clarendon Press; London-New York: Oxford University Press, 1973. Wolfson College Lectures, 1972. Contains his introduction plus items 4193, 4115, 3772, 5151, 4059, 4643, and 90.

177. Rougier, Louis. "Structuralisme." *Spectacle du Monde*, no. 80 (November 1968), pp. 125-128.

178. ————. "Le Structuralisme." *La Pensée et les Hommes*, 13 (Brussels, 1969-1970), 35-40.

179. Rubio Carracedo, J. "El Estructuralismo." *Pensamiento* (issue entitled "Tendencias actuales de la filosofía"), 29, no. 114-115 (1973), 149-174.

Method vs. doctrine; the common basis shared by Lévi-Strauss, Lacan, Foucault, Althusser, Barthes, and Dumézil; the critics: Sartre, Dufrenne, Boudon, and Cencillo.

180. Ruciński, Brunon J., and Ludwik Stomma. "Lubelskiej Szkoły Strukturalnej nie będzie." *Więź*, 14, no. 5 (1971), 127-133.

"There won't be a structuralist school at Lublin."

181. Runciman, W.G. "What is Structuralism?" *British Journal of Sociology*, 20 (September 1969), 253-265. Reprinted in *The Philosophy of Social Explanation*. Ed. Alan Ryan. London-New York: Oxford University Press, 1973, pp. 189-202.

182. Santinello, Giovanni. "Nota sul Vico e lo strutturalismo." *Studi in onore di A. Corsano*. (Università degli studi di Bari, Facoltà di lettere e filosofia) Manduria: Lacaita, 1970, pp. 693-702.

183. Sazbón, José. "El Estructuralismo en las revistas. (Una muestra significativa de "numéros especiales")" *Cuadernos de Filosofia*, 11 (sic for 13) (1973), 557-564.

184. Schaff, Adam. *Szkice o strukturalizmie*. Warsaw: Ksiażka i Wiedza, 1975.

185. Schechter, Rebecca. "Canadian Pioneer Cookery--A Structural Analysis." *Journal of Canadian Studies*, 12 (August 1977), 3-11.

186. Schiller, Hillel A. "From Shape to Letters." *Main Currents*, 28 (November-December 1971), 61-70.

187. Schiwy, Günther. "Strukturalismus in Paris. Mode, Methode und Ideologie." *Stimmen der Zeit*, 180, no. 8 (1967), 91-104.

188. ————. *Der französische Strukturalismus. Mode, Methode, Ideologie*. Mit einem Anhang mit Texten von de Saussure u. a. Reinbek bei Hamburg: Rowohlt, 1969, 249pp. 5th rev. ed. 1971. (Rowohlts deutsche Enzyklopädie 310/311: Sachgebiet Philosophie)

*189. ————. *Neue Aspekte des Strukturalismus*. Munich: Kösel-Verlag, 1971, 191pp.; Munich: Deutscher Taschenbuch-Verlag, 1973.

An anthology of articles he wrote from 1967-1971.

190. ————. *Nuovi aspetti dello strutturalismo*. Trans. Aniceto Molinaro. Rome: Città Nuova, 1973.

191. Scurati, Cesare. *Strutturalismo e scuola*. Brescia: La Scuola, 1973, 393pp.

192. Segre, C. "Structuralism in Italy." *Semiotica*, 4, no. 3 (1971), 215-239.

193. Selz, D.B. "Structuralism for the Non-Specialist: A Glossary and a Bibliography." *College English*, 37, no. 2 (October 1975), 160-166.

194. Serres, Michel. *Hermès ou la communication*. Paris: Presses Universitaires de France, 1968. See item 174.

195. *Soundings: An Interdisciplinary Journal*, 58, no. 2 (Summer 1975): a special issue entitled "Structuralism: An Interdisciplinary Study," ed. Susan Wittig. Rpt. in item 219. Contains items 218, 15, 3622, 3877, 5050, 4948, 4345, and 4315.

196. Sturrock, John. "Working the System: *Structuralism*, ed. Michael Lane." *New Society*, 19 March 1970, pp. 487-488.

196a. ———, ed. *Structuralism and Since: From Lévi-Strauss to Derrida*. New York: Oxford University Press, 1980, 224pp.

   Shows the development of structuralism from a method of inquiry limited to linguistics and anthropology to a worldwide fashion that has shaped an intellectual epoch by touching almost every field of thought. Clarifies the ideas of Barthes, Derrida, Foucault, Lacan, and Lévi-Strauss. Attempts to determine what is of lasting worth and originality in their work.

*197. *Les Temps Modernes*, 22, no. 246 (November 1966): issue entitled "Problèmes du structuralisme."

   Contains: (1) Jean Pouillon: Présentation: un essai de définition, pp. 769-790; (2) Marc Barbut: Sur le sens du mot structure en mathématiques, pp. 791-814; (3) A.J. Greimas: Structure et histoire, pp. 815-827; (4) Maurice Godelier: Système, structure et contradiction dans "Le Capital," pp. 828-864; (5) Pierre Bourdieu: Champ intellectuel et projet créateur, pp. 865-906; (6) Pierre Macherey: L'Analyse littéraire, tombeau des structures, pp. 907-928; (7) Jacques Ehrmann: Les structures de l'échange dans *Cinna*, pp. 929-960 (see also item 3920). For Portuguese trans., see item 4.

198. Thompson, Ewa M. "Russian Structuralist Theory." *Books Abroad*, 49 (Spring 1975), 232-238.

199. Todorov, Tzvetan. "Le Structuralisme dans les revues." *Information sur les Sciences Sociales*, 6, no. 4 (1967), 139-142.

200. Turner, Terence. "Piaget's Structuralism: Review Article." *American Anthropologist*, 75 (April 1973), 351-373.

201. Uscatescu, George. *Aporías del estructuralismo*. Madrid: Instituto de Estudios Políticos, 1971.

202. ———. "Aporias do estruturalismo." *Convivium*, 11 (São Paulo, 1972), 22-33.

203. ———. "Aporias del estructuralismo." *Estafeta Literaria*, no. 463 (1 March 1971), p. 409.

204. ———. *Genesi e vicende dello strutturalismo.* Pisa: Giardini, 1972, 135pp. (Biblioteca dell'Ussero)

205. Van Haecht, Louis. Review of J.M. Broekman's *Strukturalismus.* *Revue Philosophique de Louvain*, 70, no. 6 (May 1972), 317-318.

206. Vinaty, Tommaso. "Attraverso gli strutturalismi." Trans. Giovanni Giacopini. *Incontri Culturali*, 2 (1969), 162-185.

*207. Wahl, François, ed. *Qu'est-ce que le structuralisme?* Paris: Editions du Seuil, 1968, 446pp. Contains items 4127, 4863, 3805, 4899, and 4807. Later (1973) published in five separate volumes in the Points collection.

208. ———. *Estruturalismo e filosofia.* Trans. Alfredo Bosi and Adélia Bolle. São Paulo: Cultrix, Fundo Estadual de Cultura, 1970.

209. ———, ed. *Che cos'è lo strutturalismo? Linguistica, poetica, antropologia, psicanalisi, filosofia.* Trans. Mario Antomelli. Milan: ILI, 1971. (Campus, 1)

210. ———, ed. *Einführung in den Strukturalismus.* Trans. Eva Moldenhauer. Frankfurt am Main: Suhrkamp, 1973.

211. ———, ed. *¿Qué es el estructuralismo?* Buenos Aires: Losada, 1975.

212. Watté, Pierre. "Etes-vous structuraliste?" *La Revue Nouvelle*, 45, no. 6 (1967), 655-660.

     An overview of the various aspects of structuralism and of the paths and perspectives it opens up.

213. Weiler, A.G., ed. *Structuralisme: Voor en Tegen.* Bilthoven: Amboboeken, 1974, 149pp.

214. Weinrich, Harald. "'Strukturalimus.'" *Merkur*, 23 Jahrgang, Heft 6, nr. 254 (June 1969), 593-595.

     An overview of the movement starting with the events of May, 1968.

215. White, Hayden. "Structuralism and Popular Culture." *Journal of Popular Culture*, 7, no. 4 (Spring 1974), 759-774.

216. Wilden, Anthony. *System and Structure. Essays in Communication and Exchange.* London: Tavistock, 1972.

     A seminal work which attempts to bridge the gap between Anglo-Saxon and Continental participation in the structuralist movement. Contains: Introduction: The Scientific Discourse: Knowledge as a Commodity; (1) The Symbolic, the Imaginary, and the Real: Lacan, Lévi-Strauss, and Freud; (2) Metaphor and

Metonymy: Freud's Semiotic Model of Condensation and Displacement; (3) Death, Desire, and Repetition: Commentary on Svevo's *Confessions of Zeno*; (4) Montaigne on the Paradoxes of Individualism: A Communication about Communication; (5) The Double Bind: Schizophrenia and Gödel; (6) Beyond the Entropy Principle in Freud; (7) Analog and Digital Communication: On Negation, Signification and Meaning; (8) Epistemology and Ecology: The Difference that Makes the Difference; (9) Nature and Culture: The Emergence of Symbolic and Imaginary Exchange; (10) Critique of Phallocentrism: Daniel Paul Schreber on Women's Liberation; (11) The Structure as Law and Order: Piaget's Genetic Structuralism; (12) Ecosystem and Metasystem: A Morphogenic Model of Emergence in Open Systems; (13) Order from Disorder: Noise, Trace, and Event in Evolution and in History; (14) The Scientific Discourse as Propaganda: The Binary Opposition; (15) Language and Communication; (16) Linguistics and Semiotics: The Unconscious Structured like a Language; (17) The Ideology of Opposition and Identity: Critique of Lacan's Theory of the Mirror-stage in Childhood; Bibliography.

217. ————. "Structuralism, Communication, and Evolution." *Semiotica*, 6, no. 3 (1972), 244-256. A critical study of Piaget's *Le Structuralisme* (item 154).

218. Wittig, Susan. "The Historical Development of Structuralism." *Soundings: An Interdisciplinary Journal*, 58, no. 2 (Summer 1975), 145-166.

219. ————, ed. *Structuralism: An Interdisciplinary Study*. Pittsburgh: Pickwick Press, 1975. Originally published as item 195.

220. ————, ed. *Steps to Structure*. Englewood, N.J.: Winthrop (a subsidiary of Prentice-Hall), 1976.

221. *Yale French Studies*, no. 36-37 (1966): issue on "Structuralism," see item 68.

222. *Yale French Studies*, no. 41 (1968): issue entitled "Game, Play, Literature" deals with the structural implications of "play."

223. Yallop, Colin. "The Lord is my Goatherd; I Don't Want Him." *Interchange*, 1974, pp. 214-220.

224. Zółkiewski, Stefan. "Deux structuralismes." In *Sign, Language, Culture*. Ed. A.J. Greimas, et al. The Hague: Mouton, 1970, pp. 3-12.

225. Zumr, J. "The Evolution of Czech Structural Thought to 1930" (in Czech). *Filosofický Časopis*, 17, no. 1 (1969), 66-75.

II
WORKS BY AND ABOUT
INDIVIDUAL STRUCTURALISTS

LOUIS ALTHUSSER

PRIMARY SOURCES

1954

226. "L'Enseignement de la philosophie." *Esprit*, 22, no. 215 (1954), 858-864.

1955

227. "Essais et propos sur l'objectivité de l'histoire (lettre à Paul Ricoeur)." *Revue de l'Enseignement Philosophique*, 5, no. 4 (1955), 3-15.

1959

*228. *Montesquieu, la politique et l'histoire*. Paris: Presses Universitaires de France, 1959, 119pp. Rpt. 1964, 1969, and 1974. (Initiation Philosophique) For trans., see items 277 (Italian), 303 (English), 321 (Spanish), and 358 (English). For reviews, see items 649-653.

Contains: Avant-Propos; (1) Une révolution dans la méthode; (2) Une nouvelle théorie de la loi; (3) La dialectique de l'histoire; (4) "Il y a trois gouvernements"; (5) Le mythe de la séparation des pouvoirs; (6) Le parti pris de Montesquieu; Conclusion; Bibliographie, pp. 118-119.

1960

229. Translation of *Manifestes philosophiques. Textes choisis (1839-1845)*. By Ludwig Feuerbach. Paris: Presses Universitaires de France, 1960. See item 307 for a new edition.

230. "Les *Manifestes philosophiques*." *La Nouvelle Critique* (December 1960). Rpt. in item 244, chapter 2.

1961

231. "Sur le jeune Marx. (Questions de théorie)." *La Pensée*, no. 96 (1961), pp. 3-26. Rpt. in item 244, chapter 3.

1962

*232. "Contradiction et surdétermination." *La Pensée*, no. 106
        (December 1962), pp. 3-22. Rpt. in item 244, chapter 4. For
        English trans., see item 249.

233. "Le 'Piccolo,' Bertolazzi et Brecht: Notes sur un théâtre
        matérialiste." *Esprit*, 30, no. 312 (December 1962), 946-965.
        Rpt. in item 244, chapter 5. See also item 273.

1963

234. "Philosophie et sciences humaines." *Revue de l'Enseignement
        Philosophique*, no. 5 (June-July 1963).

235. "Les 'Manuscrits de 1844' de Karl Marx (Economie politique et
        philosophie)." *La Pensée*, no. 107 (1963), pp. 106-109.

236. Review of *Hegel et l'hégélianisme* by René Serreau. *La Pensée*,
        no. 110 (1963), pp. 153-154.

1964

237. "Problèmes étudiants." *La Nouvelle Critique*, no. 152 (January
        1964).

238. Introduction to "La Philosophie de la science de Georges
        Canguilhem." By Pierre Macherey. *La Pensée*, no. 113 (January-
        February 1964), pp. 50-74.

239. "Sur la dialectique matérialiste." *Cahiers de l'I.S.E.A.* (June
        1964). Rpt. in item 244, chapter 6.

240. "Marxisme et humanisme." *Cahiers de l'I.S.E.A.* (June 1964).
        Rpt. in item 244, chapter 7.

1965

*241. "Freud et Lacan." *La Nouvelle Critique*, no. 161-162 (December
        1964-January 1965). For trans., see items 271 (English), 294
        (Catalonian or Spanish), 295 (German), 297 (English), and
        324 (Italian). Rpt. in item 341.

242. "Note complémentaire sur l'humanisme 'réel.'" *La Nouvelle
        Critique* (March 1965). Rpt. in item 244, chapter 8.

243. "Esquisse du concept d'histoire." *La Pensée*, no. 121 (1965),
        pp. 3-21.

        On *The Capital*.

*244. *Pour Marx*. Paris: F. Maspero, 1965. 2nd ed. 1966; 6th ed. 1970.
        Contains: Préface: aujourd'hui and items 230, 231, 232, 233,

239, 240, and 242. For trans., see items 250 (Italian), 251
(Portuguese), 255 and 256 (Spanish), 263 (German), 272
(English), 278 (Catalonian or Spanish), and 328 (German). For
reviews, see items 658-666.

*245. Co-author of *Lire "Le Capital."* 2 vols. Paris: F. Maspero, 1965.
Appears in four volumes in 1968 and 1973. Cf. item 331. For
trans., see items 264 (Italian), 280 (Spanish), 281 (Dutch),
285 (English), 300 (Italian), 306 (German), 356 and 357
(English). For reviews, see items 644-648.

Volume 1 with Jacques Rancière and Pierre Macherey; volume 2
with Etienne Balibar and Roger Establet. Contains: Du *Capital*
à la philosophie de Marx and L'Objet du *Capital*.

1966

246. "Matérialisme historique et matérialisme dialectique." *Cahiers
Marxistes-Léninistes*, no. 11 (1966). See also item 279.

1967

*247. "Sur le *Contrat social.*" *Cahiers pour l'Analyse*, no. 8 (1967),
pp. 5-42. A course given at the Ecole Normale Supérieure in
1965-1966 and part an entire issue entitled "L'Impensé de
Jean-Jacques Rousseau." For English trans., see item 303.

*248. "Sur le travail théorique. Difficultés et ressources." *La
Pensée*, no. 132 (1967), pp. 3-22. For Portuguese trans., see
item 292.

The difficulties involved in a theoretical presentation of
Marxist principles have to do with the terminology of theoretical
discourse, the background of this discourse, the method, and
the theory's aspect of revolutionary newness. The sources or
resources of the presentation lie in the classical works and
the facts that practice reveals, and both aspects are brought
together through a general theory.

249. "Contradiction and Overdetermination." *New Left Review*, 41
(January-February 1967), 15-35. Trans. of item 232, preceded
by Ben Brewster's "Presentation of Althusser," pp. 11-14.

250. *Per Marx.* Intro. Cesare Luporini. Trans. F. Madonia. Rome:
Editori Riuniti, 1967. Trans. of item 244.

251. *Análise crítica da teoria marxista.* Trans. Dirceu Lindoso.
Rio de Janeiro: Ed. Zahar, 1967. Trans. of item 244.

252. *Dialética e ciências sociais.* Trans. Wanderlei Guilherme Santos.
Rio de Janeiro: Ed. Zahar, 1967. With Stalislaw Ossowski,
et al.

253. *Marxismo segundo Althusser: polêmica Althusser-Garaudy.*
     São Paulo: Ed. Sinal, 1967. With Raymond Domergue.

*254. "Cours de philosophie pour scientifiques" (mimeographed version
      for student use), 1967. For trans., see item 334. See also
      item 318.

255. *La Revolución teórica de Marx.* Trans. Marta Harnecker. Buenos
     Aires-Mexico: Siglo Veintiuno, 1967. Trans. of item 244.

1968

256. Preface to *La Revolución teórica de Marx.* Trans. Marta Harnecker.
     2nd rev. enlarged ed. Buenos Aires-Mexico: Siglo Veintiuno,
     1968. Trans. of item 244.

257. *¿Por qué una teoría revolucionaria?* Montevideo: Editorial "De
     Frente," 1968.

258. *Sobre el trabajo téorico: dificultades y recursos.* Barcelona:
     Anagrama, [1968?].

259. *Polémica sobre marxismo y humanismo.* Trans. Marta Harnecker.
     Mexico: Siglo Veintiuno, 1968. With Jorge Semprún, Michel
     Simon and Michel Verret.

     Contains articles originally published in magazines and in
     another book.

*260. "La Philosophie comme arme de la révolution." *La Pensée*, no.
      138 (1968), pp. 26-34. For trans., see items 261 (Spanish) and
      286 (English). Rpt. in item 341.

      Answers to eight questions asked by M.-A. Macchiocchi, the
      correspondent of *Unità* (February 1, 1968).

261. *La Filosofía como arma de la revolución.* Trans. Oscar Del Barco
     and Enrique Román. Córdoba, Argentina: Cuadernos de Pasado y
     Presente, c. 1968, 1972. Trans. of item 260.

*262. *Lénine et la philosophie.* Paris: Armand Colin, 1968, pp. 125-
      186. With others. Book form of the *Bulletin de la Société
      Française de Philosophie*, 62, no. 4 (1968) which deals with
      the February 24, 1968 meeting. Rpt. in item 267. For trans.,
      see items 275 (Italian), 287 (Catalonian), and 288-290
      (Spanish). Cf. item 298. For reviews, see items 636-643.

263. *Für Marx.* Trans. Karin Brachmann and Gabriele Sprigath.
     Frankfurt am Main: Suhrkamp, 1968. Trans. of item 244.

264. *Leggere Il Capitale.* Trans. R. Rinaldi and V. Oskian. Milan:
     Feltrinelli, 1968. With Etienne Balibar. Trans. of item 245
     with omissions and an enlarged section by Balibar. See also
     item 300.

1969

*265. "Lénine devant Hegel." *Hegel-Jahrbuch* (1968-1969), pp. 45-58.
For English trans., see item 297. Rpt. in item 302.

266. "Comment lire *Le Capital*?" *L'Humanité*, 23 March 1969. Rpt. in
item 341.

*267. *Lénine et la philosophie*. Paris: F. Maspero, 1969. Rpt. of item
262. For trans., see items 275 (Italian), 287 (Catalonian),
288-290 (Spanish), and 297 (English). Cf. item 298. See also
item 302.

*268. "Chronologie et avertissement." In *Le Capital, I*. By Karl Marx.
Trans. Joseph Roy. Paris: Garnier-Flammarion, 1969. For
English trans., see item 297.

269. "A propos de l'article de Michel Verret sur Mai Etudiant." *La
Pensée*, no. 145 (1969).

270. *L'Eglise aujourd'hui*. Lyon: "Lumière et Vie," 1969. With J.-M.
Domenach, M.-D. Chenu, M. Maréchal, et al.

271. "Freud and Lacan." Trans. Ben Brewster. *New Left Review*, no. 55
(May-June 1969), pp. 48-65.

A revised version of item 241, preceded by an editorial note
by Ben Brewster.

272. *For Marx*. Trans. Ben Brewster. London: Allen Lane, The Penguin
Press; New York: Pantheon Books, 1969. New York: Vintage
Books, c. 1969, 1970.

English trans. of item 244. Contains two new additions: "To
my English Readers" and a glossary of Althusserian terms (revised and amplified since the original publication) followed by
a "Letter to the Translator." Shows the young Marx as propound-
ing a humanist philosophy, but a philosophical break occurs
between the Marx of the 1840s and the later Marx.

273. *Notes on a Materialist Theater*. Urbana, Illinois: Depot Press,
c. 1969. On Carlo Bertolazzi: "El Nost Milan" and political
aspects of the theater. See also item 233.

274. Letters in *Lettere dall'interno del P.C.I. a Louis Althusser*.
By Maria Antonietta Macciocchi. Milan: Feltrinelli, 1969.
See also items 515-518.

275. *Lenin e la filosofia*. Trans. F. Madonia. Milan: Jaca Book, 1969.
Trans. of items 262 and 267. See also item 325.

276. *Leonardo Cremonini. Mostra antologica 1953-1969. Bologna, Museo
civico, 15 ottobre-15 novembre 1969*. Bologna: Alfa, 1969. With
Franco Solmi and the Ente Bolognese Manifestazioni Artistiche.

277. *Montesquieu. La Politica e la storia*. Trans. B. Menato. Rome:
Samonà e Savelli, 1969. Trans. of item 228.

278. *Per Marx.* Trans. Josef Blasco. Valencia: Garbí, 1969. Trans. of item 244.

279. Contributor to *Materialismo histórico y materialismo dialectico.* Córdoba: Cuadernos de Pasado y Presente, 1969. See also item 246.

280. *Para leer "El Capital."* Mexico: Siglo Veintiuno, 1969. With Etienne Balibar. Trans. of item 245.

281. *Enkele summiere maar nuttige vingerwijzingen bij het lezen van Marx' HET KAPITAAL.* Trans. H. van Maren. Amsterdam: Pegasus, 1969. Trans. of item 245?

1970

*282. "Sur le rapport de Marx à Hegel." In *Hegel et la pensée moderne. Séminaire dirigé par Jean Hyppolite au Collège de France (1967-1968).* Ed. Jacques D'Hondt. Paris: Presses Universitaires de France, 1970, pp. 85-111. See also items 296 and 302. For English trans., see item 303.

*283. "Idéologie et appareils idéologiques d'Etat." *La Pensée*, 6, no. 151 (June 1970), 4-38. For trans., see items 284 (Italian), 297 (English), 299 (Spanish), and 351 (German). Rpt. in item 341.

Althusser lays the groundwork for a theory of "superstructure" by presenting the concept of the ideological apparatus of the State (religion, education, family, politics, law, etc.). He then goes on to a theoretical analysis of the concept of ideology as a "representation of the imaginary relationship that individuals have with their own conditions of existence." One example given is the religious ideology of Christianity.

284. "Ideologia ed apparati ideologici di Stato." *Critica Marxista*, 8, no. 5 (1970), 23-65. Trans. of item 283.

285. *Reading Capital.* Trans. Ben Brewster. London: New Left Books; New York: Pantheon Books, 1970. London: 2nd ed., 1977.

With Etienne Balibar. English trans. of the second edition of item 245 which contains only the two essays by Althusser and Balibar which were presented as papers at a seminar on Marx's *Capital* at the Ecole Normale Supérieure in 1965, with an introduction by Althusser. Deals with the problem of reading and understanding Marx; with constructing Althusser's concepts of overdetermination, structure in dominance, structural causality, and differential historical time; and with elucidating the basic concepts of historical materialism in their light. Also discussed are the ideas of Gramsci, Della Volpe, Colletti, Sartre, and Lévi-Strauss. See also items 356 and 357.

286. "Philosophy as a Revolutionary Weapon: Interview with Louis Althusser." *New Left Review*, no. 64 (November-December 1970), pp. 3-11. Trans. of item 260, reprinted from *L'Unità* (1 February 1968).

Althusser tells what he means by "philosophy" and "science," and why it is important to study Marx's *Capital* and to fight for a precise detailed terminology.

287. *Lenin i la filosofia.* Catalonian trans. Vicent Raga. Valencia: Tres i Quatre, 1970. Trans. of items 262 and 267.

288. *Lenín y la filosofía.* Mexico: Ediciones Era, 1970. Trans. of items 262 and 267.

289. *Lenín y la filosofía.* Trans. Carlos Pérez. Buenos Aires: Tres Américas, [1970?]. Trans. of items 262 and 267.

290. *Lenín y la filosofía.* Montevideo: Fundación de Cultura Universitaria, [1970?]. Trans. of items 262 and 267.

291. *Polémica sobre la lectura de El Capital.* Bogotá: Oveja Negra, [1970?]. With Ernest Mandel. (Tiempo Crítico)

292. *Sobre o trabalho teórico.* Trans. Joaquim José Moura Ramos. Lisboa: Editorial Presença, 1970 or 1971. Trans. of item 248.

293. Essay in *Estructuralismo y psicoanálisis.* Ed. José Sazbon. Buenos Aires: Nueva Visión, 1970.

294. *Freud y Lacan.* Trans. Muria Garreta. Barcelona: Editorial Anagrama, 1970. Trans. of item 241 followed by "El objeto del psicoanalisis," a trans. of Lacan's "Reponse à des étudiants en philosophie sur l'objet de la psychanalyse." See also item 3126.

295. *Freud und Lacan.* Trans. Hanns-Henning Ritter and Herbert Nagel. Berlin: Merve Verlag, 1970. Trans. of item 241. See also item 344.

1971

296. "Sur le rapport de Marx à Hegel." In *Contemporary Philosophy: A Survey.* Ed. Raymond Klibansky. Vol. IV. *Ethics, Aesthetics, Law, Religion, Politics. Historical and Dialectical Materialism. Philosophy in Eastern Europe, Asia and Latin America (International Institute of Philosophy).* Florence: La Nuova Italia Editrice, 1971, pp. 358-377. See also item 282.

297. *Lenin and Philosophy and Other Essays.* Trans. Ben Brewster. London: New Left Books; New York: Monthly Review Press, 1971. English trans. of items 241, 265, 267, 268, 283, together with "A Letter on Art in Reply to André Daspre" (*La Nouvelle Critique,* April 1966) and "Cremonini, Painter of the Abstract" (*Démocratie Nouvelle,* August 1966).

298. "Lenin y la filosofía (1870-1924)." *Revista de Occidente,* no. 94 (1971), pp. 77-93. Cf. items 262 and 267.

299. *Ideología y aparatos ideológicos del Estado.* Mexico: Centro
      Interamericano de Libros Académicos, 1971. Trans. of item
      283.

300. *Leggere il Capitale.* Trans. R. Rinaldi and V. Oskian.
      New revised and corrected ed. Milan: Feltrinelli, 1971. With Etienne
      Balibar. Trans. of item 245. See also item 264.

                                  1972

301. "Une Erreur politique." *France Nouvelle*, 25 July and 1 August
      1972.

*302. *Lénine et la philosophie (suivi de) Marx et Lénine devant Hegel.*
      Paris: F. Maspero, 1972. Second edition of item 267. Also
      contains items 265 and 282. For trans., see items 325 (Italian),
      and 327 (German).

303. *Politics and History: Montesquieu, Rousseau, Hegel and Marx.*
      Trans. Ben Brewster. London: New Left Books; Atlantic High-
      lands, N.J.: Humanities Press, 1972. Trans. of items 228
      (pp. 9-109), 247 (pp. 111-160) and 282 (pp. 161-186). See
      also item 358.

      The first two essays criticize Marx and Rousseau as having
      been limited by the ideologies of their days. The third essay
      is a structural analysis tracing the development of Marxian
      historical materialist categories from Hegel's Logic. The
      American edition was rpt. in 1975; a second English edition
      appeared in 1977.

*304. "Reply to John Lewis (Self-Criticism)." *Marxism Today*, 16, no.
      10 (October 1972), 310-318; 16, no. 11 (November 1972), 343-
      349. For trans., see items 309 (French), 310 (Italian), and
      314 (German).

305. Essay in *Scuola, potere e ideologia.* Ed. Marzio Barbagli.
      Bologna: Il Mulino, 1972. Contains essays previously published
      in various periodicals. Bibliography, pp. 303-313. Another
      edition appeared in 1975.

306. *Das Kapital lesen, I-II.* Trans. Klaus-Dieter Thieme. 2 vols.
      Reinbek bei Hamburg: Rowohlt, 1972. German trans. of item
      245 with omissions and an enlarged section by co-author
      Etienne Balibar.

                                  1973

307. Translation of *Manifestes politiques. Textes choisis, 1839-1845.*
      By Ludwig Feuerbach. Paris: Union Générale d'Editions, 1973.
      A new edition of item 229.

308. Participant in the discussion on "Les Communistes, les intellec-
      tuels et la culture," Fête de l'*Humanité. France Nouvelle*, 18
      September 1973.

*309. *Réponse à John Lewis. L'Assaut humaniste contre le marxisme:
       pourquoi?* Paris: F. Maspero, 1973. Originally published in
       item 304 in answer to John Lewis' "The Case Althusser,"
       published in *Marxism Today*, January-February 1972. For trans.,
       see items 310 (Italian), 314 (German), and 329 (Dutch). For
       reviews, see items 667-674.

       Sees Stalinism as a form of posthumous revenge by the Second
       International.

310. *Umanesimo e stalinismo: I fondamenti teorici della deviazione
     staliniana.* Trans. Franca Papa. Bari: De Donato, 1973. Trans.
     of item 309.

311. "The Condition of Marx's Scientific Discovery." *Theoretical
     Practice*, no. 7-8 (January 1973).

312. Essay in *Antworten der Strukturalisten.* Ed. Adelbert Reif.
     Trans. Britta Reif-Willenthal and Friedrich Griese. Hamburg:
     Hoffman und Campe, 1973.

313. *Marxismus und Ideologie. Probleme der Marx-Interpretation.*
     Trans. Horst Arenz, et al. Berlin: Verlag für das Studium
     der Arbeiterbewegung, 1973.

314. *Was ist revolutionärer Marxismus? Kontroverse über Grundfragen
     marxistischer Theorie zwischen Louis Althusser und John Lewis.*
     Trans. from French by Georg Fexer. Trans. from English by
     Bernd F. Gruschwitz. Berlin: Verlag für das Studium der
     Arbeiterbewegung, 1973. With John Lewis. Edited by Horst
     Arenz, Joachim Bischoff and Urs Jaeggi. Trans. of items 304
     and 309. See also item 371.

315. "Od 'Kapitala' do marksove filosofije." *Delo*, 19, no. 12 (1973),
     1593-1617.

                                 1974

316. Four unpublished texts in *Théorie et politique: Louis Althusser.
     Avec quatre textes inédits de Louis Althusser.* By Saül Karsz.
     Paris: Fayard, 1974.

     Contains: (1) Projet de préface pour un recueil de textes
     (1968); (2) Texte ronéotypé (1970); (3) A Propos de *Lénine et
     la philosophie* et de l'article "Comment lire *Le Capital?*"; (4)
     Préface à la seconde édition en espagnol du livre de Marta
     Harnecker, *Los Conceptos elementales del materialismo histórico*,
     Mexico-Buenos Aires, 1971.

*317. *Eléments d'auto-critique.* Paris: Hachette, 1974. Includes "Sur
      l'évolution du jeune Marx." A questioning and examination of
      the "theoricist tendency" in his earlier works. For trans.,
      see items 335 (Catalonian or Spanish), 337 (German), 338
      (English), and 339 (Italian). For reviews, see items 630-635.

      On Marx, Spinoza and structuralism.

*318. *Philosophie et philosophie spontanée des savants (1967)*. Paris:
       F. Maspero, 1974. (Théorie. Cours de philosophie pour scien-
       tifiques) An amended version of item 254, the text of three
       courses given at the Ecole Normale Supérieure in 1967. For
       trans., see items 334 (Catalonian or Spanish) and 340 (Italian).
       For reviews, see items 654-655.

319.   "Justesse et philosophie." *La Pensée*, no. 176 (1974), pp. 3-8.

       A proposition in philosophy cannot be called true, only correct.
       A philosophical thesis has no object, but something at stake.

320.   "Sur la dialectique de l'évolution intellectuelle du jeune
       Marx." *Hegel-Jahrbuch*, p. vol. (1974), 128-136.

       Using the main theses developed in his earlier writings on
       Marx, Althusser tries to trace some of the decisive moments
       in Marx's thought from two viewpoints: philosophical (from
       neo-Hegelianism to a revolutionary materialism via L. Feuerbach)
       and political (from radical bourgeois liberalism to communism
       via utopian communism).

321.   *Montesquieu. La política y la historia*. Trans. María Ester
       Benítez. 2nd ed. Esplugas de Llobregat: Ariel, 1974. Trans.
       of item 228.

322.   *Para una crítica de la práctica teórica*. Trans. Santiago Funes.
       Madrid: Siglo Veintiuno de España, 1974.

323.   "Advertencia a los lectores del libro I de El Capital." In *El
       Concepto de historia*. By Pierre Vilar, Louis Althusser and
       Raúl Olmedo. Trans. and intro. Raúl Olmedo. Mexico: Departa-
       mento de Investigaciones Históricas, INAH, 1974.

324.   "Freud e Lacan." *Aut Aut*, no. 141 (1974), pp. 71-90. Trans. of
       item 241.

325.   *Lenin e la filosofia. Seguito da: Sul rapporto fra Marx e Hegel.
       Lenin di fronte a Hegel*. Trans. F. Madonia. 2. ristampa.
       Milan: Jaca Book, 1974. Trans. of item 302. See also item 275.

326.   Preface to *Lenin e la crisi delle scienze*. By Dominique Lecourt.
       Trans. F. Fistetti and A. Marchi. Rome: Editori Riuniti, 1974.

327.   *Lenin und die Philosophie. Marx und Lenin nach Hegel*. Trans.
       Klaus-Dieter Thieme. Reinbek bei Hamburg: Rowohlt, 1974.
       Trans. of item 302.

328.   *Für Marx*. Trans. Karin Brachmann and Gabriele Sprigath. Frank-
       furt am Main: Suhrkamp, 1974. Trans. of item 244.

329.   *Antwoord aan John Lewis*. Trans. Tony Vogel. Nijmegen: Social-
       istiese Uitgeverij, 1974. Trans. of item 309.

1975

330. "Dialektyka ewolucji teoretycznej młodego Marksa." *Studia Filozoficzne*, 19, no. 1 (1975), 11-18. Paper in Polish read at the 10th International Hegelian Congress held in Moscow in August 1974.

   The epistemological break which separates the young Marx from the mature Marx results from a philosophical change (from humanism to materialism) and a political change (from the petty bourgeoisie to the proletariat).

331. *Lire "Le Capital,"* I. New recast ed. Paris: F. Maspero, 1975. With Etienne Balibar. Cf. item 245.

*332. "Est-il simple d'être marxiste en philosophie?" *La Pensée*, no. 183 (1975), pp. 3-31. For Spanish trans., see item 333.

   On the occasion of his doctoral defense, Althusser summarizes and polishes the main themes of his activity as a Marxist philosopher: the final instance (how is it final and how is it instance?); Hegelian totality and the Marxian whole (the notion of inequality); the process of knowledge (Spinoza and Marx, the real object and the object of thought); theoretical humanism (Marx can only construct the science of history by breaking with himself).

333. "¿Es fácil ser marxista en filosofía?" *Ideas y Valores*, no. 42-45 (Colombia, 1973-1975), pp. 5-38. Trans. of item 332, Althusser's defense of his *doctorat d'état* held in June, 1975 at Amiens.

334. *Curso de filosofía para científicos*. Trans. Albert Roies. Barcelona: Editorial Laia, 1975. Trans. of item 254 or 318.

335. *Elementos de autocritica*. Trans. Miguel Barroso. Barcelona: Editorial Laia, 1975. Trans. of item 317.

336. Contributor to *Para una crítica del fetichismo literario*. Ed. Juan M. Azpitarte Almagro. Madrid: Akal, 1975.

337. *Elemente der Selbstkritik*. Trans. Peter Schöttler. Berlin: Verlag für das Studium der Arbeiterbewegung, 1975. Trans. of item 317.

1976

338. *Essays in Self-Criticism*. Trans. Grahame Lock. London: New Left Books; Atlantic Highlands, N.J.: Humanities Press, 1976. Trans. of item 317.

   Contains: Reply to John Lewis: Note on "The Critique of the Personality Cult"; Remark on the Category "Process Without a Subject or Goal(s)"; Elements of Self-Criticism: On the Evolution of the Young Marx; Is It Simple to be a Marxist in Philosophy?; "Something New"; Lock's 32-page introduction to the work of Althusser and a bibliography of works by and about Althusser, pp. 217-221.

339. *Elementi di autocritica.* Trans. Nazzareno Mazzini. Milan: Feltrinelli, 1976. Trans. of item 317.

340. *Filosofia e filosofia spontanea degli scienziali e altri scritti.* Trans. Francesco Fistetti. Bari: De Donato, 1976. Trans. of item 318.

*341. *Positions (1964-1975).* Paris: Editions Sociales, 1976. Contains items 241, 260, 266, 283, "Marxisme et lutte de classe," and "Soutenance d'Amiens." For trans., see items 349 (Spanish), and 351 (German). For reviews, see items 656-657.

*342. Foreword to *Lyssenko: histoire réelle d'une "science prolétarienne."* By Dominique Lecourt. Paris: F. Maspero, 1976. For trans., see items 343 (German) and 358a (English).

343. Foreword to *Lyssenko, Proletarische Wissenschaft oder Dogmatismus?* By Dominique Lecourt. Berlin: Verlag für das Studium der Arbeiterbewegung, 1976. Trans. of item 342.

344. *Freud und Lacan. Die Psychoanalyse im historischen Materialismus.* Trans. Hanns H. Ritter, et al. Berlin: Merve Verlag, 1976. (Intern. Marxist. Diskussion, 58) With Michel Tort. Trans. of item 241. See also item 295.

345. Contributor to *Textos de la nueva izquierda.* Trans. Andres Linares. Madrid: Castellote, 1976.

346. *La Transformación de la filosofiá.* Granada: Universidad de Granada, Secretariado de Publicaciones, 1976.

1977

347. *22ᵉ Congrès.* Paris: F. Maspero, 1977, 68pp. (Théorie) Remarks made 16 December 1976 during a public debate at the invitation of the Cercle de Philosophie de l'Union des Etudiants Communistes: 22ᵉ Congrès national du parti communiste français, Saint-Ouen, France, 1976. See also item 348.

348. "On the 22nd Congress of the French Communist Party." *New Left Review,* no. 104 (July 1977), pp. 3-22. See also item 347.

349. *Posiciones.* Mexico: Grijalbo, 1977. Trans. of item 341.

350. *Seis iniciativas communistas.* Trans. Gabriel Albiac. Madrid: Siglo Veintiuno de España, 1977.

351. *Ideologie und ideologische Staatsapparate. Marxismus und Philosophie.* Trans. Rolf Löper, et al. Hamburg: Verlag für das Studium der Arbeiterbewegung, 1977. Trans. of item 283 and/or 341.

352. "Tegenspraak en overdeterminatie en Over materialistiese
      dialektiek: samenvatting." In *Seminar Althusser...*, item
      369, 1977.

353. "Van het Kapitaal naar de filosofie van Marx: samenvatting."
      In *Seminar Althusser...*, item 369, 1977.

354. "Ideologie en ideologiese staatsapparaten: samenvatting." In
      Seminar Althusser..., item 369, 1977.

355. Afterword to *On the Dictatorship of the Proletariat*. By Etienne
      Balibar. Trans. Grahame Lock. Atlantic Highlands, N.J.:
      Humanities Press, 1977.

356. *Reading Capital*. Atlantic Highlands, N.J.: Humanities Press,
      1977. With Etienne Balibar. Paper text edition. Trans. of
      item 245. See also items 285 and 357.

1978

356a. *Ce qui ne peut plus durer dans le parti communiste*. Paris:
      François Maspero, 1978, 123pp. (Théorie) Cf. item 360.
      Articles originally published in *Le Monde*, 24-27 April 1978.

357. *Reading Capital*. New York: Schocken Books, Inc., 1978. With
      Etienne Balibar. Trans. of item 245. See also items 285 and
      356.

358. *Politics and History: Montesquieu, Rousseau, Hegel, Marx*. New
      York: Schocken Books, Inc., 1978. Trans. of item 228. See
      also item 303.

358a. Introduction to *Proletarian Science? The Case of Lysenko*. By
      Dominique Lecourt. Trans. Ben Brewster. Atlantic Highlands,
      N.J.: Humanities Press, 1978. Trans. of item 342.

359. *Wetenschap en ideologiekritiek: opstellen van Louis Althusser
      et al*. Ed. Harry Kunneman. Meppel: Boom, 1978.

359a. Co-author of *Discutere lo Stato: posizioni a confronto su una
      tesi di Louis Althusser*. Bari: De Donato, 1978, 338pp.
      (Dissensi, 94)

360. "What Must Change in the Party." Trans. P. Camuller. *New Left
      Review*, no. 109 (May 1978), pp. 19-45. Cf. item 356a.

SECONDARY SOURCES

Agües, F. See item 4347.

361.   Airaksinen, T. "Marxist Philosophy and Philosophical Tradition:
       Some Differences." *Annales Universitatis Turkuensis Sarja-Ser.
       B. Humaniora*, 139 (1976), 53–63.

       Why the author agrees with Althusser.

362.   Albiac, Gabriel. *Louis Althusser: cuestiones del leninismo.*
       Bilbao: Zero; Madrid: Z.Y.X., 1976.

362a. Alessandro, V. d'. "La Saggistica marxistica francese e il
       problema dell'ideologia. Dall'astrattezza della speculazione
       filosofica all'analisi delle matrici storico-sociali dell'
       ideologia borghese." *Rassegna Italiana di Sociologia*, 19,
       no. 1 (1978), 101–128.

       Examination and critique of Althusser's theory of ideology.

363.   Anonymous. "De l'affirmation à l'autocritique." *Le Monde* [*des
       Livres*], no. 9339 (24 January 1975), p. 16.

364.   ─────. *Contre Althusser.* Paris: Union Générale d'Editions,
       1974, 320pp. (10/18)

365.   ─────. "I Debiti e la sfida di L. Althusser." *Osservatore
       Romano*, 117, no. 39 (17 February 1977), 5.

366.   ─────. "Généalogie du Capital. II. L'Idéal historique."
       Recherches, no. 14 (1974), 131pp.

       A series of essays on Althusser's interpretation of Marxism.

367.   ─────. *Del idealismo "fisico" al idealismo "biológico."* 3
       Obritas de Jacques Monod, Louis Althusser y Jean Piaget.
       Barcelona: Ed. Anagrama, 1972.

368.   ─────. "On en parlera demain: Althusser à Amiens." *Le Nouvel
       Observateur*, no. 555 (30 June-6 July 1975), p. 24.

369.   ─────. *Seminar Althusser: de marxistiese filosofie en haar
       verhouding tot Spinoza en Hegel, Bachelard en Lacan.* Nijmegen:
       S.U.N., c. 1977.

       Contains: (1) S. Macintyre and K. Tribe: Althusser en de
       marxistiese theorie; (2) G. van den Brink: Moelijkheden bij het
       lezen van Althusser; (3) L. Althusser: Tegenspraak en over-
       determinatie en Over materialistiese dialektiek: samenvatting;
       (4) G. van den Brink: Enkele vragen naar aanleiding van
       Althussers opvatting van dialektiek in *Pour Marx*; (5) M.
       Godelier: System, struktuur en tegenspraak in *Het Kapitaal*:
       samenvatting; (6) W.J. Karman: Althusser en Bachelard; (7) L.
       Althusser: Van *Het Kapitaal* naar de filosofie van Marx: samen-
       vatting; (8) L. Althusser: Ideologie en ideologiese staats-

apparaten: samenvatting; (9) R. Abma and M. Janssen: Onbewuste en ideologie; (10) P. Schöttler: Elementen van zelfkritiek; (11) M. Terpstra: Althusser en Spinoza; and a bibliography of works by L. Althusser, pp. 135-138.

370. ————. "Taller Men Wear Longer Trousers." *Economist*, CCLI, no. 6817 (20 April 1974), 123-124.

371. Arenz, H., et al., eds. *Was ist revolutionärer Marxismus? Kontroverse über Grundfragen marxistischer Theorie zwischen Louis Althusser und John Lewis*. Trans. from English by Bernd F. Gruschwitz and from French by Georg Fexer. Berlin: Verlag für das Studium der Arbeiterbewegung, 1973. See also item 314.

372. *Argument (Das)*, 17, no. 94 (1975), pp. 921-984; issue entitled "Antworten auf Althusser." Contains items 471, 571, and 614.

*373. Aron, Raymond. *D'une sainte famille à l'autre, essais sur les marxismes imaginaires*. Paris: Gallimard, 1969, 319pp.

374. ————. *Marxismes imaginaires. D'une sainte famille à l'autre*. Paris: Gallimard, 1970, 377pp.

375. ————. *Los Marxismos imaginarios de Sartre a Althusser*. Trans. Martin Sagrera. Caracas: Monte Avila, 1969.

376. ————. *De uma sagrada família à outra. Ensaios sôbre Sartre a Althusser*. Trans. Luís Augusto do Rosário. Rio de Janeiro: Civilização Brasileira, 1970.

377. Arvon, Henri. "Concerning Marx's Epistemological Break." *The Philosophical Forum*, 8 (Boston, 1978), 173-185.

Critical of Althusser's treatment of the development of Marx's theory of praxis because it fails to deal with the decisive influence that Bruno Bauer and Max Stirner exerted on Marx.

378. Augé, Marc. "Les Blancs du discours: l'idéologie en général, idéologie de classe et société primitive." *Dialectiques* (special issue on Althusser), nos. 15-16 (1976), pp. 95-98.

Auzias, J.-M. See chapter 7 of items 11-14.

379. Badiou, Alain. "Le (Re)commencement du matérialisme dialectique." *Critique*, 20ᵉ année, tome 23, no. 240 (May 1967), 438-467.

On *Lire le CAPITAL* and *Pour Marx*.

380. Balibar, E. "Sur la dialectique historique. Quelques remarques à propos de *Lire le CAPITAL*." *La Pensée*, no. 170 (1973), pp. 27-47.

381. Barale, Massimo. "Sul rapporto di scienza e ideologia in Althusser." *Aut Aut*, no. 111 (1969), pp. 26-39.

382. Barthélémy-Madaule, Madeleine. "Althusser et la recherche permanente." *Europe*, 53, no. 551 (March 1975), 199-202.

On *Eléments d'autocritique*.

382a. ———. "Lyssenko, une histoire terminée." *Europe*, 56, no. 587 (1978), 190-194.

On Lecourt's *Histoire réelle d'une science prolétarienne* and Althusser's preface to it (item 342).

Bauch, G. See item 4435a.

Baudry, J.-L. See item 3815.

Baum, H. See item 2760.

383. Bayón, Miguel, and Benito Seone. *Althusser, antiestalinismo, maoísmo* ... *y P.C.F.* Madrid: M. Castellote, 1976.

Belaval, Y. See items 4436 and 4437.

384. Bellu, Elena. "Raportul dintre ştiinţă şi filozofie la L. Althusser." *Revista de Filozofie*, 23, no. 6 (1976), 733-739.

Rumanian article on the relationship between science and philosophy in Althusser.

385. Bensusan, Gérard. "Comment lire Marx." *Dialectiques*, no. 15-16 (1976), pp. 130-134.

386. Besse, Guy. "Deux questions sur un article de Louis Althusser." *La Pensée*, no. 107 (1963), pp. 52-62.

On "Contradiction et surdétermination" (item 232).

Boisset, L. See item 4934.

387. Bonvecchio, Claudio. "Nota sulla transcendenza e presenza in Althusser." *Rivista Internazionale di Filosofia del Diritto*, 53 (January-March 1976), 110-115.

388. Boschetti, Franco. *Due letture di Marx. (Roger Garaudy e Louis Althusser)*. Lugano: Edizioni Pantarei, 1970, 56pp.

389. Bottigelli, Emile. "En lisant Althusser." *Raison Présente*, no. 2 (February-April 1967), pp. 83-96.

390. Botturi, Francesco. *Struttura e soggettività. Saggio su Bachelard e Althusser*. Milan: Vita e Pensiero, 1976.

Bouché, C. See item 3885.

391. Bourdieu, P. "La Lecture de Marx ou quelques remarques critiques à propos de 'Quelques critiques à propos de *Lire le CAPITAL*.'" *Actes de la Recherche en Sciences Sociales*, no. 5-6 (1975), pp. 65-79.

392. Bozal, Valeriano, "La Problematicidad de la dialectica." *Teorema*, 1 (March 1971), 31-42.

*393. Brandt, Per Aage. "Fiktion og filosofi: Althussers noter om et materialistik teater." *Exil*, 8 årg., nr. 3-4 (31-32) (October 1975), 56-87.

394. ———. "Fiction et philosophie: les notes d'Althusser sur un théâtre matérialiste." *Revue Romane*, 12, no. 1 (1977) 14-38.

395. Brewster, Ben. "Presentation of Althusser." *New Left Review*, 41 (January-February 1967), 11-14.

Brown, P.L. See item 4447.

396. Buci-Glucksmann, Christine. "Sur la critique de gauche du Stalinisme." *Dialectiques*, no. 15-16 (1976), pp. 25-36.

397. Callinicos, Alex. *Althusser's Marxism*. London: Pluto Press, 1976.

398. Camporeale, Ignazio, and Felice M. Verde. "Resoconto di un recente debattito su 'dialettica hegeliana e dialettica marxista.'" *Sapienza*, 18 (1965), 475-497.

On Althusser's "Contradiction et surdétermination" (item 232).

399. Cardoso, Fernando H. "Althussérisme ou marxisme? A propos du concept de classe chez Poulantzas." *L'Homme et la Société*, no. 24-25 (1972), pp. 57-71.

400. Cardoso, Henrique. *Althusserismo o marxismo*. Trans. Enrique Oltra. Barcelona: A. Redondo, 1973.

401. Cardoso e Cunha, T. "Ciência e história no marxismo de Louis Althusser. I." *Vertice*, 36, no. 386-387 (1976), 147-168.

402. ———. "Ciência e história no marxismo de Louis Althusser. II. O continente história." *Vertice*, 36, no. 388-389 (1976), 232-250.

403. Châtelet, François. "Réponse à Raymond Aron: 'Il s'agit de savoir ce qu'on appelle la gauche....'" *Le Nouvel Observateur*, no. 120 (1-9 March 1967), pp. 45-46.

———. See also item 41.

404. Cheţan, Octavian. "Texte et contexte. Commentaire critique." *Revue Roumaine des Sciences Sociales, Série de Philosophie et Logique*, 15, no. 1 (1971), 83-95.

A critique of Althusser's interpretation of a passage in Marx's *Idéologie allemande*.

405. ———. "L'Humanisme et les difficultés de l'ambiguïté théorique." *Cahiers Roumains d'Etudes Littéraires*, no. 2 (1974), pp. 53-62.

Althusser's theoretical anti-humanism.

406. ———. "Humanism and the Difficulties Caused by the Theoretical Polysemanticism of This Notion" (in Russian). *Voprosy Filosofii*, no. 5 (1970), pp. 112-119.

A critique of Althusser's theoretical anti-humanism.

407. Chiari, Joseph. "Structuralism: Claude Lévi-Strauss, Michel Foucault, Louis Althusser." Chapter 10 of item 4464.

408. Coin, Jean-Pierre. "De la logique interne des déviations." *Dialectiques*, no. 15-16 (1976), pp. 161-169.

409. Comolli, G. "Althusser e la psicanalisi." *Aut Aut*, no. 141 (1974), pp. 61-70.

410. Conilh, Jean. "Lecture de Marx (Louis Althusser)." *Esprit*, 35e année, no. 360 (May 1967), 882-901.

Althusser's "symptomal" reading of Marx gives Marxist thought the creative vitality it seems to have lost.

411. Cornforth, Maurice. "Some Comments on Louis Althusser's Reply to John Lewis." *Marxism Today*, 17, no. 5 (May 1973), 139-147.

412. Corvez, Maurice. "Le Structuralisme marxiste de Louis Althusser," chapter 5 of items 49-51.

Cotroneo, G. See item 4362.

413. Cranston, Maurice. "Ideology of Althusser." *Problems of Communism*, 22 (March 1973), 53-60.

414. Crespo, Luis. "Louis Althusser en Espagne (1966-1976)." Trans. Solange Ouvrard. *Dialectiques*, no. 15-16 (1976), pp. 57-63.

Daix, Pierre. See item 2128.

D'Amico, R. See item 57.

415. De Dijn, H. "Spinoza en Althusser over ideologie." *Bijdragen*, 38 (1977), 234-247. English summary: Spinoza and Althusser on Ideology, pp. 247-248.

416. Deguy, Michel. "Althusser: Lénine et la philosophie." *Cahiers du Chemin*, no. 10 (October 1970), pp. 159-170.

417. Demailly, Lise. "Autour de l'école: Contradictions et effets du discours althussérien." *Dialectiques*, no. 15-16 (1976), pp. 105-117.

418. Deprun, Jean. "Y a-t-il une 'pratique théorique'?" *Raison Présente*, no. 6 (April-June 1968), pp. 53-60.

419. *Dialectiques*, no. 15-16 (1976): special issue on Althusser. Contains items 378, 385, 396, 408, 414, 417, 444, 459, 485, 507, 508, 529, 538, 559, 567, 575, and 599.

420. Diaz, Carlos. "Marxismos, hoy." *Pensamiento*, 29, no. 114-115 (April 1973), 195-207.

421. Di Giovanni, M. "L'Autocritica di Althusser." *Aquinas*, 18 (1975), 385-403.

422. Domenach, Jean-Marie, and Madeleine Barthélémy-Madaule. "Althusser et ses critiques." *Esprit*, no. 449 (September 1975), pp. 213-219.

423. Droit, Roger-Pol. "Pour lire Althusser..." *Le Monde* [*des Livres*], no. 9089 (5 April 1974), p. 18.

424. ———. "Le Cas Althusser." *Le Monde* [*des Livres*], no. 9339 (24 January 1975), p. 16.

    Dufrenne, M. See item 4493.

425. Duhamel, Alain. "Centrés sur les oeuvres d'Althusser et de Garaudy les débats idéologiques du parti communiste manifestent une volonté d'approfondissement." *Le Monde*, no. 6703 (2 August 1966), p. 6.

426. Dupré, Louis. "Dialectical Philosophy Before and After Marx." *New Scholasticism*, 46 (Fall 1972), 488-511.

    On *For Marx* and *Reading Capital*.

427. Džioev, O. "The Anti-historicism of Louis Althusser" (in Russian). *Macne Vestnik Serija Filosofii, Psikhologii, Ekonomikii Prava*, no. 3 (1971), pp. 7-17.

    Eagleton, T. See item 4364.

    Ela, J.-M. See item 4966.

428. Errera, Roger. "Les Exigences d'un philosophe marxiste: Louis Althusser." *Signes du Temps*, no. 11 (November 1966), pp. 18-21.

429. Estanqueiro Rocha, Acílio. "Dialéctica e ideologia em Althusser." *Revista Portuguesa de Filosofia*, 32, no. 3-4 (1976), 305-324.

429a. ———. "Acerca da dialéctica marxista: totalidade, sujeito e sociedade." *Revista Portuguesa de Filosofia*, 35 (January-June 1979), 67-92.

430. Evangelista, Walter. "Dialectique et scientificité d'après Louis Althusser." Doctoral dissertation, Institut Supérieur de Philosophie, Université Catholique de Louvain, 10 January

1974, reported in *Revue Philosophique de Louvain*, 73, no. 20
(November 1975), 713.

431. Evangelista, Walter José. "Sur deux concepts fondamentaux dans
      la recherche althussérienne." *Kriterion*, no. 69 (Belo Horizonte,
      MG, 1976), pp. 92-116.

432. Fausto, Ray. "Althussérisme et anthropologisme." *L'Homme et la
      Société*, no. 40-41 (July-September 1976; October-December
      1976), pp. 85-104.

433. Forquin, J.C. "Lecture d'Althusser." *Les Cahiers du Centre
      d'Etudes Socialistes*, no. 76-81 (1968), pp. 7-31.

434. Fougeyrollas, Pierre. "Althusser [ou] la scolastique de la
      bureaucratie." In his item 78, pp. 135-185.

435. Fraser, J. "Structuralist Analysis in Contemporary Social
      Thought. A Comparison of the Theories of Claude Lévi-Strauss
      and Louis Althusser by M. Glucksmann: extended review."
      Sociological Review, n.s. 23 (February 1975), 178-187.

436. ————. "Louis Althusser on Science, Marxism and Politics."
      Science and Society, 40, no. 4 (Winter 1976-1977), 438-464.

      Funt, D.W. See item 4520.

437. Furet, François, comp. "La Gauche meurt-elle d'avoir gagné?...
      Un Entretien avec Raymond Aron." *Le Nouvel Observateur*,
      no. 120 (1-8 March 1967), pp. 40-44.

438. Gabel, Joseph. "Hungarian Marxism." *Telos*, 25 (Fall 1975),
      185-191.

439. ————. "Signification idéologique du phénomène althussérien."
      L'Homme et la Société, no. 41-42 (July-September 1976;
      October-December 1976), pp. 105-110.

439a. Geerlandt, Robert. *Garaudy et Althusser. Le Débat dans le
      parti communiste français et son enjeu*. Paris: Presses
      Universitaires de France, 1978, 150pp. (Travaux et recherches
      de l'Université du droit et de la santé de Lille. Série
      Droit public et science politique, 2)

440. George, François. "Lire Althusser." *Les Temps Modernes*, 24,
      no. 275 (May 1969), 1921-1962.

441. ————. "Reading Althusser." *Telos*, 6 (Spring 1971), 73-98.

442. ————. "L'Efficace du vrai." *Les Temps Modernes*, 31, no. 352
      (1975), 592-623.

443. Geras, Norman. "Althusser's Marxism: An Account and Assessment."
      New Left Review, no. 71 (January-February 1972), pp. 57-86.

444. Gerratana, Valentino. "Sur les difficultés de l'analyse du
      stalinisme." Trans. Jean Rony. *Dialectiques*, no. 15-16 (1976),
      pp. 43-53.

445. ———. "Althusser and Stalinism." Trans. P. Camiller. *New
      Left Review*, no. 101-102 (February-April 1977), pp. 111-121.

446. Giner, Salvador, and Juan Salcedo. "Ideological Practice of
      Nicos Poulantzas." *European Journal of Sociology*, 17, no. 2
      (1976), 344-365.

447. Giovanni, M. di. "L'Autocritica di Althusser." *Aquinas*, 18,
      no. 3 (1975), 385-403.

448. Glucksmann, André. "Un Structuralisme ventriloque." *Les Temps
      Modernes*, 22, no. 250 (1967), 1557-1598.

      About Althusser's works on Marx.

449. ———. *Althusser: un estructuralismo ventrílocuo*. Trans.
      Jordi Mafrá. Barcelona: Ed. Anagrama, 1971.

450. ———. "A Ventriloquist Structuralism." *New Left Review*, 72
      (March-April 1972), 68-92.

451. Glucksmann, Miriam. *Structuralist Analysis in Contemporary
      Thought. A Comparison of the Theories of Claude Lévi-Strauss
      and Louis Althusser*. London-Boston: Routledge and Kegan Paul,
      1974. Originally the author's thesis at the University of
      London. Bibliography, pp. 182-193.

452. Goldstick, Danny. "On the Dialectics of the Lewis-Althusser
      Debate." *Marxism Today*, 17, no. 12 (December 1973), 381-384.

*453. ———. "Reading Althusser." *Revolutionary World*, no. 23-25
      (1977), pp. 110-132.

      The coherence of Althusser's "Marxism" is assailed from the
      standpoint of Engels' theory of knowledge.

453a. ———. "Reading Althusser" (in Polish). *Studia Filozoficzne*,
      no. 5 (1978), pp. 67-86. Trans. of item 453.

454. González Rojo, Enrique. *Para leer a Althusser*. Mexico: Diógenes,
      1974, 144pp.

455. Grampa, Giuseppe. "L'Autocritica di Louis Althusser." *Salesianum*,
      38 (1976), 87-108.

456. Grant, D.D. "The Althusser Debate." *Marxism Today*, 17, no. 8
      (August 1973), 253-256.

457. Gray, Gordon. "The Althusser Debate." *Marxism Today*, 17, no. 7
      (July 1973), 220-221.

458. Grivel, Charles. "L'Opération littéraire institutionnelle
      (Quelques thèses d'esthétique marxiste althussérienne)."
      Rapports/Het Franse Boek, 36e année, no. 2 (March 1976), 64-67.

458a. Guichard, J. "Louis Althusser ou la philosophie comme arme de
      la révolution." *Lettre*, no. 233-234 (1978), pp. 186-197.

459. Guillaume, Marc. "Requiem pour la superstructure." *Dialectiques*,
      no. 15-16 (1976), pp. 99-104.

460. Guitton, Jean. *Journal de ma vie. 1. Présence du passé.* Paris:
      Desclée de Brouwer, 1976.

461. Harrington, William. "Blood and Guts Politics from the Italian
      Left." *Tribune*, 37, no. 13 (30 March 1973), 6.

462. Hawthorn, Geoffrey. "All in the Mind." *New Society*, 16 December
      1976, pp. 581-582.

463. Heeger, R. "Louis Althussers marxistische Hermeneutik: eine
      Kritik." *Neue Zeitschrift für systematische Theologie und
      Religionsphilosophie*, 13, no. 1 (1971), 22-43.

      Hefner, R.W. See item 4312.

464. Hesse, Mary. "Criteria of Truth in Science and Theology."
      Religious Studies, 11 (December 1975), 385-400.

465. Hirst, P.Q. "Althusser and the Theory of Ideology." *Economy
      and Society*, 5, no. 4 (1976), 385-412.

      A critical discussion of Althusser's *Idéologie et appareils
      idéologiques d'Etat*. Althusser's answer to the problem of the
      reproduction of the relationships of production and his concept
      of representation are both critically evaluated.

465a. Hirst, Paul. *On Law and Ideology.* Atlantic Highlands, N.J.:
      Humanities Press, 1979, 181pp.

      On Althusser's theory of ideology and the crucial role played
      by the use of his concept of "imaginary relation."

466. Hobsbawm, Eric John. "The Structure of Capital." In his *Revolu-
      tionaries. Contemporary Essays.* New York: Pantheon Books,
      1973, pp. 142-152.

467. Howard, D. "Fétichisme, aliénation et théorie critique: ré-
      flexions sur un manuscrit de Marx publié récemment." *L'Homme
      et la Société*, no. 17 (1970), pp. 97-110.

      One cannot, as Althusser maintains, speak of a "radical
      break" between the young Marx and the Marx of the *Capital*.

468. Invitto, Giovanni. *I Filosofi dimissionari.* Lecce: Messapica,
      1974.

469. Ionescu, Ghita. "Infernal Logic." *New Society*, 22, no. 532
      (14 December 1972), 648.

470. Ipola, Emilio de. "Critique de la théorie d'Althusser sur
      l'idéologie." *L'Homme et la Société*, no. 41-42 (July-September
      1976; October-December 1976), pp. 35-70.

Jaeggi, Urs Josef Viktor. See items 108 and 4378.

471. ———. "Theorie der Geschichte: Geschichte der Theorie?" *Das Argument*, 17, no. 94 (1975), 952-975.

Jameson, F. See item 4172.

Jannoud, C. See item 4379.

471a. Jay, M. "The Concept of Totality in Lukács and Adorno." *Telos*, no. 32 (1977), pp. 117-137.

Adorno and Althusser are used to criticize Lukács' concept of totality. Adorno from inside the humanist camp and Althusser from outside come together to destroy the foundations of Lukács' thought. This strange alliance between Adorno and Althusser is explained by analyzing their relationship to Hegel.

472. Johnson, Douglas. "Philosophy and the Crisis of French Communism." *New Statesman*, 96 (7 June 1978), 14.

473. Johnson, Richard. "Strategy and Enlightenment: A Critical Study of the 'Marxisms' of Jean-Paul Sartre and Louis Althusser." *Dissertation Abstracts International*, 37, no. 12 (June 1977), 7940-A. Yale University dissertation.

474. Juarez-Paz, Rigoberto. "El Materialismo superación o abandono de la filosofía?" *Revista Latinoamericana de Filosofía*, 1 (May 1975), 57-60.

475. Kahn, Jean-François, and Georges Suffert. "Deux Philosophes secouent le vieux cocotier marxiste." *L'Express*, no. 797 (26 September-2 October 1966), pp. 99-101.

475a. Kaisergruber, David. "Les Ruses linguistiques de l'histoire. Analyse de la réponse à John Lewis de Louis Althusser." *Dialectiques*, no. 20 (1977), pp. 59-73.

475b. ———. "Althusser, une nouvelle lecture de Marx." In *Les Dieux dans la cuisine. Vingt ans de philosophie en France.* Ed. Jean-Jacques Brochier. Paris: Aubier, 1978, pp. 63-67.

476. Kaminski, Winfred. *Zur Dialektik von Substanz und Subjekt bei Hegel und Marx.* Frankfurt am Main: Haag und Herchen, 1976. Originally presented as the author's thesis, Frankfurt am Main.

477. Karhausen, L.R. "Althusser et les deux Marx." *La Pensée et les Hommes*, 18, no. 4 (Brussels, 1975-1976), 89-97.

Maintains that the epistemological break that Althusser finds in Marx is a myth.

478. Karsz, Saül. "Après Althusser." *Aletheia*, no. 6 (April 1967), pp. 232-239.

479.   ———. Théorie et politique: Louis Althusser. Avec quatre
         textes inédits de L. Althusser. Paris: Fayard, 1974, 340pp.
         Bibliography, pp. 335-340.

480.   ———. *Teoria e politica: Louis Althusser. Con quattro testi*
         inediti di Louis Althusser. Trans. A. Cairoli. Bari: Dedalo
         Libri, 1976, 382pp.

481.   ———. *Theorie und Politik, Louis Althusser. Mit 4 Texten*
         von Louis Althusser. Trans. Erika Höhnisch. Frankfurt am
         Main-Vienna: Ullstein, 1976.

482.   Kaufmann, J.N. "Structural Analysis in Contemporary Social
         Thought. A Comparison of the Theories of Claude Lévi-Strauss
         and Louis Althusser, par Miriam Glucksmann." *Dialogue,* 15,
         no. 1 (March 1976), 184-186.

483.   Kelly, Michael. "Louis Althusser and Marxist Theory." *Journal*
         of European Studies, 7 (September 1977), 189-203.

         Kintzler, J.-M. See item 4589.

484.   Kozyr-Kowalski, S. "How (Not) to Read L. Althusser?" (in Polish).
         Studia Filozoficzne, 17, no. 8 (1973), 35-69.

485.   Labica, Georges. "Pour tout capital: Lire Marx." *Dialectiques,*
         no. 15-16 (1976), pp. 149-155.

486.   Laclau, E. "The Specificity of the Political: the Poulantzas-
         Miliband Debate." Trans. E. Nash and W. Rich. *Economy and*
         Society, 4, no. 1 (1975), 87-110.

         On the Althusserian school.

         Lacroix, Jean. "Althusser et le marxisme," chapter 13, part
         II of item 4600 (1968), pp. 188-195. See also item 488.

487.   ———. "Lénine et la philosophie." *Le Monde,* no. 7524 (23-23
         March 1969), p. 11.

488.   ———. "Althusser et le marxisme." *Cahiers Universitaires*
         Catholiques, 5 (1974), 19-25.

         A summary of the general features of Althusser's thought.

489.   ———. "Thèse à Amiens: Althusser retrace son itinéraire."
         Le Monde, no. 9470 (2 July 1975), pp. 1, 20.

490.   ———. "La Philosophie: Louis Althusser." *Le Monde*
         [Aujourd'hui], no. 9739 (16-17 May 1976), p. 25.

491.   Lafrance, Y. "La Critique de la philosophie de l'Etat de Hegel
         par K. Marx (par. 261-274)." *Dialogue,* 15, no. 1 (1976),
         75-91.

         Vs. Althusser.

492. Lagueux, M. "L'Inutile insistance sur le rapport des instances."
     Dialogue, 13, no. 4 (1974), 707-721.

     A critique of Althusser, Balibar and Poulantzas.

493. Lantz, P. "Le Marxisme, Althusser et les sciences humaines."
     In *La Dialectique*. Actes du XIVe Congrès des Sociétés de
     Philosophie de Langue Française. (Nice, 1-4 September 1969)
     Paris: Presses Universitaires de France, 1969, pp. 187-190.

494. Latorre, Pasquale. *Scienza e ideologia: la sfida antistoricista
     e antiumanista di Louis Althusser*. Rome: LAS, 1976. Bibliog-
     raphy, pp. 197-208. (Studia philosphica, 7) (Publicationes
     Pontificiae universitatis Salesianae)

495. Lecercle, Jean-Jacques. "Althusser and Marxist Philosophy."
     Cambridge Review, 91, no. 2194 (30 January 1970), 80-83.

496. Lefèbvre, Henri. "Les Paradoxes d'Althusser." *L'Homme et la
     Société*, 13 (1969), 3-37. Rpt. in his item 125, pp. 371-417.

497. Levasseur, C. "L. Althusser et N. Poulantzas 'Eléments pour
     une théorie marxiste de l'idéologie.'" Thesis presented at
     the Ecole des Gradués in July 1974, Université Laval, Départe-
     ment de Science Politique, Faculté des Sciences Sociales.

498. Lévy, Bernard-Henri. "Le Meiller thème d'Althusser." *Le Nouvel
     Observateur*, no. 556 (7-13 July 1975), pp. 61-62.

499. Lewis, John. "The Althusser Case. Part 1. Marxist Humanism."
     Marxism Today, 16, no. 1 (January 1972), 23-28.

500. ———. "The Althusser Case. Part II." *Marxism Today*, 16, no.
     2 (February 1972), 43-48.

501. ———. "On the Althusser Discussion." *Marxism Today*, 18,
     no. 6 (June 1974), 168-174.

     Leyvraz, J.-P. See items 133-134.

501a. Liebich, A. "Hegel, Marx, and Althusser." *Politics and Society*,
     9, no. 1 (1979), 89-102.

502. Lipietz, A. "D'Althusser à Mao?" *Les Temps Modernes*, 29, no.
     328 (1973), 749-787.

502a. Lisbonne, B. *Des défenseurs révisionnistes de la dictature
     du prolétariat: Althusser, Balibar et compagnie*. Paris:
     Nouveau Bureau d'Edition, 1976.

502b. Livi, Antonio. *Louis Althusser. La Revolución teórica de Marx
     y Para leer El Capital*. Madrid: Magisterio Español, 1979,
     152pp.

503. Lock, Grahame. "Althusser: Philosophy as a Weapon of the Revolu-
     tion." *Cambridge Review*, 93, no. 2204 (22 October 1971), 25-28.

504.   ———. "Louis Althusser: Philosophy and Leninism." *Marxism Today*, 16, no. 6 (June 1972), 180–187.

505.   ———. "Red Reading." *Cambridge Review*, 95, no. 2219 (March 1974), 96–99.

506.   ———. "French Philosophy and the Chinese Enigma" (in Dutch). *De Gids*, no. 1–2 (1976), pp. 48–58.

        On the problem of the state.

507.   ———. "Althusser en Angleterre." Trans. Jean-Claude Chaumette. *Dialectiques*, no. 15–16 (1976), pp. 64–72.

508.   ———. "Humanisme et lutte de classes dans l'histoire du mouvement communiste." Trans. Yannick Blanc. *Dialectiques*, no. 15–16 (1976), pp. 7–24.

508a.   Longhin, Luigi. "Analisi della società negli scritti di Louis Althusser." *Fenomenologia e Società*, 1, no. 1 (1977–1978), 52–75.

509.   Lopes, Sérgio. "Ideologia e prática social." *Analise Social*, 10, no. 4 (1973–1974), 656–678.

*510.   Lowy, M. "L'Humanisme historiciste de Marx ou relire le *Capital*." *L'Homme et la Société*, no. 17 (1970), pp. 111–125.

        Althusser's "anti-humanistic" reading is in contradiction not only with those works which he throws into the purgatory of the "coupure" and the "mature" period, but also with the *Capital* itself.

511.   ———. "El Humanismo historicista de Marx, o releer el Capital." *Revista Mexicana de Ciencia Politica*, 19, no. 73 (1973), 65–74.

        A critique of Althusser.

512.   Lubasz, Heinz. "The Mandarin versus the Tribune." *The Times Higher Education Supplement*, no. 248 (23 July 1976), p. 76.

513.   Luporini, Cesare. "Réflexions sur Louis Althusser." *L'Homme et la Société*, 4 (April–June 1967), 23–36.

514.   Lyotard, J.-F. "La Place de l'aliénation dans le retournement marxiste." *Les Temps Modernes*, 25, no. 277–278 (1969), 92–160.

        The Marxist interpretation that Althusser gives constitutes a new alienation, not by what it signifies, but in its very position of discourse.

*515.   Macchiocchi, Maria Antonietta. *Lettere dall'interno del P.C.I. a Louis Althusser*. Milan: Feltrinelli, 1969.

        A collection of letters exchanged between Macchiocchi and Althusser from February, 1968 through March, 1969. Macchiocchi, a former journalist, describes how she became a candidate for the Communists in Naples and won her seat in the 1968 election. See also item 274.

516. ————. *Lettres de l'intérieur du Parti, le parti communiste, les masses et les forces révolutionnaires pendant la campagne electorale à Naples en mai 1968.* Paris: F. Maspero, 1970.

517. ————. *Letters from Inside the Italian Communist Party to Louis Althusser.* Trans. Stephen M. Hellman. 2nd ed. London: New Left Books, 1973.

518. ————. *Letters from Inside the Italian Communist Party to Louis Althusser.* Atlantic Highlands, N.J.: Humanities Press, 1975.

519. MacRae, Donald. "Marx Men." *New Society,* 15, no. 382 (22 January 1970), 145-146.

520. Madelin, H. "De l'idéologie à l'utopie." *Projet,* no. 56 (1971), pp. 728-738.

Part of the issue entitled "Anatomie politique des Français," this article examines the function of ideology in Marx, Engels, Althusser, and Marcuse. Utopia is defined as the fabric of social dynamics.

521. Mandel, Ernest. *Contra Althusser.* Trans. Ramón Ballester. Barcelona: Madragora, 1975.

522. Manieri, Maria Rosaria. "Una Lettura disideologizzante di Marx: L. Althusser." *Logos,* no. 2 (1971), pp. 227-275.

522a. Manschot, H. "Althussers filosofisch structuralisme." *Wijsgerig Perspectief op Maatschappij en Wetenschap,* 19 (1978-1979), 16-22.

523. Mantovani, Giuseppe. "Sul marxismo strutturalista di Althusser." *Rivista di Filosofia Neo-Scolastica,* 59 (1967), 726-751.

524. Mariano Júnior, Júlio. "Uma leitura de Althusser." *Reflexão,* 2 (1977), 443-461.

525. Marín Morales, José Alberto. "Montesquieu, visto por Louis Althusser." *Arbor,* 90 (1975), 247-264.

Martano, G. See item 4638.

McDonell, D.J. See item 2214.

526. Mehlman, J. "Teaching Reading: The Case of Marx in France." *Diacritics,* 6, no. 4 (1976), 10-18.

On item 565.

527. Milanesi, V. "Althusser, Garaudy, Goldmann: antiumanismo e umanismo teorico nel marxismo francese contemporaneo." *Studia Patavina. Rivista di Scienze Religiose,* 23, no. 2 (1976), 297-324.

Millet, L., et al. See Items 147-149.

528. Minogue, K.R. "Recent Discussions from Machiavelli to Althusser:
      Review Article." *Political Studies*, 23 (March 1975), 95-100.

      Miščevic, N. See item 4386.

529. Montanari, M., and F. Fistetti. "Transition révolutionnaire
      et dialectique matérialiste: historicisme et anti-historicisme
      dans le marxisme italien." Trans. C. Lazzeri, Y. Blanc, and
      D. Kaisergruber. *Dialectiques*, no. 15-16 (1976), pp. 73-80.

530. Moravia, Sergio. "Althusser, il filosofo che condanna la
      filosofia." *Tuttolibri*, no. 36 (10 July 1976), p. 4.

531. Morot-Sir, Edouard. "Louis Althusser à la recherche d'une
      théorie marxiste," section 4 of chapter 5 of his item 4653,
      pp. 78-81.

532. Munišić, Z. "Ideologies and Althusser's Philosophy of Sciences.
      I" (in Serbo-Croatian). *Delo*, 19, no. 12 (1973), 1618-1631.

533. Murguia, A. "Anotacion acerca del tema del hombre nuevo."
      Stromata, 29 (Argentina, October-December 1973), 533-536.

534. Mury, Gilbert. "Matérialisme et hyperempirisme." *La Pensée*,
      no. 108 (1963), pp. 38-51.

      On Althusser's item 232.

535. Nagels, Jacques. "Utilisation d'un modèle épistémologique comme
      instrument de critique (Etude de la conception althussérienne
      de la théorie de la connaissance de Marx à partir d'un modèle
      épistémologique.)." *Annales de l'Institut de Philosophie*
      (Brussels, 1972), pp. 117-181.

536. Nancy, J.-L. Review of Althusser's *Lire LE CAPITAL I-II* and
      Pour Marx. *Esprit*, 34, no. 5 (1966), 1074-1087.

536a. Nelisse, C. "Jeux et enjeux de l'idéologie." Thèse de doctorat
      troisième cycle, U.E.R. de Sociologie-Ethnologie, Université
      de Provence, 405pp. No publisher or date given, but probably
      1978 or earlier.

      One of the theories treated is Althusser's.

537. Nepi, P. "Strutturalismo e rinnovamento del marxismo contempo-
      raneo." *Studium*, 72, no. 6 (Rome, 1976), 787-802.

538. Normand, Claudine. "Pour une certitude inquiète." *Dialectiques*,
      no. 15-16 (1976), pp. 156-160.

539. Núñez Tenorio, J.R. *Humanismo, estructuralismo y marxismo:
      Sartre, Althusser, Marx*. Caracas: Ediciones de la Facultad
      de Humanidades y Educación, Universidad Central de Venezuela,
      1976, 213pp.

540. Oakley, John. "Marxism and Ideology. II. Althusser and Ideology." *Marxism Today*, 16, no. 9 (September 1972), 276-281.

541. O'Neill, John. "For Marx Against Althusser." *Human Context*, 6 (1974), 385-398.

542. ————. "Theorie und Kritik bei Marx." *Kölner Zeitschrift für Soziologie und Sozialpsychologie*, 28, no. 3 (1976), 405-425.

543. Orozco Silva, Luis Enrique. "Spécificité de la dialectique marxiste. A propos de la noétique de Louis Althusser." Doctoral dissertation, Institut Supérieur de Philosophie, Université Catholique de Louvain, 18 January 1973, reported in *Revue Philosophique de Louvain*, 71, no. 12 (November 1973), 830-832.

544. ————. "¿Marxismo o Althusseranismo?" *Razón y Fábula*, nos. 40-41 (Bogotá, 1976), pp. 7-44.

545. Otero, M.H. "Tres modalidades de immanentismo." *Dianoia*, 21, no. 21 (1975), 182-195.

546. Palma, Norman. "Het Marxisme en zijn perspektief. Dialoog met Louis Althusser en Raymond Aron." Trans. Hubert Vandenbossche. *Dialoog*, 12 (1971-1972), 232-261.

547. Panach, Emilio. "Althusser: causalidad estructural." *Teorema*, no. 4 (1971), pp. 85-96.

Parain-Vial, J. See item 3721.

548. Paris, Robert. "En deçà du marxisme." *Les Temps Modernes*, 21, no. 240 (1966), 1983-2002.

On Althusser's *Pour Marx*.

549. Peyret, Jean-François. "Althusser ou l'éternel détour." *Le Nouvel Observateur*, no. 546 (28 April-4 May 1975), pp. 72-73.

550. Pieri, Sergio. "Althusser in Italia [Rassegna bibliografica su Althusser]." *Aut Aut*, no. 135 (1973), pp. 93-110.

Pingaud, B. See item 4704.

551. Plaut, Martin. "Positivism in Poulantzas." *Telos*, Summer 1978, pp. 159-167.

Examines certain of Poulantzas' key concepts by considering their origins in Althusser. The positivism that undermines Poulantzas is traced to the scientism that Althusser adopts in his attack on humanism.

552. Ponikowski, Bogusław. "Althusser i marksizma." *Studia Filozoficzne*, no. 7 (1975), pp. 43-57.

On Althusser's *Réponse à John Lewis*.

553.   Pop, T. "The Young Marx and Feuerbach" (in Rumanian). *Studia Universitatis Babeş-Bolyai. Series Philosophia*, 18 (1973), 133-141.

       Versus Althusser.

554.   Poster, Mark. "Althusser on History Without Man." *Political Theory*, 2, no. 4 (November 1974), 393-409.

       ———. See item 4393.

555.   Poulantzas, Nicos. *Pouvoir politique et classes sociales*. 2 vols. Paris: Maspero, 1970.

       Inspired by Althusser.

556.   ———. *Les Classes sociales dans le capitalisme aujourd'hui*. Paris: Editions du Seuil, 1974.

       Inspired by Althusser.

557.   Prado Júnior, Caio. *O Estruturalismo de Lévi-Strauss [e] o marxismo de Louis Althusser*. São Paulo: Editôra Brasiliense, 1971.

558.   Projekt Klassenanalyse. *Louis Althusser. Marxistische Kritik am Stalinismus?* Berlin: Verlag für das Studium der Arbeiterbewegung, 1975.

559.   ———. "Louis Althusser--lutte contre la déchéance de la théorie de Marx." *Dialectiques*, no. 15-16 (1976), pp. 118-129.

560.   Prontera, Angelo. *Il Naufragio della libertà (Saggio su L. Althusser)*. Manduria: Lacaita, 1972. Bibliography by and about Althusser, pp. 245-255. (Biblioteca di ricerca politica, 2)

561.   Quintanilla, M.A. "Notas para una teoría postanalítica de la ciencia." *Revista de Occidente* (issue entitled "Análisis y dialéctica"), no. 138 (1974), pp. 252-282.

       Rancière, Jacques. See item 4396.

562.   ———. "Sur la théorie de l'idéologie. Politique d'Althusser." *L'Homme et la Société*, 27 (January-March 1973), 31-61. Italian trans. and rpt., item 566.

563.   ———. "Mode d'emploi pour une réédition de *Lire le Capital*." *Les Temps Modernes*, 29, no. 328 (1973), 788-807.

564.   ———. "La Nuova ortodossia di Louis Althusser." *Aut Aut*, no. 138 (1973), pp. 73-77.

565.   ———. *La Leçon d'Althusser*. Paris: Gallimard, 1974, 277pp.

566.   ————. *Ideologia e politica in Althusser*. Milan: Feltrinelli, 1974, 51pp. Trans. of item 562.

567.   Raymond, Pierre. "... Et la théorie dans la lutte des classes." *Dialectiques*, no. 15-16 (1976), pp. 137-148.

568.   Regnier, A. "Les Surprises de l'idéologie Heisenberg et Althusser." *L'Homme et la Société*, no. 15 (1970), pp. 241-253.

Part of an issue entitled "Marxisme et sciences humaines." Examines the "scientistic" conceptions of Heisenberg and Althusser; the "epistemological break" in Althusser; and how to found scientific knowledge by separating science from ideology.

569.   Revel, Jean-François. "Marx mis à la retraite par ses célibataires mêmes." In *Contrecensures. Politique, religion, culture de masse, art et critique d'art, enseignement, avant-garde, philosophie et sciences humaines, auteurs incompris, antisémitisme*. Paris: Jean-Jacques Pauvert, 1966, pp. 268-274.

On Althusser's *Pour Marx*.

570.   *Revista de Filozofie*, 22, no. 1 (1975), 45-72: section devoted to "Contemporary Opinions in the Problematic of Marxist Philosophy. Louis Althusser" (in Rumanian).

571.   Rheinberger, H.J. "Die erkenntnistheoretischen Auffassungen Althussers." *Das Argument*, 17, no. 94 (1975), 922-951.

571a.   ————. "Entwicklung als 'Prozess ohne Subjekt.'" *Hegel-Jahrbuch*, p. vol. (1976, appeared in 1978), 268-276.

The Lenin-Hegel relation as seen by Althusser.

571b.   Ricci, F. "Le Bâton courbé." *Annales de la Faculté des Lettres et Sciences Humaines de Nice*, no. 32 (1977), pp. 117-129.

"When a stick is bent in one direction, it must be bent in the other direction." This idea, which Althusser presented during his doctoral defense at Amiens as characterizing Marxism, is already in the Cartesian experience of doubting and thinking. But the question arises whether the application of counter-forces won't eventually lead to deviations.

Rivelaygue, J. See item 4740.

572.   Robert, Jean-Dominique. "Rapports de l'idéologique, du scientifique et du philosophique chez Althusser, d'après ses écrits les plus récents (1968-1970)." *Tijdschrift voor Filosofie*, 33 (June 1971), 279-382. Bibliography, pp. 376-382.

573.   ————. "Autour d'Althusser. I. Les Positions noétiques de base chez Althusser d'après M. J.-C. Forquin." *Archives de Philosophie*, 35, no. 1 (1972), 127-147.

574.   ————. "Autour d'Althusser. II. La Connaissance comme production. Critique de cette 'catégorie.'" *Archives de Philosophie*, 35, no. 4 (1972), 611-648.

575. Robin, Régine, and Jacques Guilhaumou. "L'Identité retrouvée."
     Dialectiques, no. 15-16 (1976), pp. 37-42.

576. Rocha, Acílio Estanqueiro. "Dialectica e ideologia em Althusser."
     Revista Portuguesa de Filosofia, 32 (July-December 1976),
     305-324.

577. Roies, Albert. *Lectura de Marx por Althusser*. Barcelona:
     Editorial Estela, 1971.

578. Rosio, Jean. "A Propos de l''articulation' des modes de produc-
     tion. Quelques réflexions sur le 'matérialisme' althussérien."
     Les Temps Modernes, 31, no. 358 (March 1976), 1462-1501.

579. Rostenne, P. "L'Aliénation rationaliste et la culture occiden-
     tale." *Giornale di Metafisica*, 26, no. 4 (1971), 309-330.

580. Roth, A. "Marxism and Structuralism" (in Rumanian). *Studia
     Universitatis Babeş-Bolyai. Series Philosophia*, 15 (1970),
     109-116.

581. Roudinesco, Elisabeth. "L'Autre de la théorie." *Action Poétique*,
     no. 53 (1973), pp. 1-6.

582. Rovatti, Pier Aldo. *Critica e scientificita in Marx. Per una
     lettura fenomenologica di Marx e una critica del marxismo di
     Althusser*. Milan: Feltrinelli, 1973.

583. ———. "Sartre e il marxismo strutturalistico." *Aut Aut*, no.
     136-137 (1973), pp. 41-64.

     Sartre vs. Althusser.

584. ———. "Filosofia e politica. Il caso Althusser." *Aut Aut*,
     no. 142-143 (1974), pp. 61-96.

585. ———. "Bruch und Grundlegung. Zu einer phänomenologischen
     Kritik an Althusser." Trans. B. Waldenfels. In *Phänomenologie
     und Marxismus*. Band I. Konzepte und Methoden. Eds. Bernhard
     Waldenfels, Jan M. Broekman and Ante Pažanin. Frankfurt am
     Main: Suhrkamp Verlag, 1977, pp. 178-196.

586. Rowinski, C. "History-Diachrony (Against Althusser)" (in
     Polish). *Studia Filozoficzne*, no. 6 (1976), pp. 95-110.

587. Roy, Claude. "Alice au pays de la logique." *Le Nouvel Observa-
     teur*, no. 123 (22-29 March 1967), pp. 34-35.

588. Rubio Carracedo, J. "Estructuralismo y estrategia política
     en L. Althusser." *Arbor*, 82, no. 319-320 (Madrid, 1972),
     37-50.

589. Sakagami, T. "Althusser and his Theory of Ideologies" (in
     Japanese). *Zinbun Gakuho*, 36 (1973), 165-187.

590. Samarskaia, E.A. "The Relationship between Science, Ideology and Philosophy in the Interpretation of L. Althusser" (in Russian). *Filosofskie Nauki*, 3 (Moscow, 1971), 138-145.

590a. Sánchez Vázquez, Adolfo. *Ciencia y revolución. El Marxismo de Althusser*. Madrid: Alianza Ed., 1978, 208pp.

591. Sandkühler, Hans Jörg. *Betr., Althusser: Kontroversen über den "Klassenkampf in der Theorie."* Cologne: Pahl-Rugenstein, c. 1977.

592. Saponaro, P. "Umanesimo e stalinismo." *Problemi del Socialismo*, 15, no. 16-17 (1973), 637-640.

593. Sasso, Javier. *La Fundamentación de la ciencia segun Althusser*. Montevideo: Fundación de Cultura Universitaria, 1970 (i.e., 1971), 42pp.

   Schaff, A. See items 4760-4762 and 4763.

*594. Schmidt, Alfred. *Geschichte und Struktur. Fragen einer marxistischen Historik*. Munich: Carl Hanser Verlag, 1971, 140pp.

   Versus the structuralist interpretation of the Paris Althusser school of thought.

595. ————. *Storia e struttura. Problemi di una teoria marxista della storia*. Trans. Giacomo Marramao. Bari: De Donato, 1972.

596. ————. *La Negazione della storia. Strutturalismo e marxismo in Althusser e Lévi-Strauss*. Trans. Giancarlo Bosetti. Milan: Lampugnani Nigri, 1972.

   On the structuralist attack on history.

597. Schmidt, Lars-Henrik. "Marxist Theory of Class Struggle." *Acta Sociologica*, 20, no. 4 (1977), 385-392.

   On Althusser's *Lire le Capital* and *Pour Marx*.

598. Schmied-Kowarzik, W. "Die Dialektik der Philosophie gegenüber der Praxis (Eine Antwort an Louis Althusser)." *Hegel-Jahrbuch*, p. vol. (1974, appeared in 1975), 496-507.

599. Schottler, Peter. "Les Eléments d'autocritique. Désaveu ou rectification?" Trans. Gerard Bensussan. *Dialectiques*, no. 15-16 (1976), pp. 81-92.

600. Schroeder, U. "Lo Strutturalismo althusseriano e la critica letteraria." *Agora. Filosofia e Cultura*, 3, no. 9 (Camerino, 1975), 5-18.

601. Schwartzman, David W. "Althusser, Dialectical Materialism and the Philosophy of Science." *Science and Society*, 39, no. 3 (Fall 1975), 318-330.

602. Segura Naya, Armando. "El Escamoteo del sujeto en el capitalismo
      metodologico de Althusser." *Convivium*, 43 (1974; appeared in
      1975), 55-74.

603. ————. *El Estructuralismo de Althusser.* Barcelona: Editorial
      Dirosa, 1976, 350pp. Originally the author's thesis, Barcelona,
      1974. (Colección Técnico-universitario, 4)

604. Sevilla, Sergio. "Dos Concepciones dialecticas de la historia
      de la filosofia." *Teorema*, 1 (March 1971), 129-138.

      On Althusser and Gramsci.

      Simon, J.K., ed. See item 4338.

605. Singer, B. Review of J. Rancière, *La Leçon d'Althusser* (item
      565). *Telos*, no. 25 (1975), pp. 224-233 (in English).

606. Sklair, Leslie. "Recent Developments in European Marxism." *New
      Humanist*, 88, no. 6 (October 1972), 225-226.

607. Skorupski, John. "For Marx, Against Althusser." *Granta*, 75, no.
      4 (March 1970), 18-19.

608. Sommet, J. *"Théorie et politique: Louis Althusser."* Archives
      de Philosophie, 38, no. 2 (April-June 1975), 345-346.

      Review of item 479.

609. Stevens, Peter. "Ideology and Schooling." *Educational Philosophy
      and Theory*, 8 (October 1976), 29-42.

610. Telez, Freddy. "L'Epistémologie althusserienne ou un positivisme
      délirant." *L'Homme et la Société*, no. 41-42 (July-December
      1976), pp. 71-84.

611. Téllez, F. "Emilio de Ipola y la teoría de la ideología o Marx
      contra Marx." *Ideas y Valores*, no. 42-45 (1973-1975), pp.
      39-60.

      Emilio de Ipola as a critical reader of Althusser.

612. Terray, Emmanuel. "Le Livre de Louis Althusser: un événement
      politique." *Le Monde*, no. 8893 (17 August 1973), p. 5.

613. Texier, Jacques. "Sur la détermination en dernière instance
      (Marx et/ou Althusser)." In *Sur la dialectique*. Ed. E. Balibar,
      et al. Paris: Editions Sociales, 1977, pp. 249-308.

614. Thoma-Herterich, C. "Althussers 'Selbstkritik.'" *Das Argument*
      (issue entitled "Antworten auf Althusser"), 17, no. 94 (1975),
      976-984.

      On Althusser's *Eléments d'autocritique*.

      Thomas, D. See item 5289.

Todisco, O. See item 4793.

615. Tomassini, R. "Per una discussione sulla nozione di 'ideologia.'" *Aut Aut*, no. 138 (1973), pp. 7-35.

616. Tosel, André. "Le Développement du marxisme en Europe occidentale depuis 1917: vers un recommencement du matérialisme dialectique en France et en Italie. Le Néo-léninisme d'Althusser et le retour à Lénine en Italie (1946-1968)." In item 4437, pp. 996-998.

617. ————. "Le Développement du marxisme en Europe occidentale depuis 1917: le néo-léninisme d'Althusser. Vers le recommencement d'un matérialisme dialectique rectifié." In item 4437, pp. 1013-1034.

Turner, B.S. See item 5292.

Vancourt, R. See item 4415.

618. Van de Putte, A. "Althusser's filosofische lectuur van Marx." *Wijsgerig Perspectief op Maatschappij en Wetenschap*, 17 (1976-1977), 33-49.

619. ————. "Althusser's theorie van de ideologie." *Bijdragen*, 38, no. 1 (1977), 44-69. English summary, pp. 70-71.

Differentiates between Althusser's materialistic theory of ideology and a formalistic theory. Explains the specific structural mechanism and the logic of the ideological instance by the concept "structure of interpellation." Ideologies are regional and related to class.

620. Vaquero, Pedro. *Althusser o el estructuralismo marxista* (estudio de una polémica entre marxistas). Algorta: Ed. Zero, 1970, 159pp. (Serie P, 17)

Veltmeyer, H. See item 4416.

621. Venault, Philippe. "Cela s'appelle *Digraphe*." *Magazine Littéraire*, no. 86 (March 1974), pp. 47-48.

An interview with Jean Ristat on Althusser, Barthes and Derrida.

622. Vigorelli, Amedeo. "Continuità e rottura in Marx: Su alcune recenti interpretazioni dei 'Grundrisse 1857-1858.'" *Aut Aut*, no. 145-146 (1975), pp. 118-126.

623. Vilar, Pierre, Boris Fraenkel, Robert Paris, Stanley Pullberg, et al. *Dialectique marxiste et pensée structurale* (à propos des travaux d'Althusser). Tables Rondes, 18 janvier-26 avril 1967. Paris: Etudes et Documentation Internationales, 1968. (Les Cahiers du Centre d'Etudes Socialistes, no. 76-81)

*624. Vilar, Pierre. "Histoire marxiste, histoire en construction.
        Essai de dialogue avec Althusser." *Annales Economies, Sociétés,
        Civilisations*, 28, no. 1 (1973), 165-198.

625.   ———. "Marxist History, a History in the Making: Towards a
        Dialogue with Althusser." *New Left Review*, no. 80 (July-August
        1973), pp. 65-106.

626.   Whitten, M. "The Althusser Debate." *Marxism Today*, 17, no. 11
        (November 1973), 348-351.

627.   Wrigley, John. "The Althusser Debate." *Marxism Today*, 17, no. 9
        (September 1973), 286-287.

628.   Zanchettin, Claudio. "L'Epistemologia marxista di Louis Althusser."
        Il Mulino, 21, no. 220 (March-April 1972), 257-280.

        Zardoya, J.M. See item 4824.

629.   Zuckerkandl, F. "Rencontre avec Louis Althusser." *Synthèses*,
        22, no. 256-257 (October-November 1967), 32-40.

REVIEWS

Eléments d'autocritique
(item 317)

630.   Anonymous. Review of *Essays in Self-Criticism. Books and Bookmen*,
        22 (July 1977), 51.

631.   ———. Review of *Essays in Self-Criticism. Choice*, 14 (November
        1977), 1228.

632.   ———. Review of *Essays in Self-Criticism. Journal of Politics*,
        40 (May 1978), 557.

633.   ———. Review of *Eléments d'autocritique. Times Literary
        Supplement*, 22 August 1975, p. 942.

633a. Arriaga de Castro, F. "Sobre as autocríticas de Althusser."
        Vertice, 37, no. 392-393 (Coimbra, 1977), 32-37.

634.   Canning, J.C., and J.D. Cockcroft. Review of *Essays in Self-
        Criticism. Monthly Review*, 30 (January 1979), 55-62.

635.   Tabaroni, N. Review of *Elementi di autocritica. Rivista Inter-
        nazionale di Filosofia del Diritto*, 53 (1976), 438-439.

See also items 363, 382, 447, 455, and 614.

Lénine et la philosophie
(items 262 and 267)

636. Anonymous. Review of *Lenin and Philosophy....* *Choice*, 9 (December 1972), 1300.

637. ————. Review of *Lenin and Philosophy....* *Kirkus Reviews*, 40 (1 June 1972), 644.

638. ————. Review of *Lenin and Philosophy....* *Times Literary Supplement*, 3 December 1971, p. 1503.

639. B., T.J. Review of *Lenin and Philosophy....* *Studies in Soviet Thought*, 12 (1972), 402.

640. Faracovi, Ornella Pompeo. Review of *Lenin e la filosofia*. *Rivista di Filosofia*, 61 (January-March 1970), 83-87.

641. G., E. Review of *Lenin i la filosofia*. *Teorema*, no. 4 (1971), pp. 136-138.

642. Lunardi, A. Review of *Lenin e la filosofia*. *Logos*, 2 (1970), 309-315.

643. Müller, G.H. Review of *Lenin und die Philosophie*. *Philosophischer Literaturanzeiger*, 28 (1975), 269-272.

See also item 487.

Lire le CAPITAL
(item 245)

644. Agües, F. Review of *Lire le CAPITAL, I-II*. *Teorema*, no. 3 (1971), pp. 133-134.

645. Anonymous, Review of *Reading Capital*. *Times Literary Supplement*, 22 January 1971, p. 84.

646. Dupré, Louis. Review of *Reading Capital*. *Commonweal*, 95 (10 December 1971), 260.

647. Kaplan, L.S. Review of *Reading Capital*. *Library Journal*, 96 (15 September 1971), 2777.

648. Müller, U. "Althussers strukturalistische Umdeutung des Kapital." *Das Argument*, 17, no. 1-2 (1975), 85-92.

See also items 379, 380, 391, 426, 502b, 510, 511, 536, 563, and 597.

Montesquieu, la politique et l'histoire
(item 228)

649. Anonymous. Review of *Politics and History*. *Choice*, 12 (January 1976), 1458.

650.   ———. Review of *Politics and History*. *Times Literary Supplement*, 15 June 1973, p. 667.

651.   ———. Review of *Politics and History*. *Contemporary Sociology*, 6 (March 1977), 252.

652.   Federici, Silvia. Review of *Montesquieu*.... *Telos*, 4 (Fall 1969), 236-240.

653.   O'Hagan, Timothy. Review of *Politics and History*. *Mind*, 84 (January 1975), 151-153.

Philosophie et philosophie spontanée des savants
(item 318)

654.   Anonymous. Review of *Philosophie et*.... *Times Literary Supplement*, 22 August 1975, p. 242.

655.   Tabaroni, N. Review of *Filosofia e filosofia spontanea*....
Rivista Internazionale di Filosofia del Diritto, 53 (1976), 571-572.

Positions
(item 341)

656.   Buci-Glucksmann, C. "Philosophie et luttes de classe. Du 'Capital' à l'Etat." *La Nouvelle Critique*, no. 94 (1976), pp. 81-84.

657.   Höhn, G. Review of *Positions* and *Reponse à John Lewis*. *Philosophischer Literaturanzeiger*, 30 (1977), 157-161.

657a.   Margolin, J.-C. Review of *Positions*. *Revue de Synthèse*, 99 (1978), 396-397.

Pour Marx
(item 244)

658.   Anonymous. Review of *For Marx*. *Economist*, 234 (7 March 1970), 49.

659.   ———. Review of *For Marx*. *Encounter*, 41 (October 1973), 86.

660.   ———. Review of *For Marx*. *Sociological Review*, n.s. 21 (August 1973), 491.

661.   ———. Review of *For Marx*. *Times Literary Supplement*, 16 April 1970, p. 436.

662.   ———. Review of *For Marx*. *Times Literary Supplement*, 15 December 1972, p. 1526.

663. Ardagh, John. Review of *For Marx*. *Book World*, 11 October 1970, p. 18.

664. Kaplan, L.S. Review of *For Marx*. *Library Journal*, 95 (15 March 1970), 1032.

665. Paim, A. Review of *Análise crítica*.... *Revista Brasileira de Filosofia*, 18 (1968), 97-99.

666. Spounal, J. Review of *Pour Marx* (in Czech). *Filosofický Časopis*, 15, no. 4 (1967), 544-551.

See also items 379, 426, 536, 548, 569, and 597.

Réponse à John Lewis
(item 309)

667. Droit, Roger-Pol. "Théorie marxiste: Louis Althusser--Staline en question." *Le Monde [des Livres]*, no. 8880 (2 August 1973), p. 11.

668. ———. "Théorie marxiste: Louis Althusser--Staline en question." *Le Monde (hebdomadaire)*, no. 1293 (2-8 August 1973), p. 12.

669. Florian, R. "Controversies in Contemporary Marxist Philosophy (On Althusser's *Réponse à John Lewis*)" (in Rumanian). *Revista de Filozofie*, 21, no. 1 (1974), 57-72.

670. G[aley], M[atthieu]. "Louis Althusser descend dans l'arène." *L'Express*, no. 1150 (23-29 July 1973), p. 54.

671. Makarius, Michel I. "La Non-réponse d'Althusser." *L'Homme et la Société*, no. 31-32 (January-June 1974), pp. 259-266.

672. Milhaud, Gérard. "Marxisme et communisme: sur le dernier ouvrage de Louis Althusser." *Europe*, no. 539 (March 1974), pp. 288-292.

673. Nemo, Philippe. "Althusser est-il maoïste?" *Le Nouvel Observateur*, no. 456 (6-12 August 1973), p. 47.

674. Rovatti, P.A. "L'Autocritica degli althusseriani." *Aut Aut*, no. 138 (1973), pp. 65-73.

See also items 411, 475a, 552, and 657.

ROLAND BARTHES

PRIMARY SOURCES

1952

675. "Jean Cayrol et ses romans." *Esprit*, 20, no. 3 (March 1952), 482-499.

676. "Le Monde où l'on catche." *Esprit*, October 1952. Rpt. in item 700.

1953

677. *"Le Prince de Hombourg* au T.N.P." *Les Lettres Nouvelles*, 1, no. 1 (March 1953), 90-97.

  On Jean Vilar.

678. "L'Arlésienne du catholicisme." *Les Lettres Nouvelles*, no. 9 (November 1953), pp. 1162-1165.

679. "Le Monde objet." *Les Lettres Nouvelles*, June 1953. Rpt. in item 739, pp. 19-28.

*680. *Le Degré zéro de l'écriture.* Paris: Editions du Seuil, 1953, 125pp. (Pierres Vives) Rpt. in items 751 and 838. For trans., see items 713 (German), 768 (Swedish), 776 (English), 781 (Spanish), 791 (English), 792 (Danish), 812 (English), and 836 (Portuguese). For reviews, see items 1288-1294.

  Rpts. "Le Degré zéro de l'écriture," *Combat*, 1 August 1947; "Faut-il tuer la grammaire?" *Combat*, 26 September 1947; and "Pour un langage réel," *Combat*, 9, 16, 23 November, 7, 14 December 1950.

1954

*681. Editor of *Michelet par lui-même.* Paris: Editions du Seuil, 1954, 189pp. (Ecrivains de toujours) Rpt. in 1965 and in item 872. See also items 839 and 860. For Italian trans., see item 867a.

682. "Le Silence de Don Juan." *Les Lettres Nouvelles*, no. 12 (February 1954), pp. 264-267.

683.   "Fin de Richard II." *Les Lettres Nouvelles*, no. 13 (March 1954),
        pp. 425-429.

684.   "Phénomène ou mythe?" *Les Lettres Nouvelles*, no. 22 (December
        1954), pp. 951-953.

*685.   "Littérature objective." *Critique*, no. 86-87 (July-August 1954),
        pp. 581-582. Rpt. in item 739, pp. 29-40. See also items 840
        and 759. For English trans., see item 712.

        On Robbe-Grillet's *Les Gommes* and *Trois visions réfléchies*.

                                  1955

686.   "Le Théâtre de Baudelaire." In *Baudelaire: Oeuvres complètes*.
        Paris: Club du Meilleur Livre, 1955, tome I, pp. 1077-1088.
        A preface written in 1954 and rpt. in item 739, pp. 41-47.

687.   "Mère Courage aveugle." *Théâtre Populaire*, 1955. Rpt. in item
        739, pp. 48-50.

688.   "La Révolution brechtienne." Editorial in *Théâtre Populaire*,
        no. 11 (January-February 1955). Rpt. in item 739, pp. 51-52.

*689.   "Littérature littérale." *Critique* (September-October 1955), pp.
        820-826. Rpt. in item 739, pp. 63-70. For English trans., see
        item 712.

        On Robbe-Grillet's *Le Voyeur*, 1955.

690.   "Les Maladies du costume de théâtre." *Théâtre Populaire*, no. 12
        (March-April 1955). Rpt. in item 739, pp. 53-62.

691.   "Comment représenter l'antique." *Théâtre Populaire*, no. 15
        (September-October 1955). Rpt. in item 739, pp. 71-79.

        On Barrault's production of *L'Orestie*.

692.   "Propos sur Claudel." *Théâtre Populaire*, no. 11 (1955). Co-
        authors are J.-L. Barrault, B. Dort, J. Duvignaud, and J. Paris.

693.   "Nautilus et bateau ivre." *Les Lettres Nouvelles*, 3, no. 27
        (May 1955), 790-792. See also item 758.

        On Jules Verne.

694.   "La Mangeuse d'hommes." *Guilde du Livre. Bulletin Mensuel*, 20,
        no. 6 (June 1955), 226-228.

694a.   "Du nouveau en critique." *Esprit*, no. 23 (November 1955), pp.
        1778-1781.

        On Jean-Pierre Richard.

*695. "A l'avant-garde de quel théâtre?" *Théâtre Populaire*, May 1956.
       Rpt. in item 739, pp. 80-83. For English trans., see item 813.

696.   "La Littérature selon Minou Drouet." *Les Lettres Nouvelles*, no.
       34 (January 1956), pp. 153-160.

697.   "The People's Theatre." *Adam, International Review*, 24, no. 253
       (1956), 14.

698.   "Les Tâches de la critique brechtienne." *Arguments*, no. 1 (December 1956-January 1957). Rpt. in item 739, pp. 84-89.

1957

699.   "'Vouloir nous brûle ...'" *Bref*, 1957. Rpt. in item 739, pp.
       90-93.

       On Vilar's production of Balzac's *Le Faiseur*.

699a. Preface to *Quelques promenades dans Rome, suivi de Les Cenci*.
       By Stendhal. Lausanne: Guilde du Livre, 1957, pp. 11-21.

*700. *Mythologies*. Paris: Editions du Seuil, 1957, 270pp. (Pierres
       Vives) Rpt. in item 800. For trans., see items 749 (German),
       849 (English), 881 (Italian), and 905 (Dutch). For reviews,
       see items 1348-1374.

       A semiological theory of the contemporary myths found in today's
       mass culture. Rpts. item 676; "Visages et figures," *Esprit*,
       July 1953; "Jules César au cinéma," *Lettres Nouvelles*, January
       1954; "L'Ecrivain en vacances," *France-Observateur*, 9 September
       1954 (for English trans., see item 757); and "Petites mythologies
       du mois," *Lettres Nouvelles*, November and December 1954, each
       month of 1955, and January through May 1956.

1958

701.   "Quand les critiques sont dans la pièce (Entretien sur *Paolo
       Paoli*)." *La Nouvelle Critique*, 10, no. 94 (March 1958), 90-
       105. Co-authors are Arthur Adamov, et al.

702.   "Roger Planchon à Villeurbanne, théâtre de demain." *Spectacles*,
       no. 1 (March 1958), pp. 45-51. Co-author is Frédéric Towarnicki.

703.   "Alfred Jarry: *Ubu* (TNP, 1958)." *Théâtre Populaire*, no. 3 (May
       1958), pp. 80-83.

704.   "Le Dernier des écrivains heureux." *Actualité Littéraire*, March
       1958, and Preface to *Romans et contes*. By Voltaire. Paris:
       Editions du Club des Libraires de France, 1958. Rpt. in item
       739, pp. 94-100; also in *Romans et contes*. Paris: Gallimard,
       1976. (Folio, 876)

704a. Preface to *Iphigénie*. By Racine. In *Théâtre de Racine*. Paris:
       Club des Libraires de France, 1958, tome II. Rpt. in *Sur Racine*,
       item 730.

705. "Il n'y a pas d'école Robbe-Grillet." *Arguments*, 1958. Rpt. in
      item 739, pp. 101-105.

      On *La Modification*.

                                    1959

706. "Littérature et métalangage." *Phantomas*, no. 13 (Brussels,
      January 1959). Rpt. in item 739, pp. 106-107.

707. "Tacite et le baroque funèbre." *L'Arc*, no. 6 (Spring 1959). Rpt.
      in item 739, pp. 108-111.

708. "La Sorcière." Preface to *La Sorcière*. By Michelet. Paris: Le
      Club Français du Livre, 1959. Rpt. in item 739, pp. 112-124.

709. "*Le Soulier de Satin*, mise en scène au Théâtre du Palais-Royal."
      Théâtre Populaire, no. 33 (1959), pp. 121-123.

709a. "Langage et vêtement." *Critique*, no. 142 (March 1959), pp. 242-
      252.

710. "*Les Trois Mousquetaires*, d'après Dumas, mise-en-scène de Roger
      Planchon." *Théâtre Populaire*, no. 36 (third quarter 1959),
      pp. 47-49.

*710a. "Sept photos modèles de *Mère Courage*." *Théâtre Populaire*, no.
      35 (third quarter 1959). For English trans., see item 778.

711. "Zazie et la littérature." *Critique*, 12e année, tome XV, no.
      147-148 (August-September 1959), 675-681. Rpt. in item 739,
      pp. 125-131.

      On *Zazie dans le métro*.

712. "Alain Robbe-Grillet." *Evergreen Review*, 2, no. 5 (1959), 113-
      126. Trans. of items 685 and 689.

713. *Am Nullpunkt der Literatur. Objektive Literatur. Zwei Essays*.
      Düsseldorf: Claassen Verlag, 1959. Trans. of item 680.

                                    1960

714. "Ecrivains et écrivants." *Arguments*, no. 20 (fourth quarter 1960).
      Rpt. in item 739, pp. 147-154.

      On the function of the writer.

714a. Preface to *Théâtre*. By Racine. Paris: Club Français du Livre,
      1960, tomes XI and XII. (Théâtre Classique) Rpt. in *Sur Racine*,
      item 730. Cf. item 760.

715. "*Je* n'est pas un autre: Yves Velan." *Critique*, 13e année, 16,
      no. 153 (February 1960), 99-104. Rpt. as "Ouvriers et pasteurs"
      in item 739, pp. 132-137.

716.   "Le Bleu est à la mode cette année: note sur la recherche des
        unités signifiantes dans le vêtement de mode." *Revue Française
        de Sociologie*, 1 (1960), 147-162.

        Using examples borrowed from the description of women's clothing
        in fashion magazines, Barthes studies the methodological premises
        of a structural analysis of fashion and reviews the operations
        needed to establish a "lexicon" of fashion.

717.   "Jean Genet: Le Balcon (mise en scène Peter Brook)." *Théâtre
        Populaire*, no. 38 (2nd quarter 1960), pp. 96-98.

718.   "Le Problème de la signification au cinéma." *Revue Internationale
        de Filmologie*, 10, no. 32-33 (January-June 1960).

719.   "La Réponse de Kafka." *France Observateur*, 24 March 1960. Rpt.
        in item 739, pp. 138-142.

        On Marthe Robert's *Kafka* (Gallimard, 1960).

720.   "Sur *La Mère* de Brecht." *Théâtre Populaire*, no. 39 (third quarter
        1960). Rpt. in item 739, pp. 143-146.

720a.   Preface to *Mère Courage*. By Brecht. Paris: L'Arche, 1960.

                                    1961

721.   Editor of *Maximes et réflexions*. By François, duc de La Roche-
        foucauld. Paris: Club Français du Livre, 1961, 1966.

722.   "La Littérature, aujourd'hui." *Tel Quel*, no. 7 (Fall 1961), pp.
        32-41. Rpt. in item 739, pp. 155-166.

        Answers to questions asked by *Tel Quel* in 1961.

*723.   "Le Message photographique." *Communications*, 1 (1961), 127-138.
        For English trans., see item 920.

        At first sight the photograph, as an entirely analogical re-
        production of something real, seems to constitute a paradoxal
        message, a *codeless message*. However, parasitic meanings on the
        connotative level develop on this message and can be classified.

724.   "Le Théâtre français d'avant-garde." *Le Français dans le Monde*,
        no. 2 (June-July 1961), pp. 10-15.

725.   "Pour une psycho-sociologie de l'alimentation contemporaine."
        Annales, no. 5 (September-October 1961), pp. 977-986.

        An outline of the tasks of a psycho-sociology of contemporary
        alimentation when subjected to semiological analysis. Following
        Lévi-Strauss' suggestions on "*gustèmes*," Barthes gives several
        examples of probable variants of the meaning of food.

726.   Review of *Folie et déraison: Histoire de la folie a l'âge
        classique* by Michel Foucault. *Critique*, 17, no. 174
        (November 1961), 915-922. Rpt. in item 739, pp. 167-174 under
        the title "De part et d'autre."

1962

*727. "Littérature et discontinu." *Critique*, no. 185 (October 1962),
      pp. 817-829. Rpt. in item 739, pp. 175-187. See also item 841.
      For English trans., see item 850.

      On Michel Butor's *Mobile*.

727a. "Sociologie et sociologique." *Social Science Information*, 1,
      no. 4 (1962), 114-122.

728. "Structure du fait-divers." *Médiations*, no. 5 (1962), pp. 27-36.
      Rpt. in item 739, pp. 188-197.

729. "L'Imagination du signe." *Arguments*, no. 27-28 (1962). Rpt. in
      item 739, pp. 206-212.

1963

*730. *Sur Racine*. Paris: Editions du Seuil, 1963, 171pp. (Pierres
      Vives) For trans., see items 747 (English) and 767 (Italian).
      For reviews, see items 1489-1492.

      Rpts. items 704a; 714a; "La Relation d'autorité chez Racine,"
      Lettres Nouvelles, no. 15 (10 June 1959); and "Histoire et
      littérature: à propos de Racine," *Annales*, no. 3 (May 1960).

731. Co-author of *France, mère des arts? Aspects présents de l'activité
      intellectuelle et artistique en France*. Paris: Julliard, 1963.

732. Preface to *Les Romans de Robbe-Grillet*. By Bruce Morrissette.
      Paris: Editions de Minuit, 1963. A new enlarged edition of
      this work was published in 1971. Preface rpt. in item 739,
      pp. 198-205, under the title of "Le Point sur Robbe-Grillet?"

*733. "L'Activité structuraliste." *Les Lettres Nouvelles*, no. 32
      (February 1963). Rpt. in item 739, pp. 213-220. For English
      trans., see item 779.

734. "La Bruyère: du mythe à l'écriture." In *Les Caractères ou Les
      moeurs de ce siècle*. By Jean de La Bruyère. Paris: Union
      Générale d'Editions, 1963. Rpt. in item 739, pp. 221-237.

735. "La Métaphore de l'oeil." *Critique*, 15ᵉ année, no. 195-196
      (August-September 1963), 770-777. The entire issue was entitled
      "Hommage à Georges Bataille." Rpt. in item 739, pp. 238-245.

736. "Les Deux critiques." *Modern Language Notes*, 78, no. 5 (December
      1963), 447-452. Rpt. in item 739, pp. 246-251.

      The two kinds of literary criticism in France.

*737. "Criticism as Language." *Times Literary Supplement*, 27 September
      1963, pp. 739-740. Rpt. in item 739, pp. 252-257 under the
      title of "Qu'est-ce que la critique?" For Norwegian trans.,
      see item 750.

1964

738. "Littérature et signification." *Tel Quel*, no. 16 (Winter 1964),
      pp. 3-17. Rpt. in item 739, pp. 258-276.

      Nine questions answered in *Tel Quel*.

*739. *Essais critiques*. Paris: Editions du Seuil, 1964, 278pp. (Tel
      Quel) Contains "Préface" plus items 679, 685, 686, 687, 688,
      689, 690, 691, 695, 698, 699, 704, 705, 706, 707, 708, 711,
      714, 715, 719, 720, 722, 726, 727, 728, 729, 732, 733, 734,
      735, 736, 737, and 738. For trans., see items 767 (Italian),
      769 (Catalonian or Spanish), 783 (Norwegian), and 848 (English).
      For reviews, see items 1314-1323.

740. "La Nature." In *Les Corps étrangers*. By Jean Cayrol. Paris:
      Union Générale d'Editions, 1964.

741. "La Nature." In *Les Corps étrangers*. *Pour un romanesque lazaréen*.
      By Jean Cayrol. Paris: Editions du Seuil, 1964.

*741a. *La Tour Eiffel*. Paris: Delpire, 1964. (Le Génie du lieu) With
      André Martin. For trans., see items 822 (German) and 924d
      (English). For reviews, see items 1498a-1498g.

742. "Image, raison, déraison." In *Encyclopédie; ou, Dictionnaire
      raisonné des sciences. L'Univers de l'Encyclopédie*. Paris:
      Les Libraires Associés, 1964, tome I.

743. "Les Sciences humaines et l'oeuvre de Lévi-Strauss." *Annales.
      Economies. Sociétés. Civilisations*, 19e année, no. 6 (November-
      December 1964), 1085-1086.

744. "La Cuisine du sens." *Le Nouvel Observateur*, n.s., no. 4 (10
      December 1964), pp. 29-30.

      On semiology, Ferdinand de Saussure and *Communications*, no. 4.

*745. "Eléments de sémiologie." *Communications*, no. 4 (November 1964),
      pp. 91-136. Also printed in *Recherches sémiologiques*. Paris:
      Editions du Seuil, 1964, pp. 91-136. Later rpt. in item 751.
      For trans., see items 766 (Italian), 775 (English), 790
      (English), 812 (English), 835 (Spanish), and 837 (Portuguese).
      For reviews, see items 1295-1298.

*746. "Rhétorique de l'image." *Communications*, no. 4 (November 1964),
      pp. 40-50. Also printed in *Recherches sémiologiques*. Paris:
      Editions du Seuil, 1964, pp. 40-50. For English trans., see
      item 920.

747. *On Racine*. Trans. Richard Howard. New York: Hill and Wang, 1964.
      Trans. of item 730. Rpt. in item 922.

748. "Robbe-Grillet Today." In *On Contemporary Literature: An Anthol-
      ogy of Critical Essays on the Major Movements and Writers of
      Contemporary Literature*. New York: Avon Books, 1964, pp. 511-
      519.

749. *Mythen des Alltags.* Trans. Helmut Scheffel. Frankfurt am Main: Suhrkamp, c. 1964, 1970, 1974. Trans. of item 700.

750. "Hva er kritikk?" *Vinduet*, 18 årgang, nr. 4 (1964), 272-274. Trans. by Storm Michael Wiik of item 737 in item 739.

1965

*751. *Le Degré zéro de l'écriture. (Suivi de:) Eléments de sémiologie.* Paris: Gonthier, c. 1964, 1965. Rpts. items 680 and 745. For trans., see items 766 (Italian), 775 (English), 780 (English), 790 (English), 812 (English), 835 (Spanish), and 837 (Portuguese). For reviews, see items 1288-1294 and 1295-1298.

752. "La Voyageuse de nuit." In *La Vie de Rancé.* By François Auguste René Châteaubriand. Paris: Union Générale d'Editions, 1965.

752a. "Le Théâtre grec." In *Histoire des spectacles.* Paris: Editions Gallimard, 1965, pp. 513-536. (Encyclopédie de la Pléiade)

753. Response in "Les Réactions (écrivains interrogés sur Céline)." *Le Nouvel Observateur*, n.s., no. 15 (25 February 1965), pp. 27-28.

754. "Le Théâtre." *Esprit*, n.s., no. 338 (May 1965), pp. 834-836.

755. "Drame, poème, roman." *Critique*, no. 218 (July 1965), pp. 591-603. Rpt. in item 785.

   On Philippe Sollers' *Drame.*

756. "Si ce n'est toi ..." *Le Nouvel Observateur*, no. 52 (10-16 November 1965), p. 29.

   On Picard's *Nouvelle critique ou nouvelle imposture* and Duvignaud's article in the 3-9 November 1965 issue of *Le Nouvel Observateur.*

757. "Writers on Vacation." Trans. Richard Howard. *The Nation*, no. 20, 13 December 1965, p. 474. Partial trans. of item 700.

758. "Nautilus och den berusade båten." *Ord och Bild*, 74:e årgang, no. 1 (1965), 7-8. See also item 693.

1966

759. "Objective Literature: Alain Robbe-Grillet." In *Two Novels.* By Alain Robbe-Grillet. Trans. Richard Howard. New York: Grove Press, 1965. Trans. of item 685.

760. Editor of *Théâtre* of Jean Baptiste Racine. 2 vols. Paris: Club Français du Livre, 1965-1966. Cf. item 714a.

*761. *Critique et vérité*. Paris: Editions du Seuil, 1966, 79pp. (Tel
       Quel) For trans., see items 782 (German), 795 (Italian), 796
       (Catalonian), 820 (Portuguese), and 851 (Spanish). For reviews,
       see items 1285-1287.

       Barthes' reply to Picard's *Nouvelle critique ou nouvelle
       imposture*.

*762. "Introduction à l'analyse structurale des récits." *Communications*,
       no. 8 (November 1966), pp. 1-27. Also printed in *Recherches
       sémiologiques: l'analyse structurale du récit*. Paris: Editions
       du Seuil, 1966, pp. 1-27. Rpt. in item 916. For trans., see
       items 794 (Italian), 816 (Spanish), 902 (English), and 920
       (English).

       A theory based on linguistics can lead to a description and
       classification of narratives.

763. "Les Vies parallèles." *La Quinzaine Littéraire*, no. 1, 15 March
       1966, p. 11.

       On G.D. Painter's *Marcel Proust. 1. Les Années de jeunesse*.

764. "Condition féminine: la mode, stratégie du désir." *Le Nouvel
       Observateur*, no. 71, 23-29 March 1966, pp. 28-29. Co-authors
       are Henri Lefèbvre and Jean Duvignaud.

       A possible preparation for item 772.

765. "Situation du linguiste." *La Quinzaine Littéraire*, no. 5, 15
       May 1966, p. 20.

       On E. Benveniste's *Problèmes de linguistique générale*.

766. *Elementi di semiologia*. 6th ed. Turin: G. Einaudi, 1966. Rpt.
       1971. Trans. of item 745 which is part of item 751.

767. *Saggi critici*. Turin: G. Einaudi, 1966. Trans. of items 730 and
       739.

                                    1967

768. *Litteraturens nollpunkt*. Trans. Gun och Nils A. Bengtsson.
       Stockholm: Staffanstorp, Cavefors, 1966. Trans. of item 680.

769. *Ensayos críticos*. Trans. Carlos Pujol. Barcelona: Editorial Seix
       Barral, c. 1966, 1967. Trans. of item 739.

770. "Proust et les noms." In *To Honor Roman Jakobson. Essays on the
       Occasion of His Seventieth Birthday, 11 October 1966*. The
       Hague-Paris: Mouton, 1967, vol. I, pp. 150-158. Rpt. in items
       824 and 838.

*771. "L'Analyse rhétorique." In *Littérature et société. Problèmes de
       méthodologie en sociologie de la littérature*. Colloque organisé
       conjointement par l'Institut de Sociologie de l'Université
       Libre de Bruxelles et l'Ecole Pratique des Hautes Etudes (6e

section) de Paris du 21 au 23 mai 1964. Brussels: Editions de
l'Institut de Sociologie, Université Libre de Bruxelles, 1967,
pp. 31-45. For trans., see item 797.

772. *Système de la mode*. Paris: Editions du Seuil, 1967, 327pp. For
reviews, see items 1493-1498.

This work, begun in 1957 and ended in 1963, is a structural
analysis of women's clothing as described in today's fashion
magazines. Barthes considers it as a work of applied semiology,
an attempt to see fashion as a system of meaning.

772a. Preface to *Verdure*. By Antoine Gallien. Paris: Editions du Seuil,
1967. (Ecrire)

773. "Le Discours de l'histoire." *Information sur les Sciences Sociales*,
6, no. 4 (August 1967), 65-76.

774. "L'Arbre du crime." *Tel Quel*, no. 28 (1967), pp. 23-37. Also in
Oeuvres complètes du marquis de Sade. Paris: Tchou, 1967, tome
XVI, pp. 511-532.

For Sade, there is eroticism only if the crime is subjected
to the system of spoken language. The "language" of the crime
or new code of love is just as elaborate as the courtly code.
The units of this code are carefully determined and named by
Sade himself.

775. *Elements of Semiology*. Trans. Annette Lavers and Colin Smith.
London: Jonathan Cape Editions, 1967. Trans. of item 745 which
is part of 751.

776. *Writing Degree Zero*. Trans. Annette Lavers and Colin Smith.
London: Jonathan Cape Editions, 1967. Trans. of item 680 with
a note on the author and a selected bibliography.

777. "Science versus Literature." *Times Literary Supplement*, no.
3422, 28 September 1967, pp. 897-898. Rpt. in item 815.

778. "Seven Photo Models of Mother Courage." Trans. H.F. Bernays.
Drama Review, 12 (Fall 1967), 44-55. Trans. of item 710a.

779. "Structuralist Activity: Diseases of Costume." Trans. R. Howard.
Partisan Review, 34, no. 2 (Winter 1967), 82-97. Trans. of
item 733 from item 739.

780. "Writing and Revolution." Trans. June Guicharnaud. *Yale French
Studies*, no. 39 (1967) [Literature and Revolution, ed. Jacques
Ehrmann], pp. 77-84. Partial trans. of item 751.

781. *El Grado cero de la escritura*. Buenos Aires: Editorial Jorge
Alvarez, c. 1967. Trans. of item 680.

782. *Kritik und Wahrheit*. Trans. Helmut Scheffel. Frankfurt am Main:
Suhrkamp, 1967. Trans. of item 761.

783.   "Forord." Trans. Storm Michael Wiik. *Vinduet*, 21. årgang, nr. 4
       (1967), 252-256. Trans. of the preface of item 739.

784.   "Čo je kritika? Kritika a pravada; Litteraturá a víjznam."
       Slovenské Pohl'ady, Ročník 83, no. 8 (August 1967), 113-122.

784a. "Une Problématique du sens." *Cahiers Média*, Service d'Edition
       et de Vente des Productions de l'Education Nationale, no. 1
       (1967-1968), pp. 9-22.

                                    1968

785.   "Drame, poème, roman." In *Théorie d'ensemble*. By Michel Foucault,
       et al. Paris: Editions du Seuil, 1968, pp. 25-40. Rpts. item
       755.

       On Philippe Sollers' *Drame*.

*786. "L'Effet du réel." *Communications*, no. 11 (1968), pp. 84-89.
       Also printed in *Recherches sémiologiques: Le vraisemblable*.
       Paris: Editions du Seuil, 1968, pp. 84-89. For Spanish trans.,
       see item 817.

*787. "La Mort de l'auteur." *Mantéia*, no. 5 (1968), pp. 12-17. For
       English trans., see item 920.

       On Mallarmé and Proust.

788.   "Le Refus d'hériter." *Le Nouvel Observateur*, no. 181, 30 April-7
       May 1968), p. 35.

       On Sollers' *Logiques* and *Nombres*.

*789. "Leçon d'écriture." *Tel Quel*, no. 34 (Summer 1968), pp. 28-33.
       For English trans., see item 920.

790.   *Elements of Semiology*. Trans. Annette Lavers and Colin Smith.
       New York: Hill and Wang, 1968, 1977. Trans. of item 745 which
       is part of 751.

       A concise and systematic presentation of the fundamentals of
       semiology as a science of signs, this work begins with a review
       of Saussurian linguistics. Part 2 defines the functional terms
       of signifier-signified-signification. Part 3 explains the use of
       the two axes of language--the syntagm and the system--and their
       applications. The last part formulates the larger systems of
       meta-language and connotation. Also contains a bibliography and
       index.

791.   *Writing Degree Zero*. Trans. Annette Lavers and Colin Smith. New
       York: Hill and Wang, 1968, 1977. Trans. of item 680.

       Contains essays which date from 1953 and which attempt to
       define the essence of writing, modes of writing, distinctions
       in novelistic writing based on political, historical and personal
       exigencies. Also contains a 20-page introduction by Susan Sontag.

791a. "Società, immaginazione, pubblicità." In *Pubblicità e Televisione*. Rome: Ed. RAI, 1968, pp. 164-174.

792. *Letteraturens nulpunkt*. Trans. Hans-Jørgen Andersen. Copenhagen: Rhodos, 1968. Trans. of item 680.

793. "Linguistique et littérature." *Langages*, no. 12 (1968-1969), pp. 3-8.

1969

794. "Introduzione all'analisi strutturale dei racconti." In *L'Analisi del racconto*. Milan: V. Bompiani, 1969, pp. 5-46. Trans. of item 762.

795. *Critica e verità*. Turin: G. Einaudi, c. 1969. Trans. of item 761.

796. *Crítica i veritat*. Barcelona: Llibres de Sinera, 1969. Trans. of item 761.

797. *Literatura y sociedad. Problemas de metodología en sociología de la literatura*. Trans. R. de la Iglesia. Barcelona: M. Roca, 1969. Co-authors are Henri Lefèbvre, Lucien Goldmann, et al. Trans. of item 771.

798. *Das Denken von Sade*. Munich: Carl Hanser, 1969. Co-authors are H. Damisch, P.I. Klossowski, Ph. Sollers, and M. Tort.

799. *Literatur oder Geschichte*. Trans. Helmut Scheffel. Frankfurt am Main: Suhrkamp, 1969, 1970.

Contains nine essays by Barthes.

1970

800. *Mythologies*. Paris: Editions du Seuil, 1970. Double volume in the "Points" collection. Rpts. item 700.

*801. *S/Z*. Paris: Editions du Seuil, 1970, 278pp. (Tel Quel) Rpt. in item 907. For trans., see items 879 (English), 900 (English), and 906 (German). For reviews, see items 1430-1466.

Based on work done during a seminar at the Ecole Pratique des Hautes Etudes in 1968 and 1969. Contains 93 short texts and 3 appendices in which Barthes approaches a text in the four medieval roles of scriptor, compilator, commentator and auctor. This participation in what Barthes calls "the pluralization of criticism," the structural analysis of narrative and the science of the text will lead to the collective construction of a liberating theory of what is meaningful.

802. *L'Empire des signes*. Geneva: Albert Skira, 1970, 155pp. (Les Sentiers de la Création) For reviews, see items 1299-1307.

On travel in Japan.

803.   Co-author of *Itinéraire de Roger Planchon*. Paris: Editions de l'Arche, 1970.

803a. Preface to *La Fuite en Chine (René Leys*, de Victor Segalen). By Bernard Minoret and Danielle Vézolles. Paris: Christian Bourgois, 1970.

*804. "Le Troisième sens: notes de recherche sur quelques photogrammes de S.M. Eisenstein." *Cahiers du Cinéma*, no. 222 (July 1970). For English trans., see item 920.

*805. "Musica practica." *L'Arc*, no. 40 (February 1970). For English trans., see item 920.

       On Beethoven.

806.   "L'Analyse structurale du récit: à propos d'Actes X-XI." *Recherches de Science Religieuse*, 58 (January-March 1970), 17-37. Rpt. in item 826.

807.   "L'Ancienne rhétorique, aide-mémoire." *Communications*, 16 (December 1970), 172-229. Published in Paris by the Editions du Seuil.

808.   "Critique à pied d'oeuvre." *Le Figaro Littéraire*, no. 1242, 9-15 March 1970, pp. 21-22.

       On *S/Z*.

808a. Preface to *Eden Eden Eden*. By Pierre Guyotat. Paris: Editions Gallimard, 1970.

809.   "*L'Etranger*, roman solaire." In *Les Critiques de notre temps et Camus*. Ed. Jacqueline Lévi-Valensi. Paris: Editions Garnier, 1970, pp. 60-64.

809a. Preface to *Encyclopédie Bordas*, tome VIII: L'Aventure littéraire de l'humanité (I). Paris: Bordas, 1970.

810.   "Par où commencer?" *Poétique. Revue de Théorie et d'Analyse Littéraire*, no. 1 (1970), pp. 3-9. Rpt. in item 838.

       On Jules Verne's *L'Ile mystérieuse*.

810a. "Masculin, féminin, neutre." In *Echanges et communications. Mélanges offerts à Claude Lévi-Strauss*. Ed. J. Pouillon. The Hague: Mouton, 1970, pp. 893-907.

811.   "La Linguistique du discours." In *Sign, Language, Culture*. Ed. A.J. Greimas, et al. The Hague: Mouton, 1970, pp. 580-584.

812.   *Writing Degree Zero and Elements of Semiology*. Trans. Annette Lavers and Colin Smith. Boston: Beacon Press, 1970. Trans. of item 751. Contains a long preface by Susan Sontag.

813.   "The Avant-Garde of What Theatre?" *Ark*, no. 46 (Spring 1970), pp. 20-21. Trans. of item 695.

814. "To Write: An Intransitive Verb?" In *The Languages of Criticism and the Sciences of Man. The Structuralist Controversy.* Ed. Richard Macksey and Eugenio Umberto Donato. Baltimore, Maryland: Johns Hopkins Press, 1970, 1972, pp. 134-145.

815. "Science versus Literature." In *Introduction to Structuralism.* Ed. Michael Lane. New York: Basic Books, 1970, pp. 410-416. Rpts. item 777.

816. Co-author of *Análisis estructural del relato.* Trans. Beatriz Dorriots. Buenos Aires: Editorial Tiempo Contemporáneo, 1970. Trans. of item 762, the entire issue.

817. Contributor to *Lo Verosímil.* Trans. Beatriz Dorriots. Buenos Aires: Editorial Tiempo Contemporáneo, 1970. Trans. of item 786, the entire issue.

818. Contributor to *Estructuralismo y literatura.* Comp. José Sazbón. Buenos Aires: Ediciones Nueva Visión, 1970.

819. Contributor to *Estructuralismo y sociología.* Buenos Aires: Ediciones Nueva Visión, [1970?].

820. *Crítica e verdade.* São Paulo: Editôra Perspectiva, 1970. Trans. of item 761.

821. *Erté (Romain de Tirtoff). Testo di Roland Barthes. Seguido dai ricordi di Erté.* Trans. Giovanni Mariotti. Parma: F.M. Ricci, 1970 & 1972. Published in French, English and Italian. German edition published by Echter in Würzburg. See also item 901. For reviews, see items 1308-1313.

822. *Der Eiffelturm.* Trans. Helmut Scheffel. Munich: Rogner & Bernhard, 1970. With André Martin. Trans. of item 741a.

1971

*823. *Sade, Fourier, Loyola.* Paris: Editions du Seuil, 1971. For trans., see items 871 (German) and 914 (English). For reviews, see items 1467-1488.

824. "Proust et les noms." In *Les critiques de notre temps et Proust.* Ed. Jacques Bersani. Paris: Editions Garnier Frères, 1971, pp. 158-169. Rpts. item 770. Rpt. in item 838.

825. "Adamov et le langage." In *Arthur Adamov.* By René Gaudy. Paris: Stock, 1971, pp. 129-133.

825a. "Réflexions sur un manuel." In *L'Enseignement de la littérature.* Paris: Plon, 1971, pp. 170-177.

826. "L'Analyse structurale du récit. A propos d'Actes 10-11." In *Exégèse et herméneutique.* Paris: Editions du Seuil, 1971, pp. 181-204 and discussion, pp. 239-265. Rpts. item 806.

827. "Réponses." In *Roland Barthes*. Paris: Tel Quel, 1971, pp. 89-107.

827a. Preface, in Italian, to *Aziyadé*. By Pierre Loti. Parma: Franco-
      Maria Ricci, 1971. (Morgana) Cf. items 838 and 845.

828. "Ecrivains, intellectuels, professeurs." *Tel Quel*, no. 47 (Fall
      1971), pp. 3-18. For English trans., see item 920.

828a. "Letter to *Sub-Stance*." *Sub-Stance*, 1, no. 0 (March 1971), v.

*829. "Changer l'objet lui-même." *Esprit*, 39, no. 402 (1971), 613-616.
      Part of a special issue entitled "Le Mythe aujourd'hui." For
      English trans., see item 920.

      After "demystifying" mythical language and revealing its
      ideological meaning in *Mythologies* (item 700), Barthes tries
      to go beyond this dissociation of the sign and undermine and
      destroy the sign itself by including myth in a general theory
      of language.

829a. "Digressions." *Promesse*, no. 29 (Spring 1971), pp. 15-32.

*830. "De l'oeuvre au texte." *Revue d'Esthétique*, 24, no. 3 (July-
      September 1971), 225-32. For English trans., see item 920.

      Statements about method, genres, the sign, the plural, filia-
      tion, reading, and pleasure.

831. "Une Idée de recherche." *Paragone*, anno XXII, n. 260 (October
      1971), 25-30.

831a. "Action Sequence." In *Patterns of Literary Style*. Ed. Joseph
      Strelka. University Park, Pa.: Pennsylvania State University
      Press, 1971, pp. 5-14.

832. "Style and its Image." In *Literary Style: A Symposium*. Ed. and
      trans. (in part) Seymour Chatman. New York: Oxford University
      Press, 1971, pp. 3-10. Proceedings of the International Sym-
      posium on Literary Style held in Bellagio, Italy in 1969.

832a. "A Conversation with Roland Barthes." *Signs of the Times*. Cam-
      bridge: Granta, 1971, pp. 41-55.

      An interview with Stephen Heath.

833. "On Bunraku." Trans. S. MacDonald. *Drama Review*, 15 (Spring
      1971), 76-82.

834. "Languages at War in a Culture at Peace." *Times Literary Supple-
      ment*, no. 3632, 8 October 1971, pp. 1203-1204.

835. *Elementos de semiología*. Madrid: Alberto Corazón, 1971. Trans.
      of item 745 which is part of item 751.

836. *A Grau zero de escritura*. Trans. Anne Arnichaud and Alvaro
      Lorencini. São Paulo: Cultrix, 1971. Trans. of item 680.

837. *Elementos de semiologia*. Trans. Izidoro Blikstein. São Paulo:
      Editôra Cultrix, 1971. Trans. of item 745 which is part of item
      751.

1972

*838. *Le Degré zéro de l'écriture. (Suivi de) Nouveaux essais critiques.*
Paris: Editions du Seuil, 1972. (Points) Contents include items
680, 770, 810, 824, and "Pierre Loti: *Aziyadé*" (item 845;
cf. item 827a). For trans., see items 854 (Portuguese) and
868 (Spanish).

839. Contributing editor to *Michelet.* Aix-en-Provence: L'Arc no. 52,
[1972?], 89pp. See items 681 and 860.

840. "Littérature objective." In *Les Critiques de notre temps et le
nouveau roman.* Ed. Réal Ouellet. Paris: Editions Garnier
Frères, 1972, pp. 67-73. See also item 685.

On Robbe-Grillet.

841. "Littérature et discontinu." In *Les Critiques de notre temps et
le nouveau roman.* Ed. Réal Ouellet. Paris: Editions Garnier
Frères, 1972, pp. 140-143. See also item 727.

On Michel Butor.

*842. "La Lutte avec l'Ange: analyse textuelle de *Genèse* 32, 23-33."
In *Analyse structurale et exégèse biblique. Essais d'interprétation.* By Roland Barthes, François Bovon, Franz J. Leenhardt, Robert Martin-Achard, and Jean Starobinski. Neuchâtel:
Delachaux et Niestlé, 1972. For English trans., see items
880 and 920. For reviews, see items 1277-1284.

843. "*Le Balcon*: mise en scène de Peter Brook au Théâtre du Gymnase."
Obliques, no. 2 (1972), pp. 37-38.

On Jean Genet.

*844. "Le Grain de la voix." *Musique en Jeu*, 9 (1972). For English
trans., see item 920.

845. "Le Nom d'Aziyadé." *Critique*, no. 297 (February 1972), pp. 103-
117. See also items 838 and 827a.

On Pierre Loti.

846. "Lettre à Jean Ristat [21 March 1972]." *Les Lettres Françaises*,
no. 1429 (29 March-4 April 1972), p. 3.

On Derrida.

847. "Le Retour du poéticien." *La Quinzaine Littéraire*, no. 150
(16-31 October 1972), pp. 15-16.

On Gérard Genette's *Figures III.*

848. *Critical Essays.* Trans. Richard Howard. Evanston, Illinois:
Northwestern University Press, 1972. Trans. of item 739.

Contains (in alphabetical order): Authors and Writers;
Baudelaire's Theater; The Brechtian Revolution; The Diseases
of Costume; The Imagination of the Sign; Kafka's Answer; La
Bruyère; The Last Happy Writer; The Last Word on Robbe-Grillet?;

Literal Literature; Literature and Discontinuity; Literature
and Metalanguage; Literature and Signification; Literature Today;
The Metaphor of the Eye; Mother Courage Blind; Objective Litera-
ture; On Brecht's Mother; Preface; Putting on the Greeks; La
Sorcière; The Structuralist Activity; Structure of the Fait-Divers;
Tacitus and the Funerary Baroque; Taking Sides; The Tasks of
Brechtian Criticism; There is no Robbe-Gillet School; The Two
Criticisms; What is Criticism?; Whose Theater? Whose Avant-Garde?;
"Will burns us ..."; Workers and Pastors; The World as Object;
Zazie and Literature.

849. *Mythologies*. Trans. Annette Lavers. London: Jonathan Cape; New
      York: Hill and Wang, 1972. Trans. of item 700. Rpt. in item
      865.

      Contains 28 of the original *Mythologies* written between 1954
      and 1956 together with the 50-page essay "Myth Today." Social
      phenomena such as films, wrestling matches, detergents, and
      strip-tease are seen as part of a contemporary reality which
      is determined by history. Barthes presents both an ideological
      critique of the language of "mass culture" and an analysis of
      that language.

850. "Literature and Discontinuity." Trans. Richard Howard. *Salmagundi*,
      no. 18 (Winter 1972), pp. 82-93. Trans. of item 727. See also
      item 848.

851. *Crítica y verdad*. Trans. José Bianco. Buenos Aires: Siglo Vein-
      tiuno Argentina Editores, 1972. Trans. of item 761.

852. Contributor to *Literatura y sociedad*. 2nd ed. Barcelona: Ediciones
      Martínez Roca, 1972.

853. Contributor to *Estructuralismo e historia*. Ed. José Sazbón.
      Buenos Aires: Ediciones Nueva Visión, 1972.

854. *Novo ensaios críticos, seguidos de grau zero da escritura*. Trans.
      Heloysa de Lima Dantas, Anne Arnichaud and Álvaro Lorencini.
      São Paulo: Editôra Cultrix, c. 1972, 1974. Trans. of item 838.

                                1973

*855. *Le Plaisir du texte*. Paris: Editions du Seuil, 1973. (Tel Quel)
      For trans., see 884 (Spanish), 887 (German), 899 (English),
      903 (Italian), and 913 (English). For reviews, see items
      1375-1404.

      A series of short paragraphs in which Barthes attempts to
      answer the question: "What do we enjoy in the text?" On Bachelard,
      Lacan, Proust, Sollers, and others.

856. *Dialogue avec Jean Ristat*. Paris: Les Editeurs Français Réunis,
      1973.

857. Contributor to *L'Express va plus loin avec ces théoriciens.*
Paris: R. Laffont, 1973.

A collection of interviews.

858. *Bernard Réquichot.* Brussels: La Connaissance, 1973. With Marcel
Billot and Alfred Pacquement. A trilingual catalog in German,
French and English was also published by M. Weber of Geneva
under the title of *Das Werk von Bernard Requichot.*

859. *Sémiotique narrative et textuelle.* Paris: Larousse, 1973. With
Sorin Alexandrescu, Claude Bremond, A.J. Greimas, et al.

860. Contributing editor to *Michelet: un inédit de Michelet.* Aix-en-
Provence: *L'Arc* no. 52, 1973, 96pp. See items 681, 839 and 872.

*861. "Les Sorties du texte." In *Bataille.* Ed. Philippe Sollers. Paris:
Union Générale d'Editions, 1973, pp. 49-73. For Italian trans.,
see item 882.

Barthes' paper and the discussion following it at a colloquium
held in the Centre Culturel International de Cerisy-la-Salle
from June 29 to July 9, 1972. The colloquium was directed by
Sollers and entitled "Vers une révolution culturelle: Artaud,
Bataille."

862. "L'Inconnu n'est pas le n'importe quoi, dialogue avec Roland
Barthes et Jean Ristat." In *L'Entrée dans la baie et la prise
de la ville de Rio de Janeiro en 1711, tragi-comédie.* By Jean
Ristat. Paris: Les Editeurs Français Réunis, 1973.

862a. "Texte (Théorie du)." In *Encyclopaedia Universalis*, vol. 15
(1973), pp. 1013-1017. Paris: Encyclopaedia Universalis France,
1968.

*863. "Diderot, Brecht, Eisenstein." *Revue d'Esthétique*, 26 (April-
December 1973), 185-191. For English trans., see item 920.

864. "Comment travaillent les écrivains. Roland Barthes: 'un rapport
presque maniaque avec les instruments graphiques.'" *Le Monde
[des Livres]*, no. 8928 (27 September 1973), p. 24.

Jean-Louis de Rambures' interview of Barthes.

865. *Mythologies.* Trans. Annette Lavers. St. Albans: Granada Publishing Limited, 1973, 158pp. A Paladin Books rpt. of item 849.

866. "The Structuralist Activity." In *European Literary Theory and
Practice.* Ed. Vernon W. Gras. New York: Dell, 1973.

867. "Racinian Man (excerpt)." In *European Literary Theory and Practice.* Ed. Vernon W. Gras. New York: Dell, 1973.

867a. *Michelet.* Naples: Guida, 1973, 185pp. (Il Sagittario, no. 15)
Trans. of item 681.

868. *El Grado cero de la escritura, seguido de Nuevos ensayos críticos*.
      Trans. Nicolás Rosa. Buenos Aires: Siglo Veintiuno Editores,
      1973. Trans. of item 838.

869. "Über die Semiologie der Mode und der Literatur. Ein Gespräch
      mit Raymond Bellour." In *Antworten der Strukturalisten*. Ed.
      Adelbert Reif. Trans. Britta Reif-Willenthal and Friedrich
      Griese. Hamburg: Hoffmann und Campe, 1973, pp. 11-24.

870. "Vergnügen-Schreiben-Lesen. Ein Gespräch mit Jean Ristat." In
      Antworten der Strukturalisten. Ed. Adelbert Reif. Trans. Britta
      Reif-Willenthal and Friedrich Griese. Hamburg: Hoffmann und
      Campe, 1973, pp. 25-42.

871. *Sade, Fourier, Loyola*. Trans. Maren Sell and Jürgen Hoch. Frank-
      furt: Suhrkamp, 1973, 1974. Trans. of item 823.

                                   1974

872. *Michelet*. Paris: Editions du Seuil, 1974, 191pp. (Ecrivains de
      Toujours, 19) Rpts. item 681; see also items 839 and 860.

873. *Ecrire, pour quoi? Pour qui*. Paris: Presses Universitaires de
      Grenoble, 1974 or 1975. With Pierre Barbéris, Michel Butor,
      et al.

874. "Premier texte: en marge du Criton." *L'Arc*, no. 56 (Aix-en-
      Provence, 1974), pp. 3-7. Part of special issue on Barthes.

875. "Au séminaire." *L'Arc*, no. 56 (Aix-en-Provence, 1974), pp.
      48-56. Part of special issue on Barthes.

876. "Bibliographie." *L'Arc*, no. 56 (Aix-en-Provence, 1974), pp.
      91-95. Bibliography of works by Barthes. Part of special issue
      on Barthes.

877. "Pourquoi j'aime Benveniste." *La Quinzaine Littéraire*, no. 185
      (15-30 April 1974), pp. 3-4.

      Review of Benveniste's *Problèmes de linguistique générale*,
      tome II.

878. "Roland Barthes contre les idées reçues." *Figaro Littéraire*,
      no. 1471 (27 July 1974), pp. i, iv, 7, 10.

      Interview given to Claude Jannoud.

879. *S-Z*. Trans. Richard Miller. New York: Hill and Wang, 1974.
      Preface by Richard Howard. Trans. of item 801.

      Considers the text of Balzac's "Sarrasine" in sections ranging
      in length from several sentences to a single word, then analyzes
      these "lexias" by "codes" and "voices."

880. Co-author of *Structural Analysis and Biblical Exegesis: Inter-
      pretational Essays*. Trans. Alfred M. Johnson, Jr. Pittsburgh:

Pickwick Press, 1974. Trans. of item 842. Contains a bibliography on pp. 110-164.

881. *Miti d'oggi*. Trans. Lidia Lonzi. Turin: G. Einaudi, 1974. Trans. of item 700.

882. Article in *Bataille. Verso una rivoluzione culturale*. Ed. Philippe Sollers. Bari: Dedalo Libri, 1974. Trans. of item 861.

883. *El Proceso de la escritura*. Buenos Aires: Calden, 1974.

884. *El Placer del texto*. Trans. Nicolás Rosa. Buenos Aires: Siglo Veintiuno Editores, 1974. Trans. of item 855.

885. Contributor to *La Semiología*. Buenos Aires: Editorial Tiempo Contemporáneo, 1974 or before.

886. *La Teoría*. Barcelona: Editorial Anagrama, 1974 or before.

887. *Die Lust am Text*. Trans. Traugott König. Frankfurt am Main: Suhrkamp, 1974. Trans. of item 855.

888. *Sprache, Zeichen, Kommunikation*. Trans. Ulrich Köppen. Frankfurt am Main: Suhrkamp, 1974. With Claude Bremond, Tzvetan Todorov, and Christian Metz.

889. *Alors la Chine?* Paris: Christian Bourgois, 1975, 14pp. Excerpted from the May 24, 1974 issue of *Le Monde*. See also item 908. For review, see item 1276.

On China, description and travel.

1975

*890. *Roland Barthes par Roland Barthes*. Paris: Editions du Seuil, 1975. (Ecrivains de Toujours) For English trans., see item 921. For reviews, see items 1406-1429.

Contains a bibliography of works by Barthes from 1942 to 1974 on pp. 185-187, a biography of the major dates of his life and photographs.

891. Preface to *Les Pousse-au-jouir du maréchal Pétain*. By Gérard Miller. Paris: Editions du Seuil, 1975.

892. Preface to *Physiologie du goût*. By Jean Anthelme Brillat-Savarin. Paris: Hermann, 1975.

"Brings together his love of pleasure, his liking for wood and his continued interest in the existential thematics of substances."--Thody, 1977.

893. "Vingt mots-clé pour Roland Barthes." *Magazine Littéraire*, no. 97 (February 1975), pp. 28-37.

Remarks gathered by Jean-Jacques Brochier.

894. "Littérature/enseignement: Entretien avec Roland Barthes."
      Pratiques, no. 5 (February 1975), pp. 15-21.

895. "Fragments." *Le Monde [des Livres]*, no. 9357 (14 February 1975),
      p. 16.

896. "Barthes puissance trois." *Quinzaine Littéraire*, no. 205 (1-15
      March 1975), pp. 3, 5.

      On item 890.

897. "Roland Barthes met le langage en question." *Figaro Littéraire*,
      no. 1520 (5 July 1975), pp. 1, III: 11, 13.

      Interview given to Laurent Kissel.

898. "Réflexions sur *Souvenirs d'en-France*: Ce qui est bon ..." *Le
      Monde [des Arts et des Spectacles]*, no. 9535 (18 September
      1975), p. 17. See also item 912.

      On André Techine.

899. *The Pleasure of the Text*. Trans. Richard Miller. New York: Hill
      and Wang, 1975. Trans. of item 855. See also item 913.

      Reflections on the pleasures of reading and the erotic nature
      of writing. Also includes a four-page note on the text by
      Richard Howard.

900. *S-Z*. Trans. Richard Miller. London: Jonathan Cape, 1975. Trans.
      of item 801.

901. *Erte*. Trans. William Weaver. Limited ed. New York: Rizzoli
      International, 1975. See item 821.

902. "An Introduction to the Structural Analysis of Narrative."
      Trans. L. Duisit. *New Literary History*, 6, no. 2 (Winter 1975),
      237-272. Trans. of item 762.

903. *Il Piacere del testo*. Trans. Lidia Lonzi. Turin: G. Einaudi,
      1975. Trans. of item 855.

904. "Linguaggio come teatro e teatro del linguaggio (conversazione
      con Roland Barthes di Giuseppe Recchia)." *Altri Termini*, nuova
      serie, n. 8 (June 1975), pp. 55-62.

905. *Mythologieën*. Trans. C. Jongenburger. Amsterdam: De Arbeiderspers,
      1975. Trans. of item 700.

906. *S/Z*. Trans. Jürgen Hoch. Frankfurt am Main: Suhrkamp, 1975.
      Trans. of item 801.

1976

907. *S/Z*. Paris: Editions du Seuil, 1976. (Points) Rpts. item
      801.

908. *Et la Chine?* Paris: Christian Bourgois Editeur, 1976, 16pp. See also item 889.

909. Contributor to *La Sociologie de l'art et sa vocation interdisci-plinaire*. Paris: Denoël-Gonthier, 1976.

    A university colloquium organized in memory of Pierre Francastel.

910. "Le Chant romantique." *Gramma*, no. 5 (1976), pp. 164-169.

    Unlike the distribution of voices in opera which comes from the Oedipus God, that of the *lied* is almost unisexual. It mani-fests the song of the loving body, similar for each sex and addressed to no one in particular.

911. "Qu'en pensent les écrivains?... [de la réforme de l'orthographe]." *Le Monde de l'Education*, no. 13 (January 1976), pp. 16-18. Co-authors are Herve Bazin and Jean Dutourd.

912. "Ce qui est bon ..." *Avant-Scène-Cinéma*, no. 166 (February 1976), p. 5. Excerpted from item 898.

913. *The Pleasure of the Text*. Trans. Richard Miller. London: Jonathan Cape, 1976, 67pp. Trans. of item 855. See also item 899.

914. *Sade, Fourier, Loyola*. Trans. Richard Miller. New York: Hill and Wang, 1976. Trans. of item 823.

    Instead of summarizing the writings of the three authors, Barthes examines the language that each uses and shows that they formulate new languages. Sade invents a code of erotic pleasure; Fourier constructs a perfect society on paper; and Loyola is a "logo-technician" of the relationship between the individual and God. Their texts are instances of languages which subvert histor-ical and social contexts and establish new possibilities of meaning.

1977

*915. *Fragments d'un discours amoureux*. Paris: Editions du Seuil, 1977. (Tel Quel) For English trans., see item 924. For reviews, see items 1323a-1341a.

    Commentaries on a series of words (in alphabetical order) which evoke or arise in the lover's discourse: e.g., s'abîmer, absence, adorable, affirmation, altération, angoisse,... union, vérité, vouloir-saisir.

915a. *Leçon inaugurale faite le vendredi 7 janvier 1977*. Paris: Collège de France, c. 1977, 30pp. Chaire de sémiologie litté-raire.

916. "Introduction à l'analyse structurale des récits." In *Poétique du récit*. By Roland Barthes, Wolfgang Kayser, Wayne C. Booth, and Philippe Hamon. Paris: Editions du Seuil, 1977, pp. 7-57. Rpts. item 762. For review, see item 1405.

917.   "Roland Barthes au Collège de France: portrait d'un sémiologue
       en artiste." *Le Monde [Aujourd'hui]*, no. 9938 (9-10 January
       1977), p. 14.

       Excerpts of Barthes's inaugural lesson.

918.   "A quoi sert un intellectuel? Un entretien avec Roland Barthes."
       Le Nouvel Observateur, no. 635 (10-16 January 1977), pp. 64-
       68, 74.

       Interview given to Bernard-Henri Lévy.

919.   "Roland Barthes--*Fragments d'un discours amoureux*." *Art Press
       International*, no. 7 (May 1977), pp. 4-7.

       Interview given to Jacques Henric on 5 April 1977.

920.   *Image, Music, Text*. Ed. and trans. Stephen Heath. New York:
       Hill and Wang; London: Fontana, 1977, 220pp. For reviews,
       see items 1342-1347.

       Contains: The Photographic Message, pp. 15-31, trans. of item
       723; Rhetoric of the Image, pp. 32-51, trans. of item 746; The
       Third Meaning: Research Notes on some Eisenstein Stills, pp.
       52-68, trans. of item 804; Diderot, Brecht, Eisenstein, pp. 69-
       78, trans. of item 863; Introduction to the Structural Analysis
       of Narratives, pp. 79-124, trans. of item 762; The Struggle with
       the Angel: Textual Analysis of Genesis 32:22-32, pp. 125-141,
       trans. of item 842; The Death of the Author, pp. 142-148, trans.
       of item 787; Musica Practica, pp. 149-154, trans. of item 805;
       From Work to Text, pp. 155-164, trans. of item 830; Change the
       Object Itself: Mythology Today, pp. 165-169, trans. of item 829;
       Lesson in Writing, pp. 170-178, trans. of item 789; The Grain
       of the Voice, pp. 179-189, trans. of item 844; Writers, Intel-
       lectuals, Teachers, pp. 190-215, trans. of item 828; a translator's
       note, a list of sources and an index.

921.   *Roland Barthes*. Trans. Richard Howard. London: Macmillan; New
       York: Hill and Wang; Toronto: McGraw-Hill Ryerson Limited,
       1977. Trans. of item 890, with bibliography omitted.

       Contains photographs, a brief chronology of Barthes's life,
       and a series of passages, arranged in roughly alphabetical order,
       dealing with the shifts and contradictions in his work.

922.   *On Racine*. Trans. Richard Howard. New York: Octagon Books, 1977.
       Rpts. item 747.

923.   Contributor to "Reputations Revisited." *Atlas World Press Review*,
       24, no. 5 (May 1977), 50.

1978

923a. Contributor to *Prétexte, Roland Barthes*. Ed. Antoine Compagnon.
       Paris: Union Générale d'Editions, 1978, 443pp. (10/18, no.
       1265) Colloquium organized by the Centre culturel international
       de Cerisy-la-Salle, 22-29 June 1977.

924. *A Lover's Discourse: Fragments*. Trans. Richard Howard. New York:
      Hill and Wang, 1978, 234pp. Trans. of item 915.

924a. Editor of *Wilhelm von Gloeden*. Naples: Amelio, 1978, 59pp.

      Introductory text in English, French and Italian to an exhibit
      of Baron von Wilhelm von Gloeden's photography of the nude.
      XXI Festival dei due mondi, Incontri internazionali d'arte.

                                  1979

924b. *Sollers écrivain*. Paris: Editions du Seuil, c. 1979, 88pp.

924c. "Toward a Psychosociology of Contemporary Food Consumption." In
      Food and Drink in History. Ed. Robert Forster and Orst Ranum.
      Trans. Elborg Forster and Patricia M. Ranum. Baltimore, Md.:
      Johns Hopkins University Press, 1979, pp. 166-173.

      Selections from *Annales. Economies. Sociétés. Civilisations.*,
      volume 5.

924d. *The Eiffel Tower and Other Mythologies*. Trans. Richard Howard.
      New York: Hill and Wang, 1979, 152pp. Trans. of item 741a and
      twenty-eight short essays.

924e. "Barthes on Theatre." Trans. P.W. Mathers. *Theatre Quarterly*,
      9 (Spring 1979), 25-30.

924f. Contributor to "Entretiens sur Roger Laporte." *Digraphe*, no.
      18-19 (1979), pp. 176-203.

      Part of a special issue on Roger Laporte. Transcription of a
      broadcast devoted to his work, his conception of writing and his
      reflections on music.

                          SECONDARY SOURCES

925. Adamov, Arthur. *Ici et maintenant*. Paris: Gallimard, 1964.

     Albérès, R.-M. See item 3853.

     Aletheia. See item 3. Includes an interview with Barthes on
       pp. 213-219.

     Allemand, A. See item 4269.

     Allen, D.G. See item 4422.

926. Allombert, Guy, et al. "Les Artistes devant la politique [en-
     quête]." *Arts*, n.s., no. 10 (1-7 December 1965), pp. 10-11.

     Alter, R. See item 3856.

Améry, J. See item 4425.

Andreev, L. See item 4271.

Anonymous. See items 3859 and 4915.

927. ———. "La Balle au bond." *Le Nouvel Observateur*, no. 78
     (11–17 May 1966), p. 34.

928. ———. [Bibliographie]. *Magazine Littéraire*, no. 97 (February
     1975), pp. 22–23.

929. ———. Biography of Roland Barthes. *Current Biography*, 40
     (February 1979), 3–6. Also in *Current Biography Yearbook*,
     1979, pp. 20–24.

930. ———. "Les Bruits de la ville." *Le Nouvel Observateur*, no.
     57 (15–21 December 1965), pp. 28–29.

931. ———. "Les Bruits de la ville." *Le Nouvel Observateur*, no.
     70 (16–22 March 1966), pp. 30–31.

932. ———. "Civil War Among the Critics." *The Times Literary
     Supplement*, no. 3336 (3 February 1966), p. 83.

     On the Barthes-Picard debate.

933. ———. "Au Collège de France: M. Roland Barthes occupera la
     chaire de sémiologie littéraire." *Le Monde*, no. 9735 (12
     May 1976). Cf. items 956 and 961.

934. ———. "Confessions d'un 'barthomane' anglais." *Le Monde [des
     Livres]*, no. 9357 (14 February 1975), p. 17.

935. ———. "Crisis in Criticism: the Picard-Barthes Debate."
     The Times Literary Supplement, 5 (1966), 163–171. Reprinted
     in *T.L.S. 5. Essays and Reviews from THE TIMES LITERARY
     SUPPLEMENT, 1966*. London: Oxford University Press, 1967,
     pp. 163–171.

     On Barthes's *Critique et Vérité*.

936. ———. "Crisis in Criticism." *The Times Literary Supplement*,
     no. 3356 (23 June 1966), pp. 545–546.

     On Picard's *Nouvelle critique ou nouvelle imposture*, Barthes's
     Critique et Vérité, Doubrovsky's *Pourquoi la nouvelle critique?*,
     and Lanson's *Essais de méthode, de critique et d'histoire
     littéraire*.

937. ———. "Dates." *Le Monde [des Livres]*, no. 9357 (14 February
     1975), p. 16.

938. ———. "Deep Waters." *The Times Literary Supplement*, no. 3424
     (12 October 1967), p. 960.

     On Barthes and Lévi-Strauss.

939. ———. "Les Ecrits de Roland Barthes." *Magazine Littéraire*,
     no. 97 (1975), pp. 20–23.

940. ———. "Entretien avec Roland Barthes." *Aletheia* (see item 3), no. 4 (May 1966), pp. 213-218.

941. ———. "Entretien--Roland Barthes et le *Système de la mode:* 'Tout objet culturel est imprégné de langage humain.'" *Le Monde [des Livres]*, no. 6926 (19 April 1967), p. vi.

    Remarks gathered by Frédéric Gaussen.

942. ———. "L'Esprit et la lettre." *Le Nouvel Observateur*, no. 126 (12-18 April 1967), p. 42.

943. ———. "L'Esprit et la lettre." *Le Nouvel Observateur*, no. 127 (19-26 April 1967), p. 38.

944. ———. "The Ever-Moving Finger." *The Times Literary Supplement*, no. 3782 (30 August 1974), p. 934.

945. ———. "*L'Express* va plus loin avec Roland Barthes." *L'Express*, no. 985 (25-31 May 1970), pp. 70-80.

946. ———. *L'EXPRESS va plus loin avec Roland Barthes [et al.]*. Paris: Editions Robert Laffont, 1973, 465pp. See item 955.

    On Barthes and Lévi-Strauss.

    ———. See also item 3420.

947. ———. "Ladies as Letters." *The Times Literary Supplement*, no. 3736 (12 October 1973), p. 1256.

    On Barthes's *Erté.*

    ———. See also item 4827.

948. ———. "Lektüre als Kritik bei Roland Barthes." In *Gesellschaft Literatur Lesen. Literaturrezeption in theoretischer Sicht*. By Manfred Naumann, et al. Berlin-Weimar: Aufbau-Verlag, 1973, pp. 164-178.

    ———. See also items 4272 and 3861.

949. ———. "Modern Charlatanism. III. Frozen Labyrinths. Roland Barthes." *Cambridge Review*, 198, no. 2230 (30 January 1976), 87-93.

    ———. See also item 4273.

950. ———. "Peint par lui-même et quelques autres: Roland Barthes 'écrivain de toujours.'" *Le Monde*, no. 9357 (14 February 1975), p. 1.

951. ———. "Le Plaisir de Barthes." *N.D.L.R.: Ecriture/Peinture*, no. 1 (Summer 1976), p. 61.

952. ———. "The Pleasures of Logolysis." *The Times Literary Supplement*, no. 3656 (24 March 1972), p. 330. (Tel Quel, 1971).

On Barthes's *Sade, Fourier, Loyola*; *Mythologies*; and *Roland Barthes*.

953. ————. "Portrait [of Roland Barthes]." *Le Maclean*, 15 (Montreal, May 1975), p. 8.

————. See also items 4274 and 4275.

954. ————. *Roland Barthes*. Paris: Tel Quel, 1971. Bibliography, pp. 126–132. Rpts. *Tel Quel*, no. 47 (Fall 1971). See also item 1232.

955. ————. "Roland Barthes." In *L'EXPRESS va plus loin avec Roland Barthes [et al.]*. Paris: Editions Robert Laffont, 1973, pp. 153–188. See item 946.

956. ————. "Roland Barthes au Collège de France--Portrait du sémiologue en artiste." *Le Monde (hebdomadaire)*, no. 1472 (13–19 January 1977), p. 9. Cf. item 933 and 961.

957. ————. "Roland Barthes et la 'nouvelle critique.'" *Vie et Langage*, no. 220 (July 1970), p. 369.

958. ————. "Roland Barthes par ses textes." *Magazine Littéraire*, no. 97 (February 1975), p. 8.

959. ————. "La Semaine." *Arts et Loisirs*, no. 27 (30 March–5 April 1966), p. 11.

————. See also item 4276.

960. ————. "Structure and Society." *The Times Literary Supplement*, no. 3318 (30 September 1965), pp. 863–865.

On Barthes, Goldmann, Lévi-Strauss, et al.

961. Anquetil, Gilles. "Roland Barthes au Collège de France: la saveur du savoir." *Nouvelles Littéraires*, 55, no. 2567 (13–20 January 1977), p. 10. Cf. items 933 and 956.

962. Arbasino, Alberto. "Roland Barthes." In *Sessanta posizioni*. By Alberto Arbasino. Milan: Feltrinelli Editore, 1971, pp. 48–55.

963. *L'Arc*, no. 56 (Aix-en-Provence, 1974): issue on Roland Barthes. Contains items 990, 1000, 1001, 1007, 1008, 1020, 1022, 1027, 1055, 1061, 1148, 1206, 1210, 1275, and a bibliography, pp. 91–95.

964. Assad, Maria L. "La Lecture comme mythe." *Esprit Créateur*, 14 (Winter 1974), 333–341.

965. Atkins, John. "Judging a Novel." *Books and Bookmen*, 15, no. 1 (October 1969), 25–27.

966. Auclair, Georges. "Faits divers et 'Pensée naïve.'" *Critique*, no. 197 (October 1963), pp. 893-906.

967. B., J. "Barthes au Collège." *Magazine Littéraire*, no. 121 (February 1977), p. 37.

Balmas, E. See item 4278.

968. Bassy, Alain-Marie. "Du texte à l'illustration: pour une sémiologie des étapes." *Semiotica*, 11, no. 4 (1974), 297-334.

969. Bateson, F.W. "Is Your Structuralism Really Necessary?" *New Review*, 2, no. 14 (London, May 1975), 55-58.

970. Baudry, Jean-Louis. "La Tragédie racinienne: une oeuvre ouverte." *Tel Quel*, no. 15 (Fall 1963), pp. 65-67.

971. Béguin, Albert. "Pré-critique." In *Création et destinée. I. Essais de critique littéraire: L'Ame romantique allemande. L'Expérience poétique. Critique de la critique.* By Albert Béguin. Paris: Editions du Seuil, 1973, pp. 245-251.

972. Behar, Jack. "Notes on Literature and Culture." *Centennial Review*, 18, no. 3 (Summer 1974), 197-220.

973. Bellenger, Yvonne. "La Querelle de la 'nouvelle critique'; Proust et Montaigne à la défense de Barthes." *Le Monde*, no. 6492 (27 November 1965), p. 13.

974. Bellour, Raymond. "Entretien avec Roland Barthes." *Les Lettres Françaises*, no. 1172 (2-8 March 1967), pp. 1, 12-13.

975. ———. "*S/Z* et (ou) l'empire des signes." *Les Lettres Françaises*, no. 1335 (20-26 May 1970), pp. 3-7.

Interview with Barthes.

976. ———. "Entretien avec Roland Barthes." In *Le Livre des autres*. By Raymond Bellour. Paris: Editions de l'Herne, 1971, pp. 162-174.

977. ———. "Deuxième entretien avec Roland Barthes." In *Le Livre des autres*. By Raymond Bellour. Paris: Editions de l'Herne, 1971, pp. 240-259.

978. ———. "La Clé des champs." *Magazine Littéraire*, no. 97 (February 1975), pp. 15-18.

979. Ben Jalloun, Tahar. "Une Lecture politique de Barthes." *Le Monde [des Livres]*, no. 8928 (27 September 1973), p. 24.

980. Berggren, Tobias. "Roland Barthes' analysemetoder." *Bonniers Litterära Magasin*, årg. 40, nr. 2 (1971), 113-127.

Bergonzi, B. See item 22.

981. Berl, Emmanuel. "'Anciens' contre 'modernes,' un match nul."
      Preuves, no. 184 (June 1966), 73-79.

      On the Barthes-Picard debate.

      Bermejo, J.M. See item 5133.

      Bersani, J., et al. See item 3871.

982. Bersani, Leo. "Criticism, French Style: From Bachelard to
      Barthes." *Partisan Review*, 4, no. 2 (1967), 215-232.

      ————. See also item 3873.

      Bettetini, G. See item 3816.

983. Biasi, Gian-Paolo. "Rhetorical Questions from James Bond to
      Dante." *Diacritics*, 1, no. 1 (Fall 1971), 3-7.

      Biles, J.I. See item 3874.

      Blanchard, J.M. See item 3875.

984. Blanchot, Maurice. *Le Livre à venir*. Paris: Gallimard, 1971,
      c. 1959.

985. Bloc-Michel, Jean. "Barthes-Picard: Troisième rond." *Le Nouvel
      Observateur*, no. 72 (30 March-5 April 1966), pp. 34-35.

      On Barthes's *Critique et vérité*.

      Boisdeffre, P. de. See item 3879.

986. Boncenne, Pierre. "Un 'Sujet incertain'?" *Lire*, February 1977,
      p. 13.

      Bonnefis, Philippe. See item 5209.

987. ————. "La Pratique du sens dans le texte de Roland Barthes."
      Beiträge zur Analyse des sozialen Wortschatzes ... [no. 371],
      (Halle 1975), pp. 71-77.

      Bonnefoy, Claude. See item 4282.

988. ————. "Pour le plaisir." *Nouvelle Littéraires*, 51e année,
      no. 2371 (1973), 6.

989. Bonzon, A. "La Polémique Barthes-Picard." In *La Nouvelle critique
      et Racine*. By A. Bonzon. Paris: Editions A.-G. Nizet, 1970,
      pp. 178-182. See also items 4283 and 2764.

      Bouazis, C. See item 5134.

990. Bouttes, Jean-Louis. "A travers et à tors." *L'Arc*, no. 56 (1974),
      pp. 57-62.

991. Braun, Lev. *Witness of Decline. Albert Camus, Moralist of the
      Absurd*. Rutherford, Madison, Teaneck, N.J.: Fairleigh Dickinson
      University Press, 1974.

992. Bréchon, Robert. "Barthes et son double." *Colóquio-Letras*, núm. 32 (July 1976), pp. 26-30.

Brewster, B. See item 3818.

————, et al. See also item 5135.

993. Brincourt, André. "Un Peu de savoir et le plus de saveur possible." *Figaro Littéraire*, no. 1600 (15-16 January 1977), pp. 1, 13.

994. Brochier, Jean-Jacques. "Vingt mots-clés pour Roland Barthes." *Magazine Littéraire*, no. 97 (February 1975), pp. 28-37.

995. Brooke-Rose, Christine. "Letter from Paris: Ganging Up." *Spectator*, 236, no. 7709 (27 March 1976), p. 26.

996. Brooks, Peter. "An Erotics of Art." *New York Times Book Review*, 14 September 1975, p. 38.

    On *Pleasure of the Text* and *S/Z*.

997. Bruch, Jean-Louis. "Un Essai sur le style et l'écriture littéraire." *La Revue du Caire*, 16ᵉ année, no. 163 (October 1953), 233-237.

————. See also item 4287.

Bruézière, M. See item 4288.

Bruns, G.L. See item 4831.

998. Buchan, Tom. "Writing versus Literature: An Introduction to the Work of Roland Barthes." *Scottish International*, no. 2 (April 1968), pp. 8-18.

999. Buffat, Marc. "Le Simulacre: notes pour une diachronie." In *Roland Barthes*. Paris: Tel Quel, 1971, pp. 108-114.

1000. Burch, Noël. "Barthes et le Japon." *L'Arc*, no. 56 (1974), pp. 40-44.

1001. Burgelin, Olivier. "Le Double système de la mode." *L'Arc*, no. 56 (1974), pp. 8-16.

1002. Burgess, Anthony. "Short Sharp Stimulants." *The Sunday Times*, no. 7532 (8 October 1967), p. 32.

1003. Burkart, Angelika. "Zwischenspiel: Mythen des Alltags." *Beiträge zur romanischen Philologie*, heft 1 (1973), pp. 21-53.

1004. ————. "Sartre und Roland Barthes." *Beiträge zur romanischen Philologie*, 13, no. 1-2 (1974), 77-116.

    On their different conceptions of literary writing.

1004a. ――――. "Roland Barthes zwischen Brecht und Robbe-Grillet.
        (Literaturkritik 1954-1958)." *Beiträge zur romanischen
        Philologie*, Heft 1 (1976), pp. 9-31.

1004b. Burnier, Michel Antoine, and Patrick Rambaud. *Le Roland Barthes
        sans peine.* Paris: A. Balland, 1978.

1005.   Butor, Michel. "La Fascinatrice." *Les Cahiers du Chemin*, no. 4
        (October 1968), pp. 20-55.

1006.   Calvet, Louis-Jean. *Roland Barthes: un regard politique sur le
        signe.* Paris: Petite Bibliothèque Payot, 1973.

1007.   ――――. "Une Sémiologie politique." *L'Arc*, no. 56 (1974),
        pp. 25-29.

1008.   ――――. "Logophile et logothète." *L'Arc*, no. 56 (1974), pp.
        45-47.

1009.   ――――. *"Roland Barthes. Un regard politique sur le signe."*
        Sub-stance, no. 10 (1974 [1975]), pp. 192-193.

        An anonymous review of item 1006; not by Calvet.

1010.   ――――. "Barthes: l'amont, l'aval (structuralisme et sémio-
        logie)." *Magazine Littéraire*, no. 97 (February 1975), pp.
        13-14.

1011.   Caminade, Pierre. *Image et métaphore. Un problème de poétique
        contemporaine.* Paris: Bordas, 1970.

1012.   Camus, Albert. "Letter to Roland Barthes on *La Peste.*" In
        Lyrical and Critical. By Albert Camus. Trans. Philip Thody.
        London: H. Hamilton, 1967, pp. 253-255.

1013.   Carassus, Emilien. *Le Mythe du dandy.* Paris: Librairie Armand
        Colin, 1971.

        Carduner, J. See item 3901.

1014.   Carontini, E., and D. Peraya. "La Sémiologie comme translinguis-
        tique: le projet de R. Barthes." In *Le Projet Sémiotique.
        Eléments de sémiotique générale.* By E. Carontini and D.
        Peraya. Paris: Jean-Pierre Delarge, 1975, pp. 103-132.

1015.   Caute, David. *The Illusion. An Essay on Politics, Theatre and
        the Novel.* London: Panther Books Ltd., 1972.

1016.   Certeau, Michel de. "Faire de l'histoire: Problèmes de méthodes
        et problèmes de sens." *Recherche de Science Religieuse*, t.
        58, no. 4 (October-December 1970), 481-520.

1017.   Chabrol, Claude. *Le Récit féminin.* The Hague: Mouton, 1971.

        A thesis prepared under the direction of Barthes and influ-
        enced by Greimas.

1018. Champagne, Roland A. "La Chanson de Roland: A Study of Roland Barthes' *Le Degré Zéro de l'Ecriture.*" *Delta Epsilon Sigma Bulletin*, 17, no. 3 (October 1972), 78-87.

————. See also item 3905a.

Châtelet, F. See item 41.

1019. Chatman, Seymour. "On the Formalist-Structuralist Theory of Character." *Journal of Literary Semantics*, no. 1 (1972), pp. 57-79.

————. See also items 3906 and 4833.

1020. Chevrier, Jean-François. "La Puissance de l'inutile." *L'Arc*, no. 56 (1974), pp. 63-69.

Clancier, A. See item 4874.

1021. Clark, John G. "*La Conscience critique*. By Georges Poulet." *French Studies*, 28, no. 3 (July 1974), 355-356.

1022. Clément, Catherine, and Bernard Pingaud. "Au Lecteur." *L'Arc* no. 56 (1974), pp. 1-2.

1023. Cockburn, Alexander. "In Praise of Treachery." *New Statesman*, 74, no. 1909 (13 October 1967), 477.

Communications. See item 5140.

1023a. Compagnon, Antoine, ed. *Prétexte, Roland Barthes*. Paris: Union Générale d'Editions, 1978, 443pp. (10/18, no. 1265) Colloquium organized by the Centre culturel international de Cerisy-la-Salle, 22-29 June 1977.

Cormeau, N. See item 3694.

Corti, M., et al. See item 4291.

1024. Cournot, Michel. "La Zuppa pavese." *Le Nouvel Observateur*, no. 84 (22-28 June 1966), pp. 38-39.

1025. Cox, C.B., and A.E. Dyson, eds. *Word in the Desert. THE CRITICAL QUARTERLY Tenth Anniversary Number*. London-New York-Toronto: Oxford University Press, 1968.

1026. ————. *The Twentieth-Century Mind. History, Ideas and Literature in Britain*. London-Oxford-New York: Oxford University Press, 1972.

Culler, J. See item 4836.

1027. Dadoun, Roger. "Marches barthésiennes." *L'Arc*, no. 56 (1974), pp. 37-39.

1028. Daix, Pierre. "Structuralisme et sémiologie." *Les Lettres Françaises*, no. 1243 (31 July-6 August 1968), pp. 12-13.

Interview with Barthes.

1028a. Dauga, Jean. "Le 'Nouveau roman' ou le triomphe de Trissotain." *La Revue Universelle des Faits et des Idées*, December 1976, pp. 62-74.

On Barthes and Robbe-Grillet.

1029. Dausendschön, U. "Über Roland Barthes, Exercitia spiritualia und die strukturalistische Tätigkeit." *Sprache im Technischen Zeitalter*, 43 (1972), 245-249.

1030. Davidson, Hugh M. "The Critical Position of Roland Barthes." *Contemporary Literature*, 9, no. 3 (Summer 1968), 367-376.

1031. ———. "The Critical Position of Roland Barthes." In 4294, ed. L.S. Dembo, pp. 93-102.

1032. ———. "Sign, Sense, and Roland Barthes." In item 4833, ed. Seymour Chatman, pp. 29-50.

1033. ———. "Sign, Sense, and Roland Barthes." In *Literary Criticism: Idea and Act. The English Institute, 1939-1972. Selected Essays*. Ed. William Kurtz Wimsatt. Berkeley: University of California Press, 1974, pp. 228-241.

Degeorge, Fernande M. See item 3912.

Degrés. See items 3913 and 3915.

1034. Delbouille, Paul. "Sens littéral et interprétations symboliques. A propos des débats sur la Nouvelle Critique." *Cahiers d'Analyse Textuelle*, no. 8 (1966), pp. 107-125.

Delbouille rises up against the contempt of theorists (Barthes and Doubrovsky) for literary meaning. He sides with Picard and defends the value of a textual analysis based on respect for the word and not deformed by an abusive "psychoanalysis."

1035. D[elbouille], P. "Sur la lisibilité de Roland Barthes." *Cahiers d'Analyse Textuelle*, no. 17 (1975), pp. 131-135.

Demougin, J. See item 4295.

Denat, A. See item 4296.

1036. Detweiler, Robert. "The Moment of Death in Modern Fiction." *Contemporary Literature*, 13, no. 3 (Summer 1972), 269-294.

1037. Diéguez, Manuel de. *L'Ecrivain et son langage*. Paris: Gallimard, 1960.

1038. Donley, Michael. "Structures/Strictures." *Dutch Quarterly Review of Anglo-American Letters*, 5, no. 4 (1975), 283-294.

1039. Dort, Bernard. "Barthes: un défi au theatre." *Magazine Littéraire*, no. 97 (February 1975), pp. 10-11.

Doubrovsky, S. See item 4301.

1040. Duckworth, A.M. "Kermode, Frank: *The Classics: Literary Images of Permanence and Change.*" *Nineteenth Century Fiction*, 31, no. 3 (December 1976), 239-333.

1041. Dumur, Guy. "Portrait: avez-vous lu Barthes?" *Le Nouvel Observateur*, no. 373 (3-9 January 1972), pp. 36-37.

1042. Duncan, Catherine, and François Peraldi. "Discourse of the Erotic--The Erotic in the Discourse." *Meanjin Quarterly*, 33, no. 1 (March 1974), 62-71.

Dupeyron, G. See item 4302.

1043. Dupriez, B. *L'Etude des styles ou la commutation en littérature.* Paris-Montreal-Brussels: Didier, 1969.

Duvignaud, J. See item 3703.

1044. Duvignaud, Jean. "Littérature: Barthes." *Nouvelle Revue Française*, no. 269 (May 1975), pp. 93-95.

1045. Eberbach, Margaret. "Roland Barthes's Pleasure Primer." In *Twentieth Century Fiction. Essays for Germaine Brée.* Ed. George Stambolian. New Brunswick, N.J.: Rutgers University Press, 1975, pp. 252-264.

Eckert, C.W. See item 3823.

Eco, U. See item 2788.

1046. Egebak, Niels. "Strukturalisme og ideologi. Introduktion til Roland Barthes." *Vinduet*, 18. årgang, nr. 4 (1964), 266-271.

————. See also item 3704.

1047. Ehrmann, Jacques. "L'Emprise des signes." *Semiotica*, 7, no. 1 (1973), 49-76.

On Barthes's *L'Empire des signes* and *S/Z*.

1048. Eile, Stanisław. *Swiatopoglad powiesci.* Wrocław-Warsaw-Draków-Gdansk: Zaklad Narodowy Imienia Ossolinskich, 1973.

1049. Epshtein, M. "Kritika v Konflikte s tvorshestvom." *Voprosy Literatury*, 18 (February 1975), 131-168.

1050. Ezine, Jean-Louis. "Sur la sellette. Roland Barthes." *Nouvelles Littéraires*, 53e année, no. 2468 (13-19 January 1975), 3.

1050a. Fages, Jean-Baptiste. *Comprendre Roland Barthes.* Toulouse: Privat, 1979, 230pp. (Pensée)

1051.   Faye, J.-P. "Roland Barthes, une critique fabuleuse." *Lettres Françaises*, no. 1023 (2-8 April 1964), p. 5.

1052.   Fayolle, R. "Raymond Picard: *Nouvelle Critique ou nouvelle imposture*." *Revue d'Histoire Littéraire de la France,* 67e année, no. 1 (January-February 1967), 175-179.

1053.   Fiedler, Leslie A. "Intellectual Uncles." *The Guardian*, no. 37,716 (13 October 1967), p. 961.

        Filippetti, A., et al. See item 3927.

1054.   Finas, Lucette. "Barthes, ou le pari sur une nouvelle forme de raison." *La Quinzaine Littéraire,* no. 3 (15 April 1966), p. 15.

1055.   Finkelkraut, Alain. "Savoirs-vivre." *L'Arc*, no. 56 (1974), pp. 70-77.

1056.   Fisson, Pierre. "Pierre Fisson mène l'enquête sur le roman: Dominique Rolin, René Fallet, Roland Barthes." *Le Figaro Littéraire*, no. 863 (13 October 1962), p. 3.

1056a. Fitch, Brian T. "A Critique of Roland Barthes' Essay on Bataille's Histoire de l'oeil." In *Interpretation of Narrative*. Ed. Mario J. Valdés and Owen J. Miller. Toronto: University of Toronto Press, 1978, pp. 48-57. Paper read at the International Colloquium on the Interpretation of Narrative held at the University of Toronto, 24-27 March 1976.

1057.   Florenne, Yves. "Revue des revues: Sade dans le texte et dans les marges; Racine et la querelle des anciens et modernes." *Le Monde*, no. 6905 (25 March 1967), p. 13.

1058.   Founau, Pierre-Jean. "Vivre avec Barthes." *Nouvelle Revue Française*, no. 247 (July 1973), pp. 95-97.

        Fowlie, W. See item 4303.

        Francq, H.G. See item 4304.

1059.   Freedman, Richard. "Like Talk at a Terribly Serious Cocktail Party." *Chicago Tribune Book World*, III, no. 16 (20 April 1969), p. 5.

        Funt, D.W. See item 4520.

1060.   Funt, David. "Roland Barthes and the *Nouvelle Critique*." *Journal of Aesthetics and Art Criticism*, 26, no. 3 (Spring 1968), 329-340.

        G., P.-M. See item 85.

1061.   Gaillard, Françoise. "Roland Barthes 'sémioclaste'?" *L'Arc*, no. 56 (1974), pp. 17-24.

1061a. ———. "Literary Code(s) and Ideology: Towards a Contestation
of Semiology." *Sub-stance*, 5, no. 15 (February 1977), 68-81.

Fetishization of the code; catch-all code; Barthes and the
loss of difference and ideological value of texts through
(de)structuring operations accomplished by the reader's subjectivity.

Galard, J. See item 4841.

1062. Gardair, Jean-Michel. "Ritratti critici di contemporanei: Roland
Barthes." *Belfagor*, anno XXIII, n. 1 (31 January 1968),
50-77.

1063. ———. "Les Anciens et les modernes." *Critique*, no. 272
(January 1970), pp. 25-31.

1064. Genette, Gérard. "La Rhétorique et l'espace du langage."
Tel Quel, no. 19 (Fall 1964), pp. 44-54.

1065. ———. "L'Homme et les signes." *Critique*, 16e année, tome 21,
no. 213 (February 1965), 99-114.

On Barthes's *Essais Critiques*.

1066. ———. "L'Envers des signes." In *Figures, essais*. Paris:
Editions du Seuil, 1966, pp. 185-204. See also item 4305 and
Figures I. Paris: Editions du Seuil, 1976, a new edition.

Georgin, R. See item 3939.

1067. Gheude, Michel. "La Sémioclastie de Roland Barthes." In
L'Oeuvre ouverte. Ed. André Helbo. Brussels: *Degrés*, 1973,
pp. k/1 - k/4. A special issue of *Degrés*, 1ère année, no. 1
(January 1973).

1068. Giacchetti, Claudine. "La Structure narrative des nouvelles
de Maupassant." *South Central Bulletin*, 37, no. 3 (Fall 1977),
104.

Gillan, G. See item 4538a.

1069. Girard, René. "Racine, poète de la gloire." *Critique*, no. 205
(June 1964), pp. 483-506.

On Barthes's *Sur Racine* and Goldmann's *Le Dieu caché*.

González, J.E. See item 3944.

Grimaud, M. See item 4885.

1070. Grimm, Jürgen. "R. Barthes. Der formalistische Strukturalismus."
In his (et al.) *Einführung in die französische Literaturwissenschaft*. Stuttgart: J.B. Metzlersche Verlagsbuchhandlung,
1976, pp. 139-144.

Grotzer, P. See item 4310.

1071.   Gugliemi, Joseph. "Picard, Barthes et la critique en question."
        Cahiers du Sud, 61, no. 387-388 (April-June 1966), 326-329.

1072.   Guilbert, Jean-Claude. "Les Nouveaux maîtres à penser de la
        jeunesse." *Combat*, no. 7318 (24 January 1968), 8-9.

Guillén, C. See item 3948.

1073.   Guissard, Lucien. "Un Débat passionné: Nouvelle critique ou
        nouvelle imposture?" *La Croix*, 10 December 1965, p. 5.

        On the Barthes-Picard debate.

Guyon, F. See item 4311.

1074.   Hahn, Pierre. "L'Existentialisme vingt ans après: Déclin ou
        renaissance?" *Arts et Loisirs*, no. 26 (23-29 March 1966),
        pp. 10-11.

        Interviews with Barthes, Goldmann and others.

Hamon, P. See item 5164.

Hanhardt, J.G., et al. See item 3825.

1075.   Hanrez, Marc, ed. *Espagne d'écrivains. Guerre civile*. Paris:
        Pantheon Press France--Les Dossiers H, 1975.

1076.   Harari, Josué V. "The Maximum Narrative: An Introduction to
        Barthes's Recent Criticism." *Style*, Winter 1974, pp. 56-77.

1076a. ————. "Changing the Object of Criticism: 1965-1978." *MLN*,
        94 (May 1979), 784-796.

        On *Image, Music, Text*.

1077.   Hassan, Ihab. "Beyond a Theory of Literature: Intimations of
        Apocalypse?" *Comparative Literature Studies*, 1, no. 4
        (College Park, 1964), 261-271.

1078.   ————. "The Literature of Silence: From Henry Miller to
        Beckett and Burroughs." *Encounter*, 28, no. 1 (January 1967),
        74-82.

1079.   ————. *The Dismemberment of Orpheus. Towards a Postmodern
        Literature*. New York: Oxford University Press, 1971.

1080.   Hatzfeld, Helmut. "The Leading French Stylisticians of the
        Twentieth Century." *Style*, 8, no. 1 (Winter 1974), 3-17.

Hawkes, T. See item 5165.

1081.   Hayman, David. "Poisoned Wells." *Novel*, 8, no. 3 (Spring, 1975),
        274-276.

1082.   Heath, Stephen. "Roland Barthes and Semiology." In *Languages*.
        Ed. Anthony Rudolf. London: Circuit Magazine, 1969, pp. 9-12.

        This is part of the special issue of *Cambridge Opinion* and
        Circuit, Summer, 1969, on Barthes, Lacan, Lévi-Strauss, and
        others.

1083.   ————. "Orders of Discourse." *Atlantis*, no. 4 (September
        1972), pp. 66-74.

1084.   ————. *The Nouveau Roman: A Study in the Practice of Writing*.
        London: Elek Books Ltd., 1972.

*1085. ————. *Vertige du déplacement. Lecture de Barthes*. Paris:
        Fayard, 1974.

1086.   ————. "Changer de langue." *Magazine Littéraire*, no. 97
        (February 1975), pp. 18-19.

1086a. ————. *L'Analisi sregolata: lettura di Roland Barthes*. Trans.
        Patrizia Lombardo. Bari: Dedalo Libri, 1977, 200pp. (Collana
        bianca, 13) Trans. of item 1085.

1087.   Hector, Josette. "Roland Barthes: la mise en volume de l'écri-
        ture." *Synthèses*, 27e année, no. 309-310 (March-April 1972),
        82-86.

        Hempfer, K.W. See item 3956.

1088.   Henderson, B. "Segmentation." *Film Quarterly*, 31 (Fall 1977),
        57-65.

1089.   Henrie, Jacques. "Roland Barthes au Collège de France." *Art
        Press International*, no. 5 (March 1977), p. 5.

1090.   Heppenstall, Rayner. "Special Notices." *London Magazine*, 16,
        no. 2 (June-July 1976), 106-107.

        On item 913.

1091.   Hill, Leslie. "The Shroud of Barthes." *The Times Higher Educa-
        tion Supplement*, no. 316 (25 November 1977), p. 15.

        Hopkins, M.F. See item 3962.

1092.   Isou, Isidore. *Les Pompiers du nouveau roman, Sarraute, Robbe-
        Grillet, Butor, Simon, Beckett, Ionesco, Barthes, C. Mauriac*.
        Paris: "Lettrisme," 1971; Centre de Créativité, Editions
        Lettristes, 1977. Extracted from *Poésie Nouvelle*, no. 4-5
        (July-December 1958); *Lettrisme*, 17 January 1971.

1093.   Itterbeek, Eugene van. *Tekens van leven. Beschouwingen over
        het schrijverschap*. Brussels-The Hague: Manteau, 1969.

        Jaeggi, U.J.V. See items 108 and 4378.

        Jameson, F. See item 4172.

1094. Jarrett-Kerr, Martin, C.R. "The Conditions of Tragedy." *Comparative Literature Studies*, 2, no. 4 (1965), 363-374.

1095. J[ean], R[aymond]. "Le Japon comme écriture." *Le Monde [des Livres]*, no. 7874 (9 May 1970), p. III.

1096. Johansen, Hans Boll. *Den moderne roman i Frankrig. Analyser og synteser*. Copenhagen: Akademisk Forlag, 1970.

1097. Joncherie, Roger. "A propos d'une critique 'nouvelle.'" *La Nouvelle Critique*, 7ᵉ année, no. 69 (November 1955), 169-180.

1098. Jones, Robert Emmet. "L'Ecole structuraliste: Roland Barthes," part 2 of chapter 4 of item 4316, pp. 221-250.

1099. Josipovici, Gabriel. "Structures of Truth: The Premises of the French New Criticism." *The Critical Quarterly*, 10, no. 1-2 (Spring-Summer 1968), 72-88.

1100. ———. *The World and the Book. A Study of Modern Fiction*. London: Macmillan, 1971.

1101. Josselin, Jean-François. "Voulez-vous jouer avec Balzac?" *Le Nouvel Observateur*, no. 286 (4-10 May 1970), pp. 41-42.

Kahn, J.-F. See item 112.

Kampits, P. See item 4585.

1102. Kanters, Robert. "Roland Barthes et le mythe de Racine." *Le Figaro Littéraire*, no. 903 (10 August 1963), p. 2.

1103. ———. "Critique de la critique." *Le Figaro Littéraire*, no. 1063 (1 September 1966), p. 5.

1104. ———. "Roland Barthes et le lac des signes." *Le Figaro Littéraire*, no. 1252 (18-24 May 1970), pp. 20-21.
   On Barthes's *L'Empire des signes* and *S/Z*.

1105. ———. "Roland Barthes." In his *L'Air des lettres, ou Tableau raisonnable des lettres françaises d'aujourd'hui*. Paris: Grasset, 1973, pp. 323-328.

1106. ———. [Roland Barthes]. *Le Figaro Littéraire*, no. 1520 (5 July 1975), I: 11.

1106a. Kenner, Hugh. "Decoding Roland Barthes." *Harper's*, 261, no. 1563 (August 1980), 68-71.
   Barthes's obituary.

1107. Kermode, Frank. "In Parvo." *The Listener*, 78, no. 2011 (12 October 1967), 474.

1108. ———. "The Uses of the Codes." In item 4833, pp. 51-79.

1108a. Kevelson, Roberta. "A Restructure of Barthes's Readerly Text." *Semiotica*, 3 (1976), 253-267.

1109. Kittang, Atle. *Literaturkritiske problem. Teori og analyse.* Bergen-Oslo-Tromsφ: Universitetsforlaget, 1976.

1110. Koch, Stephen. "Melancholy King of the Cats." *Saturday Review*, 2 September 1978, pp. 32-34, 36.

    Krieger, M., and L.S. Dembo. See item 4319.

1111. Kristeva, Julia. "Le Sens et la mode." *Critique*, 20, no. 247 (December 1967), 1005-1031.

    An analysis and commentary of Barthes's *Système de la mode*; how Barthes uncovers the secret functioning of the symbolic machine.

1112. ———. "Comment parler à la littérature." In item 954, pp. 27-49.

1113. Laffly, Georges. "Le Goût et les critiques." *La Revue des Deux Mondes*, no. 15 (1 August 1967), pp. 335-349.

1114. Lafon, Francis. "Poètes, romanciers et critiques." *Français dans le Monde*, no. 118 (January 1976), 55-57.

1115. Laporte, Roger. "L'Empire des signifiants." *Critique*, 28, no. 302 (July 1972), 583-594. Reprinted in *Quinze Variations sur un thème biographique. Essais.* By Roger Laporte. Paris: Flammarion, 1975, pp. 145-157.

    On Barthes's *L'Empire des signes.*

1116. Lapouge, Gilles. "Entretien. Voyage autour de Roland Barthes." *La Quinzaine Littéraire*, no. 130 (1-15 December 1971), pp. 3-4.

1117. Lavers, Annette. "En traduisant Barthes." In item 954, pp. 115-125.

1118. ———. "A Mode of Knowledge." *The Times Literary Supplement*, no. 3829 (1 August 1975), p. 878.

    On *S/Z* and *Roland Barthes par Roland Barthes*, Culler's *Structuralist Poetics*, and Calvet's *Roland Barthes.*

1119. Le Clec'h, Guy. "Roland Barthes se considère comme le vrai gardien des valeurs rationales." *Le Figaro Littéraire*, 20e année, no. 1017 (14-20 October 1965), 4.

    Lefebve, M.-J. See item 3981.

1120. Lefèbvre, Henri. *Le Langage et la société.* Paris: Gallimard, 1966.

1121.   Léonard, Albert. *La Crise du concept de littérature en France au XXe siècle.* Paris: Librairie José Corti, 1974.

1122.   Leroy, Claude. "L'Ecrivain en habit dandy." *Revue des Sciences Humaines,* fasc. 150 (April-June 1973), pp. 261-276.

1123.   Le Sage, Laurent. "The New French Literary Critics." *The American Society Legion of Honor Magazine,* 37, no. 2 (1966), 75-86.

————.   "Roland Barthes." In item 4322, pp. 36-46.

1124.   Lewis, Philip. "Language and French Critical Debate." *Yale French Studies,* no. 45 (1970), pp. 154-165.

1125.   Lobet, Marcel. "La Vie littéraire." *Revue Générale Belge,* 89e année, no. 10 (15 October 1953), 1007-1013.

1126.   Lodge, David. "Metaphor and Metonymy in Modern Fiction." *Critical Quarterly,* 17, no. 1 (Spring 1975), 75-93.

1127.   ————.   "The Novel and the Nouvelle Critique." In his *The Modes of Modern Writing: Metaphor, Metonymy, and the Typology of Modern Literature.* Ithaca, New York: Cornell University Press, 1977, pp. 57-71.

1128.   Louit, Robert. "Le Discours du mythologue." *Magazine Littéraire,* no. 97 (February 1975), pp. 11-12.

1129.   Lydenberg, Robin. "Cut-Up: Negative Poetics in William Burroughs and Roland Barthes." *Comparative Literature Studies,* 14 (December 1978), 414-430.

1130.   Magliola, Robert. "The Phenomenological Approach to Literature: Its Theory and Methodology." *Language and Style,* 5, no. 2 (Spring 1972), 79-99.

————.   See also item 4626.

1131.   Major, Jean-Louis. "Le Philosophe comme critique littéraire." *Dialogue,* 4, no. 2 (September 1965), 230-242.

1132.   Maldavsky, David. *Teoría literaria general. Enfoque multidisciplinario.* Buenos Aires: Edit. Paidós, 1974.

1133.   Mall, James P. "Reviews." *Modern Language Journal,* 58, no. 7 (November 1974), 360-361.

1134.   Mambrino, Jean. "D'un cahier de poésie: des chants et des hommes." *Etudes,* June 1973, pp. 879-888.

Marchán, S. See item 3713.

Martin, G.D. See item 3994.

1135. Matignon, Renaud. "Roland Barthes: 'Je ne crois pas aux influences.'" *France Observateur*, 15, no. 728 (16 April 1964), 14.

An interview with Barthes.

1136. Mauriac, Claude. "Raymond Picard contre Roland Barthes: la réponse de la critique universitaire à la nouvelle critique." *Le Figaro*, 139e année, no. 6588 (3 November 1965), 24.

1137. ———. "Roland Barthes." In *L'Allitérature contemporaine*. Paris: Editions Albin Michel, 1969, c. 1958, pp. 215-232.

1138. McClendon, Wendell Eudell. "Paul Valery on Language and the Novel." *Dissertation Abstracts International*, 33, no. 9 (March 1973), 5186-A. Indiana University dissertation.

McFadden, G. See item 4852.

1139. McMullen, Roy. "The Rear Guard of the Avant-Garde: Roland Barthes." *Horizon*, 17, no. 2 (Spring 1975), 32-37.

Melenk, H. See item 4642.

1140. Mellac, Guy de, and Margaret Eberbach. *Barthes*. Paris: Editions Universitaires/Delarge, 1972. (Psychothèque, 12)

Merrell, Floyd. See items 4645 and 4646.

1141. Meschonnic, Henri. "Le Langage est une maladie." *Les Cahiers du Chemin*, no. 23 (1975), pp. 74-134.

1142. ———. *Le Signe et le poème*. Paris: Gallimard, 1975.

1142a. Michalczyk, John J. "Robbe-Grillet, Michelet, and Barthes: From *La Sorcière* to *Glissements progressifs du plaisir*." *The French Review*, December 1977, pp. 233-244.

1143. Michel, François. "A propos de Michelet." *La Nouvelle Critique*, 6e année, no. 58 (September-October 1954), 201-204.

1144. Miguelez, Roberto. "Théorie du discours et théorie de l'histoire." *Dialogue*, 13, no. 1 (March 1974), 53-70.

1144a. Milet, A. "Roland Barthes ou le paquet japonais." *La Foi et le Temps*, 8 (1978), 133-178.

Millet, L., et al. See items 147-149.

1145. Milošević, Nikola. "Rolan Bart izmedu egzistencijalizma i formalizma." In his *Ideologija, psihologija, i stvarataštvo*. Belgrade: Novinsko Izdavačko Preduzeće Duga, 1972, pp. 41-60.

Minguet, P. See item 4853.

1146. Molino, Jean. "Sur la méthode de Roland Barthes." *La Linguistique*, no. 2 (1970), pp. 141-154.

Montalbetti, J. See item 4330.

1147. Morawski, Stefan. "Mimesis." *Semiotica*, 2, no. 1 (1970), 35-58.

1148. Moreau, Jean A. "Plaisir du texte, plaisir du style." *L'Arc*, no. 56 (1974), pp. 78-82.

1149. Morris, Christopher D. "Barthes and Lacan: The World of the Moebius Strip." *Critique*, 17, no. 1 (1975), 69-77.

1150. Mouillaud, M. "Le Nouveau roman: tentative de roman et roman de la tentative." *Revue d'Esthétique*, fasc. 3 and 4 (August-December 1964), pp. 228-263.

Mounin, Georges. See item 4208.

————. "La Sémiologie de Roland Barthes." In his item 5176, pp. 189-197.

1151. Naumann, Manfred, et al. *Gesellschaft Literatur Lesen. Literaturrezeption in theorischer Sicht*. Berlin-Weimar: Aufbau Verlag, 1975, c. 1973.

1152. Naville, P. "Recherches pour une sémiologie de l'image optique." *Epistémologie sociologique*, no. 9 (1970), pp. 95-119.

A critique of the work of Barthes, not in its origins (Saussure) but in its integration with linguistics and in its semiology. An opposite approach is proposed starting with semiological material and inventing its own rules of signification.

1153. Nichols, Stephen G., Jr. "Roland Barthes." *Contemporary Literature*, 10, no. 1 (Winter 1969), 136-146.

————. See also item 4332.

Niculescu, R. See item 5178.

Niel, A. See item 4005.

1154. Norris, Christopher. "Les Plaisirs des clercs: Barthes's Latest Writings." *British Journal of Aesthetics*, 14, no. 3 (Summer 1974), 250-257.

1155. ————. "Roland Barthes: The View form Here." *Critical Quarterly*, 20 (Spring 1978), 27-43.

La Nouvelle Critique. See item 4009.

1156. Nuñez Ladeveze, Luis. "El Binarismo de Roland Barthes." In his *Crítica del discurso literario*. Madrid: Cuadernos para el Dialogo, 1974, pp. 319-324.

1157. Olmi, Massimo. "Rissa tra i critici." *Fiera Letteraria*, 41, no. 8 (3 March 1966), 14-15.

1158. Onimus, Jean. "L'Homme égaré: notes sur le sentiment d'égarement dans la littérature actuelle." *Etudes*, 283, no. 12 (December 1954), 320-329.

1159. Osowski, Judy. "The Structuralist Concept of Form: Roland Barthes, Georges Poulet, and J. Hillis Miller." *The Modern Schoolman*, 49, no. 4 (May 1972), 349-355.

1160. P., B. "Le Réflexe de réduction." *La Quinzaine Littéraire*, no. 43 (15-31 January 1968), pp. 10-12.

1161. Palomo, Dolores. "Scholes, Barthes and Structuralist Criticism." *Modern Language Quarterly*, 36, no. 2 (June 1975), 193-206.

On Barthes's *S/Z* and Scholes' *Structuralism in Literature*.

Parain-Vial, J. See item 3720.

1162. Pascal, Roy. "Narrative Fictions and Reality." *Novel*, 11, no. 1 (Fall 1977), 40-50.

On Sartre and Barthes.

1163. Pasquet, Sylvaine. "Les Ecrits de Roland Barthes." *Magazine Littéraire*, no. 97 (February 1975), pp. 20-22.

1164. Pasternack, Gerhard. *Theoriebildung in der Literaturwissenschaft. Einführung in Grundfragen des Interpretations-pluralismus.* Munich: Wilhelm Fink, 1975.

On Barthes and Saussure.

1165. Patrizi, Giorgio. "Le Aporie del testo nell'ultimo Barthes." *Il Ponte*, 31, no. 7-8 (July-August 1975), 832-835.

1166. ————. *Roland Barthes o le peripezie della semiologia.* Rome Istituto della Enciclopedia Italiana, 1977, 176pp. (Biblioteca biographica, 18)

1167. Perrone-Moisès, Leyla. "Le Langage de Roland Barthes." *La Quinzaine Littéraire*, no. 191 (16-31 July 1974), pp. 23-24.

1168. ————. "L'Intertextualité critique." *Poétique*, no. 27 (1976), pp. 372-384.

1169. Perros, Georges. "Barthes étoilé." In his *Papiers collés II.* Paris: Gallimard, 1973, pp. 292-295.

1170. Perruchot, Claude. "The Liberation of Writing." Trans. Harriett Watts. *Boston University Journal*, 22, no. 3 (Fall 1974), 36-42.

1171. Petitjean, Gérard. "Les Grands prêtres de l'université française." *Le Nouvel Observateur*, no. 543 (7-13 April 1975), pp. 52-57.

1172. Piatier, Jacqueline. "La 'Nouvelle critique' est-elle une 'imposture'?" *Le Monde (hebdomadaire)*, no. 888 (27 October 1965), p. 10.

   On item 1175.

1173. P[iatier], J[acqueline]. "Zoologie fantastique: cheval de bataille et bouc émissaire." *Le Monde*, no. 6552 (5 February 1966), p. 12.

1174. ———. "La Querelle de la 'nouvelle critique': Roland Barthes répond à Raymond Picard." *Le Monde*, no. 6606 (9 April 1966), p. 11.

   On Barthes's *Critique et vérité*.

*1175. Picard, Raymond. *Nouvelle critique ou nouvelle imposture*. Paris: Jean-Jacques Pauvert, 1965.

1176. ———. "Racine et la 'nouvelle critique.'" *Revue des Sciences Humaines*, n.s., fasc. 117 (January–March 1965), pp. 29–49.

1177. ———. "La Nouvelle critique? Une imposture, un délire ..." *Le Figaro Littéraire*, 20, no. 1016 (7–13 October 1965), 10.

1178. ———. "Un Nihilisme confortable." *Le Nouvel Observateur*, no. 74 (13–19 April 1966), pp. 50–51.

   Comment on Barthes's *Critique et vérité*.

1179. ———. "Magical Criticism." *New Statesman*, 72, no. 1844 (15 July 1966), 88.

1180. ———. *New Criticism or New Fraud?* Trans. Frank Towne. Pullman: Washington State University Press, 1969, 47pp.

1181. Pierssens, Michel. "Le *S/Z* de Roland Barthes: l'avenir du 'texte.'" *Sub-stance*, no. 1 (Fall 1971), pp. 37–48.

   A review of Barthes's main concepts; a brief survey of the main issues in French new criticism.

1182. Pingaud, Bernard. "Critique traditionnelle et nouvelle critique." *La Nef*, 24, no. 29 (January–March 1967), 41–56.

1183. Pivot, Bernard. "A la demande de Roland Barthes la page 187 d'*Immédiatement* a été arrachée sans délai." *Le Figaro Littéraire*, no. 1342 (4 February 1972), II: 14.

1184. ———. "Blanche Epiphanie et Roland Barthes." *Lire*, no. 21 (May 1977), pp. 9–10.

1185. Pizzorusso, Arnaldo. *Teorie litterarie in Francia. Ricerche sei-settecenesche*. Pisa: Nistri-Lischi, 1968.

1186. Plett, Heinrich F. *Textwissenschaft und Textanalyse. Semiotik, Linguistik, Rhetorik*. Heidelberg: Quelle & Meyer, 1975.

1187. Pleynet, Marcelin. "Dedicace." In item 954, pp. 50-63.

1188. Plottel, Jeanine Parisier. "Names, Spaces, Signs." *Centerpoint*, 1, no. 3 (Spring 1975), 67-70.

   On Barthes and Saussure.

1189. *Poésie/Ecriture*, no. 7 (January 1976): issue entitled "Lecture productive." Vieux-Lyon: Editions de l'Ollave, 1976.

1190. Pollmann, Leo. *Literaturwissenschaft und Methode.* Band I. Theoretischer Teil und Methodengeschichtlicher Überblick. Band II. Gegenwartsbezogener systematisch-kritischer Teil. Frankfurt: Athenäum, 1971.

1191. Pommier, Jean. "La Querelle." *Revue d'Histoire Littéraire de la France*, 67, no. 1 (January-March 1967), 82-96.

   Poole, R. See items 165 and 4709.

1192. Poulet, Georges. "Roland Barthes." In his *La Conscience critique*. Paris: Librairie José Corti, 1971, pp. 267-272.

1193. Poulet, Robert. "La Relève de Tamerlan." *Ecrits de Paris*, no. 325 (May 1973), pp. 91-96.

   Prieto, L.J. See item 5181.

1194. Raillard, Georges. "Clés pour le 'nouveau roman.'" *Le Français dans le Monde*, no. 17 (June 1963), pp. 20-21.

1195. ————. "Les Anciens et les modernes." *Le Français dans le Monde*, no. 39 (March 1966), pp. 46-48.

   On the Barthes-Picard debate.

1196. Rambures, Jean-Louis de. "Comment travaillent les écrivains. Roland Barthes. Propos recueillis par Jean-Louis de Rambures." *Le Monde [des Livres]*, 27 September 1973, p. 24.

1197. Rawicz, Piotr. "*Eden, Eden, Eden*, de Pierre Guyotat: sur trois préfaces." *Le Monde [des Livres]*, no. 8000 (3 October 1970), p. 16.

1198. Reed, Walter L. "The Problem with a Poetics of the Novel." *Novel*, 9, no. 2 (Winter 1976), 101-113.

   Reif, Adelbert. "Roland Barthes." In item 172, pp. 9-10. See also items 869 and 870.

1199. Rella, Franco. "Pratica letteraria e ideologia (note su alcuni testi)." *Nuova Corrente*, no. 57-58 (1972), pp. 136-152.

1200. Revel, Jean-François. "J'ai cherché à ouvrir une discussion." *La Quinzaine Littéraire*, no. 3 (15 April 1966), pp. 14-15.

1201. ———. "Le Fantasme anonyme." *L'Express*, no. 1006 (19-25
       October 1970), p. 67.

       Ricardou, J. See item 4333.

1201a. Rice, Donald. "Theological Pornography: A Non-Reading of
       Klossowski's *Roberte ce soir*." *Sub-stance*, 4, no. 10 (Fall
       1974), 39-45.

       Discusses Roberte using the methods of Barthes and others to
       show the essentially different universe of literature/criticism
       at work in the novel.

       Ricoeur, P. See item 4735.

1202. Rimmon, Shlomith. "Barthes' 'Hermeneutic Code' and Henry James's
       Literary Detective: Plot-Composition in 'The Figure in the
       Carpet.'" *Hebrew University Studies in Literature*, 1, no. 2
       (Fall 1973), 183-207.

1203. Ristat, Jean. "Plaisir/écriture/lecture." *Les Lettres Françaises*,
       no. 1422, pp. 5-8.

1204. ———. "Plaisir/écriture/lecture: entretien avec Roland
       Barthes." In his *Qui sont nos contemporains*. Paris: Gallimard,
       1975, pp. 248-265.

1205. ———. *L'Entrée dans la baie et la prise de la ville de Rio
       de Janeiro en 1711. Tragi-comédie. Suivi de l'Inconnu n'est
       pas n'importe quoi. Dialogue avec Roland Barthes*. Paris:
       Les Editeurs Français Réunis, 1973.

1206. Rivière, Jean-Louis [Loup]. "Mises en scène d'Orphée." *L'Arc*,
       no. 56 (1974), pp. 83-86.

1207. Robbe-Grillet, Alain, et al. "Barthes par les autres." *Le Monde
       [des Livres]*, no. 9357 (14 February 1975), p. 17.

1208. Robinet, André. "La Mode à la mode." *Les Nouvelles Littéraires*,
       no. 2077 (22 June 1967), p. 4.

1209. [Roche, Denis]. "Le 96ème Titre de collection 'Ecrivains de
       toujours': Roland Barthes écrit un livre sur ... Roland
       Barthes." *27, Rue Jacob*, no. 183 (February 1975), p. 11.

       An interview with Barthes.

1209a. Roger, Philippe. "Roland Barthes. Le Texte: science, plaisir."
       In *Les Dieux dans la cuisine. Vingt ans de philosophie en
       France*. Ed. Jean-Jacques Brochier. Paris: Aubier, 1978, pp.
       68-77.

       Romani, B. See item 4334.

1210. Ronat, Mitsou. "Alternative." *L'Arc*, no. 56 (1974), pp. 30-36.
       See also item 1211.

1211. ———. "Alternative (à Roland Barthes)." In his *La Langue manifeste. Littérature et théories du langage.* Paris: *Action Poétique*, 1975, pp. 43-52. Part of a supplement to *L'Action Poétique*, no. 63 (1975). See also item 1210.

1212. Rosenbaum, Jonathan. "Rivière & Cie. I. *Duelle.*" *Film Comment*, 12, no. 5 (September-October 1976), 2-29.

1213. Rosenthal, Peggy. "Deciphering *S/Z.*" *College English*, 37, no. 2 (October 1975), 125-144.

   Sees Barthes's *S/Z* as offering ways of approaching critical problems not well dealt with in Anglo-American criticism.

1214. Roudiez, Leon S. "The Reader as Subject." *Semiotext(e)*, 1, no. 3 (1975), 69-80.

   Roudinesco, E. See item 581.

1215. Roux, Dominique de. *Maison [jaune].* Paris: Christian Bourgois, Editeur, 1969.

   Russell, L. See item 3836.

1216. Rutten, M. "De Derde weg van de kritiek." *Speigel der Letteren*, 13, no. 4 (1970-1971), 241-275.

   On Barthes and Picard.

   Šabouk, S. See item 3728.

   Said, E.W. See item 4336.

1217. Saint-Onge, Paule. "The Writer: His Art as He Sees It." *Canadian Author and Bookman*, 40, no. 3 (Spring 1965), 6-7.

1218. Salvi, Sergio. "Barthes e la scrittura poetica." *Letteratura*, anno XXV (IX nuova serie), n. 51 (May-June 1961), vi-x.

   Sanders, S. See item 4031.

1219. Sarduy, Severo. "Tanger." In item 954, pp. 86-88.

1220. Sartre, Jean-Paul. "Sartre at Seventy: An Interview (with Michael Contat)." Trans. Paul Aster and Lydia Davis. *New York Review of Books*, 22, no. 13 (3 August 1975), 10, 12-17.

1220a. Savage, N.D. "Rencontre avec Roland Barthes." *French Review*, 52 (February 1979), 432-439.

1221. Scarpati, Claudio. "La 'Nouvelle critique': la Sorbona contra Roland Barthes." *Vita E Pensiero*, 50, no. 4 (April 1967), 385-392.

   Schiwy, G. See items 189, 190, and 4034.

1222. Schmidt, Albert-Marie. "Un Grand commis aux écritures." In his
       Chroniques de Réforme, 1945-1966. Lausanne: Editions Rencontre,
       1970, pp. 248-252.

1223. Schober, Rita. *"Im Banne der Sprache." Strukturalismus in der
       Nouvelle Critique, speziell bei Roland Barthes.* Halle (Saale):
       Mitteldeutscher Verlag, 1968.

1224. ————. *Von der wirklichen Welt in der Dichtung. Aufsätze zur
       Theorie und Praxis des Realismus in der französischen Literatur.*
       Berlin-Weimar: Aufbau-Verlag, 1970.

1225. Schulze, Joachim. "Kurze Beschreibung und Erklärung von
       Maupassants Erzählung." *Literatur in Wissenschaft und Unter-
       richt*, Band VIII, Heft 3 (1975), 148-161.

1226. Schwartz, Danielle. "Barthes, le langage et le pouvoir." *La
       Nouvelle Critique*, no. 106 (August-September 1977), pp. 55-57.

1227. Sénart, Philippe. "La Critique: de Barbey d'Aurevilly à Roland
       Barthes." *Combat*, no. 6240 (16 July 1964), p. 7.

1228. ————. "La Critique: Roland Barthes--Jacques Vier--Henri
       Clouard." *Combat*, no. 6797 (28 April 1966), p. 7.

1229. Seymour-Smith, Martin. "Cape of Good Hope." *Spectator*, 221,
       no. 7329 (13 December 1968), 849-850.

1230. Shepler, Frederic J. "Peeking through the Keyhole with Barthes."
       New Boston Review, 1, no. 4 (Spring 1976), 26-29.

       On Barthes's *S/Z, The Pleasure of the Text*, and *Sade, Fourier,
       Loyola.*

       Silverstein, N. See item 3839.

       Simon, John K., ed. See item 4338.

1231. Simon, Pierre-Henri. "Actif et passif de l'année 1966." *Le
       Monde*, no. 6830 (28 December 1966), pp. 10-11.

1231a. Slăvescu, Micaela. "Lecture d'une lecture: Roland Barthes."
       Cahiers Roumains d'Etudes Littéraires, no. 4 (1977), pp. 96-
       104.

1232. Sollers, Philippe, et al. *Roland Barthes.* Paris: Editions du
       Seuil, 1971. A special issue of *Tel Quel*, no. 47; bibliography,
       pp. 126-132. See also item 954.

1233. ————. "R.B." In item 954, pp. 19-26.

1234. Sollers, Philippe. "R.B." In his *Sul materialismo.* Milan:
       Feltrinelli, 1973, pp. 111-121.

*1235. ————. *Sur le matérialisme.* Paris: Editions du Seuil, 1974.

1236.   ———. "Pour Barthes." *Magazine Littéraire*, no. 97 (February 1975), p. 9.

1237.   Soto Verges, Rafael. "Ciencias sociales." *Estafeta Literaria*, no. 522 (15 August 1973), pp. 1438-1439.

On *El Libro de los otros* by Raymond Bellour.

1238.   ———. "Literatura mágica." *Estafeta Literaria*, no. 545 (1 August 1974), pp. 4-7.

1239.   Squarotti, Giorgio Barberi. "Arte e società: tre indicazioni." *Questioni*, no. 1-2 (January-April 1958), pp. 48-54.

Steinwachs, G. See item 4050.

1240.   Štěpánková, Julie. "Za novou kritiku." *Česká Literatura*, no. 15 (1967), pp. 39-46.

1241.   Streit, Edward Arnold. "From Proust to Richard: French Thematic and Phenomenological Criticism." *Dissertation Abstracts International*, 34, no. 6 (December 1973), 3433-3434A. Yale University dissertation.

1242.   Sturrock, John. "Roland Barthes: A Profile." *New Letters*, 1, no. 2 (May 1974), 13-21.

———. See items 196a and 4862.

1243.   Sur, Jean. "Duel critique." *La Table Ronde*, no. 220 (May 1966), pp. 103-107.

On the Barthes-Picard debate.

1244.   Sutton, Geneviève. "Racine et la critique contemporaine." *South Atlantic Bulletin*, 34, no. 3 (May 1969), 1-4.

On Barthes, Picard and others.

1245.   Szanto, George H. *Narrative Consciousness. Structure and Perception in the Fiction of Kafka, Beckett, and Robbe-Grillet.* Austin-London: University of Texas Press, 1972.

1246.   Tans, J. "Itterbeek, Eugène van: *Tekens van leven. Beschouwingen over het schrijverschap.*" *Revue d'Histoire Littéraire de la France*, 70, no. 3 (May-June 1970), 539-540.

Taranienko, Z. See item 4053.

1247.   Texier, Jean C. "Roland Barthes: la duplicité critique." *Combat*, no. 8562 (27 January 1972), p. 9.

1248.   Theis, Raimund. "Roland Barthes." In *Französische Literaturkritik der Gegenwart in Einzeldarstellungen.* Ed. Wolf-Dieter Lange. Stuttgart: A. Kröner, 1975, pp. 252-278.

1249. Thibaudeau, Jean. "Livres à emporter: nouvelle littérature."
       France Observateur, 15, no. 740 (9 July 1964), 13-14.

1250. Thody, Philip, ed. *Camus: Lyrical and Critical Essays*. Trans.
       Ellen Conroy Kennedy. New York: Knopf, 1968; Random House,
       1970.

1251. ————. *Roland Barthes: A Conservative Estimate*. Atlantic
       Highlands, N.J.: Humanities Press; London: Macmillan, 1977.

       Summarizes the milieu, major ideas and development of Barthes.

1252. Tilliette, Xavier. "La Querelle des critiques." *Etudes*, Septem-
       ber 1966, pp. 228-234.

       About Barthes, Picard and Doubrovsky.

1253. Tixier, Max. "Logique du poème." *Courrier du Centre Inter-
       national d'Etudes Politiques*, no. 100 (n.d.), pp. 3-13.

1254. Todorov, Tzvetan. "Le Langage à Baltimore." *La Quinzaine
       Littéraire*, no. 17 (1-15 December 1966), p. 25.

1254a. ————. "Reflections on Literature in Contemporary France."
       Trans. B. Braunrot. *New Literary History*, 10 (Spring 1979),
       511-531.

1255. Toynbee, Philip. "Semantic Frontiersmen." *The Observer*, no.
       9205 (17 December 1967), p. 21.

1256. Turnell, Martin. "Men and Ideas: The Criticism of Roland
       Barthes." *Encounter*, 26, no. 2 (February 1966), 30-36.

1257. ————. "Kritika Rolanda Barthesa." *Slovenské Pohl'ady*, Ročník
       83, no. 8 (August 1967), 105-113. A translation of item 1256.

1258. Ulmer, Gregory L. "Fetishism in Roland Barthes's Nietzschean
       Phase." *Papers on Language and Literature*, 14 (Summer 1978),
       334-355.

1259. Uphaus, Robert W. "Book Reviews." *Criticism*, 16, no. 1 (Winter
       1974), 73-77.

       Uscatescu, G. See items 203 and 4063.

1260. Uscatescu, Jorge. "Espacio, tiempo, imagen." *Estafeta Literaria*,
       no. 502 (15 October 1972), pp. 4-9.

1261. Velan, Yves. "Barthes." In item 4338, pp. 311-339.

       Venault, P. See item 621.

1262. Vidal, Gore. "American Plastic: The Matter of Fiction." *New
       York Review of Books*, 23, no. 12 (15 July 1976), 31-39. Rpt.
       in his *Matters of Fact and of Fiction. Essays, 1973-1976*.
       New York: Random House, 1977, pp. 99-126.

1262a. Villena, Luis Antonio de. "Entrevista. Roland Barthes e il
       placer como inteligencia." *Insula*, no. 385 (December 1978),
       p. 4.

       Vogel, A. See item 3842.

1263. Wagener, Françoise. "Un Livre de Franco Maria Ricci: la
       rencontre de Barthes et d'Erté." *Le Monde [des Livres]*, no.
       8992 (13 December 1973), p. 21.

1264. Wahl, François. "Le Code, la roue, la réserve." In item 954,
       pp. 64-85.

1265. Wakeman, John, ed. Biography of Roland Barthes. *World Authors,
       1950-1970: A Companion Volume to Twentieth-Century Authors*.
       New York: H.W. Wilson Company, 1975, pp. 121-122.

1266. Waldrop, Rosmarie. "Signs and Wonderings." *Comparative Litera-
       ture*, 27, no. 4 (Fall 1975), 344-354.

       Watkins, E. See item 4345.

1267. Watson, George. "Old Furniture and 'Nouvelle Critique.'"
       Encounter, 44, no. 2 (February 1975), 48-54.

1268. Weber, Jean-Paul. "Correspondance." *Revue d'Histoire Littéraire
       de la France*, 68, no. 2 (March-April 1968), 342-343.

       On Barthes and Picard.

1269. Weightman, John. "The Paris Scene." *The Observer*, no. 9070
       (2 May 1965), p. 27; no. 9071 (9 May 1965), p. 32.

1270. ———. "Incest with Mother." *New Society*, 20 October 1977,
       pp. 131-132.

       Weinmann, Robert. "Zwischen Soziologie und Formalismus. (Roland
       Barthes)." In his item 4069, pp. 286-297.

       Weinrich, H. See item 4071.

       Wellek, R. See item 4072.

       White, H.C. See item 5122.

       White, H.V. See items 215 and 4073.

1271. Wood, Michael. "Rules of the Game." *New York Review of Books*,
       23, no. 3 (4 March 1976), 31-34.

       On Barthes's *Sade, Fourier, Loyola*; *The Pleasure of the Text*;
       L'Empire des Signes; *S/Z*.

       Yon, A.F. See item 4346.

       Zaborski, A. See item 5126.

Zand, N. See item 3847.

1272. Zéraffa, Michel. "Petites mythologies pour grandes personnes."
       La Parisienne, no. 45 (June 1957), pp. 750-752.

       ————. See also item 4866.

1273. Zilli, L. "La Critica strutturalista: Roland Barthes." In item
       4278, pp. 61-79, 115-123.

       Zimmer, C. See item 3848.

1274. Zumthor, P. "Texte et société." *Semiotica*, 7, no. 3 (1973),
       282-284.

       Review of item 1017.

1275. Zuppinger, Renaud. "Notes étourdies écrites pendant un séminaire
       de Roland Barthes." *L'Arc*, no. 56 (1974), pp. 87-90.

                                    REVIEWS

                             Alors la Chine?
                                (item 889)

1276. Leys, Simone. *Contrepoint*, no. 21 (1976), pp. 191-192.

                   Analyse structurale et exégèse biblique
                           (items 842 and 4915)

1277. Graystone, G. *The Catholic Biblical Quarterly*, 35 (October
       1973), 516-517.

1278. Isambert, F.A. *Archives de Sciences Sociales des Religions*,
       18, no. 35 (1973), 174-175.

1279. Kapelrud, A.S. *Norsk Teologisk Tidsskrift*, 75, no. 1 (1974),
       87-88.

1280. Kieffer, R. *Svensk Teologisk Kvartalskrift*, 48, no. 3 (1972),
       127-128.

1281. Lamouille, A. *Revue Thomiste*, 73, no. 3 (1973), 469-471.

1282. Lys, D. *Etudes Théologiques et Religieuses*, 48, no. 1 (1973),
       105-107.

1283. Meschonnic, H. *Les Cahiers du Chemin*, 21 (1974), 184-202.

1284. Montagnini, Felice. "Analisi strutturale ed esegesi biblica."
       Humanitas, 30, no. 4 (April 1975), 350-351.

Critique et vérité
(item 761)

1285. Egebak, Niels. "Roland Barthes: *Critique et vérité*." *Revue Romane*, 1, no. 1-2 (1966), 128-131.

1286. Grivel, Ch. "Roland Barthes, *Critique et vérité*, essai." *Neophilologus*, 51, no. 1 (January 1967), 78-79.

1287. Nourissier, François. "*Critique et vérité*, essai de Roland Barthes." *Les Nouvelles Littéraires*, no. 2016 (21 April 1966), p. 2.

See also items 935, 936, 985, 1174, and 1178.

Le Degré zéro de l'écriture
(item 680)

1288. Anonymous. Review of *Writing Degree Zero*. *Choice*, 5 (February 1969), 1584.

1289. ————. Review of *Writing Degree Zero*. *Publishers Weekly*, 197 (2 February 1970), 91.

1290. Lawson, David. Review of *Writing Degree Zero*. *Library Journal*, 93 (15 May 1968), 2007.

1291. Merton, Thomas. "Writing as Temperature." *Sewanee Review*, 77, no. 3 (Summer 1969), 535-542.

1292. Nadeau, Maurice. *Les Lettres Nouvelles*, 1, no. 5 (July 1953), 591-599.

1293. Pautasso, Sergio. "Scrittura 'grado zero.'" *L'Europa Letteraria*, 2, no. 7 (February 1961), 153-155.

1294. Theissen, Siegfried. "Wat noemt Roland Barthes *Le Degré zéro de l'écriture?*" *De Vlaamse Gids*, 54, no. 8-9 (August-September 1970), 10-13.

See also item 1018.

Eléments de sémiologie
(items 745 and 751)

1295. Anonymous, Review of *Elements of Semiology*. *Choice*, 6 (May 1969), 353.

1296. Cevasco, G.A. Review of *Elements of Semiology*. *Library Journal*, 93 (15 December 1968), 4654.

1297. Duncan, Robert. "*Kopóltús*: Notes on Roland Barthes, *Elements of Semiology*." *Credences*, no. 1 (1974?), pp. 2-6.

1298.   Segre, C. "Roland Barthes: *Elementi di semiologia*; *Saggi critici.*" *Strumenti Critici*, 1, fasc. 1 (October 1966), 89–91.

See also item 1289.

L'Empire des signes
(item 802)

1299.   Berthier, Philippe. "Les Sentiers de la création." *Bulletin des Lettres*, no. 321 (15 October 1970), pp. 281–282.

1300.   Bigongiari, Piero. "*Il Giappone, scrittura vivente*, di Roland Barthes." *Approdo Letterario*, no. 55–56 (September–December 1971), pp. 227–230.

1301.   Choay, Françoise. "L'Emploi des signes." *La Quinzaine Littéraire*, no. 94 (1–15 May 1970), p. 5.

1302.   Cornu, Marcel. "Roland Barthes: *L'Empire des signes.*" *La Pensée*, no. 152 (August 1970), pp. 148–149.

1303.   D., G. "Un Japon mallarméen." *Le Nouvel Observateur*, no. 286 (4–10 May 1970), p. 42.

1304.   Duranteau, Josane. "Roland Barthes ou l'empire des signes." *L'Education*, no. 68 (21 May 1970), pp. 27–28.

1305.   Gallégo, Julián. "Crítica." *Revista de Occidente*, 32, no. 95 (February 1971), 243–246.

1306.   Mellac, Guy de. "Métaphores du vide: *L'Empire des signes*, de Roland Barthes." *Sub-stance*, no. 1 (Fall 1971), pp. 31–36.

1307.   Perros, Georges. "Roland Barthes: *L'Empire des signes.*" *Cahiers du Chemin*, no. 11 (January 1971), pp. 101–104.

See also items 975, 1047, 1104, 1115, and 1271.

Erté
(item 821)

1308.   Anonymous. *Art in America*, 64 (January 1976), 23.

1309.   ———. *Atlantic Monthly*, 237 (January 1976), 98.

1310.   ———. *Library Journal*, 100 (1 November 1975), 2040.

1311.   ———. *Newsweek*, 86 (8 December 1975), 94.

1312.   ———. *Saturday Review*, 3 (29 November 1975), 22.

1313.   ———. *Village Voice*, 20 (15 December 1975), 65.

See also item 947.

Essais critiques
(item 739)

1314. Anonymous. Review of *Critical Essays*. *Christian Century*, 89 (26 April 1972), 488.

1315. ———. Review of *Critical Essays*. *Drama Review*, 19 (June 1975), 140.

1316. ———. Review of *Critical Essays*. *The New York Times*, 121 (30 June 1972), 33.

1317. Diéguez, Manuel de, and J. Dhaenens. "Les Deux méthodes." *Le Monde*, no. 5978 (4 April 1964), p. 11.

1318. Klein, Richard. "Roland Barthes: *Mythologies* and *Critical Essays*." *Partisan Review*, 40, no. 2 (Spring 1973), 294-301.

1319. Majault, Joseph. "Barthes: *Essais critiques*." *L'Education Nationale*, no. 21 (4 June 1964), p. 20.

1320. Picard, Raymond. "M. Barthes et la 'critique universitaire.'" *Le Monde*, no. 5960 (14 March 1964), p. 12.

1321. Simon, Pierre-Henri. "*Almagestes*, par Alain Badiou; *Essais critiques*, de Roland Barthes." *Le Monde*, no. 5981 (8 April 1964), pp. 8-9.

1322. ———. "La Critique du langage. Alain Badiou et Roland Barthes." In his *Diagnostic des lettres françaises contemporaines*. Brussels: La Renaissance du Livre, 1966, pp. 413-419.

1323. Velan, Yves. "Les Essais critiques de Roland Barthes." *Gazette de Lausanne*, 18-19 July 1964, p. 14.

See also items 1065, 1298, and 1371.

Fragments d'un discours amoureux
(item 915)

1323a. Anonymous. Review of *A Lover's Discourse*. *Book World (Washington Post)*, 9 (19 August 1979), 13.

1323b. ———. Review of *A Lover's Discourse*. *Choice*, 16 (November 1979), 1164.

1323c. ———. Review of *A Lover's Discourse*. *Christian Science Monitor*, 71 (13 August 1979), B-5.

1324. ———. *French Review*, 51 (April 1978), 769.

1325. ———. Review of *A Lover's Discourse*. *Guardian Weekly*, 120 (22 April 1979), 21.

1326.   ———. Review of *A Lover's Discourse*. *Kirkus Reviews*, 46
          (15 June 1978), 669.

1326a. ———. Review of *A Lover's Discourse*. *Listener*, 102 (2 August
          1979), 155.

1326b. ———. Review of *A Lover's Discourse*. *Observer* (London),
          22 April 1979, p. 37.

1327.   ———. Review of *A Lover's Discourse*. *Publishers' Weekly*,
          214 (10 July 1978), 123.

1328.   ———. Review of *A Lover's Discourse*. *The Spectator*, 242
          (31 March 1979), 25.

1329.   ———. *World Literature Today*, 52 (Summer 1978), 432.

1329a. Bachellier, Jean Louis. *Sub-stance*, no. 17 (Fall 1977), pp.
          169-170.

1330.   Bonnefoy, Claude. "Entretien. Barthes en bouffées de langage."
          Les Nouvelles Littéraires, 55, no. 2581 (21-28 April 1977), 9.

1331.   Chapelan, Maurice. "De Stendhal à Roland Barthes." *Le Figaro
          Littéraire*, no. 1623 (25-26 June 1977), p. III:19.

1332.   Davis, Douglas. "The Language of Love." *Newsweek*, 92 (18
          December 1978), 96.

1332a. Delany, Paul. Review of *A Lover's Discourse*. *Canadian Forum*,
          59 (June 1979), 32-33.

1333.   Delcourt, Xavier. "Les Mille façons de dire 'Je t'aime.'"
          La Quinzaine Littéraire, no. 255 (1-15 May 1977), p. 4.

1334.   Galey, Matthieu. "La Carte tendre de Roland Barthes." *L'Express*,
          no. 1353 (13-19 June 1977), pp. 69-70.

1335.   Gamarra, Pierre. "Discours amoureux, amour du roman." *Europe*,
          55, no. 578-579 (June-July 1977), 208-209.

1335a. Grier, Peter. Review of *A Lover's Discourse*. *Christian Science
          Monitor*, 10 January 1979, p. 19.

1336.   Hartman, G.H. Review of *A Lover's Discourse: Fragments* and
          Image/Music/Text. *The New York Times Book Review*, 84 (4
          February 1979), 12-13 ff.

1336a. Kuczkowski, Richard. Review of *A Lover's Discourse*. *Library
          Journal*, 103 (August 1978), 1510.

1337.   Merkin, D. Review of *A Lover's Discourse: Fragments*. *New
          Leader*, 61 (23 October 1978), 14.

1338.   Poirot-Delpech, Bertrand. *Le Monde*, no. 10012 (8 April 1977),
          pp. 11, 14; *Le Monde (hebdomadaire)*, no. 1484 (7-13 August
          1977), p. 12.

1339. ———. "Language of Love." *The Manchester Guardian Weekly*,
          117, no. 2 (10 July 1977), 14.

1339a. Raphael, Frederic. Review of *A Lover's Discourse*. *New Statesman*,
          97 (4 May 1979), 648.

1340. Ron, M. *The New Republic*, 178 (25 March 1978), 28-30.

1341. Sturrock, John. "In the Words of the Lover." *The Times Literary
          Supplement*, no. 3930 (8 July 1977), p. 824.

1341a. Vine, R. Review of *A Lover's Discourse*. *The Georgia Review*,
          33 (Winter 1979), 918-922.

See also items 1110 and 1184.

Image/Music/Text
(item 920)

1342. Anonymous. *Choice*, 15 (September 1978), 857.

1342a. ———. *Journal of Aesthetics and Art Criticism*, 37 (Winter
          1978), 235.

1342b. ———. *Modern Fiction Studies*, 24 (Winter 1978-1979), 612.

1342c. ———. *The New York Times Book Review*, 4 February 1979, p. 12.

1343. ———. *The Times Educational Supplement*, 13 January 1978,
          p. 18.

1344. Flores, Ralph. *Library Journal*, 103 (1 May 1978), 973.

1345. Hough, Graham. "The Importation of Roland Barthes." *The Times
          Literary Supplement*, no. 3950 (9 December 1977), p. 1443.
          Also on Thody's item 1251.

1346. Larrieu, Kay and Duane. *Best Sellers*, 38 (July 1978), 130.

1347. Sturrock, John. *New Statesman*, 94 (14 October 1977), 514.
          Calls this work the best and cheapest introduction to
          Barthes's career as a slayer of contemporary myths.

See also items 1076a, 1336 and 1429.

Mythologies
(item 700)

1348. Anonymous. *Hudson Review*, 26 (Summer 1973), 411.

1349. ———. *Journal of Aesthetics and Art Criticism*, 31 (Summer
          1973), 563.

1350. ———. *Kirkus Reviews*, 40 (1 April 1972), 435.

1351. ———. *Newsweek*, 81 (1 January 1973), 54.

1352. ———. *New Yorker*, 48 (9 September 1972), 128.

1353. ———. *New York Review of Books*, 18 (18 May 1972), 37.

1354. ———. *The New York Times*, 121 (30 June 1972), 32.

1355. ———. *The New York Times Book Review*, 3 December 1972, p. 68.

1356. ———. *Publishers' Weekly*, 201 (24 April 1972), 44.

1357. ———. *Publishers' Weekly*, 203 (7 May 1973), 68.

1358. ———. *Spectator*, 228 (18 March 1972), 440.

1359. ———. *Spectator*, 231 (15 September 1973), 348.

1360. Barden, Garrett. *Philosophical Studies*, 21 (1973), 249-256.

1361. Berger, Arthur Asa. *Clio*, 2, no. 2 (February 1973), 192-193.

1362. Berger, John. "Mythical Speech." *New Society*, 19, no. 491 (24 February 1972), 407-408.

1363. Culler, Jonathan. *Journal of the British Society for Phenomenology*, 4 (May 1973), 171-173.

1364. Furbank, P.N. "The Lonely Mythologue." *Listener*, 88, no. 2265 (24 August 1972), 246-247.

1365. Lys, D. *Etudes Théologiques et Religieuses*, 48, no. 1 (1973), 110.

1366. Merler, Grazia. *West Coast Review*, 7, no. 3 (January 1973), 66-68.

1367. Pateman, Trevor. *Human Context*, 5 (Spring 1973), 245-249.

1368. Poster, Mark. *Library Journal*, 97 (1 November 1972), 3606.

1369. Prendergast, Christopher. "Myth, Ideology and Semioclastics." *Cambridge Review*, 93, no. 2208 (2 June 1972), 170-174.

1370. Ricks, Christopher. "Adman's Friend." *The Sunday Times*, no. 7760 (5 March 1972), p. 35.

1371. Said, E.W. *The New York Times Book Review*, 30 July 1972, p. 5.

1372. Sharpe, Eric J. *Critical Quarterly*, 15, no. 4 (Winter 1973), 272-283.

1373. Velan, Yves. *Les Lettres Nouvelles*, 5, no. 51 (July-August 1957), 113-119.

1374. Weightman, John. "The Myth is the Message." *Observer*, no. 9424 (12 March 1972), p. 30.

See also items 952 and 1318.

Le Plaisir du texte
(item 855)

1375. Ackroyd, Peter. "Academe." *The Spectator*, 236 (14 February 1976), 24.

1376. Anonymous. "Joyful Reading." *The Times Literary Supplement*, no. 3720 (22 June 1973), p. 713.

1377. ————. Review of *The Pleasure of the Text*. *Books and Bookmen*, 22 (October 1976), 63.

1378. ————. Review of *The Pleasure of the Text*. *Kirkus Reviews*, 43 (1 April 1975), 409.

1379. ————. Review of *The Pleasure of the Text*. *The New York Times Book Review*, 7 December 1975, p. 70.

1380. ————. Review of *The Pleasure of the Text*. *Sewanee Review*, 85 (January 1977), 153.

1381. ————. "Romance." *Choice*, 12, no. 9 (November 1975), 1175.

1382. Aron, Jean-Paul. "Roland Barthes: *Le Plaisir du texte*." *Les Cahiers du Chemin*, no. 19 (October 1973), pp. 134-142.

1382a. Bugliani, R. Review of *Il Piacere del testo*. *Nuova Corrente*, no. 70 (1976), pp. 176-181.

1383. Chapelan, Maurice. "Lecture(s) de Roland Barthes." *Le Figaro Littéraire*, no. 1396 (17 February 1973), II:16.

1384. Culler, Jonathan. Review of *The Pleasure of the Text*. *Yale Review*, 65 (December 1975), 261.

1385. Cumming, John. "The Use of a Book." *The Tablet*, 230, no. 7080 (13 March 1976), 258-260.

1386. De Ley, Herbert. "The Erotics of Reading." *Book Forum*, 2, no. 2 (Spring 1976), 319-320.

1387. Di Girolamo, Giacomo. "Le Plaisir du texte d'après Roland Barthes." *Culture Française* (Bari, November-December 1973), pp. 339-344.

1388.   Faulks, Sebastian. "This Way for Bliss." *The Sunday Times*,
        no. 7969 (7 March 1976), p. 39.

1389.   Gardair, Jean-Michel. "Roland Barthes: *Le Plaisir du texte.*"
        Paragone, 24, no. 282 (August 1973), 109-112.

1390.   Hayman, Ronald. Review of *The Pleasure of the Text. Encounter*,
        47 (July 1976), 71.

1391.   Josselin, Jean-François. "Texte-shops." *Le Nouvel Observateur*,
        no. 434 (6-12 March 1973), p. 63.

1392.   Kermode, Frank. "Facets, Bubbles, Phylacteries." *New Statesman*,
        85, no. 2198 (4 May 1973), 660-661.

1393.   Lentegre, Marie-Louise. "Il Lettore perverso." *Il Verri*, no.
        11 (October 1975), pp. 93-97.

1394.   Moreau, Jean A. "Heurs." *Critique*, 29, no. 314 (July 1973),
        583-595.

1395.   Nadeau, Maurice. "Le Petit Kamasutra de Roland Barthes." *La
        Quinzaine Littéraire*, no. 160 (16-31 March 1973), pp. 3-4.

1396.   Newton-de Molina, David. "Roland Barthes: *Le Plaisir du texte.*"
        Modern Language Review, 69, no. 2 (April 1974), 362-365.

1397.   Palencia, E.F. Review of *The Pleasure of the Text. Library
        Journal*, 100 (1 June 1975), 1129.

1398.   Poirot-Delpech, Bertrand. "Pour une érotique de la lecture: le
        petit *Kamasutra* de Roland Barthes." *Le Monde [des Livres]*,
        no. 8737 (15 February 1973), p. 17.

1399.   ————. "Pour une érotique de la lecture: le petit *Kamasutra*
        de Roland Barthes." *Le Monde (hebdomadaire)*, no. 1269 (15-
        21 February 1973), p. 20.

1400.   Rinaldi, Angelo. "Barthes réhabilite le plaisir de lire."
        L'Express, no. 1128 (19-25 February 1973), pp. 72-73.

1401.   Sabatier, Robert. "Par delà vice et vertu, le plaisir du texte."
        Les Nouvelles Littéraires, 51, no. 2376 (9-15 April 1973), 2.

1402.   Theroux, Paul. "Bliss." *New Statesman*, 91, no. 2344 (20 February
        1976), 232-233.

1403.   Weightman, John. "The Voluptuous Modernist." *The Observer*,
        no. 9629 (London, 22 February 1976), p. 27.

1404.   West, Philip J. "Barthes/Barth: Textual/Sexual." *Salmagundi*,
        no. 37 (Spring 1977), pp. 133-139.

See also items 996, 1148, 1230, 1271, 1420, and 1464.

Poétique du récit
(item 916)

1405. Lys, Daniel. *Etudes Théologiques et Religieuses*, 52, no. 3
       (1977), 457-458.

Roland Barthes par Roland Barthes
(item 890)

1406. Anonymous. Review of *Roland Barthes*. *Booklist*, 73 (15 July
       1977), 1690.

1407. —————. Review of *Roland Barthes*. *Book World (Washington Post)*,
       15 January 1978, p. F-6; 3 December 1978, p. E-10.

1408. —————. Review of *Roland Barthes*. *Books West*, 1 (October
       1977), 44.

1409. —————. Review of *Roland Barthes*. *Choice*, 14 (December 1977),
       1344.

1409a. —————. Review of *Roland Barthes*. *Modern Fiction Studies*,
       24 (Winter 1978-1979), 612.

1410. —————. Review of *Roland Barthes*. *Modern Language Journal*,
       62 (March 1978), 147.

1411. —————. Review of *Roland Barthes*. *The New York Review of Books*,
       23 (4 March 1976), 31.

1412. —————. Review of *Roland Barthes*. *Village Voice*, 22 (11 July
       1977), 60.

1413. Arcy, Philippe d'. "Roland Barthes sur Roland Barthes." *Bulletin
       des Lettres*, 36, no. 369 (15 June 1975), 231-232.

1414. Bachellier, Jean-Louis. "La Grenure du texte." *Sub-stance*,
       no. 13 (1976), pp. 163-164.

1415. Bayley, J. Review of *Roland Barthes*. *The Listener*, 98 (27
       October 1977), 542.

1416. Bersani, Jacques. "Etude: Barthes par lui-même. Un livre de
       plaisir." *Le Monde [des Livres]*, no. 9357 (14 February 1975),
       p. 16; *Le Monde (hebdomadaire)*, no. 1373 (13-19 February
       1975), p. 12.

1417. Bourniquel, Camille. "*Roland Barthes* par Roland Barthes."
       Esprit, no. 445 (April 1975), pp. 616-618.

1418. Bouttes, Jean-Louis. "Faux comme la vérité." *Critique*, 31,
       no. 341 (1975), 1024-1052.

1419. Bowman, Frank Paul. "Roland Barthes par Roland Barthes et
       Charles Fourier." *Romanic Review*, 69 (May 1978), 236-241.

1419a. Cesbron, G. *Les Lettres Romanes*, November 1977, pp. 369-371.

1420. Delany, P. Review of *The Pleasure of the Text* and *Roland
       Barthes*. *Partisan Review*, 45, no. 3 (1978), 466-470.

1421. Fernandez, Dominique. "Barthes et son secret." *L'Express*, no.
       1233 (24 February-2 March 1975), pp. 66-67.

1422. Josselin, Jean-François. "Roland Barthes, voyageur du désir."
       Le Nouvel Observateur, no. 537 (24 February-2 March 1975),
       pp. 60-61.

1423. Kanters, Robert. "A Roland Barthes pour toujours." *Le Figaro
       Littéraire*, no. 1502 (1 March 1975), p. III:17.

1424. Kermode, Frank. Review of *Roland Barthes*. *The New York Times
       Book Review*, 7 August 1977, p. 13.

1425. Lys, Daniel. *Etudes Théologiques et Religieuses*, 51, no. 2
       (1976), 224.

1426. Masterson, G.A. Review of *Roland Barthes*. *Library Journal*, 102
       (1 September 1977), 1761.

1426a. McDonald, J. Review of *Roland Barthes*. *Cross Currents*, 29
       (Spring 1979), 94-99.

1427. McGraw, Betty. "Roland Barthes: *Barthes par lui-même*." *French
       Review*, 49, no. 3 (February 1976), 427-428.

1428. Rey, Alain. "Le Corps aux miroirs." *Critique*, 31, no. 341
       (October 1975), 1015-1023.

1429. Thiher, A. Review of *Roland Barthes*. *Modern Fiction Studies*,
       24 (Winter 1978-1979), 612-615.

See also items 952, 1118, and 1209.

S/Z
(item 801)

1430. Anonymous. *Choice*, 12 (April 1975), 226.

1431. ———. *Hudson Review* 30 (Winter 1977-1978), 587.

1432. ———. *Kirkus Reviews*, 42 (15 July 1974), 768.

1433. ———. *The New York Review of Books*, 23 (4 March 1976), 31.

1434. ———. *Village Voice*, 19 (21 November 1974), 50.

1435. ———. "Sensuous and Systematic." *The Times Literary Supplement*, no. 3569 (23 July 1970), p. 804.

1436. Bassoff, Bruce. "Roland Barthes or the Critic as Underground Man--A Review Essay." *Southern Humanities Review*, 11, no. 1 (Winter 1977), 63-66.

1437. Bayley, John. "Balzac Possessed." *The New York Review of Books*, 20, no. 15 (4 October 1973), 25.

1438. Benevelli, Elio. "Strutturalismo e/o scritturalismo. (A proposito di *S/Z* di Roland Barthes)." *Strumenti Critici*, 7, no. 21-22 (October 1973), 257-268.

1439. Bergonzi, Bernard. Review of *S/Z*. *Encounter*, 45 (July 1975), 52-57.

1440. Berthier, Philippe. "Roland Barthes: *S/Z*." *Bulletin des Lettres*, no. 321 (15 October 1970), p. 305.

1441. Campbell, G.W. Review of *S/Z*." *Humanities Association Review*, Winter 1976, p. 61.

1442. Citron, Pierre. "Deux points de vue sur *S/Z*: Balzac lu par Roland Barthes. Une méthode qui accentue le côté subjectif de toute lecture." *Le Monde [des Livres]*, no. 7874 (9 May 1970), p. III.

1443. Culler, Jonathan. "Roland Barthes: *S/Z*." *Modern Language Review*, 66, no. 1 (January 1971), 191-192.

1444. ———. Review of *S/Z*. *Yale Review*, 64 (Summer 1975), 606.

1445. Eggen, Einar. "Barthes/Balzac--en presentasjon." *Edda*, 71, no. 3 (1971), 181-188.

1446. Emond, Paul. "Roland Barthes: *S/Z*." *Lettres Romanes*, 25, no. 3 (August 1971), 324-330.

1447. Gardair, Jean-Michel. "Roland Barthes: *S/Z*." *Paragone*, no. 244 (June 1970), pp. 120-127.

1448. Guenther, F. "Roland Barthes: *S/Z*." *Poetics*, no. 1 (1973), pp. 113-117.

1449. Jean, Raymond. "Deux points de vue sur *S/Z*: Balzac lu par Roland Barthes. Le 'Commentaire' comme forme 'active' de la critique." *Le Monde [des Livres]*, no. 7874 (9 May 1970), p. III.

1450. Keener, F.M. Review of *S/Z*. *Library Journal*, 99 (August 1974), 1951.

1451. Lodge, David. "Meaning of Meanings." *Tablet*, 229, no. 7033 (19 April 1975), 361-362.

1452. Luccioni, Gennie. "Roland Barthes: *S/Z*." *Esprit*, 38, no. 393 (June 1970), 1199-1202.

1453. Lys, Daniel. Review of *S/Z*. *Etudes Théologiques et Religieuses*, 51, no. 4 (1976), 550-551.

1454. Margolin, J.-C. Review of *S/Z*. *Les Etudes Philosophiques*, no. 2 (1970), pp. 225-226.

1455. Marshall, Donald. "Roland Barthes: *S/Z*." *Partisan Review*, 42, no. 3 (1975), 469-474.

1456. Marty, Robert. "Re-lire Balzac (ou le suicide de la parole)." *Encres Vives*, no. 70-71 (Winter 1971), pp. 35-40.

1457. May, Derwent. "Code in the Head." *The Listener*, 93, no. 2398 (20 March 1975), 379-380.

1458. Partridge, Eric. "Roland Barthes: *S/Z*." *Books and Bookmen*, 21, no. 7 (April 1976), 66.

1459. Raphael, Frederic. "The Heart of Art." *The Sunday Times*, no. 7922 (13 April 1975), p. 40.

1460. Rella, Franco. "Roland Barthes: *S/Z*." *Nuova Corrente*, no. 52 (1970), pp. 209-210.

1461. Silverstein, Norman. "Film and Language, Film and Literature." *Journal of Modern Literature*, 2, no. 1 (September 1971), 154-160.

1462. Sollers, Philippe. "Sollers parle de Barthes." *La Quinzaine Littéraire*, no. 90 (1-15 March 1970), pp. 22-23.

1463. Sturrock, John. "No Balzac at All." *New Statesman*, 90, no. 2316 (8 August 1975), 176.

1464. Updike, John. Review of Barthes's *S/Z* and *Pleasure of the Text*. *New Yorker*, 51 (24 November 1975), 189-194.

1465. Vannier, Bernard. "Balzac à l'encan." *Critique*, no. 302 (July 1972), pp. 610-622.

1466. Weightman, John. "Logos Unlimited." *Observer*, no. 9587 (27 April 1975), p. 34.

See also items 975, 996, 1047, 1104, 1118, 1161, 1181, 1213, 1230, and 1271.

Sade, Fourier, Loyola
(item 823)

1467. Amette, Jacques-Pierre. "Roland Barthes: *Sade, Fourier, Loyola*." *Nouvelle Revue Française*, no. 230 (February 1972), pp. 92-93.

1468. ———. "Apprendre à lire." *La Quinzaine Littéraire*, no. 132 (1-15 January 1972), pp. 15-16.

1469. Anonymous. Review of *Sade, Fourier, Loyola*. *Book World (Washington Post)*, 11 April 1976, p. 2.

1470. ————. Review of *Sade, Fourier, Loyola*. *Kirkus Reviews*, 44 (15 January 1976), 98.

1471. ————. Review of *Sade, Fourier, Loyola*. *The Spectator*, 238 (15 October 1977), 22.

1472. ————. Review of *Sade, Fourier, Loyola*. *Virginia Quarterly Review*, 53 (Winter 1977), 9.

1473. ————. "*Sade, Fourier, Loyola*, trans. Richard Miller." *Choice*, 13, no. 8 (October 1976), 993.

1474. Appleyard, J.A. Review of *Sade, Fourier, Loyola*. *Commonweal*, 103, no. 21 (8 October 1976), 669.

1475. Bory, Jean-Louis. "Roland Barthes a inventé une nouvelle manière de lire les livres." *Paris-Match*, no. 1185 (22 January 1972), p. 64.

1476. Duvernois, Pierre. "L'Emportement de l'écriture." *Critique*, no. 302 (July 1972), pp. 595-609.

1477. Fiore, Silvana. "Barthes continua a sorprendere tutti: Sade, Fourier, Loyola, 'inventori' di linguaggio." *Informatore Librario*, 7, no. 12 (December 1977), 27.

1478. Helbo, André. "Roland Barthes: *Sade, Fourier, Loyola*." In his *Théorie et pratique du code (I)*. Brussels: Degrés, 1974, pp. h/1-h/2. Part of a special issue of *Degrés*, 2, no. 6 (April 1974).

1479. Jannoud, Claude. "Roland Barthes réunit dans une même lecture Sade le maudit, Fourier l'utopiste et Loyola le jésuite." *Le Figaro Littéraire*, no. 1333 (3 December 1971), p. IV.

1480. Lalou, Etienne. "Trois maniaques de génie." *L'Express*, no. 1069 (3-9 January 1972), p. 61.

1481. Luccioni, Gennie. "Roland Barthes: *Sade, Loyola, Fourier*." *Esprit*, no. 413 (April-May 1972), pp. 885-887.

1482. Margolin, Jean-Claude. "Roland Barthes: *Sade, Fourier, Loyola*." *Les Etudes Philosophiques*, January-March 1972, pp. 69-70.

1483. Ormesson, Jean d'. "Logothètes et littérature." *Les Nouvelles Littéraires*, 49, no. 2309 (24 December 1971-2 January 1972), 8.

1484. Palencia, E.F. Review of *Sade, Fourier, Loyola*. *Library Journal*, 101 (15 April 1976), 1020.

1485.   Riffaterre, Michael. "Sade, or Text as Fantasy." *Diacritics*,
        2, no. 3 (Fall 1972), 2-9.

1486.   Savater, Fernando. "Crítica." *Revista de Occidente*, 38, no.
        113-114 (August-September 1972), 344-347.

1487.   Sturrock, John. "'Words.'" *New Statesman*, 94, no. 2430 (14
        October 1977), 514.

1488.   Updike, John. "Texts and Men." *New Yorker*, 52, no. 33 (4
        October 1976), 148-150.

See also items 952, 1230, and 1271.

                            Sur Racine
                            (item 730)

1489.   Anonymous. "*On Racine*. Trans. by Richard Howard." *Choice*, 1,
        no. 12 (February 1965), 560-561.

1490.   Cornu, Marcel. "Roland Barthes: *Sur Racine*." *La Pensée*,
        nouvelle série, no. 113 (February 1964), pp. 128-129.

1491.   Remacle, Madeleine. "A propos de l'essai de R. Barthes *Sur
        Racine*." *Cahiers d'Analyse Textuelle*, no. 17 (1975), pp.
        92-109.

1492.   Simon, Pierre-Henri. "De Roland Barthes. *Sur Racine*." In his
        Diagnostic des lettres françaises contemporaines. Brussels:
        La Renaissance du Livre, 1966, pp. 402-406.

See also item 1069.

                        Système de la mode
                            (item 772)

1493.   Anonymous. "Matrix and Myth." *The Times Literary Supplement*,
        no. 3407 (15 June 1967), pp. 521-522.

1494.   Finas, Lucette. "Entre les mots et les choses." *La Quinzaine
        Littéraire*, no. 28 (15-31 May 1967), pp. 3-4.

1495.   Luccioni, Gennie. "Roland Barthes: *Système de la mode*." *Esprit*,
        35, no. 363 (September 1967), 338-340.

1496.   Nairn, Tom. "Fashionable Structures." *New Statesman*, 74,
        no. 1900 (11 August 1967), 174.

1497.   Revel, Jean-François. "Le Rat et la mode." *L'Express*, no. 831
        (22-28 May 1967), p. 43.

1498. Van Rossum-Guyon, F.M.H. "Over Roland Barthes *Système de la mode.*" *Wijsgerig Perspectief op Maatschappij en Wetenschap,* 14, no. 4 (1973-1974), 210-223.

See also items 941 and 1111.

La Tour Eiffel
(item 741a)

1498a. Anonymous. Review of *The Eiffel Tower and Other Mythologies. Choice,* 16 (December 1979), 1297.

1498b. ————. Review of *The Eiffel Tower and Other Mythologies. Kirkus Reviews,* 47 (15 July 1979), 828.

1498c. ————. Review of *The Eiffel Tower and Other Mythologies. Publishers' Weekly,* 216 (23 July 1979), 144.

1498d. ————. Review of *The Eiffel Tower and Other Mythologies. Village Voice,* 24 (17 September 1979), 44.

1498e. Beatty, Jack. Review of *The Eiffel Tower and Other Mythologies. New Republic,* 181 (20 October 1979), 38.

1498f. Clark, Jeff. Review of *The Eiffel Tower and Other Mythologies. Library Journal,* 104 (15 October 1979), 2216.

1498g. Gilman, Richard. Review of *The Eiffel Tower and Other Mythologies. The New York Times Book Review,* 84 (4 November 1979), 11 ff.

JACQUES DERRIDA

PRIMARY SOURCES

1962

*1499. Translation of and introduction to *L'Origine de la géométrie*. By Edmund Husserl. Paris: Presses Universitaires de France, 1962. 2nd rev. ed. 1974. For English trans., see item 1610. For reviews, see items 1879a, 1879b and 1880.

1963

1500. "Force et signification." *Critique*, no. 193 (June 1963), pp. 483-499; no. 194 (July 1963), pp. 619-636. Rpt. in item 1521, pp. 9-49.

On Jean Rousset's *Forme et signification: essais sur les structures littéraires de Corneille à Claudel* (Paris: José Corti, 1962).

1501. "Cogito et histoire de la folie" [Réflexions ayant comme point de départ le livre de Michel Foucault: *Folie et déraison. Histoire de la folie à l'âge classique*. Paris: Plon, 1961]. *Revue de Métaphysique et de Morale*, 68 (1963), 460-494. Rpt. in item 1521, pp. 51-97. See also item 1504.

1502. Review of *Lebenswelt und Geschichte. Grundzüge der Spätphilosophie Edmund Husserls*. By Hubert Hohl. Freiburg-Munich: Karl Alber, 1962. *Les Etudes Philosophiques*, 18 (1963), 95-96.

1503. Review of *Phänomenologische Psychologie. Vorlesungen Sommersemester, 1925*. Herausgegeben von Walter Biemel. The Hague: Martinus Nijhoff, 1962. *Les Etudes Philosophiques*, 18 (1963), 203-206.

1964

1504. "A propos de *Cogito et histoire de la folie*." *Revue de Métaphysique et de Morale*, 69 (1964), 116-119.

On item 1501.

1505. "Edmond Jabès et la question du livre." *Critique*, 20, no. 201 (February 1964), 99-115. Rpt. in item 1521, pp. 99-116.

1506. "Violence et métaphysique. Essai sur la pensée d'Emmanuel
Levinas." *Revue de Métaphysique et de Morale*, 69 (1964),
322-354, 425-473. Rpt. in item 1521, pp. 117-228.

1507. Co-translator, with Roger Martin, of "Les Frontières de la
théorie logique." By W.V. Quine. In *Perspectives sur la
philosophie nord-américaine, I*. Paris: Presses Universitaires
de France, 1964, pp. 191-208. *Les Etudes Philosophiques*,
19, no. 2 (1964).

1508. Translator of "Le Monde-de-la-vie et la tradition de la philosophie américaine." By Marvin Farber. In *Perspectives sur
la philosophie nord-américaine, I*. Paris: Presses Universitaires de France, 1964, pp. 209-219. *Les Etudes Philosophiques*,
19, no. 2 (1964).

1509. Review of *Edmund Husserl's Theory of Meaning*. By J.N. Mohanty.
The Hague: Martinus Nijhoff, 1964. *Les Etudes Philosophiques*,
19 (1964), 617-619.

1965

1510. "'Genèse et structure' et la phénoménologie." *Entretiens sur
les notions de genèse et de structure*. Ed. Maurice de
Gandillac, Lucien Goldmann and Jean Piaget. Centre culturel
international de Cerisy-la-Salle, July-August 1959. Paris-
The Hague: Mouton, 1965, pp. 243-60. Rpt. in item 1521, pp.
229-251.

1511. "La Parole soufflée." *Tel Quel*, no. 20 (Winter 1965), pp. 41-
67. Rpt. in item 1521, pp. 253-292.

On Antonin Arnaud.

1512. Review of *The Idea of Phenomenology*. By Edmund Husserl. Trans.
William P. Alston and George Nakhnikian. The Hague: Martinus Nijhoff, 1964. *Les Etudes Philosophiques*, 20 (1965),
538.

1513. Review of *The Paris Lectures*. By Edmund Husserl. Trans. Peter
Koestenbaum. The Hague: Martinus Nijhoff, 1964 [1965].
Les Etudes Philosophiques, 20 (1965), 539.

1514. Review of *The Formation of Husserl's Concept of Constitution*.
By Robert Sokolowski. The Hague: Martinus Nijhoff, 1964.
Les Etudes Philosophiques, 20 (1965), 557-558.

1966

1515. "De la grammatologie. I-II." *Critique*, 21, no. 223 (December
1965), 1016-1042; 22, no. 224 (January 1966), 23-53. Rpt.
and developed in the first part of item 1522. See also
item 1519.

Commentary and philosophical reflection on M.V. David's
*Le Débat sur les écritures et l'hiéroglyphe au XVIIe et XVIIIe
siècles* (1965), A. Leroi-Gourhan's *Le Geste et la parole* (1965),
and *L'Ecriture et la psychologie des peuples* (1963).

*1516. "Freud et la scène de l'écriture." *Tel Quel*, no. 26 (Summer
        1966), pp. 10-41. Paper read in Dr. Green's seminar at the
        Institut de Psychanalyse in March 1966. Rpt. in item 1521,
        pp. 293-340. For English trans., see items 1558 and 1567.

*1517. "Le Théâtre de la cruauté et la clôture de la représentation."
        Critique, 22, no. 230 (July 1966), 595-618. Paper read at
        Parma, April 1966, at the Antonin Arnaud Colloquium (Festival
        International de Théâtre Universitaire). Rpt. in item 1521,
        pp. 341-368. For English trans., see item 1617a.

 1518. "Avertissement." *Cahiers pour l'Analyse*, no. 4 (September-
        October 1966), pp. iii-iv. Introduction to an entire issue
        entitled "Lévi-Strauss dans le 18ème siècle."

 1519. "Nature, culture, écriture. La Violence de la lettre de Lévi-
        Strauss à Rousseau." *Cahiers pour l'Analyse*, no. 4 (Septem-
        ber-October 1966), pp. 1-45.

        The text of two classes of a course given at the Ecole Normale
        Supérieure in 1965-1966 under the title of "Ecriture et Civili-
        sation." Item 1515 contains the main points of the introduc-
        tion announcing the systematic intention of this course. See
        part two of item 1522 for comparison.

                                    1967

*1520. "De l'économie restreinte à l'économie générale: un hégélianisme
        sans réserve." In *Georges Bataille*. Ed. Henri Ronse. Aix-
        en-Provence: *L'Arc*, no. 32 (May 1967), pp. 24-44. Rpt. in
        item 1521, pp. 369-407. For English trans., see item 1601.

*1521. *L'Ecriture et la différence*. Paris: Editions du Seuil, 1967.
        Contains items 1500, 1501, 1505, 1506, 1510, 1511, 1516,
        1517, 1520, the French version of item 1542, and chapter XI
        entitled "Ellipse," pp. 429-436. For trans., see items 1548
        (Italian), 1560 (German), 1569 (Serbo-Croatian), and 1616a
        (English). For reviews, see items 1862-1870.

*1522. *De la grammatologie*. Paris: Les Editions de Minuit, 1967. For
        trans., see items 1537 (Italian), 1549 (Spanish), 1574
        (English), 1577 (German), and 1600 (English). For reviews,
        see items 1844-1857.

        Contains: Avertissement; Première Partie: L'Ecriture avant
        la lettre; Exergue; (1) La Fin du livre et le commencement
        de l'écriture; (2) Linguistique et grammatologie; (3) De la
        grammatologie comme science positive; Deuxième Partie: Nature,
        culture, écriture; Introduction à l'"époque de Rousseau"; (1)
        La Violence de la lettre: de Lévi-Strauss à Rousseau;

(2) "... Ce dangereux supplément ..."; (3) Genèse et structure de l'*Essai sur l'origine des langues*; (4) Du supplément à la source: la théorie de l'écriture. Cf. items 1515 and 1519.

*1523. La *Voix et le phénomène*. *Introduction au problème du signe dans la phénoménologie de Husserl*. Paris: Presses Universitaires de France, 1967. 2nd ed. 1972. 3rd ed. 1976. For trans., see items 1534 (Italian) and 1566 (English), pp. 1-104. For reviews, see items 1883-1892.

Contains: Introduction; (1) Le Signe et les signes; (2) La Réduction de l'indice; (3) Le Vouloir-dire comme soliloque; (4) Le Vouloir-dire et la représentation; (5) Le Signe et le clin d'oeil; (6) La Voix qui garde le silence; (7) Le Supplément d'origine.

*1524. "La Forme et le vouloir-dire. Note sur la phénoménologie du langage." *Revue Internationale de Philosophie*, 81, no. 3 (September 1967), 277-299. Rpt. in item 1553, pp. 185-207. For English trans., see item 1566, pp. 107-128.

Husserl's attempt at an eidetics of language in *Ideen I*.

*1525. "La Linguistique de Rousseau." *Revue Internationale de Philosophie*, 82, no. 4 (1967), 443-62. For Spanish trans., see item 1576.

Rousseau's thinking on language, the sign, the origin of languages, and the relationships between speech and writing mark him as a forerunner of modern linguistics. This article is an early version of "Le Cercle linguistique de Genève" published in item 1553, pp. 165-184.

1526. "Implications: entretien avec Henri Ronse." *Les Lettres Françaises*, no. 1211 (6-12 December 1967), pp. 12-13. Rpt. in item 1554, pp. 9-24.

1527. Review of *Zur Phänomenologie des inneren Zeitbewusstseins*. By Edmund Husserl. Ed. R. Boehm. The Hague: Martinus Nijhoff, 1966. *Les Etudes Philosophiques*, 22 (1967), 94.

1528. Review of *Studien zur Phänomenologie 1930-1939*. By Eugen Fink. The Hague: Martinus Nijhoff, 1966. *Les Etudes Philosophiques*, 22 (1967), 549-550.

1968

1529. "La Pharmacie de Platon, I-II." *Tel Quel*, no. 32 (Winter 1968), pp. 3-48; no. 33 (Spring 1968), pp. 18-59. Rpt. in item 1552, pp. 69-197.

*1530. "Ousia et Grammè: note sur une note de *Sein und Zeit*." In *L'Endurance de la pensée. Pour saluer Jean Beaufret*. Ed. Marcel Jouhandeau. Paris: Plon, 1968, pp. 219-266. Rpt. in item 1553, pp. 31-78. For trans., see items 1541 (English), 1550 (Spanish), and 1603 (German).

1531.   "Sémiologie et grammatologie, entretien avec Julia Kristeva."
        Information sur les Sciences Sociales, 7 (3 June 1968),
        135-148. Rpt. in item 1554, pp. 25-50 and item 1544.

*1532. "La 'Différance.'" *Bulletin de la Société Française de Philo-
        sophie*, 62, no. 3 (July-September 1968), 73-101. Paper read
        at a meeting of the Société held in the Amphithéâtre Michelet
        of the Sorbonne on January 27, 1968. Rpt. in item 1553, pp.
        1-29. For trans., see item 1566 (English), pp. 129-162,
        and item 1603 (German). See also item 1533.

1533.   "La 'Différance.'" In *Théorie d'ensemble*. Paris: Editions du
        Seuil, 1968, pp. 41-66. Rpts. item 1532.

1534.   *La Voce e il fenomeno. Introduzione al problema del segno nella
        fenomenologia di Husserl*. Trans. G. Dalmasso. Milan: Jaca
        Book, 1968. Trans. of item 1523.

                                      1969

1535.   "La Dissémination." *Critique*, 25, no. 261 (February 1969),
        99-139; no. 262 (March 1969), 215-249. Rpt. in item 1552,
        pp. 319-407.

        On Philippe Sollers' *Nombres*.

*1536. "The Ends of Man." Trans. Edouard Morot-Sir, et al. *Philosophy
        and Phenomenological Research*, 30, no. 1 (1969), 31-57. Paper
        read at a French-American philosophers' conference on Language
        and Human Nature, SUNY Conference Center, Oyster Bay, Long
        Island, October 18-19, 1968. Rpt. in item 1553, pp. 129-164.
        For German trans., see item 1603.

        Analyzes the anthropological conceptions of Hegel, Husserl
        and Heidegger as opposed to post-war French philosophers who
        badly interpreted them.

1537.   *Della grammatologia*. Milan: Jaca Book, 1969. Trans. of item
        1522.

                                      1970

1538.   "Le Puits et la pyramide. Introduction à la sémiologie de
        Hegel." In *Hegel et la pensée moderne. Séminaire dirigé par
        Jean Hyppolite au Collège de France* (1967-1968). Ed. Jacques
        D'Hondt. Paris: Presses Universitaires de France, 1970,
        pp. 27-83. Paper given January 16, 1968. Rpt. in item 1553,
        pp. 79-127.

1539.   "D'un texte à l'écart." *Les Temps Modernes*, 25, no. 284 (March
        1970), 1546-1552.

        On J. Garelli's *L'Ecart du maintenant et l'extension de
        l'esprit*.

1540.   "La Double séance." *Tel Quel*, no. 41 (Spring 1970), pp. 3-43;
        no. 42 (Summer 1970), pp. 3-45. Rpt. in item 1552, pp. 199-
        317. See also item 1543.

        On Mallarmé.

1541.   "'*Ousía* and *Grammé*': A Note to a Footnote in *Being and Time*."
        Trans. Edward S. Casey. In *Phenomenology in Perspective*. Ed.
        F.J. Smith. The Hague: Martinus Nijhoff, 1970, pp. 54-93.
        Trans. of item 1530.

*1542. "Structure, Sign and Play in the Discourse of the Human
        Sciences." In *The Languages of Criticism and the Sciences
        of Man. The Structuralist Controversy*. Ed. Richard Macksey
        and Eugenio Umberto Donato. Baltimore, Md.: Johns Hopkins
        University Press, 1970, pp. 247-265; discussion, pp. 265-270.
        Paper read at the colloquium on October 21, 1966. Rpt. in item
        1521, pp. 409-428. For Serbo-Croatian trans., see item 1569.

1971

1543.   *La Double séance*. Paris: Tel Quel, 1971, 88pp. Cf. item 1540.

1544.   "Sémiologie et grammatologie: entretien avec Julia Kristeva."
        In *Essays in Semiotics. Essais de Sémiotique*. Ed. Julia
        Kristeva, Josette Rey-Debove, and Donna Jean Unicker. The
        Hague-Paris: Mouton, 1971, pp. 11-17. Rpts. item 1531.

*1545. "La Mythologie blanche. La Métaphore dans le texte philosophi-
        que." *Poétique*, no. 5 (1971), pp. 1-52. Rpt. in item 1553,
        pp. 247-324. For English trans., see item 1575.

*1546. "Positions. Entretien avec Jean-Louis Houdebine et Guy Scar-
        petta." *Promesse*, nos. 30-31 (Fall and Winter 1971), pp.
        5-62. Rpt. in item 1554, pp. 51-133. For English trans., see
        items 1555 and 1568.

*1547. "Le Supplément de copule. La Philosophie devant la linguistique."
        Langages, 24 December 1971, pp. 14-39. Rpt. in item 1553,
        pp. 209-246. For English trans., see items 1587 and 1602.

1548.   *La Scrittura e la differenza*. Trans. Gianni Pozzi. Turin: G.
        Einaudi, 1971. Trans. of item 1521.

1549.   *De la gramatología*. Buenos Aires: Siglo Veintiuno Argentina
        Editores, 1971. Trans. of item 1522.

1550.   *Tiempo y presencia. Ousia y grammé*. Trans. Patricio Marchant.
        Santiago de Chile: Editorial Universitaria, 1971. Trans.
        of item 1530.

1551.   "Les Sources de Valéry: qual, quelle." *MLN*, 87, no. 4 (May
        1972), 563-599. Paper given November 6, 1971 at Johns Hopkins
        University for the 100th anniversary of Valéry's birth. This
        issue of *MLN* was published as *Paul Valéry* in 1972 by the
        Johns Hopkins University Press. Article rpt. in item 1553,
        pp. 325-363.

1552.   *La Dissémination*. Paris: Editions du Seuil, 1972. Contains:
        Hors livre: préfaces, pp. 7-67 and items 1529, 1540 and
        1535. For reviews, see items 1858-1861. English trans. forth-
        coming by University of Chicago Press.

1553.   *Marges de la philosophie*. Paris: Editions de Minuit, 1972.
        Contains: Tympan by Michel Leiris, pp. i-xxv and items 1532,
        1530, 1538, the original French version of item 1536 (dated
        12 May 1968), and items 1525, 1524, 1547, 1545, 1551, and
        1561. For reviews, see items 1878-1879.

*1554. *Positions. Entretiens avec Henri Ronse, Julia Kristeva, Jean-
        Louis Houdebine, Guy Scarpetta*. Paris: Editions de Minuit,
        1972. Contains items 1526, 1531, and 1546. For Italian trans.,
        see item 1589. For reviews, see items 1881-1882.

1555.   "Positions." *Diacritics*, 2, no. 4 (Winter 1972), 35-43.
        Partial trans. of item 1546. See also item 1568.

1556.   [Edmond Jabès aujourd'hui.] *Nouveau Cahiers*, 8ᵉ année, no. 31
        (Winter 1972-1973), 56.

1557.   Interview with Lucette Finas: "Avoir l'oreille de la philosophie."
        La Quinzaine Littéraire, no. 152 (16-30 November 1972), pp.
        13-16. Rpt. in *Ecarts: quatre essais à propos de Jacques
        Derrida*. By Lucette Finas, et al. Paris: Fayard, 1973, pp.
        303-312.

1558.   "Freud and the Scene of Writing." Trans. Jeffrey Mehlman. *Yale
        French Studies* (issue entitled "French Freud: Structural
        Studies in Psychoanalysis"), no. 48 (1972), pp. 74-117.
        Trans. of item 1516. Rpt. in item 1567.

1559.   *Dos Ensayos*. Trans. Eugenio Trías and Alberto González Troyano.
        Barcelona: Anagrama, 1972. For review, see item 1871.

1560.   *Die Schrift und die Differenz*. Trans. R. Gasché. Frankfurt
        am Main: Suhrkamp Verlag, 1972, 1975, 1977. Trans. of item
        1521.

*1561. "Signature, événement, contexte." *La Communication, II. Actes
        du XVᵉ Congrès de l'Association des Sociétés de Philosophie
        de Langue Française. Université de Montréal, 1971*. Montreal:

Editions Montmorency, 1973, pp. 49-76. Rpt. in item 1553, pp. 365-393. For trans., see items 1603 (German) and 1611 (English).

1562. "Glas." *L'Arc* (issue on Jacques Derrida), no. 54 (1973), pp. 4-15. Excerpts of this article appeared in *La Quinzaine Littéraire*, no. 172 (1973), pp. 23-36. Cf. item 1570.

1563. "L'Archéologie du frivole." In Condillac's *Essai sur l'origine des connaissances humaines*. Ed. Charles Porset. Paris: Editions Galilée, 1973, pp. 9-95. Rpt. in items 1569a and 1591.

1564. Anonymously. "Aphorismes ou 'textuels'" and "En marge de Rousseau." *Le Monde [des Livres]*, no. 8838 (14 June 1973), p. 22.

*1565. "La Question du style." In *Nietzsche aujourd'hui? I. Intensités*. Paris: Union Générale d'Editions, 1973, pp. 235-287; discussion, pp. 288-299. For modified version and English, Italian and German trans., see items 1592 and 1614.

1566. *Speech and Phenomena, and Other Essays on Husserl's Theory of Signs*. Trans. David B. Allison. Evanston, Ill.: Northwestern University Press, 1973.

Contains: a preface by Newton Garver, pp. ix-xxix; a translator's introduction, pp. xxxi-xlii; and trans. of items 1523, 1524 and 1532.

1567. "Freud and the Scene of Writing." Trans. and intro. Jeffrey Mehlman. *L'Arc* (issue on Jacques Derrida), no. 54 (1973), pp. 73-117. Rpt. of item 1558.

1568. "Positions." *Diacritics*, 3, no. 1 (Spring 1973), 33-46. Partial trans. of item 1546. See also item 1555.

Interview with J.-L. Houdebine.

1569. "Struktura, znak i igra u govoru nauka o čoveku." *Delo*, 19, no. 12 (1973), 1477-1495. Serbo-Croatian trans. of item 1542 or of the last chapter of item 1521.

1974

1569a. *L'Archéologie du frivole*. Paris: Editions Galilée, 1974. (Palimpseste) Rpt. of item 1563. See item 1591 for new edition, table of contents and reviews.

1570. *Glas*. Paris: Editions Galilée, 1974. Cf. item 1562. For reviews, see items 1872-1877.

1571. "Mallarmé." In *Tableau de la littérature française. De Madame de Staël à Rimbaud*. Paris: Gallimard, 1974, pp. 368-379.

1572. "Le Parergon." *Digraphe*, no. 2 (1974), pp. 21-57.

1573.   "Le Sans de la coupure pure. (Le Parergon II)." *Digraphe*,
        no. 3 (1974), pp. 5-31.

1574.   "Linguistics and Grammatology." *Sub-stance*, no. 10 (1974),
        pp. 127-181. Trans. of second chapter of part one of item
        1522 by Gayatri Chakravorty Spivak. See also item 1600.

1575.   "White Mythology: Metaphor in the Text of Philosophy." *New
        Literary History* (issue on Metaphor), 6, no. 1 (Autumn
        1974), 5-74. Trans. of item 1545.

1576.   "La Lingüística de Rousseau." In *El origen de las lenguas*.
        By Jean-Jacques Rousseau. Buenos Aires: Ediciones Calden,
        1974 or earlier. Trans. of item 1525.

1577.   *Grammatologie.* Trans. Hans J. Rheinberger and Hanns Zischler.
        Frankfurt am Main: Suhrkamp Verlag, 1974. Trans. of item
        1522.

                                1975

1578.   "Economimesis." In *Mimesis des articulations*. By Sylviane
        Agacinski, Jacques Derrida, et al. Paris: Aubier-Flammarion,
        1975, pp. 55-93.

1579.   Text of *Valerio Adami: le voyage du dessin accompagné par +
        R (par dessus le marché)*. Paris: Maeght, 1975. See also
        items 1580 and 1581.

1580.   "+ R (par dessus le marché)." In *Derrière le miroir*, no. 214
        (May 1975), pp. 1-23. See also items 1579 and 1581.

1581.   "Inédit + R (par dessus le marché)." *Quinzaine Littéraire*,
        no. 211 (1-15 June 1975), pp. 14-16. See also items 1579 and
        1580.

*1582. "Le Facteur de vérité." *Poétique* (issue on Littérature et
        philosophie melées), no. 21 (1975), pp. 96-147. For English
        trans., see item 1586.

        Commentary on Lacan's *Séminaire sur la lettre volée*; what
        psychoanalysis does with literature and how it seeks truth
        in it.

1583.   "Pour la philosophie." *La Nouvelle Critique*, no. 84 (1975),
        pp. 25-29. Rpt. in item 1607.

1584.   "Response to Questions on the Avant-Garde." *Digraphe*, no. 6
        (October 1975), pp. 152-153.

1585.   "La Philosophie refoulée." *Le Monde de l'Education*, no. 4
        (1975), pp. 14-15. An extract of item 1606.

        Haby's (the minister of education) offensive against philos-
        ophy must not just elicit the reflex of defending the tradi-

tional institution. It must also lead philosophers to re-examine content and what is at stake in teaching their discipline.

1586. "Purveyor of Truth." Trans. Willis Domingo, et al. *Yale French Studies* (issue on Graphesis: Perspectives in Literature and Philosophy), no. 52 (1975), pp. 31-113. Trans. of item 1582.

1587. "The Copula Supplement." Trans. David B. Allison. In *Dialogues in Phenomenology*. Ed. Don Ihde and Richard M. Zaner. The Hague: Martinus Nijhoff, 1975, pp. 7-48. Trans. of item 1547. See also item 1602.

1588. *El Pensamiento de Antonin Artaud*. Buenos Aires: Ediciones Calden, 1975, 124pp. With Julia Kristeva. (Colección el Hombre y el Mundo, 18)

1589. *Posizioni. Colloqui con Henri Ronse, Julia Kristeva, Jean-Louis Houdebine, Guy Scarpetta e Lucette Finas*. Ed. Giuseppe Sertoli. Trans. M. Chiappini and G. Sertoli. Verona: Bertani, 1975, 156pp. (Il Lavoro crítico: filosofia, 6) Trans. of item 1554.

1590. Article in *Theorie-Literatur-Praxis. Arbeitsbuch zur Literatur-theorie seit 1970*. Ed. Richard Brütting and Bernhard Zimmer-man. Frankfurt am Main: Athenaion, 1975.

1976

1591. *L'Archéologie du frivole*. Paris: Denoël-Gonthier, 1976. A new edition of item 1569a. Rpts. item 1563. For reviews, see items 1841-1843.

Contains: (1) Première seconde--la métaphysique; (2) L'Après-coup de génie; (3) Imaginer--la doublure des concepts et le roman de la force; (4) Note marginale ou remarque--les deux pages volantes; (5) Introduction à l'*Essai sur l'origine des connaissances humaines*--la frivolité même; Biographie de E. Bonnot de Condillac.

*1592. *Eperons: les styles de Nietzsche. Spurs: Nietzsche's Styles*. Venice: Corbo e Fiore, c. 1976; Paris: Flammarion, 1977, 129pp. See also item 1614. See item 1617d for American edi-tion. For reviews, see items 1843a and 1843b.

Modified version and English, Italian and German trans. of item 1565. Includes "Coup sur coup: introduction à Eperons" by Stefano Agosti and drawings by François Loubrieu.

1593. Reply in *Aujourd'hui, Rimbaud...: enquête de Roger Munier*. Paris: Lettres Modernes, 1976.

*1594. "Fors: les mots anglés de Nicolas Abraham et Maria Torok." In *Cryptonymie: le verbier de l'"homme aux loups."* By Nicolas Abraham and Maria Torok. Paris: Aubier-Montaigne/ Flammarion, 1976, pp. 7-73. For English trans., see item 1615.

1595.   "Où commence et comment finit un corps enseignant?" In *Châtelet,
        Derrida, Foucault, Lyotard, Serres. Politiques de la philosophi*
        Ed. Dominique Grisoni. Paris: Bernard Grasset, 1976, pp. 55-97.

1596.   "Entre crochets. Entretien avec Jacques Derrida. Première
        partie." *Digraphe*, no. 8 (April 1976), pp. 97-114. See item
        1609 for second part of the interview.

1597.   "Pas I." *Gramma: Lire Blanchot I*, nos. 3-4 (1976), pp. 111-215.

1598.   "Signéponge." *Digraphe*, no. 8 (April 1976), pp. 17-39. See
        item 1604.

1599.   "Où sont les chasseurs de sorcières?" *Le Monde*, 1 July 1976.

1600.   *Of Grammatology*. Trans. Gayatri Chakravorty Spivak. Baltimore:
        Johns Hopkins University Press, 1976. Trans. of item 1522.

1601.   "From Restricted to General Economy. A Hegelianism without
        Reserves." Trans. Alan Bass. *Semiotext(e)*, 2, no. 2 (1976),
        25-55. Trans. of item 1520.

1602.   "Supplement of Copula: Philosophy before Linguistics." Trans.
        James Creech and Josué Harari. *Georgia Review*, 30 (Fall
        1976), 527-564. Trans. of item 1547; to be reprinted in the
        forthcoming *Textual Strategies: Criticism in the Wake of
        Structuralism*, ed. Josué Harari. See also item 1587.

1603.   *Randgänge der Philosophie*. Trans. Gerhard Ahrens, Henriette
        Beese, and Eva Brückner-Pfaffenberg. Frankfurt-Berlin-Vienna:
        Ullstein, 1976. Contains trans. of items 1532, 1530, 1536,
        and 1561, all part of item 1553.

1977

1604.   "Signéponge." In *Ponge Inventeur et Classique. Colloque de
        Cerisy*. Paris: Union Générale d'Editions, 1977, pp. 115-
        144. Discussion, pp. 145-151. Differs from item 1598. Both
        are extracts of a work in progress.

1605.   "L'Age de Hegel." In *Qui a peur de la philosophie?* By the
        Groupe de Recherches sur l'Enseignement Philosophique (GREPH).
        Paris: Flammarion, 1977, pp. 73-107.

1606.   "La Philosophie et ses classes." In *Qui a peur de la philoso-
        phie?* By the Groupe de Recherches sur l'Enseignement Philos-
        ophique (GREPH). Paris: Flammarion, 1977, pp. 445-450. For
        an extract of this article, see item 1585.

1607.   "Réponses à *La Nouvelle Critique*." In *Qui a peur de la philo-
        sophie?* By the Groupe de Recherches sur l'Enseignement
        Philosophique (GREPH). Paris: Flammarion, 1977, pp. 451-
        458. Rpts. item 1583.

1608. Preface to Warburton's *Essai sur les hiéroglyphes*. Paris: Aubier-Flammarion, 1977.

1609. "Ja, ou le faux-bond (Suite)." *Digraphe*, no. 11 (March 1977), pp. 83-121. See item 1596 for the first part of this interview.

Derrida answers questions on *Glas* (item 1570) and talks about upcoming works on Marxism, the practice of deconstruction and the notion of ideology.

1610. *Edmund Husserl's Origin of Geometry: An Introduction*. Ed. David B. Allison. Trans. John P. Leavey. Stony Brook, N.Y.: Nicolas Hays, 1977; Boulder, Colo.: Great Eastern Book Co. (distributor), 1978; Hassocks, Sussex: The Harvester Press, 1978. See item 1499. Derrida bibliography, pp. 181-193.

1611. "Signature, Event, Context." Trans. Samuel Weber and Jeffrey Mehlman. In *Glyph I. Johns Hopkins Textual Studies*. Ed. Samuel Weber and Henry Sussman. Baltimore: Johns Hopkins University Press, 1977, pp. 172-197. Trans. of item 1561. See item 1612.

1612. "Limited Inc." In *Glyph 2. Johns Hopkins Textual Studies*. Ed. Samuel Weber and Henry Sussman. Baltimore: Johns Hopkins University Press, 1977, pp. 162-254. English trans. of item 1613 which is the sequel to item 1611.

Responds to the criticisms of John Searle published in *Glyph 1*.

1613. *Limited Inc.: Supplement to Glyph 2*. Baltimore: Johns Hopkins University Press, 1977. This is the 81-page French version of item 1612 written in anticipation of its translation.

1614. "The Question of Style." Trans. Reuben Berezdivin. In *The New Nietzsche: Contemporary Styles of Interpretation*. Ed. David B. Allison. New York: Dell Publishing, 1977, pp. 176-189. Excerpts and trans. of items 1565 and 1592.

1615. "Fors: the Anglish Words of Nicolas Abraham and Maria Torok." Trans. Barbara Johnson. *Georgia Review*, 31, no. 1 (Spring 1977), 64-116. Trans. of item 1594.

1978

1615a. *La Vérité en peinture*. Paris: Flammarion, 1978, 440pp. (Champs, no 57. Champ philosophique) Drawn, in part, from various journals and publications of 1968-1978.

1615b. *Gérard Titus-Carmel: The Pocket Size Tlinget Coffin*. Paris: Centre Georges Pompidou, 1978, 73pp. Text of an exhibit held at the Centre National d'Art et de Culture Georges Pompidou, Musée National d'Art Moderne, 1 March to 10 April 1978.

1615c. "Le Retrait de la métaphore." *Poésie*, no. 7 (1978), pp. 103-
       126.

1616. "Scribble: pouvoir/écrire." In *Essai sur les hiéroglyphes des
       Egyptiens.* By William Warburton. Trans. Léonard Des Malpeines.
       Paris: Aubier-Montaigne/Flammarion, 1978. (Palimpseste)

1616a. *Writing and Difference.* Trans. and intro. Alan Bass. London:
       Routledge and Kegan Paul; Chicago: University of Chicago
       Press, 1978, 342pp. Trans. of item 1521.

1616b. "Coming Into One's Own." In *Psychoanalysis and the Question
       of the Text.* Ed. Geoffrey H. Hartman. Baltimore, Md.: Johns
       Hopkins University Press, 1978, pp. 114-148. (Selected papers
       from the English Institute, 1976-1977, new series no. 2)

       On chapter two of Freud's *Beyond the Pleasure Principle.*

1617. "Restitutions of Truth to Size, *De la vérité en pointure.*"
       Trans. John P. Leavey. *Research in Phenomenology*, 8 (1978),
       1-44. A portion of this text was read at Columbia University
       in the Fall of 1977. A French version was to be published
       in *Macula.*

1617a. "Theater of Cruelty and the Closure of Representation."
       Theater, 9 (Summer 1978), 7-19. Trans. of item 1517.

1617b. "Becoming Woman." *Semiotext(e)*, 3 (1978), 128-137.

       On Nietzsche.

1617c. "Speech and Writing According to Hegel." Trans. Alfonso Lingis.
       Man and World, 11, no. 1-2 (1978), 107-130.

1617d. *Spurs: Nietzsche's Styles--Eperons: les styles de Nietzsche.*
       Intro. Stefano Agosti. Eng. trans. Barbara Harlow. Drawings
       by François Loubrieu. Chicago: University of Chicago Press,
       1979, c. 1978, 165pp. First American edition of item 1592.

                                  1979

1617e. "Du tout." *Cahiers Confrontation*, no. 1 (Paris, 1979), pp.
       63-77.

       R. Major questions Derrida on *Glas* and other texts thematic-
       ally related to the psychoanalytic theory, movement or insti-
       tution.

1617f. "Ce qui reste à force de musique." *Digraphe*, no. 18-19 (1979),
       pp. 165-174. Part of a special issue on Roger Laporte.

       Derrida reflects on the unattainable essence of the "economy"
       of writing; on Laporte's *Fugue* and *Supplément.*

SECONDARY SOURCES

1618. Abel, Lionel. "Jacques Derrida: His 'Difference' with Meta-
       physics." *Salmagundi*, no. 25 (Winter 1974), pp. 3-21.

1619. Abrams, M.H. "The Limits of Pluralism II. The Deconstructive
       Angel." *Critical Inquiry*, 3 (1977), 425-438.

1620. Accame, Lorenzo. *La Decostruzione e il testo*. Florence: Nuova
       Società Editoriale G.C. Sansoni, 1976.

       On Derrida's *Grammatologie*, Plato's *Cratylus*, language and
       philosophy.

1620a. Aćin, J. "To Be, To Think, To Speak" (in Serbo-Croatian).
       Delo, 23, no. 10 (Yugoslavia, 1977), 17-30.

       With the second Meditation of Descartes as a starting point,
       Aćin discusses various solutions to the problem of ontologico-
       grammatical parallelism. Derrida is one of those treated.

1621. Agosti, Stefano. "Coup sur coup. Introduction à *Eperons*,"
       preface to Derrida's *Eperons. Les Styles de Nietzsche*.
       Venice: Corbo e Fiore, 1976. English trans. by Barbara Harlow,
       "Coup upon Coup. An Introduction to *Spurs*" in ibid. See item
       1592.

1622. Allison, David Blair. Translator's preface to Derrida's *Speech
       and Phenomena: And Other Essays on Husserl's Theory of Signs*.
       Evanston, Ill.: Northwestern University Press, 1973, xxxi-xliii.
       See item 1566.

1623. ———. "Derrida's Critique of Husserl: The Philosophy of
       Presence." Dissertation: The Pennsylvania State University,
       1974.

1624. ———. "Derrida and Wittgenstein: Playing the Game." *Research
       in Phenomenology*, 8 (1978), 93-109.

1625. Altieri, Charles F. "Northrop Frye and the Problem of Spiritual
       Authority." *Publications of the Modern Language Association
       of America*, 87, no. 5 (1972), 964-975.

       On how Derrida and Foucault could be criticized by Frye.

1626. ———. "Wittgenstein on Consciousness and Language: A Chal-
       lenge to Derridan Literary Theory." *MLN*, 91 (December 1976),
       1397-1423.

       Ames, V.M. See item 3689.

       Anonymous. See items 5128, 4272 and 2064.

1627. ———. "La Crise du signe et de l'impérialisme: Trotsky/
       Derrida." *Scription Rouge*, no. 5 (September-November 1973).

1628. ———. "Echos et nouvelles." *Le Monde [des Livres]*, no.
       9035 (1 February 1974), p. 15.

1629. ———. "A propos de *L'Arc*, no. 54." *La Quinzaine Littéraire*,
       no. 175 (1973).

1630. ———. "Scription, matérialisme dialectique: Derrida-Marx."
       Scription Rouge, no. 1 (May 1972).

1631. ———. "Le Territoire des autres." *L'Arc* (issue on Derrida),
       no. 54 (1973), pp. 2-3.

1632. *L'Arc*, no. 54 (Aix-en-Provence, 1973): issue on Jacques
       Derrida. Contains items 1631, 1648, 1656, 1658, 1658a, 1695,
       1714, 1731, 1735, 1747, 1753, 1780, and bibliography.

1633. Backès-Clément, Catherine. "La Dissémination: la méthode
       déplacée." *Les Lettres Françaises*, no. 1429 (29 March-4 April
       1972), pp. 4-5.

       Balmas, E. See item 4278.

1634. Bandera, Cesáreo. "The Crisis of Knowledge in *La Vida es
       sueño*." *Sub-stance*, no. 7 (Fall 1973), pp. 27-47.

1635. ———. "Literature and Desire: Poetic Frenzy and the Love
       Potion." *Mosaic*, 8 (Winnipeg, Winter 1975), 33-52.

       Barthes, R. See item 846.

1635a. Bass, Alan. "Writing and Difference: A Translation of Eight
       Essays from *L'Ecriture et la différence* by Jacques Derrida,
       with Introduction and Notes." *Dissertation Abstracts
       International*, 36, no. 10 (April 1976), 6662A. Johns Hopkins
       University, 1975.

1636. Beigbeder, Marc. "La Grammatologie de Jacques Derrida." In
       Contradiction et nouvel entendement. Paris: Bordas, 1972.

       Benamou, M. See item 4829.

1637. Benoist, Jean-Marie. "Actualité d'Adler." *Adam. International
       Review*, 35th year, nos. 340-342 (1970), 42-45.

1638. ———. "L'Inscription de Derrida." *La Quinzaine Littéraire*,
       no. 182 (1974), pp. 18-19.

1639. ———. "Le Colosse de Rhodes ou quelques remarques à propos
       de *Glas* de Jacques Derrida." *Art Vivant*, no. 54 (December
       1974-January 1975), pp. 37-38.

1640. Berezdivin, Ruben. "Gloves: Inside-Out." *Research in Phenomen-
       ology*, 8 (1978), 111-126.

       Bersani, L. See item 3873.

Beyssade, J.M. See item 2084.

1641.   Bonnefoy, Claude. "Un Nouveau philosophe, Jacques Derrida, met en question toute la pensée contemporaine." *Arts-Loisirs*, no. 87 (June 1967), pp. 31-33, 35.

On *L'Ecriture et la différence*.

1642.   ———. "La Clôture et sa transgression." *Opus International*, 3 (1967).

1643.   Booth, Wayne C. "The Limits of Pluralism I. 'Preserving the Exemplar': or, How Not to Dig our Own Graves." *Critical Inquiry*, 3 (1977), 404-423.

1644.   Bothezat, T. "Lecturer to visit Baltimore." *The Sun* (Baltimore), 2 February 1968.

Bouazis, C. See item 5134.

1644a. Bouchard, G. "Le Signe saussurien et la métaphysique occidentale selon Jacques Derrida." *The Canadian Journal of Research in Semiotics. Le Journal Canadien de Recherche Sémiotique*, 6, no. 1-2 (1978-1979), 147-169.

Discusses Derrida's critique of Saussure in *De la grammatologie* and the attempt to show that Saussure's theory of signs cannot be reduced to the metaphysical tradition.

1645.   Boyer, Philippe. "Déconstruction: le désir à la lettre." *Change* (issue on La Destruction), 1, no. 2 (1969), 127-148. Rpt. in *L'Ecarté(e) (fiction théorique)*. By Philippe Boyer. Paris: Editions Seghers/Lafont, 1973, pp. 209-234.

1646.   ———. "Le Point de la question." *Change* (issue on L'Imprononçable: l'écriture nomade), no. 22 (1975), pp. 41-72.

1647.   Brague, Rémi. "En marge de 'La Pharmacie de Platon' de Jacques Derrida." *Revue Philosophique de Louvain*, 71, no. 10 (May 1973), 271-277.

Broekman, Jan M. See item 30, pp. 91-94, 101-104.

Brown, P.L. See items 4447 and 4448.

1648.   Buci-Glucksmann, Christine. "Déconstruction et critique marxiste de la philosophie. A propos d'une lecture de Hegel: *Marges de la philosophie*. *L'Arc*, no. 54 (1973), pp. 20-32.

1649.   Catesson, J. "Note sur le sens du mot Réalité." *Revue de Métaphysique et de Morale*, 72, no. 3 (1967), 374-378.

Critical remarks on Derrida's ideas in item 1506.

1650.   ———. "A propos d'une pensée de l'intervalle." *Revue de Métaphysique et de Morale*, 74, no. 1 (1969), 74-90.

Reflection on birth and death, the beginning and the end, and the gap which separates them (regarding the analyses of Derrida).

Caws, M.A. See item 3905.

1651.   Champagne, Roland A. "Un Déclenchement: The Revolutionary Implications of Philippe Sollers' *Nombres* for a Logocentric Western Culture." *Sub-stance*, no. 7 (Fall 1973), pp. 101-111.

1652.   ————. "The Resurrection of Thoth, the God of Writing: Jacques Derrida's Arguments for the *Machine à Ecrire*." *Centrum*, 2, no. 1 (Spring 1974), 5-13.

1653.   Châtelet, François. "Qui est Jacques Derrida? La Métaphysique dans sa clôture." *Le Nouvel Observateur-Spécial Littéraire*, no. 210 bis (20 November-20 December 1968), pp. 26-27.

1654.   Chumbley, Robert. "'Delfica' and 'la différance': Patterning an Inscription by Nerval." *South Central Bulletin*, 33, no. 3 (October 1973), 131.

1655.   ————. "'Delfica' and 'La Différance': Toward a Nervalian System." *Sub-stance*, no. 10 (1974), pp. 33-37.

1656.   Cixous, Hélène. "L'Essort de plusje." *L'Arc*, no. 54 (1973), pp. 46-52.

1657.   Clemens, Eric. "Sur Derrida: alternance et dédoublement." *TXT*, cahier no. 5 (1972).

1658.   Clément, Catherine. "Le Sauvage." *L'Arc*, no. 54 (1973), pp. 1-2.

1658a. ————. "A l'écoute de Derrida." *L'Arc*, no. 54 (1973), pp. 16-19.

1659.   Conley, Tom. "Reviews." *Modern Language Journal*, 59, no. 8 (December 1975), 459-460.

Crémant, Roger. See item 54.

1660.   Culler, Jonathan. "Commentary." *New Literary History* (issue "On Metaphor."), 6, no. 1 (Fall 1974), 219-229.

————. See also item 4836.

Dadoun, R. See item 55.

Daix, P., et al. See item 56.

1661.   Damisch, Hubert. "Ceci (donc)." *Les Lettres Françaises*, no. 1429 (29 March-4 April 1972), p. 6.

1662.   Dauenhauer, Bernard P. "On Speech and Temporality: Jacques Derrida and Edmund Husserl." *Philosophy Today*, 18, no. 3 (Fall 1974), 171-180.

1663. Deese, James. "Mind and Metaphor: A Commentary." *New Literary History*, 6, no. 1 (Fall 1974), 211-217.

1664. Deguy, Michel. "Husserl en seconde lecture." *Critique*, 19, no. 192 (May 1963), 434-448.

1665. Delacampagne, Christian. "La Lettre retrouvée: un coup porté à la métaphysique." *Le Monde [des Livres]*, no. 8838 (14 June 1973), p. 22.

1666. ————. "Autour de Derrida: Condillac et la 'frivole.'" *Le Monde [des Livres]*, no. 8998 (20 December 1973), p. 24.

1667. ————. "Derrida et Deleuze." *Le Monde*, 30 April 1976, p. 28.

1668. ————. "Six auteurs, une voix anonyme." *Le Monde*, 30 April 1976, p. 28.

De Man, Paul. See Man, Paul de.

Detweiler, R. See item 1036.

1669. Detweiler, Robert. "Jacques Derrida: Phenomenology and Structuralism." In his *Story, Sign, and Self: Phenomenology and Structuralism as Literary Critical Methods* (item 4299), pp. 187-191.

Donato, E. See item 65.

1670. D[roit], R[oger]-P[ol]. "Dix ans de lecture. Philosophie: mort et renouveau." *Le Monde [des Livres]*, no. 9976 (25 February 1977), p. 22.

On Deleuze and Derrida.

1671. Dufrenne, Mikel. "Pour une philosophie non-théologique." In his *Le Poétique*. 2nd ed. Paris: Presses Universitaires de France, 1973, pp. 7-57.

Duval, R. See item 4495.

Eco, Umberto. "La Structure et l'absence." In his *La Structure absente* (item 5148).

1672. Ehrmann, Jacques. "Sur le jeu et l'origine, où il est surtout question de *La Dissémination* de Jacques Derrida." *Sub-stance*, no. 7 (Fall 1973), pp. 113-123.

1673. Escarpit, Robert. *L'Ecrit et la communication*. Paris: Presses Universitaires de France, 1973, pp. 17, 22, 44, 64-66.

1674. Falconer, Graham, and Henri Mitterand, eds. *La Lecture socio-critique du texte romanesque. Textes, Pierre Barbéris, Jacques Derrida ... et al.* Toronto: Hakkert & Co., 1975.

1675. Felman, Shoshana. "Madness and Philosophy or Literature's
       Reason." *Yale French Studies* (issue on "Graphesis: Perspec-
       tives in Literature and Philosophy"), no. 52 (1975), pp.
       206-228.

1676. Ferguson, Frances C. "Reading Heidegger: Paul De Man and
       Jacques Derrida." *Boundary 2*, 4, no. 2 (Winter 1976), 593-
       610.

1677. Ferguson, M.W. "Saint Augustine's Region of Unlikeness: The
       Crossing of Exile and Language." *The Georgia Review*, 29,
       no. 4 (Winter 1975), 842-864.

1678. Finas, Lucette. "Entretien. Jacques Derrida: 'avoir l'oreille
       de la philosophie.'" *La Quinzaine Littéraire*, no. 152
       (16-30 November 1972), pp. 13-16.

1679. ————. "Derrida 'marque' Valéry." *La Quinzaine Littéraire*,
       no. 152 (16-30 November 1972), pp. 16-17.

1680. ————, et al. *Ecarts. Quatre essais à propos de Jacques
       Derrida*. Paris: Fayard, 1973. Contains items 1681, 1724, 1732,
       and 1802.

1681. ————. "Le Coup de D. e(s)t judas." In *Ecarts....* (item 1680),
       pp. 9-105.

1682. ————. "Etude, Jacques Derrida: le déconstructeur." *Le
       Monde [des Livres]*, no. 8838 (14 June 1973), pp. 22-23.

1683. F[inas], L[ucette]. "Elaboration." and "Indécidables." *Le
       Monde [des Livres]*, no. 8838 (14 June 1973), p. 23.

1684. Flieger, Jerry Aline. "Implication of the Comic Mode in Con-
       temporary French Literature." *Dissertation Abstracts Inter-
       national*, 38, no. 2 (August 1977), 824-825-A. University of
       California, Berkeley, dissertation.

1684a. Florián, V. "Jacques Derrida y la oposición naturaleza/cultura."
       Ideas y Valores, no. 46-47 (Bogotá, 1976), pp. 45-52.

1685. Fontaine-De Visscher, Luce. "Des privilèges d'une grammatologie."
       Revue Philosophique de Louvain, 67, no. 95 (August 1969),
       461-475.

1686. Foucault, Michel. "Une Petite pédagogie." *Le Monde*, 14 June
       1973, p. 23. Excerpt from "Mon corps, ce papier, ce feu,"
       appendix to *Histoire de la folie à l'âge classique*, new
       edition (item 1971), pp. 583-603.

1687. Frank, M. "Eine fundamental-semiologische Herausforderung der
       abendländischen Wissenschaft." *Philosophische Rundschau*, no.
       no. 1-2 (1976), pp. 1-16.

       On two of Derrida's works in German: *Grammatologie* and *Die
       Schrift und die Differenz*.

1688. Garelli, Jacques. "L'Ecart du maintenant et l'extension de l'esprit." *Les Temps Modernes*, 25, no. 281 (December 1969), 874-896.

1689. ————. "Le Flux et l'instant." *Les Temps Modernes*, 26, no. 283 (February 1970), 1239-1263.

1690. ————. "De quelques erreurs statistiques." *Les Temps Modernes*, 26, no. 286 (May 1970), 1929-1936.

1691. Garver, Newton. Preface to Jacques Derrida's *Speech and Phenomena* ... (item 1566), pp. ix-xxix.

1692. ————. "Derrida on Rousseau on Writing." *The Journal of Philosophy*, 74, no. 11 (November 1977), 663-673.

   Rousseau's claim (in his *Essay on the Origin of Languages*) that writing entails the corruption of speech is of special interest to Derrida, who counters with the even more bizarre claim that writing is prior to speech.

1693. [Genet, Jean]. "Une Lettre de Jean Genet." *Les Lettres Françaises*, no. 1429 (29 March-4 April 1972), p. 14.

   Gillet-Stern, S. See item 4539.

1694. Gillibert, Jean. "A propos de *Freud et la scène de l'écriture*." *Les Lettres Françaises*, no. 1429 (29 March-4 April 1972), p. 8.

1695. Giovannangeli, Daniel. "La Question de la littérature." *L'Arc*, no. 54 (1973), pp. 81-86.

1696. ————. "Code et différence impure." *Littérature*, no. 12 (1973), pp. 93-106.

1697. ————. "Vers un dépassement de la phénoménologie et du structuralisme. La Réflexion sur la littérature dans la pensée de Jacques Derrida." Dissertation, Université de Mons, Belgium, 1974.

1698. ————. "Jacques Derrida. Une Pensée de la répétition." *Annales de l'Institut de Philosophie* (Brussels, 1976), pp. 193-211.

1699. Girard, René. "Lévi-Strauss, Frye, Derrida and Shakespearean Criticism." *Diacritics*, 3, no. 3 (Fall 1973), 34-38.

1700. Goux, Jean-Joseph. "Du graphème au chromosome." *Les Lettres Françaises*, no. 1429 (29 March-4 April 1972), pp. 6-7.

   Graff, G. See item 4308a.

1701. Granel, Gérard. "Jacques Derrida et la rature de l'origine." *Critique*, 20e année, no. 246 (November 1967), 887-905. Rpt. in his *Traditionis traditio*. Paris: Gallimard, 1972, pp. 154-175.

On Derrida's *De la grammatologie*, *L'Ecriture et la différence*, and *La Voix et le phénomène*.

1702.   Greisch, Jean. "La Crise de l'herméneutique. Réflexions méta-
        critiques sur un débat actuel." In his (et al.) *La Crise
        contemporaine: du modernisme à la crise des herméneutiques*.
        Paris: Beauchesne, 1973, pp. 135-190.

1702a. ————. *Herméneutique et grammatologie*. Paris: Centre National
        de Recherche Scientifique, C.H.S.D., 1977, 233pp. (Phénomén-
        ologie et Herméneutique)

        Greisch's way of relating hermeneutics and grammatology is
        comparable to that of Derrida.

1703.   Grene, Marjorie. "Life, Death, and Language: Some Thoughts on
        Wittgenstein and Derrida." *Partisan Review*, 43, no. 2 (1976),
        265-279. Rpt. in her *Philosophy In and Out of Europe*.
        Berkeley: University of California Press, 1976, pp. 142-154.

1704.   ————. "On the Use and Abuse of Deconstruction." *The Journal
        of Philosophy*, 74, no. 11 (November 1977), p. 682.

1705.   Guibal, Francis. "Philosophie, langage, écriture." *Etudes*, no.
        336 (May 1972), pp. 769-781.

        Hanhardt, J.G., et al. See item 3825.

1705a. Hans, James S. "Derrida and Freeplay." *MLN*, 94 (May 1979),
        809-826.

        On *Of Grammatology*.

1706.   Hartman, Geoffrey H. "Monsieur Texte: On Jacques Derrida, His
        Glas." *Georgia Review*, 29, no. 4 (Winter 1975), 759-797.

1707.   ————. "Monsieur Texte II: Epiphony in Echoland." *Georgia
        Review*, 30, no. 1 (Spring 1976), 169-204.

1708.   ————. "Crossing Over: Literary Commentary as Literature."
        Comparative Literature, 28, no. 3 (Summer 1976), 257-276.

1708a. ————. "Psychoanalysis: The French Connection." In his (ed.)
        Psychoanalysis and the Question of the Text. Baltimore, Md.:
        Johns Hopkins University Press, 1978, pp. 86-113.

        On Derrida's *Glas*; on Lacan.

        Hawkes, T. See item 5165.

1709.   Heath, Stephen. "Of Derrida." *Canto*, Winter 1977, pp. 174-181.

1710.   Hector, J. "Jacques Derrida: la clôture de la métaphysique."
        Techniques Nouvelles, no. 6 (June 1972).

        Hefner, R.W. See item 4312.

Hempfer, K.W. See item 3956.

1711. Hollier, Denis. "La Copulation labyrinthique (un détail d'interférences)." *Les Lettres Françaises*, no. 1429 (29 March-4 April 1972), pp. 14-15.

1712. Irigaray, Luce. "Le V(i)ol de la lettre." *Tel Quel*, no. 39 (Fall 1969), pp. 64-77.

1713. Itzkowitz, Kenneth. "Differance and Identity." *Research in Phenomenology*, 8 (1978), 127-143.

1714. Jabès, Edmond. "Lettre à Jacques Derrida sur la question du livre." *L'Arc*, no. 54 (1973), pp. 59-64.

1715. Jacob, André. "De la socio-analyse à la grammatologie," chapter 12 of his *Introduction à la philosophie du langage*. Paris: Gallimard, 1976, pp. 306-332.

1715a. Jaimes, F. "Jacques Derrida o el pensamiento de la diferencia." *Franciscanum*, 21, no. 61 (Bogotá, Colombia, 1979), 5-25.

Jameson, F. See item 4172, pp. 173-186.

1716. Janicaud, Dominique. "Presence and Appropriation: Derrida and the Question of an Overcoming of Metaphysical Language." *Research in Phenomenology*, 8 (1978), 67-75.

1717. Jannoud, Claude. "Sur Hegel et Genet: l'évangile selon Derrida." *Le Figaro Littéraire*, no. 1489 (30 November 1974), IV: 15, 18.

1718. Johnson, Barbara. "Frame of Reference: Poe, Lacan, Derrida." *Yale French Studies*, no. 55-56 (1977), pp. 457-505.

1718a. ————. "The Frame of Reference: Poe, Lacan, Derrida." In *Psychoanalysis and the Question of the Text*. Ed. Geoffrey H. Hartman. Baltimore, Md.: Johns Hopkins University Press, 1978, pp. 149-171.

On Derrida's "The Purveyor of Truth" and Lacan's "Seminar on the Purloined Letter."

1719. Jouffroy, Alain. *La Fin des alternances*. Paris: Gallimard, 1970.

1720. *The Journal of Philosophy*, 74, no. 11 (November 1977): issue on "Symposium: The Philosophy of Jacques Derrida." See items 1692, 1704, and 1810.

1721. Kerr, Fergus. "Derrida's *Wake*." *New Blackfriars*, 55, no. 653 (October 1974), 449-460.

1722. Klein, Richard. "Prolegomenon to Derrida." *Diacritics*, 2, no. 4 (Winter 1972), 29-34.

1723. ————. "The Blindness of Hyperboles: The Ellipses of Insight."
      Diacritics, 3, no. 2 (Summer 1973), 33-44.

1724. Kofman, Sarah. "Un Philosophe 'Unheimlich.'" In item 1680,
      pp. 107-204.

      Krieger, M. See items 4318-4320.

1725. Kristeva, Julia. *La Révolution du langage poétique. L'Avant-
      garde à la fin du XIXe siècle: Lautréamont et Mallarmé.*
      Paris: Editions du Seuil, 1974, pp. 129-134.

      Künzli, R.E. See item 4597.

1726. Kurtz, Paul Winter, ed. *Language and Human Nature: A French-
      American Philosophers' Dialogue.* St. Louis, Mo.: Warren H.
      Green, 1971.

1726a. La Capra, D. "Habermas and the Grounding of Critical Theory."
      History and Theory, 16, no. 3 (1977), 237-264.

      Shows the relation between the way Habermas proceeds and
      certain aspects of Derrida's thought.

      Lacroix, Jean. "Ecriture et métaphysique selon Jacques Derrida,"
      chapter 6, part III of his item 4600 (1968), pp. 240-249.

1727. Laferrière, Daniel. "The Writing Perversion." *Semiotica*, 18
      (1976), 217-233.

1728. Lamberti, Amato. "Il Luogo del senso e o del discorso." *Altri
      Termini*, nuova serie, n. 8 (June 1975), pp. 63-85.

1729. Lamizet, Bernard, and Frederic Nef. "Entrave double: le glas
      et la chute (sur *Glas* de J. Derrida)." *Gramma*, no. 2 (April
      1975), pp. 129-150.

1730. Laporte, Roger. "'Les *Blancs* assument l'importance' (Mallarmé)."
      Les Lettres Françaises, no. 1429 (29 March-4 April 1972),
      p. 5.

1731. ————. "Bief." *L'Arc*, no. 54 (1973), pp. 65-70.

1732. ————. "Une Double stratégie." In item 1680, pp. 205-264.

1733. Lapouge, Gilles. "Six philosophes occupés à déplacer la
      philosophie à propos de la mimesis." *La Quinzaine Littéraire*,
      no. 231 (1976), p. 23.

1734. Larmore, C. "Reading Russell, Readying Derrida." *Cambridge
      Review*, 95, no. 2219 (March 1974), 89-93.

1735. Laruelle, François. "Le Texte quatrième. L'Evénement textuel
      comme simulacre." *L'Arc*, no. 54 (1973), pp. 38-45.

1736. ———. "Le Style di-phallique de Jacques Derrida." *Critique*, 31, no. 334 (1975), 320-339. On *Glas*.

1737. ———. "La Scène du vomi ou comment ça se détraque dans la théorie." *Critique*, 32, no. 347 (April 1976), 265-279.

1738. ———. *Machines textuelles: déconstruction et libido d'écriture*. Paris: Editions du Seuil, 1976.

1739. ———. *Le Déclin de l'écriture. Suivi d'entretiens avec Jean-Luc Nancy, Sarah Kofman, Jacques Derrida, Philippe Lacoue-Labarthe*. Paris: Aubier-Flammarion, 1977.

Lavers, A. See item 4611.

1740. ———. "A Theory of Writing." *The Times Literary Supplement*, 15 (February 1968), p. 153.

1741. Leavey, John. "Derrida and Dante: Differance and the Eagle in the Sphere of Jupiter." *MLN*, 91 (January 1976), 60-68.

1742. ———. "Undecidables and Old Names," translator's preface to item 1610, pp. 1-21.

1743. ———, and David B. Allison. "A Derrida Bibliography." *Research in Phenomenology*, 8 (1978), 145-160.

1744. Lévesque, Claude. "L'Etrangeté (du) texte. De Freud à Blanchot." *Sub-stance*, no. 7 (Fall 1973), pp. 73-88.

1745. ———. "The World-Remoteness of the Text." *Analecta Husserliana*, 5 (1976), 53-70.

1746. ———. *L'Etrangeté du texte: essais sur Nietzsche, Freud, Blanchot et Derrida*. Montreal: VLB, 1976; Paris: Union Générale d'Editions, 1978, 274pp.

1747. Levinas, Emmanuel. "Tout autrement." *L'Arc*, no. 54 (1973), pp. 33-37. Rpt. in his *Noms propres. Agnon, Buber, Celan, Delhomme, Derrida, Jabès, Kierkegaard, Lacroix, Laporte, Max Picard, Proust, Van Breda, Wahl*. Montpellier: Fata Morgana, 1976, pp. 81-89. Also rpt. in *Les Dieux dans la cuisine. Vingt ans de philosophie en France*. Ed. Jean-Jacques Brochier. Paris: Aubier, 1978, pp. 105-112.

1748. Levine, Suzanne Jill. "Discourse as Bricolage." *Review*, no. 13 (Winter 1974), pp. 32-37.

1749. ———. "Writing as Translation: *Three Trapped Tigers* and *A Cobra*." *MLN*, 90, no. 2 (March 1975), 265-277.

1750. Lévy, Bernard-Henri. "Derrida n'est pas un gourou." *Magazine Littéraire*, no. 88 (May 1974), pp. 60-62.

1750a. Libertson, Joseph. "Bataille and Communication: Savoir, Non-savoir, Glissement, Rire." *Sub-stance*, 4, no. 10 (Fall 1974), 47-65.

On Derrida and Bataille.

1751. Lingis, Alphonso. "Differance in the Eternal Recurrence of the Same." *Research in Phenomenology*, 8 (1978), 77-91.

1752. Logan, Marie-Rose. "Graphesis ..." *Yale French Studies* (issue on "Graphesis: Perspectives in Literature and Philosophy"), no. 52 (1975), pp. 4-15.

1753. Lotringer, Sylvère. "Le Dernier mot de Saussure." *L'Arc*, no. 54 (1973), pp. 71-80.

       Saussure via Derrida.

1754. Macann, Christopher. "Jacques Derrida's Theory of Writing and the Concept of Trace." *Journal of the British Society for Phenomenology*, 3, no. 2 (May 1972), 197-200.

1755. MacCabe, Colin. "Readings in French." *Cambridge Review*, 95, no. 2219 (March 1974), 86-89.

1756. Malmberg, Bertil. "Derrida et la sémiologie. Quelques notes marginales." *Semiotica*, 11, no. 2 (1974), 189-199.

       Man, Paul de. "The Rhetoric of Blindness: Jacques Derrida's Reading of Rousseau." In item 4329, pp. 102-141.

       ————. "Literary History and Literary Modernity." In item 4329, pp. 142-165.

1757. ————. "Rhétorique de la cécité: Derrida lecteur de Rousseau." Trans. Jean-Michel Rabeate and Bernard Esmein. *Poétique*, no. 4 (1970), pp. 455-475.

       Martinet, J. See item 5174.

1758. Massey, Irving. *The Uncreating Word. Romanticism and the Object*. Bloomington and London: Indiana University Press, 1970.

1759. McDonald, David. "Derrida and Pirandello: A Post-Structuralist Analysis of Six Characters in Search of an Author." *Modern Drama*, 20 (December 1977), 421-437.

1759a. McGraw, Betty R. "(De)Constructing Consciousness. The 'Subject' in Phenomenology, Structuralism, and 'Left Bank Semiotics.'" *Research Studies*, 45, no. 4 (1977), 224-235.

1760. McLaughlen, Kathleen Blamey. "Reading Anew: A Study of Critical Methods Through the Texts of Jacques Derrida." *Dissertation Abstracts International*, 36, no. 7 (January 1976), 4478-A. University of California at Davis dissertation.

1761. Mecchia, R. "L'Interpretazione della linguistica saussuriana e la duplice nozione di 'scrittura' in Jacques Derrida." *Lingua e Stile*, 11, no. 1 (1976), 91-99.

       On Derrida's critique of Saussure.

Mehlman, Jeffrey. See item 3997.

1762. ————. "Orphée scripteur: Blanchot, Rilke, Derrida." *Poétique*, no. 20 (1974), pp. 458-482.

1763. Melville, Stephen. "Situation of Writing." *Chicago Review*, 29 (Fall 1977), 103-116.

1764. Merlin, Frédéric. "Derrida ou la philosophie en éclats." *Les Nouvelles Littéraires*, no. 2415 (7 January 1974), p. 15.

1765. Meschonnic, Henri. "L'Ecriture de Derrida." *Les Cahiers du Chemin*, no. 24 (1975), pp. 137-180.

————. "L'Ecriture de Derrida." In his item 1142, pp. 401-492.

1766. Miers, Paul. "Avertissement: Fourfold Vortex Formulations of Difference in Derridian Cryptograms." *MLN*, 92 (December 1977), 1049-1051.

1766a. ————. "Language, Literature, and the Limits of Theory." *Bulletin of the Midwest MLA*, 10, no. 1 (1977), 29-37.

1767. Miller, J. Hillis. "Williams' *Spring and All* and the Progress of Poetry." *Daedalus*, 99 (Spring 1970), 405-434.

1768. ————. "Geneva or Paris? The Recent Work of Georges Poulet." *University of Toronto Quarterly*, 29, no. 3 (April 1970), 212-228.

1769. ————. "Tradition and Difference." *Diacritics*, 2, no. 4 (Winter 1972), 6-13.

1770. ————. "Deconstructing the Deconstructers." *Diacritics*, 5, no. 2 (Summer 1975), 24-31.

1771. ————. "Stevens' Rock and Criticism as Cure, II." *The Georgia Review*, 30, no. 2 (Summer 1976), 330-348.

1772. ————. "Beginning with a Text." *Diacritics*, 6, no. 3 (Fall 1976), 2-7.

1773. ————. "The Limits of Pluralism III: The Critic as Host." *Critical Inquiry*, 3 (1977), 439-447.

Millet, L., et al. See items 147-149.

1774. Mohanty, Jitendra N. "On Husserl's Theory of Meaning." *Southwestern Journal of Philosophy*, 5 (Fall 1974), 229-244.

On Derrida's criticism of Husserl.

1775. [Montefiore, Alan]. "Conversations with Philosophers--Alan Montefiore Looks with Brian Magee at the Work Done by Foreign Philosophers." *Listener*, 85, no. 2188 (4 March 1971), 267-271.

1776. Mottram, Eric. "No Centre to Hold: A Commentary on Derrida."
       Curtains, May 1977, pp. 38-57.

       Müller, H.J. See item 4003.

1777. Nemo, Philippe. "L'Aventure collective d'un chercheur solitaire:
       Derrida et le GREPH." *Les Nouvelles Littéraires*, no. 2519
       (12 February 1976).

1778. Noferi, Adelia. "Il *Canzoniere* del Petrarca: scrittura del
       desiderio e desiderio della scrittura." *Paragone*, no. 296
       (October 1974), pp. 3-24.

       La Nouvelle Critique. See item 4009.

1779. Ollier, Claude. "Ouverture." *Les Lettres Françaises*, no. 1429
       (29 March-4 April 1972), pp. 11-13.

1780. ————. "Pulsion." *L'Arc*, no. 54 (1973), pp. 53-58.

1780a. Orr, Leonard. "A Derrida Checklist." *Sub-stance*, no. 22 (1979),
       pp. 107-111.

1781. Pachet, Pierre. "Une Entreprise troublante." *La Quinzaine
       Littéraire*, no. 197 (1 November 1974), pp. 19-20.

1782. Paquet, Marcel. "Essai sur l'absolu." In *Morale et Enseignement.
       Annales de l'Institut de Philosophie*. Brussels: Université
       Libre de Bruxelles, 1972, pp. 77-115.

1783. Parret, Herman. "Jacques Derrida. Een wijsbegeerte van de
       schriftuur." *Tijdschrift voor Filosofie*, 30 (1968), 3-81.
       Includes a French summary, "Une Philosophie de l'écriture,"
       pp. 79-81.

1784. ————. "Over de 'notie' van schriftuur." *Tijdschrift voor
       Filosofie*, 34, no. 3 (1972), 525-549. See also item 1787.

       On Derrida's *La Dissémination*.

1785. ————. "Over de 'notie' van grens." *Tijdschrift voor Filosofie*,
       35, no. 2 (1973), 363-388. See also item 1787.

1786. ————. "Grammatology and Linguistics. A Note on Derrida's
       Interpretation of Linguistic Theories." *Poetics*, 4, no. 1
       (March 1975), 107-127.

1787. ————. *Het Denken van de grens. Vier opstellen over Derrida's
       grammatologie*. Leuven, Belgium: Acco, 1975.

       Contains: De grammatologie als wending van de wijsbegeerte;
       Het gramma en de ontwichting van de taal; item 1785 and item
       1784.

1788. Pavel, Toma. "Linguistique et phénoménologie du signe (Réflex-
       ions à propos de la philosophie de J. Derrida)." *Studi Italiani
       di Linguistica Teoretica ed Applicata*, 1 (1972), 51-68.

1789.   Pazura, S. "The Textual Revolution of Tel Quel or Diagonal
            Theater" (in Polish). *Studia Estetyczne*, 9 (Warsaw, 1972),
            313-339.

1790.   Penel, A. "Comment échapper à la philosophie? Jacques Derrida
            met en question la pensée occidentale." *La Tribune de Genève*,
            15 November 1967.

1790a. Peretti della Rocca, Cristina De. "'Ereignis' y 'Différance.'
            Derrida, interprète de Heidegger." *Annales del Seminario de
            Metafisica*, 12 (1977), 115-131.

        Perruchot, C. See item 1170.

        Petitjean, G. See item 1171.

        Pettit, P. See item 4700.

1791.   Pierssens, Michel. "Literature ... and Philosophy? The
            Dissemination of Derrida. Introduction." *Sub-stance*, no. 7
            (Fall 1973), pp. 3-7.

        ————. See also item 3330.

1792.   Poirot-Delpech, B. "Maîtres à dé-penser." *Le Monde*, 30 April
            1976, p. 21.

1793.   Pollock, Michèle R. "Georges Bataille: Literature and Sovereign-
            ty." *Sub-stance*, no. 7 (Fall 1973), pp. 49-71.

        Poole, R. See item 165.

1794.   Popkin, Richard. "Comments on Professor Derrida's Paper."
            *Language and Human Nature: A French-American Philosophers'
            Conference* (October 18-19, 1968; SUNY Conference Center,
            Oyster Bay, Long Island, I-II). *Philosophy and Phenomenological
            Research*, 30, no. 1 (1969-1970), 58-65.

        On item 1536.

1795.   Probst, Alain. "Une Critique de la métaphysique occidentale:
            la philosophie de Jacques Derrida." *La Revue Réformée*, 24,
            no. 93 (Société Calviniste de France, 1973), 29-43.

        Follows Derrida in the chronological succession of his works.

1796.   Raffi, M.E. "Le Ultime tendenze." In *Orientamenti sulla moderna
            critica*. Ed. Enea Balmas. Milan: La Viscontea, 1975, pp. 81-
            94.

1797.   Rassam, J. "La Déconstruction de la métaphysique selon M.
            Derrida ou le retour au nominalisme le plus moyenâgeux
            (suite aux journées de Toulouse 1974)." *Revue de l'Enseigne-
            ment Philosophique*, 25, no. 2 (1975), 1-8.

1798. Reeder, Claudia Gene. "Maurice Roche: l'écriture en jeu."
       Dissertation Abstracts International, 37, no. 8 (February
       1977), 5172-A. Dissertation, University of Wisconsin,
       Madison, 1976.

       Also on Derrida.

1799. *Research in Phenomenology*, 8 (1978): issue entitled "Reading(s)
       of Jacques Derrida." Contains items 1624, 1640, 1616, 1713,
       1716, 1743, 1751, and 1822.

1800. Rey, Jean-Michel. "La Scène du texte." *Critique*, 25, no. 271
       (1969), 1059-1073.

1801. ———. "De Saussure à Freud." *Les Lettres Françaises*, no.
       1429 (29 March-4 April 1972), pp. 9-10.

1802. ———. "Note en marge sur un texte en cours." In item 1680,
       pp. 265-322.

       Ricoeur, Paul. See item 4735, pp. 362-374.

1803. Riddel, Joseph. *The Inverted Bell: Modernism and the Counter-
       poetics of William Carlos Williams*. Baton Rouge: Louisiana
       State University Press, 1974.

1804. ———. "A Miller's Tale." *Diacritics*, 5, no. 3 (Fall 1975),
       56-65.

1805. ———. "Scriptive Fate/Scriptive Hope." *Diacritics*, 6, no. 3
       (Fall 1976), 14-23.

1806. ———. "From Heidegger to Derrida to Change: Doubling and
       (Poetic) Language." *Boundary 2*, 4, no. 2 (Winter 1976),
       571-592.

1807. Ristat, Jean. "Le Fil(s) perdu." *Les Lettres Françaises*, no.
       1429 (29 March-4 April 1972), pp. 13-14.

1808. Roger, Philippe. "Les Philosophes saisis par la politique:
       un nouvel art de l'abordage." *Les Nouvelles Littéraires*,
       no. 2532 (13 May 1976), pp. 8-9.

1809. Ronse, Henri. "Entretien avec Jacques Derrida." *Les Lettres
       Françaises*, no. 1211 (6-12 December 1967), pp. 12-13.

1810. Rorty, Richard. "Derrida on Language, Being, and Abnormal
       Philosophy." *The Journal of Philosophy*, 74, no. 11 (1977),
       673-681.

1811. ———. "Philosophy as a Kind of Writing: An Essay on Derrida."
       New Literary History, 10 (Fall 1978), 141-160.

       Roudiez, L.S. See item 1214.

1812. Roudinesco, Elisabeth. "A propos du 'concept' de l'écriture.
       Lecture de Jacques Derrida." In *Littérature et idéologies*.

     Colloque de Cluny II, 2, 3, 4 April 1970. Paris: *La Nouvelle Critique*, 1971, pp. 219-230.

1813. ———. "De Derrida à Jung: une tradition." In *Un Discours au réel*. Paris: Mame, 1973.

1813a. Ruegg, Maria. "End(s) of French Style: Structuralism and Post-Structuralism in the American Context." *Criticism*, 21 (Summer 1979), 189-216.

1813b. Ryan, M. "The Question of Autobiography in Cardinal Newman's *Apologia Pro Vita Sua*." *Georgia Review*, 31, no. 3 (1977), 672-699.

     According to Ryan, Newman's *Apologia* is founded on a Derridian distinction between good and bad writing.

1814. Said, Edward W. See item 4336. Said's comments on Derrida were rpt. in his *Beginnings: Intention and Method*. New York: Basic Books, 1975, pp. 339-343.

1815. ———. "Contemporary Fiction and Criticism." *Tri-Quarterly*, no. 33 (Spring 1975), pp. 231-256.

1816. Santiago, Silviano, and the Departamento de Letras da Pontifícia Universidade Católica, Rio de Janeiro. *Glossário de Derrida*. Rio de Janeiro: Livraria F. Alves Editora, 1976, 95pp.

1817. Scarpetta, Guy. "Brecht et la Chine." *La Nouvelle Critique* (issue entitled *Littérature et idéologies*. Colloque de Cluny, II), 39b (1970), 231-236.

1818. Schérer, René. "Philosophie et Communication." In his (ed.) *La Communication, II. Actes du XVe Congrès de l'Association des Sociétés de Philosophie de Langue Française. Université de Montréal, 1971*. Montreal: Editions Montmorency, 1973, pp. 393-431. Part of a round table discussion which included Derrida. See also item 1561.

1819. ———. "Clôture et faille dans la phénoménologie de Husserl." *Revue de Métaphysique et de Morale*, 73 (July-September 1968), 344-360.

1820. Schumann, Karl. "Verschijning en niet-tegenwoordigheid, Derrida over metafysica en fenomenologie." *Tijdschrift voor Filosofie*, 30 (March 1968), 159-163.

1821. Searle, John R. "Reiterating the Differences: A Reply to Derrida." In *Glyph I: Johns Hopkins Textual Studies*. Ed. Samuel Weber and Henry Sussman. Baltimore: Johns Hopkins University Press, 1977, pp. 198-208.

     On item 1611.

1822. Silverman, Hugh J. "Self-Decentering: Derrida Incorporated." *Research in Phenomenology*, 8 (1978), 45-65.

160

Individual Structuralists

Simon, John K., ed. See item 4338.

1823. Singevin, Charles. "La Pensée, le langage, l'écriture et l'être."
      Revue Philosophique de la France et de l'Etranger, 162, no.
      2 (April–June 1972), 129-148; 162, no. 3 (July–September
      1972), 273-288.

1824. Smith, F. Joseph. "Jacques Derrida's Husserl Interpretation."
      Philosophy Today, 11, no. 2 (Summer 1967), 106-123.

1824a. Smock, Ann. "Re-turning Dissemblance: Readings of Two Poems by
       Michel Deguy." *Sub-stance*, 4, no. 10 (Fall 1974), 17-31.

       On "Marche qui déplie ..." ("Blasons") and "Un Homme las"
       ("Epigrammes") from a Derridian viewpoint.

1825. Sollers, Philippe. "Un Pas sur la lune." *Tel Quel*, no. 39
      (Fall 1969), pp. 3-12.

1826. ———. "A Step on the Moon." *The Times Literary Supplement*,
      no. 3526 (25 September 1969), pp. 1085-1087.

      On Derrida's *La Grammatologie*.

1827. [———]. "Entretien avec Philippe Sollers: 'Transformer le
      statut même de la littérature.'" *Le Monde [des Livres]*, no.
      8838 (14 June 1973), p. 23.

1828. Spivak, Gayatri Chakravorty. Translator's preface to Derrida's
      Of Grammatology. Baltimore: The Johns Hopkins University
      Press, 1976, pp. ix-lxxxvii.

1829. Steinmetz, Jean-Luc. "La Mort de l'auteur de droit divin."
      Magazine Littéraire, no. 47 (December 1970), p. 19.

      Steinwachs, Gisela. See item 4050.

      Sturrock, J. See item 196a.

1829a. *Sub-stance*, no. 7 (Fall 1973): issue dealing with "Jacques
       Derrida and Philosophy"; no. 10 (Fall 1974): issue dealing
       with "Jacques Derrida: Grammatology."

1830. Thévenin, Paule. "Le Hors-lieu." *Les Lettres Françaises*, no.
      1429 (29 March-4 April 1972), pp. 10-11.

1831. Thomas, Johannes. "Jacques Derrida." In *Französische Literatur-
      kritik der Gegenwart in Einzeldarstellungen*. Ed. Wolf-Dieter
      Lange. Stuttgart: A. Kröner, 1975, pp. 234-251.

1832. Toubeau, Hélène. "La Pharmakon et les aromates." *Critique*, 28,
      no. 303-304 (August-September 1972), 681-706.

      On Derrida's *La Dissémination*.

1833. Toyosaki, Kōichi. *Suppléments mobiles*. Tokyo: Editions Epaves,
      1975.

1834. Trinh, Minh Ha Thi. "Un Art sans oeuvre ou l'anonymat dans les arts contemporains." *Dissertation Abstracts International*, 38, no. 6 (December 1977), 3492-3493-A. Dissertation, University of Illinois at Urbana-Champaign.

Deals with Derrida and others.

Venault, P. See item 621.

1835. Vuarnet, Jean-Noël. "Jacques Derrida." *Littérature de notre temps. Recueil 4*. Paris: Casterman, 1970.

1836. ————. "Sans titre." *Les Lettres Françaises*, no. 1429 (29 March-4 April 1972), pp. 3-4.

1837. Vuilleumier, J. "L'Irruption du dehors dans le dedans." *La Tribune de Genève*, 1-2 October 1966.

1838. Wahl, François. "L'Ecriture avant la parole?" *La Quinzaine Littéraire*, no. 4 (1 May 1966), pp. 14-15.

————. See also item 4807.

Waldrop, R. See item 1266.

1838a. Weber, Samuel. "It." In *Glyph 4*. Ed. Samuel Weber and Henry Sussman. Baltimore, Md.: Johns Hopkins University Press, 1978, pp. 1-31.

1839. White, Hayden. "Criticism as Cultural Politics." *Diacritics*, 6, no. 3 (Fall 1976), 8-13.

————. See also item 4073.

Wilden, A. See item 216, pp. 395-400, 458-459.

Wyschogrod, E. See item 4821.

1840. Zaner, Richard M. "Discussion of Jacques Derrida, 'The Ends of Man.'" *Philosophy and Phenomenological Research*, 32, no. 3 (March 1972), 384-389. See also 30, no. 1 (1969), 31-57.

REVIEWS

L'Archéologie du frivole
(items 1569a and 1591)

1841. Delacampagne, C. "Derrida hors de soi." *Critique*, 30, no. 325 (1974), 503-514.

1842. Duchesneau, François. *Dialogue*, 14 (Canada, December 1975), 704-706.

1843. Stéfan, Jude. *Les Cahiers du Chemin*, no. 28 (15 October 1976),
       pp. 157-159.

                       De la grammatologie
                          (item 1522)

1844. Anonymous. Review of Derrida's *Of Grammatology*. *Choice*, 14
       (July 1977), 673.

1845. ———. Review of Derrida's *Of Grammatology*. *Encounter*, 50
       (March 1978), 44.

1846. ———. Review of Derrida's *Of Grammatology*. *French Review*,
       51 (April 1978), 741.

1846a. Berns, Egide E. "De Grammatologie van J. Derrida." *Wijsgerig
       Perspectief op Maatschappij en Wetenschap*, 19 (1978-1979),
       5-11.

1847. Châtelet, François. "Mort du livre?" *La Quinzaine Littéraire*,
       no. 37 (15-31 October 1967), p. 3.

1848. Dalmasso, G. Review of Derrida's *Della grammatologia*. *Rivista
       di Filosofia Neo-Scolastica*, 61 (1969), 331.

1848a. Davidson, H.M. Review of Derrida's *Of Grammatology*. *Comparative
       Literature*, 31 (Spring 1979), 167-169.

1849. Declève, Henri. *Dialogue*, 9, no. 3 (December 1970), 499-502.

1850. Donoghue, Denis. Review of Derrida's *Of Grammatology*. *The
       New Republic*, 176, no. 16 (April 1977), 32-34.

1850a. Filippov, L.I. "The Grammatology of Jacques Derrida" (in
       Russian). *Voprosy Filosofii*, no. 1 (1978), n.p.

1851. Gelley, Alexander. "Form as Force." *Diacritics*, 2, no. 1
       (Spring 1972), 9-13.

1852. Kuczkowski, Richard. Review of Derrida's *Of Grammatology*.
       Library Journal, 102 (15 February 1977), 495.

1853. Lacroix, Jean. "La Philosophie: la parole et l'écriture."
       Le Monde, no. 7107 (18 November 1967), p. 13.

1854. M., A. *Nice-Matin*, 12 January 1968.

1855. Man, Paul de. *Annales de la Société J.J. Rousseau*, 1969, p. 442.

1856. O'Hara, Daniel. Review of Derrida's *Of Grammatology*. *Journal
       of Aesthetics and Art Criticism*, 36 (Spring 1978), 361-364.

1856a. Poole, R. Review of Derrida's *Of Grammatology*. *Notes and
       Queries*, 26 (April 1979), 188-190.

1856b. Riddel, J.N. Review of Derrida's *Of Grammatology* and Foucault's
       Language, Counter-Memory, Practice. Contemporary Literature,
       20 (Spring 1979), 237-250.

1857. Wood, Michael. "Deconstructing Derrida." *New York Review of
       Books*, 24, no. 3 (3 March 1977), 27-30.

See also items 1620, 1644a, 1685, 1687, 1701, 1705a, 1715, 1786, 1787,
1826, 1828, 1829a, and 1864.

La Dissémination
(item 1552)

1858. Brykman, Geneviève. *Revue Philosophique de la France et de
       l'Etranger*, 164, no. 2 (April-June 1974), 256.

1859. Goux, Jean-Joseph. *Les Lettres Françaises*, no. 1455 (11-17
       October 1972), p. 15.

1860. Margolin, Jean-Claude. *Les Etudes Philosophiques*, 28 (1973),
       389-90.

1861. Míguez, José Antonio. "Derrida, Jacques: *La Diseminación*."
       Arbor, 92, no. 360 (December 1975), 127-128.

See also items 1633, 1672, 1784, 1791, and 1832.

L'Ecriture et la différence.
(item 1521)

1862. Agosti, Stefano, *Strumenti Critici*, no. 5 (February 1968),
       pp. 133-136.

1863. Anonymous. *Bulletin Critique du Livre Français*, nos. 260-261
       (August-September 1967).

1863a. ———. Review of Derrida's *Writing and Difference. Choice*,
       16 (June 1979), 543.

1864. ———. "A Theory of Writing." *The Times Literary Supplement*,
       no. 3442 (15 February 1968), p. 153.

1864a. Barnouw, J. Review of Derrida's *Writing and Difference. The
       Review of Metaphysics*, 33 (September 1979), 172-174.

1865. Bertherat, Yves. *Esprit*, 35ᵉ année, no. 364 (October 1967),
       698-700.

1865a. Cain, W.E. Review of Derrida's *Writing and Difference. The
       Sewanee Review*, 87 (Fall 1979), xciii-xciv ff.

1866. Engelhardt, H. Review of Derrida's *Die Schrift und die Differenz.
       Philosophischer Literaturanzeiger*, 27 (1974), 82-88.

1867.   Jacob, André. *Les Etudes Philosophiques*, 22 (1967), 464.

1867a. Maller, M.P. Review of Derrida's *Writing and Difference* and
        Edmund Husserl's *The Origin of Geometry*. *Library Journal*,
        104 (1 January 1979), 110.

1868.   Noguez, Dominique. *Nouvelle Revue Française*, no. 178 (October
        1967), p. 720.

1869.   Panaccio, C. *Dialogue*, 7 (1968-1969), 657-661.

1869a. Quinton, A. Review of Derrida's *Writing and Difference*. *New
        Statesman*, 98 (17 August 1979), 240-242.

1870.   Wahl, François. "Forcer les limites." *La Quinzaine Littéraire*,
        no. 32 (15-31 July 1967), pp. 18-20.

See also items 1641, 1687, and 1701.

Dos Ensayos
(item 1559)

1871.   Bermejo, José María. "Filosofía." *Estafeta Literaria*, no. 497
        (1 August 1972), pp. 1034-1035.

Eperons: les styles de Nietzsche. Spurs: Nietzsche's Styles
(item 1592)

1871a. Anonymous. Review of Derrida's *Spurs*. *Choice*, 16 (December
        1979), 1291.

1871b. Gordon, David. Review of Derrida's *Spurs*. *Library Journal*,
        104 (1 October 1979), 2102.

Glas
(item 1570)

1872.   Anquetil, Gilles. "*Glas*, le nouveau livre de J. Derrida." *Les
        Nouvelles Littéraires*, no. 2457 (28 October-3 November 1974),
        p. 9.

1873.   Delacampagne, Christian. "Le 'premier' livre de Jacques
        Derrida: Hegel et Gabrielle." *Le Monde [des Livres]*, no.
        9321 (3 January 1975), p. 12.

1874.   Loriot, P. *Le Nouvel Observateur*, no. 256 (9-15 December 1974).

1875.   Merlin, Frédéric. "Après Mallarmé, pour qui sonne le glas."
        Les Nouvelles Littéraires, 53e année, no. 2461 (25 November-
        1 December 1974), p. 10.

1876.   Parenti, Claire. *Magazine Littéraire*, no. 96 (January 1975),
        p. 38.

1877.   Spivak, Gayatri Chakravorty. *"Glas*-Piece: A *compte rendu."*
        Diacritics, 7, no. 3 (Fall 1977), 22-43.

See also items 1617e, 1706, 1708a, 1729, 1736, and 1857.

                    Marges de la philosophie
                         (item 1553)

1878.   De Greef, Jan. "De la métaphore (à propos de la *Mythologie
        blanche,* de Derrida)." *Cahiers de Littérature et de Linguis-
        tique Appliquée,* no. 3-4 (Kinshasha, 1971), 45-50.

1879.   Margolin, Jean-Claude. "Les Marginalia de Derrida." *Revue de
        Synthèse,* no. 73-74 (January-June 1974), p. 102.

See also items 1648 and 1881.

             Translation of and introduction to Husserl's
                    L'Origine de la géométrie
                         (item 1499)

1879a. Anonymous. Review of Edmund Husserl's *The Origin of Geometry.*
        Choice, 16 (April 1979), 236.

1879b. Barnouw, J. Review of Edmund Husserl's *Origin of Geometry. The
        Review of Metaphysics,* 33 (September 1979), 168-172.

1880.   Jacob, André. Review of Edmund Husserl's *L'Origine de la
        géométrie. Les Etudes Philosophiques,* 18 (1963), 464.

See also item 1867a.

                         Positions
                         (item 1554)

1881.   Jacob, André. Review of Derrida's *Positions* and *Marges. Les
        Etudes Philosophiques,* 28 (1973), 389.

1882.   Mecchia, R. Review of Derrida's *Posizioni. Bollettino biblio-
        grafico per le scienze morali e sociali,* no. 33-36 (Rome,
        1976), pp. 314-315.

                    La Voix et le phénomène
                         (item 1523)

1883.   Anonymous. Review of *Speech and Phenomena. Choice,* 10 (June
        1973), 634.

1884.   Benoist, J.-M. "'Présence' de Husserl." *Les Etudes Philoso-
        phiques,* no. 4 (1969), pp. 528-531.

1885. Clifford, P. Review of *Speech and Phenomena*. *The Journal of the British Society for Phenomenology*, 6 (1975), 203.

1886. Collins, M.L. Review of *Speech and Phenomena*. *Library Journal*, 98 (15 May 1973), 1586.

1887. Galay, J.-L. *Studia Philosophica*, 28 (1968), 232-235.

1888. Jacob, André. *Les Etudes Philosophiques*, 23 (1968), 224-225.

1889. Mays, W. *Philosophy*, 44 (1969), 77-79.

1890. Paez, Alicia. *Cuadernos de Filosofia*, 10 (January-June 1970), 204-206.

1891. Robert, Jean-Dominique. "Voix et phénomène: A propos d'un ouvrage récent." *Revue Philosophique de Louvain*, tome 66, no. 90 (May 1968), 309-324.

1892. Sokolowski, R. Review of *Speech and Phenomena*. *Review of Metaphysics*, 27 (1973-1974), 123-124.

See also item 1701.

MICHEL FOUCAULT

1949

1893. *Sur l'emploi de la pénicilline par voie buccale.* Paris:
[Université] Faculté de Médecine, thèse, 1949, no. 1025.

1954

1894. Introduction and notes to *Le Rêve et l'existence.* By Ludwig
Binswanger. Trans. Jacqueline Verdeaux. Paris-Bruges: Desclée
de Brouwer, 1954.

*1895. *Maladie mentale et personnalité.* Paris: Presses Universitaires
de France, 1954. (Initiation Philosophique, no. 12) See item
1898 for subsequent editions. For Spanish trans., see item 2002.

1958

1896. Translation, with Daniel Rocher, of *Le Cycle de la structure.*
(Der Gestaltkreis). By Viktor von Weizsäcker. Paris: Desclée
de Brouwer, 1958.

1961

*1897. *Folie et déraison: histoire de la folie à l'âge classique.*
Paris: Plon, 1961. For trans., see items 1909 (Italian),
1918 (English), 1925 (English), 1926 (Spanish), 1946 (German),
and 2027 (Dutch). For abridged editions, see items 1910,
1957 and 1996. For other editions, see items 1971 and 2014.
For reviews, see items 2298-2322.

1962

*1898. *Maladie mentale et psychologie.* Paris: Presses Universitaires
de France, 1962. This is the second edition of item 1895.
3rd ed. 1966. For trans., see items 1937 (German) and
2022 (English). For reviews, see items 2349-2350.

1899. Editor of *Rousseau, juge de Jean-Jacques. Dialogues.* Paris:
Armand Colin, 1962; London: H. Pordes, n.d. (Bibliothèque
de Cluny)

1900.   "Dire et voir chez Raymond Roussel." *Lettre Ouverte*, no. 4
        (Summer 1962), pp. 38-51. Cf. item 1902.

1901.   "Un Si cruel savoir." *Critique*, no. 182 (1962), pp. 567-611.

                                    1963

1902.   *Raymond Roussel*. Paris: Gallimard, 1963.   (Le Chemin) Cf. items
        1900 and 1904.

        Contains: (1) Le Seuil et la clef; (2) Les Bandes du billard;
        (3) Rime et raison; (4) Aubes, mine, cristal; (5) La Métamorphose
        et le labyrinthe; (6) La Surface des choses; (7) La lentille
        vide; (8) Le Soleil enfermé.

*1903. *Naissance de la clinique. Une Archéologie du regard médical.*
        Paris: Presses Universitaires de France, 1963. For trans.,
        see items 1988 (English), 1990 (German), and 2003 (Spanish).
        For other edition, see item 1970. For reviews, see items 2406-
        2426.

1904.   "La Métamorphose et le labyrinthe." *La Nouvelle Revue Française*,
        11e année, no. 124 (April 1963), 638-661. Cf. chapter five
        of item 1902.

*1905. "Préface à la transgression." *Critique* (issue entitled "Hommage
        à Georges Bataille"), 15e année, nos. 195-196 (August-Septem-
        ber 1963), 751-769. For English trans., see item 2033.

1906.   "Guetter le jour qui vient." *La Nouvelle Revue Française*, 11^e
        année, no. 130 (October 1963), 709-716.

        On Roger Laporte's *La Veille*.

1907.   "Distance, aspect, origine." *Critique*, no. 198 (November 1963),
        pp. 931-945. Rpt. in item 1928.

        On Ph. Sollers' *L'Intermédiaire*, M. Pleynet's *Paysage en deux*
        and J.-L. Baudry's *Les Images*.

*1908. "Le Langage à l'infini." *Tel Quel*, no. 15 (Fall 1963), pp.
        44-53. For English trans., see item 2033.

1909.   *Storia della follia*. Milan: Rizzoli, 1963. Trans. of item 1897.

                                    1964

1910.   *Histoire de la folie à l'âge classique*. Paris: Union Générale
        d'Editions, 1964, c. 1961. (10/18) Abridged edition of item
        1897. See also items 1957 and 1996.

1911.   Translation of *Anthropologie du point de vue pragmatique*. By
        Emmanuel Kant. Paris: J. Vrin, 1964. 2nd ed. 1970.

1912.   "La Prose d'Actéon." *La Nouvelle Revue Française*, 12e année,
        no. 135 (March 1964), 444-459.

1913. "Le Langage de l'espace." *Critique*, no. 203 (April 1964), pp. 378-382. Rpt. in item 1973.

On Laporte's *La Veille*, Le Clézio's *Le Procès-verbal*, Ollier's *Eté indien* and Butor's *Description de San Marco*.

1914. Chaired the "Débat sur le roman." *Tel Quel* (special issue entitled "Une Littérature nouvelle? Décade de Cerisy, septembre 1963"), no. 17 (Spring 1964), pp. 12-54.

1915. Participant in the "Débat sur la poésie." *Tel Quel* (special issue entitled "Une Littérature nouvelle? Décade de Cerisy, septembre 1963"), no. 17 (Spring 1964), pp. 69-82.

1916. "Pourquoi réédite-t-on l'oeuvre de Raymond Roussel? Un Précourseur de notre littérature moderne." *Le Monde*, no. 6097 (22 August 1964), p. 9.

1917. "Le *Mallarmé* de J.-P. Richard." *Annales. Economies. Sociétés. Civilisations*, 19e année (1964), 996-1004.

1965

1918. *Madness and Civilization. A History of Insanity in the Age of Reason*. Trans. Richard Howard. New York: Random House; New York: Pantheon Books, 1965. Trans. of item 1897. See also item 1925 and New York: Vintage Books, 1973 which rpts. the edition published by Pantheon.

Rather than give a historical review of the concept of madness, Foucault tries to recreate, mostly from original documents, mental illness, folly and unreason as they must have existed in their time, place and proper historical perspective at the end of the sixteenth century and during the seventeenth and eighteenth centuries.

1966

*1919. *Les Mots et les choses. Une Archéologie des sciences humaines*. Paris: Gallimard, 1966. For trans., see items 1927 (Italian), 1934 (Spanish), 1935 (Portuguese), 1952 (English), 1969 (German), and 1994 (Dutch). For reviews, see items 2370-2405.

1920. "La Pensée du dehors." *Critique* (issue on Maurice Blanchot), 17e année, 22, no. 229 (June 1966), 523-546. Also published in *Maurice Blanchot*. Paris: Editions de Minuit, 1966, pp. 523-546.

1921. "L'Arrière-fable." *L'Arc* (issue on Jules Verne), no. 29 (1966), pp. 5-12.

*1922. "La Prose du monde." *Diogène*, no. 53 (1966), pp. 20-41. For English trans., see item 1923.

1923.   "The Prose of the World." *Diogenes*, no. 53 (Spring 1966), pp.
        17-37. Trans. of item 1922.

                                  1967

1924.   Edition critique and introduction, with Gilles Deleuze, to
        Nietzsche. Oeuvres philosophiques complètes. V. Le Gai savoir.
        Fragments posthumes [inédits], 1881-1882. Texte et variantes
        établis par G. Colli et M. Montinari. Trans. Pierre Klossowski.
        Paris: Gallimard, 1967. See also items 1958, 2007 and 2029.

1925.   *Madness and Civilization. A History of Insanity in the Age of*
        Reason. Trans. Richard Howard. New York: New American Library;
        London: Tavistock; Toronto: Random House, 1967. Trans. of
        item 1897. See also item 1918.

1926.   *Historia de la locura en la época clásica.* Trans. Juan José
        Utrilla. Mexico: Fondo de Cultura Económica, 1967. Trans.
        of item 1897.

1927.   *Le Parole e le cose. Un'Archeologia delle scienze umane.* Con
        un saggio critico di Georges Canguilhem. Trans. E. Panaitescu.
        Milan: Rizzoli, 1967. Trans. of item 1919.

                                  1968

1928.   "Distance, aspect, origine." In *Théorie d'ensemble.* Paris:
        Editions du Seuil, 1968, pp. 11-24. Rpts. item 1907.

1929.   "Une Mise au point de Michel Foucault." *La Quinzaine Littéraire*,
        no. 47 (15-31 March 1968), p. 21.

*1930. "Réponse à une question." *Esprit*, 36e année, no. 371 (May
        1968), 850-874. For Italian trans., see item 1965.

1931.   "Réponse au Cercle d'épistémologie." *Les Lettres Françaises*,
        no. 1240 (10-16 July 1968), pp. 3-6. Cf. item 1932.

*1932. "Réponse au Cercle d'épistémologie." *Cahiers pour l'Analyse*,
        no. 9 (1968), pp. 9-40. Cf. item 1931. For Italian trans.,
        see item 1965.

1933.   "Correspondance. A propos des 'Entretiens sur Foucault.'"
        La Pensée, no. 139 (1968), pp. 114-119. With J. Stefanini.
        Refers to an article in *La Pensée*, no. 137 (February 1968).

        Contains: (1) une lettre de Foucault à Jacques Proust; (2)
        une série d'observations de Foucault au sujet des intérpreta-
        tions de J. Stefanini; and (3) la réponse de J. Stefanini.

1934.   *Las Palabras y las cosas. Una arqueología de las ciencias*
        humanas. Trans. Elsa Cecilia Frost. Mexico: Siglo Veintiuno,
        1968. 2nd ed. 1969; 3rd ed. 1971; 4th ed. 1972. Trans. of
        item 1919.

1935. *As Palavras e as coisas. Uma Arqueologia das ciências humanas.*
       Trans. António Ramos Rosa. Lisboa: Portugália Editora, 1968.
       Trans. of item 1919.

1936. Text(s) in *Estruturalismo. Antologia de textos teóricos [por]
       Foucault [et al].* Comp. Eduardo Prado Coelho. Trans. Maria
       Eduarda Reis Colares, et al. Lisboa: Portugália Editora,
       1968.

1937. *Psychologie und Geisteskrankheit.* Trans. Anneliese Botond.
       Frankfurt am Main: Suhrkamp, 1968 and 1973. Trans. of item
       1898.

1969

*1938. *L'Archéologie du savoir.* Paris: Gallimard, 1969. For trans.,
       see items 1953 (Spanish), 1964 (Italian), 1977 (English),
       and 1989 (German). For reviews, see items 2278-2297.

1939. Preface to *Grammaire générale et raisonnée.* By Arnaud and
       Lancelot. Paris: Republications Paulet, 1969.

1940. Preface to *Grammaire génératrice.* By André Brisset. Paris:
       Republications Paulet, 1969.

*1941. *Qu'est-ce qu'un auteur?* Paris: Armand Colin, 1969, pp. 73-104.
       With Lucien Goldmann and Jacques Lacan, et al. Rpt. from
       the *Bulletin de la Société Française de Philosophie*, 63,
       no. 3 (1969), which was the February 22, 1969 meeting. For
       English trans., see items 2012 and 2033.

1942. "Hommage à Jean Hyppolite (1907-1968)." *Revue de Métaphysique
       et de Morale*, 74, no. 2 (1969), 131-136. Address given during
       the commemorative session held at the Ecole Normale Supérieure
       on January 19, 1969.

1943. "Ariane s'est pendue." *Le Nouvel Observateur*, no. 229 (31
       March-6 April 1969), pp. 36-37.

       On Gilles Deleuze's *Différence et répétition.*

1944. "Michel Foucault explique son dernier livre." *Magazine Litté-
       raire*, no. 28 (April-May 1969), pp. 23-25.

       Remarks gathered by J.-J. Brochier on item 1938.

1945. "La Arqueología del Saber. Introducción." *Convivium*, 30 (1969),
       69-83.

1946. *Wahnsinn und Gesellschaft. Eine Geschichte des Wahns im Zeit-
       alter der Vernunft.* Trans. Ulrich Köppen. Frankfurt am Main:
       Suhrkamp, 1969, 1973. Trans. of item 1897.

1970

1947. Preface to *Oeuvres complètes. I. Premiers écrits, 1922-1940.
       Histoire de l'oeil, L'Anus solaire, Sacrifices, Articles.*
       By Georges Bataille. Paris: Gallimard, 1970.

1948. "Sept propos sur le septième ange." Preface to *La Grammaire
       logique. Suivi de "La Science de Dieu."* By Jean-Pierre
       Brisset. New ed. Paris: Tchou, 1970.

1949. "La Situation de Cuvier dans l'histoire de la biologie." In
       Georges Cuvier. Journées d'études organisées par l'Institut
       d'Histoire des Sciences de l'Université de Paris les 30 et
       31 mai 1969 pour le bicentenaire de la naissance de G. Cuvier
       [*Revue d'Histoire des Sciences et de Leurs Applications,* 23,
       no. 1 (1970)]. Paris: Presses Universitaires de France, 1970,
       pp. 63-92.

       Discussion of this article by François Dagognet, pp. 49-62.

*1950. "Theatrum philosophicum." *Critique,* 26, no. 282 (1970), 885-
       908. For trans., see items 1980 (Catalonian or Spanish) and
       2033 (English).

       On G. Deleuze's *Différence et répétition* and *Logique du sens.*

 1951. "Il y aura scandale, mais...." *Le Nouvel Observateur,* no. 304
       (7-13 September 1970), p. 40. Rpt. in item 1972.

       On Pierre Guyotat's *'Eden, 'Eden, 'Eden.*

1952. *The Order of Things. An Archaeology of the Human Sciences.*
       Trans. A.M. Sheridan Smith. London: Tavistock, 1970, 1974;
       New York: Pantheon Books, c. 1970, 1971; Random House/Vintage
       Books, c. 1970, 1973. Trans. of item 1919.

       A structualist intellectual history that attempts to show
       under what conditions the human sciences (biology, economics
       and linguistics or life, labor and language) arose. Foucault
       takes these as having been invented at the beginning of the
       modern period and views natural history, the analysis of wealth
       and general grammar as their classical analogues. Paracelsus,
       Condillac, Nietzsche and Mallarmé are seen as types or repre-
       sentatives of the late Renaissance, classical and modern periods.

1953. *La Arqueología del saber.* Trans. Aurelio Garzón del Camino.
       Mexico: Siglo Veintiuno, 1970. Trans. of item 1938.

1954. *Nietzsche, Freud, Marx.* Trans. Alberto González Troyano.
       Barcelona: Ed. Anagrama, 1970.

                                  1971

1955. *Leçon inaugurale faite le 2 décembre 1970.* Paris: Le Collège
       de France, 1971. Chaire d'histoire des systèmes de pensée:
       leçon inaugurale 53. Rpt. in item 1956.

*1956. *L'Ordre du discours. Leçon inaugurale au Collège de France
       prononcée le 2 décembre 1970.* Paris: Gallimard, 1971.
       Rpts. item 1955. For trans., see items 1961 (English), 1977
       (English), 1979 (Italian), 1998 (German), 2001 (Catalonian or
       Spanish), 2028 (Dutch), and 2035 (German). For reviews,
       see items 2427-2429.

1957. *Folie et déraison. Histoire de la folie à l'âge classique.*
Paris: Plon, 1971, c. 1961. (10/18) Another abridged edition
of item 1897. See also items 1990 and 1996.

1958. Introduction, with Gilles Deleuze, to *Oeuvres philosophiques
complètes.* Tome VII. *Par delà bien et mal. La Généalogie de
la morale.* By Friedrich Nietzsche. Trans. Cornélius Heim,
et al. Paris: Gallimard, 1971. See also items 1924, 2007
and 2029.

*1959. "Nietzsche, la généalogie, l'histoire." In *Hommage à Jean
Hyppolite.* By Suzanne Bachelard, et al. Paris: Presses
Universitaires de France, 1971, pp. 145-171. For English
trans., see item 2033. For Spanish trans., see item 2039d.

1960. "Lettre de Michel Foucault." *La Pensée*, no. 159 (1971), pp.
141-142.

1961. "The Discourse on Language." Trans. Rupert Swyer. *Social
Science Information*, April 1971, pp. 7-30. Rpt. in item
1977. Trans. of item 1956.

1962. "Monstrosities in Criticism." Trans. Robert J. Matthews.
Diacritics, 1, no. 1 (Fall 1971), 57-60.

1963. "Foucault Responds." *Diacritics*, 1, no. 2 (Winter 1971), 60.

Foucault's reply to Steiner's statements on p. 5 of same
issue.

1964. *L'Archeologia del sapere.* Trans. Giovanni Bogliolo. Milan:
Rizzoli, 1971. Trans. of item 1938.

1965. *Due riposte sull'epistemologia.* Trans. M. De Stefanis. Milan:
Lampugnani Nigri, 1971. Trans. of items 1932 and 1930.

1966. *Scritti letterari.* Trans. Cesare Milanese. Milan: Feltrinelli,
1971, 155pp. (Critica Letteraria: I Fatti e Le Idee, 216)
For review, see item 2430.

1967. Contributor to *Estruturalismo e teoria da linguagem.* Petrópolis:
Editora Vozes, 1971.

1968. Contributor to *O Homem e o discurso (a arqueologia de Michel
Foucault).* Rio de Janeiro: Tempo Brasileiro, 1971.

Contains Foucault's interview with Rouanet and Merquior,
Lecourt's article on item 1938, Escobar's article on scientific
discourse and ideological discourse (item 1919), and Rouanet
on the grammar of homicide.

1969. *Die Ordnung der Dinge. Eine Archäologie der Humanwissenschaften.*
Trans. Ulrich Köppen. Frankfurt am Main: Suhrkamp, 1971 and
1974. Trans. of item 1919.

1972

1970. *Naissance de la clinique. Une Archéologie du regard médical.*
       Paris: Presses Universitaires de France, 1972. Second revised
       edition of item 1903. 3rd ed. 1975.

1971. *Histoire de la folie à l'âge classique. [Suivi de] Mon corps,
       ce papier, ce feu [et] La Folie, l'absence d'oeuvre.* Paris:
       Gallimard, 1972. New edition of item 1897.

1972. "Il y aura scandale, mais...." In *Littérature interdite.* By
       Pierre Guyotat. Paris: Gallimard, 1972, pp. 161-162. Rpts.
       item 1951.

1973. "Le Langage de l'espace." In *Les Critiques de notre temps et
       le nouveau roman.* Ed. Réal Ouellet. Paris: Editions Garnier
       Frères, 1972, pp. 118-120. Rpts. item 1913.

1974. "Les Intellectuels et le pouvoir: un débat entre Gilles Deleuze
       et Michel Foucault." *Le Nouvel Observateur,* no. 391 (8-14
       May 1972), pp. 68-70.

       On Deleuze's *L'Anti-Oedipe.* Cf. item 1975.

*1975. "Les Intellectuels et le pouvoir: entretien entre Michel
       Foucault et Gilles Deleuze." *L'Arc* (issue on Deleuze), no.
       49 (1972), pp. 3-10. Cf. item 1974. For English trans.,
       see item 1987.

1976. "Piéger sa propre culture." *Figaro Littéraire,* no. 1376 (30
       September 1972), p. iv.

       On Gaston Bachelard.

1977. *The Archaeology of Knowledge.* Trans. A.M. Sheridan Smith.
       London: Tavistock; New York: Pantheon Books; New York:
       Irvington Publications, 1972. Contains trans. of items 1938
       and 1956 (item 1961). See also item 2021.

       On the nature of change and the object of historical inquiry.
       Foucault wants to articulate the history of the unconscious,
       to decenter history away from human subjects and their projects,
       to expose the discontinuity of change and the poly-dimensional-
       ity of historical regions.

1978. "History, Discourse and Discontinuity." *Salmagundi,* no. 20
       (Summer-Fall 1972), pp. 225-248.

       Interview with Foucault.

1979. *L'Ordine del discorso.* Trans. Alessandro Fontana. Turin: G.
       Einaudi, 1972. Trans. of item 1956.

1980. *Theatrum philosophicum. [Followed by] Repetición y diferencia.*
       By Gilles Deleuze. Trans. Francisco Monge. Barcelona: Ed.
       Anagrama, 1972. Trans. of item 1950.

1981.   *Neuer Faschismus, neue Demokratie: über die Legalität des*
        Faschismus im Rechstsstaat. Berlin: Wagenbach, 1972. With
        A. Geismar and A. Glucksmann. Articles taken from a special
        issue of *Les Temps Modernes,* no. 310 (1972).

                              1973

*1982. *Ceci n'est pas une pipe. Deux lettres et quatre dessins de*
        René Magritte. Montpellier: Fata Morgana, 1973. For German
        trans., see item 1997.

*1983. Editor of *Moi, Pierre Rivière, ayant égorgé ma mère, ma soeur*
        et mon frère ... un cas de parricide au XIXe siècle. By
        Blandine Barret-Kriegal, et al. Paris: Gallimard, 1973. For
        trans., see items 2011 (English) and 2013 (German). For re-
        views, see items 2351-2369.

        This work is the outcome of a joint research project by a
        seminar at the Collège de France.

1984.   Text of *Rebeyrolle.* Paris: Maeght, 1973.

        Catalog of Paul Rebeyrolle's exhibit of Dogs in Art.

1985.   *C'est demain la veille.* Paris: Editions du Seuil, 1973. With
        Herbert Marcuse, et al. Articles from *Actuel Nova Press,*
        November 1971-October 1972.

1986.   "Sectorisation, mixité, formation continue. Exposé-débat
        présenté le 14 novembre 1972 par un groupe d'étude inter-
        hôpitaux." *L'Information Psychiatrique,* 49, no. 6 (1973),
        555-572.

1987.   "The Intellectuals and Power. A Discussion between Michel
        Foucault and Gilles Deleuze." *Telos,* no. 16 (1973), pp.
        103-109. Trans. of item 1975.

1988.   *The Birth of the Clinic. An Archaeology of Medical Perception.*
        Trans. A.M. Sheridan Smith. London: Tavistock; New York:
        Pantheon Books, 1973. Trans. of item 1903. See also New York:
        Vintage Books, 1975, c. 1973 which rpts. the edition published
        by Pantheon.

        Examines how classical medicine, which saw transcendent
        diseases analyzed into a nosology of species and classes, gave
        way to the nineteenth-century positivist medicine of empirical
        observation, the "clinic."

1989.   *Archäologie des Wissens.* Trans. Ulrich Köppen. Frankfurt am
        Main: Suhrkamp, 1973. Trans. of item 1938.

1990.   *Die Geburt der Klinik. Eine Archäologie des ärztlichen Blicks.*
        Trans. Walter Seitter. Munich: Hanser, 1973. Trans. of item
        1903. See also item 2024.

1991. "Die Ordnung der Dinge. Ein Gespräch mit Raymond Bellour." In
      Antworten der Strukturalisten. Comp. Adelbert Reif. Trans.
      Britta Reif-Willenthal and Friedrich Griese. Hamburg: Hoffmann
      und Campe, 1973, pp. 147-156. Cf. item 2076.

1992. "Über verschiedene Anten Geschichte zu schreiben. Ein Gespräch
      mit Raymond Bellour." In *Antworten der Strukturalisten*.
      Comp. Adelbert Reif. Trans. Britta Reif-Willenthal and
      Friedrich Griese. Hamburg: Hoffmann und Campe, 1973, pp.
      157-175. Cf. item 2077.

1993. "Strukturalismus und Geschichte. Ein Gespräch mit Jean-Pierre
      El Kabasch." In *Antworten der Strukturalisten*. Comp. Adelbert
      Reif. Trans. Britta Reif-Willenthal and Friedrich Griese.
      Hamburg: Hoffmann und Campe, 1973, pp. 176-184.

1994. *De Woorden en de Dingen. Een Archeologie van de Mensweten-
      schappen*. Bilthoven: Ambo, 1973. Trans. of item 1919.

1995. "Uvod u Arheologiju Znanja." *Delo*, 19, no. 12 (1973), 1538-
      1555.

                                   1974

1996. *Folie et déraison. Histoire de la folie à l'âge classique*.
      Paris: Union Générale d'Editions, 1974, c. 1961. (10/18)
      New abridged edition of item 1897. See also items 1910 and
      1957.

1997. *Dies ist keine Pfeife*. Ill. René Magritte. Munich: Hanser,
      1974. Trans. of item 1982.

1998. *Die Ordnung des Diskurses. Inauguralvorlesung am Collège de
      France, vom 2. Dezember 1970*. Trans. Walter Seitter. Munich:
      Hanser, 1974. Trans. of item 1956. See also item 2035.

1999. *Schriften zur Literatur*. Trans. Karin von Hofer and Anneliese
      Botond. Munich: Nymphenburger Verlagshandlung, 1974.

      A selection of articles which originally appeared in French
      in various periodicals.

2000. *Von der Subversion des Wissens*. Trans. Walter Seitter. Munich:
      Hanser, 1974. For review, see item 2479.

2001. *El Orden del discurso*. Trans. Alberto González Troyano.
      Barcelona: Tusquets, 1974. Trans. of item 1956.

2002. *Enfermedad mental y personalidad*. Buenos Aires: Editorial
      Paidós, 1974 or earlier. (Biblioteca del Hombre Contemporáneo)
      Trans. of item 1895.

2003. *El Nacimiento de la clínica*. Mexico: Siglo Veintiuno, 1974
      or 1967. Trans. of item 1903.

1975

*2004. *Surveiller et punir. Naissance de la prison.* Paris: Gallimard, 1975. For trans., see items 2026 (German) and 2034 (English). For reviews, see items 2431-2478.

2005. "La Peinture photogénique." Preface to *Le Désir est partout, Fromanger.* Paris: La Galerie Jeanne Bucher, 1975, pp. 1-11. From the catalog of the Exposition Fromanger, Galerie Jeanne Bucher, Paris, 27 February-29 March 1975.

2006. Preface to *De la prison à la révolte. Essai-témoignage.* By Serge Livrozet. Paris: Mercure de France, 1975.

2007. General introduction, with Gilles Deleuze, to Nietzsche's *Oeuvres philosophiques complètes.* vol. I, 2 and vol. VIII, 2. Paris: Gallimard, 1975. See also items 1924, 1958, and 2029.

2008. "Entretien: des supplices aux cellules." *Le Monde [des Livres],* no. 9363 (21 February 1975), p. 16.

Remarks gathered by Roger-Pol Droit.

2009. "Foucault et les historiens." *Magazine Littéraire,* no. 101 (June 1975), pp. 10-13.

Conversation with Jacques Revel; remarks gathered by Raymond Bellour.

2010. "Entretien sur la prison: le livre et sa méthode." *Magazine Littéraire,* no. 101 (June 1975), pp. 27-33.

Remarks gathered by J.-J. Brochier.

2011. Editor of *I, Pierre Rivière, Having Slaughtered my Mother, my Sister, and my Brother...: A Case of Parricide in the Nineteenth Century.* By Blandine Barret-Kriegal, et al. Trans. Frank Jellinek. New York: Pantheon Books, 1975. Trans. of item 1938.

On June 3, 1835 a 20-year-old peasant from Normandy killed his mother, sister and brother with a pruning hook. This work presents three viewpoints on the question of what is to be done with a person who commits such a crime. Provided are: (1) the legal proceedings in Rivière's case; (2) his autobiography composed in prison; (3) a collection of modern essays on the case by Foucault's seminar at the Collège de France.

2012. "What Is an Author?" Trans. J. Venit. *Partisan Review,* 42, no. 4 (1975), 603-614. Trans. of a slightly abridged version of item 1941.

2013. *Der Fall Rivière. Materialen zum Verhältnis von Psychiatrie und Strafjustiz.* Trans. Wolf H. Leube. Frankfurt: Suhrkamp, 1975. Trans. of item 1983.

1976

2014.   *Histoire de la folie à l'âge classique*. Paris: Gallimard,
         1976, 583pp. (Tel, 9) Another edition of item 1897.

*2015.   *Histoire de la sexualité. Tome I. La Volonté de savoir*. Paris:
         Gallimard, 1976. For trans., see items 2036 (German) and
         2039 (English). For reviews, see items 2323-2341.

2016.   Contributor to *Les Machines à guérir*. [Aux origines de l'hôpital
         moderne]. Paris: Institut de l'Environnement, 1976.

2017.   Explains *Surveiller et punir* in *Châtelet, Derrida, Foucault,
         Lyotard, Serres. Politiques de la philosophie*. Ed. Dominique
         Grisoni. Paris: Bernard Grasset, 1976.

2018.   Preface to *En attendant le grand soir*. By WIAZ. Paris: Denoël,
         1976.

2019.   Preface, with Pierre Vidal-Naquet, to *L'Affaire Mirval ou
         Comment le récit abolit le crime*. By Bernard Cuau. Paris:
         Presses d'Aujourd'hui, 1976.

2020.   *La Naturaleza humana. Justicia o poder?* Valencia: Departamento
         de Lógica y Filosofía de la Ciencia, Universidad de Valencia,
         1976, 88pp. With Noam Chomsky. See also item 4465.

2021.   *The Archaeology of Knowledge*. Trans. A.M. Sheridan Smith.
         New York: Harper and Row, 1976. Another edition of item 1977.

2022.   *Mental Illness and Psychology*. Trans. Alan Sheridan. New York:
         Harper and Row, 1976. Trans. of item 1898.

2023.   "Politics of Crime." Trans. M. Horwitz. *Partisan Review*, 43,
         no. 3 (1976), 453-459.

         Interview with Foucault.

2024.   *Die Geburt der Klinik. Eine Archäologie des ärztlichen Blicks*.
         Trans. Walter Seitter. Ed. Henning Ritter and Wolf Lepenies.
         Frankfurt am Main-Vienna: Ullstein Taschenbuch, 1976. Another
         edition of item 1990.

2025.   *Mikrophysik der Macht. Über Strafjustiz, Psychiatrie und Medizin*.
         Trans. Walter Seitter, et al. Berlin: Merve Verlag, 1976.

2026.   *Überwachen und Strafen. Die Geburt des Gefängnisses*. Trans.
         Walter Seitter. Frankfurt am Main: Suhrkamp, 1976, 395pp.
         Trans. of item 2004.

2027.   *Geschiedenis van de waanzin: in de zeventiende en achttiende
         eeuw*. Trans. C.P. Heering-Moorman. Meppel: Boom, 1976.
         Trans. of item 1897.

2028.   *De Orde van het vertoog*. Trans. C.P. Heering-Moorman. Amsterdam:
         Boom Meppel, 1976, 63pp. Trans. of item 1956.

1977

2028a. Editor of *Politiques de l'habitat: 1800-1850*. Paris: CORDA
[Comité de la Recherche et du Développement en Architecture],
1977, 324pp. In conjunction with the Equipe de recherches
de la chaire d'histoire des systèmes de pensée, Collège de
France.

2028b. Preface to *Les Juges Kaki*. By Mireille Debard and Jean-Luc
Hennig. Paris: Alain Moreau, 1977, 297pp.

2029. Introduction, with Gilles Deleuze, to *Oeuvres philosophiques
complètes*. Vol. I tome I. *La Naissance de la tragédie. Fragments posthumes. Automne 1869-printemps 1872*. By Friedrich
Nietzsche. Trans. Michel Haar, et al. Paris: Gallimard,
1977. See also items 1924, 1958 and 2007.

2030. "L'Oeil du pouvoir." Preface [conversation with Jean-Pierre
Barou and Michelle Perrot] to *Le Panoptique*. By Jeremy
Bentham. Paris: P. Belfond, 1977.

2030a. "Enfermement, psychiatrie, prison." *Change*, no. 32-33 (1977),
pp. 76-110. With D. Cooper.

*2031. "Foucault: non au sexe roi." *Le Nouvel Observateur*, no. 644
(12-21 March 1977), pp. 92-93, 95, 98, 100, 105, 113, 124,
130.

Interview with Bernard-Henri Lévi. For English trans., see
item 2032.

2031a. "Vérité et pouvoir. Entretien avec M. Fontanal." *L'Arc*, no.
70 (Aix-en-Provence, 1977), pp. 16-26. In issue entitled
"La Crise dans la tête."

2032. "Power and Sex: An Interview with Michel Foucault." *Telos*, no.
32 (1977), pp. 152-161. With B.-H. Lévi. Trans. of item 2031
by D.J. Parent.

2032a. Preface to *My Secret Life* [Récit de la vie sexuelle d'un Anglais
de l'époque victorienne]. Trans. Christian Charnaux, et al.
Paris: Les Formes du Secret, 1977. (Documents)

2033. *Language, Counter-Memory, Practice. Selected Essays and Interviews*. Ed. Donald F. Bouchard. Trans. Donald F. Bouchard and
Sherry Simon. Ithaca, N.Y.: Cornell University Press; Oxford:
Basil Blackwell & Mott, 1977, 240pp. For reviews, see items
2342-2348.

Contains: Fantasia of the Library; The Father's "No"; History of Systems of Thought; Language to Infinity (item 1908);
Nietzsche, Genealogy, History (item 1959); A Preface to Transgression (item 1905); Theatrum Philosophicum (item 1950); What
Is an Author? (item 1941).

2034. *Discipline and Punish. The Birth of the Prison*. Trans. Alan
Sheridan. New York: Pantheon Books, 1977, 333pp. Trans. of
item 2004.

Foucault explains why present-day arguments about the failures
of penal institutions are as old as the modern prison itself.
Torture of the body gave way to punishment of the soul through
rehabilitation, but these failures remain an inherent part of
an institution which never functions to eliminate criminals
but only to define, refine or perpetuate crime. Prisons are a
concentrated expression of a discipline that has spread throughout schools, armies, factories, and hospitals since the 17th
century; they epitomize the ways people are controlled and
repressed today.

2035. *Die Ordnung des Diskurses. Inauguralvorlesung am Collège de
      France, 2. Dezember 1970.* Trans. Walter Seitter. Frankfurt
      am Main-Vienna: Ullstein, 1977. Trans. of item 1956. See
      also item 1998.

2036. *Sexualität und Wahrheit. I. Der Wille zum Wissen.* Trans. Ulrich
      Raulf and Walter Seitter. Frankfurt am Main: Suhrkamp, 1977.
      Trans. of item 2015.

2037. Contribution to *Hexenwahn. Studien zur Entwicklung und Ver-
      selbständigung eines kulturellen Deutungsmusters. Arbeits-
      titel.* Frankfurt am Main: Suhrkamp, 1977. With Claudia
      Honegger, et al.

2038. *Der Faden ist gerissen.* With Gilles Deleuze. Trans. Walter
      Seitter and Ulrich Raulf. Berlin: Merve Verlag, 1977.
      (Internationale marxistische Diskussion, no. 68)

                                    1978

2038a. Editor of *Herculine Barbin, dite Alexina B.* Paris: Gallimard,
       1978, 160pp. (Les Vies Parallèles)

2038b. Conversations in *Le Livre des autres: entretiens avec Michel
       Foucault...[et al.].* By Raymond Bellour. Paris: Union
       Générale d'Editions, 1978, 444pp. (10/18, no. 1267)

2039. *The History of Sexuality. I. An Introduction.* Trans. Robert
       Hurley. New York: Pantheon Books, 1978. Trans. of item 2015.

       Foucault explores why we feel compelled to continually
       analyze and discuss sex and examines the social and mental
       mechanisms of power that cause us to direct the question of
       what we are to the question of our sexuality. The extension
       of sex into all areas of life began in the Victorian era and
       results in a society which molds how we view our bodies, our
       sex and our human possibilities.

2039a. "The West and the Truth of Sex." *Sub-stance*, no. 20 (Fall
       1978), pp. 5-8.

       Our society seems dedicated to the "expression," rather than
       the repression, of sex. Instead of erotic art the West has
       evolved a science of sex.

2039b. *Dispositive der Macht. Über Sexualität, Wissen und Wahrheit.*
       Berlin: Merve Verlag, 1978, 232pp. (Internationale marx-
       istische Diskussion, 77)

2039c. *Sexo, poder, verdad: conversaciones con Michel Foucault.* Ed.
       Miguel Morey. 1st ed. Barcelona: Materiales, 1978, 280pp.
       (Cuadernos Materiales, 8)

       Contains "Guía para la lectura de Foucault," pp. 261-280.

2039d. *Nietzsche, la genealogía, la historia.* Trans. José Vázquez.
       Valencia: Pre-Textos, 1978, 40pp. Trans. of item 1959.

2039e. "Precisazioni sul potere. Riposta ad alcuni critici." *Aut Aut*,
       no. 167-168 (1978), pp. 3-11. A February, 1978 interview on
       Surveiller et punir.

2039f. "La 'Governamentalità.'" *Aut Aut*, no. 167-168 (1978), pp. 12-29.

       On the art of governing in the 16th, 17th and 18th centuries.

                            SECONDARY SOURCES

       Albérès, R.M. See item 3852.

2040. Albury, W.R., and D.R. Oldroyd. "From Renaissance Mineral Studies
       to Historical Geology, in the Light of Michel Foucault's *The
       Order of Things.*" *The British Journal for the History of Sci-
       ence*, 10 (November 1977), 187-215.

       Altieri, C.F. See item 1625.

2041. Améry, Jean. "Wider den Strukturalismus. Das Beispiel des
       Foucault." *Merkur*, 27 (1973), 468-482.

2042. ————. "Michel Foucaults Vision des Kerker-Universums." *Merkur*,
       31, no. 4 (Stuttgart, April 1977), 389-394.

       ————. See also item 4425.

2043. Amiot, Michel. "Le Relativisme culturaliste de Michel Foucault."
       Les Temps Modernes, 22e année, no. 248 (January 1967), 1271-1298.

       Examines and evaluates the ideas in *Les Mots et les choses*;
       on the distinction and opposition between scientific and non-
       scientific knowledge; on the contemporary rejection of this dis-
       tinction by scientists; on the forms of knowledge generated by
       the human sciences.

2044. Amulree, Lord. "Evolution of the Clinic." *Books and Bookmen*,
       19, no. 4 (January 1974), 53-54.

2045. Andreani, E. "La Musique et les mots." *Romantisme*, no. 5 (1973),
       pp. 37-51.

2046.   Anonymous. "Après Foucault." *Le Nouvel Observateur*, no. 132
        (24-30 May 1967), p. 39.

2047.   ——. "Bibliographie." *Le Monde [des Livres]*, no. 9363 (21
        February 1975), p. 17.

2048.   ——. "En bref." *Le Nouvel Observateur*, no. 229 (31 March-
        6 April 1969), p. 39.

2049.   ——. "Che cos'è lei professore Foucault?" *La Fiera Lette-
        raria*, anno XLII, n. 39 (28 September 1967), 11-15.

2050.   ——. *La Conception idéologique de L'HISTOIRE DE LA FOLIE de
        Michel Foucault*. Journées annuelles de *L'Evolution Psychiatri-
        que*, 6 et 7 décembre 1969 (*L'Evolution Psychiatrique*, t. 36,
        fasc. 2, avril-juin 1971). Toulouse: Edouard Privat, 1971, pp.
        221-428.

2051.   ——. "Correspondance. A propos des *Entretiens sur Foucault*."
        La Pensée, no. 139 (1968), pp. 114-119.

        On *Les Mots et les choses*. Cf. item 2071.

2052.   ——. "L'Esprit et la lettre." *Le Nouvel Observateur*, no.
        227 (17-23 March 1970), p. 43.

2053.   ——. "L'Esprit et la lettre." *Le Nouvel Observateur*, no.
        231 (14-20 April 1969), p. 41.

2054.   ——. "Foucault comme des petits pains." *Le Nouvel Observateur*
        no. 91 (10-16 August 1966), p. 29.

2055.   ——. *O Homem e o discurso. Entrevista com Michel Foucault,
        e artigos: Dominique Lecourt, A Arqueologia e o saber. Carlos
        Henrique de Escobar, Discurso científico e discurso ideológico.
        Sergio Paulo Rouanet, A Gramática do homicídio*. Rio de Janeiro:
        Ed. Templo Brasileiro, 1971.

2056.   ——. "L'Homme à apprendre." *Le Nouvel Observateur*, no. 78
        (11-17 May 1966), p. 33.

        On Foucault and Gallimard's new collection "Bibliothèque des
        Sciences Humaines."

        ——. See also item 4867.

2057.   ——. "Informations: après Francfort." *La Quinzaine Littéraire*
        no. 14 (15-31 October 1966), p. 14.

2058.   ——. "Isolated Intellectuals." *Economist*, CCXXVIII, no. 6522
        (August 24, 1968), p. 37.

2059.   ——. "Las Meninas." *Revista de Occidente*, 18, no. 52 (July
        1967), 34-52.

2060.   ——. "Michel Foucault." In *C'est demain la veille. Entretiens
        [d'] Actuel avec Michel Foucault; ... Gilles Deleuze et Félix
        Guattari; ...*. Paris: Editions du Seuil, 1973, pp. 19-43.

2061. ————. "Un Philosophe militant." *Le Monde [des Livres]*, no. 9363 (21 March 1975), p. 17.

————. See also item 4275.

2062. ————. "Rendre à Sartre ce qui est à Sartre...." *Le Monde [des Livres]*, no. 7214 (23 March 1968), p. II.

2063. ————. "De Sartre à Foucault." *Le Monde [des Livres]*, no. 9274 (8 November 1974), p. 18.

2064. ————. "Selon Michel Foucault: 'une petite pédagogie.'" *Le Monde [des Livres]*, 8838 (14 June 1973), p. 23.

2065. ————. "Structuralism in the Streets." *The Times Literary Supplement*, no. 3469 (22 August 1968), p. 897.

2066. ————. "La Vie littéraire." *Le Monde [des Livres]*, no. 10006 (1 April 1977), p. 16.

Aron, See item 374.

2067. Askenazi, Joël. "Michel Foucault et les lendemains de l'homme." *Nouveaux Cahiers*, 3e année, no. 9 (Spring 1967), 16-19.

2067a. Autonomova, N.S. "From the 'Archéologie du savoir' to the 'Généalogie du pouvoir'" (in Russian). *Voprosy Filosofii*, no. 2 (1978), pp. 144-152.

Auzias, J.-M. See chapter 8 of items 11-14.

2068. B., M. "En suivant le cours de Foucault." *Esprit*, 35, no. 6 (1967), pp. 1066-1069.

2069. Bakker, Reinout. *Het anonieme denken. Michel Foucault en het structuralisme*. Baarn: Het Wereldvenster, 1973.

2070. ————. "Het Filosoferen van Michel Foucault." In *Structuralisme: voor en tegen*. Ed. A.G. Weiler. Bilthoven: Amboboeken, 1974.

2071. Balan, B., et al. "Entretiens sur Foucault." *La Pensée*, no. 137 (January-February 1968), pp. 3-37. On *Les Mots et les choses*. Cf. item 2051.

Balmas, E. See item 4278.

2072. Baltheiser, Karl. "Die Wegbereiter der linguistischen Strukturalismus und dessen sprachphilosophische Aspekte bei Foucault." Doctoral dissertation, Salzburg, 1971, 197pp.

2073. Barou, Jean-Pierre, and Michelle Perrot. "Un Entretien avec Michel Foucault. L'Oeil du pouvoir." *Nouvelles Littéraires*, 55e année, no. 2578 (31 March-7 April 1977), 6-7.

Bauch, J. See item 4435a.

*2074. Baudrillard, Jean. *Oublier Foucault*. Paris: Editions Galilée,
        1977, 87pp. (L'Espace Critique)

2075.   ————. *Olvidar a Foucault*. Trans. José Vazquez. Valencia:
        Pre-Textos, 1978.

        Belaval, Y. See item 4436.

2076.   Bellour, Raymond. "Entretien: Michel Foucault, 'les mots et
        les choses.'" *Les Lettres Françaises*, no. 1125 (31 March-6
        April 1966), pp. 3-4. Rpt. in *Le Livre des autres*. By
        Raymond Bellour. Paris: Edition de l'Herne, 1971, pp. 135-
        144. Another edition of *Le Livre des autres* was published by
        the Union Générale d'Editions in 1978. (10/18, no. 1267)
        Cf. item 1991.

2077.   ————. "Deuxième entretien avec Michel Foucault: sur les
        façons d'écrire l'histoire." *Les Lettres Françaises*, no.
        1187 (15-21 June 1967), pp. 6-9. Rpt. in *Le Livre des autres*.
        By Raymond Bellour. Paris: Edition de l'Herne, 1971, pp. 189-
        207. Another edition of *Le Livre des autres* was published by
        the Union Générale d'Editions in 1978. (10/18, no. 1267)
        Cf. item 1992.

2078.   ————. "Entretien avec Pierre Francastel: interprétation
        de la peinture et structuralisme." *Les Lettres Françaises*,
        no. 1181 (4-10 May 1967), pp. 30-31, 34.

2079.   ————. "L'Homme, les mots." *Magazine Littéraire*, no. 101
        (June 1975), pp. 20-23.

2080.   Berl, Emmanuel. *A contretemps*. Paris: Gallimard, 1969.

2081.   Bertels, C.P. "Michel Foucault." In *Filosofen van de 20ᵉ eeuw*.
        Ed. C.P. Bertels and E. Petersma. Assen-Amsterdam: Van Gorcum,
        1972; Amsterdam-Brussels: Intermediair, 1972, pp. 211-223.

2082.   Bertherat, Yves. "La Pensée folle." *Esprit*, 35, no. 360 (May
        1967), pp. 862-881.

2083.   Bertrand, Pierre. *L'Oubli: révolution ou mort de l'histoire*.
        Ouvrage publié avec le concours du conseil canadien de re-
        cherches sur les humanités. Paris: Presses Universitaires
        de France, 1975.

2084.   Beyssade, Jean Marie. "Mais quoi ce sont des fous. Sur un
        passage controversé de la première méditation." *Revue de
        Métaphysique et de Morale*, 78 (July-September 1973), 273-294.

        Blegen, J.C. See item 3876.

        Bogliolo, H. See item 4440.

2085.   Bondy, François. "Der Mensch ist tot—es lebe di Episteme!
        Michel Foucault." In *Der Rest ist Schreiben. Schriftsteller*

als *Aktivisten, Aufklärer und Rebellen*. By F. Bondy. Vienna-Munich-Zurich: Europa-Verlag, 1972, pp. 180-186.

B[onitzer], P[ascal], et al. See item 3817.

Bonnefis, P. See item 5209.

2086. Bonnefoy, Claude. "Un Jeune philosophe: Michel Foucault." *Arts et Loisirs*, no. 35 (25-31 May 1966), p. 8.

2087. ————. "L'Homme est-il mort? Un Entretien avec Michel Foucault." *Arts et Loisirs*, no. 38 (15-21 June 1966), pp. 8-9.

On Foucault and Sartre.

2088. ————. "André Breton-Michel Foucault: 'c'était un nageur entre deux mots.'" *Art et Loisirs*, no. 54 (5-11 October 1966), pp. 8-9.

Interview with Foucault.

Bouchard, Donald F. See item 2033.

2089. Brochier, J.-J. "Entretien de Michel Foucault avec J.-J. Brochier." *Magazine Littéraire*, no. 28 (April-May 1969).

2090. Brodeur, Jean-Paul. "McDonell on Foucault's Philosophical Method. Supplementary Remarks." *Canadian Journal of Philosophy*, 7 (September 1977), 555-568.

Brosse, J. See item 3893.

2091. Broustra, J. "Quelques questions à Michel Foucault." *Le Nouvel Observateur*, no. 438 (2-8 April 1973), p. 10.

Brown, P.L. See items 4447 and 4448.

2092. Brown, Robert. "The Idea of Imprisonment." *The Times Literary Supplement*, 16 June 1978, p. 658.

Bruézière, Maurice. See item 4288.

2093. ————. "Les Philosophes-essayistes: G. Bachelard, M. Merleau-Ponty, C. Lévi-Strauss, M. Foucault." In *Histoire descriptive de la littérature contemporaine*. Tome II. Les Grands genres. By Maurice Bruézière. Paris: Berger-Levrault, 1976, pp. 337-343.

Bukowski, J. See item 4419.

2094. Burgelin, Pierre. "L'Archéologie du savoir." *Esprit*, 35e année, no. 360 (May 1967), 843-861.

An analysis of Foucault's *Les Mots et les choses*.

2095. Burguière, André. "Michel Foucault: la preuve par l'aveu." *Le Nouvel Observateur*, no. 633 (31 January-6 February 1977), pp. 64-66.

2096.   Cabral de M Machado, Roberto. "A arqueologia do saber e a
        constitutição das ciências humanas." *Discurso*, 5 (1974),
        87-118.

2097.   Cacciari, Massimo. "Razionalità e irrazionalità nella critica
        del politico in Deleuze e Foucault." *Aut Aut*, no. 161 (Sep-
        tember-October 1977), pp. 119-133.

2097a. Cancino-P., Cesar Augusto. "Analítica del poder en Michel
        Foucault." *Franciscanum*, 20 (Bogotá, 1978), 105-127.

2098.   Canguilhem, Georges. "Mort de l'homme ou épuisement du cogito?"
        Critique, 20e année, 24, no. 242 (July 1967), 599-618.

        On Foucault's *Les Mots et les choses*.

2099.   ———. Introduction to *Le Parole e le cose. Un'Archeologia
        delle scienze umane*. By Michel Foucault. Trans. E. Panaitescu.
        Milan: Rizzoli, 1967.

        Carduner, J. See item 3901.

2100.   Carroll, David. "Subject of Archeology, or the Sovereignty of
        the Episteme." *MLN*, 93 (May 1978), 695-722.

*2101. Caruso, Paolo. *Conversazioni con Claude Lévi-Strauss, Michel
        Foucault, Jacques Lacan*. Milan: U. Mursia, 1969.

2102.   ———. *Conversaciones con Lévi-Strauss, Foucault y Lacan*.
        Trans. F. Serra Cantarell. Barcelona: Editorial Anagrama,
        1969.

2103.   Castro, Américo. "El Quijote, taller de existencialidad."
        Revista de Occidente, 18, no. 52 (July 1967), 1-33.

2104.   Cavaillès, R. "L'Epistémologie en question." *Annales publiées
        trimestriellement par l'Université de Toulouse-Le Mirail*,
        9, no. 6 (1973), Philosophie, II, 103-109.

2105.   Cavazzoni, Ermanno. "Michel Foucault: *Surveiller et punir; Moi,
        Pierre Rivière....*" *Il Verri*, no. 11 (October 1975), pp.
        119-123.

        Caws, P. See item 36.

2106.   Le Cercle d'Epistémologie. "A Michel Foucault. Sur l'archéolo-
        gie des sciences." *Cahiers pour l'Analyse*, no. 9 (1968), pp.
        5-8. Foucault's reply on pp. 9-40.

2107.   ———. "Nouvelles questions." *Cahiers pour l'Analyse*, no. 9
        (1968), pp. 41-44.

2108.   Certeau, Michel de. "Le Noir soleil du langage: Michel Foucault."
        In *L'Absent de l'histoire*. By Michel de Certeau. Tours:
        Repères-Mame, 1973, pp. 115-132.

————. See also items 2379 and 1016.

2109. Chalumeau, Jean-Luc. *La Pensée en France. De Sartre à Foucault.* Paris: F. Nathan, 1974.

2110. Chapsal, Madeleine, ed. "Entretien: Michel Foucault." *La Quinzaine Littéraire*, no. 5 (15 May 1966), pp. 14-15.

2111. Châtelet, François. "Les Nouveaux prophètes." *Le Nouvel Observateur*, no. 94 (31 August-6 September 1966), p. 28.

2112. ————. "Le Fantôme du 'cyberanthrope.'" *Le Nouvel Observateur*, no. 180 (24-30 April 1968), p. 40.

————. See also item 41.

Chiari, J. See item 407.

2113. Clavel, Maurice. "Un Manifestant bien éléve." *Le Nouvel Observateur*, no. 424 (23-29 December 1972), p. 56.

2114. Coelho, Eduardo Prado, comp. *Estruturalismo: antologia de textos teóricos [por] Foucault [et al.].* Trans. Maria Eduarda Reis Colares, et al. Lisboa: Portugalia Editora, 1968.

2115. Comfort, Alex. "Breakdown and Repair." *The Guardian*, no. 37,578 (5 May 1967), p. 7.

2116. Cooper, David. "Crosscurrents-VIII. Poetic Injustice." *The Times Literary Supplement*, no. 3413 (27 July 1967), p. 687.

2117. Corradi, Enrico. "La Storiografia archeologica di Michel Foucault." *Rivista Rosminiana di Filosofia e di Cultura*, 69, no. 4 (1975), 323-330.

2118. ————. *Filosofia della morte dell'uomo. Saggio sul pensiero di Michel Foucault.* Milan: Vita e Pensiero, 1977. (Filosofia e Scienze Umane, 14) Bibliography, pp. 259-278.

2119. Corvez, Maurice. "Le Structuralisme de Michel Foucault." *Revue Thomiste*, 68, no. 1 (January-March 1968), 101-124.

————. "Le Structuralisme anthropologique de Michel Foucault," chapter 2 of items 49-51.

2120. Crahay, Franz. "Perspective(s) sur les philosophies de la Renaissance." *Revue Philosophique de Louvain*, 72 (November 1974), 655-677.

2121. Cranston, Maurice. "Michel Foucault." *Encounter*, 30, no. 6 (May 1968), 34-42.

2122. ————. "Les 'Périodes' de Michel Foucault." *Preuves*, 18e année, no. 209-210 (August-September 1968), 65-75.

2123.   ————. "The Spirit of Knowledge." *The Sunday Times*, no. 7784
        (20 August 1972), p. 30.

2124.   ————. "Michel Foucault: A Structuralist View of Reason and
        Madness." In *The Mask of Politics, and Other Essays*. By
        Maurice William Cranston. La Salle, Ill.: Library Press,
        distributed by Open Court Publishing Co., 1973, pp. 137-155.

        Crémant, Roger. See item 54.

2125.   Daix, Pierre. "Sartre est-il dépassé?" *Les Lettres Françaises*,
        February 1967, pp. 1168-1169.

2126.   ————. "Du structuralisme. I.- Le Divorce avec la philosophie."
        Les Lettres Françaises, no. 1226 (20-26 March 1968), pp. 5-7.

2127.   ————. "Du structuralisme (suite). II.- Mort de l'homme ou
        fin de l'anthropocentrisme." *Les Lettres Françaises*, no. 1227
        (27 March-2 April 1968), pp. 9-10.

2128.   ————. "Structure du structuralisme (II), Althusser et Fou-
        cault." *Les Lettres Françaises*, no. 1239 (3-9 July 1968),
        pp. 7, 11.

2129.   ————. "Michel Foucault et Georges Duby au Collège de France."
        Les Lettres Françaises, no. 1363, pp. 3-4.

2130.   D'Alessandro, Lucio. "Potere e pena nella problematica di
        M. Foucault." *Rivista Internazionale di Filosofia del Diritto*,
        53 (July-September 1976), 415-429.

2131.   D'Amico, Robert. "Introduction to the Foucault-Deleuze Dis-
        cussion." *Telos*, no. 16 (Summer 1973), pp. 101-102.

2132.   ————. Review of Foucault's *Discipline and Punish*; *La Volonté
        de savoir*; and *Language, Counter-Memory, Practice*. *Telos*, 36
        (Summer 1978), 169-183.

2133.   Daumezon, G., et al. "Michel Foucault et l'histoire de la folie."
        L'Evolution Psychiatrique, 36 (1971), 227-241.

        Degrés. See items 3914 and 3915.

2134.   Deleuze, Gilles. *Un Nouvel archiviste*. Montpellier: Fata Morgana,
        1972, 52pp.

        On Foucault's *Les Mots et les choses*.

2135.   ————, and Félix Guattari. *Capitalisme et schizophrénie*.
        L'Anti-Oedipe. Paris: Editions de Minuit, 1972.

2136.   Denat, Antoine. "Critique littéraire et langage philosophique."
        In his *Vu des antipodes* ... (item 4296), pp. 28-47.

2137.   Derrida, Jacques. "Cogito et histoire de la folie." In his
        L'Ecriture et la différence (item 1521), pp. 51-97; *Writing
        and Difference* (item 1616a), pp. 31-63.

2138. D'Hondt, J. "L'Idéologie de la rupture." *Revue de Théologie et de Philosophie*, 21, no. 4 (Lausanne, 1971), 253-262.

2139. Domenach, Jean-Marie. "Une Nouvelle passion." *Le Nouvel Observateur*, no. 88 (20-26 July 1966), pp. 26-27.

2140. ———. "Le Système et la personne." *Esprit*, 35, no. 360 (May 1967), 771-780.

Donato, Eugenio. See item 65.

2141. D[roit], R[oger]-P[ol]. "Hérodote et Foucault." *Le Monde [des Livres]*, no. 9643 (23 January 1976), p. 14.

2142. Dufrenne, Mikel. "Le Structuralisme et l'anti-humanisme." *Le Monde [des Livres]*, no. 7452 (28 December 1968), p. 3.

———. See also item 4493.

Duvignaud, J. See item 3703.

2143. Duvivier, Roger. "La Mort de don Quichotte et l'*Histoire de la folie*." *Marche Romane*, 20 (Liège, 1970), 69-83.

Ela, J.-M. See item 4966.

2144. El Kabbach, Jean-Pierre. "Foucault répond à Sartre." *La Quinzaine Littéraire*, no. 46 (1-15 March 1968), pp. 20-22.

2145. El Kordi, M. "L'Archéologie de la pensée classique selon Michel Foucault." *Revue d'Histoire Economique et Sociale*, 51, no. 3 (1973), 309-335.

2146. Enthoven, Jean-Paul. "Crimes et châtiments." *Le Nouvel Observateur*, no. 538 (3-9 March 1975), pp. 58-59.

2147. Escobar, Carlos Henrique de. "Discurso científico e discurso ideológico." In Anonymous. *O Homen e o discurso...* (item 2055).

2147a. Ewald, François. "Foucault, une pensée sans aveu." In *Les Dieux dans la cuisine. Vingt ans de philosophie en France*. Ed. Jean-Jacques Brochier. Paris: Aubier, 1978, pp. 45-53.

2148. Ezine, Jean-Louis. "Sur la sellette: Michel Foucault." *Les Nouvelles Littéraires*, 53e année, no. 2477 (17-23 March 1975), 3.

2149. Felman, Shoshana. "*Aurélia* ou 'le livre infaisable.' De Foucault à Nerval." *Romantisme*, 3 (1972), 43-55.

———. See also item 1675.

2150. Ferreira, Virgilio. "Questionario a Foucault e a algum estruturalismo." *O Tempo e o Modo*, 56 (1968), 17-27.

2151. Finas, Lucette. "Michel Foucault: 'Les Rapports de pouvoir passent à l'intérieur des corps.'" *La Quinzaine Littéraire*, no. 247 (1-15 January 1977), pp. 4-6.

2152. Flynn, Bernard Charles. "Michel Foucault and the Husserlian Problematic of a Transcendental Philosophy of History." *Philosophy Today*, 22 (Fall 1978), 224-238.

       Husserl's transcendental philosophy of history in *The Crisis of European Sciences and Transcendental Phenomenology* vs. Foucault's conception of history as radically discontinuous and without immanent teleology in his *The Order of Things* and *The Archaeology of Knowledge*.

2153. Fontaine, José. "Foucault et Baudrillart. Deux méditations sur le pouvoir." *Revue Nouvelle*, 67 (Brussels, 1978), 79-85.

       On Foucault's *Histoire de la sexualité*, v. 1 and Baudrillart's *Oublier Foucault*.

2154. Franck, Robert. "Où est la vérité?" *Dialogue*, 17 (Canada, 1978), 286-319.

       Francovich, G. See items 79 and 80.

2155. Frullini, Andrea. "Foucault, un Proust in filosofia." *Tempo Presente*, anno XII, n. 2 (February 1967), 58-61.

       Funt, D.W. See item 4520.

       Furet, F. See item 84.

       Garaudy, Roger. See items 4522 and 4523.

2156. Geertz, Clifford. "Stir Crazy." *New York Review of Books*, 24 (26 January 1978), 3-4ff.

       Gerbault, R. See item 4535.

       Gillet-Stern, S. See item 4539.

2156a. Giuntoli, Franco. *Misticismo e figure del potere-sapere in Michel Foucault*. Pisa: Giardini, 1976, 29pp. (Università di Pisa. Facoltà di lingue e lettere straniere. Pubblicazioni della Cattedra di filosofia, 2)

2157. Giusberti, Fiorella. "Michel Foucault: archeologia o dossologia?" *Il Mulino*, 22, no. 228 (July-August 1973), 627-647.

2158. Gorga, Maria Antonietta. "Il Motivo dell''altro' nella filosofia di Michel Foucault." *Logos*, 3, no. 1 (1971), 83-108.

2159. Gotroneo, Girolano. "Foucault et il trionfo della parole." *Studi Francesi*, 12 (1968), 434-453.

       On Foucault's *Les Mots et les choses*.

Gozzi, G. See item 5251.

Gramont, S. de. See item 3541.

2160. Grande, Maurizio. "Topografia e discorso (Su *L'Archeologia del sapere* di M. Foucault)." *Nuova Corrente*, no. 66 (1975), pp. 84-108.

Greckij, M.N. See item 4549.

2161. Greene, J.C. "Les Mots et les choses." *Information sur les Sciences Sociales*, 6, no. 4 (1967), 131-138.

*2162. Guédez, Annie. *Foucault*. Paris: Editions Universitaires/Delarge, 1972. (Psychothèque, 15)

2163. ————. *Che cosa ha veramente detto Foucault*. Trans. Augusto Menzio. Rome: Ubaldini, 1973.

2163a. Guédon, Jean-Claude. "Michel Foucault: The Knowledge of Power and the Power of Knowledge." *Bulletin of the History of Medicine*, Summer 1977, pp. 245-277.

Guilbert, J.-C. See item 1072.

2164. Gutiérrez, Rafael. "Michel Foucault: los laberinthos del estructuralismo." *Insula*, no. 349 (December 1975), pp. 1, 12.

2165. Hacking, Ian. "The Archeology of Knowledge." *Cambridge Review*, 93, no. 2208 (2 June 1972), 166-170.

2165a. ————. "Michel Foucault's Immature Science." *Nous*, 13 (March 1979), 39-51.

On the basic assumptions of Foucault's "archaeology of knowledge," using the terminology and concepts of current American philosophy of science. Comparisons and contrasts with Quine and Kuhn are made. Concludes with a brief application of Foucault's methodology to philosophical problems about "incommensurability" and "natural kinds."

Hanhardt, J.G., et al. See item 3825.

2166. Harvard-Watts, John. "Michel Foucault." *The Times Literary Supplement*, no. 3570 (31 July 1970), p. 855. See also item 2282.

2166a. Hattiangadi, J.N. "Language Philosophy. Hacking: Foucault." *Dialogue*, 17 (1978), 513-528.

2167. Hayman, Ronald. "Cartography of Discourse? On Foucault." *Encounter*, 47, no. 6 (December 1976), 72-75.

Heath, S. See item 1084.

2168.   Hector, Josette. "Michel Foucault et l'histoire." *Synthèses*,
        27e année, no. 309-310 (March-April 1972), 86-88.

        Heusch, Luc de. See item 3761.

2169.   Hodgson, Godfrey. "All the Eggheads in One Basket." *The Sunday
        Times Magazine*, 16 April 1967, pp. 41, 43-44, 46.

2170.   Huppert, George. "*Divinatio et eruditio*: Thoughts on Foucault."
        History and Theory, 13, no. 3 (1974), 191-207.

        On *Les Mots et les choses*. When applied to sixteenth-century
        France, Foucault's method yields unsatisfactory results.

2171.   ————. "*Divinatio et eruditio*: beschouwingen over Foucault."
        De Gids, no. 7-8 (1975), 503-514.

2172.   Hutcheon, Linda. "The Outer Limits of the Novel: Italy and
        France." *Contemporary Literature*, 18, no. 2 (Spring 1977),
        198-216.

2173.   Jacerme, Pierre. *La "Folie" de Sophocle à l'anti-psychiatrie*.
        Paris: Bordas, 1975, c. 1974.

        Jacob, A. See item 4576.

2174.   Jacob, André. "Annie Guédez: *Foucault*; Michel Cressole: *Deleuze*;
        Pierre V. Zima: *Goldmann*." *Les Etudes Philosophiques*, no. 3
        (July-September 1975), 375-376.

        Jaeggi, U.J.V. See item 4378.

2175.   Jambet, Christian. "L'Unité d'une pensée: une intérrogation sur
        les pouvoirs." *Le Monde [des Livres]*, no. 9363 (21 February
        1975), p. 17.

2176.   ————. "Bibliographie." *Magazine Littéraire*, no. 101 (June
        1975), pp. 24-26.

        Jameson, F. See item 4172.

2177.   Japiassú, Hilton F. "Idéia de uma 'Arqueologia' das ciências
        humanas segundo Michel Foucault." *Convivium*, S.P., 13 (1974),
        415-430.

2177a. Jara, José. "El Hombre y su diferencia histórica." *Revista
        Venezolana di Filosofia*, 1979, pp. 53-90.

        Kahn, J.-F. See item 112.

        Kampits, P. See item 4585.

        Krause-Jensen, E. See item 4593.

*2178. Krémer-Marietti, Angèle. *Foucault et l'archéologie du savoir.
        Présentation, choix de textes, bibliographie*. Paris: Seghers,
        1974. Bibliography, pp. 237-242.

2179. ————. *Michel Foucault, der Archäologe des Wissens. Mit Texten von Michel Foucault.* Trans. Gerhard Ahrens. Frankfurt-Vienna-Berlin: Ullstein, 1976. (Ullstein-Buch, 3302)

Krieger, M., and Dembo., L.S. See item 4319.

Kritzman, L.D. See item 4594.

Künzli, R.E. See item 4597.

2179a. Kurzweil, Edith. "Michel Foucault." *Theory and Society*, Fall 1977, pp. 395-420.

2180. Kwant, R.C. "Foucault en de Menswetenschappen." *Tijdschrift voor Filosofie*, 37 (July 1975), 294-326.

2181. L., M. "Foucault et Deleuze aux *Cahiers.*" *Le Monde [des Arts et des Spectacles]*, no. 9957 (3 February 1977), p. 14.

2182. Lacharité, Normand. "Les Conditions de possibilité du savoir: deux versions structuralistes de ce problème." *Dialogue*, 7, no. 3 (December 1968), 359-373.

2183. ————. "Archéologie du savoir et structures du langage scientifique." *Dialogue*, 9, no. 1 (June 1970), 35-53.

2184. Lacouture, Jean. "Au Collège de France: le cours inaugural de M. Michel Foucault--éloge du discours interdit." *Le Monde*, no. 8053 (4 December 1970), p. 8.

2185. Lacroix, Jean. "La Signification de la folie selon Michel Foucault," chapter 4, part III of his item 4600 (1966), pp. 208-215; (1968), pp. 222-230.

2186. Langlois, J. "Michel Foucault et la mort de l'homme." *Science et Esprit*, 21, no. 2 (1969), 209-230.

Examines his "archeology of knowledge" according to *Les Mots et les choses.*

2187. Lapointe, François H. "Michel Foucault: A Bibliographic Essay." *The Journal of the British Society for Phenomenology*, 4 (May 1973), 195-197.

2188. ————, and Walter Seitter. "Bibliographie der Schriften über Michel Foucault." *Philosophisches Jahrbuch*, 81, no. 1 (1974), 202-207.

2189. ————, and Claire Lapointe. "Michel Foucault: A Bibliographic Essay." *Diálogos*, 10, no. 26 (April 1974), 153-157.

2190. ————. "A. Foucault's Writings; B. Supplement to Bibliography on Foucault" (item 2189). *Diálogos*, 11, no. 29-30 (November 1977), 245-254.

Lavers, A. See item 4611.

Le Blond, J.-M. See item 5269.

2191.   Le Bon, Sylvie. "Un Positiviste désespéré: Michel Foucault."
        Les Temps Modernes, 22, no. 248 (1967), 1299-1319.

        A critique of the archeology of the human sciences that
        Foucault undertook in his *Les Mots et les choses*. Unable to do
        away with history, Foucault proposes not to think about it.
        Furthermore, he goes against the logical demands of his method
        in order to save the fundamental positivism of his thought.

2192.   Lecourt, Dominique. "Sur l'archéologie et le savoir (à propos
        de Michel Foucault)." *La Pensée*, no. 152 (August 1970),
        pp. 69-87. Rpt. in a modified version in her item 2193, pp.
        98-133.

*2193. ―――. *Pour une critique de l'épistémologie (Bachelard,
        Canguilhem, Foucault)*. Paris: F. Maspero, 1972.

2194.   ―――. *Per una critica dell'epistemologia. Bachelard,
        Canguilhem, Foucault*. Trans. Francesco Fistetti. Bari: De
        Donato, 1973.

2195.   ―――. *Kritik der Wissenschaftstheorie. Marxismus und Episte-
        mologie (Bachelard, Canguilhem, Foucault)*. Trans. Irmela Neu
        and Georg Fexer. Berlin: Verlag für das Studium der Arbeiter-
        bewegung, 1974.

2196.   ―――. *Marxism and Epistemology: Bachelard, Canguilhem and
        Foucault*. Trans. Ben Brewster. Atlantic Highlands, N.J.:
        Humanities Press; London: New Left Books, 1975. Trans. of
        item 2193 and her *L'Epistémologie historique de Gaston
        Bachelard* (Paris: J. Vrin, 1969).

2197.   Leland, Dorothy. "On Reading and Writing the World: Foucault's
        History of Thought." *Clio*, 4, no. 2 (February 1975), 225-243.

        On *L'Archéologie du savoir*.

2198.   Lemaigre, B. "Michel Foucault, ou les malheurs de la raison et
        les prospérités du langage." *Revue des Sciences Philosophiques
        et Théologiques*, 51, no. 3 (July 1967), 440-460.

        A critical analysis of *Les Mots et les choses*.

2199.   Lemaire, Frans. "Essai sur la pensée impensable. Malraux, Fou-
        cault, Blanchot...." *Synthèses*, 24, no. 271-272 (1969), 42-
        47.

        On the unthinkable fringe attached to all thought, whether it
        be applied to art (Malraux), writing (Blanchot), or to knowledge
        and its manifestations (Foucault).

2200.   Lemert, Charles, and Garth Gillan. "The New Alternative in
        Critical Sociology: Foucault's Discursive Analysis." *Cultural
        Hermeneutics*, 4 (December 1977), 309-320.

Tendencies toward a subjectivization of recent critical social and sociological theories are analyzed. Foucault's structural archeological method is outlined with special attention to his *Archeology of Knowledge* and *The Order of Things*. The critical aspects of Foucault's formal thought are also examined.

2200a. Lenoci, Michele. "Maurice Clavel: Annuncio di fede e rinascita dell'uomo." *Rivista di Filosofia Neo-Scholastica*, 71 (January-March 1979), 112-142.

2200b. Léonard, J. "L'Historien et le philosophe. A propos de *Surveiller et punir. Naissance de la prison.*" *Annales Historiques de la Révolution Française*, 49, no. 228 (1977), 163-181.

Le Sage, Laurent. "Michel Foucault." In his item 4322, pp. 76-78.

2201. Lévy, Bernard-Henri. "Le Système Foucault." *Magazine Littéraire*, no. 101 (June 1975), pp. 7-9.

2202. Levy, Zeev. "The Structuralist Epistemology of Michel Foucault" (in Hebrew). *Iyyun: A Hebrew Philosophical Quarterly*, 25, no. 1-2 (January-April 1974), 39-57.

Leyvraz, J.-P. See items 133 and 134.

2203. Lojacono, Ettore. "Le Choix philologique de l'histoire et l'archéologie du savoir." *Annales de l'Institut de Philosophie* (Brussels, 1973), pp. 143-163. Includes a bibliography of Foucault, pp. 164-166.

2204. Loriot, Patrick. "Trois Nouveaux collégiens." *Le Nouvel Observateur*, no. 267 (22-28 December 1969), p. 34.

2205. Lourenço, Eduardo. "Michel Foucault ou o fim do humanismo." *O Tempo e o Modo*, 56 (1968), 8-16.

2206. Lyautney, P. *Foucault*. Paris: Editions Universitaires, 1973. (Classiques de XXe siècle)

2207. Mandrou, R. "Histoire sociale et histoire des mentalités." *La Nouvelle Critique*, no. 49 (January 1972).

2208. Marcus, Steven. "Madness, Literature, and Society." In his *Representations: Essays on Literature and Society*. New York: Random House, 1975, pp. 137-160.

On Foucault's *Madness and Civilization*.

2209. Margolin, Jean-Claude. "L'Homme de Michel Foucault." *Revue des Sciences Humaines*, n.s. 32, fasc. 128 (October-December 1967), 497-521.

On *Les Mots et les choses*.

2210. ———. "Tribut d'un antihumaniste aux études d'Humanisme et Renaissance--Note sur l'oeuvre de M. Foucault." *Bibliothèque d'Humanisme et de Renaissance*, 29, no. 3 (1967), 701-711.

Takes chapter 1 of *Histoire de la folie* ... and chapter 2 of
Les Mots et les choses and shows their interest for a thematic
study of the Renaissance and a renewal of the ideas applied
to it.

2211.   ————. "La Méthode des *Mots et des choses* dans le *De pueris
         instituendis* d'Erasme (1529) et l'*Orbis sensualium pictus*
         de Comenius (1658)." *Organon*, no. 12-13 (1976-1977), pp. 69-
         86.

         Massey, I. See item 1758.

2212.   Mauriac, Claude. *Les Espaces imaginaires*. Paris: Bernard
         Grasset, 1975.

2213.   ————. "Foucault et Deleuze." *Le Figaro Littéraire*, no.
         1544 (20 December 1975), II: 16.

2214.   McDonell, Donald J. "Savoir, Epistémé, Enoncé: A Clarification
         of Some of the Major Concepts in the Work of Michel Foucault."
         Doctoral dissertation, Institut Supérieur de Philosophie,
         Université Catholique de Louvain, 16 December 1972, reported
         in *Revue Philosophique de Louvain*, tome 71, no. 12 (November
         1973), 827-828.

         Also on Althusser and Kuhn in relation to Foucault.

2215.   ————. "On Foucault's Philosophical Method." *Canadian Journal
         of Philosophy*, 7 (September 1977), 537-553.

         An examination of Foucault's works shows that he is a special
         type of historian concerned with discontinuity, and not with
         continuity, in history. After a study of Foucault's major con-
         cepts, it is shown that by going beyond the subjective point
         of view, it is possible to discover the historical *a priori*
         set of "statements," i.e., the set of conditions making the
         appearance of statements possible.

2216.   McMullen, Roy. "Michel Foucault." *Horizon*, 11, no. 4 (Fall
         1969), 36-39.

2216a.   Megill, Allan. "Foucault, Structuralism, and the Ends of
         History." *Journal of Modern History*, 51 (September 1979),
         451-503.

2217.   Melandri, Enzo. "Michel Foucault: l'epistemologia delle
         scienze umane." *Lingua e Stile*, 2, no. 1 (1967), 75-96.

         On *Les Mots et les choses*.

2218.   ————. "Note in margine all'*episteme* di Foucault." *Lingua
         e Stile*, 5, no. 1 (1970), 145-156.

         On *Les Mots et les choses*.

2219.   Miel, Jan. "Ideas or Epistemes: Hazard versus Foucault." *Yale
         French Studies*, 49 (1973), 231-245. Part of a special issue

entitled "Science, Language and the Perspective Mind: Studies in Literature and Thought from Campanella to Bayle."

2220. Migliorini, Ermanno. "Siamo natri ieri." *La Fiera Letteraria*, 42, no. 48 (30 November 1967), 29-30.

Minguelez, R. See item 1144.

Miller, J.H. See item 1772.

Millet, L., et al. See items 147-149.

2221. Milošević, N. "Michel Foucault and Oswald Spengler" (in Serbo-Croatian). *Izraz. Časopis za Književnu i Umetnicku Kritiku*, 19, no. 11-12 (1975), 423-425.

Miščevic, N. See item 4386.

2222. Monteiro, João Paulo. "Discurso téorico e discurso retórico." *Discurso*, 4 (1973), 79-93.

2223. Morawe, B. Interview with Foucault about prison revolts and their causes. *Dokumente. Zeitschrift für uebernatiōnale Zusammenarbeit* (issue entitled "Die strafende Gesellschaft"), 29, no. 2 (1973), 109-137.

Mounin, G. See item 4208.

2224. Mundwiler, Leslie. "Williams, Breton, Marcuse, Foucault." *Open Letter*, 2nd series, no. 5 (Summer 1973), pp. 54-68.

2225. Murguía, Adolfo. "Acerca de la muerte de la filosofía." *Revista de Occidente*, 39, no. 116 (November 1972), 234-243.

2226. Nemo, Philippe. "Au Collège de France. Le Pouvoir pris en flagrant-délit par Foucault." *Les Nouvelles Littéraires*, 54, no. 2515 (15 January 1976), 6-7.

2227. Nikolova, M. "The Problem of the 'Death' of Man in the Philosophy of Structuralism" (in Bulgarian). *Filosofska Mis'l*, 28, no. 6 (1972), 65-74.

————. See also item 4671.

2228. Noiray, André, ed. *La Philosophie. De Hegel à Foucault. Du marxisme à la phénoménologie*. Paris: Culture, Art, Loisirs; Tournai: Académie du Livre, 1969. (Les Dictionnaires du Savoir Moderne, 1)

2229. Núñez, L. "Escenario nuevo para la filosofía." *Estafeta Literaria*, no. 513 (1 April 1973), p. 1296.

2229a. Nye, Robert A. "Crime in Modern Societies: Some Research Strategies for Historians." *Journal of Social History*, 11 (Summer 1978), 491-507.

2229b. O'Brien, Patricia. "Crime and Punishment as Historical Problem."
       Journal of Social History, 11 (Summer 1978), 508-520.

       O'Malley, J.B. See item 4676.

2230. Ormesson, J. d'. "Passage de l'homme ou les avatars du savoir."
       Nouvelle Revue Française, 15, no. 171 (1967), 477-490.

       On Foucault's archeology of the human sciences; an examination
       of the main themes of *Les Mots et les choses*.

2231. Pelorson, Jean-Marc. "Michel Foucault et l'Espagne." *La Pensée*,
       no. 152 (August 1970), 88-89.

       A critical analysis of the Spanish examples in *Histoire de
       la folie* ... and *Les Mots et les choses*.

       Petitjean, G. See item 1171.

2232. Petrisor, M. "Structural Correlations in the Thought of Michel
       Foucault" (in Rumanian). *Revista de Filozofie*, 16, no. 2
       (1969), 247-259.

2233. Piatier, Jacqueline, and Jean-Louis Ferrier. "Reading Round
       the World." *The Sunday Times*, no. 7492 (1 January 1967),
       p. 17.

2233a. Pieretti, A. "Il Paradosso di Foucault." *Studium*, 74, no. 6
       (Rome, 1978), 799-808.

       On the death of man in the human sciences.

2234. Pingaud, Bernard. "Interview: Sartre répond." *La Quinzaine
       Littéraire*, no. 14 (15-31 October 1966), pp. 4-5.

       ————. See also item 4704.

       Pöhler, E. See item 4708.

       Poole, R. See item 165.

       Poster, M. See item 4393.

2235. Pratt, Vernon. "Foucault and the History of Classification
       Theory." *Studies in History and Philosophy of Science*, 8,
       no. 2 (1977), 163-171.

2236. Puder, Martin. "Der böse Blick des Michel Foucault." *Neue
       Rundschau*, 83, no. 2 (1972), 315-324.

       Raffi, M.E. See item 1796.

2237. Rassam, Joseph. *Michel Foucault. Las Palabras y las cosas.*
       Madrid: Ed. Magisterio Español, 1978, 144pp. (Crítica
       Filosófica)

Reif, Adelbert. "Michel Foucault." In item 172, pp. 143-145.

2238. Reiter, Josef. "Der 'endgültige' Tod Gottes. Zum Strukturalismus von M. Foucault." *Salzburger Jahrbuch für Philosophie*, 14 (1970 appeared 1971), 111-125.

2238a. Rella, Franco. *Il Mito dell'altro. Lacan, Deleuze, Foucault.* Milan: Feltrinelli, 1978, 66pp. (Opuscoli marxisti, 26)

————. See also item 1199.

2239. Revault d'Allones, Olivier. "Michel Foucault: les mots contre les choses." *Raison Présente*, no. 2 (February-April 1967), pp. 29-41. Rpt. in item 4350, pp. 13-37.

Riddel, J. See item 1805.

Rivelaygue, J. See item 4740.

2240. Rodríguez Monegal, Emir. "Borges y nouvelle critique." *Revista Iberoamericana*, 38, no. 80 (July-September 1972), 367-390.

2240a. Rojas-R., Carlos. "Foucault, una respuesta general al marxismo." *Pucara*, no. 3 (Cuenca, 1977), pp. 187-193.

2241. Rousseau, G.S. "Whose Enlightenment? Not Man's: The Case of Michel Foucault." *Eighteenth-Century Studies*, 6, no. 2 (Winter 1972-1973), 238-256.

On Foucault's *Les Mots et les choses*.

2242. Ruprecht, Hans-George. "Mémoire(r) poésie: Mythe et 'pratique discursive.'" *Canadian Review of Comparative Literature*, 2, no. 1 (Spring 1975), 97-110.

2243. Russo, François. "L'Archéologie du savoir de Michel Foucault." *Archives de Philosophie*, 36, no. 1 (January-March 1973), 69-105.

2244. ————. "*L'Archeologia del sapere* di Michel Foucault." *La Civiltà Cattolica*, anno 124, vol. 3, no. 2954 (21 July 1973), 117-129.

Said, E.W. See items 4236 and 4336.

2245. Said, Edward W. "Michel Foucault as an Intellectual Imagination." *Boundary 2*, 1, no. 1 (Fall 1972), 1-36.

2246. ————. "An Ethics of Language." *Diacritics*, 4, no. 2 (Summer 1974), 28-37.

On Foucault's *Archeology of Knowledge* and *Discourse on Language*.

2247. ————. "Interview." *Diacritics*, 6, no. 3 (Fall 1976), 30-47.

2248. Santos, M.I. "Busqueda de un nuevo espacio para la emergencia
       del hombre." *Stromata*, 29 (Argentina, July-September 1973),
       215-339.

       Schiwy, G. See items 189 and 190.

2249. Sedgwick, Peter. "Mental Illness *is* Illness." *Salmagundi*, no.
       20 (Summer-Fall 1972), pp. 196-224.

2250. Seem, Mark Douglas. "Liberation of Difference: Toward a Theory
       of Anti-Literature." *New Literary History*, 5, no. 1 (October
       1973), 119-133.

2251. ————. "The Logic of Power: An Essay on G. Deleuze, M. Fou-
       cault and F. Guattari." *Dissertation Abstracts International*,
       37, no. 5 (November 1976), 2950-A. S.U.N.Y. at Buffalo
       dissertation.

       Serres, M. See item 194.

2252. Sharratt, Bernard. "Notes after Foucault." *New Blackfriars*,
       53, no. 625 (June 1972), 251-264.

2253. Simon, J. "Das Neue in der Geschichte." *Philosophisches Jahrbuch*,
       79, no. 2 (1972), 269-287.

2254. Simon, John K. "A Conversation with Michel Foucault." *Partisan
       Review*, 38, no. 2 (1971), 192-201.

       An interview.

       ————. See also item 4338.

2255. ————. "Michel Foucault on Attica: An Interview." *Telos*,
       no. 19 (1974), pp. 154-161.

       An interview held in April, 1972.

       Simon, P.H. See item 1231.

2256. Sini, Carlo. *Il Problema della storia in Foucault: filosofia
       della storia. Anno accademico 1972-1973.* L'Aquila: Centro
       Tecnico Culturale ed Assistenziale, 1973, 121pp.

2257. ————. "Il Problema della verità in Foucault." *Pensiero*, 19,
       no. 1-2 (1974), 20-45.

2258. Sloterdijk, P. "Michel Foucaults strukturale Theorie der
       Geschichte." *Philosophisches Jahrbuch*, 79, no. 1 (1972),
       161-184.

       On Foucault's *Archéologie du savoir*.

2258a. Smock, Ann. "'Où est la loi?': Law and Sovereignty in *Aminadab*
       and *Le Très-Haut*." *Sub-stance*, no. 14 (September 1976), pp.
       99-116.

2259.   Sokolov, R.A. "Inside Mind." *Newsweek*, 77 (25 January 1971), 88.
        A portrait.

2260.   Sorin, Raphael. "Le Pendule de Foucault...." *Bizarre*, 1964,
        pp. 75-76.

        Soto Verges, R. See items 1237 and 1238.

2261.   [Steiner, George]. "Steiner Responds to Foucault." *Diacritics*,
        1, no. 2 (Winter 1971), 59.

        Steinwachs, G. See item 4050.

2262.   Struyker Boudier, Henk. *Inleiding in het mediese denken van
        J.H. van den Berg en M. Foucault.* Kolleges mediese filosofie
        (Sun werk-uitgave). Nijmegen: Socialistiese Uitgeverij
        Nijmegen, 1975.

        Sturrock, J. See item 196a.

2263.   Tatarkiewicz, A. "Foucault and Velasquez" (in Polish). *Studia
        Estetyczne*, 8 (Warsaw, 1971), 223-242. Polish trans. of the
        first chapter of *Les Mots et les choses* with a critique.

2264.   Testa, Aldo. *Le Parole e gli uomini. Risposta a Foucault.*
        Bologna: Cappelli, 1968. (Biblioteca di Scienze Umane, 4)

        Thomas, D. See item 5289.

        Todisco, O. See item 4793.

2265.   Toyosaki, Kō ichi. *Suna no kao.* Japan, 1975.

2266.   Trías, Eugenio. "Presentación de la obra de Michel Foucault."
        Convivium, 30 (1969), 55-68.

2267.   ————. *Filosofía y carnaval.* Barcelona: Editorial Anagrama,
        1970, 81pp.

2268.   Trías Mercant, Sebastián. *Hombre y filosofía a nivel arqueológico.*
        Palma de Mallorca: n.p., 1973?, 58pp.

2269.   ————. "El Ser del hombre y el ser del lenguaje." *La Ciudad
        de Dios*, 190, no. 1 (1976), 97-113.

2270.   Valdinoci, S. "Etude Critique: les incertitudes de l'archéologie:
        Archè et archive." *Revue de Métaphysique et de Morale*, 83
        (January-March 1978), 73-101.

        Examines the relationship between the archeology of Husserl
        and that of Foucault. Concludes that Foucault remains dependent
        on a problematic of foundation; his critique does not begin
        a positive era; it is stuck in the Husserlian question of which
        it remains theoretically derivative.

2271.   Venault, Philippe. "Histoires de...." *Magazine Littéraire*,
        no. 101 (June 1975), pp. 14-19.

2272.   Verley, Etienne. "L'Archéologie du savoir et le problème de la
        périodisation." *Dix-Huitieme Siècle*, no. 5 (1973), pp. 151-
        162.

        Vogel, A. See item 3842.

2273.   Wald, H. "A Decomposition of the Notion of Man?" (in Rumanian).
        Revista de Filozofie, 14, no. 8 (1967), 903-912.

        Starting with the ideas expressed in *Les Mots et les choses*,
        Wald shows that man only disappears in conceptions which refuse
        to make the transition from structure to essence and which
        subsume the logical into the historical.

2274.   White, Hayden V. "Foucault Decoded: Notes from Underground."
        History and Theory, 12, no. 1 (1973), 23-54. Rpt. in his
        Tropics of Discourse. Essays in Cultural Criticism. Baltimore,
        Md.: Johns Hopkins University Press, 1979, pp. 230-260.

        On Foucault and Foucault's *The Order of Things. An Archaeology
        of the Human Sciences*.

        ————. See also item 1839.

2275.   Williams, K. "Unproblematic Archaeology." *Economy and Society*,
        3, no. 1 (1974), 41-68.

        On Foucault's *Archéologie du savoir*.

2275a. Wright, Gordon. "Foucault in Prison." *Stanford French Review*,
        Spring 1977, pp. 71-78.

        Wyschogrod, E. See item 4821.

2276.   Ysmal, C. "Histoire et archéologie. Note sur la recherche de
        Michel Foucault." *Revue Française de Science Politique*, 22,
        no. 4 (1972), 775-804.

        Zardoya, J.M. See item 4824.

2277.   Zoïla, A.F. "Michel Foucault, anti-psychiatre?" *Revue Inter-
        nationale de Philosophie*, 32 (1978), 59-74.

                              REVIEWS

                       L'Archéologie du savoir
                            (item 1938)

2278.   Anonymous. "Análisis y definición." *Hispano Americano*, 59, no.
        1516 (24 May 1971), 58.

2279. ————. Review of *The Archaeology of Knowledge*. *Kirkus Reviews*, 40 (15 July 1972), 834.

2280. ————. Review of *The Archaeology of Knowledge*. *The New York Review of Books*, 20 (17 May 1973), 37.

2281. ————. Review of *The Archaeology of Knowledge*. *The Times Literary Supplement*, 9 June 1972, p. 663.

2282. ————. "The Contented Positivist: Michel Foucault and the Death of Man" [illustrated portrait]. *The Times Literary Supplement*, no. 3566 (2 July 1970), pp. 697–698.

2283. Brocher, Jean-Louis. "Michel Foucault explique son dernier livre." *Magazine Littéraire*, no. 28 (April–May 1969), pp. 23–25.

2284. Caws, Peter. Review of *The Archaeology of Knowledge*. *The New York Times Book Review*, 22 October 1972, p. 6.

2285. Châtelet, François. "L'Archéologie du savoir." *La Quinzaine Littéraire*, no. 72 (1–15 May 1969), pp. 3–4.

2286. Cichowicz, Stanislaw. "Archéologie du savoir." *Pamietnik Literacki*, 63, no. 2 (1972), 360–368.

2287. Cranston, Maurice. "Digging in the Junkyards of Our Past." *Washington Post Book World*, 7, no. 44 (29 October 1972), 3.

2288. Culler, Jonathan. Review of *The Archaeology of Knowledge*. *Yale Review*, 62 (Winter 1973), 290.

2289. Daix, Pierre. "Du journalisme de Flaubert de Foucault." *Les Lettres Françaises*, no. 1284 (21–27 May 1969).

2290. Deledalle, Gérard. Review of *L'Archéologie du savoir*. *Journal of the History of Philosophy*, 10 (October 1972), 495–502.

2291. Deleuze, Gilles. "Un Nouvel archiviste." *Critique*, 26, no. 274 (March 1970), 195–209.

2292. Duvignaud, Jean. "Ce qui parle en nous, pour nous, mais sans nous." *Le Nouvel Observateur*, no. 232 (21–27 April 1969), pp. 42–43.

2293. Kremer-Marietti, Angèle. Review of *L'Archéologie du savoir*. *Revue de Métaphysique et de Morale*, 75 (1970), 355–360.

2294. Parain, Brice. "Michel Foucault: *L'Archéologie du savoir*." *Nouvelle Revue Française*, 17 (November 1969), 726–733.

2295. Poster, Mark. Review of *The Archaeology of Knowledge*. *Library Journal*, 97 (1 September 1972), 2736.

2296. Shaffer, E.S. Review of *The Archaeology of Knowledge. Studies
       in History and Philosophy of Sciences*, 7 (1976), 269-275.

2297. Watté, Pierre. "Michel Foucault ou la fin de l'histoire." *La
       Revue Nouvelle*, 26ᵉ année, 52, no. 10 (October 1970), 309-311.

See also items 2096, 2152, 2160, 2178-2179, 2183, 2192, 2197, 2200,
2243-2244, 2246, 2258, 2272, and 2275.

               Folie et déraison. Histoire de la folie ...
                            (item 1897)

2298. Anonymous. "Un Mundo loco, loco." *Hispano Americano*, 52, no.
       1331 (6 November 1967), 85.

2299. ————. Review of *Madness and Civilization. Christian Century*,
       82 (16 June 1965), 780.

2300. ————. Review of *Madness and Civilization. Sociological
       Review*, n.s. 19 (November 1971), 634.

2301. Atherton, John. "In Praise of Folly." *Partisan Review*, 32
       (1965), 441-444.

2302. Bakker, Reinout. Review of *Geschiedenis van de waanzin....
       Wijsgerig Perspectief op Maatschappij en Wetenschap*, 16
       (1975-1976), 400-404.

2303. Bloomquist, Harold. Review of *Madness and Civilization. Library
       Journal*, 90 (July 1965), 3062.

2304. Cauthen, Nelson R. Review of *Madness and Civilization. Human
       Context*, 7 (1975), 628-631.

2305. Engelhardt, S. Review of *Wahnsinn und Gesellschaft. Philo-
       sophisches Jahrbuch*, 79 (1972), 219-222.

2306. Freeman, Hugh. "Anti-Psychiatry through History." *New Society*,
       9, no. 240 (4 Mary 1967), 665-666.

2307. Friedenberg, E.Z. Review of *Madness and Civilization. New York
       Times Book Review*, 22 August 1965, p. 6.

2308. Gay, Peter. Review of *Madness and Civilization. Commentary*,
       40 (October 1965), 93.

2309. Gorer, Geoffrey. "French Method and Madness." *The Observer*,
       no. 9171 (23 April 1967), p. 30.

2310. Laing, R.D. "Sanity and 'Madness'--1. The Invention of Madness."
       New Statesman, 73, no. 1892 (16 June 1967), 843.

2311. Leach, Edmund. "Imprisoned by Madmen." *The Listener*, 77, (8
       June 1967), 752-753.

2312. Marcus, Steven. "In Praise of Folly." *The New York Review of Books*, 7, no. 7 (3 November 1966), 6, 8, 10.

2313. ————. "In Praise of Folly [a corrected version]." *The New York Review of Books*, 7, no. 8 (17 November 1966), 36-39.

2314. Nemo, Philippe. *Le Nouvel Observateur*, no. 404 (7-13 August 1972), p. 39.

2315. Nuñez, L. "Historia de la locura en la época clásica." *Estafeta Literaria*, no. 502 (15 October 1972), p. 1116.

2316. P[almier], J[ean]-M[ichel]. *Le Monde [des Livres]*, no. 8606 (15 September 1972), p. 16.

2317. Reider, Norman. Review of *Madness and Civilization*. *Nation*, 201 (5 July 1965), 22.

2318. Richman, Geoffrey. "Beware of False Prophets." *The Tribune*, 31, no. 34 (25 August 1967), 10.

2319. Rousseau, G.S. Review of *Madness and Civilization*. *Eighteenth-Century Studies*, 4, no. 1 (Fall 1970), 90-95.

2320. [Scruton, Roger]. "Roger Scruton on Madness and Death." *The Spectator*, 227, no. 7476 (9 October 1971), 513.

Also on *The Order of Things*.

2321. Simon, John K. *"Histoire de la folie à l'âge classique."* *Modern Language Notes*, 78 (January 1963), 85-88.

2322. Thom, Achim. Review of *Wahnsinn und Gesellschaft*. *Deutsche Zeitschrift für Philosophie*, 20 (1972), 1066-1069.

See also items 2050, 2133, 2208, 2210 and 2231.

Histoire de la sexualité
(item 2015)

2322a. Adamowski, T.H. Review of *The History of Sexuality*. *Canadian Forum*, 59 (June 1979), 40-42.

2323. Adams, M.V. Review of *The History of Sexuality*. *Commentary*, 67 (March 1979), 84-87.

2324. Anonymous. Review of *Histoire de la sexualité*. *Observer* (London), 2 January 1977, p. 25.

2324a. ————. Review of *The History of Sexuality*. *Book World (Washington Post)*, 7 January 1979, p. E-1.

2325. ————. Review of *The History of Sexuality*. *Choice*, 15 (February 1979), 1727.

2325a. ———. Review of *The History of Sexuality*. *Chronicle of
        Higher Education*, 17 (8 January 1979), R-10.

2325b. ———. Review of *The History of Sexuality*. *Critic*, 37 (March
        1979), 7.

2325c. ———. Review of *The History of Sexuality*. *Guardian Weekly*,
        120 (22 April 1979), 21.

2325d. ———. Review of *The History of Sexuality*. *History: Reviews
        of New Books*, 8 (October 1979), 3.

2325e. ———. Review of *The History of Sexuality*. *Listener*, 102
        (2 August 1979), 155.

2325f. ———. Review of *The History of Sexuality*. *Observer* (London),
        8 April 1979, p. 37.

2325g. ———. Review of *The History of Sexuality*. *Publishers Weekly*,
        216 (26 November 1979), 51.

2325h. ———. Review of *The History of Sexuality*. *Spectator*, 242
        (31 March 1979), 20.

2325i. ———. Review of *The History of Sexuality*. *Village Voice*,
        24 (19 March 1979), 81.

2326. ———. "Six Volumes de Michel Foucault: une histoire de la
        sexualité." *Le Monde*, no. 9885 (5 November 1976), p. 1.

2326a. Ariès, P. "A propos de *La Volunté de savoir*." *Arc*, no. 70
        (1977), pp. 27-32. Issue is entitled "La Crise dans la tête."

2327. Brincourt, André. "Le Goulag du sexe." *Le Figaro Littéraire*,
        no. 1600 (15-16 January 1977), pp. 1, 17.

2327a. Conrad, Peter. Review of *The History of Sexuality*. *New States-
        man*, 97 (30 March 1979), 451-452.

2328. Droit, Roger-Pol. "*La Volonté de savoir*, de Michel Foucault:
        le pouvoir et le sexe." *Le Monde*, no. 9968 (16 February
        1977), pp. 1, 18.

2329. Feldman, Jacqueline. "Michel Foucault: *Histoire de la sexualité.
        1. La Volonté de savoir*." *Cahiers Internationaux de Sociologie*,
        63 (July-December 1977), 370-373.

2329a. Gilbert, A.N. Review of *The History of Sexuality*. *American
        Historical Review*, 84 (October 1979), 1020.

2329b. Harkness, J. Review of *The History of Sexuality*. *Society*, 16
        (September 1979), 82ff.

2330. Kenny, Denis. Review of *The History of Sexuality*. *Library
        Journal*, 103 (15 October 1978), 2127.

2331. Kunkel, F.L. Review of *The History of Sexuality*. *America*, 140 (7 April 1979), 291.

2332. Lasch, C. Review of *The History of Sexuality*. *Psychology Today*, 12 (November 1978), 147ff.

2333. Lavoie, M. Review of *Histoire de la sexualité*. *Laval Théologique et Philosophique*, 33 (1977), 321-326.

2333a. Mehl, R. Review of *Histoire de la sexualité*. *Revue d'Histoire et de Philosophie Religieuses*, 58 (1978), 472-473.

2334. Poirier, Richard. Review of *The History of Sexuality*. *The New York Times Book Review*, 84 (14 January 1979), 1ff.

2335. Robinson, Paul. Review of *The History of Sexuality*. *The New Republic*, 179 (28 October 1978), 29-32.

   Calls it a fraud and an intellectual embarrassment.

2335a. Sennett, R. Review of *The History of Sexuality*. *New Yorker*, 55 (16 July 1979), 101-106.

2336. Simon, J. Review of *The History of Sexuality*. *New Leader*, 61 (4 December 1978), 6-7.

2337. Turkle, Sherry. Review of *The History of Sexuality*. *Nation*, 228 (27 January 1979), 92-94.

2337a. Vera, Hernan. Review of *The History of Sexuality*. *Contemporary Sociology*, 8 (July 1979), 589.

2337b. Wassmer, T. Review of *The History of Sexuality*. *Best Sellers*, 39 (April 1979), 35.

2338. Welsch, W. Review of *Histoire de la sexualité*. *Philosophischer Literaturanzeiger*, 30 (1977), 350-354.

2339. White, Hayden. "The Archeology of Sex." *The Times Literary Supplement*, no. 3921 (6 May 1977), p. 565.

2340. Wolton D. "Qui veut savoir?" *Esprit*, no. 7-8 (1977), pp. 36-47.

2341. Zinner, Jacqueline. Review of *Histoire de la sexualité*. *Telos*, 36 (Summer 1978), 215-225.

See also item 2132.

Language, Counter-Memory, Practice
(item 2033)

2342. Anonymous. Review of *Language, Counter-Memory, Practice*. *Book World* (*Washington Post*), 29 January 1978, p. L1.

2343. ———. Review of *Language, Counter-Memory, Practice*. *Choice*, 15 (March 1978), 64.

2343a. ———. Review of *Language, Counter-Memory, Practice*. *Contemporary Sociology*, 8 (March 1979), 318.

2343b. ———. Review of *Language, Counter-Memory, Practice*. *Criticism*, 20 (Summer 1978), 324.

2343c. ———. Review of *Language, Counter-Memory, Practice*. *Journal of Aesthetics and Art Criticism*, 37 (Spring 1979), 369.

2344. ———. Review of *Language, Counter-Memory, Practice*. *Kirkus Reviews*, 45 (15 August 1977), 897.

2344a. Barnouw, J. Review of *Language, Counter-Memory, Practice*. *The Review of Metaphysics*, 32 (June 1979), 750-752.

2345. Daniels, P.T. Review of *Language, Counter-Memory, Practice*. *Library Journal*, 102 (15 October 1977), 2162.

2346. Ellrich, R.J. Review of *Language, Counter-Memory, Practice*. *Modern Language Journal*, 62 (April 1978), 206.

2347. Judovitz, D. Review of *Language, Counter-Memory, Practice*. *MLN*, 93 (May 1978), 755-758.

2347a. O'Meara, Maureen. Review of *Language, Counter-Memory, Practice*. *Sub-stance*, no. 21 (Winter 1978-1979), pp. 160-161.

2348. Prince, G. Review of *Language, Counter-Memory, Practice*. *Criticism*, 20 (Summer 1978), 324-325.

See also items 1856b, 2092 and 2132.

Maladie mentale et psychologie
(item 1898)

2349. Huard, P. *Revue de Synthèse*, 88 (1967), 94-95.

2350. Schaerer, R. *Revue de Théologie et de Philosophie*, 103 (1970), 63.

Moi, Pierre Rivière ...
(item 1983)

2351. Anonymous. Review of *I, Pierre Rivière....* *American Journal of Sociology*, 82 (July 1976), 256.

2352. ———. Review of *I, Pierre Rivière....* *Booklist*, 71 (1 May 1975), 884.

2353. ————. Review of *I, Pierre Rivière....* *Choice*, 12 (October 1975), 1079.

2354. ————. Review of *I, Pierre Rivière....* *Contemporary Psychology*, 21 (June 1976), 440.

2355. ————. Review of *I, Pierre Rivière....* *Esquire*, 84 (July 1975), 24.

2356. ————. Review of *I, Pierre Rivière....* *Kirkus Reviews*, 43 (15 February 1975), 212.

2357. ————. Review of *I, Pierre Rivière....* *The New York Times Book Review*, 7 December 1975, p. 55.

2358. ————. Review of *I, Pierre Rivière....* *Partisan Review*, 43 (Summer 1976), 489.

2359. ————. Review of *I, Pierre Rivière....* *Publishers Weekly*, 207 (3 March 1975), 66.

2360. Bobango, G.J. Review of *I, Pierre Rivière....* *Best Sellers*, 35 (May 1975), 37.

2361. Bowler, R.L. Review of *I, Pierre Rivière....* *Library Journal*, 100 (1 April 1975), 684.

2362. De Feo, Ronald. Review of *I, Pierre Rivière....* *National Review*, 27 (29 August 1975), 950.

2363. Delaney, Paul. "The Prisoner's Confession was a Verboballistic Invention." *The New York Times Book Review*, 18 May 1975, pp. 31-32.

2364. Galey, Matthieu. "L'Intelligence et l'idiot--*Moi, Pierre Rivière, ayant égorgé ma mère, ma soeur et mon père...*, Michel Foucault;..." *Réalités*, no. 336 (January 1974), pp. 82-83.

2365. Gallo, Max. "Histoire d'une folie." *L'Express*, no. 1162 (15-21 October 1973), pp. 59-60.

2366. Kanters, Robert. "La Mort triomphait dans cette voix étrange." *Le Figaro Littéraire*, no. 1435 (17 November 1973), p. V: 19.

2367. Menard, Jacques. "Michel Foucault: *Moi, Pierre Rivière....*" *Cahiers du Chemin*, no. 20 (15 January 1974), pp. 159-164.

2368. Orgogoso, Isabelle. "*Moi, Pierre Rivière...*, présenté par Michel Foucault." *Esprit*, no. 3 (March 1974), pp. 532-533.

2369. Roudinesco, Elisabeth. "Le Schreber du pauvre." *Action Poétique*, no. 57 (1974), pp. 64-69.

See also item 2105.

Les Mots et les choses
(item 1919)

2370. Albérès, R.-M. "L'Homme n'est plus dans l'homme." *Les Nouvelles Littéraires*, no. 2035 (1 September 1966), p. 5.

2371. Anonymous. Review of *The Order of Things*. *Kirkus Reviews*, 38 (15 December 1970), 1365.

2372. ――――. Review of *The Order of Things*. *Publishers Weekly*, 198 (16 November 1970), 74.

2373. ――――. Review of *The Order of Things*. *Science and Society*, 35 (Winter 1971), 490.

2374. ――――. Review of *The Order of Things*. *Spectator*, 227 (9 October 1971), 513.

2375. Bortolaso, G. Review of *Le Parole e le cose*. *La Civiltà Cattolica* 120, no. 1 (1969), 574-577.

2376. Bossy, John. "Abstract Acrobat." *New Statesman*, 81, no. 2098 (4 June 1971), 775.

2377. Caws, Peter. "Language as the Human Reality." *New Republic*, 164, no. 13 (27 March 1971), 28-32.

2378. Ceppa, L., and C. Pianciola. Review of *Le Parole e le cose*. *Revista di Filosofia*, 59 (1969), 214-222.

2379. Certeau, Michel de. "Les Sciences humaines et la mort de l'homme." *Etudes*, 326, no. 3 (March 1967), 344-360.

2380. Chapsal, Madeleine. "Is Man Dead?" *Atlas*, 12, no. 3 (September 1966), 58-59.

2381. Châtelet, François. "L'Homme, ce Narcisse incertain." *La Quinzaine Littéraire*, no. 2 (1 April 1966), pp. 19-20.

2382. Cotroneo, G. "Michel Foucault e il trionfo della parola." *Studi Francesi*, no. 36 (1968), pp. 434-453.

2383. Cranston, Maurice. *Book World*, 14 February 1971, p. 5; 5 December 1971, p. 27.

2384. Culler, Jonathan. "Words and Things: Michel Foucault." *Cambridge Review*, 92, no. 2200 (29 January 1971), 104-105.

2385. Deleuze, Gilles. "L'Homme, une existence douteuse." *Le Nouvel Observateur*, no. 81 (1-7 June 1966), pp. 32-34.

2386. Dias de Lima, Altino. "Fundando as ciências humanas." *Brotéria*, 86 (1968), 643-656.

2387. Dubarle, Dominique. Review of *Les Mots et les choses*. *Signes du Temps*, no. 12 (December 1966), pp. 26-28.

2388. Girardin, Benoit. "'Les Mots et les choses,' à propos du livre de Michel Foucault." *Freiburger Zeitschrift für Philosophie und Theologie*, 16 (1969), 92-99.

2389. Gorga, M.A. Review of *Le Parole e le cose*. *Logos*, 1, no. 2 (1969), 443-444.

2390. Harding, D.W. Review of *The Order of Things*. *The New York Review of Books*, 17 (12 August 1971), 21.

2391. Howard, Richard. "Our Sense of Where We Are." *Nation*, 213, no. 1 (5 July 1971), 21-22.

2392. Jahoda, M. Review of *The Order of Things*. *Science Studies*, 2 (1972), 99-101.

2393. Kanters, Robert. "Tu causes, tu causes, est-ce tout ce que tu sais faire?" *Le Figaro Littéraire*, no. 1053 (23 June 1966), p. 5.

2394. Lacroix, Jean. "Fin de l'humanisme?" *Le Monde*, no. 6657 (9 June 1966), 13.

2395. Larson, J.L. Review of *The Order of Things*. *Isis*, 64 (1973), 246-247.

2396. Norbrook, David. Review of *The Order of Things*. *The Oxford Literary Review*, Spring 1975, p. 12.

2397. Perreault, J.M. Review of *The Order of Things*. *Library Journal*, 96 (1 February 1971), 482.

2398. Saldanha, N.N. Review of *Les Mots et les choses*. *Revista Brasileira de Filosofia*, 21 (1971), 344-348.

2399. ————. Review of *Les Mots et les choses*. *Archiv für Rechts- und Sozialphilosophie*, 58 (1972), 600-604.

2400. Sokolov, R.A. Review of *The Order of Things*. *Newsweek*, 77 (25 January 1971), 88.

2401. Soler Ferrandez, M.J. Review of *Las Palabras...*. *Teorema*, 1 (March 1971), 157-158.

2402. Steiner, George. "The Mandarin of the Hour--Michel Foucault." *The New York Times Book Review*, 28 February 1971, pp. 8, 28-31.

2403. Thom, Achim. Review of *Les Mots et les choses*. *Deutsche Zeitschrift für Philosophie*, 20 (November 1972), 96-100.

2404. Van Laere, F. Review of *Les Mots et les choses*. *Cahiers Internationaux du Symbolisme*, 14 (1967), 91-93.

2405.   Wurms, Pierre. "Un Best-seller: Michel Foucault--*Les Mots et
        les choses*." *Die Neueren Sprachen*, Band 67, Heft 11 (November
        1968), 561-564.

See also items 2040, 2043, 2051, 2071, 2076, 2094, 2098, 2099, 2106,
2107, 2134, 2152, 2159, 2161, 2170, 2177, 2186, 2191, 2198, 2200,
2209-2211, 2217-2218, 2230-2231, 2237, 2241, 2263, 2273, 2274, and
2320.

                          Naissance de la clinique
                               (item 1903)

2406.   Anonymous. "Notes on Current Books." *Virginia Quarterly Review*,
        51, no. 2 (Spring 1975), xlix, lxviii, lxxx, lxxxi.

2407.   ————. Review of *The Birth of the Clinic*. *American Journal of
        Sociology*, 80 (May 1975), 1503.

2408.   ————. Review of *The Birth of the Clinic*. *Book World* (*Wash-
        ington Post*), 16 February 1975, p. 4.

2409.   ————. Review of *The Birth of the Clinic*. *Choice*, 11 (March
        1974), 114.

2410.   ————. Review of *The Birth of the Clinic*. *Kirkus Reviews*, 41
        (1 July 1973), 725.

2411.   ————. Review of *The Birth of the Clinic*. *Library Journal*, 98
        (1 June 1973), 1849.

2412.   ————. Review of *The Birth of the Clinic*. *The New York Review
        of Books*, 22 (22 January 1976), 18.

2413.   ————. Review of *The Birth of the Clinic*. *Publishers Weekly*,
        204 (2 July 1973), 76.

2414.   ————. Review of *The Birth of the Clinic*. *Science and Society*,
        39 (Summer 1975), 235.

2415.   ————. Review of *The Birth of the Clinic*. *The Times Literary
        Supplement*, 1 February 1974, p. 107.

2416.   ————. Review of *The Birth of the Clinic*. *Village Voice*, 18
        (22 November 1973), 27.

2417.   Aronson, A.L. Review of *The Birth of the Clinic*. *Yale Review*,
        63 (March 1974), 473.

2418.   Caws, Peter. Review of *The Birth of the Clinic*. *New Republic*,
        169 (10 November 1973), 28.

2419.   Dagognet, François. *Critique*, 21 (1965), 436-437.

2420.   Howe, Marguerite. "Open Up a Few Corpses." *Nation*, 218, no. 4
        (26 January 1974), 117-119.

2421. Lasch, Christopher. "After the Church the Doctors, After the Doctors Utopia." *The New York Times Book Review*, 24 February 1974, p. 6.

2422. Mainetti, José Alberto. Review of *The Birth of the Clinic*. *Journal of Medicine and Philosophy*, 2 (March 1977), 77-83.

2423. Mullin, R. Review of *The Birth of the Clinic*. *Heythrop Journal*, 19 (October 1978), 426.

2424. Rousseau, G.S. Review of *The Birth of the Clinic*. *Philological Quarterly*, Fall 1975, p. 790.

2425. Vossenkuhl, W. Review of *Die Geburt der Klinik*. *Philosophisches Jahrbuch*, 82 (1975), 413-416.

2426. Zeldin, Theodore. "An Archaeologist of Knowledge." *New Statesman*, 86, no. 2229 (7 December 1973), 861-862.

See also item 2044.

L'Ordre du discours
(item 1956)

2427. G., F. *Revue de l'Institut de Sociologie*, no. 3 (1972), pp. 596-597.

2428. O., L.E. Review of *El Orden del discurso*. *Razón y Fábula*, no. 40-41 (Bogotá, 1976), pp. 169-170.

2429. Ver Eecke, W. *Review of Metaphysics*, 26 (1972-1973), 534-535.

See also items 2184 and 2246.

Scritti letterari
(item 1966)

2430. Magrini, G. *Annali della Scuola Normale Superiore di Pisa*, 2 (1972), 1038-1043.

Surveiller et punir
(item 2004)

2431. Anonymous. Review of *Discipline and Punish*. *Booklist*, 74 (15 February 1978), 964.

2432. ———. Review of *Discipline and Punish*. *Books and Bookmen*, 23 (April 1978), 20; (May 1978), 59.

2433. ———. Review of *Discipline and Punish*. *Book World* (Washington Post), 29 January 1978, p. L1.

2434.   ———. Review of *Discipline and Punish*. *Choice*, 15 (May 1978),
        471.

2435.   ———. Review of *Discipline and Punish*. *Guardian Weekly*, 117
        (18 December 1977), 18.

2436.   ———. Review of *Discipline and Punish*. *Kirkus Reviews*, 45
        (15 October 1977), 1124.

2436a. ———. Review of *Discipline and Punish*. *The New York Times
        Book Review*, 25 February 1979, p. 41.

2437.   ———. Review of *Discipline and Punish*. *Publishers Weekly*,
        212 (7 November 1977), 75.

2438.   ———. Review of *Surveiller et punir*. *Publishers Weekly*, 44
        (Spring 1977), 293.

2439.   ———. Review of *Surveiller et punir*. *The Times Literary
        Supplement*, 26 September 1975, p. 1090.

2440.   Barham, P. Review of *Discipline and Punish*. *Sociology*, 13
        (January 1979), 111-115.

2441.   Bettinger, Sven-Claude. "Die Struktur der Strafjustiz." *Dokumente*
        32, no. 1 (March 1976), 80-81.

2442.   Blot, Jean. "Michel Foucault: *Surveiller et punir*." *Nouvelle
        Revue Française*, no. 276 (December 1975), pp. 89-92.

2443.   Bynagle, Hans. Review of *Discipline and Punish*. *Library Journal*,
        102 (1 December 1977), 2442.

2444.   Clemons, Walter. Review of *Discipline and Punish*. *Newsweek*, 91
        (2 January 1978), 61.

2445.   Cohen, Stanley. Review of *Discipline and Punish*. *Contemporary
        Sociology*, 7 (September 1978), 566.

2446.   Coles, R. Review of *Discipline and Punish*. *New Yorker*, 54 (29
        January 1979), 95-98.

2447.   De Feo, Ronald. Review of *Discipline and Punish*. *National
        Review*, 30 (17 March 1978), 359.

2448.   Deleuze, Gilles. "Ecrivain non: un nouveau cartographe."
        Critique, 30, no. 343 (December 1975), 1207-1227.

2449.   Di Piero, W.S. Review of *Discipline and Punish*. *Commonweal*,
        105 (12 May 1978), 313-315.

2450.   D[roit], R[oger]-P[ol]. "Michel Foucault et la naissance des
        prisons." *Le Monde [des Livres]*, no. 9363 (21 February 1975),
        p. 16.

2451. Ewald, François. "Anatomie et corps politique." *Critique*, 30, no.
       343 (December 1975), 1228-1265.

2452. Fernandez Zoila, Adolfo. "La Machine à fabriquer des délinquants."
       La Quinzaine Littéraire, no. 206 (16-31 March 1975), pp. 3, 5.

2453. Gallo, Max. "La Prison selon Michel Foucault." *L'Express*,
       no. 1233 (24 February-2 March 1975), pp. 65-66.

2454. Geertz, Clifford. Review of *Discipline and Punish*. *The New York
       Review of Books*, 24 (26 January 1978), 3-4ff.

2454a. Goldstein, J. Review of *Discipline and Punish*. *The Journal of
       Modern History*, 51 (March 1979), 116-118.

2455. Goodman, D. Review of *Discipline and Punish*. *Cross Currents*,
       28 (Fall 1978), 378-382.

2456. Harding, D.W. "Towards Total Control of Man." *The Listener*,
       98, no. 2539 (15 December 1977), 802-803.

2456a. Hillyard, P. Review of *Discipline and Punish*. *Community Develop-
       ment Journal*, 14 (April 1979), 163-165.

2456b. Hoffman, R.L. Review of *Discipline and Punish*. *The Historian*,
       41 (February 1979), 332-333.

2457. Hussain, A. Review of *Discipline and Punish*. *Sociological
       Review*, n.s. 26 (November 1978), 932-939.

2458. Jackson, Bruce. Review of *Discipline and Punish*. *The Nation*,
       226 (4 March 1978), 250-251.

2459. Kanters, Robert. "Crimes et châtiments." *Le Figaro Littéraire*,
       no. 1501 (22 February 1975), p. III: 17.

2460. Kaplan, R. Review of *Discipline and Punish*. *Commentary*, 65
       (May 1978), 83-86.

2461. Kurzweil, Edith. "Law and Disorder." *Partisan Review*, 44, no.
       2 (1977), 293-297.

2462. Laslett, Peter. "Under Observation." *New Society*, 42, no. 791
       (1 December 1977), 474-475.

2463. Locke, R. Review of *Discipline and Punish*. *The New York Times
       Book Review*, 83 (26 March 1978), 3ff.

2464. Lucas, Colin. "Power and the Panopticon." *The Times Literary
       Supplement*, no. 3837 (26 September 1975), p. 1090.

2465. McConnell, Frank. Review of *Discipline and Punish*. *The New
       Republic*, 178 (1 April 1978), 32-34.

2466. McHugh, G. Review of *Discipline and Punish*. *New Catholic World*,
       221 (November-December 1978), 283.

2467. Meyer, Philippe. "La Correction paternelle ou l'état, domicile de la famille." *Critique*, 30, no. 343 (December 1975), 1266-1276.

2468. Morris, T. Review of *Discipline and Punish. The Tablet*, 232 (London, 25 March-1 April 1978), 304.

2469. Nemo, Philippe. "D'une prison à l'autre." *Le Nouvel Observateur*, no. 374 (10-16 January 1972), pp. 40-41.

2470. Rothman, D.J. Review of *Discipline and Punish. The New York Times Book Review*, 83 (19 February 1978), 1ff.

2471. Roustang, François. "La Visibilité est un piège." *Les Temps Modernes*, 31, no. 356 (March 1976), 1567-1579.

2472. Russell, George. Review of *Discipline and Punish. Time*, 111 (6 February 1978), 92.

2472a. Shelley, L.I. Review of *Discipline and Punish. American Journal of Sociology*, 84 (May 1979), 1508-1510.

2472b. Singer, R. Review of *Discipline and Punish. Crime and Delinquency* 25 (July 1979), 376-379.

2473. Stinchcomb, J.D. Review of *Discipline and Punish. Christian Science Monitor*, 70 (15 March 1978), 26, 34.

2474. Storr, Anthony. "When Punishment Is Itself a Crime." *The Sunday Times*, no. 8059 (4 December 1977), p. 40.

2475. Tarbet, D.W. Review of *Discipline and Punish. Eighteenth-Century Studies*, 11 (Summer 1978), 509-514.

2476. Versele, S.C. Review of *Surveiller et punir. Revue de l'Institut de Sociologie*, no. 3-4 (Brussels, 1975), pp. 481-482.

2477. Ward, S. Review of *Discipline and Punish. Best Sellers*, 38 (May 1978), 50.

2478. White, H. Review of *Surveiller et punir. American Historical Review*, 82 (June 1977), 605-606.

See also items 2092, 2105, 2132, 2146, and 2200b.

Von der Subversion des Wissens
(item 2000)

2479. Vossenkuhl, W. *Philosophisches Jahrbuch*, 82 (1975), 416-419.

LUCIEN GOLDMANN

PRIMARY SOURCES

1945

*2480. *Mensch, Gemeinschaft und Welt in der Philosophie Immanuel Kants. Studien zur Geschichte der Dialektik.* Zurich-New York: Europa Verlag, 1945. Goldmann's doctoral dissertation in philosophy at the University of Zurich. For trans., see items 2487 (French) and 2696 (English).

2481. "Un Grand polémiste: Karl Krauss." *Lettres*, 3, no. 4 (Geneva, 1945), 166-173. Rpt. in item 2529.

1947

2482. "Marxisme et psychologie. La psychologie de Jean Piaget." *Critique*, 3, no. 13-14 (1947), 115-124. Rpt. in item 2529.

On Piaget's *La Psychologie de l'intelligence.*

2483. "La Philosophie classique et la bourgeoisie occidentale." *La Revue Socialiste: Culture-Doctrine-Action*, n.s. no. 12, (June 1947), pp. 49-64. Rpt. in item 2487.

1948

2484. Translation of *Psychologie des Intelligenz*. By Jean Piaget. Zurich: Rascher Verlag, 1948, 247pp. Originally *Psychologie de l'intelligence.*

2485. "Matérialisme dialectique et histoire de la philosophie." *Revue Philosophique de la France et de l'Etranger*, no. 4-6 (1948), pp. 160-179. Rpt. in item 2529.

2486. "Les Conditions sociales et la vision tragique du monde." In *Echanges Sociologiques*. Ed. Cercle de Sociologie de la Sorbonne. Paris: Centre de Documentation Universitaire, 1948, pp. 81-91.

2487. *La Communauté humaine et l'univers chez Kant*. Paris: Presses Universitaires de France, 1948, 271pp. (Etudes sur la Pensée Dialectique et son Histoire) Author's trans. of item 2480. See also items 2603 and 2696.

Contains: Préface; Introduction; Première Partie: (1) La
Philosophie classique et la bourgeoisie occidentale (item
2483); (2) La Catégorie de la totalité dans la pensée kantienne
et dans la philosophie en général; (3) La Période pré-classique;
Deuxième Partie: (1) La Philosophie critique et ses problèmes;
(2) Que puis-je savoir?; (3) Que dois-je faire?; (4) Qu'ai-je
le droit d'espérer?; Conclusion: Qu'est-ce que l'homme? Kant
et la philosophie contemporaine.

1949

2488.   "Goethe et la révolution française." *Etudes Germaniques*, no.
        2-3 (1949). Rpt. in item 2529.

2489.   Translation, with André Frank, of *Goethe et son époque*. By
        Georg Lukács. Paris: Nagel, 1949, 351pp. (Pensées)

2490.   Translation, with Michel Butor, of *Brève histoire de la litté-
        rature allemande du XVIII*e *siècle à nos jours*. By Georg
        Lukács. Paris: Nagel, 1949, 353pp. (Pensées)

1950

2491.   "Georg Lukács: l'essayiste." *Revue d'Esthétique*, 3 (1950),
        82-95. Rpt. in item 2529.

*2492. "Matérialisme dialectique et histoire de la littérature."
        Revue de Métaphysique et de Morale, 55 (1950), 283-301. Rpt.
        in item 2529. For trans., see items 2579 (German) and 2732
        (English).

2493.   "Pascal et la pensée dialectique." *Empédocle, Revue Littéraire
        Mensuelle*, 2, no. 7 (January 1950), 47-61.

1952

*2494. *Sciences humaines et philosophie*. Paris: Presses Universitaires
        de France, 1952, 147pp. (Nouvelle Encyclopédie Philosophique,
        no. 53) See also item 2593. For trans., see items 2528
        (Spanish), 2546 (Italian), 2601 (Catalonian), 2635 (Spanish),
        2653 (English), 2684 (Portuguese), and 2702 (German). For
        reviews, see items 2967-2969.

        Contains: Introduction, pp. 1-2; (1) La Pensée historique
        et son objet, pp. 3-16; (2) La Méthode en sciences humaines,
        pp. 17-79; (3) Les Grandes Lois de structure, pp. 80-127; (4)
        Expression et forme, pp. 128-136; Appendice, pp. 137-145.

2495.   "Thèses sur l'emploi du concept de 'vision du monde' en histoire
        de la philosophie." In *L'Homme et l'histoire* [Actes du VIe
        Congrès des Sociétés de Philosophie de Langue Française.
        Strasbourg, 10-14 septembre 1952]. Paris: Presses Universi-
        taires de France, 1952, pp. 399-403.

1953

2496.   "Remarques sur la théorie de la connaissance." In *Actes du XIe Congrès International de Philosophie*. Bruxelles: 20-26 août 1953. Vol II: Epistémologie. Amsterdam: North Holland Publishing Company; Louvain: Editions Nauwelaerts, 1953, pp. 90-95.

2497.   "L'Epistémologie de Jean Piaget." *Synthèses*, 7, no. 82 (March 1953), 161-173. Rpt. in item 2529.

2498.   "Remarques sur le Jansénisme: la vision tragique du monde et la noblesse de robe." *Bulletin de la Société d'Etude du XVIIe Siècle*, no. 19 (1953), pp. 23-54. Rpt. as "Vision tragique du monde et nobless de robe" in item 2529.

2499.   "Phèdre," a lecture given at the Ecole de théâtre Jean Deschamps in 1953 and rpt. in item 2529.

1954

2500.   "Au Sujet du 'plan' des *Pensées* de Pascal." *Bulletin de la Société d'Etude du XVIIe Siècle*, no. 23 (1954), pp. 597-604. With Jacques Chevalier.

1955

2501.   "'Port Royal,' d'Henri de Montherlant, mise en scène de Jean Meyer, à la Comédie-Française." *Théâtre Populaire*, no. 11 (January-February 1955), pp. 86-88.

*2502.   *Le Dieu caché. Etude sur la vision tragique dans LES PENSEES de Pascal et dans le théâtre de Racine*. Paris: Gallimard, c. 1955, 1956, 1959, 1976, 451pp. (Bibliothèque des Idées) Thesis presented at the University of Paris. For trans., see items 2547 (Italian), 2578 (English), 2634 (Catalonian or Spanish), 2701 (Italian), and 2718 (German). See also item 2625. For reviews, see items 2914-2923.

1956

*2503.   *Jean Racine, dramaturge*. Paris: L'Arche, 1956, 159pp. (Les Grands Dramaturges, 13) See also items 2666 and 2688. For English trans., see item 2706. For reviews, see items 2933-2935.

        Contains: Dates significatives, pp. 7-9; (1) Structure de la tragédie racinienne, pp. 10-38; (2) Port-Royal, Racine et le Jansénisme, pp. 39-58; (3) L'Homme, pp. 59-84; (4) Evolution du théâtre racinien, pp. 85-147; Bibliographie, pp. 148-150; Répertoire des mises en scène, pp. 151-158.

2504.   Editor of and Preface to *Correspondance de Martin de Barcos, Abbé de Saint-Cyran, avec les abbesses de Port Royal et les*

principaux personnages du groupe janséniste. Paris: Presses
Universitaires de France, 1956, 629pp. Thèse complémentaire
pour le doctorat ès lettres présentée à la Faculté des Lettres
de l'Université de Paris. Volume 4 of the Publications de
l'Institut Français d'Amsterdam.

2505.   "Le 'Pari' est-il écrit 'pour le libertin'?" In *Blaise Pascal.*
L'Homme et l'oeuvre. Paris: Editions de Minuit, 1956. Written
in 1954 and rpt. in item 2529.

2506.   Discussion participant on a paper by Claude Lévi-Strauss in
Sur les rapports entre la mythologie et le rituel (Séance
du 26 mai 1956). *Bulletin de la Société Française de Philos-*
ophie, 50, no. 3 (July-September 1956), 123-124.

2507.   "Bérénice ou le tragique racinien." *Théâtre Populaire*, no. 20
(September 1956), a text read on the Radio-Télévision Fran-
çaise by Sylvia Montfort and later rpt. in item 2529 as
"Bérénice."

1957

2508.   "Philosophie et scientisme." In *Chacun peut-il philosopher?*
Paris: La Nef de Paris Editions, 1957, 24pp. (Cercle Ouvert,
9) By Lucien Goldmann, François Châtelet, Maurice de Gandillac,
Jean Wahl, and Robert Misrahi.

2509.   Discussion participant in *La Mémoire* (Séance du 1er décembre
1956). [*Bulletin de la Société Française de Philosophie*, 50,
no. 4 (1956), 205-206.] Paris: Armand Colin, 1957, pp. 161-
224.

2510.   "'L'Hôtel du libre échange' de Georges Feydeau et Marie
Desvallières, avec la compagnie Grenier-Hussenot, au Théâtre
Marigny." *Théâtre Populaire*, no. 22 (January 1957), p. 87.

2511.   "Un Bilan désabusé. A propos de Fritz Sternberg: *Kapitalismus*
und Sozialismus vor dem Weltgericht; *Marx und die Gegenwart*."
Arguments, 1, no. 2 (February-March 1957).

2512.   Discussion participant in *Descartes*. Paris: Les Editions de
Minuit, 1957, pp. 55, 138-139, 257-259, 270-271, 477.
(Cahiers de Royaumont. Philosophie, no. 11)

2513.   "*Le Dieu caché*, 'La Nouvelle Critique' et le marxisme." *Les*
Temps Modernes, 12, no. 134 (1957), 1617-1627. Rpt. in item
2651 and in item 2665, pp. 475-490.

        Reply to Crouzet's review of item 2502 in *La Nouvelle*
        Critique of November 1956.

2514.   "Propos dialectiques." *Les Temps Modernes*, 13, no. 137-138
(1957), 235-254. Rpt. in item 2529.

        On J.-F. Revel's *Pourquoi des philosophes?* and H. Chambre's
        Le Marxisme en Union Soviétique.

2515. "Propos dialectiques. Y a-t-il une sociologie marxiste?" *Les
       Temps Modernes*, 13, no. 140 (October 1957), 729-751. Rpt.
       in item 2529.

2516. [Réponse à M. Rubel]. *Les Temps Modernes*, 13 (1957), 1141-1144.

       Goldmann's answer to Rubel's article on pp. 1138-1141.

2517. "La Nature de l'oeuvre." *Les Etudes Philosophiques*, 12, no. 3
       (1957), 139-143. Part of a special issue entitled *L'Homme
       et ses oeuvres*, Actes du IXe Congrès des Sociétés de Philos-
       ophie de Langue Française. Rpt. in item 2529.

2518. "A propos du 'Karl Krauss' de W. Kraft." *Allemagne d'Aujourd'hui*,
       no. 2 (1957), rpt. in item 2529.

2519. "A propos de 'La Maison de Bernarda' de F. Garcia Lorca."
       Théâtre Populaire, no. 24 (May 1957). Rpt. in item 2529.

2520. "Quelques remarques sur la philosophie de T.A. Adorno." *Allemagne
       d'Aujourd'hui*, no. 6 (November-December 1957), pp. 94-96.

2521. "Phèdre. Remarques sur la mise en scène." *Bref*, no. 11 (Decem-
       ber 1957). Rpt. in item 2529.

                                 1958

2522. Discussion participant on a paper by Gabriel Marcel in *L'Etre
       devant la pensée interrogative* (Séance du 25 janvier 1958).
       Bulletin de la Société Française de Philosophie, 52, no. 1
       (January-March 1958), 26.

2523. Discussion participant on a paper by Georges Gurvitch in
       Structures sociales et multiplicité du temps (Séance du 31
       janvier 1958). *Bulletin de la Société Française de Philosophie*,
       52, no. 3 (July-December 1958), 130-133.

2524. "Le Matérialisme dialectique est-il une philosophie?" *Revue
       Internationale de Philosophie*, 12, no. 3-4 (1958), 249-264.
       Rpt. in item 2529.

2525. "Propos dialectiques. Morale et droit naturel." *Les Temps
       Modernes*, 13, no. 143-144 (1958), 1453-1469. Rpt. in item
       2529.

       On Pierre Bigo's *Marxisme et humanisme. Introduction à
       l'oeuvre économique de Karl Marx*.

2526. "Problèmes de théorie critique de l'économie." *Les Temps
       Modernes*, 13, no. 147-148 (1958), 2210-2231. Rpt. in item
       2529.

2527. "Faust, de...." *Théâtre Populaire*, 32 (1958), 139-140.

2528.   *Las Ciencias humanas y la filosofía.* Buenos Aires: Ediciones
        Galatea Nueva Visión, 1958, 122pp. Trans. of item 2494.

                                    1959

*2529. *Recherches dialectiques.* Paris: Gallimard, 1959, 356pp.
        (Bibliothèque des Idées) For trans., see items 2560 (Spanish),
        2602 (German), and 2624 (German). For reviews, see items
        2965-2966.

        Contains: I. Problèmes de méthode: items 2524, 2485, 2492,
        2530, 2550, 2482, 2497, and 2517; II. Analyses concrètes: items
        2498, 2505, 2507, 2499, 2521, 2488, 2481, 2518, and 2519; III.
        Chroniques: items 2491, 2514, 2515, 2525, and 2526; and a Post-
        face, pp. 343-353.

2530.   "La Réification." *Les Temps Modernes,* 14, no. 156-157 (1959),
        1433-1474. Rpt. in item 2529. See also item 2642.

2531.   "L'Apport de la pensée marxiste à la critique littéraire."
        Arguments, 3, no. 12-13 (January-March 1959), 44-46.

                                    1960

2532.   "Liberté et valeur." In *Atti del XII Congresso Internazionale
        di Filosofia* (Venezia, 12-18 settembre 1958), *Vol. III:
        Libertà e valore.* Florence: Sansoni, 1960, pp. 183-185.

2533.   Contributor to "Discussioni." In *Atti del XII Congresso Inter-
        nazionale di Filosofia* (Venezia, 12-18 settembre 1958). *Vol.
        II: L'Uomo e la natura. Discorsi della seduta inaugurale.*
        Florence: Sansoni, 1960, pp. 485-511.

2534.   Preface to *Les Origines du socialisme allemand.* By Jean Jaurès.
        Paris: François Maspero, 1960, pp. 11-28.

2535.   "*Phèdre,* de Racine et *Nathan le Sage,* de Lessling, mises en
        scène de H.K. Zeiser et K.H. Stroux, avec le Schauspielhaus
        de Düsseldorf, au Théâtre des Nations." *Théâtre Populaire,*
        no. 38 (1960), pp. 110-111.

2536.   "Etre et dialectique." In *L'Etre* [*Les Etudes Philosophiques,* 15,
        no. 2 (April-June 1960), 161-320]. Paris: Presses Universi-
        taires de France, 1960, pp. 205-212.

2537.   "Jean Jaurès, la question religieuse et le socialisme." *Bulletin
        de la Société d'Etudes Jaurésiennes,* 1, no. 1 (June 1960),
        6-12.

*2538. "Une Pièce réaliste: Le Balcon de Genet." *Les Temps Modernes,*
        15, no. 171 (June 1960), 1885-1896. For German trans., see
        item 2548.

2539. "Sur la peinture de Chagall. Réflexions d'un sociologue."
       Annales. Economies, Sociétés, Civilisations, 15, no. 4
       (July-August 1960), 667-683. Rpt. in item 2665, pp. 415-444.
       Cf. item 2585.

                                 1961

2540. "Civilisation et économie." In *L'Histoire et ses interpréta-
       tions*. Entretiens autour de Arnold Toynbee sous la direction
       de Raymond Aron. Paris-The Hague: Mouton, 1961, pp. 76-90;
       discussion, p. 98. Paper read on Monday, 14 July 1958.

2541. "L'Esthétique du jeune Lukács." *Médiations*, no. 1 (1961),
       pp. 9-21. Rpt. in items 2664 and 2705.

*2542. "Marx, Lukács, Girard et la sociologie du roman." *Médiations*,
       no. 2 (1961), pp. 143-153. Text which served as a basis for
       item 2566, later rpt. in item 2569, pp. 21-57. For Spanish
       trans., see item 2561.

2543. Discussion participant on papers by J.-G. Gurvitch and Ch.
       de Lauwe in *Quel avenir attend l'homme?* Paris: Presses Uni-
       versitaires de France, 1961, pp. 167-168 and 247. At the
       Rencontre internationale de Royaumont, 17-20 May 1961.

2544. "Le Problème du mal. A propos de *Rodogune* et de l'*Annonce faite
       à Marie*." *Médiations*, no. 3 (Fall 1961), pp. 167-175. Rpt.
       in item 2665, pp. 135-151.

       On Claudel.

2545. "La Démocratie économique et la création culturelle." *Revue
       de l'Institut de Sociologie*, 34 (Brussels, 1961), 239-258.
       Paper read at the IIIe Colloque de l'Association Internationale
       des Sociologues de Langue Française, Geneva, 1960.

2546. *Scienze umane e filosofia*. Trans. M. Rago. Milan: G. Feltrinelli,
       1961, 169pp. Trans. of item 2494.

2547. *Pascal e Racine. Studio sulla visione tragica nei Pensieri di
       Pascal e nel teatro di Racine*. Trans. Luciano Amodio and
       Franco Fortini. Milan: Lerici, 1961. Trans. of item 2502.
       See also item 2701.

2548. "*Der Balkon* von Jean Genet--ein realistisches Stück." *Theater
       und Zeit*, 8, nr. 9 (May 1961), 161-167. Trans. of item 2538.

                                 1962

2549. "Les Deux avant-gardes." *Médiations*, no. 4 (Winter 1961-1962),
       pp. 63-83. Rpt. in item 2665, pp. 179-208. Incorporated in
       item 2566.

       On Roger Planchon and Alain Robbe-Grillet.

2550.   "Le Concept de structure significative en histoire de la cul-
        ture." In *Sens et usages du terme structure dans les sciences
        humaines et sociales*. Paris-The Hague: Mouton, 1962. Written
        in 1958. Rpt. in item 2529.

2551.   Discussion participant in *La Philosophie analytique* (Cahiers
        de Royaumont. Philosophie, no. IV). Paris: Editions de Minuit,
        1962, pp. 330-380.

2552.   Study in *Connaissance de Racine*. Ed. Jean-Louis Barrault. Paris:
        Gallimard, 1962.

2553.   "Structure de la tragédie racinienne." In *Le Théâtre tragique*.
        Ed. Jean Jacquot. Paris: C.N.R.S., 1962. A paper read at
        the Colloque d'Anvers, 19-22 June 1959.

2554.   "Problèmes d'une sociologie du roman." *Cahiers Internationaux
        de Sociologie*, nouvelle série, 9e année, 32 (January-June
        1962), 61-72. See also item 2563.

2555.   "Marilyn, ce négatif de notre temps." *France-Observateur*, no.
        644 (6 September 1962), pp. 21-22.

2556.   "Introduction aux premiers écrits de Georges Lukács." *Les
        Temps Modernes*, 18, no. 195 (August 1962), 254-280. Rpt.
        as "Les Ecrits du jeune Lukács," postface to *La Théorie du
        roman*. By G. Lukács. Paris: Gonthier, 1963. See item 2559.

2557.   "La Place d'*Andromaque* dans l'oeuvre de Racine." *Les Cahiers
        de la Compagnie Madeleine Renaud--Jean-Louis Barrault*, no.
        40 (November 1962), pp. 107-119.

2558.   "Diderot, la pensée des 'Lumières' et la dialectique." *Médecine
        de France*, no. 136 (1962), pp. 33-40.

2559.   Introduction to *Teoria del romanzo. Saggio storico-filosofico
        sulle forme della grande epica*. By György Lukács. Trans.
        F. Saba Sardi. Milan: Sugar Editore, 1962. See item 2556.

2560.   *Investigaciones dialécticas*. Trans. Eduardo Vásquez. Caracas:
        Ediciones del Instituto de Filosofía, Facultad de Humanidades
        y Educación, Universidad Central de Venezuela, 1962. Trans.
        of item 2529.

2561.   "Marx, Lukács, Girard y la sociología de la novela." Trans.
        Guillermo Sucre. *Cultura Universitaria*, no. 78-79 (Caracas,
        1962), pp. 13-25. Trans. of item 2542.

1963

2562.   "Lumières et dialectique." In *Utopies et institutions au XVIIIe
        siècle: le pragmatisme des Lumières*. Ed. Pierre Francastel.
        Paris-The Hague: Mouton, 1963, pp. 305-314. Written in June
        1959, this paper was read at a colloquium held in Nancy, 23-
        26 June 1959.

2563. "Introduction aux problèmes d'une sociologie du roman." In
       Problèmes d'une sociologie du roman. Nouveau roman et réalité.
       [*Revue de l'Institut de Sociologie*, 36, no. 2 (1963), 225-
       467.] Brussels: Les Editions de l'Institut de Sociologie,
       Université Libre de Bruxelles, 1963, pp. 225-242. Rpt. in
       item 2564; item 2569, pp. 13-37; item 2581, pp. 19-57. See
       also item 2554.

2564. *Introduction aux problèmes d'une sociologie du roman.* Brussels:
       Université Libre de Bruxelles, 1963, pp. 225-242. Rpts.,
       under separate cover, item 2563.

2565. "Introduction à une étude structurale des romans de Malraux."
       In *Problèmes d'une sociologie du roman. Nouveau roman et
       réalité.* [*Revue de l'Institut de Sociologie*, 36, no. 2 (1963),
       225-467.] Brussels: Les Editions de l'Institut de Sociologie,
       Université Libre de Bruxelles, 1963, pp. 285-392. Rpt. in
       item 2569, pp. 39-180; item 2581, pp. 59-277; and item 2672.
       See also item 2568.

*2566. "Nouveau roman et réalité." In *Problèmes d'une sociologie du
       roman. Nouveau roman et réalité.* [*Revue de l'Institut de
       Sociologie*, 36, no. 2 (1963), 225-467.] Brussels: Les Editions
       de l'Institut de Sociologie, Université Libre de Bruxelles,
       1963, pp. 449-467. Rpt. in item 2569, pp. 181-209; item 2581,
       pp. 279-324. Cf. items 2542, 2549 and 2703. For Norwegian
       trans., see item 2580.

2567. Discussion participant in *Les Sciences humaines et la philosophie*
       (Séance du 24 novembre 1962). [*Bulletin de la Société Fran-
       çaise de Philosophie*, 57, no. 3 (1963), 92-95.] Paris: Armand
       Colin, 1963, pp. 65-116.

2568. "L'Individu, l'action et la mort dans *Les Conquérants* de Mal-
       raux." *Médiations*, no. 6 (Summer 1963), pp. 69-94. See also
       item 2565.

                                    1964

*2569. *Pour une sociologie du roman.* Paris: Gallimard, 1964, 229pp.
       (Bibliothèque des Idées, no. 93) Contains items 2563 (item
       2564), 2565, 2566, and "La Méthode structuraliste génétique
       en histoire de la littérature," pp. 211-229, rpt. in item
       2581, pp. 335-372. Rpt. in item 2581. Cf. item 2604. For
       trans., see items 2622 (Italian), 2685 (German), 2731
       (English), and 2733 (Spanish). For reviews, see items 2951-
       2964.

2570. Preface to *L'Abbé Le Roy et ses amis. Essai sur le jansénisme
       extrémiste intramondain.* By Gérard Namer. Paris: Service
       d'Edition et de Vente des Publications de l'Education
       Nationale, 1964, pp. 7-8.

2571.   "Messages de France: Marcel Bataillon, ..., Lucien Goldmann,
        ..., Paul Ricoeur." In *Hommage à Gaston Berger*. Gap: Editions
        Ophrys, 1964, pp. 113-131. (Publications de la Faculté des
        Lettres d'Aix-en-Provence, 42)

2572.   Discussion participant in *Littérature et stylistique--Les
        Visages de la critique depuis 1920-Molière. Cahiers de
        l'Association Internationale des Etudes Françaises*, no. 16
        (March 1964), pp. 289 and 294. XVᵉ Congrès de l'Association
        Internationale des Etudes Françaises, Collège de France,
        25-27 July 1963.

2573.   "A propos du 'Le Mariage' de Gombrowicz." *France-Observateur*,
        no. 718 (6 February 1964), p. 1.

2574.   "Les Deux critiques." *Le Monde*, no. 5984 (11 April 1964), p. 13.

        On Barthes's *Essais critiques*.

2575.   "L'*Immortelle* est de retour." *France Observateur*, 15, no. 751
        (24 September 1964), 15-16. With Anne Olivier. Rpt. in item
        2581, pp. 325-333.

        On Robbe-Grillet.

*2576. "Socialisme et humanisme." *Diogène*, no. 46 (1964), pp. 88-107.
        For English trans., see item 2577. Rpt. in item 2664.

2577.   "Socialism and Humanism." *Diogenes*, no. 46 (Summer 1964), pp.
        82-102. Trans. of item 2576.

2578.   *The Hidden God. A Study of the Tragic Vision in the Pensees of
        Pascal and the Tragedies of Racine*. Trans. Philip Thody. New
        York: Humanities Press; London: Routledge and Kegan Paul,
        1964. Trans. of item 2502.

        Pascal and Racine are regarded as the key figures in the
        politico-theological crisis which convulsed mid-17th century
        France: a crisis involving (1) the disintegration of the tra-
        ditional social order; (2) the dissolution of the Thomist world
        view; and (3) certain mundane conflicts between the Court and
        the social stratum to which Pascal and Racine belonged, the
        noblesse de la robe. Goldmann concludes that Jansenism should
        be understood as the ideology of the *noblesse de robe* in its
        struggle against the Court and the Jesuits.

2579.   "Dialektischer Materialismus und Literaturgeschichte." *Die
        Neue Rundschau*, 75. Jahrgang, Heft 2 (1964), 214-229. Trans.
        of item 2492.

2580.   "Ny Roman og virkelighet." Trans. Storm Michael Wiik. *Vinduet*,
        18. årgang, nr. 2 (1964), 116-126. Trans. of item 2566.

1965

*2581. *Pour une sociologie du roman*. Revised and enlarged ed. Paris:
        Gallimard, 1965 and 1970, 373pp. (Idées, no. 93) Rpts. item
        2569 with three notes and item 2575. For trans., see items
        2685 (German), 2731 (English), and 2733 (Spanish).

2582.   "L'Importance du concept de conscience possible pour la communi-
        cation." In *Le Concept d'information dans la science con-
        temporaine* (Cahiers de Royaumont. Information et Cyberné-
        tique). Paris: Gauthier-Villars; Les Editions de Minuit, 1965,
        pp. 47-57. Rpt. in item 2687.

2583.   Discussion participant on "L'Homme et la machine." By Norbert
        Wiener. In *Le Concept d'information dans la science contempo-
        raine* (Cahiers de Royaumont. Information et Cybernétique).
        Paris: Gauthier-Villars; Les Editions de Minuit, 1965, pp.
        106-132.

*2584. "Introduction générale." In *Entretiens sur les notions de
        "genèse" et de "structure."* (Congrès, Centre Culturel Inter-
        national de Cerisy-la-Salle, juillet-août 1959) Ed. Maurice
        de Gandillac, Lucien Goldmann and Jean Piaget. Paris-The
        Hague: Mouton, 1965, pp. 7-16. Rpt. in item 2664 as "Genèse
        et structure." For Spanish trans., see item 2592.

*2585. "A propos de quelques réflexions structuralistes sur le peintre
        Chagall." In *Entretiens sur les notions de "genèse" et de
        "structure."* (Congrès, Centre Culturel International de
        Cerisy-la-Salle, juillet-août 1959) Ed. Maurice de Gandillac,
        Lucien Goldmann and Jean Piaget. Paris-The Hague: Mouton,
        1965, pp. 161-165. Cf. item 2539. For Spanish trans., see
        item 2660.

2586.   "Les Interdépendances entre la société industrielle et la
        création littéraire." UNESCO, 1965. Unpublished at this time,
        but later rpt. in item 2687.

*2587. "Valéry et la dialectique. A propos de *Mon Faust*." *Médecine
        de France*, no. 163 (1965), pp. 33-40. Rpt. in item 2665, pp.
        153-169. For Italian trans., see item 2623.

2588.   "Ces Intellectuels sans attache--A propos de Karl Korsch:
        Marxisme et philosophie." *Le Nouvel Observateur*, n.s. no. 17
        (11 March 1965), p. 26.

*2589. "Valéry: *Monsieur Teste*." Conference given at the O.R.T.F.,
        September 1965 and rpt. in item 2665, pp. 171-178. For
        Italian trans., see item 2623. Also appears in item 2616.

2590.   "Le Livre et la lecture dans les sociétés industrielles modernes."
        Le Drapeau (Montreal, October 1965).

2591.   "To the Memory of Paul Alexander Baran. A Collective Portrait."
        Monthly Review, 16, no. 11 (March 1965).

A short death notice dedicated to the memory of this Marxist
thinker who died in 1964.

2592. "Génesis y estructura." Trans. Alfredo Chacon. *Cultura Univer-
       sitaria*, no. 89 (Caracas, 1965), pp. 189-198. Trans. of item
       2584.

                                    1966

*2593. *Sciences humaines et philosophie*. Paris: Gonthier, 1966, 151pp.;
        1971, 170pp. (Médiations, 46) New edition of item 2494 with
        a new preface dedicated to the memory of Lucien Sebag. For
        English trans., see item 2653. The 1971 edition also contains
        "Structuralisme et création littéraire," pp. 151-165 and a
        short biography established by Goldmann's wife Annie, p. 167.

2594. "Jean Piaget et la philosophie." In *Jean Piaget et les sciences
       sociales. A l'occasion de son 70e anniversaire. [Cahiers
       Vilfredo Pareto*, no. 10 (November 1966)] Geneva: Librairie
       Droz, 1966, pp. 5-23. Cf. items 2724 and 2740. See also item
       2716.

2595. "Les Rapports de la pensée de Georges Lukács avec l'oeuvre de
       Kierkegaard." In *Kierkegaard vivant*. (Colloque organisé par
       l'UNESCO à Paris du 21 au 23 avril 1964) Paris: Gallimard,
       1966, pp. 125-164. (Idées, 106)

2596. "Sur le problème de l'objectivité en sciences sociales." In
       *Psychologie et épistémologie génétique. Thèmes piagétiens.
       Hommage à Jean Piaget avec une bibliographie complète de ses
       oeuvres*. Paris: Dunod, 1966, 421pp. (Sciences du Comporte-
       ment, 1)

2597. Discussion participant in *La Littérature à l'heure du livre de
       poche*. (Une table ronde du Centre du Livre de Masse dans le
       cadre de la Semaine de Recherche et d'Action culturelle de
       Bordeaux, 26 octobre 1965) Bordeaux: Sobodi, 1966.

*2598. "Le Théâtre de Genet. Essai d'étude sociologique." Conference
        given at the Westdeutscher Rundfunk, Cologne, 1966 and rpt.
        in item 2665, pp. 299-339 and item 2667, pp. 9-34. Cf. items
        2599 and 2607. For trans., see items 2632 (English), 2636
        (Spanish), and 2682 (English). See also item 2646.

        On the dialectic understood as genetic structuralism.

2599. "Le Théâtre de Genet et ses études sociologiques." *Cahiers de
       la Compagnie Madeleine Renaud--Jean-Louis Barrault*, no. 57
       (November 1966), pp. 90-125. Cf. item 2598.

2600. "Structuralisme, marxisme, existentialisme." *L'Homme et la
       Société*, no. 2 (October-December 1966), pp. 105-124.

       Rpts., almost totally, an interview given to Ilija Bojovic
       of the Belgrade radio-television, a Serbo-Croatian trans.
       of which was to appear in *Socijalism*, no. 9 (Belgrade, September

1966) and a Slovenian trans. of which was to appear in *Odjek*,
no. 21 (Sarajevo, 1 November 1966).

2601. *Ciències humanes i filosofía*. Trans. Augus Gil. Barcelona:
Edicions 62, 1966, 45pp. Trans. of item 2494.

2602. *Dialektische Untersuchungen*. Trans. Ingrid Peters and Gisela
Schöning. Neuwied-Berlin: Luchterhand, 1966. Trans. of item
2529. See also item 2624.

1967

*2603. *Introduction à la philosophie de Kant*. Paris: Gallimard, 1967,
311pp. (Idées, 146) A new edition of item 2487 with a new
preface dated May 1967 and the preface from the 1948 edition.
For trans., see items 2480 (German), 2707 (Italian), and
2725 (Spanish). For reviews, see items 2924-2932.

*2604. "Le Structuralisme génétique en sociologie de la littérature."
In *Littérature et société. Problèmes de méthodologie en
sociologie de la littérature*. Colloque organisé conjointement
par l'Institut de Sociologie de l'Université Libre de Bruxelles
et l'Ecole Pratique des Hautes Etudes (6e section) de Paris
du 21 au 23 mai 1964. Brussels: Editions de l'Institut de
Sociologie, Université Libre de Bruxelles, 1967, pp. 195-
211 and debate, pp. 211-222. Cf. item 2569. For Catalonian
or Spanish trans., see item 2661.

2605. "Conditions de l'interprétation dialectique." In *L'Ambivalence
dans la culture arabe*. Ed. Jean-Paul Charnay. Paris: Anthropos,
1967, pp. 356-358.

*2606. "Epistémologie de la sociologie." In *Logique et connaissance
scientifique*. Ed. Jean Piaget. Paris: Gallimard, Encyclopédie
de la Pléiade, 1967, pp. 992-1016. For English trans., see
item 2738.

The principles of dialectical sociology generalized in genetic
structuralism assume the possibility of conceptualizing and
integrating genesis into the process of scientific knowledge,
not by studying isolated facts but by studying the processes
of structuration.

2607. "Le Théâtre de Genet. Essai d'étude sociologique." In *Contributions à la sociologie de la connaissance*. Paris: Anthropos,
1967, pp. 141-154. Cf. item 2598.

2608. "Actualité de la pensée de Karl Marx." *L'Homme et la Société*,
no. 4 (April-June 1967), pp. 37-48.

2609. Participant in the debate on the "Sociologie de la 'construction nationale' dans les Nouveaux Etats." (VIe Colloque
de l'Association Internationale des Sociologues de Langue
Française, Royaumont, 28-30 octobre 1965) *Revue de l'Institut
de Sociologie*, no. 2-3 (Brussels, 1967), pp. 558-561.

2610. "Micro-structures dans les vingt-cinq premières répliques des
       Nègres de Jean Genet." *Modern Language Notes*, 82, no. 5
       (December 1967), 531-548. Rpt. in item 2665, pp. 341-367 and
       item 2667, pp. 35-52.

       Written with others as part of a team effort of the Centre
       de Sociologie de la Littérature at the Université Libre de
       Bruxelles. A revised version was published in the *Revue de
       l'Institut de Sociologie*, no. 3 (1969), pp. 363-380.

2611. "La Pensée des 'Lumières.'" *Annales. Economies, Sociétés,
       Civilisations*, 22 (1967), 752-779. A partial trans. of item
       2637, later rpt. in item 2665.

2612. "Possibilités d'action culturelle à travers les mass-media."
       Paper read at the Séminaire International "Mass-media et
       création imaginaire" sous le patronage de l'Institut de
       Sociologie de l'Art (Faculté des Lettres de Tours) et l'Asso-
       ciation Internationale pour la Liberté de la Culture, Fondation
       CINI, Venise, octobre 1967. Rpt. in item 2687.

2613. "La Sociologie de la littérature. Situation actuelle et pro-
       blèmes de méthode." *Revue Internationale des Sciences Sociales*,
       19, no. 4 (1967), 531-534. Rpt. in item 2664. Cf. item 2619.

*2614. "Le Sujet de la création culturelle." *L'Homme et la Société*,
       no. 6 (1967), pp. 3-16. Rpt. in item 2664, item 2669, pp.
       193-211 and in *Revue de Sociologie* (Université de Montréal,
       1967). For English trans., see item 2655.

*2615. "Le Théâtre de Gombrowicz." *Paragone: Letteratura*, nuova serie,
       18, no. 212/32 (October 1967), 3-20. Rpt. in item 2665, pp.
       265-289. For English trans., see item 2681.

2616. "Valéry: Monsieur Teste." In *Critical Spirit, Essays in Honor
       of Herbert Marcuse*. Ed. Kurt H. Wolff and Barrington Moore,
       Jr. Boston: Beacon Press, 1967. Rpts. item 2589. Also rpt.
       in item 2665.

2617. "The World of Genet, Sartre and Gombrowicz." In *The Literature
       of the Western World*. London: Aldus Book Ltd., 1967?.

2618. "Ideology and Writing." *The Times Literary Supplement*, no.
       3422 (28 September 1967), pp. 903-905.

2619. "Sociology of Literature: Status and Problems of Method."
       International Social Science Journal, 19, no. 4 (1967),
       493-516. Cf. item 2613.

2620. *Dialéctica e cultura*. Trans. Luiz Fernando Cardoso. Rio de
       Janeiro: Ed. Paz e Terra, 1967. For review, see item 2913.

2621. *Pascal*. Trans. Lisa Baruffi. Milan: Compagnia Edizioni Inter-
       nazionali, 1967. (I Protagonisti, VI)

2622. *Per una sociologia del romanzo.* Trans. G. Buzzi. Milan: V.
       Bompiani, 1967. Trans. of item 2569.

2623. *L'Illuminismo e la societa moderna. Storia e funzione attuale
       dei valori di "libertà," "eguaglianza," "tolleranza."* Trans.
       Gian Giacomo Cagua. Turin: G. Einaudi, 1967. Trans. of "Die
       Aufklärung und die moderne Gesellschaft," item 2587 and item
       2589. Cf. item 2637.

2624. *Weltflucht und Politik. Dialektische Studien zu Pascal und
       Racine.* Neuwied-Berlin: Luchterhand, 1967. A partial trans.
       of item 2529 (items 2498, 2505 and 2499 or 2521). See also
       item 2602.

       Contains: Pascal und Port Royal; Bemerkungen über den Jansen-
       ismus: Tragische Weltsicht und Amtsadel; Ist die Wette "für
       den Freigeist" geschrieben?; Phaidra.

                                  1968

2625. Participant in the discussion on "Hérésie et société au XVIIe
       siècle: le cas janséniste." In *Hérésies et sociétés dans
       l'Europe pré-industrielle--XIe-XVIIIe siècles.* (Communications
       et débats du Colloque de Royaumont, 27-30 mai 1962) Ed.
       Jacques Le Goff. Paris-The Hague: Mouton, 1968, 484pp.
       (Civilisations et Société, 1)

       Goldmann's remarks (pp. 341-342) do not appear in this volume,
       but there is a note indicating that they were based on chap-
       ters V ("Visions du monde et classes sociales," pp. 97-114)
       and VI (Jansénisme et noblesse de robe," pp. 115-156) of the
       second part of his *Le Dieu caché* (item 2502). The discussion
       which followed his remarks is included.

2626. Participant in the debate on "Structure et histoire." In *Raison
       Présente*, no. 7 (July-September 1968), pp. 50-53. See also
       item 2671.

2627. Participant in the discussion on "La Différance." By Jacques
       Derrida. *Bulletin de la Société Française de Philosophie*
       (séance du 27 janvier 1968), 62, no. 3 (July-September 1968),
       101-120.

2628. "Les Sciences humaines doivent-elles intégrer la philosophie?"
       *Cahiers du Centre Economique et Social de Perfectionnement
       des Cadres, Fédération Nationale des Syndicats d'Ingénieurs
       et des Cadres supérieurs*, 1968 (3e trimestre), pp. 9-32. A
       conference given by Goldmann at the 16th session, second
       cycle on "Recherche et science de l'homme."

2629. "Pourquoi les étudiants?" *L'Homme et la Société*, no. 8 (1968),
       pp. 3-7. Part of a round table of the same title held on 23
       May 1968.

2630. "Débat sur l'autogestion." In *Autogestion, études, débats, documents,* cahier no. 7 (Paris, December 1968), pp. 57-61 and 64-71. The main passages of remarks by Goldmann and Serge Mallet at a round table organized by *Le Nouvel Observateur,* 6 July 1968.

2631. "La Croyance en Dieu." Conversation with Michèle Georges in *L'Express,* no. 892 (12 August 1968).

2632. "The Theatre of Genet: A Sociological Study." Ed. R. Schechner. Trans. P. Dreyfus. *Drama Review,* 12, no. 2 (Winter 1968), 51-61. Trans. of item 2598. Cf. item 2680.

2633. "La Denuncia sociologica e culturale." Written in 1967, edited by B. Navelet from a recording of Goldmann's conference at La Biennale di Venezia, 1968: *Participazione, denuncia esorcismo nel teatro d'oggi.* Italian trans. by Ernesto Rubin de Cervin.

2634. *El Hombre y el absoluto. "Le Dieu caché."* Trans. Juan Ramón Capella. Barcelona: Ed. Península, 1968. Trans. of item 2502.

2635. *Las Ciencias humanas y la filosofía.* Trans. Josefina Martínez Alinari. Buenos Aires: Ediciones Nueva Visión, 1968, 1970, 120pp. Trans. of item 2494.

2636. *El Teatro de Jean Genet: ensayo de estudio sociológico.* Caracas: Monte Avila Editores, 1968. Trans. of item 2598.

*2637. *Der christliche Bürger und die Aufklärung.* Neuwied: Hermann Luchterhand Verlag, 1968. See item 2611. For French trans. by Irene Petit, see item 2665, pp. 1-133. For English trans., see item 2714. See also items 2661 and 2623. For reviews, see items 2896-2907.

1969

2638. "Réflexions sur la pensée de Herbert Marcuse." In *Marcuse, cet inconnu.* [*La Nef,* no. 36 (January-March 1969)] Paris: J. Tallandier, 1969. Rpt. in item 2664. Cf. items 2663 and 2700.

2639. *Qu'est-ce qu'un auteur?* Paris: Armand Colin, 1969. With Michel Foucault, Jacques Lacan, et al. Rpt. from the *Bulletin de la Société Française de Philosophie,* 63, no. 3 (1969), which was the February 22, 1969 meeting.

2640. "Idéologie et marxisme." In *Le Centenaire du CAPITAL. Exposés et entretiens sur le marxisme.* Paris-The Hague: Mouton, 1969, pp. 297-341. Dated 19 July 1967.

2641. "La Révolte des lettres et des arts dans les civilisations avancées." In *Liberté et organisation dans le monde actuel.* By J. de Bourbon-Busset, et al. Brussels: Desclée de Brouwer, 1969, pp. 245-279. Dated 1968. Rpt. in item 2687.

2642. "Premessa." *Ideologie*, no. 8 (1969), pp. 122-125. A previously
       unpublished preface, dated April 1969, to "La Réification,"
       an article which appeared in items 2530 and 2529. Trans. by
       Giusi Oddo.

2643. "Le Théâtre de Genet: Essai d'étude sociologique (1966)."
       Revue de l'Institut de Sociologie (issue entitled "Sociologie
       de la littérature: recherches récentes et discussions"), no.
       3 (1969), pp. 337-362. Rpt. in item 2667. See also item 2598.

2644. Co-author of "Eloges III de Saint-John Perse." *Revue de l'Insti-
       tut de Sociologie* (issue entitled "Sociologie de la littéra-
       ture: recherches récentes et discussions"), no. 3 (1969),
       pp. 399-408. Rpt. in item 2665, pp. 369-379 and item 2667,
       pp. 53-59.

2645. "*La Gloire des Rois* de Saint-John Perse." *Revue de l'Institut
       de Sociologie* (issue entitled "Sociologie de la littérature:
       recherches récentes et discussions"), no. 3 (1969), pp.
       389-397. Rpt. in item 2665, pp. 381-392 and item 2667, pp.
       61-80.

2646. "Notes sur quatre films de Godard, Buñuel, et Pasolini." *Revue
       de l'Institut de Sociologie* (issue entitled "Sociologie de
       la littérature: recherches récentes et discussions"), no. 3
       (1969), pp. 475-477. Rpt. in item 2667, pp. 147-149.

2647. "Les Chats de Baudelaire." *Revue de l'Institut de Sociologie*
       (issue entitled "Sociologie de la littérature: recherches
       récentes et discussions"), no. 3 (1969), pp. 409-425. With
       Norbert Peters. Rpt. in item 2665, pp. 393-399, and in item
       2667.

2648. "Note sur deux romans de Marie-Claire Blais." *Revue de l'Insti-
       tut de Sociologie* (issue entitled "Sociologie de la littéra-
       ture: recherches récentes et discussions"), no. 3 (1969),
       pp. 515-523. Rpt. in item 2665, pp. 401-414 and item 2667,
       pp. 187-195.

2649. "Réponse à MM. Elsberg et Jones." *Revue de l'Institut de Soci-
       ologie* (issue entitled "Sociologie de la littérature: re-
       cherches récentes et discussions"), no. 3 (1969), pp. 539-
       551. Rpt. in item 2665, pp. 445-465 and item 2667, pp. 211-
       223.

2650. "Réponse à MM. Picard et Daix." *Revue de l'Institut de Sociologie*
       (issue entitled "Sociologie de la littérature: recherches
       récentes et discussions"), no. 3 (1969), pp. 553-557. Rpt.
       in item 2665, pp. 467-473 and item 2667, pp. 225-229.

2651. "Le Dieu caché, la 'Nouvelle Critique' et le marxisme." *Revue
       de l'Institut de Sociologie* (issue entitled "Sociologie de
       la littérature: recherches récentes et discussions"), no. 3
       (1969), pp. 559-568. Rpts. item 2513; see also item 2667,
       pp. 231-240.

2652. "La Mort d'Adorno." *La Quinzaine Littéraire*, no. 78 (1-15
      September 1969), pp. 25-26.

2653. *The Human Sciences and Philosophy*. Trans. Hayden V. White and
      Robert Anchor. London: Jonathan Cape, 1969. Trans. of item
      2593. Also contains a general editor's note, a selected
      bibliography and a note on the author.

2654. "Criticism and Dogmatism in Literature." In *The Dialectics of
      Libération*. London: Penguin Books, 1969. English trans. of
      "Critique et dogmatisme dans la création littéraire" by
      Ilona Halberstadt, rpt. in item 2664.

2655. "The Subject of the Cultural Creation." In *Boston Studies in
      the Philosophy of Science, IV. Proceedings of the Boston
      Colloquium for the Philosophy of Science, 1966*. Ed. Robert
      S. Cohen and M.W. Wartofsky. Dordrecht: D. Reidel; New York:
      Humanities Press, 1969, pp. 241-260. Trans. of item 2614.

2656. *L'Ideologia tedesca e le Tesi su Feuerbach*. Trans. Nicola De
      Vito. Rome: Samonà e Savelli, 1969. On Marx's *Die deutsche
      Ideologie* and *Thesen über Feuerbach*. See also item 2664.

2657. Editor of the catalogue for the exhibit by Antonio Bueno and
      Silvio Loffredo at the Galerie G 30, Paris. *Eco d'Arte*,
      no. 6 (June 1969).

2658. *Litteratura y sociedad. Problemas de metodología en sociología
      de la litteratura*. Trans. R. de la Iglesia. Barcelona: M.
      Roca, 1969. With Roland Barthes, Henri Lefèbvre, et al.
      Trans. of item 2604.

2659. *Marxismo, dialéctica y estructuralismo*. Buenos Aires: Ediciones
      Calden, 1969.

2660. *Las Nociones de estructura y génesis*. Buenos Aires: Editorial
      Protea, 1969. With Maurice Patronnier de Gandillac, Jean
      Piaget, et al. Trans. of item 2585.

2661. *La Ilustración y la sociedad actual*. Trans. Julieta Fombona.
      Caracas: Monte Avila, 1969. Trans. of item 2637.

2662. "El Poeta del sub-proletariado." *Primer Acto*, no. 113 (October
      1969), pp. 20-24. On Jean Genet.

2663. "Das Denken Herbert Marcuses." *Soziale Welt*, 20, no. 3 (1969),
      pp. 257-273. Cf. items 2638 and 2700.

1970

*2664. *Marxisme et sciences humaines*. Paris: Gallimard, 1970, 361pp.
       (Folio/Idées, no. 228, double volume) For trans., see items
       2715 (Italian) and 2735 (Spanish). For reviews, see items
       2947-2950.

Contains: Préface (September 1970); items 2584; 2654; 2613; 2614; "Conscience réelle et conscience possible. Conscience adequate et fausse conscience" (paper read at the IVe Congrès Mondial de Sociologie, 1959); "Philosophie et sociologie dans l'oeuvre du jeune Marx" (previously published in *Annali dell'Istituto Giangiacomo Feltrinelli*, 7 [Milan, 1964-1965]; "L'Idéologie allemande et les Thèses sur Feuerbach" (previously published in *L'Homme et la Société*, no. 7 (1968) and in item 2656); "Economie et sociologie: à propos du 'Traité d'Economie politique' d'Oscar Lange" (previously published in *L'Homme et la Société*, no. 14 [1969]; "Pour une approche marxiste des études sur le marxisme" (previously published in *Annales. Economies, Sociétés, Civilisations*, no. 1 [1963]; item 2541; "Jean-Paul Sartre: question de méthode" (previously published in *L'Année Sociologique*, 1961); item 2638; item 2576; "De la rigueur et de l'imagination dans la pensée socialiste" (previously published in *Praxis*, no. 2-3 [1965]; and item 2677.

2665. *Structures mentales et création culturelle*. Paris: Editions Anthropos, 1970, 493pp. (Sociologie et Connaissance) See also items 2667 and 2719. Contains items 2637, 2544, 2587, 2589, 2549, 2673, 2615, 2674, 2598, 2610, 2644, 2645, 2647, 2648, 2539, 2649, 2650, and 2513. For reviews, see items 2746 and 2756.

2666. *Racine: essai*. Paris: L'Arche, 1970, 134pp. A new edition of item 2503 without bibliography and the Répertoire de mises en scène. (Travaux, 2) Cf. item 2688. For reviews, see items 2933-2935.

*2667. Contributor to *Sociologie et littérature. Recherches récentes et discussions*. Brussels: Editions de l'Institut de Sociologie, Université Libre de Bruxelles, 1970. See also item 2665. Rpts. items 2598, 2610, 2643, 2644, 2645, 2646, 2647, 2648, 2649, 2650, and 2651 (item 2513). For trans., see items 2709 (Rumanian), 2721 (Italian), and 2726 (Spanish).

2668. Contributor to *Pensée dialectique et sujet transindividuel* (Séance du 28 février 1970). [*Bulletin de la Société Française de Philosophie*, 64, no. 3 (1970)] Paris: Armand Colin, 1970, pp. 73-120. Rpt. in item 2687.

2669. *Critique sociologique et critique psychanalytique*. Brussels: Editions de l'Institut de Sociologie, Université Libre de Bruxelles, 1970. Contains a rpt. of item 2614, which is also rpt. in 2664.

2670. Preface to *La Dialectique de l'objet économique*. By Fernand Dumont. Paris: Editions Anthropos, 1970, pp. vii-xiv.

2671. "Structure sociale et conscience collective des structures." In *Structuralisme et marxisme*. Paris: Union Générale d'Editions, 1970. (10/18, no. 485 & 486) Previously published in item 2626.

Part of a colloquium organized by *Raison Présente* and directed
by Victor Leduc. February 23, 1968 was devoted to "Structure
sociale et histoire," and Goldmann's remarks may be found on
pp. 145-146, 156, 174-175, 193-194, 197-198, and 200-204.

2672. "Introduction à une étude structurale des romans de Malraux."
       In *Les Critiques de notre temps et Malraux*. Ed. Pol Gaillard.
       Paris: Editions Garnier Frères, 1970, pp. 159-161. Rpts. item
       2565.

2673. "Problèmes philosophiques et politiques dans le théâtre de
       Jean-Paul Sartre. L'Itinéraire d'un penseur." *L'Homme et la
       Société*, no. 17 (July-September 1970), pp. 5-34. Excerpted
       from item 2665, pp. 209-264. Cf. item 2683.

*2674. "A propos d'*Opérette* de Gombrowicz." *La Quinzaine Littéraire*,
       no. 88 (1-15 February 1970), pp. 21-22. Rpt. in item 2665,
       pp. 291-297. For English trans., see item 2682.

2675. "La Théorie," conversation with Brigitte Devismes. *VH 101*, no.
       2 (Summer 1970).

2676. "Interview sur le structuralisme pour la radio finlandaise."
       January, 1970.

*2677. "Pouvoir et humanisme." *Praxis*, 1970, pp. 24-44. Rpt. in item
       2664. For English trans., see items 2697, 2720 and 2744.

2678. "Structuralisme génétique et analyse stylistique." In *Linguaggi
       nella societa nella technica*. Milan: Edizioni di Comunità,
       1970, pp. 143-161.

       Includes a discussion of item 2644.

2679. "Structure: Human Reality and Methodological Concept." In *The
       Language of Criticism and the Science of Man. The Structuralist
       Controversy*. Ed. Richard Macksey and Eugenio U. Donato.
       Baltimore, Md.: Johns Hopkins Press, 1970, pp. 98-110. The
       French original is still unpublished.

2680. "The Theater of Genet: A Sociological Study." In *The Theater
       of Jean Genet. A Casebook*. By Richard N. Coe. New York: Grove
       Press, 1970, pp. 220-238. Trans. of item 2598. Cf. item 2632.

2681. "Theatre of Gombrowicz." Trans. P. Dreyfus. *Drama Review*, 14,
       no. 3 (1970), 102-112. Trans. of item 2615, rpt. in item 2665.

2682. "Notes on Operetta." Trans. S. Mac Donald. *Drama Review*, 14,
       no. 3 (1970), 113-115. Trans. of item 2674, rpt. in item 2665.

2683. "The Theatre of Sartre." *Drama Review*, 15, no. 1 (Fall 1970),
       102-119. Cf. item 2673.

2684. *Ciências humanas e filosofia. O que é filosofia*. Trans. Lupe
       Cotrim Garaude and José Arthur Giannotti. São Paulo: Difusão
       Européia do Livro, 1970. Trans. of item 2494.

2685. *Soziologie des modernen Romans*. Trans. Lucien Goldmann and
       Ingeborg Fleischhauer. Neuwied-Berlin: Luchterhand, c. 1970.
       Trans. of item 2581. Cf. item 2710.

2686. *Dialektiek en maatschappijkritiek*. Meppel: Boom, 1970. With
       G. Harmsen, J. van Santen and H. Schweppenhäuser. A publica-
       tion of the first part of a congress of this title held in
       Nijmegen, 6-8 February 1969.

1971

*2687. *La Création culturelle dans la société moderne*. Paris: Denoël-
       Gonthier, 1971, 184pp. (Bibliothèque Médiations, 84) A
       posthumous publication which rpts. items 2582, pp. 7-24;
       2612, pp. 25-45; 2641, pp. 47-93; 2586, pp. 95-119; 2668,
       pp. 121-154; and 2694, pp. 155-181. For trans., see items
       2708 (Portuguese), 2737 (English), and 2742 (English). For
       reviews, see items 2908-2912.

2688. *Situation de la critique racinienne: essai*. Paris: L'Arche,
       1971. (Travaux, 16) Cf. items 2503 and 2666.

2689. *Problèmes d'une sociologie du roman*. 3rd ed. Brussels: Univer-
       sité Libre de Bruxelles, 1971. With Natalie Sarraute.

2690. "Littérature (Sociologie de la)." In *Encyclopaedia Universalis*,
       vol. 10 (1971), pp. 7-10. Paris: Encyclopaedia Universalis
       France, 1968.

2691. "Lukács (György)." In *Encyclopaedia Universalis*, vol. 10
       (1971), pp. 138-140. Paris: Encyclopaedia Universalis France,
       1968.

2692. Trans. of "Novalis et la philosophie romantique de la vie."
       By G. Lukács. *Romantisme*, no. 1-2 (1971), pp. 13-24. Trans.
       of one of the essays of *Die Seele und die Formen*. Berlin:
       Fleishel, 1911, pp. 91-117.

2693. "Sujet et objet en sciences humaines." *Raison Présente*, no. 17
       (January-March 1971), pp. 83-101.

2694. "La Dialectique aujourd'hui." *L'Homme et la Société*, no. 19
       (1971), pp. 193-206. Rpt. in item 2687, pp. 155-181. The
       text of a paper read at the summer school of Korçula,
       Yugoslavia at the end of August 1970.

2695. "Révolution et bureaucratie (July 1970)." *L'Homme et la Soci-
       été*, no. 21 (July-September 1971). During the colloquium at
       Cabris on "Sociologie et Révolution," July 1970.

2696. *Immanuel Kant*. Trans. Robert Black. New York: Humanities Press;
       London: New Left Books, 1971. An English trans. based mostly
       on item 2603 but which also refers to item 2480; also con-
       tains the preface to item 2603 and excerpts from the prefaces
       to items 2487 and 2480.

Goldmann focuses on Kant's thesis that man is limited and
striving for realization of the absolute, the totality. The
dualism that exists between man and the totality can only be
reconciled in the community at the logical, aesthetic and
practical levels. Goldmann points out that Kant's doctrine,
with its emphasis on man in a communal setting, provides the
foundation for the dialectical philosophy of Hegel, Marx and
much of modern philosophy.

2697. *Power and Humanism.* Nottingham: Bertrand Russell Peace Founda-
        tion Ltd., 1971. A fourteen-page pamphlet which translates
        item 2677. See also items 2720 and 2744.

2698. "Reflections on History and Class Consciousness." In *Aspects
        of History and Class Consciousness.* By G. Lukács. Ed. I.
        Meszaros. London: Routledge and Kegan Paul, 1971. Dated
        January 1970 and trans. by Peter France, the French original
        is still unpublished.

2699. "Eppur si muove." *The Spokesman,* no. 15-16 (August-September
        1971). Dated February 1969 and trans. by Tom Wengraf. See
        also item 2720.

2700. "Understanding Marcuse." *Partisan Review,* 38, no. 3 (1971),
        247-262. Cf. items 2638 and 2663.

2701. *Il Dio nascoto. Studio sulla visione tragica nei Pensieri di
        Pascal e nel teatro di Racine.* Bari: Laterza, 1971. Trans.
        of item 2502. See also item 2547.

2702. *Gesellschaftswissenschaften und Philosophie.* Trans. Friedrich
        Griese. Frankfurt am Main: Europäische Verlagsanstalt;
        Vienna: Europa-Verlag, 1971. Trans. of item 2494.

                                1972

2703. "Nouveau roman et réalité." In *Les Critiques de notre temps
        et le nouveau roman.* Ed. Réal Ouellet. Paris: Editions
        Garnier Frères, 1972, pp. 77-81. Cf. item 2566.

2704. "Tradition, vérité et histoire." In *Truth and Historicity.*
        Ed. Hans-Georg Gadamer. (International Institute of Philos-
        ophy. Entretiens in Heidelberg, 12-16 September 1969.) The
        Hague: Martinus Nijhoff, 1972, pp. 52-57. This work appears
        in both English and French editions.

2705. "L'Esthétique du jeune Lukács." In *The New Hungarian Quarterly*
        (issue on "In Memoriam Gyorgy Lukács 1885-1971"), 13, no. 47
        (1972), 3-167. Pagination is for entire issue. Rpts. item
        2541.

2706. *Racine.* Trans. Alastair Hamilton. Intro. Raymond Williams.
        Cambridge: Rivers Press Ltd., 1972. Trans. of item 2503 or
        2666.

2707. *Introduzione a Kant. Uomo, comunità e mondo nella filosofia di Immanuel Kant.* Trans. S. Mantovani and V. Messana. Milan: Sugar, 1972. Trans. of item 2603.

2708. *A Criação cultural na sociedade moderna.* Trans. Rolando Roque da Silva. São Paulo: Difusão Européia do Livro, 1972. Trans. of item 2687.

2709. *Sociologia literaturii.* Trans. Florica Neagoe. Bucarest: Editura Politica, 1972. Trans. of item 2667.

2710. *Soziologie des Romans.* 2nd ed. Darmstadt: Luchterhand, 1972, 258pp. (Soziologische Texte, Band 61) Cf. item 2685.

1973

*2711. *Lukács et Heidegger. Fragments posthumes établis et présentés par Youssef Ishaghpour.* Paris: Denoël-Gonthier, 1973, 182pp. (Méditations, 112) For trans., see items 2734 (Spanish), 2736 (German), 2739 (English), and 2743 (English). For reviews, see items 2936-2946.

Contains: Avant-propos by Y. Ishaghpour, pp. 5-56; Introduction à Lukács et Heidegger, written in August 1970, was to be the start of a book on their early writings, pp. 57-87; Cours de l'année 67-68 (a course on Lukács and Heidegger given during the winter term at the VIe section of the Ecole Pratique des Hautes Etudes): (1) Réification, *Zuhandenheit* et praxis, pp. 91-105; (2) Totalité, être et histoire, pp. 106-120; (3) Possibilité objective et conscience possible, pp. 121-139; (4) Sujet-objet et fonction, pp. 140-162; (5) L'actualité de la question du sujet, pp. 163-176.

2712. "Lukács et Heidegger." *Revue de l'Institut de Sociologie*, nos. 3-4 (1973), pp. 503-523. Rpt. in item 2728.

2713. "Deuxième colloque international sur la sociologie de la littérature, Royaumont. Discussion extraite des actes du colloque." *Revue de l'Institut de Sociologie*, nos. 3-4 (1973), pp. 525-542. With T.W. Adorno. Rpt. in item 2729. Adorno trans. from German by Rainer Rochlitz.

2714. *The Philosophy of the Enlightenment. The Christian Burgess and the Enlightenment.* Trans. Henry Maas. Cambridge, Mass.: M.I.T. Press; London: Routledge and Kegan Paul, 1973. Trans. of item 2637.

Originally written in 1960 as a chapter for a German history of Christian thought, and published in 1968 as item 2637. A French version appeared in item 2665. This trans. follows the German text with additions and corrections from the French edition. Contains: (1) The Structure of the Enlightenment, pp. 1-49; (2) The Enlightenment and Christian Belief, pp. 50-82; (3) The Enlightenment and the Problems of Modern Society, pp. 83-97; Index, pp. 99-100.

2715. *Marxismo e scienze umane.* Intro. Jacques Leenhardt. Trans.
       R. Minore. Rome: Newton Compton Italiana, 1973. Trans. of
       item 2664.

2716. *Jean Piaget e le scienze sociali. Con un'autobiografia di Jean
       Piaget. Saggi di L. Goldmann e altri.* Florence: La Nuova
       Italia, 1973. See item 2594.

2717. *Kultur in der Mediengesellschaft.* Trans. Linde Birk. Frankfurt
       am Main: S. Fischer, 1973.

2718. *Der verborgene Gott. Studie über der tragische Weltanschauung
       in den Pensees Pascals und im Theater Racines.* Trans. Hermann
       Baum and Karl H. Klär. Neuwied: Luchterhand, 1973, 604pp.
       (Soziologische Texte, Band 87) Trans. of item 2502.

                                  1974

2719. *Structures mentales et création culturelle.* Paris: Union Générale
       d'Editions, 1974. Rpts. item 2665.

2720. *Power and Humanism.* Trans. Brian Trench and Tom Wengraf.
       Nottingham: Spokesman Books, 1974. Originally published as
       item 2697, this 52-page edition also includes the text of
       Eppur si muove (item 2699), trans. by Tom Wengraf. See also
       item 2744.

2721. Contributor to *Sociologia della letteratura.* Rome: Newton
       Compton Italiana, 1974. Trans. of item 2667.

2722. *La Creazione culturale. Saggi di sociologia della communicazione.*
       Trans. D. Novacco. Rome: A. Armando, 1974.

2723. Introduction to *Teoria del romanzo. Saggio storico-filosofico
       sulle forme della grande epica.* By György Lukács. Trans.
       Francesco Saba Sardi. Milan: Garzanti, 1974.

2724. *Jean Piaget y las ciencias sociales.* Trans. Miguel Angel
       Quintanilla. Salamanca: Sígueme, 1974. Cf. item 2594.

2725. *Introducción a la filosofía de Kant.* Trans. José Luis Etcheverry.
       Buenos Aires: Amorrortu Ed., 1974. Trans. of item 2603.

2726. Contributor to *Sociología de la creación literaria.* Buenos
       Aires: Ediciones Nueva Visión, 1974 or earlier. Trans. of
       item 2667?

2727. Preface to *Die Ursprünge des Sozialsmus in Deutschland. Luther,
       Kant, Fichte und Hegel.* By Jean Jaurès. Trans. Erika Höhnisch
       and Klaus Sonnendecker. Frankfurt am Main-Vienna: Ullstein,
       1974.

1975

2728. "Lukács et Heidegger." In *Lucien Goldmann et la sociologie de la littérature. Hommage à Lucien Goldmann*. Brussels: Editions de l'Université de Bruxelles, 1975, pp. 11-31. Rpts. item 2712.

2729. "Discussion extraite des actes du colloque. Deuxième Colloque International sur la Sociologie de la Littérature, Royaumont." In *Lucien Goldmann et la sociologie de la littérature. Hommage à Lucien Goldmann*. Brussels: Editions de l'Université de Bruxelles, 1975, pp. 33-50. With Th. W. Adorno. Rpts. item 2713. Adorno trans. from German by Rainer Rochlitz.

2730. "Le Dieu caché." In *Le Paradoxe de Phèdre, suivi de Le Paradoxe constitutif du roman*. By Eric L. Gans. Paris: Nizet, 1975.

2730a. "Un Grand polémiste." *Herne*, no. 28 (1975), pp. 107-111.

On Karl Krauss.

2731. *Towards a Sociology of the Novel*. Trans. Alan Sheridan. London: Tavistock, 1975 and 1977. Trans. of item 2569/2581.

2732. "Dialectical Materialism and Literary History." *New Left Review*, no. 92 (1975), pp. 39-51. Trans. of item 2492.

2733. *Para una sociología de la novela*. 2nd ed. Madrid: Ayuso, 1975, 240pp. Trans. of item 2569/2581.

2734. *Lukács y Heidegger. Hacia una filosofía nueva*. Trans. José Luis Etcheverry. Buenos Aires: Amorrortu Ed., 1975. Trans. of item 2711.

2735. *Marxismo y ciencias humanas*. Trans. Noemí Fiorito. Buenos Aires: Amorrortu Ed., 1975. Trans. of item 2664.

2736. *Lukács und Heidegger*. Trans. Rainer Rochlitz. Darmstadt-Neuwied: Luchterhand, 1975. Trans. of item 2711.

1976

2737. *Cultural Creation in Modern Society*. Trans. Bart Grahl. St. Louis: Telos Press, 1976. Trans. of item 2687. See also item 2742.

2738. "The Epistemology of Sociology." *Telos*, 20 (Winter 1976-1977), 201-210. Trans. of item 2606.

2739. *Lukács e Heidegger. Fragmenti postumi a cura di Youssef Ishaghpour*. Trans. Emanuela Dorigotti Volpi. Verona: Bertani, 1976. Trans. of item 2711.

2740. Contributor to *Jean Piaget--Werk und Wirkung*. Munich: Kindler Verlag, 1976. Cf. item 2594.

1977

2741. Texts in *Le Structuralisme génétique. L'Oeuvre et l'influence de Lucien Goldmann*. Ed. Annie Goldmann, Michel Lowy, and Sami Naïr. Paris: Denoël-Gonthier, 1977.

2742. *Cultural Creation in Modern Society*. Intro. William Mayrl. Trans. Bart Grahl. Oxford: B. Blackwell, 1977. Trans. of item 2687. See also item 2737. Bibliography, pp. 146-173.

2743. *Lukács and Heidegger. Towards a New Philosophy*. Trans. William Q. Boelhower. London-Boston: Routledge and Kegan Paul, 1977, 112pp. Trans. of item 2711.

2744. *Power and Humanism*. Atlantic Highlands, N.J.: Humanities Press, 1977. Trans. of item 2677. See also items 2697 and 2720.

SECONDARY SOURCES

2744a. Abbou, J. "Literature and Ideology: Problems." *Revue Française d'Etudes Américaines*, no. 3 (1977), pp. 73-78.

2745. Adolfsson, Eva. "Lucien Goldmann." *Bonniers Litterära Magasin*, Årg. 37, Nr. 7 (September 1970), 466-477.

2746. Akoun, André. "Hommage à Lucien Goldmann." *La Quinzaine Littéraire*, no. 112 (16-28 February 1971), pp. 19-20.

   On Goldmann's *Marxisme et sciences humaines* and *Structures mentales et création culturelle*.

   Albérès, R.-M. See item 3853.

   Allen, D.G. See item 4422.

2747. Andreatta, Alberto. "Contributi per uno studio dell'assiologia." *Rivista Internazionale di Filosofia del Diritto*, 49, no. 1 (January-March 1972), 3-28. Goldmann's *L'Illuminismo e la società moderna* (Turin, 1967) vs. F. Venturi's *Utopia e riforma nell'illuminismo* (Turin, 1970).

2748. Angenot, Marc. "The Classical Structures of the Novel: Remarks on Georg Lukács, Lucien Goldmann, and René Girard." *Genre*, 3, no. 3 (September 1970), 205-213.

2749. Anonymous. "Cross Purposes." *The Times Literary Supplement*, no. 3422 (28 September 1967), pp. 851-852.

2750. ———. "French Studies: I. A Marxist on Pascal." *The Hibbert Journal*, 63, no. 250 (Spring 1965), 133-135.

   ———. See also item 3861.

2751.   ————. "Lucien Goldmann." *Indice*, núm. 278-279 (1-15 November 1970), p. 50.

2752.   ————. "Lucien Goldmann (1913-1970)." *Praxis*, 7, no. 3-4 Yugoslavia, 1970), 281-282.

2753.   ————. *Lucien Goldmann et la sociologie de la littérature. Hommage à Lucien Goldmann.* Brussels: Editions de l'Université de Bruxelles, 1975. Rpts. item 2867.

   Contains: (1) Roger Lallemand: En guise d'introduction, pp. 7-10; (2) Lucien Goldmann: Lukács et Heidegger [excerpted from item 2711], pp. 11-31 (3) Lucien Goldmann and Th. W. Adorno: Discussion extraite des actes du second colloque international sur la sociologie de la littérature tenu à Royaumont, pp. 33-50; (4) Herbert Marcuse: Some General Remarks on Lucien Goldmann, pp. 51-52; (5) Jean Piaget: Bref témoignage, pp. 53-55; (6) Jean Duvignaud: Goldmann et la "vision du monde," pp. 57-62; (7) J. Leenhardt: A propos de "Marxisme et sciences humaines," pp. 63-69; (8) G. Lukács: Remarques sur la théorie de l'Histoire littéraire [trans. Georges Kassai; previously unpublished manuscript, dated 1910], pp. 71-103; (9) Eric Kohler: Le Hasard littéraire, le possible et la nécessité, pp. 105-120; (10) Annie Goldmann: "Salammbô" ou l'Histoire absente, pp. 121-132; (11) Agnès Krutwig Caers and the Groupe de travail du Centre de Sociologie de la Littérature (Brussels): La vision du monde dans les "Petits Poèmes en prose" de Ch. Baudelaire, pp. 133-147; (12) Geneviève Mouillaud: Roman (article d'un dictionnaire de la sociologie de la littérature en préparation sous la direction de L. Goldmann), pp. 149-157; (13) L. and N. Rudich: "Eugénie Grandet," martyr du capitalisme, pp. 159-177; (14) Youssef Ishaghpour: "Citizen Kane" et les antinomies de la pensée bourgeoise, pp. 179-220; (15) Françoise Gaillard: Le Roi est mort. Note sur la vision du monde dans un drame de Eugène Ionesco, pp. 221-240; (16) E. Esaer: G. Lukács--L. Goldmann: l'Aventure discursive, pp. 240-343; (17) Eduard Tell: Bibliographie de Lucien Goldmann, pp. 345-364.

2754.   ————. "Mort de Lucien Goldmann." *Les Lettres Françaises*, no. 1354 (7-13 October 1970), p. 2.

2755.   ————. "Obituary [of Lucien Goldmann, 1913-1970, French sociologist]." *New York Times*, 10 October 1970, p. 29.

2756.   ————. "A Portrait of the Artist as a Midwife: Lucien Goldmann and the 'Transindividual' Subject." *The Times Literary Supplement*, 70 (26 November 1971), 1465-1466.

   On Goldmann's *Structures mentales...*, *Marxisme et sciences humaines*, and *La Création culturelle dans la société moderne.* Cf. item 2774.

   ————. See also items 3862 and 4275.

2757.   ————. *Sainte-Beuve et la critique littéraire contemporaine. Actes du colloque tenu à Liège du 6 au 8 octobre 1969.* Paris: Société d'Edition "Les Belles Lettres," 1972.

———. See also item 4276.

2758.   ———. *Le Structuralisme génétique. L'Oeuvre et l'influence de Lucien Goldmann.* Paris: Denoël/Gonthier, 1977.

———. See also item 960.

Balmas, E. See item 4278.

2759.   Barilli, Renato. "Le Teorie di Goldmann sul romanzo." *Europa Letteraria*, anno VI, n. 34 (March-April 1965), 95-107.

2760.   Baum, Hermann. "Humanismus und Ideologie bei Lucien Goldmann und Louis Althusser." *Philosophisches Jahrbuch*, 79, no. 1 (1972), 184-198.

2761.   ———. *Lucien Goldmann, Marxismus contra Vision Tragique?* Stuttgart-Bad Cannstatt: Frommann-Holzboog, 1974. Bibliography, pp. 201-207.

Béguin, Albert. See item 4280.

Bersani, J., et al. See item 3871.

2762.   Birchall, Ian, and Miriam Glucksmann. "Communication." *New Left Review*, no. 59 (January-February 1969), pp. 110-112.

2763.   Boelhower, William Quentin. "The Genetic Structuralism of Lucien Goldmann: The Status and Problems of Method." *Dissertation Abstracts International*, 38, no. 2 (August 1977), 781-A. Marquette University dissertation.

2764.   Bonzon, A. "Lucien Goldmann et la critique sociologique." In *La Nouvelle critique et Racine.* By A. Bozon. Paris: Editions A.-G. Nizet, 1970, pp. 21-23. See also items 4283 and 989.

Bouazis, C. See item 3884.

2765.   Brady, Patrick. "Socio-criticism as Genetic Structuralism: Value and Limitations of the Goldmann Method." *L'Esprit Créateur*, 14, no. 3 (Fall 1974), 207-218.

Brée, G., et al. See item 4285.

2766.   Brereton, Geoffrey. "The Tragic Sense of Life." In *Principles of Tragedy: A Rational Examination of the Tragic Concept in Life and Literature.* By G. Brereton. London: Routledge and Kegan Paul, 1968; Coral Gables, Florida: University of Miami Press, 1969, pp. 56-74.

On Goldmann's *The Hidden God.*

2767.   Brouwers, Bert. "Herman Gorter: bolangrijk literatuursocioloog avant la lettre." *Nieuw Vlaams Tijdschrift*, 21, no. 9 (September 1969), 918-931.

2768. Bručar, M. "Lucien Goldmann and Genetic Structuralism" (in Rumanian). *Revista de Filozofie*, 18, no. 12 (Bucharest, 1971), 1549-1570.

Bruézière, M. See item 4288.

2769. Brûle, M. "L'Oeuvre ouverte de Lucien Goldmann." *Sociologie et Sociétés*, 3, no. 1 (1971), 3-14.

Busino, G. See item 5223.

2770. Caraël, Michel. Interview with Lucien Goldmann. *Mai*, no. 6 (Brussels, June-July 1969), pp. 38-40.

Discusses the May 1968 movement and new possibilities for an overall questioning of advanced capitalist society.

2771. Carballo, Emmanuel. "Novela y sociedad." *Hispano Americano*, 53, no. 1369 (9 July 1968), 47-48.

2772. Castella, Charles. *Structures romanesques et vision sociale chez Maupassant*. Paris: Editions de l'Age d'Homme, 1972.

Work dedicated to the memory of G. Lukács and L. Goldmann.

Caute, D. See item 1015.

2773. Caute, David. "After Lukács: The Literary Criticism of Lucien Goldmann." In *Collisions. Essays and Reviews*. By David Caute. London: Quartet Books, 1974, pp. 208-218.

2774. ———. "A Portrait of the Artist as a Midwife: Lucien Goldmann and the 'Transindividual Subject.'" In *Collisions. Essays and Reviews*. By David Caute. London: Quartet Books, 1974, pp. 219-227. Cf. item 2756.

2774a. Colman, S.J. "Margaret Atwood, Lucien Goldmann's Pascal, and the Meaning of Canada." *University of Toronto Quarterly*, 48 (Spring 1979), 245-262.

2775. Colucci, F. "Marxismo e storicismo." *Rivista di Studi Crociani*, 11, no. 1 (1974), 76-84.

2776. Comoth, René. "La Querelle des critiques." *Rivista di Studi Crociani*, 6, fasc. 3 (July-September 1969), 334-338.

2777. Corredor, Eva Schaeffer. "Georg Lukacs as Critic of French Literature, or the Literary Text as a Pretext." *Dissertation Abstracts International*, 36, no. 6 (December 1975), 3748-3749-A.

2778. Crispini, Franco. *Lo Strutturalismo dialettico di Lucien Goldmann*. Naples: Libreria Scientifica Editrice, 1970. Bibliography of works by Goldmann, pp. 111-114.

Daix, Pierre. See item 4293.

2779. Demetz, P. "Transformations of Recent Marxist Criticism: Hans Mayer, Ernst Fischer, Lucien Goldmann." In *The Frontiers of Literary Criticism*. Ed. David H. Malone. Los Angeles: Hennessey & Ingalls, 1974, pp. 75-92.

Demougin, J. See item 4295.

2780. De Paz, Alfredo. "Alcune tendenze attuali nella sociologia della letteratura e nella critica sociologia." *Il Mulino*, 21, no. 221 (May-June 1972), 552-570.

2781. Di Nardo, Armando. "Il Metodo strutturale in Lucien Goldmann." In *Studi in Onore di Arturo Massolo*. Ed. Livio Sichirollo. Urbino: Argalía, 1967, pp. 665-677. Rpts. *Studi Urbinati di Storia, Filosofia e Letteratura*, 41, nuova serie B, no. 1-2 (1967).

Donato, E. See item 3917.

Donley, M. See Item 1038.

Doubrovsky, S. See item 4301.

2782. Dumont, Fernand. "Lucien Goldmann." *Cahiers Internationaux de Sociologie*, 50 (1971), 143-146.

Dupeyron, G. See item 4302.

Duvignaud, J. See item 3703.

2783. Duvignaud, Jean. "Mort de Lucien Goldmann, élève de Lukács et théoricien de la 'Nouvelle Critique.'" *Le Monde*, no. 8002 (6 October 1970), p. 26.

2784. ―――. "Portrait: a la recherche de la raison perdue." *Le Nouvel Observateur*, no. 309 (12-18 October 1970), pp. 43-44.

2785. ―――, and A. Guédez, eds. "Trois penseurs sans idéologie." *Cause Commune*, 2, no. 6 (1973), 9-20.

On B. Groethuysen, M. Raphael and L. Goldmann, three philosophers who espouse neither liberalism nor orthodox Marxism.

2786. ―――. "Goldmann et la 'vision du monde.'" *Revue de l'Institut de Sociologie*, no. 3-4 (1973), pp. 549-554. See also item 2753.

2787. Eagleton, Terry. "Form and Content: Goldmann and Genetic Structuralism." In his *Marxism and Literary Criticism* (item 4364), pp. 32-34.

2788. Eco, Umberto. "Crosscurrents--IV. Sociology and the Novel." *The Times Literary Supplement*, no. 3422 (28 September 1967), pp. 875-876.

2789.   Esaer, E. "G. Lukács--L. Goldmann: l'aventure discursive. I.
        Lecture sémantique d'un discours néo-hégélien matérialiste."
        Revue de l'Institut de Sociologie, no. 3-4 (1973), pp. 733-
        785. See also item 2753.

2790.   ————. G. Lukács--L. Goldmann: l'aventure discursive. II.
        Lecture sémantique d'un discours néo-hégélien matérialiste."
        Revue de l'Institut de Sociologie, no. 1 (1974), pp. 165-215.
        See also item 2753.

2791.   Fehér, F. "Le Roman est-il un genre problématique? (Contribu-
        tion à la théorie du roman)." *Acta Litteraria Academiae
        Scientiarum Hungaricae*, 15, no. 1-2 (1973), 123-158.

2791a. ————. "Lucien Goldmann, the 'Mère Récipient' of Georg
        Lukács." *Philosophy and Social Criticism* [formerly *Cultural
        Hermeneutics*], no. 1 (1979), pp. 1-24.

2792.   Ferreras, Juan Ignacio. *Teoria y praxis de la novela. La
        última aventura de Don Quijote*. Paris: Ediciones Hispano-
        americanas, 1970.

        Work inspired by Goldmann.

2793.   ————. "La Sociología de Lucien Goldmann." *Revista de
        Occidente*, 35, no. 105 (December 1971), 317-336.

2794.   ————. *La Novela de ciencia ficción. Interpretación de una
        novela marginal*. Madrid: Siglo Veintiuno de España Editores,
        1972.

        Work inspired by Goldmann.

2795.   ————. "La Muerte de Descartes." *Cuadernos Hispanoamericanos*,
        no. 289-290 (1974), pp. 270-302.

2796.   Ferrier, Jean-Louis. "Le Philosophe sortit à 3 heures." *Express*,
        no. 864 (8-14 January 1968), pp. 43-44.

        Filippetti, A., et al. See item 3927.

        Florenne, Y. See item 1057.

        Fowlie, W. See item 4303.

2797.   Furter, Pierre. "La Pensée de Georges Lukács en France." *Revue
        de Théologie et de Philosophie*, 3ᵉ série, 11, no. 4 (1961),
        353-361.

2798.   Geelen, Jan van. "Het Goedkope boek: Frankrijk." *Litterair
        Paspoort*, 21, no. 197 (June-July 1966), 131-134.

        Girard, R. See item 1069.

2799.   Glucksmann, Miriam. "Lucien Goldmann: Humanist or Marxist?"
        New Left Review, no. 56 (July-August 1969), pp. 49-62.

Goldmann, Annie. See item 3824.

2800.   ———, Michel Lowy, and Sami Naïr, eds. *Le Structuralisme
         génétique: l'oeuvre et l'influence de Lucien Goldmann.* Paris:
         Denoël/Gonthier, 1977, 282pp. (Bibliothèque Médiations, 159)

2801.   Gorin, Jean-Pierre. "Colloque à Royaumont: Sociologues et
         psychanalystes en quête du fait littéraire." *Le Monde*, no.
         6510 (18 December 1965), p. 13.

2802.   Gossman, Lionel. "Lucien Goldmann--1913-1970." *Modern Language
         Notes*, 86, no. 4 (May 1971), 453-455.

2803.   Goytisolo, Juan. "Litteratur og politik." *Vinduet*, 18, no. 1
         (1964), 50-53.

2804.   Grimm, Jürgen. "L. Goldmann. Der genetische Strukturalismus."
         In his (et al) *Einführung in die französische Literaturwissen-
         schaft.* Stuttgart: J.B. Metzlersche Verlagsbuchhandlung,
         1976, pp. 155-162.

2805.   Guarin, B.T., and R.F. Tovar. "I. Análisis de contenido. II.
         Método estructural genético." *Centro de Investigaciones
         Sociales. Documentos de Trabajo*, no. 1 (Bogota, 1973), pp.
         65-84.

2806.   Guitton, Jean. *Journal de ma vie. 2. Avenir du présent.* Paris:
         Desclée de Brouwer, 1976.

         Hahn, P. See item 1074.

2807.   Hansen, Olaf. "Hermeneutik und Literatursoziologie. Zwei
         Modelle: Marxistische Literaturtheorie in Amerika, Zum
         Problem der 'American Studies.'" In *Literatursoziologie. I.
         Begriff und Methodik.* Ed. Joachim Bark. Stuttgart-Berlin-
         Cologne-Mainz: Verlag W. Kohlhammer, 1974, pp. 114-126.

2808.   Hathorn, J.M., and David Gervais. "Lucien Goldmann." *The Times
         Literary Supplement*, no. 3643 (24 December 1971), pp. 1607-
         1608.

2809.   heyndels, Ralph. "Réflexion sur la notion de 'cohérence' dans
         la théorie de Lucien Goldmann." *Revue de l'Université de
         Bruxelles*, no. 1-2 (1974), pp. 3-23.

2810.   ———. "Vision du monde et réification. Réflexion sur la
         sociologie de la littérature de Lucien Goldmann." *Revue de
         l'Institut de Sociologie*, no. 4 (Brussels, 1974), pp. 593-
         617.

2810a.   ———. "Théorie de la religion et marxisme tragique chez
         Lucien Goldmann." *Problèmes d'Histoire du Christianisme*, 7
         (Brussels, 1976-1977), 87-102.

2811. Hobson, Harold. "A Dearth of Dialectic." *The Sunday Times*, no. 7393 (24 January 1965), p. 41.

2812. Hoeges, Dirk. "Lucien Goldmann." In *Französische Literaturkritik der Gegenwart in Einzeldarstellungen*. Ed. Wolf-Dieter Lange. Stuttgart: A. Kröner, 1975, pp. 208-233.

2813. Huaco, G.A. "Ideology and Literature." *New Literary History*, 4, no. 3 (1973), 421-436.

2814. Huertas Vazquez, Eduardo. "A propósito de Goldmann: génesis y cultura." *Cuadernos Hispanoamericanos*, no. 256 (April 1971), pp. 121-133.

2815. Iljenko, B. "Vision of the World, Cultural Creation, Class Consciousness, Socio-economic Life, and the Theory of Lucien Goldmann" (in Serbo-Croatian). *Delo*, 21, no. 4 (1975), 713-731.

Jacob, A. See item 2174.

Jaeggi, U.J.V. See item 108.

2816. Jones, Robert Emmet. "L'Ecole structuraliste: Lucien Goldmann," part 1 of chapter 4 of his item 4316, pp. 187-220.

2817. Kittang, Atle. "Teoretiske forutsetningar for Lucien Goldmanns litteratursosiologi." In his item 1109, pp. 73-99.

2818. Krémer-Marietti, Angele. "Hommage à Lucien Goldmann." *La Quinzaine Littéraire*, no. 112 (16-28 February 1971), pp. 18-19.

2819. Krynen, J. "Critique marxiste et spiritualité chrétienne: Le Dieu caché de Pascal est-il un Dieu tragique?" In *Baroque. Revue Internationale* (issue on "Idees et philosophies au temps du baroque"), no. 7 (1974), pp. 85-92.

Maintains that Goldmann's positive answer to this question is wrong.

2820. Labbé, Y. "Humanisme et religion chez L. Goldmann, J.-P. Sartre et H. Duméry." *Concilium*, no. 86 (1973), pp. 121-127.

2821. Lalou, Renée. "Feuilleton littéraire: ce mystérieux Monsieur Racine." *Hommes et Mondes*, 11e année, no. 119 (June 1956), 433-438.

2822. Lanza, D. "Alla ricerca del tragico." *Belfagor. Rassegna di Varia Umanita*, 31, no. 1 (1976), 33-64.

2823. Lattarulo, Leonardo. "Sul metodo di Lucien Goldmann." *Filosofia e Società*, no. 2 (Rome, 1974), pp. 317-322.

2824. Laurenson, Diana, and Alan Swingewood. *The Sociology of Literature*. London: MacGibbon and Kee, 1971; London: Paladin, 1972, c. 1971.

2825.   Leenhardt, Jacques. "Psicocritica e sociologia della letteratura."
        Nuova Corrente, no. 51 (1970), pp. 5-20.

2826.   ————. "Pour une esthétique sociologique: Essai de construc-
        tion de l'esthétique de Lucien Goldmann." *Revue d'Esthétique*,
        24, fasc. II (April-June 1971), 113-128.

2827.   ————. "Introduction à la sociologie de la littérature."
        Mosaic, 5, no. 2 (Winter 1971-1972), 1-10.

2828.   ————. "Towards a Sociological Aesthetic: An Attempt at Con-
        structing the Aesthetic of Lucien Goldmann." *Sub-stance*
        (issue on Socio-Criticism), no. 15 (1976), pp. 94-104.

2829.   Lentini, O. "Lucien Goldmann (Bucarest 1913-Parigi 1970)."
        Sociologia. Rivista di Studi Sociali, 4, no. 3 (1970), 169-
        171.

        A death notice in which Goldmann is briefly situated in the
        context of French intellectuals.

        Le Sage, Laurent. "Lucien Goldmann." In his item 4322, pp. 87-93.

2830.   Levin, Harry. "Towards a Sociology of the Novel." In his
        Refractions. Essays in Comparative Literature. New York:
        Oxford University Press, 1966, pp. 239-249.

2831.   Linze, Jacques-Gérard. "Lectures de vacances et notes sur
        l'état du roman." *Revue Générale. Lettres, Arts et Sciences
        Humaines*, no. 8-9 (September 1974), pp. 29-43.

2832.   Lobet, Marcel. "Racine, Claudel, Mauriac." *Revue Générale
        Belge*, 92e année, no. 7 (15 July 1956), 1591-1594.

2833.   Lovell, Terry. "Weber, Goldmann and the Sociology of Beliefs."
        Archives Européennes de Sociologie, 14, no. 2 (1973), 304-
        323.

2834.   Lowy, Michel. *La Théorie de la révolution chez le jeune Marx*.
        Paris: Maspero, 1970. (Bibliothèque socialiste, 18)

        Work inspired by Goldmann.

2835.   ————, and Sami Naïr. *Lucien Goldmann ou la dialectique de la
        totalité. Présentation, choix de textes, bibliographie*.
        Paris: Editions Seghers, 1973. (Philosophes de tous les
        temps, 84)

2836.   MacIntyre, Alasdair C. "Pascal and Marx: On Lucien Goldmann's
        Hidden God." In his *Against the Self-Images of the Age:
        Essays on Ideology and Philosophy*. New York: Schocken, 1971,
        pp. 76-87.

2837.   Marchese, A. "La Sociologia della letteratura." *Humanitas*, 31,
        no. 3 (Brescia, 1976), 214-224.

2838. Marcuse, Herbert. "A Reply to Lucien Goldmann." *Partisan Review*, no. 4 (Winter 1971-1972), pp. 397-400.

On item 2700.

2839. ———. "Some General Remarks on Lucien Goldmann." *Revue de l'Institut de Sociologie*, no. 3-4 (1973), pp. 543-544. Rpt. in item 2753.

2840. Marin Morales, José Alberto. "Ideas estéticas de Lucien Goldmann en su entronque con las de Lukacs." *Arbor*, 78, no. 302 (February 1971), 15-29.

Milanesi, V. See item 527.

2841. Montgomery, J.W. "The French Contribution: Goldmann." *Christianity Today*, 17 (14 September 1973), 57-58.

2842. Morawski, Stefan. *L'Absolu et la forme. L'Esthétique d'André Malraux*. Trans. Yolande Lamy-Grun. Paris: Klincksieck, 1972.

2843. Morse, David, and Sandy Petrey. "Literature and History in Contemporary French Scholarship." *Clio*, 5, no. 1 (Fall 1975), 37-54.

2844. Mouillaud, Geneviève. *Le Rouge et le Noir de Stendhal, le roman possible*. Paris: Larousse, 1972. (Thèmes et Textes de Larousse Université)

A work inspired by Goldmann.

Mouillaud, M. See item 1150.

2845. Mulhern, Francis. "Introduction to Goldmann." *New Left Review*, no. 92 (July-August 1975), pp. 34-38.

2846. Naïr, Sami. "Le Cheminement d'une pensée." *La Quinzaine Littéraire*, no. 112 (16-28 February 1971), pp. 20-21.

2847. Namer, Gérard. "Lucien Goldmann (1913-1970)." *Revue Philosophique de la France et de l'Etranger*, 95 (1970), 506-507.

Narskij, I.S. See item 4387.

2848. Nicoletti, Gianni. *Saggi e idee di letteratura francese*. Bari: Adriatica, 1965.

2849. ———. "Sociologia e letteratura." *Letteratura*, no. 74-75 (March-June 1965), pp. 158-160.

2850. Nuñez Ladeveze, Luis. "La Estructura significativa en Goldmann." In his *Crítica del discurso literario*. Madrid: Cuadernos para el Diálogo, 1974, pp. 250-256.

2851. ———. "La Concepción del mundo en Goldmann." In his *Crítica del discurso literario*. Madrid: Cuadernos para el Diálogo, 1974, pp. 256-262.

2852. ————. "La Apuesta Sebag-Pascal-Goldmann." In his *Crítica del discurso literario*. Madrid: Cuadernos para el Diálogo, 1974, pp. 304-312.

2853. Nykrog, Per. "Lucien Goldmann." *Kritik*, no. 1 (1967), pp. 39-49.

2854. Ormesson, Jean d'. "Un Collègue à l'Unesco sur Kierkegaard vivant." *Le Monde*, no. 5996 (25 April 1964), p. 13.

2855. Palmier, Jean-Michel. "Goldmann vivant." *Praxis*, 8, no. 3-4 (1971), 567-624. See also items 2856 and 2857.

2856. ————. "Goldmann vivant." *Raison Présente*, no. 20 (October-December 1971), pp. 45-80. See also items 2855 and 2857.

2857. ————. "Goldmann vivant. II. Problèmes théoriques de la méthode génétique et dialectique en sociologie de l'art et de la littérature; III. Socialisme ou barbarie." *Raison Présente*, no. 21 (January-March 1972), pp. 25-47. See also items 2855 and 2856.

2858. ————. "Goldmann." In *Esthétique et marxisme*. By O. Revault d'Allonnes et al. Paris: Union Générale d'Editions, 1974, pp. 107-188.

2859. ————. "Lucien Goldmann, sociologue de la litterature." *Le Monde [des Livres]*, no. 9461 (20 June 1975), p. 16.

       A review of item 2753.

2860. Parenti, Roberto. "Goldmann e l'illuminismo." *Rivista Critica di Storia della Filosofia*, 23 (1968), 202-205.

2861. Piaget, Jean. "Bref témoignage." *Revue de l'Institut de Sociologie*, no. 3-4 (Brussels, 1973), pp. 545-547. Rpt. in item 2753.

2862. Pianori, R. "Critica esistenzialista e marxista: Jean-Paul Sartre e Lucien Goldmann." In *Orientamenti sulla moderna critica*. Ed. Enea Balmas. Milan: Ediz. La Viscontea, 1975, pp. 23-37.

2863. Pincott, R. "The Sociology of Literature." *Archives Européennes de Sociologie*, 11, no. 1 (1970), 177-195.

       The approach of Lukács and Goldmann, while interesting and while allowing even the application of the concept of a tragic vision of the world to the authors of ancient Greece, is not very rigorous and cannot be generalized. A truly scientific method of structuralist approach is necessary.

       Pingaud, B. See item 1182.

2864. Pleydell-Pearce, A.G. "Art and Praxis." *The British Journal of Aesthetics*, 15, no. 1 (Winter 1975), 3-13.

Pollman, L. See item 1190.

2865.   Poole, Roger C. "Communauté ou communication?" *Revue de
        Métaphysique et de Morale*, 73 (July-August 1968), 307-327.

Poster, M. See item 4393.

2865a. Pratola, V. "Marx: coscienza e rivoluzione." *Giornale Critico
        della Filosofia Italiana*, 8, no. 2 (1977), 223-255.

Quaghebeur, M. See item 4714.

Rella, F. See item 1199.

2866.   Reverdin, Henri. "IXe Congrès des Sociétés de Philosophie de
        Langue Française--Aix-en-Provence, 2-5 septembre 1957."
        Revue de Théologie et de Philosophie, 3e série, tome 7, no.
        4 (1957), 296-298.

2867.   *Revue de l'Institut de Sociologie*, no. 3-4 (Brussels, 1973),
        499-806: issue entitled "Hommage à Lucien Goldmann." Rpt.
        as item 2753.

Ricardou, J. See item 4333.

2868.   Robert, J.-D. "Lucien Goldmann ou la dialectique de la totalité."
        Archives de Philosophie, tome 39, cahier 2 (April-June 1976),
        337.

        On item 2835.

2869.   ————. "Le Problème de la spécificité de la 'scientificité'
        des sciences de l'homme." *Tijdschrift voor Filosofie*, 39
        (December 1977), 677-704.

        A typology of recent positions on the problem of the scien-
        tific specificity of the human sciences in the thought of
        Goldmann, G.G. Granger and J. Ladrière.

2869a. ————. "Objet et sujet collectif dans les sciences humaines
        chez Lucien Goldmann." *Laval Théologique et Philosophique*,
        35 (June 1979), 117-193.

2870.   Roelens, R. "Les Avatars de la médiation dans la sociologie
        de Lucien Goldmann." *L'Homme et la Société*, no. 15 (1970),
        pp. 295-316.

        Part of an issue devoted to "Marxisme et sciences humaines."
        Challenges Goldmann's methodology, particularly in his writings
        on the sociology of literature. Examines the significance and
        limits of his notion of "vision of the world."

2870a. Roggerone, G.A. "Premesse illuministiche della teoria demo-
        cratica." *Bollettino di Storia della Filosofia dell'Univer-
        sità degli studi di Lecce*, 3 (1975, appeared in 1977), 167-
        200.

        Goldmann's is one of the interpretations discussed.

2871.   Rubel, Maximilien. "Mise au point non-dialectique." *Les Temps Modernes*, 13 (1957), 1138-1141.

Reply to item 2516.

2872.   Saccà, A. "Ipotesi per una sociologia della letteratura." *Revue Internationale de Sociologie*, 10, no. 1 (1974), 48-66.

2873.   Sahay, A. "Sociological Analysis of Philosophical Notions." *Sociological Analysis*, 3, no. 3 (1973), 75-82.

2874.   Saint-Martin, Fernande. "Lucien Goldmann et le nouveau roman." *Liberté*, 8, no. 4 (July-August 1966), 94-101.

2875.   Sanders, S. "Towards a Social Theory of Literature." *Telos*, no. 18 (1973-1974), pp. 107-121.

2876.   Sayre, Robert. "Lucien Goldmann and the Sociology of Culture." *Praxis*, 1, no. 2 (Winter 1976), 129-148.

Schiwy, G. See items 189 and 190.

Schulze, J. See item 1225.

2877.   Silbermann, Alphons. "Literaturphilosophie, soziologische Literaturästhetik oder Literatursoziologie." In *Literatursoziologie. I. Begriff und Methodik*. Ed. Joachim Bark. Stuttgart-Berlin-Cologne-Mainz: Verlag W. Kohlhammer, 1974, pp. 148-157.

Simon, J.K. See item 4338.

Starobinski, J. See item 4340.

Steiner, G. See items 4048-4049.

2878.   Swingewood, A. *The Novel and Revolution*. London-Basingstoke: Macmillan, 1975.

2879.   Tarrab, Gilbert. "La Sociologie du théâtre et de la littérature d'après Lucien Goldmann." *Sociologie et Sociétés*, 3, no. 1 (May 1971), 15-24.

The two major difficulties of Goldmann's analysis are to understand the work (examine its internal structures) and to explain it (how it fits into the globalizing socio-economic structure).

2880.   Tell, Eduard. "Bibliographie de Lucien Goldmann." *Revue de l'Institut de Sociologie*, no. 3-4, (Belgium, 1973), pp. 787-806. Rpt. in item 2753.

2881.   Tertulian, Nicolas. "Genèse et structure." *Revue d'Esthétique*, 25 (July-September 1972), 279-285.

2882. Tremaine, Louis. "Literary Sociology and the African Novel:
      The Theories of Sunday Anozie and Lucien Goldmann." *Research
      in African Literature*, 9 (Spring 1978), 31-45.

2883. Tulloch, J.C. "Sociology of Knowledge and the Sociology of
      Literature." *The British Journal of Sociology*, 27, no. 2
      (1976), 197-210.

2884. Valentine, J. "Perennial Issues in the Sociology of Ideas."
      *Sociological Analysis and Theory. A Discussion Journal of
      Research and Ideas*, 5, no. 3 (1975), 301-330.

2885. Vantuch, A. "Lucien Goldmann sociológ nielen románu." *Slovenské
      Pohl'ady*, 82, no. 7 (1966), 95-100.

      Weinmann, Robert. "Historische 'Bedeutungskritik.' (Lucien
      Goldmann)." In item 4069, pp. 297-310.

2886. White, Hayden V. "The Tasks of Intellectual History." *The
      Monist*, 53 (October 1969), 606-630.

2887. Williams, Raymond. "Literature and Sociology: In Memory of
      Lucien Goldmann." *New Left Review*, no. 67 (May-June 1971),
      pp. 3-18.

      A review of the theory and major concepts in Goldmann (collec-
      tive mental structures, vision of the world, forms of conscious-
      ness); the weakness in his explanation of secondary changes;
      the notion of "collective subject" needs clarification as does
      the structure of the genesis of consciousness.

2888. ———. "Lucien Goldmann and Marxism's Alternative Tradition."
      The Listener, 87, no. 2243 (23 March 1972), 275-276.

*2889. Zéraffa, Michel. *Roman et société*. Paris: Presses Universitaires
      de France, 1971.

2890. ———. *Fictions. The Novel and Social Reality*. Trans. Catherine
      Burns and Tom Burns. Harmondsworth, Middlesex: Penguin Books,
      1976. Trans. of item 2889.

*2891. Zima, Pierre V. *Goldmann: dialectique de l'immanence*. Paris:
      Editions Universitaires/Delarge, 1973, 135pp. (Psychothèque,
      22)

2892. ———. *Le Désir du mythe. Une Lecture sociologique de Marcel
      Proust*. Paris: Nizet, 1973, 319pp.

      An interpretation according to Goldmann's method of genetic
      structuralism.

2893. ———. "Le Philosophe exilé." *Les Lettres Nouvelles*, no. 5
      (December 1972-January 1973), pp. 76-79.

2894. ———. *Goldmann*. Trans. Ramón Ballester. Barcelona: Madragora,
      1975.

2895.   ———. "Le Caractère double du texte ou le désespoir des
         glossateurs." *Les Lettres Nouvelles*, 4 (1975), 112–137.

                              REVIEWS

                 Der christliche Bürger und die Aufklärung
                              (item 2637)

2896.   Anonymous. Review of *The Philosophy of the Enlightenment*.
         Christian Century, 91 (20 February 1974), 212.

2897.   ———. Review of *The Philosophy of the Enlightenment*. *Choice*,
         11 (September 1974), 960.

2898.   ———. Review of *The Philosophy of the Enlightenment*. *The
         Times Literary Supplement*, 7 December 1973, p. 1498.

2899.   ———. "The Rise of the Individual." *Economist*, 249, no.
         6793 (3 November 1973), 134–135.

2900.   C., M. Review of *L'Illuminismo e la societa moderna*. *Rivista
         Internazionale di Filosofia del Diritto*, 45 (1968), 176.

2901.   Flew, Antony. "Promising." *The Times Educational Supplement*,
         no. 3061 (25 January 1974), 28.

2902.   Kasachkoff, T. Review of *The Philosophy of the Enlightenment*.
         Philosophical Studies, 23 (Maynooth, n.d.), 262–265.

2903.   Kern, W. *Theologie und Philosophie*, 44 (1969), 466–468.

2904.   Levi, A. Review of *The Philosophy of the Enlightenment*. *The
         Heythrop Journal*, 16 (1975), 207–208.

2905.   Mayrl, William W. Review of *The Philosophy of the Enlightenment*.
         Telos, 27 (Spring 1976), 199–208.

2906.   Parkinson, G.H.R. Review of *The Philosophy of the Enlightenment*.
         Philosophy, April 1975, p. 215.

2907.   Parsons, Howard L. Review of *The Philosophy of the Enlighten-
         ment*. *Philosophy and Phenomenological Research*, 35 (September
         1974), 125–126.

See also item 2747.

13

La Création culturelle dans la société moderne
(item 2687)

2908. Crispini, F. *Logos*, no. 1 (1972), pp. 144-145.

2909. Mauriac, Claude. "La Fin de l'angoisse et de l'espérance."
        Le Figaro Littéraire, no. 1329 (5 November 1971), p. IV: 26.

2910. Phillipson, M. Review of *Cultural Creation in Modern Society*.
        Sociological Review, n.s. 26 (August 1978), 669-671.

2911. Rodriguez, Ileana, and Marc Zimmerman. Review of *Cultural
        Creation in Modern Society*. *Telos*, 28 (Summer 1976), 199-214.

2912. Routh, J.C. Review of *Cultural Creation in Modern Society*.
        Sociology, 12 (September 1978), 595-596.

See also item 2756.

Dialética e cultura
(item 2620)

2913. Macedo Soares, F. *Revista Brasileira de Filosofia*, 18 (1968),
        226-227.

Le Dieu caché
(item 2502)

2914. Anonymous. Review of *The Hidden God*. *The Times Literary Supple-
        ment*, 5 November 1964, p. 996.

2915. Béguin, Albert. "Note conjointe sur M. Goldmann et la méthode
        'globale.'" *Esprit*, 24, no. 12 (1956), 874-880.

2916. Grimsley, Ronald. "*The Hidden God...*, by Lucien Goldmann...."
        Philosophical Books, 6, no. 1 (January 1965), 10-12.

2917. Johnson, Carol. Review of *The Hidden God*. *Commonweal*, 83 (17
        December 1965), 352.

2918. Julien-Eymard d'Angers, P. "A propos d'une thèse marxiste sur
        les *Pensées* de Pascal." *Etudes Franciscaines*, n.s. 7, no. 17
        (December 1956), 172-178.

2919. Lichtheim, George. "From Pascal to Marx." *New Statesman*, 68,
        no. 1747 (4 September 1964), 322-323. Rpt. in his *The
        Concept of Ideology, and Other Essays*. New York: Random
        House, 1967, pp. 276-281.

2920. MacIntyre, Alasdair. "Pascal and Marx: On Lucien Goldmann's
        Hidden God." *Encounter*, 23, no. 4 (October 1964), 69-72,
        74, 76.

2921. Schauder, Karlheinz. "Strukturalistische Literaturbetrachtung.
       Lucien Goldmann: *Der verborgene Gott.*" *Frankfurter Hefte*,
       30, Heft 7 (1975), 67-70.

2922. Turnell, Martin. "Tragic Vision." *The Listener*, 72, no. 1853
       (1 October 1964), 519.

2923. Weightman, John. "The Veiled Face of God." *The Observer*, no.
       9028 (12 July 1964), p. 22.

See also item 2766.

Introduction à la philosophie de Kant
(item 2603)

2924. A., L. d'. *Rivista Internazionale di Filosofia del Diritto*,
       45 (1968), 176-177.

2925. Anonymous. "Kantian Dialectics." *The Times Literary Supplement*,
       no. 3657 (31 March 1972), p. 359.

2926. ―――――. Review of *Immanuel Kant*. *Catholic Library World*, 44
       (December 1972), 279.

2927. ―――――. Review of *Immanuel Kant*. *Choice*, 10 (March 1973), 115.

2928. Crispini, F. Review of *Introduzione a Kant*. *Logos*, 4 (1972),
       522-526.

2929. Madden, Kathleen. Review of *Immanuel Kant*. *Library Journal*,
       97 (1 September 1972), 2736.

2930. Marsh, James L. Review of *Immanuel Kant*. *Modern Schoolman*,
       50 (May 1973), 388-390.

2931. Oedingen, Karlo. Review of *Immanuel Kant*. *Kant-Studien*, Band
       65, Heft 3 (1974), 322-325.

2932. Williams, Bernard. "Goldmann on Kant." *Cambridge Review*, 93,
       no. 2208 (2 April 1972), 163-166.

Jean Racine, dramaturge
(items 2503 and 2666)

2933. Anonymous. "Racine Club de Paris." *The Times Literary Supple-
       ment*, no. 3658 (7 April 1972), p. 399.

2934. ―――――. Review of *Racine*. *The Times Literary Supplement*, 23
       February 1973, p. 218.

2935. Barnwell, H.T. Review of *Racine*. *French Studies*, July 1976,
       p. 323.

Lukács et Heidegger ...
(item 2711)

2936. Anonymous. Review of *Lukács and Heidegger*. *Choice*, 15 (September 1978), 887.

2937. Armour, Leslie. Review of *Lukács and Heidegger*. *Library Journal*, 103 (1 April 1978), 756.

2938. Barden, Garrett. Review of *Lukács et Heidegger*. *Human Context*, 7 (1975), 611-613.

2939. Cohen, Olivier. "Un Franc-tireur de la dialectique." *La Quinzaine Littéraire*, no. 174 (1-15 November 1973), pp. 25-26.

2940. Gounelle, A. *Etudes Théologiques et Religieuses*, 50, no. 1 (1975), 121-122.

2941. Höhn. G. *Philosophischer Literaturanzeiger*, 28 (1975), 33-36.

2942. Homann, U. Review of *Lukács und Heidegger*. *Philosophischer Literaturanzeiger*, 30 (1977), 141-144.

2943. Lévy, Bernard-Henri. *Le Nouvel Observateur*, no. 465 (8-14 October 1973), p. 58.

2943a. O'Connor, T. Review of *Lukács and Heidegger*. *Philosophical Studies*, 26 (1977), 274-277.

2943b. Opincar, Charles M. "The Heidegger and Lukacs Collaboration." *Research in Phenomenology*, 9 (1979), forthcoming.

2944. Palmier, Jean-Michel. "*Lukács et Heidegger*, selon Goldmann." *Le Monde [des Livres]*, no. 8952 (25 October 1973), p. 24.

2945. Pasqualotto, G. Review of *Lukács e Heidegger*. *Aut Aut*, no. 155-156 (1976), pp. 256-259.

2946. Sheehan, Thomas J. Review of *Lukács and Heidegger*. *Review of Metaphysics*, 32 (September 1978), 136-137.

Marxisme et sciences humaines
(item 2664)

2947. Baum, H. *Philosophisches Jahrbuch*, 82 (1975), 433-442.

2948. Crispini, F. *Logos*, no. 1 (1972), pp. 142-144.

2949. Desolre, G. *Revue de l'Institut de Sociologie*, no. 4 (1971), pp. 577-583.

2950. Leenhardt, J. "A propos de *Marxisme et sciences humaines*." *Revue de l'Institut de Sociologie*, no. 3-4 (1973), pp. 555-561. Rpt. in *Lucien Goldmann et la sociologie de la litté-*

rature. *Hommage à Lucien Goldmann*. Brussels: Editions de
l'Université de Bruxelles, 1975, pp. 63-69.

See also items 2746 and 2756.

Pour une sociologie du roman
(item 2569)

2951. Amorós, Andrés. "La 'Sociología de la novela' de Goldmann."
        Cuadernos Hispanoamericanos, no. 184 (April 1965), 173-177.

2952. Anonymous. Review of *Towards a Sociology of the Novel*. *Sociological Review*, 23 (November 1975), 944.

2953. ———, Review of *Towards a Sociology of the Novel*. *The Times
        Literary Supplement*, 14 October 1977, p. 1176.

2954. Arnaud-Matech, L. *La Revue Socialiste*, n.s. no. 185 (July 1965),
        pp. 214-216.

2955. Bourbon Busset, Jacques de. "La Fonction de l'irréel: *Pour
        une sociologie du roman*. *La Table Ronde*, no. 204 (January
        1965), pp. 85-88.

2956. Braine, John. "The Prof and the Pro." *Books and Bookmen*, 20,
        no. 8 (May 1975), 48-49.

2957. Châtelet, François. "Autopsie du héros." *Le Nouvel Observateur*,
        no. 43 (8-15 September 1965), p. 24.

2958. Davey, E.R. Review of *Towards a Sociology of the Novel*. *Journal
        of European Studies*, 8 (December 1978), 293-294.

2959. Fiore, Silvana. "Considerazioni sulla *Sociologia del romanzo*
        di Lucien Goldmann." *Rivista di Studi Crociani*, 12, no. 3
        (July-September 1975), 329-335.

2960. Grover, Frederick. "Lucien Goldmann: *Pour une sociologie du
        roman*." *MLN*, 80, no. 3 (May 1965), 382-388.

2961. Grover, P.R. "Towards a Sociology of Literature?" *Cambridge
        Review*, 89, no. 2131 (22 October 1966), 45-47.

2962. Laurenson, Diana, and Alan Swingewood. "Lucien Goldmann and
        the Study of Literature." *New Society*, 14, no. 362 (4 September 1969), 354-356.

2963. Simon, Pierre-Henri. "Encore le nouveau style." *Le Monde
        (hebdomadaire)*, no. 843 (10-16 December 1964), p. 10.

2964. Sucre, Guillermo. *Revista Nacional de Cultura*, no. 166 (October-December 1964), pp. 138-140.

Recherches dialectiques
(item 2529)

2965.   Flam, Léopold. *Revue Belge de Philologie et d'Histoire*, 40
(1962), 177-178.

2966.   Mueller, Fernand-Lucien. *Revue de Théologie et de Philosophie*,
98, no. 1 (1965), 59-60.

Sciences humaines et philosophie
(item 2494)

2967.   Anonymous. "The Dialectics of Pedestrianism." *The Times Literary
Supplement*, no. 3501 (3 April 1969), p. 344.

2968.   Rex, John. "Subject and Objectivity." *New Society*, 13, no. 337
(13 March 1969), 414.

2969.   Rinciman, W.H. "Sociologists and the Truth." *The Listener*, 81,
no. 2086 (20 March 1969), 389-390.

Structures mentales et création culturelle
(item 2665)

See items 2746 and 2756.

JACQUES LACAN

PRIMARY SOURCES

1926

2970. "Fixité du regard par hypertonie, prédominant dans le sens vertical, avec conservation des mouvements automatico-réflexes; aspect spécial du syndrome de Parinaud par hyper-tonie associé à un syndrome extrapyramidal avec troubles pseudo-bulbaires." *Revue Neurologique* (Séance de la Société de Neurologie, 2 novembre 1926), no. II (1926), pp. 410-418. With Alajouanine and Delafontaine. Later rpt. in "Révision des mouvements associés des globes oculaires (contribution à l'étude de la dissociation des activités volontaires et réflexes)." By Alajouanine and Delafontaine. *Revue Neurologique*, février 1931.

1928

2971. "Abasie chez une traumatisée de guerre." *Revue Neurologique* (Séance de la Société de Neurologie, 2 novembre 1928), no. I (1928), pp. 233-237. With Trénel.

2972. "Roman policier. Du délire type hallucinatoire chronique au délire d'imagination." (résumé par Reiller, Société Psychi-atrique de Paris, 26 avril 1928) *Revue Neurologique*, no. I (1928), pp. 738-739. With J. Lévy-Valensi and P. Meignant. Also appeared in *Annales médico-psychologiques*, no. I (1928), pp. 474-476 and *L'Encéphale*, no. 5 (1928), pp. 550-551.

1929

2973. "Syndrome comitio-parkinsonien encéphalitique." (résumé par Marchand, Société clinique de médecine mentale, 17 juin 1929) *Revue Neurologique*, no. II (1929), p. 128. With L. Marchand and A. Courtois. Also appeared in *Annales médico-psychologiques*, no. II (1929), p. 185 and was summarized by P. Meignant in *L'Encéphale*, no. 7 (1929), p. 672.

2974. "Paralysie générale avec syndrome d'automatisme mental." (Société Psychiatrique de Paris, 20 avril 1929) *L'Encéphale*, no. 9 (1929), pp. 802-803. With G. Heuyer.

1930

2975. "Paralysie générale prolongée." (Société Psychiatrique de Paris, 19 décembre 1929) *L'Encéphale*, no. 1 (1930), pp. 83-85. With R. Torgowla.

2976. "Psychose hallucinatoire encéphalitique." (résumé par Marchand, Société clinique de médecine mentale, 17 novembre 1930) *Annales médico-psychologiques*, no. I (1930), pp. 284-285. With A. Courtois. A résumé by P. Schiff also appeared in *L'Encéphale*, no. 4 (1930), p. 331 under the title of "Psychose hallucinatoire chronique."

1931

2977. "Troubles mentaux homochromes chez deux frères hérédosyphiliques." (Séances de la Société de Psychiatrie du 20 novembre 1930) *L'Encéphale*, no. I (1931), pp. 151-152. With P. Schiff and Mme. Schiff-Wertheimer. Cf. item 2979.

2978. "Crises toniques combinées de protrusion de la langue et de trismus se produisant pendant le sommeil chez une parkinsonienne post-encéphalitique. Amputation de la langue consécutive." (Société de Psychiatrie, Paris, 20 novembre 1930) *L'Encéphale*, no. 2 (1931), pp. 145-146. With P. Schiff and Mme. Schiff-Wertheimer. Summarized by Baruk in *Annales médico-psychologiques*, no. II (1930), p. 420.

2979. "Troubles mentaux homochromes chez deux frères hérédosyphilitiques." (Société de Psychiatrie, Paris, 20 novembre 1930) *L'Encéphale*, no. 2 (1931), pp. 151-154. With P. Schiff and Mme. Schiff-Wertheimer. Cf. item 2977.

2980. "Structures des psychoses paranoïaques." *Semaine des Hôpitaux de Paris*, juillet 1931, pp. 437-445.

2981. "Folies simultanées." (Société médico-psychologique, 21 mai 1931) *Annales médico-psychologiques*, no. I (1931), pp. 483-490. With H. Claude and P. Migault. Summarized by Courbon in *L'Encéphale*, no. 7 (1931), p. 557.

2982. "Troubles du langage écrit chez une paranoïaque présentant des éléments délirants du type paranoïde (schizographie)." (Société médico-psychologique, 12 novembre 1931) *Annales médico-psychologiques*, no. II (1931), pp. 407-408. With J. Lévy-Valensi and P. Migault. Summary of a paper which was published in its entirety in item 2984. Also summarized by Courbon under the title "Délire et écrits à type paranoïde chez une malade à présentation paranoïaque." *L'Encéphale*, no. 10 (1931), p. 821.

2983. "Parkinsonisme et syndromes démentiels (protrusion de la langue dans un cas)." (Société médico-psychologique, 12 novembre 1931) *Annales médico-psychologiques*, 1931, pp. 418-428. With

H. Ey. Summarized by Courbon in *L'Encéphale*, no. 10 (1931), p. 822.

2984. "Ecrits 'inspirés': schizographie." *Annales médico-psycholo-giques*, no. II (1931), pp. 508-522. With J. Lévy-Valensi and P. Migault. For summary, see item 2982.

1932

2985. "Spasme de torsion et troubles mentaux post-encéphalitiques." (Société médico-psychologique, 19 mai 1932) *Annales médico-psychologiques*, no. I (1932), pp. 546 and 551. With H. Claude and P. Migault. Summarized by Courbon in *L'Encéphale*, no. 6 (1932), p. 544.

2986. Translation of "De quelques mécanismes névrotiques dans la jalousie, la paranoïa et l'homosexualité." By Sigmund Freud. *Revue Française de Psychanalyse*, no. 3 (1932), pp. 391, 401.

2987. *De la psychose paranoïaque dans ses rapports avec la personnali-té*. Paris: Librairie E. Le François, 1932. Lacan's thesis for the Doctorat en Médecine, Faculté de Médecine de Paris, 1932, no. 530. Rpt. in item 3176.

1933

2988. "Hiatus irrationalis." *Le Phare de Neuilly*, nos. 3-4 (1933), p. 37. Rpt. in item 3184.

2989. "Un Cas de démence précocissime." (Société médico-psychologique, 9 mai 1933) *Annales médico-psychologiques*, no. I (1933), pp. 620-624. With H. Claude and G. Heuyer. Summarized by Courbon in *L'Encéphale*, no. 6 (1933), p. 469.

2990. "Un Cas de perversion infantile par encéphalite épidémique précoce diagnostiqué sur un syndrome moteur fruste." (Société médico-psychologique, 13 juillet 1933) *Annales médico-psycho-logiques*, no. II (1933), pp. 221-223. With G. Heuyer. Sum-marized by Courbon in *L'Encéphale*, no. 8 (1933), p. 617.

2991. "Alcoolisme subaigu à pouls ou ralenti. Co-existence du syn-drome d'automatisme mental." (Société médico-psychologique, 27 novembre 1933) *Annales médico-psychologiques*, no. II (1933), pp. 531-546. With G. Heuyer. Summarized by Courbon in *L'Encéphale*, no. 1 (1934), p. 53.

2992. "Le Problème du style et la conception psychiatrique des formes paranoïaques de l'expérience." *Le Minotaure*, no. 4 (1933), pp. 68-69.

2993. "Motifs du crime paranoïaque. Le Crime des soeurs Papin." *Le Minotaure*, nos. 3-4 (1933), pp. 25-28. Rpt. in item 3137.

2994. "Importance des troubles du caractère dans l'orientation pro-
       fessionelle." Compte rendu du Congrès international pour
       la protection de l'enfance, 1933. With G. Heuyer. Seemingly
       unpublished.

2995. Compte rendu de la 84e assemblée de la Société suisse de psy-
       chiatrie tenue à Nyons-Prangins, les 7 et 8 octobre 1933, et
       consacré au problème des hallucinations. *L'Encéphale*, Novem-
       ber 1933, pp. 686-695.

1934

2996. Participant in the discussion on "La Psychanalyse et le
       développement intellectuel." By Jean Piaget. (VIIIe Congrès
       des psychanalystes de langue française, 19 décembre 1933)
       Revue Française de Psychanalyse, no. 1 (1934), p. 1934.

1935

2997. Participant in the discussion on "Conflits instinctuels et
       bisexualité." By Ch. Odier. (Société Psychanalytique de Paris,
       20 novembre 1934) *Revue Française de Psychanalyse*, no. 4
       (1935), p. 683.

2998. Participant in the discussion on "Quelques réflexions sur le
       suicide." By Dr. Friedman. (Société Psychanalytique de Paris,
       18 décembre 1934) *Revue Française de Psychanalyse*, no. 4
       (1935), p. 686.

2999. Review of *Hallucinations et délire*. By H. Ey. *Evolution Psychi-
       atrique*, no. 1 (1935), pp. 87-91.

3000. Participant in the discussion on "Psychanalyse d'un crime in-
       compréhensible." By P. Schiff. (Société Psychanalytique
       de Paris, 18 novembre 1935) *Revue Française de Psychanalyse*,
       no. 4 (1935), pp. 690-691.

1936

3001. Review of *Le Temps vécu. Etudes phénoménologiques et psycho-
       logiques*. By E. Minkowski. *Recherches Philosophiques*, no. 4
       (1935-1936), pp. 121-131.

3002. Participant in the discussion on "A propos de trois cas d'ano-
       rexie mentale." By O. Codet. (Société Psychanalytique de
       Paris, 18 juin 1935) *Revue Française de Psychanalyse*, no. 1
       (1936), p. 127.

3003. "Au-delà du 'Principe de réalité.'" *Evolution Psychiatrique*
       (special issue of Freudian studies), no. 3 (1936), pp. 67-
       86. Written at Marienbad and Noirmoutier, August-October
       1936. Rpt. in item 3086, pp. 73-92.

1937

3004. "The Looking-Glass-Phase." *International Journal of Psycho-
       analysis*, no. 1 (1937), p. 78. Cf. items 3022, 3023 and 3187.

       Only the title of Lacan's paper is mentioned since he did not
       hand in a summary of it. The paper entitled *"Le Stade du miroir*
       (Théorie d'un moment structurant et génétique de la constitution
       de la réalité, conçu en relation avec l'expérience et la doc-
       trine psychanalytique),"* was read on August 3, 1936 during the
       fourteenth International Psychoanalytic Congress held in
       Marienbad, 2-7 August 1936.

1938

3005. Participant in the discussion on "Vues paléobiologiques et
       biopsychiques." By M. Bonaparte. (Société Psychanalytique
       de Paris, 19 janvier 1937) *Revue Française de Psychanalyse*,
       no. 3 (1938), p. 551.

3006. Participant in the discussion on "Deuil et mélancolie." By D.
       Lagache. (Société Psychanalytique de Paris, 25 mai 1937)
       Revue Française de Psychanalyse, no. 3 (1938), pp. 564-565.

3007. Participant in the discussion on "L'Origine du masochisme et
       la théorie des pulsions." By M. Loewenstein. *Revue Française
       de Psychanalyse*, no. 4 (1938), pp. 750-752. At the Xe Con-
       férence des Psychanalystes de Langue Française, 21 and 22
       February 1938.

3008. "La Famille: le complexe, facteur concret de la pathologie
       familiale. Les Complexes familiaux en pathologie." In
       Encyclopédie Française, tome 8 sur la Vie Mentale. Ed. H.
       Wallon. Paris: Larousse, 1938, no. 40, pp. 3-16; no. 42,
       pp. 1-8.

1939

3009. Lacan's own summary of his paper "De l'impulsion au complexe."
       (Société Psychanalytique de Paris, 25 octobre 1938) *Revue
       Française de Psychanalyse*, no. 1 (1939), pp. 137-141.

       Includes the discussion on it.

1945

3010. "Le Temps logique et l'assertion de certitude anticipée. Un
       Nouveau Sophisme." *Cahiers d'Art*, 1940-1944, pp. 32-42. Ac-
       tually written in March 1945, though the journal dates are
       listed as such. Rpt. in item 3086, pp. 197-213.

1946

3011. "Le Nombre treize et la forme logique de la suspicion." *Cahiers
       d'Art*, 1945-1946, pp. 389-393.

1947

3012. "La Psychiatrie anglaise et la guerre." *Evolution Psychiatrique*,
       no. 1 (1947), pp. 293-318.

       Includes discussion.

1948

3013. "L'Agressivité en psychanalyse." (Rapport théorique présenté
       au XIe Congrès des Psychanalystes de Langue Française,
       Bruxelles, mi-mai 1948) *Revue Française de Psychanalyse*, no.
       3 (1948), pp. 367-388. Rpt. in item 3086, pp. 101-124 with a
       slightly modified first sentence.

3014. "Essai sur les réactions psychiques de l'hypertendu." *Congrès
       Français de Chirurgie*, 1948, pp. 171-176. Cf. item 3031.

       The Congress was held on 4-9 October 1948. A report on Le
       Traitement chirurgical de l'hypertension artérielle was written
       by S. Blondin and A. Weiss with the collaboration of C. Rou-
       villois and J. Lacan. The text on the psychic factors of arterial
       hypertension was written by Lacan.

1949

3015. Participant in the discussion on "La Délinquance névrotique."
       By F. Pasche. (Société Psychanalytique de Paris, 17 février
       1948) *Revue Française de Psychanalyse*, no. 3 (1949), p. 315.

3016. Participant in the discussion on "Mère phallique et mère cas-
       tratrice." By J. Leuba. (Société Psychanalytique de Paris,
       20 avril 1948) *Revue Française de Psychanalyse*, no. 3 (1949),
       p. 317.

3017. Participant in the discussion on "Psychanalyse des principaux
       syndromes psychosomatiques." By M. Ziwar. (Société Psych-
       analytique de Paris, 19 octobre 1948) *Revue Française de
       Psychanalyse*, no. 3 (1949), p. 318.

3018. Participant in the discussion on "Remarques méthodologiques sur
       la socio-analyse." By M. Shentoub. (Société Psychanalytique
       de Paris, 14 décembre 1948) *Revue Française de Psychanalyse*,
       no. 3 (1949), p. 319.

3019. Co-author of "Règlement et doctrine de la Commission de
       l'Enseignement déléguée par la Société Psychanalytique de
       Paris." *Revue Française de Psychanalyse*, no. 4 (1949), pp.
       426-435.

3020. Co-author, in the same Commission de l'Enseignement, of "Les
       Conseillers et conseillères d'enfants agréés par la Société
       Psychanalytique de Paris." *Revue Française de Psychanalyse*,
       no. 4 (1949), pp. 436-441.

3021. Participant in the discussion on "Le Problème de la thérapeu- -
       tique en médecine psychosomatique." By R. Held. (Société Psych-
       analytique de Paris, 20 juin 1949) *Revue Française de Psych-
       analyse*, no. 4 (1949), p. 446.

*3022. "Le Stade du miroir comme formateur de la fonction du Je, telle
       qu'elle nous est révélée dans l'expérience psychanalytique."
       Revue Française de Psychanalyse, 13, no. 4 (1949), pp. 449-
       455. Rpt. in item 3086, pp. 93-100. Paper read at the XVIe
       Congrès International de Psychanalyse held in Zurich, 17
       July 1949. Cf. item 3004. See item 3023 for English abstract.
       For English trans., see item 3104.

3023. "The Mirror-Stage, Source of the I-Function, as Shown by Psycho-
       Analytic Experience." *International Journal of Psychoanalysis*,
       30 (1949), 203.

       Lacan's abstract of item 3022.

3024. Participant in discussion on "A propos de la poupée-fleur."
       By F. Dolto. (Société Psychanalytique de Paris, 18 octobre
       1949) *Revue Française de Psychanalyse*, no. 4 (1949), p. 566.

3025. Participant in discussion on "Psyché dans la nature, ou les
       limites de la psychogenèse." By M. Bonaparte. (Société
       Psychanalytique de Paris, 16 novembre 1949) *Revue Française
       de Psychanalyse*, no. 4 (1949), p. 570.

3026. Participant in the discussion on "Incidences thérapeutiques
       de la prise de conscience de l'envie de pénis dans des cas
       de névrose obsessionnelle féminine." By M. Bouvet. (Société
       Psychanalytique de Paris, 20 décembre 1949) *Revue Française
       de Psychanalyse*, no. 4 (1949), pp. 571-572.

1950

3027. "Propos sur la causalité psychique." In *Le Problème de la
       psychogenèse des névroses et des psychoses*. By Lucien Bonnafé,
       Henri Ey, Sven Follin, Jacques Lacan, and Julien Rouart.
       Bruges-Paris: Desclée de Brouwer, 1950, pp. 123-165. Allocu-
       tion finale, pp. 215-216. Paper read on 28 September 1946
       during the Journées Psychiatriques at Bonneval. Rpt. in item
       3086, pp. 151-194 without the "Allocution finale."

1951

3028. "Introduction théorique aux fonctions de la psychanalyse en criminologie." *Revue Française de Psychanalyse*, 15, no. 1 (1951), pp. 5-29. With M. Cénac. "Réponses aux questions," pp. 84-88. Paper read at the XIIe Conférence des Psychanalystes de Langue Française, 29 mai 1950. Rpt. in item 3086, pp. 125-149 without the "réponses aux questions."

1952

3029. "Intervention sur le transfert." *Revue Française de Psychanalyse*, nos. 1-2 (1952), pp. 154-163. Remarks made at the XIVe Conférence des Psychanalystes de Langue Française, 1951. Rpt. in item 3086, pp. 215-226 with a brief new introduction and without two short passages.

1953

3030. "Some Reflections on the Ego." *International Journal of Psycho-Analysis*, 34 (1953), 1-17. Paper read before the British Psychoanalytical Society, 2 May 1951.

3031. "Considérations psychosomatiques sur l'hypertension artérielle." *Evolution Psychiatrique*, no. 3 (1953), pp. 397-409. With R. Lévy and H. Danon-Boileau. Cf. item 3014.

3032. *Le Mythe individuel du névrose ou "Poésie et vérité" dans la névrose*. Paris: Centre de Documentation Universitaire, 1953. A thirty-page mimeographed text of a speech given by Lacan before the Collège Philosophique, not corrected by the author.

3033. Participant in the discussion on "Sur la théorie des instincts," a theoretical report by M. Benassy, and on "Le Moi dans la névrose obsessionelle, relations d'objets et mécanismes de défense," a clinical report by M. Bouvet, both given during the XVe Conférence des Psychanalystes de Langue Française, Paris, 1952 and announced in the *Revue Française de Psychanalyse*, no. 4 (1952), p. 592; however, Lacan's remarks were not published. See *Revue Française de Psychanalyse*, nos. 1-2 (1953), p. 212.

3034. "Le Stade du miroir en action," avec projection du film de Gesell "La Découverte de soi devant le miroir." A conference given by Lacan before the Société Psychanalytique de Paris on May 19, 1953 and announced in the *Revue Française de Psychanalyse*, no. 3 (1953), p. 369, but not published.

1955

3035. Participant in the discussion on "Psychanalyse et philosophie." By J. Favez-Boutonnier. (Société Française de Philosophie, 25 janvier 1955) Discussion summarized by Lacan. *Bulletin* de la *Société Française de Philosophie*, 49, no. 1 (1955), 37-41.

3036.   "Variantes de la cure-type." In *Encyclopédie Médico-chirurgicale,* Psychiatrie, tome III, 2-1955, fasc. 37812-C 10.

Written during Easter 1955 and withdrawn from the encyclopedia in 1960, this article was rpt. in item 3086, pp. 323-362 with brief new introduction and a rewritten first chapter.

1956

*3037.   "Fonction et champ de la parole et du langage en psychanalyse, (Rapport du Congrès de Rome tenu à l'Istituto di Psicologia della Università di Roma les 26 et 27 septembre 1953)." In *La Psychanalyse* [Recherche et enseignement freudiens de la Société Française de Psychanalyse], *vol. 1* [consacré au thème spécial de l'usage de la parole et des structures de langage dans la conduite et dans le champ de la psychanalyse et dirigé par Jacques Lacan. Travaux des années 1953-1955]. Paris: Presses Universitaires de France, 1956, pp. 81-166. For English trans., see items 3103, 3178 and 3187.

Subsequent references to *La Psychanalyse* will list only the volume and the year. Several paragraphs of the article cited here were rewritten and rpt. in item 3086, pp. 237-322, preceded by a new introductory text "Du sujet enfin en question," pp. 229-236, written in 1966.

3038.   "Actes du Congrès de Rome." *La Psychanalyse*, 1 (1956), 202-211 and 242-255.

Lacan's address and his answers to remarks made during discussions. See item 3037 for details.

3039.   "Le Symbolique, l'imaginaire et le réel." A conference before the Société Française de Psychanalyse on July 8, 1953, announced in *La Psychanalyse*, 1 (1956), 288-290 but seemingly unpublished. Cf. item 3048.

3040.   "Introduction au commentaire de Jean Hyppolite sur la *Verneinung* de Freud." (Séminaire de technique freudienne du 10 février 1954) *La Psychanalyse*, 1 (1956), 17-28. Rpt., together with item 3041, in 3086, pp. 369-399, preceded by a new introductory text "D'un dessin," pp. 363-367, written in 1966.

*3041.   "Réponse au commentaire de Jean Hyppolite sur la *Verneinung* de Freud." (Séminaire de technique freudienne du 10 février 1954) *La Psychanalyse*, 1 (1956), 41-58. Rpt., together with item 3040, in 3086, pp. 369-399, preceded by a new introductory text "D'un dessin," pp. 363-367, written in 1966. For Italian trans., see item 3166.

3042.   "Psychanalyse et cybernétique, ou: de la nature du langage." A conference before the Société Française de Psychanalyse on June 22, 1955, announced in *La Psychanalyse*, 1 (1956), 288-290 but seemingly unpublished.

3043. Participant in the Colloquium on Mental Anorexia, Société
      Française de Psychanalyse, November 28, 1955, announced in
      La Psychanalyse, 1 (1956), 288-290 but seemingly unpublished.

3044. Translation of "Logos." By Martin Heidegger. *La Psychanalyse*, 1
      (1956), 59-79.

*3045. "La Chose freudienne ou Sens du retour à Freud en psychanalyse."
      Evolution Psychiatrique, no. 1 (1956), pp. 225-252. Rpt. in
      item 3086, pp. 401-436 with one rewritten paragraph. An ex-
      panded version of a conference given at the neuropsychiatric
      clinic of Vienna, November 7, 1955. For Italian trans., see
      item 3154.

3046. Participant in the discussion on "Sur les rapports entre la
      mythologie et le rituel." By Claude Lévi-Strauss. (Société
      Française de Philosophie, 21 mai 1956) *Bulletin de la Société
      Française de Philosophie*, no. 3 (1956), pp. 110-119.

      Includes the response by Lévi-Strauss.

3047. "Situation de la psychanalyse et formation du psychanalyste
      en 1956." The first version exists only in off-print; the
      second version in *Les Etudes Philosophiques* (special issue
      commemorating the centenary of Freud's birth), 11, no. 4
      (1956), 567-584. Rpt. in item 3086, pp. 459-491, which gives
      both versions.

3048. "Fetishism: The Symbolic, the Imaginary and the Real." In
      Perversions: Psychodynamics and Therapy. Ed. S. Lorand and
      M. Balint. New York: Random House; London: Ortolan Press,
      1956, pp. 265-276. With W. Granoff. Cf. item 3039.

                                1957

*3049. "Le Séminaire sur 'la lettre volée.'" *La Psychanalyse*, 2 (1957),
      1-44. For English trans., see item 3153.

      Given before the Société Française de Psychanalyse on April
      26, 1955; written and dated mid-May, mid-August 1956 at
      Guitrancourt-San Casciano. Rpt. in item 3086, pp. 9-61, pre-
      ceded by a new introduction entitled "Ouverture de ce recueil";
      the introduction to the first version is placed after the text
      and preceded by a "Présentation de la suite" and followed by
      a "Parenthèse des parenthèses," both written in 1966.

3050. A summary of Lacan's remarks after "Phénoménologie de Hegel
      et psychanalyse." By J. Hyppolite. (Société Française de
      Psychanalyse, 11 janvier 1955) *La Psychanalyse*, 3 (1957),
      32 (note).

3051. Participant in the discussion on "Réflexions sur le 'Wo Es war,
      soll Ich werden' de Freud." By A. Hesnard. (Société Française
      de Psychanalyse, 6 novembre 1956) *La Psychanalyse*, 3 (1957),
      323-324.

3052. Participant in the discussion on "Fascination de la conscience
       par le Moi." By D. Lagache. (Société Française de Psychanalyse
       8 janvier 1957) *La Psychanalyse*, 3 (1957), 329.

*3053. "L'Instance de la lettre dans l'inconscient ou la raison depuis
       Freud." *La Psychanalyse*, 3 (1957), 47-81. Rpt. in item 3086,
       pp. 493-528 with several additional notes. For English trans.,
       see items 3091 and 3125.

       Given at the Amphithéâtre Descartes of the Sorbonne on May
       9, 1957, at the request of the Groupe de Philosophie de la
       Fédération des Etudiants ès Lettres; written version is dated
       14-26 May 1957.

3054. "La Relation d'objet et les structures freudiennes." *Bulletin
       de Psychologie*, tome X, no. 7 (1956-1957), 426-430; no. 10,
       602-605; no. 12, 742-743 and no. 14, 851-854; tome XI, no. 1
       (1957-1958), 31-34.

       J.B. Pontalis' report on Lacan's seminar of 21 November 1956
       to 3 July 1957.

3055. "La Psychanalyse et son enseignement." (Société Française de
       Philosophie, 23 février 1957) *Bulletin de la Société Fran-
       çaise de Philosophie*, 51, no. 2 (1957), 65-104. Includes
       debate. Rpt. in item 3086, pp. 437-458 without debate.

                                    1958

3056. "D'une question préliminaire à tout traitement possible de la
       psychose." *La Psychanalyse*, 4 (1958), 1-50. Rpt. in item
       3086, pp. 531-583.

       Refers to the seminar of the first two quarters of 1955-1956.
       Written in December 1957 and January 1958.

3057. Participant in the discussion on "Le Rendez-vous avec le
       psychanalyste." By. G. Favez. (Société Française de Psych-
       analyse, 5 février 1957) *La Psychanalyse*, 4 (1958), 308-313.

3058. Participant in the discussion on "Abandon et névrose." By J.
       Favez-Boutonnier. (Société Française de Psychanalyse, 7 mai
       1957) *La Psychanalyse*, 4 (1958), 318-320.

3059. Participant in the discussion on "La Psychothérapie des
       schizophrènes." By P. Matussek. (Société Française de Psych-
       analyse, 4 juin 1957) *La Psychanalyse*, 4 (1958), 332.

*3060. "Les Formations de l'inconscient." *Bulletin de Psychologie*,
       tome XI, nos. 4-5 (1957-1958), 293-296; tome XII, nos. 2-3
       (1958-1959), 182-192; no. 4, 250-256. For Spanish trans.,
       see item 3127.

       J.B. Pontalis' report on Lacan's seminar of 6 June 1957 to
       June 1958.

3061. "Jeunesse de Gide ou la lettre et le désir." *Critique*, 11^e
       année, no. 131 (April 1958), 291-315. Rpt. in item 3086, pp.
       739-764. Cf. item 3128.

       On books by Jean Delay and Jean Schlumberger.

1959

*3062. "Le Désir et son interprétation." *Bulletin de Psychologie*,
       tome XIII, no. 5 (1959-1960), 263-272 and no. 6, 329-335.
       Cf. item 3189. For Spanish trans., see item 3127.

       J.B. Pontalis' report on Lacan's seminar of 12 November 1958
       to 11 February 1959.

1960

3063. "A la mémoire d'Ernest Jones: sur sa théorie de symbolisme."
       La Psychanalyse, 5 (1960), 1-20. Written at Guitrancourt,
       January-March 1959. Rpt. in item 3086, pp. 697-717 with "D'un
       syllabaire après coup," pp. 717-724, added.

3064. "L'Ethique de la psychanalyse." The seventeen-page typed re-
       transcription of two conferences which Lacan gave at the
       Facultés Universitaires Saint-Louis, Brussels, in 1960.
       Seemingly unpublished.

1961

3065. "La Direction de la cure et les principes de son pouvoir."
       La Psychanalyse, 6 (1961), 149-206. Rpt. in item 3086, pp.
       585-645.

       First report on the Colloque International de Royaumont
       held at the invitation of the Société Française de Psychanalyse,
       10-13 July 1958. An account of what Lacan really said about
       his report is given by J.B. Pontalis in *Bulletin de Psychologie*,
       tome XII, nos. 2-3 (1958-1959), 160-162.

3066. "Remarques sur le rapport de Daniel Lagache: 'Psychanalyse et
       structure de la personnalité.'" *La Psychanalyse*, 6 (1961),
       111-147. Report at the Colloque de Royaumont, 10-13 July
       1958; definitive version, Easter 1960. Rpt. in item 3086,
       pp. 647-684.

3067. Participant in the discussion on "L'Idée de rationalité et la
       règle de justice." By C. Perelman. (Société Française de
       Psychanalyse, 23 avril 1960) *Bulletin de la Société Française
       de Philosophie*, 55, no. 1 (1961), 29-33. Rewritten by Lacan
       in June 1961 and rpt. in item 3116, pp. 889-892, under the
       title of "La Métaphore du sujet."

3068. "Maurice Merleau-Ponty." *Les Temps Modernes* (special issue on
       Merleau-Ponty), 17e année, no. 184-185 (August-October 1961),
       245-254. Rpt. in item 3183?

3069. "Kant avec Sade." *Critique*, 19, no. 191 (1963), 289–313. Rpt.
       in item 3086, pp. 765–790 without the long introductory note;
       also rpt. as the postface to item 3080, pp. 551–577.

       This article, written in September 1962, was to be the preface
       to *La Philosophie dans le boudoir*. Paris: Editions du Cercle
       du Livre Précieux, 1963, vol. 15.

1964

3070. "Propos directifs pour un Congrès sur la sexualité féminine."
       (Colloque International de Psychanalyse, 5–9 septembre 1960,
       à l'Université Municipale d'Amsterdam) *La Psychanalyse*, 7
       (1964), 3–14. Written two years before the congress and rpt.
       in item 3086, pp. 725–736.

3071. "Du Trieb de Freud et du désir du psychanalyste" (résumé). In
       Tecnica e casistica. Tecnica, escatologia e casistica. Atti
       del Convegno indetto dal Centro Internazionale di Studi
       Umanistici e dall'Istituto di Studi Filosofici. Roma, 7–12
       Gennaio 1964. Ed. Enrico Castelli. Rome: Istituto di Studi
       Filosofici; Padua: Cedam, 1964, pp. 51–53; discussion, pp.
       55–60. Rpt. in item 3086, pp. 851–854 without the discussion
       but with an introductory note.

3072. Participant in the discussion on "Technique et non-technique
       dans l'interprétation." By Paul Ricoeur. In *Tecnica e
       casistica* (see item 3071), p. 44.

3073. Participant in the discussion on "Notes pour une épistémologie
       de la santé mentale." By Alphonse De Waelhens. In *Tecnica
       e casistica* (see item 3071), pp. 87–88.

3074. Participant in the discussion on "Morale tradizionale e Società
       contemporanea." By Filiasi Carcano. In *Tecnica e casistica*
       (see item 3071), p. 106.

3075. Participant in the discussion on "Casuistique et morales
       modernes de situation." By R. Marlé. In *Tecnica e casistica*
       (see item 3071), p. 117.

1965

3076. "Hommage fait à Marguerite Duras, du ravissement de Lol. V.
       Stein." In *Marguerite Duras. La Provinciale de Tourgueniev.*
       [*Cahiers de la Compagnie Madeleine-Renaud--Jean-Louis
       Barrault*, no. 52] Paris: Gallimard, 1965, pp. 7–15.

1966

3077.   "La Signification du phallus. Die Bedeutung des Phallus."
        Conference given in German on May 9, 1958 at the Max Planck
        Institute of Munich, at the invitation of Professor P. Matussek.
        Published in 1966, without modification but with a short
        introduction, in item 3086, pp. 685-695.

*3078.   "Subversion du sujet et dialectique du désir dans l'inconscient
        freudien." (Commission à un Congrès réuni à Royaumont par
        les soins des Colloques Philosophiques Internationaux sous
        le titre "La Dialectique" sur l'invitation de Jean Wahl, du
        19 au 23 septembre 1960). Published in 1966 in item 3086,
        pp. 793-827 with an additional concluding note. For English
        trans., see item 3187.

3079.   "Position de l'inconscient." In L'*Inconscient* (VIᵉ Colloque
        de Bonneval). Ed. Henri Ey. Paris: Desclée de Brouwer, 1966,
        pp. 159-170.

        Remarks made during a congress on the Freudian unconscious
        at the Bonneval hospital, 31 October-2 November 1960. These
        remarks were condensed in March 1964 at the request of Henri
        Ey and later rpt. in item 3086, pp. 829-850 with a brief in-
        troduction and a concluding note.

3080.   "Kant avec Sade," postface to *Oeuvres complètes du Marquis de
        Sade. Vol. II, tome III, Justine--La Philosophie dans le
        boudoir.* Paris: Cercle du Livre Précieux, 1966, pp. 551-577.
        Rpts. item 3069.

3081.   "La Science et la vérité." *Cahiers pour l'Analyse* (Cercle
        d'Epistémologie de l'Ecole Normale Supérieure), nos. 1-2
        (1966), pp. 7-30.

        Stenography of the opening lecture of his 1965-1966 seminar
        on "L'Objet de la psychanalyse" at the Ecole Normale Supérieure
        in his position as Chargé de Conférences of the VIᵉ section of
        the Ecole Pratique des Hautes Etudes. Dated December 1, 1965,
        this article was rpt. in item 3086, pp. 855-877.

3082.   "Les Graphes de Jacques Lacan," commentés par Jacques-Alain
        Miller. *Cahiers pour l'Analyse,* nos. 1-2 (1966), pp. 169-177.

        Refers to various passages and graphs in Lacan's *Ecrits* (see
        items 3086 and 3116); published as a supplement to item 3081.

*3083.   "Réponses à des étudiants en philosophie sur l'objet de la
        psychanalyse." *Cahiers pour l'Analyse,* no. 3 (May-June 1966),
        pp. 5-13. For Catalonian or Spanish trans., see item 3126.

        Questions asked by a group of students from the Faculté des
        Lettres de Paris, February 19, 1966, and rpt. by the Cercle
        d'Epistémologie de l'Ecole Normale Supérieure. The text was
        edited by M.G. Contesse and deals with the issue of why
        psychoanalysis as a science will be structuralist.

3084.   Participant in the round table at the Collège de Médecine on
        "La Place de la psychanalyse dans la médecine." *Cahiers du
        Collège de Médecine*, no. 12 (1966), pp. 761-774. The February
        16, 1966 meeting at the Salpêtrière presided by Mme. J. Aubry,
        with H.P. Klots, Mme. G. Raimault and P. Royer. Rpt. in item
        3092.

3085.   Presentation of *Ponctuation de Freud.* [with the *Mémoires d'un
        névropathe* by D.P. Schreber. Trans. Paul Duquenne.] *Cahiers
        pour l'Analyse*, no. 5 (November-December 1966), pp. 69-72.

*3086. *Ecrits.* Paris: Editions du Seuil, 1966. (Le Champ Freudien)
        See item 3116 for later edition. For trans., see items 3136
        (Spanish), 3155 (Spanish), 3168 (German), 3172 (Italian),
        3173 (Spanish), 3179-3180 (German), and 3187 (English). For
        reviews, see items 3384-3401.

        A collection of articles previously published or unpublished,
        with additional explanatory notes such as "Ouverture de ce
        recueil," etc. Contains items 3003, 3010, 3013, 3022, 3027,
        3028, 3029, 3036, 3037, 3040, 3041, 3045, 3047, 3049, 3053,
        3055, 3056, 3061, 3063, 3065, 3066, 3069, 3070, 3071, 3077,
        3078, 3079, and 3081. See also item 3093.

3087.   "Retour à Freud" [présentation de F.W.]. *La Quinzaine Littéraire*,
        no. 15 (1-15 November 1966), pp. 4-5.

3088.   "Entretien avec J. Lacan." *Les Lettres Françaises*, no. 1159
        (1-7 December 1966), pp. 1, 16 and 17.

        Conversation with P. Daix on November 26, 1966.

3089.   "Un Psychanalyste s'explique ... Auteur mystérieux et prestigi-
        eux: Jacques Lacan veut que la psychanalyse 'redevienne la
        peste.'" *Le Figaro Littéraire*, no. 1076 (1 December 1966),
        p. 11.

        Conversation with G. Lapouge.

3090.   Five-page mimeographed retranscription of an interview given
        at the R.T.B. (Radio Télévision Belge), December 14, 1966.
        Seemingly unpublished.

3091.   "Insistence of the Letter in the Unconscious." Trans. Jan Miel.
        Yale French Studies, nos. 36-37 (1966), pp. 112-147. Trans.
        of item 3053. Rpt. in item 3125. Part of a special issue on
        Structuralism.

                                    1967

3092.   "Psychanalyse et médecine." *Lettres de l'Ecole Freudienne*
        (Bulletin intérieur de l'Ecole Freudienne de Paris), no. 1
        (1967), pp. 34-61. Rpts. item 3084.

3093.   "Petit discours à l'O.R.T.F." *Recherches*, nos. 3-4 (1967), pp.
        5-9.

A conversation broadcast December 2, 1966 in the context of the Matinées de France-Culture as part of G. Charbonnier's program "Sciences et Techniques." On the publication of item 3086.

3094. "La Logique du fantasme." *Lettres de l'Ecole Freudienne*, no. 1 (1967), pp. 1, 11-17; no. 2, pp. 7-23; no. 3, pp. 3-33; no. 4, pp. 2-23; no. 5 (1968), pp. 62-108.

J. Nassif's report on Lacan's seminar of 16 November 1966 to 21 June 1967.

1968

3095. "Proposition du 9 octobre 1967 sur le psychanalyste de l'Ecole." *Scilicet* [Paris: Editions du Seuil], no. 1 (1968), pp. 14-30. See item 3109. For reviews, see items 3404-3405.

3096. "Discours de clôture des Journées sur les psychoses chez l'enfant" (Paris, 22 October 1967). *Recherches*, December 1968 (special issue on "Enfance aliénée [II]). pp. 143-152. Rpt. in item 3138.

3097. "La Méprise du sujet supposé savoir." *Scilicet*, no. 1 (1968), pp. 31-41. Paper read at the Institut Français de Naples, 14 December 1967.

3098. "De Rome 53 à Rome 67: la psychanalyse. Raison d'un échec." *Scilicet*, no. 1 (1968), pp. 42-50. Paper read at the Magistero of the University of Rome, 15 December 1967 at 6 P.M.

3099. "De la psychanalyse dans ses rapports avec la réalité." *Scilicet*, no. 1 (1968), pp. 51-59. Paper read at the Institut Français de Milan, 18 December 1967 at 6:30 P.M.

A short note on his stay in Italy and the papers read there, p. 60.

3100. "Introduction de Scilicet au titre de la revue de l'Ecole Freudienne de Paris." *Scilicet*, no. 1 (1968), pp. 3-13.

3101. "Jacques Lacan commente la naissance de Scilicet." (Entretien avec R. Higgins) *Le Monde*, 16 March 1968.

3102. A brief commentary on the *L'Arc* issue devoted to Freud. *Scilicet*, no. 1 (1968), pp. 173-177. Also contains "Notes prises aux présentations de malades du Dr Lacan à l'Hôpital Sainte-Anne."

3103. *Language of the Self. The Function of Language in Psychoanalysis.* Trans. with notes and commentary by Anthony Wilden. Baltimore, Md.: Johns Hopkins Press, 1968. Rpt. in item 3178. For reviews, see items 3402-3403.

Trans. of item 3037 together with Wilden's "Lacan and the Discourse of the Other," pp. 159-311, and a bibliography, pp.

313-322. An attempt to understand Freud in the light of Lévi-
Strauss' structural anthropology and Roman Jakobson's structural
linguistics. Also deals with the Hegelian and Heideggerian
antecedents to Lacan's theory of language and Lévi-Strauss'
concept of "symbolic function" which Lacan was the first to
integrate into psychoanalytical theory.

3104.   "The Mirror-Phase as Formative of the Function of the I."
        Trans. Jean Roussel. *New Left Review*, no. 51 (September-
        October 1968), pp. 71-77. Trans. of item 3022.

                                 1969

3105.   Participant in discussions at the Congrès de l'Ecole Freudienne
        in Strasbourg on "Psychanalyse et Psychothérapie," October
        12, 1968. *Lettres de l'Ecole Freudienne*, no. 6 (1969), pp.
        42-48.

3106.   Participant in the discussion on "Thérapeutique-Psychanalyse-
        Objet" by P. Benoit and on "Du désir d'être psychanalyste:
        ses effets au niveau de la pratique psychothérapeutique de
        'l'élève-analyste'" by M. Ritter. *Lettres de l'Ecole Freudi-
        enne*, no. 6 (1969), pp. 39, 92-94.

3107.   Participant in the discussion on "Qu'est-ce qu'un auteur?"
        By Michel Foucault. (Société Française de Philosophie, 22
        February 1969) *Bulletin de la Société Française de Philosophie*,
        63, no. 3 (1969), p. 104.

3108.   Answer to the request for bio-bibliographical information in
        Anthologie des Psychologues Français Contemporains. By
        D. Hameline and H. Lesage. Paris: Presses Universitaires
        de France, 1969, pp. 322-323.

                                 1970

3109.   "Discours à l'Ecole Freudienne de Paris du 6 décembre 1967"
        (Réponse aux avis suscités par la proposition du 9 octobre
        1967 [item 3095]). *Scilicet*, nos. 2-3 (1970), pp. 9-24. See
        item 3122.

3110.   Participant in the discussion on "Sur le discours psychanaly-
        tique." By J. Nassif. *Lettres de l'Ecole Freudienne* (second
        issue devoted to the Strasbourg Congress, 12 October 1968),
        no. 7 (1970), pp. 40, 42-43.

3111.   Participant in the discussion on "Ce que Freud fait de l'his-
        toire: note à propos de: 'Une Névrose démoniaque au XVIIe
        siècle.'" By M. De Certeau. *Lettres de l'Ecole Freudienne*,
        no. 7 (1970), p. 84.

3112.   Participant in the discussion on "Essai de dégagement du concept
        psychanalytique de psychothérapie." By J. Rudrauf. *Lettres de
        l'Ecole Freudienne*, no. 7 (1970), pp. 136-137.

3113.   Participant in the discussion on "Stratégie de sauvetage de
        Freud." By J. Oury. *Lettres de l'Ecole Freudienne*, no. 7
        (1970), pp. 146, 151.

3114.   "Discours de J. Lacan en guise de conclusion au Congrès de
        Strasbourg" (October 13, 1968). *Lettres de l'Ecole Freudienne*,
        no. 7 (1970), pp. 157-166.

3115.   "Adresse du jury d'accueil de l'Ecole Freudienne de Paris à
        l'assemblée avant son vote (le 25 janvier 1969)." *Scilicet*,
        nos. 2-3 (1970), pp. 49-51.

*3116. *Ecrits, I-II.* Paris: Editions du Seuil, 1970. 2 vols. (Points,
        no. 5) New enlarged edition of item 3086, with a "Préface"
        dated December 14, 1969, pp. 7-12. Includes item 3067. For
        trans., see items 3136 (Spanish), 3155 (Spanish), 3168 (Ger-
        man), 3172 (Italian), 3173 (Spanish), and 3179-3180
        (German).

*3117. "Préface" (dated Christmas 1969) to *Jacques Lacan.* By Anika
        Rifflet-Lemaire. Brussels: Ch. Dessart, 1970, pp. 9-20. For
        Spanish or Catalonian trans., see item 3135.

3118.   "Teneur de l'entretien avec J. Lacan." With Anika Rifflet-
        Lemaire. In *Jacques Lacan.* By Anika Rifflet-Lemaire. Brussels:
        Ch. Dessart, 1970, pp. 401-407.

3119.   "Radiophonie." *Scilicet*, nos. 2-3 (1970), pp. 2-3, 55-99.

        Of these seven replies, four were broadcast on the R.T.B.
        (Radio-Télévision Belge), third program, on June 5, 10, 19,
        and 26, 1970 and on the O.R.T.F. (French Radio and Tele-
        vision) (France Culture station), June 7, 1970. On the relations
        between psychoanalysis, linguistics and ethnology and on the
        structural positions of discourse.

3120.   "Allocution prononcée pour la clôture du Congrès de l'Ecole
        Freudienne de Paris, le 19 avril 1970, par son directeur."
        Scilicet, nos. 2-3 (1970), pp. 391-399.

        This is the second text of the spoken version which appears
        in item 3132.

3121.   "Liminaire," or foreword to the double issue of *Scilicet*, nos.
        2-3 (1970), pp. 5-6.

3122.   "Commentaires datés du 1er octobre 1970, à la suite du discours
        à l'Ecole Freudienne de Paris du 6 décembre 1967." *Scilicet*,
        nos. 2-3 (1970), pp. 24-29. See item 3109.

3123.   "L'Envers de la psychanalyse," a 1970 unpublished work cited
        in *Jacques Lacan* (special issue no. 58 of *L'Arc* on Lacan).
        Aix-en-Provence: *L'Arc*, 1974.

3124.   "Of Structure as an Inmixing of an Otherness Prerequisite to
        any Subject Whatever." In *The Languages of Criticism and the*

Sciences of Man. The Structuralist Controversy. Ed. Richard
Macksey and Eugenio Umberto Donato. Baltimore, Md.: Johns
Hopkins Press, 1970, pp. 186-195.

3125. "The Insistence of the Letter in the Unconscious." Trans. Jan
Miel. In *Structuralism*. Ed. Jacques Ehrmann. New York: Doubleday Anchor Books, 1970, pp. 101-137. Rpts. item 3091. Trans.
of item 3053.

3126. "El Objeto del psicoanálisis." In *Freud y Lacan*. By Louis
Althusser. Trans. Muria Garreta. Barcelona: Editorial Anagrama, 1970. Trans. of item 3083. See item 294.

3127. *Las Formaciones del inconsciente, seguido de El Deseo y su
interpretación*. Intro. Charles Melman, Jan Miel and Jean
Reboul. Buenos Aires: Ediciones Nueva Visión, 1970. Trans.
of items 3060 and 3062.

1971

3128. "André et Emmanuèle." In *Les Critiques de notre temps et Gide*.
Ed. Michel Raimond. Paris: Editions Garnier Frères, 1971, pp.
119-124. Cf. item 3061.

3129. Participant in the discussion on "De la conception grecque de
l'éducation et de l'enseignement de la psychanalyse." By
Ph. Rappard. *Lettres de l'Ecole Freudienne*, no. 8 (1971),
pp. 8-10. At the Congress of the Ecole Freudienne de Paris
on "L'Enseignement de la psychanalyse," 17-19 April 1970.

3130. Participant in the discussion on "Sur l'enseignement de la
psychanalyse à Vincennes." By Montrelay and Baudry. *Lettres
de l'Ecole Freudienne* (Congress of 17-19 April 1970), no. 8
(1971), p. 187.

3131. Participant in the discussion on "Propos à prétention robora-
tive avant le Congrès." By Ch. Melman. *Lettres de l'Ecole
Freudienne* (Congress of 17-19 April 1970), no. 8 (1971),
pp. 199, 203-204.

3132. "Allocution prononcée pour la clôture du Congrès de l'Ecole
Freudienne de Paris, le 19 avril 1970, par son directeur."
Lettres de l'Ecole Freudienne, no. 8 (1971), pp. 205-217.

This is the spoken version; a second text may be found in
item 3120.

3133. "Opinion de J. Lacan sur *Un Métier de chien* roman de Dominique
Desanti." *Le Monde*, 19 November 1971, p. 17.

3134. "Lituraterre." *Littérature*, no. 3 (1971), pp. 3-10. Issue on
"Littérature et psychanalyse," 3 October 1971.

3135. Prologue to *Lacan*. By Anika Rifflet-Lemaire. Trans. Francisco
J. Millet. Barcelona: E.D.H.A.S.A., 1971. Trans. of item 3117.

3136. *Lectura estructuralista de Freud*. Trans. Tomás Segovia. Mexico:
       Siglo Veintiuno Editores, 1971. Trans. of item 3086/3116;
       1st edition in Spanish. See also items 3155 and 3173.

1972

3137. "Motifs du crime paranoïaque. Le Crime des soeurs Papin."
       Obliques, no. 2 (1972), pp. 100-103. Rpts. item 2993.

3138. "Discours de clôture des Journées sur les psychoses chez
       l'enfant." (Paris, 22 October 1967) In *Enfance aliénée*.
       Paris: Union Générale d'Editions, 1972, pp. 295-306. (10/18)
       Rpts. item 3096.

3139. Participant in the discussion on "Du roman conçu comme le dis-
       cours même de l'homme qui écrit." By Mme. Ch. Bardet-Giraudon.
       Lettres de l'Ecole Freudienne, no. 9 (1972), pp. 20-30. At
       the Congress of the Ecole Freudienne at Aix-en-Provence,
       20-23 May 1971, on "La Technique de la psychanalyse."

3140. Participant in the discussion on "A propos du désir du médecin."
       By P. Lemoine. *Lettres de l'Ecole Freudienne*, no. 9 (1972),
       pp. 69, 74-78. At the Aix-en-Provence Congress of 20-23 May
       1971.

3141. Participant in the discussion on "Contribution à l'étude du
       sens du symptôme épileptique." By J. Guey. *Lettres de l'Ecole
       Freudienne*, no. 9 (1972), pp. 151, 154, 155. At the Aix-en-
       Provence Congress of 20-23 May 1971.

3142. Participant in the discussion on "Le Psychanalyste est du côté
       de la vérité." By S. Ginestet-Elsair. *Lettres de l'Ecole
       Freudienne*, no. 9 (1972), p. 166. At the Aix-en-Provence
       Congress of 20-23 May 1971.

3143. Participant in the discussion on "A l'écoute de l'écoute." By
       A. Didier and M. Sylvestre. *Lettres de l'Ecole Freudienne*,
       no. 9 (1972), pp. 176-183. At the Aix-en-Provence Congress
       of 20-23 May 1971.

3144. Participant in the discussion on "Remarques sur la fonction de
       l'argent dans la technique analytique." By P. Mathis. *Lettres
       de l'Ecole Freudienne*, no. 9 (1972), pp. 195, 196, 202, 205.
       At the Aix-en-Provence Congress of 20-23 May 1971.

3145. Participant in the discussion on "Technique de l'intervention:
       incidence de l'automatisme de répétition de l'analyste." By
       S. Zlatine. *Lettres de l'Ecole Freudienne*, no. 9 (1972), pp.
       254, 255, 260. At the Aix-en-Provence Congress of 20-23 May
       1971.

3146. Participant in the discussion on "De l'analyse des résistances
       au temps de l'analyste." By Conté and Beirnaert. *Lettres de
       l'Ecole Freudienne*, no. 9 (1972), pp. 334, 336. At the Aix-
       en-Provence Congress of 20-23 May 1971.

3147. Participant in the discussion on "De la règle fondamentale."
       By J. Rudrauf. *Lettres de l'Ecole Freudienne*, no. 9 (1972),
       p. 374. At the Aix-en-Provence Congress of 20-23 May 1971.

3148. Participant in the discussion on "L'Objet dans la cure." By
       S. Leclaire. *Lettres de l'Ecole Freudienne*, no. 9 (1972),
       pp. 445-450. At the Aix-en-Provence Congress of 20-23 May
       1971.

3149. Participant in the discussion on "Le Moment spéculaire dans la
       cure, moment de rupture." By P. Delaunay. *Lettres de l'Ecole
       Freudienne*, no. 9 (1972), pp. 471-473. At the Aix-en-Provence
       Congress of 20-23 May 1971.

3150. "Discours de conclusion au Congrès d'Aix-en-Provence." *Lettres
       de l'Ecole Freudienne*, no. 9 (1972), pp. 507-513. May 13,
       1971, text reworked for the Aix-en-Provence Congress of the
       Ecole Freudienne on "La Technique de la psychanalyse," 20-
       23 May 1971.

3151. A 28-page typed retranscription of an address given in the
       Grande Rotonde of the Université de Louvain in Belgium,
       13 October 1972. Apparently unpublished.

3152. Retranscription (with gaps due to technical difficulties) of
       Lacan's remarks during an extraordinary session of the Ecole
       Belge de Psychanalyse, 14 October 1972. Lacan gave an inter-
       view on Belgian television the same day, but it was apparently
       unpublished.

3153. "Seminar on the Purloined Letter [with an introductory note by
       Jeffrey Mehlman]." Trans. Jeffrey Mehlman. In *Yale French
       Studies* (issue on French Freud: Structural Studies in Psycho-
       analysis, ed. Jeffrey Mehlman), no. 48 (1972), pp. 38-72.
       Trans. of item 3049.

3154. *La Cosa freudiana e altri scritti*. Trans. Giacomo Contri. Turin:
       G. Einaudi, 1972. Includes trans. of item 3045. For review,
       see item 3381.

3155. *Escritos*. Trans. by Tomás Segovia, revised and with the colla-
       boration of the author and Juan David Nasio. Mexico: Siglo
       Veintiuno Editores, 1972. Second edition, in Spanish, of item
       3086/3116; for first edition, see item 3136. See also item
       3173.

1973

*3156. *Les Quatre concepts fondamentaux de la psychanalyse. Le Sémi-
       naire, 1964, Livre XI*. Text established by Jacques-Alain
       Miller. Paris: Editions du Seuil, 1973. (Le Champ Freudian)
       A series of lectures given by Lacan at the Ecole Pratique des
       Hautes Etudes, Paris. A "Postface" dated January 1, 1973
       appears on pp. 251-254. For trans., see items 3188 (English),

3190 (Catalonian or Spanish), and 3191a (German). For reviews, see items 3242, 3377, 3392a, 3401, 3406-3407, 3410, 3411a, and 3412-3413.

3157. "L'Etourdit." *Scilicet*, no. 4 (1973), pp. 5-52. Dated 14 July 1972 from Beloeil.

3158. "Entretien avec Lacan. Propos élucidés." With B. Poirot-Delpech. *Le Monde*, 5 April 1973, p. 20.

3159. Participant in the opening session of the Journées de l'Ecole Freudienne de Paris, 29-30 September 1973. *Lettres de l'Ecole Freudienne*, no. 11 (1973), pp. 2-3.

3160. Participant in the discussion on "Sur le mode de présence des pulsions partielles dans la cure." By Conté. *Lettres de l'Ecole Freudienne*, no. 11 (1973), pp. 22-24. Journées, 29-30 September 1973.

3161. Participant in the discussion on "La Fonction du père réel." By Safouan. *Lettres de l'Ecole Freudienne*, no. 11 (1973), pp. 140-141. Journées, 29-30 September 1973.

3162. Participant in the discussion on "Articulation entre la position médicale et celle de l'analyste." By Allouch. *Lettres de l'Ecole Freudienne*, no. 11 (1973), p. 230. Journées, 29-30 September 1973.

3163. Participant in a round table discussion introduced by Clavreul. *Lettres de l'Ecole Freudienne*, no. 11 (1973), pp. 215ff. Journées de l'Ecole Freudienne, 29-30 September 1973.

3164. "Propos en guise de conclusion aux Journées de l'Ecole Freudienne de Paris." (1 October 1973). *Lettres de l'Ecole Freudienne*, no. 11 (1973), pp. 141-144.

3165. "Les Non-dupes errent," an unpublished seminar of 1973-1974, cited in *Jacques Lacan* (special issue no. 58 of *L'Arc* on Lacan). Aix-en-Provence: L'Arc, 1974, p. 63.

3166. "Riposta al commento di Jean Hyppolite sulla *Verneinung* di Freud." Trans. O. Saletti. *Nuova Corrente*, nos. 61-62 (1973), pp. 139-158. Trans. of item 3041.

3167. Contributor to *Significante y structura en el psicoanálisis*. Buenos Aires: Siglo Veintiuno Editores Argentina, 1973.

3168. *Schriften I*. Intro. Norbert Haas. Trans. Norbert Haas and Klaus Laermann. Olten-Freiburg im Breisgau: Walter, 1973. Trans. of item 3086/3116. See also items 3177, 3179 and 3180.

3169. Essay in *Antworten der Strukturalisten*. Comp. Adelbert Reif. Trans. Britta Reif-Willenthal and Friedrich Griese. Hamburg: Hoffmann und Campe, 1973.

3170. *Télévision*. Paris: Editions du Seuil, 1974. 72-page text of a
       broadcast on Lacan done by the Service de la Recherche de
       l'O.R.T.F., Christmas 1973. For review, see item 3414.

3171. Editor of and preface to *A propos de l'éveil du printemps de
       Wedekind*. Paris: Christian Bourgois, 1974.

3172. *Scritti, I-II*. Trans. Giacomo Contri. Turin: G. Einaudi, 1974.
       Trans. of item 3086/3116.

3173. *Escritos, I*. Buenos Aires: Siglo Veintiuno, 1974. Trans. of
       item 3086/3116. See also items 3136 and 3155.

*3174. *Le Séminaire de Jacques Lacan. Livre I: Les Ecrits techniques
       de Freud, 1953-1954*. Text established by Jacques-Alain
       Miller. Paris: Editions du Seuil, 1975. (Le Champ Freudien)
       For review, see item 3409. For German trans., see item 3191.

       Besides the recorded or shorthand version of this seminar
       which was used for its publication by Seuil, an unoffical or
       "pirate" version reconstructed by various witnesses also exists.

3175. *Le Séminaire de Jacques Lacan. Livre XX: Encore, 1972-1973*.
       Text established by Jacques-Alain Miller. Paris: Editions
       du Seuil, 1975. (Le Champ Freudien) For reviews, see items
       3233 and 3411.

       Besides the recorded or shorthand version of this seminar
       which was used for its publication by Seuil, an unofficial or
       "pirate" version reconstructed by various witnesses also
       exists.

3176. *De la psychose paranoïaque dans ses rapports avec la personnalité*
       [suivi de] *Premiers écrits sur la paranoïa*. Paris: Editions
       du Seuil, 1975. (Le Champ Freudien) Rpts. item 2987 and other
       early works on paranoia. For reviews, see items 3382-3383.

3177. "... Ou Pire/Introduction à l'édition allemande d'un premier
       volume des écrits." *Scilicet*, no. 5 (Paris: Editions du
       Seuil, 1975). See items 3168 and 3179.

3178. *The Language of the Self. The Function of Language in Psycho-
       analysis*. Trans. Anthony Wilden. New York: Dell, 1975.
       (A Delta Book) Rpts. item 3103, with a short but important
       preface referring readers to item 216 for clarification of
       problems in this work.

3179. *Schriften I*. Trans. Norbert Haas, Klaus Laermann, Rodolphe
       Gasché and Peter Stehlin. Frankfurt am Main: Suhrkamp, 1975.
       (Suhrkamp-Taschenbücher Wissenschaft, 137) Trans. of item
       3086/3116. See also items 3168, 3177 and 3180.

3180. *Schriften II*. Trans. Chantal Creusot and Norbert Haas. Freiburg
am Breisgau: Walter Verlag, 1975. Trans. of item 3086/3116.
See also items 3168 and 3179.

3181. Contributor to *Unabhängigkeitserklärung der Phantasie und
Erklärung der Rechte des Menschen auf seine Verrüktheit.
Gesammelte Schriften*. By Salvador Dali. Munich: Rogner &
Bernhard, n.d. [1975?].

1976

3182. "Conférences et entretiens dans des universités nord-américaines."
Scilicet, nos. 6-7 (Paris: Editions du Seuil, 1976). Lacan
at Yale University, November 24, 1975 and at Columbia University, December 1, 1975.

1977

3183. *Le Problème du style suivi de Merleau-Ponty*. Paris: Editions
des Grandes Têtes-Molles de Notre Epoque, n.d. [1977?]
(Petite Bibliothèque de la Psychanalyse) Rpts. item 3068?

3183a. "C'est à la lecture de Freud." In *Lacan. Théorie et pratiques*.
By Robert Georgin. Lausanne: Editions L'Age d'Homme/La Cité,
1977. (Cistre, 3)

3184. "Hiatus irrationalis." *Magazine Littéraire*, no. 121 (February
1977), p. 11. Rpts. item 2988.

3184a. Contributor to *Travaux et interventions*. Paris: Association
Régionale de l'Education Permanente, 1977. With Henri Claude,
P. Mignault and Henri Ey.

A collection of texts from various journals and publications,
1931-1947.

3185. "L'Impromptu de Vincennes." *Magazine Littéraire*, no. 121
(February 1977), pp. 21-25. A transcription of a recording
of Lacan at Vincennes, December 3, 1969.

3186. *La Femme n'existe pas*. An unofficial multilith edition listing
no publisher and no date circulating in Paris in February,
1977.

3187. *Ecrits: A Selection*. Trans. Alan Sheridan. New York: W.W. Norton;
London: Tavistock, 1977, 338pp. Trans. of just under half
of item 3086.

Contains trans. of items 3004, 3037, 3078 plus six other
papers dealing with various aspects of psychoanalytic theory
and practice.

3188. *The Four Fundamental Concepts of Psycho-Analysis*. Ed. Jacques-
Alain Miller. Trans. Alan Sheridan. London: Hogarth Press
(The Institute of Psycho-Analysis), 1977; New York: W.W.
Norton, 1978, 290pp. Trans. of item 3156.

3189. "Desire and Interpretation of Desire in Hamlet." Trans. J.
       Hulbert. *Yale French Studies*, nos. 55-56 (1977), pp. 11-52.
       Cf. item 3062.

3190. *Cuatro conceptos fundamentales del psicoanálisis.* Trans. Fran-
       cisco Monge. Barcelona: Barral Ed., 1977. Trans. of item
       3156.

                                    1978

3190a. *Le Séminaire de Jacques Lacan. Livre II: Le Moi dans la théorie
       de Freud et dans la technique de la psychanalyse, 1954-1955.*
       Text established by Jacques-Alain Miller. Paris: Editions du
       Seuil, 1978, 374pp. (Le Champ Freudien) For reviews, see
       items 3408 and 3408a.

3191. *Das Seminar. Buch 1 (1953-1954). Freuds technische Schriften.*
       Ed. Jacques-Alain Miller. Trans. Werner Hamacher. Olten-
       Freiburg im Breisgau: Walter, 1978, 364pp. Trans. of item
       3174.

3191a. *Das Seminar von Jacques Lacan. Buch 11: Die Vier Grundbegriffe
       der Psychoanalyse.* Ed. Jacques-Alain Miller. Trans. Norbert
       Haas. Olten-Freiburg im Breisgau: Walter, 1978, 307pp. Trans.
       of item 3156.

                             SECONDARY SOURCES

       Althusser, Louis. See items 241, 271, 294-295, 324, 344, and 369.

3192. Anonymous. "Commentary." *The Times Literary Supplement*, no.
       3516 (17 July 1969), p. 777.

3193. ———. *Le Corps, les mots, l'imaginaire.* Succursale Outremont,
       Quebec: La Barre du Jour, 1977. Special issue of *La Barre
       du Jour*, nos. 56-57 (May-August 1977).

3194. ———. "L'Esprit et la lettre." *Le Nouvel Observateur*, no.
       219 (20-26 January 1969), p. 37.

3195. ———. "L'Esprit et la lettre." *Le Nouvel Observateur*, no.
       428 (22-28 January 1973), p. 65.

3196. ———. "L'Expulsion du cours du Dr. Lacan." *Les Lettres
       Françaises*, no. 1292 (16-22 July 1969), p. 6.

3197. ———. "Healing Words: Dr. Lacan's Structuralism." *The Times
       Literary Supplement*, no. 3439 (25 January 1968), pp. 73-75;
       vol. 7 (1968), 205-218.

       ———. See item 2058.

3198. ———. "Au jour le jour: arts, lettres, spectacles." *Le Nouvel Observateur*. n.s. no. 13 (11 February 1965), pp. 26–27.

3199. ———. "Lacan classique et baroque...." *27, Rue Jacob*, no. 182 (January 1975), pp. 12–13.

———. See items 4272, 3860 and 4273.

3200. ———. "Retour à Freud: une tentative légitime?" *Le Monde [des Livres]*, no. 6866 (8 February 1967), pp. iv–v.

3201. ———. "Satisfaction au Seuil." *Le Nouvel Observateur*, no. 107 (30 November–6 December 1966), p. 37.

3202. Anzieu, Didier. "Contre: une doctrine hérétique." *La Quinzaine Littéraire*, no. 20 (15–31 January 1967), pp. 14–15.

3203. *L'Arc*, no. 58 (Aix-en-Provence, 1974): issue on Jacques Lacan. Contains items 3227, 3334, 3300, 3320, 3353, 3247, 3279, 3306, 3351, 3344, 3366, and 3303.

3204. Auguste-Etienne, J., and M. Guilbaud. "Approche de la dynamique familiale dans les perspectives lacaniennes." *Le Groupe Familial*, no. 52 (Paris, 1971), pp. 37–44.

3205. Autonomova, N.S. "The Psychoanalytic Conceptions of Jacques Lacan" (in Russian). *Voprosy Filosofii*, 11 (1973), 143–150.

Auzias, J.-M. See chapter 9 of items 11–14.

3206. Axelos, Kostas. "Et la pensée." *Le Monde [des Livres]*, no. 8779 (5 April 1973), p. 21.

3207. B., R. "Lacan." *Magazine Littéraire*, no. 75 (April 1973), p. 31.

3208. Backès, Catherine. "Lacan, ou le 'porte-parole.'" *Critique*, 21e année, no. 249 (February 1968), 136–161.

On Lacan's *Ecrits*.

3209. Backès-Clément, Catherine. "Freud et Lacan. Symbolique et production idéologique." In *Littérature et idéologies. Colloque de Cluny II. 2, 3, 4 avril 1970*. Paris: *La Nouvelle Critique*, 1971, pp. 202–207. Part of a special issue of *La Nouvelle Critique*.

3210. Baliteau, C. "La Fin d'une parade misogyne: la psychanalyse lacanienne." *Les Temps Modernes*, 30, no. 348 (1975), 1933–1953.

3211. Bär, Eugen Silas. "The Languages of the Unconscious According to Jacques Lacan." *Dissertation Abstracts International*, 32, no. 5 (November 1971), 2738-A. Yale University dissertation.

3212. ———. "The Language of the Unconscious According to Jacques Lacan." *Semiotica*, 3, no. 3 (1971), 241–268.

3213.   Barrat, Robert. "Freud est grand et Lacan est son prophète."
        Paris-Match, no. 1296 (9 March 1974), pp. 3-4, 25.

        Barthes, R. See item 855.

        Baudry, J.-L. See item 3815.

        Belaval, Y. See item 4437.

3214.   Bellour, Raymond. "Les Exigences de l'oeuvre complete: notes
        sur l'oeuvre et sa critique." *Les Lettres Françaises*, no.
        1217 (17-23 January 1968), pp. 9-11.

        Benoist, J.-M. See item 1637.

3215.   Bensaïd, Norbert. "Les Psychanalystes et leurs complexes."
        Le Nouvel Observateur, no. 416 (30 October-5 November 1972),
        pp. 74-75, 79, 81, 84, 88, 93, 96, 101.

3216.   Berl, Emmanuel. "Nos rapports avec la psychanalyse: Freud,
        Jung, Lacan." *Preuves*, no. 194 (April 1967), pp. 72-80.

3217.   Bertherat, Yves. "Freud avec Lacan ou la science avec le
        psychanalyste." *Esprit*, 35e année, no. 366 (December 1967),
        pp. 979-1003.

        Bogliolo, H. See item 4440.

3218.   Boon, M.C. "Class-struggle in Psychoanalysis" (in Serbo-Croa-
        tian). *Delo*, 22, no. 11 (1976), 93-103.

3219.   Boyer, Philippe. "Le Roi du fou, le fou de roi." *Change*, no. 12
        (September 1972), pp. 177-200.

3220.   ——————. *L'Ecarté(e) (fiction théorique)*. Paris: Editions
        Seghers/Laffont, 1973.

3220a. Bruss, Neal H. "Re-Stirring the Waters; or, The Voice that Sees
        the World as Patients." *The Massachusetts Review*, 20 (Summer
        1979), 337-354.

3221.   Cabanne, Pierre. *Le Siècle de Picasso. 2. La Guerre. Le Parti.
        La Gloire. L'Homme seul (1937-1973)*. Paris: Denoël, 1975.

3222.   Cancrini, Luigi. "Jacques Lacan: psicoanalisi e strutturalismo."
        La Cultura, 6 (1968), 184-220.

        Caruso, Paolo. See items 2101-2102.

3223.   Chapsal, Madeleine. "La Parole de Lacan." *Express*, no. 1185
        (25-31 March 1974), pp. 47.

        Châtelet, F. See item 41.

3224. Chazaud, Jacques. "Contre Lacan." In *Psychanalyse et créativité culturelle*. By Jacques Chazaud. Toulouse: Edouard Privat, 1972, pp. 113-134.

Cipolli, C. See item 4873.

3225. Clavel, Maurice. "Un Lacanien chrétien." *Le Nouvel Observateur*, no. 547 (5-11 May 1975), p. 59.

On P. Nemo's *L'Homme structural*, 1975.

3226. ————. "La Pomme et le pissenlit." *Le Nouvel Observateur*, no. 502 (24-30 June 1974), pp. 60-61.

3227. Clément, Catherine. "Un Numéro." *L'Arc*, no. 58 (1974), pp. 1-3.

3228. ————. *Le Pouvoir des mots: symbolique et idéologique*. Paris: Mame, 1974.

3229. ————. "Lettre à Lacan ou l'oiseau pris." *Magazine Littéraire*, no. 121 (February 1977), pp. 18-20.

3230. ————. *Miroirs du sujet*. Paris: 10/18 Inédit, 1975.

3230a. ————. "Jacques Lacan. Scénario pour un western théorique." In *Les Dieux dans la cuisine. Vingt ans de philosophie en France*. Ed. Jean-Jacques Brochier. Paris: Aubier, 1978, pp. 56-62.

3231. Comolli, G. "Desiderio e bisogno. Note critiche a Lacan e Deleuze/Guattari." *Aut Aut*, no. 139 (1974), pp. 21-44. Milan Colloquium, 8-9 May 1973.

Conley, Tom. See item 1659.

3232. Cooper, David. "Sanity and 'Madness'--2: Who's Mad Anyway?" *New Statesman*, 73, no. 1892 (16 June 1967), 844-845.

3233. Cornaz, Laurent. "Jacques Lacan: *Encore*." *Action Poétique*, no. 61 (2nd quarter, 1975), pp. 192-194.

3234. Corvez, Maurice. "Le Structuralisme de Jacques Lacan." *Revue Philosophique de Louvain*, tome 66, no. 90 (May 1968), 282-308.

————. "Le Structuralisme psychanalytique de Jacques Lacan," chapter 4 of items 49-51.

3235. ————. "El Estructuralismo de Jacques Lacan." *Revista de Psicología General y Aplicada*, 26, no. 113 (1971), 711-741.

Crémant, R. See item 54.

3236. Daix, Pierre. "Entretien avec Jacques Lacan." *Les Lettres Françaises*, no. 1159 (1-7 December 1966), pp. 1, 16-17.

3237.   ———. "L'Expulsion du cours du Dr. Lacan." *Les Lettres*
         Françaises, no. 1290 (2-8 July 1969), p. 3.

         Dayan, Daniel. See item 3821, pp. 23-25.

         Deleuze, G., et al. See item 2135.

3238.   De Tollenaere, M. "The Origin of Language" (in Dutch). *Tijd-*
         schrift voor Filosofie, 37, no. 2 (1975), 187-210.

3239.   De Waelhens, Alphonse. "Phénoménologie des relations humaines.
         J. Lacan: la famille." Mimeographed course notes circulated
         by the Cercle de Philosophie, Université Catholique de
         Louvain, 1969-1970.

*3240.   ———. *La Psychose*. Paris-Louvain: Béatrice Nauwelaerts,
         1972.

3241.   ———. *Schizophrenia. A Philosophical Reflection on Lacan's*
         Structuralist Interpretation. Trans. W. Ver Eecke. Pittsburgh:
         Duquesne University Press, 1978, 261pp. Trans. of item 3240.

3242.   Diéguez, Manuel de. "Les Quatre concepts fondamentaux de la
         psychanalyse par J. Lacan." *Nouvelle Revue Française*, no.
         248 (August 1973), pp. 78-90.

         Donato, E. See item 65.

         Dufrenne, M. See item 4493.

3242a.   Durand, R. "Les Signes de la vérité: imaginaire et symbolique
         dans 'Benito Cereno.'" *Revue Française d'Etudes Américaines*,
         no. 3 (1977), pp. 47-59.

         Melville's work interpreted psychoanalytically using the
         Lacanian concepts of the imaginary and the symbolic.

*3243.   Fages, Jean-Baptiste. *Comprendre Jacques Lacan*. Toulouse:
         Edouard Privat, 1971.

3244.   ———. *Che cosa ha veramente detto Lacan*. Trans. Orio
         Buonomini. Rome: Ubaldini, 1972.

3245.   ———. *Para comprender a Lacan*. Trans. Matilde Horne. Buenos
         Aires: Amorrortu, 1973.

3246.   Fanon, Frantz. "Le Trouble mental et le trouble neurologique
         (1951)." *Information Psychiatrique*, 51, no. 10 (December
         1975), 1079-1082 and 1085-1090.

3247.   Felman, Shoshana. "La Méprise et sa chance." *L'Arc*, no. 58
         (1974), pp. 40-48.

3248.   Fernandez, Dominique. *L'Arbre jusqu'aux racines. Psychanalyse*
         et création. Paris: Bernard Grasset, 1972.

3249. ———. "Lacan, héritier nº 1 de Freud?" *Express*, no. 1127 (12-18 February 1973), pp. 75-76.

3250. Finas, Lucette. "Jacques Lacan: un discours irréductible." *Le Monde [des Livres]*, no. 7828 (14 March 1970), p. 11.

3251. Finkelstein, Haim. "Dali's Paranoia-Criticism or the Exercise of Freedom." *Twentieth Century Literature*, 21, no. 1 (February 1975), 59-71.

3251a. Fischer, Eileen. "Discourse of the Other in Not I: A Confluence of Beckett and Lacan." *Theater*, 10 (Summer 1979), 101-103.

3252. Forrester, John. "Mirror, Mirror on the Wall, Who is Truest of Them All?" *The Times Higher Education Supplement*, no. 313 (4 November 1977), p. 12.

3253. Fougeyrollas, Pierre. "Lacan [ou] la pantomime petite-bourgeoise." In his item 78, pp. 81-134.

3254. Francioni, Mario. "La Psicolinguistica freudiana secondo Lacan. La Struttura alienante della soggettività e del linguaggio." *Filosofia*, 24, no. 1 (January 1973), 35-52.

3255. ———. "I Significanti nell'inconscio secondo Lacan. La Lettera e la metafora dal desiderio al linguaggio." *Filosofia*, 24, no. 4 (October 1973), 425-448.

3256. ———. "Bibliografia di Jacques Lacan." *Filosofia*, 24, no. 4 (October 1973), 448-452.

3257. ———. *Psicanalisi linguistica ed epistemologia in Jacques Lacan.* (Filosofia della Scienza, 34) Turin: Edizioni di Filosofia, 1973; (Lezioni e Seminari) Turin: Boringhieri, 1978, 81pp.

3258. Frappat, Bruno. "La Reprise du séminaire de psychanalyse: lorsque Lacan paraît." *Le Monde [des Arts et des Spectacles]*, no. 9896 (18 November 1976), p. 34.

3259. G., F. "L'Affaire Lacan." *Express*, no. 940 (14-20 July 1969), p. 38.

3260. Gallop, J. "The Ghost of Lacan, the Trace of Language." *Diacritics*, 5, no. 4 (1975), 18-24.

On J. Mitchell's *Psychoanalysis and Feminism*.

3261. Gauthier, Yvon. "Die Sprache und der andere Schauplatz über die Sprachtheorie Lacans." In *Akten XIV. Internationalen Kongresses für Philosophie* (Vienna, 2-9 September 1968, III). Vienna: Herder, 1968, pp. 412-413.

3262. Georgin, Robert. *Le Temps freudien du verbe.* Lausanne: Editions L'Age d'Homme, 1973.

Revised version of the author's thesis, Paris-Vincennes. Also deals with Lévi-Strauss.

————. See also item 3939.

3263.   ————. *Lacan. Théorie et pratiques*. Lausanne: Editions L'Age d'Homme/La Cité, 1977, 118pp. (Cistre, 3)

Gerbault, R. See item 4535.

3264.   Gilbert, R. "Notes sur le langage, après Jacques Lacan." *Société Alfred Binet et Théodore Simon*, no. 551 (1976), pp. 54-73.

Gimeno, F.C. See items 4882 and 4883.

3265.   Giroud, Françoise. "Quand l'autre était dieu." *L'Express*, no. 887 (8-14 July 1968), p. 35.

3265a.   Godino Cabas, Antonio. *Curso y discurso de la obra de Jacques Lacan*. Buenos Aires: Helguero, 1977, 298pp.

3266.   Gorin, Jean-Pierre. "Le Freudisme à la recherche de son statut." *Le Monde [des Livres]*, no. 6866 (8 February 1967), p. iv.

Green, André. See item 4884.

3267.   ————. "L'Objet (a) de J. Lacan, sa logique et la théorie freudienne." *Cahiers pour l'Analyse*, no. 3 (May-June 1966), pp. 15-37.

3268.   Grenet, Paul B. "Science, nescience, conscience." *Revue Thomiste*, 72 (July-September 1972), 439-454.

Grimaud, M. See items 4885 and 4885a.

3269.   Grisoni, Dominique. "Politique de Lacan." *Magazine Littéraire*, no. 121 (February 1977), pp. 25-27.

Hanhardt, J.G., et al. See item 3825.

Hartman, G.H. See item 1708a.

Hefner, R.W. See item 4312.

3270.   Held, René R. "Lacanisme sauvage." *Le Nouvel Observateur*, no. 420 (27 November-3 December 1972), pp. 3-4.

3271.   ————. "Un Praticien: 'et si l'inconscient n'était pas structuré....'" *Le Monde [des Livres]*, no. 8779 (5 April 1973), p. 21.

3272.   Herrmann, Claudine. *Les Voleuses de langues*. Paris: Editions des Femmes, 1976.

*3273. Hesnard, Ange Louis Marie. *De Freud à Lacan*. Paris: Editions
    E.S.F., 1970; 3rd ed., 1977.

3274. ————. *De Freud a Lacan*. Trans. Carmen Cienfuegos. Barcelona:
    Ed. Martinez Roca, 1976.

3275. H[iggins], R[obert]. "Jacques Lacan commente la naissance de
    Scilicet." *Le Monde [des Livres]*, no. 7208 (16 March 1968),
    p. VI.

3276. Houdebine, Jean-Louis. "Méconnaissance de la psychanalyse dans
    le discours surréaliste." *Tel Quel*, no. 46 (Summer 1971),
    pp. 67-82.

3277. Hyppolite, Jean. "Commentaire parlé sur la *Verneinung*, de Freud."
    La Psychanalyse, no. 1 (1956), pp. 29-39.

3278. ————. "Phénoménologie de Hegel et psychanalyse." *La Psychana-
    lyse*, no. 3 (1957), pp. 17-32.

3279. Irigaray, Luce. "La 'Mécanique' des fluides." *L'Arc*, no. 58
    (1974), pp. 44-55.

3280. Jaccard, Roland. "Etude: le phénomène Lacan." *Le Monde [des
    Livres]*, no. 8779 (5 April 1973), p. 20.

    Jameson, F. See item 4172.

3281. Jameson, Fredric. "Imaginary and Symbolic in Lacan: Marxism,
    Psychoanalytic Criticism, and the Problem of the Subject."
    Yale French Studies, no. 55-56 (1977), pp. 338-395.

3282. Jarry, André. "Saussure 'détourné.'" *Le Monde [des Livres]*,
    no. 8779 (5 April 1973), p. 17.

    Johnson, B. See items 1718 and 1718a.

    Kahn, J.-F. See item 112.

    Kampits, Peter. See item 4585.

    Kintzler, J.-M. See item 4589.

3282a. Kremer-Marietti, Angèle. *Lacan et la rhétorique de l'inconscient*.
    Paris: Aubier-Montaigne, 1978, 250pp.

    Perhaps the best general introduction to Lacan.

3283. Lacoue-Labarthe, Philippe, and Jean-Luc Nancy. *Le Titre de la
    lettre: une lecture de Lacan*. Paris: Editions Galilée, 1973.

    Lacroix, Jean. "La Psychanalyse de Jacques Lacan," chapter 7,
    part III of his item 4600 (1968), pp. 250-259.

3284. Laguardia, Eric. "Lacan's Full and Empty Words, and Literary
    Discourse." In *Actes du VIe Congrès de l'Association Inter-*

nationale de Littérature Comparée. Stuttgart: Erich Bieber, 1975, pp. 757-760.

3285.   Lainé, Pascal. "Jacques Lacan, lecteur de Freud." *Magazine Littéraire,* no. 12 (November 1967), pp. 21-22.

3286.   Lang, Hermann. *Die Sprache und das Unbewusste. Jacques Lacans Grundlegung der Psychoanalyse.* Frankfurt am Main: Suhrkamp, 1973. Originally the author's thesis, Heidelberg, "Das Problem der Sprache bei Jacques Lacan." Bibliography, pp. 305-326.

3287.   Laplanche, J. *Hölderlin et la question du père.* Paris: Bibliothèque de Psychanalyse et de Psychologie Clinique, 1961.

3288.   ———, and S. Leclaire. "L'Inconscient." *Les Temps Modernes,* no. 183 (July 1961), pp. 81-129.

3289.   Lapouge, Gilles. "Sartre contre Lacan." *Le Figaro Littéraire,* no. 1080 (29 December 1966), p. 4.

3290.   ———. "Jacques Lacan veut que la psychanalyse 'redevienne la peste.'" *Le Figaro Littéraire,* no. 1076 (1 December 1966), p. 11.

3291.   Lavers, Annette. "Freud in His Own Write. Language in Lacan." In *Languages.* Ed. Anthony Rudolf. London: Circuit Magazine, 1969, pp. 31-37. Part of a special issue of *Cambridge Opinion* and *Circuit,* Summer 1969.

        ———. See also item 4611.

3292.   ———. "Some Aspects of Language in the Work of Jacques Lacan." *Semiotica,* 3, no. 3 (1971), 269-279.

3293.   Lebovici, S. "A propos de quelques ouvrages récents sur les psychoses de l'enfant." *La Psychiatrie de l'Enfant,* 14, no. 1 (1971), 311-314.

        One of the approaches treated is that of Lacan and his school.

3294.   Leclaire, C. "A propos de la 'Cure-Type en Psychanalyse' de M. Bouvet." *Evolution Psychiatrique,* 1956, pp. 515, 540.

3295.   ———. "A la recherche des principes d'une psychothérapie des psychoses." *Evolution Psychiatrique,* 1958, pp. 377-411.

3296.   ———. "L'Obsessionnel et son désir." *Evolution Psychiatrique,* 1959, pp. 324-409.

3297.   ———. "Point de vue économique en psychanalyse." *Evolution Psychiatrique,* 1965, pp. 189-213. Trans. in summary by D. Plain as "The Economic Standpoint: Recent Views." *International Journal of Psycho-Analysis,* 45 (1965), 324-330.

3298. Leclaire, S. "Sur les rapports entre la mythologie et le rituel." *Bulletin de la Société Française de Philosophie*, 50, no. 2 (July-September 1956).

This covers the session of 26 May 1956 in which Lacan, Goldmann, Jean Wahl, Merleau-Ponty and others took part.

3299. Le Gaufey, Guy. "L'Archéologue de l'inconscient." *Le Nouvel Observateur*, no. 434 (6-12 March 1973), p. 62.

3300. Levallois-Colot, Anne. "Voyez comme l'on danse..." *L'Arc*, no. 58 (1974), pp. 21-24.

3301. Loriot, Patrick. "Le Discours de l'autre." *Le Nouvel Observateur*, no. 105 (16-22 November 1966), p. 46.

3302. Lotringer, Sylvère. "The 'Subject' on Trial." *Semiotext(e)*, 1, no. 3 (1975), 3-8.

3303. Lowe, Catherine. "*Salammbô* ou la question de l'autre de la parole." *L'Arc*, no. 58 (1974), pp. 83-88.

3304. *Magazine Littéraire*, no. 121 (February 1977): on Lacan. Contains items 3359, 3343, 3184, 3347, 3367, 3229, 3185, 3269, and 3376.

3305. Malrieu, Philippe. "De quelques oublis de Jacques Lacan: problèmes de méthode." *Raison Présente*, no. 5 (November/December 1967-January 1968), pp. 21-34.

3306. Mannoni, Maud. "Le Malentendu." *L'Arc*, no. 58 (1974), pp. 56-61.

3307. Mannoni, Octave. "Eclairages: la question fondamentale." *Le Monde [des Livres]*, no. 8779 (5 April 1973), p. 17.

3308. Masotta, Oscar. *Introducción a la lectura de Jacques Lacan*. Buenos Aires: Editorial Proteo, 1970; Corregidor, 1974. (Biblioteca Campo Freudiano. Ser. Temas y Problemas del Psicoanálisis, 1)

3309. ————, et al. *Temas de Jacques Lacan*. Buenos Aires: Ediciones Nueva Visión, 1971.

3310. McKenna, R. "Jacques Lacan: An Introduction." *The Journal of the British Society for Phenomenology*, 7, no. 3 (1976), 189-197.

Presenting Lacan to a non-French, non-psychoanalytic public.

3311. Mehlman, Jeffrey. "The 'Floating Signifier': From Lévi-Strauss to Lacan." *Yale French Studies*, no. 48 (1972), pp. 10-37.

————. "Appendix II." In his item 3997, pp. 229-238.

————. "Appendix III." In his item 3997, pp. 239-240.

3312. ————. "Poe Pourri: Lacan's Purloined Letter." *Semiotext(e)*,
       1, no. 3 (1975), 51-68.

3313. Melman, Charles. "Pour Lacan: Retour à Freud." *La Quinzaine
       Littéraire*, no. 20 (15-31 January 1967), pp. 13-14.

3314. ————. "Autour de Lacan." *Le Nouvel Observateur*, no. 419
       (20-26 November 1972), p. 3.

       Merrell, F. See items 4645 and 4646.

3315. Miel, Jan. "Jacques Lacan and the Structure of the Unconscious."
       In item 68, pp. 104-111. See also item 69.

3316. Miller, Jacques-Alain. "Les Graphes de Jacques Lacan." *Cahiers
       pour l'Analyse*, no. 1 and 2 (1966), supplement, pp. 169-177.

3317. [————]. "Lacan à Rome et à Vincennes." *Le Monde [des Livres]*,
       no. 9285 (22 November 1975), p. 16.

       Millet, L., et al. See items 147-149.

3318. Mitchell, Juliet. *Psychoanalysis and Feminism*. New York: Pan-
       theon Books, 1974.

       Follows Lacan in debiologizing Freud's analytical theory.

3319. Moersch, Emma. "Zum Begriff des Unbewussten bei Jacques Lacan."
       Psyche, 28 (Heidelberg, 1974), 328-339.

       Montefiore, A. See item 1775.

3320. Montrelay, Michele. "Le Saut du loup." *L'Arc*, no. 58 (1974),
       pp. 25-30.

3321. Mooij, Antoine. *Taal en verlangen. Lacans theorie van de
       psychoanalyse*. Meppel: Boom, 1975, 1976.

       Morris, C.D. See item 1149.

3322. Mounin, Georges. "Quelques traits du style de Jacques Lacan."
       La Nouvelle Revue Française, 17, no. 193 (January 1969),
       84-92.

3323. ————. "Quelques traits du style de Jacques Lacan." In *Litté-
       rature et idéologies. Colloque de Cluny II. 2, 3, 4 avril
       1970*. Paris: *La Nouvelle Critique*, 1971, pp. 181-188.

3324. ————. "Un Linguiste: 'Du sens des mots.'" *Le Monde [des
       Livres]*, no. 8779 (5 April 1973), p. 21.

       ————. See also item 5176.

3325. Moyaert, Paul. "De Metafoor en de metonymie als basisstrukturen
       van de taal bij J. Lacan." *Tijdschrift voor Filosofie*, 38
       (September 1976), 436-457. French summary, p. 457.

3325a. ————. "Jacques Lacan: de menselijke begeerte en de begeerte van de Ander." *Wijsgerig Perspectief op Maatschappij en Wetenschap*, 19 (1978-1979), 11-15.

Nichols, S.G. See item 4332.

Nikolova, M. See item 4671.

Noferi, A. See item 1778.

La Nouvelle Critique. See item 4009.

*3326. Palmier, Jean-Michel. *Lacan, le symbolique et l'imaginaire.* Paris: Editions Universitaires/Delarge, 1969. (Psychothèque, 1)

Contains: Introduction; (1) Le Stade du miroir et la formation du "Je"; (2) La Suprématie de la parole et du signifiant; (3) Les Formations de l'inconscient; (4) Le Désir et son interprétation; (5) Situation de la psychanalyse selon Jacques Lacan; Appendice; Bibliographie (pp. 147-154).

3327. ————. *Guida a Lacan. Il simbolico e l'immaginario.* Trans. Maria Grazia Meriggi. Milan: Biblioteca Universale Rizzoli, 1974.

3328. Palokane, Greg. "Books." *Film Comment*, 11, no. 5 (September-October 1975), 62-63.

Petitjean, G. See item 1171.

3329. Picon, Gaëtan. "Les Formes de l'esprit: L'expérience d'écrire." *Le Monde*, no. 7216 (26 March 1968), p. 11.

3330. Pierssens, Michel. "Questions sur le signifiant en littérature." *Sub-stance*, no. 3 (Spring 1972), pp. 23-29.

Pingaud, B. See item 2234.

3330a. Pirard, Regnier. "Si l'inconscient est structuré comme un langage...." *Revue Philosophique de Louvain*, tome 77, 4e série, no. 36 (November 1979), 528-568. French and English summaries on p. 568.

3331. [Poirot-Delpech, Bertrand]. "En d'autres termes: ça veut dire quoi?" *Le Monde [des Livres]*, no. 8779 (5 April 1973), p. 20.

3332. Pontalis, J.-B. "Freud aujourd'hui." *Les Temps Modernes*, nos. 124-125-126 (May-July 1956), pp. 1666-1680; 1890-1902; 174-186.

————. See also items 3054, 3060, 3062, and 3065.

Poster, Mark. See item 4393.

3333. Pratola, Vittorio. "L'Inconscio." *Giornale Critico della Filoso-
       fia Italiana*, 55 (July-September 1976), 331-386.

3334. Rabant, Christiane. "La Bête chanteuse." *L'Arc*, no. 58 (1974),
       pp. 15-20.

3334a. Ragland, Mary Eloise. "The Language of Laughter." *Sub-stance*,
       5, no. 13 (May 1976), 91-106.

       The unconscious as a subjective self (Lacan) and Freud on
       wit, the comic and humor.

3335. Rambaudi, D. "Linguaggio metaforico e scoperta scientifica."
       Giornale di Metafisica, 30, no. 5-6 (1975), 641-656.

3336. Reboul, J. "Jacques Lacan et les fondements de la psychanalyse."
       Critique, 18 (1962), 1056-1067.

3336a. Reeves, A. "Lacan's World." *Heythrop Journal*, 20 (January 1979),
       65-71.

3337. Rella, Franco. "Il Divano di Santa Teresa." *Aut Aut*, no. 148
       (July-August 1975), pp. 135-146.

       ————. See also item 2238a.

3338. Richard, Michel, J.M. Fournier, and J.F. Skrzypczak. *La Psychol-
       ogie et ses domaines, de Freud à Lacan, pratique et critique
       de la psychologie*. Lyon: Editions Chronique Sociale de
       France, 1971 and 1978; Paris: Editions du Cerf, 1978, 308pp.

*3339. Rifflet-Lemaire, Anika. *Jacques Lacan*. Brussels: Charles
       Dessart, 1970, 419pp. Includes a preface by Jacques Lacan
       (items 3117 and 3118) and an introduction by Antoine Vergote.
       Bibliography, pp. 409-415.

3340. ————. *Introduzione a Jacques Lacan*. Trans. Roberto Eynard.
       Rome: Astrolabio, 1970.

3341. ————. *Lacan*. Trans. Francisco J. Millet. Barcelona: EDHASA,
       1971.

3341a. ————. *Jacques Lacan*. Trans. David Macey. Boston: Routledge
       and Kegan Paul, 1977, 266pp.

       A summary of Lacan's basic ideas with emphasis on his concep-
       tions of language and their application in psychoanalysis.

       Rivelaygue, J. See item 4740.

3342. Robinet, André. "Lacan-Roi." *Les Nouvelles Littéraires*, no.
       2058 (9 February 1967), pp. 1, 11.

3343. Romet, Gilles. "Un Démon pensant." *Magazine Littéraire*, no. 121
       (February 1977), pp. 10-11.

3344. Ronat, Mitsou. "Enonciation et 'grammaire' de l'inconscient." *L'Arc*, no. 58 (1974), pp. 73-78.

3345. Rosolato, G. "Sémantique et altérations du langage." *Evolution Psychiatrique*, 1956, pp. 865-899.

Useful for a consideration of the Lacanian viewpoint on the problem of meaning.

3346. ————. "Le Symbolique." *La Psychanalyse*, no. 5 (1959), pp. 225-233.

A clarification of Lacan's linguistic vocabulary.

3347. Rouanet, Marc. "Lacan et Freud: expérience d'un savoir et division du sujet." *Magazine Littéraire*, no. 121 (February 1977), pp. 12-13.

3348. Roudinesco, Elisabeth. "L'Inconscient et ses lettres." *Action Poétique*, no. 45 (1970?), pp. 46-68.

3349. ————. "L'Action d'une métaphore. Remarques à propos de la théorie du signifiant chez Jacques Lacan." *La Pensée*, no. 162 (April 1972), pp. 54-73.

3350. ————. "Raymond Roussel, le folklore breton et l'enfant-roi pervers." *Action Poétique*, no. 50 (1972), pp. 65-87.

————. See also item 581.

3351. ————. "Cogito et science du réel ou l'assèchement du Zuyderzée." *L'Arc*, no. 58 (1974), pp. 62-72.

3352. ————. "Jacques Lacan: linguistique et linguisterie (linguy-sterie)." *Cahiers de Poétique Comparée*, 2, no. 1 (1975), 35-44.

On "le signifiant, le sujet, la science, l'amour, et le discours."

3353. Rousseau-Dujardin, Jacqueline. "Du temps, qu'entends-je?" *L'Arc*, no. 58 (1974), pp. 31-39.

3354. Roussel, Jean. "Introduction to Jacques Lacan." *New Left Review*, no. 51 (September-October 1968), pp. 63-70.

Rowinski, C. See item 4747.

Safouan, M. See items 4899-4901.

Said, E.W. See item 4236.

Schiwy, G. See items 189 and 190.

3355. Schneiderman, Stuart. "Afloat with Jacques Lacan." *Diacritics*, 1, no. 2 (Winter 1971), 27-34.

3355a. ———. "The Saying of Hamlet." *Sub-stance*, 3, no. 8 (Winter
        1973-1974), 77-88.

        Who is speaking, to whom, and about what in *Hamlet*? On Lacan
        and psychoanalysis.

3356. ———. "Most Controversial Freudian Since Freud." *Psychology
        Today*, 11 (April 1978), 50-52ff. A portrait.

3357. Sharpe, Ella. "An Examination of Metaphor." In *The Psychoanalytic
        Reader*. Ed. Robert Fliess. London: The Hogarth Press, 1950.

        According to Safouan, the Lacanian theory of metaphor largely
        concurs with that of Sharpe: the literary meaning of any meta-
        phor remains indestructible in the same sense that Freud says
        that desire is indestructible.

        Silverman, H.J. See item 4771.

        Simon, J.K. See item 4338.

3358. Slonim, Marc. "Basic Freud?" *The New York Times Book Review*,
        28 May 1967, pp. 31-32.

3359. Sollers, Philippe. "Hommage à Lacan." *Magazine Littéraire*, no.
        121 (February 1977), p. 9.

3359a. Souza, Remy de. "Uma 'chave' para Lacan?" *Revista Brasileira de
        Filosofia*, 28 (1978), 80-82.

        Steinwachs, G. See item 4050.

        Sturrock, J. See item 196a.

3360. Sublon, Roland. "Psychanalyse, symbole et signifiant." *Revue
        des Sciences Religieuses*, 52 (April 1978), 159-181.

3361. Svejgaard, Erik. "Overføringen og den ubevidste realitets
        ageren." *Exil*, 8, no. 3-4 [31-32] (October 1975), 125-178.

3362. Thom, Martin. "The Unconscious Structured Like a Language."
        Economy and Society, 5, no. 4 (1976), 435-469.

        An examination of Lacan's reading of the Freudian unconscious
        and its transposition from the structural linguistics of
        Saussure and Jakobson. Lévi-Strauss's interpretation of the
        concept of "symbolic order" is also discussed.

3363. ———. "Return to Freud." *New Society*, 41, no. 770 (7 July
        1977), 35.

3364. Thoma-Herterich, Christa. "Orakel und Wahrheit: Jacques Lacan."
        In her *Zur Kritik der Psychokritik*. Bern: Herbert Lang;
        Frankfurt: Peter Lang, 1976, pp. 133-162. Bibliography, pp.
        377-388.

3365. Tort, M. "De l'interprétation ou la machine herméneutique." *Les Temps Modernes*, no. 237 (February 1966), pp. 1461-1493.

   Turkle, S. See item 4905 for Lacan's contribution to the emergence of a "psychoanalytic culture" in France.

3366. Tytell, Pamela. "Lacune aux U.S.A." *L'Arc*, no. 58 (1974), pp. 79-82.

3367. ————. "Lacan et l'anglais tel qu'on le parle." *Magazine Littéraire*, no. 121 (February 1977), pp. 14-18.

3368. Van Laere, François. "Lacan ou le discours de l'inconscient." *Synthèses*, 22, no. 251-252 (April-May 1967), 82-88.

3369. Verstraeten, Pierre. "L'Homme du plaisir chez Hegel et l'homme du désir chez Lacan." *Revue de l'Université de Bruxelles*, no. 3-4 (1976), pp. 351-394.

3369a. Weber, Samuel M. *Rückkehr zu Freud. Jacques Lacans Ent-stellung der Psychoanalyse*. Frankfurt am Main-Vienna: Ullstein, 1978, 144pp. (Ullstein-Buch, 3437)

3370. Wieland, J.H. "De Psychoanalyse van Jacques Lacan." *Tijdschrift voor Filosofie*, 36, no. 3 (September 1974), pp. 483-520. French summary, p. 520.

   The key ideas in Lacan's *Ecrits*.

*3371. Wilden, Anthony G. "Freud, Signorelli and Lacan: The Repression of the Signifier." *American Imago*, 23, no. 4 (Winter 1966), 332-366.

3372. ————, comp. "Jacques Lacan: A Partial Bibliography." In item 68, pp. 263-268. See also item 69.

3373. ————. Introduction to and translation of *The Language of the Self: The Function of Language in Psychoanalysis*. By Jacques Lacan. Baltimore: Johns Hopkins Press, 1968.

3374. ————. "Jacques Lacan's Structuralism: Libido as Language." *Psychology Today*, May 1972, pp. 40, 42, 85-86, 89.

   Discusses Lacan's structuralism as drawing on the thought of Lévi-Strauss and yielding an interpretation of Freud in which the unconscious is structured as a language.

3375. ————. "Freud, Signorelli et Lacan: le refoulement du signifiant." *Revue de Psychologie et des Sciences de l'Education*, 8 (Liège, 1973), 427-464. Summary, pp. 464-465.

   ————. See also item 216, especially chapters 1, 10, 16, and 17.

3376. Wolf, Michel de. "(Lacan:) Essai de bibliographie complète." *Magazine Littéraire*, no. 121 (February 1977), pp. 28-36.

3377. Wollheim, Richard. "Cabinet of Dr. Lacan." *New York Review of Books*, 25 (25 January 1979), 36-45.

On Lacan's *Ecrits: A Selection* and *Four Fundamental Concepts of Psychoanalysis*.

Yale French Studies. See item 4910.

3378. Ysseling, Samuel. "Filosofie en Psychoanalyse. Enige opmerkinger over het denken van M. Heidegger en J. Lacan." *Tijdschrift voor Filosofie*, 31 (June 1969), 261-289.

In both Heidegger and Lacan, man is within a discourse of which he is not the master. Both look for what is not thought as the principle for structuring discourse.

3379. ————. "Structuralism and Psychoanalysis in the Work of Jacques Lacan." *International Philosophical Quarterly*, 10, no. 1 (March 1970), 102-117.

Zardoya, J.M. See item 4824.

3380. Zenoni, A. "Métaphore et métonymie dans la théorie de Lacan." *Cahiers Internationaux du Symbolisme*, no. 31-32 (1976), pp. 187-198.

Žižek, S. See item 4825.

REVIEWS

La Cosa freudiana ...
(item 3154)

3381. Tomasello, Paolo. *Rivista di Filosofia*, 63 (1972), 355-362.

De la psychose paranoïaque ...
(item 3176)

3382. Anonymous. *The Times Literary Supplement*, 18 July 1975, p. 797.

3383. Louvain, François. "Jacques Lacan et le président Schreber." *Magazine Littéraire*, no. 99 (April 1975), pp. 58-61.

Ecrits
(item 3086)

3384. Anonymous. Review of *Ecrits: A Selection*. *Booklist*, 74 (1 November 1977), 439.

3385. ————. Review of *Ecrits: A Selection*. *Choice*, 14 (February 1978), 1711.

3386. ————. Review of *Ecrits: A Selection*. *Encounter*, 50 (March 1978), 44.

3387. ————. Review of *Ecrits: A Selection*. *Psychology Today*, 11 (December 1977), 162.

3388. Barham, P. Review of *Ecrits: A Selection*. *Sociology*, 13 (January 1979), 111-115.

3389. Châtelet, François. "Rendez-vous dans deux ans." *Le Nouvel Observateur*, no. 113 (11-17 January 1967), pp. 38-39.

3390. Dubarle, Dominique. "Psychanalyse et philosophie du langage: les *Ecrits* de Jacques Lacan." *Signes du Temps*, no. 3 (March 1967), pp. 24-26.

3391. Fallet, René. "Page 547." *Le Canard Enchaîné*, 52, no. 2418 (22 February 1967), 7.

3392. Gauthier, Yvon. "Langage et psychanalyse: à propos des *Ecrits* de Jacques Lacan." *Dialogue*, 7, no. 4 (March 1969), 633-638.

3392a. Heaton, J.M. Review of *Ecrits: A Selection* and *The Four Fundamental Concepts of Psychoanalysis*. *The Journal of the British Society for Phenomenology*, 9 (1978), 204-205.

3393. King, R. Review of *Ecrits: A Selection*. *Georgia Review*, 32 (Winter 1978), 926-930.

3394. Kuczkowski, Richard. Review of *Ecrits: A Selection*. *Library Journal*, 102 (15 October 1977), 2168.

3395. Kurzweil, E. Review of *Ecrits: A Selection*. *Partisan Review*, 45, no. 4 (1978), 642-646.

3396. Lacroix, Jean. "Les *Ecrits* de Lacan ou retour à Freud." *Le Monde*, no. 6827 (24 December 1966), p. 11.

3397. Lanteri-Laura, G. *Revue d'Histoire et de Philosophie Religieuses*, 47 (1967), 397-399.

3398. Leavy, Stanley A. "L'Ecole freudienne." *The New York Times Book Review*, 2 October 1977, pp. 10, 38-39.

3398a. Ragland Sullivan, M.E. Review of *Ecrits: A Selection*. *Sub-stance*, no. 21 (Winter 1978-1979), pp. 166-173.

3399. Salinas, José Lázaro. "Visión de conjunto." *Hispano Americano*, 59, no. 1539 (1 November 1971), 61.

3400. Schneiderman, Stuart. "Books Considered." *The New Republic*, 177, no. 20 (12 November 1977), 34-35.

3401. Scruton, Roger. "Incantations of the Self." *The Times Literary Supplement*, no. 3984 (11 August 1978), p. 909.

On *Ecrits: A Selection*, *Four Fundamental Concepts of Psychoanalysis*, and *Le Séminaire: le moi dans la théorie de Freud et
dans la technique de la psychanalyse*.

See also items 3208, 3370 and 3377.

The Language of the Self: The Function ...
(item 3103)

3402.   Anonymous. *Choice*, 5 (January 1969), 1509.

3403.   De Rosis, Louis. *Library Journal*, 93 (1 December 1968), 4570.

Scilicet
(items 3095ff.)

3404.   Anonymous. "Tu que je cherche..." *Le Nouvel Observateur*, no.
        173 (6-12 March 1968), p. 29.

3405.   Chapsal, Madeleine. "Lacan invite dans le champ freudien."
        L'Express, no. 881 (6-12 May 1968), pp. 43-44.

Le Séminaire ...
(items 3156, 3174, 3175, and 3190a)

3406.   Anonymous. Review of *The Four Fundamental Concepts of Psycho-
        analysis*. *Booklist*, 74 (15 July 1978), 1706.

3407.   ———. Review of *The Four Fundamental Concepts of Psycho-
        analysis*. *Choice*, 15 (October 1978), 1131.

3408.   ———. Review of *Le Séminaire, book 2*. *The Guardian Weekly*,
        118 (7 May 1978), 14.

3408a. Beirnaert, L. Review of *Le Séminaire. Livre II*. *Etudes*, no. 350
        (January 1979), p. 135.

3409.   Jannoud, Claude. "Jacques Lacan en séminaire." *Le Figaro Litté-
        raire*, no. 1499 (8 February 1975), p. III: 15.

3410.   Margolin, Jean-Claude. "Jacques Lacan: *Le Séminaire*, liv. XI."
        Etudes Philosophiques, no. 4 (October-December 1975), pp.
        497-498.

3411.   ———. Review of *Le Séminaire vol. I, vol. XX*. *Revue de Syn-
        thèse*, 97 (1976), 345-346.

3411a. Tourney, G. Review of *The Four Fundamental Concepts of Psycho-
        analysis*. *American Journal of Psychiatry*, 136 (July 1979),
        1000-1001.

3412.   Van Ness, J. Review of *The Four Fundamental Concepts of Psycho-
        analysis*. *Best Sellers*, 38 (July 1978), 116.

3413. Warren, Neil. Review of *The Four Fundamental Concepts of Psycho-analysis*. *Encounter*, 50 (March 1978), 56-57.

See also items 3233, 3242, 3377, 3392a, and 3401.

Télévision
(item 3170)

3414. Champagne, Roland A. "Reviews." *Modern Language Journal*, 59, no. 7 (November 1975), 397.

AN UPDATE OF WORKS ON CLAUDE LEVI-STRAUSS

Abel, L. See item 1618.

3415. Adams, Phoebe. Review of *Tristes Tropiques*. *Atlantic Monthly*, 233 (April 1974), 120.

Aletheia. See item 3.

Aligada, G.R. See item 3737.

3415a. Allison, David. "Structuralism Revisited. Lévi-Strauss and Diachrony." In *Cross-Currents in Phenomenology*. Ed. Ronald Bruzina and Bruce Wilshire. The Hague-Boston: Martinus Nijhoff, 1978, pp. 51-65. (Selected Studies in Phenomenology and Existential Philosophy, 7)

Ames, V.M. See item 3689.

3416. Anonymous. "A l'Académie Française: M. Claude Lévi-Strauss seul candidat au fauteuil de Montherlant." *Le Monde*, no. 8821 (25 May 1973), p. 42.

3417. ————. "Anthropology's Pope." *The Times Literary Supplement*, no. 3453 (2 May 1968), pp. 445-447.

3418. ————. "The Anti-Structuralists." *The Times Literary Supplement*, no. 3750 (18 January 1974), p. 58.

3419. ————. "Claude Lévi-Strauss Prix Erasme." *Le Monde [des Livres]*, no. 8749 (1 March 1973), p. 21.

————. See also items 938 and 945.

3420. ————. "At the Frontier: Claude Lévi-Strauss and Roland Barthes." *T.L.S. 6. Essays and Reviews from THE TIMES LITERARY SUPPLEMENT, 1967*. London-New York-Toronto: Oxford University Press, 1968, pp. 35-40.

————. See also item 4867.

3421. ————. "Institut: M. Claude Lévi-Strauss candidat à l'Académie Française." *Le Monde*, no. 8733 (10 February 1973), p. 25.

————. See also items 2058 and 4827.

3422. ──────. *Lévi-Strauss dans le dix-huitième siècle.* Paris: Le
       Cercle d'Epistémologie de l'Ecole Normale Supérieure, 1966.
       (Cahiers pour l'Analyse, 4)

3423. ──────. *Lévi-Strauss dans le dix-huitième siècle: sommaire.*
       Paris: Société du Graphe, imprimés et diffusés par les Edi-
       tions du Seuil, 1972, 88pp. (Cahiers pour l'Analyse, 4)
       Rpts. item 3422.

       ──────. See also item 4272.

3424. ──────. "M. Claude Lévi-Strauss est élu à l'Académie Française."
       Le Monde, no. 8822 (26 May 1973), p. 14.

3425. ──────. "Du Musée de l'Homme au Collège de France." *Le Monde*,
       no. 8822 (26 May 1973), p. 14.

3426. ──────. "Myths and Supermyths." *Economist*, 247, no. 6765 (21
       April 1973), 114-115.

       On *From Honey to Ashes.*

       ──────. See also item 4273.

3427. ──────. "Orpheus with his Myths: The Importance of Lévi-
       Strauss." *The Times Literary Supplement*, 4 (1965), 79-91.

3428. ──────. "Le Prince Bernhard des Pays-Bas a remis le prix Erasme
       à M. Claude Lévi-Strauss." *Le Monde*, no. 8826 (31 May 1973),
       p. 21.

       ──────. See also items 3862 and 4275.

3429. ──────. Review of *Anthropologie structurale, deux. American
       Anthropologist*, 78 (March 1976), 145.

3429a. ──────. Review of *Myth and Meaning. Book World* (*Washington
       Post*), 1 July 1979, p. F-2.

3429b. ──────. Review of *Myth and Meaning. Christian Century*, 96
       (19 September 1979), 898.

3429c. ──────. Review of *Myth and Meaning. New Statesman*, 96 (22
       December 1978), 885.

3430. ──────. Review of *The Origin of Table Manners. Economist*, 269
       (25 November 1978), 125-126.

3430a. ──────. Review of *The Origin of Table Manners. Guardian Weekly*,
       119 (26 November 1978), 22.

3430b. ──────. Review of *The Origin of Table Manners. Sociology:
       Reviews of New Books*, 6 (March 1979), 62.

3430c. ──────. Review of *The Origin of Table Manners. Village Voice*,
       24 (5 February 1979), 72.

3430d. ———. Review of *The Origin of Table Manners*. *Virginia Quarterly Review*, 55 (Summer 1979), 110.

3431. ———. Review of *Structural Anthropology, vol. 2*. *Booklist*, 72 (1 June 1976), 1380.

3432. ———. Review of *Structural Anthropology, vol. 2*. *Christian Century*, 93 (9 June 1976), 579.

3433. ———. Review of *Structural Anthropology, vol. 2*. *Contemporary Sociology*, 7 (March 1978), 139.

3434. ———. Review of *Structural Anthropology, vol. 2*. *Economist*, 263 (16 April 1977), 126.

3435. ———. Review of *Structural Anthropology, vol. 2*. *Kirkus Reviews*, 43 (15 December 1975), 1415.

3436. ———. Review of *Structural Anthropology, vol. 2*. *Library Journal*, 101 (1 March 1976), 733.

3437. ———. Review of *Structural Anthropology, vol. 2*. *The New York Times Book Review*, 14 March 1976, p. 23.

3438. ———. Review of *Structural Anthropology, vol. 2*. *Partisan Review*, 45 (Winter 1978), 142.

3439. ———. Review of *Structural Anthropology, vol. 2*. *Reviews in Anthropology*, 5 (Winter 1978), 117.

3440. ———. Review of *Structural Anthropology, vol. 2*. *Science Books and Films*, 12 (December 1976), 130.

3441. ———, Review of *Structural Anthropology, vol. 2*. *The Times Educational Supplement*, 16 December 1977, p. 20.

3442. ———. Review of *Tristes Tropiques*. *Books and Bookmen*, 19 (February 1974), 20.

3443. ———. Review of *Tristes Tropiques*. *Booklist*, 70 (15 April 1974), 892.

3444. ———. Review of *Tristes Tropiques*. *Book World* (*Washington Post*), 28 April 1974, p. 4.

3445. ———. Review of *Tristes Tropiques*. *Choice*, 11 (June 1974), 640.

3445a. ———. Review of *Tristes Tropiques*. *Georgia Review*, 33 (Fall 1979), 688.

3446. ———. Review of *Tristes Tropiques*. *The Listener*, 90 (20 December 1973), 857.

3447. ———. Review of *Tristes Tropiques*. *The National Observer*, 13 (2 March 1974), 17.

3448. ———. Review of *Tristes Tropiques*. *The New York Times*, 123 (21 February 1974), 31.

3449. ———. Review of *Tristes Tropiques*. *The Observer*, 13 January 1974, p. 25.

3450. ———. Review of *Tristes Tropiques*. *Psychology Today*, 8 (July 1974), 88.

3451. ———. Review of *Tristes Tropiques*. *Publishers Weekly*, 205 (21 January 1974), 80.

3452. ———. Review of *Tristes Tropiques*. *The Times Literary Supplement*, 22 February 1974, p. 188.

3453. ———. Review of *La Voie des masques*. *The Times Literary Supplement*, 12 March 1976, p. 286.

3454. ———. "*Structural Anthropology*, vol. 2, trans. by M. Layton." *Choice*, 13, no. 4 (June 1976), 560.

———. See also items 2065, 960 and 370.

3455. Araújo, M.L. de. Review of *L'Homme nu. Mythologiques IV*. *Revista da Faculdade de Letras. Série de Filosofia*, 1, no. 2-3 (1971), 275-282; 2, no. 1-2 (1972), 107-122.

Armstrong, N. See item 3866.

3456. Arregui, C. Review of *Anthropologie structurale*. *Cuadernos Uruguayos de Filosofía*, 5 (1968), 167-169.

Aubenque, P. See items 4429-4430.

3457. Backès-Clément, Catherine. *Lévi-Strauss. Presentación y antología de textos*. Trans. Margarita Latorre. Barcelona: Anagrama, 1974.

3458. Badcock, C.R. "The Ecumenical Anthropologist. Solutions to Some Persistent Problems in Theoretical Sociology Found in the Works of Claude Lévi-Strauss." *The British Journal of Sociology*, 26, no. 2 (1975), 156-168.

3459. ———. *Lévi-Strauss: Structuralism and Sociological Theory*. London: Hutchinson, 1975, 125pp.; New York: Holmes & Meier, 1976, c.1975, 125pp.

3460. Barbera, Alexandre. "Lévi-Strauss: limites et vérités du structuralisme." *Défense de l'Occident*, no. 137 (April 1976), pp. 72-78.

3461.   Barksdale, Ethelbert Courtland. *The Dacha and the Duchess: An Application of Lévi-Strauss's Theory of Myth in Human Creativity to Works of 19th-Century Russian Novelists.* New York: Philosophical Library, 1974.

        Bartolomei, G. See item 3869.

3462.   Bastide, Roger. "As Estruturas elementares do parentesco." *Anhembi*, 1, no. 1 (December 1950), 52-64.

        Belaval, Y. See item 4437.

3463.   Bell, Daniel. "Lévi-Strauss and the Return to Rationalism." *The New York Times Book Review*, 14 March 1976, pp. 23-24.

3464.   Benavides, Manuel. "La Antropología estructural de Claude Lévi-Strauss." In *Antropologías del siglo XX*. Ed. Juan de Sahagún Lucas. Salamanca: Ed. Sígueme, 1976, pp. 237-258.

3465.   Ben Jelloun, Tahar. "Tristes structures." *Le Monde [des Livres]*, no. 8952 (25 October 1973), p. 25.

3466.   Benoist, Jean-Marie. "Classicism Revisited: Human Nature and Structure in Lévi-Strauss and Chomsky." In *The Limits of Human Nature* (essays based on a course of lectures given at the Institute of Contemporary Arts, London). Ed. Jonathan Benthall. New York: E.P. Dutton, 1974, c.1973, pp. 20-48.

3467.   ————. "Claude Lévi-Strauss entre deux masques." *Le Figaro Littéraire*, no. 1540 (22 November 1975), pp. I, III: 15, 17.

        On *La Voie des masques*.

3467a. ————. "Claude Lévi-Strauss Reconsiders." *Encounter*, 53 (July 1979), 19-26.

        An interview with Lévi-Strauss.

3468.   Berde, S. "Melanesian Distributive Justice." *Reviews in Anthropology*, 2, no. 4 (1975), 489-496.

3469.   Bergson, Philip. Review of *Tristes Tropiques*. *Oxford Literary Review*, Spring 1974, p. 5.

        Bermejo, J.M. See item 5133.

3469a. Bernstein, Gene M. "Lévi-Strauss's Totemism and Wordsworth's Lyrical Ballads." *Studies in Romanticism*, 18 (Fall 1979), 383-403.

        Bersani, J., et al. See item 3871.

3469b. Bessonov, B. "The Critique of 'Neo-Marxist' Falsifications of Marxist-Leninist Principles in the Study of the Historical and Philosophical Process" (in Czech). *Filosofický Časopis*, 25, no. 2 (1977), 192-198. Part of the Second International

Symposium of the Historians of the Philosophy of Socialist
Countries.

Lévi-Strauss is one of the authors treated.

Bettetini, G. See item 3816.

Biase, C. di. See item 4929.

Blau, H. See item 26.

3470. Bloemsma, B. "Nogmaals ordening van tijd en ruimte bij Lévi-
Strauss." *De Gids*, no. 9 (1975), pp. 641-648.

Bogliolo, H. See item 4440.

Boisset, L. See item 4934.

3471. Bonilla, Luis. "Ciencias sociales." *Estafeta Literaria*, no.
539 (1 May 1974), pp. 1711-1712.

On *El Futuro de los estudios del parentesco*.

3472. ———. "Ensayo." *Estafeta Literaria*, no. 566 (15 June 1975),
pp. 2142-2143.

On *La Antropología como ciencia*, ed. José E. Llobera.

3473. Boon, James A., and David M. Schneider. "Kinship vis-à-vis
Myth Contrasts in Lévi-Strauss' Approaches to Cross-Cultural
Comparison." *American Anthropologist*, 76 (December 1974),
799-817.

3473a. Boon, James A. *Del simbolismo al estructuralismo*. Trans. Eddy
Montaldo. Buenos Aires: Ed. El Ateneo, 1976, 280pp.

3474. ———. Review of *The Origin of Table Manners*. *Psychology
Today*, 12 (November 1978), 158ff.

3475. Bostoen, H. "Het Mensbeeld van Claude Lévi-Strauss." *Bijdragen.
Tijdschrift voor Filosofie en Theologie*, 35, no. 1 (1974),
82-100. French summary, pp. 99-100.

3476. ———. "Wijsgerige vragen over de antropologie van Claude
Lévi-Strauss." *Bijdragen. Tijdschrift voor Filosofie en
Theologie*, 35, no. 2 (1974), 186-201. French summary, p. 201.

3477. Boussard, Léon. "Claude Lévi-Strauss succède à Henry de Montherlant." *Nouvelle Revue des Deux Mondes*, no. 8 (August 1974),
pp. 349-352.

3478. Bram, Joseph. Review of *Tristes Tropiques*. *Library Journal*,
98 (15 November 1973), 3386.

3479. Brown, Edward J. "From Symbolism to Structuralism: Lévi-
Strauss in a Literary Tradition*, by James A. Boon." *Clio*,
4, no. 3 (June 1975), 416-419.

3480.   Brown, Richard Harvey. "Dialectic and Structure in Jean-Paul
        Sartre and Claude Lévi-Strauss." *Dialectica*, 32 (1978),
        165-184; *Human Studies*, 2 (January 1979), 1-19. English, French
        and German summaries on pp. 165-166.

        Attempting a reconciliation between Sartre's existentialism
        and Levi-Strauss's structuralism, Brown argues that dialectical
        thought generates structures, and that structuralism invites a
        dialectical method of construction.

3481.   Browne, Ray B. "*The Savage Mind* by Claude Lévi-Strauss."
        Journal of Popular Culture, 1, no. 4 (Spring 1968), 443.

        Bruézière, M. See item 2093.

3482.   Brykman, Geneviève. "J.-B. Fages: *Comprendre Lévi-Strauss*."
        Revue Philosophique de la France et de l'Etranger, 101, no. 1
        (January-March 1976), 35-37.

        Bulhof, I.N. See item 4450.

        Burgess, A. See item 1002.

3483.   Burkhart, John E. "Lévi-Strauss: Structural Anthropologist."
        Listening, 10 (Fall 1975), 32-43.

3484.   Burridge, K.O.L. "Claude Lévi-Strauss: Fieldwork, Explanation
        and Experience." *Theory and Society. Renewal and Critique in
        Social Theory*, 2, no. 4 (1975), 563-584.

3485.   Burton, J.W. "Some Nuer Notions of Purity and Danger. Dedicated
        to the Memory of E.E. Evans-Pritchard (1902-1973)." *Anthropos*,
        69, no. 3-4 (1974), 517-536.

        A critique of Lévi-Strauss.

3486.   [Caillois, Roger]. "Sous la coupole: L'Académie Française a
        reçu M. Claude Lévi-Strauss--la réponse de M. Roger Caillois."
        Le Monde [des Livres], no. 9160 (28 June 1974), pp. 21-22.

3487.   Caldiron, Orio. *Claude Lévi-Strauss. I Fondamenti teorici
        dell'antropologia strutturale*. Florence: L.S. Olschki, 1975,
        178pp. (Università di Padova: Pubblicazioni della Facoltà
        di Lettere e Filosofia, LIV)

3488.   Calinescu, Matei. "Imagination and Meaning: Aesthetic Attitudes
        and Ideas in Mircea Eliade's Thought." *The Journal of Religion*,
        57 (January 1977), 1-15.

        Also on Lévi-Strauss.

        Câmara, J.M., et al. See item 35.

3489.   Carreras, Alberto. *El Estructuralismo de Lévi-Strauss*. Valencia:
        Universidad, Facultad de Filosofia y Letras, 1972, 13pp. An
        offprint from *Saitabi*, 22 (1972), 23-35.

3490. Carroll, Michael P. "Applying Heider's Theory of Cognitive
       Balance to Claude Lévi-Strauss." *Sociometry*, 36, no. 3 (1973),
       285-301.

3491. ————. "Lévi-Strauss on the Oedipus Myth: A Reconsideration."
       American Anthropologist, 80 (December 1978), 805-814.

       Caruso, Paolo. See items 2101-2102.

       Caws, P. See item 36.

       Cencillo, L. See item 4455.

       Chabanis, C. See items 4941-4942.

3492. Chanan, Michael. "The Search for Meaning." *New Statesman*, 83,
       no. 2144 (21 April 1972), 534.

3493. Chapleevich, Eugeniush. "Tselosten li strukturnv i analiz?"
       Voprosy Literatury, 17 (July 1974), 207-236.

3494. Charbonnier, Georges. *Arte, lenguaje, etnología: entrevistas
       de Georges Charbonnier con Claude Lévi-Strauss*. Trans. Fran-
       cisco González Aramburu. Mexico: Siglo Veintiuno, 1968, 1971
       (3rd ed.). (Colección Mínima, 14)

3495. ————. *Arte, lenguaje, etnología. Entrevistas con Georges
       Charbonnier*. Havana: Instituto del Libro, 1970.

       Châtelet, F. See items 2111 and 41.

       Chiari, J. See item 407.

       Cipolli, C. See item 4873.

3496. Clark, Deborah Johnston. "Rousseau and Lévi-Strauss: Landscapes
       of Signification." *Dissertation Abstracts International*, 38,
       no. 1 (July 1977), 241-A. Johns Hopkins University disserta-
       tion.

3497. Clarke, Simon. "Lévi-Strauss's Structural Analysis of Myth."
       Sociological Review, n.s. 25, no. 4 (November 1977), 743-774.

3498. ————. "Origins of Levi-Strauss's Structuralism." *Sociology*,
       12 (September 1978), 405-439.

       Clavel, M. See item 3226.

3499. Clavier, H. "A l'aube de la religion avec l'enfant." *Revue
       d'Histoire et de Philosophie Religieuses*, 48, no. 4 (1968),
       329-354.

3500. Clément, C.B., and A. Casanova. "Un Ethnologue et la culture.
       Un Entretien avec Claude Lévi-Strauss." *La Nouvelle Critique*,
       no. 61 (1973), pp. 27-36.

3501.   Clément, Catherine. "Le Rire de Déméter." *Critique*, no. 323
        (April 1974), pp. 306-325.

        On *L'Homme nu*.

        Cockburn, A. See item 1023.

        Cohen, S. See item 5230.

        Conley, T. See item 1659.

3502.   Cook, Albert. "Lévi-Strauss and Myth: A Review of *Mythologiques*."
        MLN, 91, no. 8 (October 1976), 1099-1116.

3503.   Cooley, R. "Jung, Lévi-Strauss and the Interpretation of Myth."
        Criterion, 8 (Fall-Winter 1968-1969), 12-16.

        Corvez, M. See chapter 3 of items 49-51.

3504.   Cotellessa, Carla. "Aspetti del problema della storia in Lévi-
        Strauss," which is the appendix to *L'Emergere del problema
        della storia nell'età della sofistica*. By Carlo Sini. L'Aquila:
        Centro Tecnico Culturale ed Assistenziale, 1974.

        Cotroneo, G. See item 4362.

        Cottier, G.M.-M. See item 4474.

        Cox, C.B., et al. See item 1026.

        Crémant, R. See item 54.

        Crumrine, N.R., et al. See item 3747.

        Cruz Cruz, Juan. See item 4477.

3505.   Cuddihy, John Murray. *The Ordeal of Civility. Freud, Marx,
        Lévi-Strauss and the Jewish Struggle with Modernity*. New York:
        Basic Books, 1974, 272pp.

3506.   Cuisenier, Jean. "Le Structuralisme du mot, de l'idée et des
        outils." *Esprit*, 35, no. 360 (May 1967), 825-842.

3507.   D., J.-M. "Rites initiatiques." *Le Monde [des Livres]*, no.
        9160 (28 June 1974), p. 19.

3507a. D'Amico, R. Review of *Structural Anthropology*. *Philosophy and
        Phenomenological Research*, 40 (September 1979), 142-144.

        ————. See also item 57.

3508.   Damisch, Hubert. "L'Eclat du cuivre et sa puanteur." *Critique*,
        no. 349-350 (June-July 1976), pp. 599-625.

        On *La Voie des masques*.

3508a. Davenport, G. Review of *The Origin of Table Manners. The Hudson Review*, 32 (Fall 1979), 423-428.

3509. Da Via, Giuseppe. "Lo Strutturalismo." *Osservatore Romano*, no. 284 (9-10 December 1974), p. 3.

De George, Fernande M. See items 581 and 3912.

3510. Delacampagne, Christian. "Du Collège à l'Académie. Lévi-Strauss: suite à l'*Anthropologie structurale*." *Le Monde [des Livres]*, no. 8952 (25 October 1973), pp. 21, 25.

Deleuze, G., et al. See item 2135.

3511. Delfendahl, Bernard. "Critique de l'anthropologie savante. Claude Lévi-Strauss, homéliste et scolastique." *L'Homme et la Société*, 22 (1971), 211-235.

3512. Del Ninno, Maurizio. *L'Analisi dei miti in Cl. Lévi-Strauss: lessico metodologico*. Palermo: Stampatori Tipolitografi Associati, 1975, 61pp. (Quaderni del Circolo Semiologico Siciliano, 6) In French with introductory material in Italian.

3513. De Meireles, José Rui. "Antropologia estrutural: a proibição do incesto segundo Lévi-Strauss." *Revista Portuguesa de Filosofia*, 31, no. 3 (July-September 1975), 268-283.

3514. Demetz, Peter. "Literary Scholarship: Past and Future." *Comparative Literature Studies*, 10, no. 4 (December 1973), 364-373.

Denat, A. See item 4296.

3515. Dennis, P.A. "Lévi-Strauss in the Kindergarten: The Montessori Pre-Schooler as Bricoleur." *Revue Internationale de Pédagogie*, 20, no. 1 (1974), 3-16.

3516. Deregibus, A. Review of *Primitivi e civilizzati*, by Claude Lévi-Strauss. *Giornale di Metafisica*, 27 (1972), 225-227.

Derrida, Jacques. "Structure, Sign and Play in the Discourse of the Human Sciences." In his *Writing and Difference* (item 1616a), pp. 278-293.

3517. De Sousa Alves, Victorino. "Conceito de estrutura na lógica e na matemática." *Revista Portuguesa de Filosofia*, 32 (April-June 1976), 113-142.

Detweiler, R. See item 1036.

3518. Dickson, David. "Profile: Figures in a Structural Landscape--A Formal Study of Mankind." *The Times Higher Education Supplement*, no. 311 (21 October 1977), pp. 7 & 9.

Domenach, J.-M. See item 2140.

3519. ————. "Humanism in Question" (in Polish). *Więź*, 19, no. 3
       (1976), 5-14. Given at Lublin, 28 October 1975.

       Donato, E. See items 65 and 4300.

       Dorfles, G. See item 3700.

3520. Dörmann, J. Review of *Strukturale Anthropologie*. *Theologische
       Revue*, 65 (1969), 316-318.

3521. Douglas, Mary. *Natural Symbols. Explorations in Cosmology*.
       London: Barrie & Rockliff/The Cresset Press, 1970; Harmonds-
       worth, Middlesex: Penguin Books, 1973.

3522. Droit, Roger-Pol. "Claude Lévi-Strauss sur 'les Sentiers de
       la Création': quand les masques parlent." *Le Monde [des Livres]*,
       no. 9596 (28 November 1975), p. 19.

3523. Drossart, P. "Claude Lévi-Strauss et le corbeau d'Apollon."
       Latomus, 33, no. 4 (1974), 790-803.

       Dufrenne, M. See item 4493.

       Durand, G. See item 4838.

       Duvignaud, J. See item 3753.

       Eckert, C.W. See item 3823.

       Ela, J.-M. See item 4966.

3524. Elliot, E. Review of *Tristes Tropiques. Practical Anthropology*,
       17 (January-February 1970), 33-34.

3525. Epstein, Leslie. "Magical Mystery Tour: Ritual in the Modern
       Theater." *Partisan Review*, 36, no. 2 (1969), 251-264.

       Esprit, November 1963. See item 72.

       Etxeberria, M. See item 3756.

3526. Fages, Jean-Baptiste. *Para comprender a Lévi-Strauss*. Trans.
       Matilde Horne. Buenos Aires: Amorrortu Ed., 1974.

       Faucci, D. See item 4503.

3527. Félix-Faure, J. "M. Claude Lévi-Strauss: le structuralisme
       n'est plus à la mode depuis 1968." *Le Monde*, no. 8827 (1
       June 1973), p. 16.

       With statements by Lévi-Strauss.

3528. Fernandez, Dominique. "Lévi-Strauss: les masques parlent."
       L'Express, no. 1275 (15-21 December 1975), p. 20.

       On *La Voie des masques*.

Fiedler, L.A. See item 1053.

Fiore, S. See item 1477.

Firth, R. See item 3757.

3529. Fischer-Harriehausen, H. "Bemerkungen zur Kritik an Lévi-
Strauss." *Anthropos*, 67, no. 1-2 (1972), 272-280.

Fischer, J.B. See item 4509.

Flahault, F. See item 3928.

Flam, L. See item 4511.

Folkierska, A. See item 4512.

3530. Fougeyrollas, Pierre. "Lévi-Strauss [ou] le crépuscule de la
pensée bourgeoise." In his item 78, pp. 27-80.

Fowlie, W. See item 4303.

Francovich, G. See items 79-80.

Fraser, J. See item 435.

3531. Freilich, M. "Myth, Method and Madness." *Current Anthropology*,
16, no. 2 (June 1975), 207-226.

A critique of Lévi-Strauss with a discussion in 17 (March-
June 1976), pp. 139-142, 168-169, 336-337.

Funt, D.W. See item 4520.

Furet, F. See item 437.

G., P.-M. See item 85.

Gaboriau, M. See item 3758.

Galzigna, M. See item 4521.

Gardner, H. See items 4527-4530, 4881 and 5245-5246.

Georgin, R. See item 3262.

Gerber, R.J. See item 4536.

Gillet-Stern, S. See item 4539.

3532. Gilsenan, Michael. "Myth and the History of African Religion."
In *The Historical Study of African Religion*. Ed. Terence O.
Ranger and Isaria N. Kimambo. Berkeley: University of Cali-
fornia Press, 1972, pp. 50-70.

Gimeno, F.C. See items 4882-4883.

3532a. Giovannangeli, Daniel. "Esthétique de l'écriture. Remarques sur la philosophie de l'art de Claude Lévi-Strauss." *Cahiers Internationaux de Symbolisme*, no. 33-34 (1977), pp. 13-21.

3533. Girard, René. "Differentiation and Undifferentiation in Lévi-Strauss and Current Critical Theory." *Contemporary Literature*, 17 (Summer 1976), 404-429. Rpt. in item 4319, pp. 111-136.

3534. ————. "Violence and Representation in the Mythical Text." *MLN*, 92 (December 1977), 922-944. Rpt. in his *"To Double Business Bound." Essays on Literature, Mimesis, and Anthropology*. Baltimore, Md.: Johns Hopkins Press, 1978, pp. 178-198.

3534a. ————. "Differentiation and Reciprocity in Lévi-Strauss and Contemporary Theory." In his *"To Double Business Bound." Essays on Literature, Mimesis, and Anthropology*. Baltimore, Md.: Johns Hopkins Press, 1978, pp. 155-177.

————. See also item 1699.

3535. Glass, James M. "Schizophrenic and Primitive Thought: The Implicit and Unconscious Nature of Psychological Rebellion." *Politics and Society*, 6, no. 3 (1976), 327-345.

3536. Glean O'Callaghan, M., and C. Guillaumin. "Race et race ... la mode 'naturelle' en sciences humaines." *L'Homme et la Société*, no. 31-32 (1974), pp. 195-210.

A critique of Lévi-Strauss's *Race et culture*.

Glucksmann, M. See item 451.

3537. Goedecke, Robert. "Lévi-Strauss Out of His *Langue*." *Philosophy Today*, 22 (Spring 1978), 73-88.

Lévi-Strauss seen from the viewpoint of his English-speaking philosophic and scientific views. Several types of language are studied with regard to their structural implications. Structuralism is seen as a way out of the egocentrism and culture-centrism of modern European thought.

3538. Gómez García, Pedro. "La Estructura mitológica en Lévi-Strauss." *Teorema*, 6, no. 1 (1976), 119-146.

3539. ————. "Lévi-Strauss, frente a las escuelas antropológicas." *Teorema*, 8 (1978), 29-56.

3539a. Goodson, A.C. "Oedipus Anthropologicus." *MLN*, 94 (May 1979), 688-701.

3540. Gorer, Geoffrey. "Tour de force." *The Observer*, no. 9520 (13 January 1974), p. 25.

On *Tristes Tropiques*.

Gozzi, G. See item 5251.

3541. Gramont, Sanche de. "Says Lévi-Strauss, the Father of Struc-
        turalism, There Are No Superior Societies." *The New York
        Times Magazine*, 28 January 1968, pp. 28-40.

3542. ————. "No hay sociedades superiores." *Revista de Occident*,
        38, no. 113-114 (August-September 1972), 215-232.

Greckij, M.N. See item 4549.

Guala, C. See item 4551.

Guccione Monroy, N. See item 4552.

3543. Guiart, J. Review of *Le Totémisme aujourd'hui*. *Revue de l'His-
        toire des Religions*, 172, no. 1 (1967), 84-88.

Guillén, C. See item 3948.

3544. Habimana Makamba, Zacharie. "Problèmes de méthode en anthropo-
        logie culturelle: C. Lévi-Strauss et S. Strasser." Doctoral
        dissertation, 20 June 1974, at the Institut Supérieur de
        Philosophie, University of Louvain, Belgium. Reported in
        Revue Philosophique de Louvain, 72, no. 16 (November 1974),
        835-837.

3545. Haeffner, G. Review of *Mythologica, I-IV*. *Theologie und Philos-
        ophie*, 50 (1975), 470-472.

3546. Hameline, J.Y. "Relire Van Gennep ... Les Rites du passage."
        Maison-Dieu, 112 (Paris, 1972), 133-137.

3547. Hammel, Eugene A. *The Myth of Structural Analysis: Lévi-Strauss
        and the Three Bears*. Reading, Mass.: Addison-Wesley, 1972.

Hammond-Tooke, W.D. See item 3760.

Hamon, P. See item 5164.

Hanhardt, J.G., et al. See item 3825.

3548. Harris, Marvin. "Lévi-Strauss et la palourde. Réponse à la
        Conférence Gildersleeve de 1972." *L'Homme*, 16, no. 2-3 (1976),
        5-22.

        A critique of Lévi-Strauss.

3549. Harte, Barbara, and Carolyn Riley, eds. "Lévi-Strauss." In
        their *200 Contemporary Authors: Bio-Bibliographies of Selected
        Leading Writers of Today with Critical and Personal Side-
        lights*. Detroit: Gale, 1969, p. 169.

Hawkes, T. See item 5165.

3550. Heinrichs, Hans-Jürgen. "Die Besinnung auf das Allgemeine.
       Zu dem Werk von Claude Lévi-Strauss." *Psyche*, 30 (1976),
       170-199.

       Henriot, P. See item 4557.

       Herrmann, C. See item 3272.

3551. Heusch, Luc de. "Sens et contresens anthropologiques." *Critique*,
       no. 342 (November 1975), pp. 1136-1158. On *Anthropologie
       structurale deux*.

3552. Hopkins, Pandora. "Homology of Music and Myth: Views of Lévi-
       Strauss on Musical Structure." *Ethnomusicology*, 21 (May 1977),
       247-261.

3552a. Horák, P. "The 'Nominalist' Conception of Structure in Lévi-
       Strauss" (in Czech). *Filosofický Časopis*, 25, no. 3 (1977),
       411-428.

       Hund, W.B. See item 4574.

       Huppert, G. See Item 2170.

3553. Izumi, Yuka. "Preliminary Report on Lévi-Strauss's Conscious-
       ness about 'Social Structure'--From the Viewpoint of 'The
       Exchange Theory' and of the Reciprocity Found in *Les Formes
       élémentaires de la parenté*" (in Japanese). *Japanese Sociolog-
       ical Review*, 22, no. 4 (1972), 37-59.

       Jaeggi, U.J.V. See item 4378.

       Jameson, F. See item 4172.

       Janion, M. See item 3967.

       Jaroszewski, T.M. See item 4578.

       Johansen, J.L. See item 5005.

       Johnston, W.M. See item 4580.

3554. Josselin de Jong, P.E. de. "Voltooide symphonie: de *Mytholo-
       giques* van Lévi-Strauss." *Forum der Letteren*, 14, no. 2 (June
       1973), 95-120.

       Kampits, P. See item 4585.

3555. Kaplan, M.R. "A Note on Nutini's 'The Ideological Bases of
       Lévi-Strauss's Structuralism.'" *American Anthropologist*, 76,
       no. 1 (1974), 62-65.

3555a. Katramanov, Ju. M. "Claude Lévi-Strauss and the Problem of Man"
       (in Russian). *Voprosy Filosofii*, no. 10 (1976), pp. 133-141.

3556. Kaufmann, J.N. *"Structural Analysis in Contemporary Social Thought. A Comparison of the Theories of Claude Lévi-Strauss and Louis Althusser,* par Miriam Glucksmann." *Dialogue,* 15, no. 1 (March 1976), 184-186.

———. See also items 482, 4587 and 5258.

Kelemen, P. See item 3765.

Kermode, F. See item 1107.

Kirby, M. See item 3972.

3557. Kmita, Jerzy. "Methodological Proposals of Claude Lévi-Strauss" (in Polish). *Studia Filozoficzne,* 3 (Warsaw, 1971), 127-136.

A critique of *Anthropologie structurale.*

3558. ———. "Methodological Proposals of Claude Lévi-Strauss." *Poznań Studies in the Philosophy of the Sciences and the Humanities,* 1, no. 4 (1975), 73-82.

3559. Knapp, James F. "Myth in the Power House of Change." *Centennial Review,* 20, no. 1 (Winter 1976), 56-74.

3560. Köbben, A.J.F., et al. "Lévi-Strauss and Empirical Inquiry." *Ethnology,* 13, no. 3 (1974), 215-223.

Koppe, F. See item 3973a.

3561. Korn, F. "Terminology and 'Structure': The Dieri Case." *Bijdragen tot de Taal-, Land- en Volkenkunde,* 127, no. 1 (1971), 39-81.

The current value of the *Structures élémentaires de la parenté* as shown by an examination of one of the most important analyses undertaken by Lévi-Strauss, an "abnormal" case.

Krieger, Murray. See items 4319 and 4320.

3562. Kultgen, John. "Lévi-Strauss on Unconscious Social Structures." *The Southwestern Journal of Philosophy,* 7, no. 1 (1975), 153-159.

3563. Kunz, H. Review of *Strukturale Anthropologie. Studia Philosophica,* 28 (1968), 292.

3564. Kuper, Adam. "Lévi-Strauss and British Neo-Structuralism." In his *Anthropologists and Anthropology. The British School, 1922-1972.* New York: Pica Press, 1974, c.1973, pp. 204-226.

3565. ———. "Mushroom Culture." *New Society,* 39, no. 748 (3 February 1977), 243-244.

On *Structural Anthropology,* vol. 2.

3566.   ────. "The Dish Served Up by Lévi-Strauss." *New Society*,
         2 November 1978, pp. 28-32.

         Lacroix, Jean. See "Le Structuralisme de Claude Lévi-Strauss,"
         chapter 5, part III of his item 4600 (1968), pp. 231-239.

3566a.   Ladner, Gerhart B. "Medieval and Modern Understanding of Sym-
         bolism: A Comparison." *Speculum*, 54 (April 1979), 223-256.

3566b.   Lafrance, G. "Le Structuralisme et la philosophie des sciences
         sociales." *Canadian Journal of Philosophy*, 8, no. 4 (1978),
         665-676.

         On Lévi-Strauss and the critique of the philosophy of history
         in structuralist methodology.

3566c.   Lambrecht, Winifred. Review of *The Origin of Table Manners*.
         Library Journal, 104 (15 April 1979), 968.

3567.   Lapointe, François H. "Claude Lévi-Strauss: A Bibliographic
         Essay." *Man and World*, 6 (November 1973), 445-469.

3568.   ────, and Claire C. Lapointe. "Lévi-Strauss y sus críticos.
         Una Bibliografía." *Revista de Filosofía de la Universidad de
         Costa Rica*, 14, no. 38 (1976), 137-154.

3569.   ────. *Claude Lévi-Strauss and His Critics: An International
         Bibliography (1950-1976)*. Followed by a Bibliography of the
         Writings of Claude Lévi-Strauss. New York: Garland, 1977.

3570.   Lapouge, Gilles. "La Leçon du pissenlit." *Le Monde*, no. 8822
         (26 May 1973), p. 14.

         Laurentin, R. See item 122.

3570a.   Lawson, E. Thomas. "The Explanation of Myth and Myth as Explana-
         tion." *Journal of the American Academy of Religion*, 46, no.
         4 (December 1978), 507-523.

         Lévi-Strauss's structuralist perspective as a considerable
         theoretical advance over other interpretations of myth.

3571.   Leach, Edmund Roland. "Signification et position de l'oeuvre
         de Lévi-Strauss." *Annales. Economies, Sociétés, Civilisations*,
         19, no. 6 (November-December 1964), 1087-1115.

*3572.   ────. *Claude Lévi-Strauss*. New York: The Viking Press,
         1970, 1974 (rev. ed.).

3573.   ────. *Claude Lévi-Strauss*. Trans. H. ten Brummelhuis.
         Amsterdam: Meulenhoff, 1970.

3574.   ────. "A Critique of Yalman's Interpretation of Sinhalese
         Girls' Puberty Ceremonial." In *Echanges et communications.
         Mélanges offerts à Claude Lévi-Strauss*. Ed. Jean Pouillon
         and Pierre Maranda. The Hague: Mouton, 1970, tome II, pp.
         819-828.

Deals with three phases in the interpretation of ritual symbolism according to the explanations of Frazer, Radcliffe-Brown and Lévi-Strauss.

3575. ———. *Claude Lévi-Strauss*. Trans. Lutz-W. Wolff. Munich: Deutscher Taschenbuch-Verlag, 1971.

3576. ———. "Vico e Lévi-Strauss sull'origine dell'umanità." *Rassegna Italiana di Sociologia*, 13, no. 2 (1972), 221-233.

3577. ———. *As Idéias de Lévi-Strauss*. Trans. Álvaro Cabral. São Paulo: Cultrix/USP, 1974.

3578. ———. *Claude Lévi-Strauss*. Ed. Frank Kermode, Rev. ed. Middlesex, England: W. Drayton; Rutherford, N.J.: Penguin Books, 1976, 146pp.

3579. ———. "Oh Come, All Ye Faithful." *Spectator*, 238, no. 7775 (29 January 1977), 27-28.

On *Structural Anthropology, vol. 2*.

———. See also item 3774.

3580. Leacock, Eleanor. "Changing Family and Lévi-Strauss, or Whatever Happened to Fathers?" *Social Research*, 44 (Summer 1977), 235-259.

Le Blond, J.-M. See item 5269.

3581. Le Clézio, J.M.G. "Claude Lévi-Strauss: *L'Homme nu*." *Cahiers du Chemin*, no. 21 (15 April 1974), pp. 171-184.

3582. Lefebvre, Henri. *Ajustes de cuentas con el estructuralismo. Claude Lévi-Strauss y el nuevo eleatismo*. (Followed by Galvano della Volpe's Ajuste de cuentas con la poética estructural.) Trans. Maria Esther Benítez. Madrid: Alberto Corazón, 1969.

3583. ———. "Klod Levi-Stros i novi eleatizam" (in Serbo-Croatian). *Delo*, 19, no. 12 (1973), 1450-1476. Trans. of the first chapter of his item 125.

3584. Le Goff, Jacques, and Pierre Vidal-Naquet. "Lévi-Strauss en Brocéliande." *Critique*, 30, no. 325 (June 1974), 541-571.

A critical study of *Anthropologie structurale, deux*.

3585. Lépine, Claude. *O Inconsciente na antropologia de Lévi-Strauss*. São Paulo: Editora Atica, 1974.

Levin, D.M. See item 4614.

3586. Lévy, Bernard-Henri. "A travers textes et temps." *Le Nouvel Observateur*, no. 582 (5-11 January 1976), pp. 58-59.

Leyvraz, J.-P. See items 133-134.

3587. Lifšic, M. "Critical Remarks on the Contemporary Theory of
       Myth" (in Russian). *Voprosy Filosofii*, 8 (1973), 143-153.

3588. Lima, Augusto Guilherme Mesquitela. *Lévi-Strauss et les sciences
       humaines*. Luanda: Alliance Française, 1971, 23pp. A conference
       given at the Musée de l'Angola on 25 September 1969 and
       previously published in *Trabalho*, no. 27 (Luanda, 1970).

3589. Lipsius, Frank. Review of *Tristes Tropiques*. *Commentary*, 58
       (September 1974), 88.

3590. Littleton, C. Scott. "'Je ne suis pas ... structuraliste': Some
       Fundamental Differences between Dumézil and Lévi-Strauss."
       The Journal of Asian Studies, 34, no. 1 (November 1974), 151-
       158.

       Llewelyn, J.E. See item 4619.

3591. Locchi, G. "Histoire et sociétés: critique de Lévi-Strauss."
       Nouvelle Ecole, 17 (1972), 81-93.

       A critique of the interpretation of various myths, classical
       and others.

3592. Locher, Gottfried Wilhelm. "Claude Lévi-Strauss." In *Filosofen
       van de 20e eeuw*. Ed. C.P. Bertels and E. Petersma. Assen-
       Amsterdam: Van Gorcum; Amsterdam-Brussels: Intermediair,
       1972, pp. 199-220.

3593. Luebke, Neil R. "A Reply to Professor Feibleman." *Southwestern
       Journal of Philosophy*, 4 (Spring 1973), 25-31.

3594. MacIntyre, A. Review of *The Savage Mind*. *The Philosophical
       Quarterly*, 17 (1967), 372.

3595. Magaña Esquivel, Antonio. "El Hombre y su lenguaje." *Hispano
       Americano*, 52, no. 1335 (4 December 1967), 72.

3596. Manganelli, F. "Società e metafisica. Un Esempio di comparazione
       omologa." *Rivista di Etnografia*, 24 (1970), 88-97.

       Marc-Lipiansky, Mireille. See item 139.

       Marchán, S. See item 3713.

3597. Margolin, Jean-Claude. "Mireille Marc-Lipiansky: *Le Structural-
       isme de Lévi-Strauss*." *Revue de Synthèse*, no. 73-74 (Janu-
       ary-June 1974), pp. 100-101.

3598. Mariani, Stefania. "Struttura e storia nel pensiero di C.
       Lévi-Strauss. Studi e interpretazioni." *Bollettino Biblio-
       grafico per le Scienze Morali e Sociali*, no. 33-36 (Rome,
       1976), pp. 183-224.

       Martano, G. See item 4638.

3599. Marti, K. "Claude Lévi-Strauss." *Reformatio*, 21 (March 1972), 182-185.

3600. Martin, Graham Dunstan. "James A. Boon: *From Symbolism to Structuralism.*" *Modern Language Review*, 71, no. 1 (January 1976), 186-187.

────. See also item 3994.

3601. Martinoir, B.L. de. "Lévi-Strauss et les mythes." *La Recherche*, no. 18 (1971), pp. 1080-1081.

On *Mythologiques, IV*.

3602. Mazzeo, Antonio Carlos. "O Estruturalismo e a opção tecnocratica." *Reflexão*, 1, no. 3 (1975-1976), 79-87.

3603. McNeil, Helen. Review of *Myth and Meaning* and *The Origin of Table Manners*. *New Statesman*, 96 (22-29 December 1978), 885.

Mehlman, J. See item 3997.

Melenk, H. See item 4642.

3604. Meletinskii, E.M. "Claude Lévi-Strauss and the Structural Typology of Myth" (in Russian). *Voprosy Filosofii*, no. 7 (1970), pp. 165-173.

3605. ────. "Klod Levi-Stross, Tolko etnologiya." *Voprosy Literatury*, 15 (April 1971), 115-134.

3605a. ────. "Claude Lévi-Strauss and the Structural Typology of Myth" (in Czech). *Estetika*, 14, no. 2 (1977), 96-108.

3606. Mengod, Vicente. "*El Totemismo en la actualidad*, de C. Lévi-Strauss." *Atenea*, año 45, tomo 168, núm. 419 (January-March 1968), 227-228.

3607. Merquior, Jose Guilherme. *A Estética de Lévi-Strauss*. Trans. Juvenal Hahne Jr. Rio de Janeiro: Tempo Brasileiro, 1975, 114pp.

3608. ────. *L'Esthétique de Lévi-Strauss*. Paris: Presses Universitaires de France, 1977. (Croisées)

Merrell, F. See items 4645-4646.

Meschonnic, H. See item 1142.

Millet, L., et al. See items 147-149.

Minguelez, R. See item 1144.

3609. Minton, Helen Lou. "A Comparative Analysis of the Literary Styles of Chateaubriand and Lévi-Strauss." *Dissertation Abstracts International*, 38, no. 4 (October 1977), 2162-2163-A. Boston University dissertation.

Moore, J.H. See item 3780.

3610.   Moravia, Sergio, ed. *Lévi-Strauss e l'antropologia strutturale*.
         Florence: Sansoni, 1973.

Morawski, S. See item 2842.

3611.   Morazé, C. "Pensée sauvage et logique géométrique." In *Echanges
         et communications. Mélanges offerts à Claude Lévi-Strauss*.
         Ed. Jean Pouillon and Pierre Maranda. The Hague-Paris: Mouton,
         1970, tome 2, pp. 964-980.

         How observation in ethnography can be used as a conceptual
         tool to derive abstract notions and tie them together into a
         proposition. On *Le Cru et le cuit*.

3612.   Moreux, C. "Ideal-type et structure: un dialogue entre Weber
         et Lévi-Strauss." *Recherches Sociologiques*, 6, no. 1 (1975),
         3-49.

Morot-Sir, E. See item 4653.

Morris, W.A. See item 4002.

3613.   Mosse, G.L. Review of J.M. Cuddihy's *The Ordeal of Civility*.
         Telos, 25 (1975), 221-223.

Mounin, G. See item 5176.

3614.   Murphy, Robert F. "Remarkable Feast." *The New Republic*, 170,
         no. 20 (18 May 1974), 23-24.

         On *Tristes Tropiques*.

3615.   Nannini, Sandro. "Scienza e storia nella formazione di Lévi-
         Strauss." *Rivista di Filosofia*, 67 (July 1976), 289-313.

3616.   Narbona, Manuel Olivier. "Lévi-Strauss y las relaciones inter-
         humanas." *Estudios de Metafísica*, no. 3 (1972-1973), pp. 125-
         132.

Nathhorst, B. See item 4004.

3617.   Needham, Rodney. *Rethinking Kinship and Marriage*. London:
         Tavistock, 1971.

         A critique of Lévi-Strauss.

3617a.   Neschke-Hentschke, A. "Griechischer Mythos und strukturale
         Anthropologie. Kritische Bemerkungen zu Claude Lévi-Strauss'
         Methode der Mythendeutung." *Poetica*, 10, no. 2-3 (Munich,
         1978), 135-153.

3618.   Neu, Jerome. "Lévi-Strauss on Shamanism." *Man*, 10, no. 2
         (London, June 1975), 285-292.

3619. ———. "What is Wrong with Incest?" *Inquiry*, 19 (Spring 1976), 27-39.

Niculescu, R. See item 5178.

Nikolova, M. See item 4671.

La Nouvelle Critique. See item 4009.

3620. Norbeck, E. Review of *The Raw and the Cooked*. *Journal for the Scientific Study of Religion*, 9 (Winter 1970), 327-328.

3621. Pace, David. "The Bearer of Ashes: Claude Lévi-Strauss and the Problem of Cultural Relativism." *Dissertation Abstracts International*, 34, no. 11 (May 1974), 7164-A. Yale University dissertation.

3622. ———. "An Exercise in Structural History: An Analysis of the Social Criticism of Claude Lévi-Strauss." *Soundings: An Interdisciplinary Journal*, 58, no. 2 (Summer 1975), 182-199.

3623. Paluch, A.K. "The Notion of Structure in the Social Sciences: The Doctrine of Claude Lévi-Strauss" (in Polish). *Studia Socjologiczne*, no. 3 (1973), pp. 5-30.

Parain-Vial, J. See item 3720.

3624. Paz, Octavio. *Claude Lévi-Strauss: An Introduction*. Trans. J.S. and Maxine Bernstein. New York: Dell Publishing Co., 1974.

3624a. Petraş, I. "The Nature-Culture Relationship in Structural Anthropology" (in Rumanian). *Studia Universitatis Babeş-Bolyai. Series Philosophia*, 24, no. 1 (1979), 23-28. Includes an English summary.

3625. Petrus, Leon C. "The Word as Metaphor: An Interdisciplinary Theory." *Soundings*, 55, no. 3 (Fall 1972), 269-291.

3626. Pierre, José. "Dans les masques présentés par Lévi-Strauss, José Pierre a vu de drôles de choses." *La Quinzaine Littéraire*, no. 224 (1-15 January 1976), pp. 16-17, 30.

On *La Voie des masques*.

Pingaud, B. See items 2234 and 4704.

3627. Pirillo, N. "Struttura e storia." *Sociologia*, 5, no. 2 (1971), 169-176.

3628. Pitt-Rivers, J. "The Savage Mind." *Man*, 3, no. 2 (1968), 300-301.

3629. Podetti, Amelia. "El Problema de la historia en Lévi-Strauss." In *II° Congreso Nacional de Filosofía* tomo II. Simposios. Buenos Aires: Editorial Sudamericana, 1973, pp. 414-426.

Pöhler, E. See item 4708.

Pollmann, L. See item 1190.

Poole, R. See item 165.

3630. Pop, E. "Structuralist Ideas in the Anthropology of Lévi-Strauss" (in Rumanian). *Studia Universitatis Babeş-Bolyai. Series Philosophia*, 18 (1973), 105–112.

Poster, Mark. See item 4393.

Pouwer, J. See item 3788.

Prado Júnior, C. See item 557.

3631. Remotti, Francesco. *Estructura e historia. La Antropología de Lévi-Strauss*. Trans. Francesco Serra Cantarell. Barcelona: Edit. A. Redondo, 1972.

3632. Rheims, Maurice. "La Voie des masques." *Nouvelle Revue des Deux Mondes*, no. 3 (March 1976), pp. 588–598.

3633. Rhoads, E. "Little Orphan Annie and Lévi-Strauss. The Myth and the Method." *Journal of American Folklore*, 87, no. 344 (1974), 149–154.

Ricardou, J. See item 4333.

Ricoeur, P. See items 4724–4725.

Rivelaygue, J. See item 4740.

Robert, J. See item 5071.

Robert, J.-D. See item 3791.

3634. Rocha, Acílio Estanqueiro. "O Estruturalismo de Lévi-Strauss: significação do 'estrutural inconsciente.'" *Revista Portuguesa de Filosofia*, 32, no. 2 (April–June 1976), 171–206.

3635. Rosenberg, Aubrey. "The Temperamental Affinities of Rousseau and Lévi-Strauss." *Queen's Quarterly*, 82, no. 4 (Winter 1975), 543–555.

3636. Rosner, K. "The Work of Lévi-Strauss as a Source of Inspiration in Aesthetic Research" (in Polish). *Studia Estetyczne*, 9 (1972), 283–312.

The structural method of Lévi-Strauss and the semiotic definition of art it implies.

3637. Rota, A.F. "A proposito dell'oggettivita delle scienze dell'-uomo in Claude Lévi-Strauss." *Rivista di Filosofia Neo-Scolastica*, 68, no. 1 (1976), 85–93.

3638. Rotondaro, Fred. Review of *Tristes Tropiques*. *Best Sellers*, 34 (15 April 1974), 33.

Rowinski, C. See item 4747.

Roy, C. See item 632.

Rubio, J. See item 4750.

3639. Rubio Carracedo, José. *Lévi-Strauss: estructuralismo y ciencias humanas*. Madrid: Ediciones Istmo, c.1976, 368pp. (Biblioteca de estudios críticos, 4: Sección Antropología)

3640. Ryan, Michael. "Self-De(con)struction." *Diacritics*, 6, no. 1 (1976), 34-41.

3641. Ryklin, M. "Rousseau, Rousseauism and the Fundamental Concepts of Structural Anthropology." *International Social Science Journal*, 30, no. 3 (1978), 605-617.

3642. Salazar Cárdenas, Rafael. "El Hombre total." *Libro Anual*, 2 (ISEE, Mexico, 1973-1974), 181-191.

3643. Saliba, J.A. Review of *Structural Anthropology, vol. 2*. *America*, 134 (8 May 1976), 411-412.

3644. Salzano, Giorgio. "The Concept of Mind in the Thought of Claude Lévi-Strauss." *Dissertation Abstracts International*, 38, no. 5 (November 1977), 2853-A. Drew University dissertation.

3645. Samaranch, Francisco. *"Sentidas y usos del término estructura en las ciencias del hombre."* *Torre*, 20, no. 75-76 (January-June 1972), 260-266.

Sartre, J.-P. See item 4754.

3646. Scarduelli, Pietro. "Lévi-Strauss e il Terzo Mondo, con un' antologia di testi di Lévi-Strauss." *Quaderni di Terzo Mondo*, no. 4 (1974), pp. 1-80. Rpt. as item 3647.

On the limits of structuralism.

3647. ————. *Lévi-Strauss e il Terzo Mondo. Con un'antologia di testi di Claude Lévi-Strauss*. Milan: Centro Studi Terzo Mondo, 1974, 80pp. Rpts. item 3646.

Schaff, A. See items 4760-4763.

Schiwy, G. See items 189, 190 and 4034.

Schmalenberg, E. See item 5086.

Schober, R. See item 1447.

Scholes, R.E. See item 4036.

Scholte, B. See items 3799–3800.

3648.   Scholte, Bob, and Yvan Simons. "Lévi-Strauss and *la pensée leachéenne*." *Semiotica*, 6, no. 3 (1972), 289–294.

3649.   Schwimmer, Erik. "Myth and the Ethnographer: A Critique of Lévi-Strauss." In *Phenomenology, Structuralism, Semiology* (item 4531), pp. 162–185.

Seymour-Smith, M. See item 1452.

3650.   Shalvey, Thomas. *Claude Lévi-Strauss: Social Psychotherapy and the Collective Unconscious*. Amherst: The University of Massachusetts Press, 1979, 180pp.

Contains: (1) The Intellectual Context, pp. 1–6; (2) The Logic of the Unconscious, pp. 7–20; (3) The Lévi-Straussian Interpretation of the Unconscious, pp. 21–51; (4) There are No Privileged Societies, pp. 52–57; (5) Rousseau and Lévi-Strauss, pp. 58–81; (6) Lévi-Strauss and Marx, pp. 82–95; (7) Some Issue and Criticisms, pp. 96–120; (8) Lévi-Strauss: Last of the Scholastics, pp. 121–140; Selected Bibliography and Index.

Silverman, H.J. See item 4771.

3651.   Silverstone, Roger. "Ernst Cassirer and Claude Lévi-Strauss. Two Approaches to the Study of Myth." *Archives des Sciences Sociales des Religions*, 21, no. 41 (1976), 25–36.

Simon, J.K. See item 4338.

3652.   Simonis, Yvan. *Claude Lévi-Strauss o la 'Pasión del incesto' (Introducción al estructuralismo)*. Trans. Juan A. Méndez. Barcelona: Ed. Cultura Popular, 1969.

3653.   ———. Review of *L'Homme nu*. *Recherches Amérindiennes au Québec. Bulletin d'Information*, 2, no. 1 (1972), 33–36.

———. See also item 4773.

3654.   Soto Verges, Rafael. "Ciencias sociales." *Estafeta Literaria*, no. 558 (15 February 1975), p. 2013.

On the Spanish trans. of Catherine Backès-Clément's *Lévi-Strauss*.

———. See also items 1237–1238.

3655.   Sozzi, Lionello. *Il Primitivismo nella letteratura francese da Gonnerville a Lévi-Strauss*. Turin: G. Giappichelli, 1976, 369pp.

Spivey, R.A. See item 5096.

3656.   Staude, J.R. "From Depth Psychology to Depth Sociology: Freud, Jung and Lévi-Strauss." *Theory and Society. Renewal and Critique in Social Theory*, 3, no. 3 (1976), 303–338.

3657. Steiner, George. *Nostalgia for the Absolute*. Toronto: Canadian Broadcasting Corporation, 1974. Massey Lectures, 14th series.

3658. ————. "The Lost Garden." *New Yorker*, 50, no. 15 (3 June 1974), 100-108.

    On *Tristes Tropiques*.

3659. ————. "Lévi-Strauss and the Marriage Market." *The Sunday Times*, no. 8022 (20 March 1977), p. 40.

    Steinwachs, G. See item 4050.

    Stinchcombe, A.L. See item 5287.

    Strenski, I. See item 3808.

3660. ————. "Grammatical and Reductionist Explanations of Myth in Lévi-Strauss." *Philosophy Today*, 21, no. 1 (1977), 74-83.

    Lévi-Strauss explains the make up of myths in two contrary ways: grammatically and reductively. Both methods eliminate myth as a reality.

    Sturrock, John. See items 196a and 4862.

3661. ————. "Systems and Brothers." *New Review*, 1, no. 4 (London, July 1974), 77-78.

3662. Swanson, G.E. "Orpheus and Star Husband: Meaning and the Structure of Myths." *Ethnology*, 15, no. 2 (1976), 115-133.

    Tajima, S. See item 4787.

3663. Tam, Nathaniel. "Pansies for Thoughts: Reflections on the Work of Claude Lévi-Strauss." *The Listener*, 77 (11 May 1967), 618-619, 635.

    Taranienko, Z. See items 4053 and 4790.

    Tarkowska, E. See item 5288.

3664. Tissot, G. Review of *L'Homme nu*. *Studies in Religion/Sciences Religieuses*, 3, no. 4 (1973-1974), 365-367.

    Todisco, O. See item 4793.

    Topolski, J. See items 5290-5291.

3665. Townsend, C. Review of *La Voie des masques*. *Man*, 13 (December 1978), 688-689.

    Toynbee, P. See item 1255.

3666. Tucci, G. "Stagione di Lévi-Strauss." *Rivista di Etnografia*, 20 (1966), 126-128.

On the success of Lévi-Strauss's work in Italy; an analysis of his thought.

3667. Ueno, Chizuko. "The Epistemological Model of the Structuralism in Claude Lévi-Strauss" (in Japanese). *Shakaigaku Hyoron/ Japanese Sociological Review*, 26, no. 2 (November 1975), 2-17.

3667a. Updike, John. Review of *The Origin of Table Manners*. *New Yorker*, 55 (30 July 1979), 85-88.

3668. Urrutia, B. "Lévi-Strauss and Mormonism." *American Anthropologist*, 76, no. 2 (1974), 342-343.

        Uscatescu, G. See item 203.

3669. Van Baal, J. "The Part of Women in the Marriage Trade: Objects or Behaving as Objects?" *Bijdragen*, 126, no. 2 (1970), 289-308.

        A critical analysis of the thesis defended by Lévi-Strauss in *Les structures élémentaires de la parenté* according to which women are among the objects used in transactions among men.

        ————. See also item 3812.

3669a. Van Dyne, Larry. "A Titan of Anthropology." *The Chronicle of Higher Education*, 13 March 1978, p. 7.

        On Lévi-Strauss's reception of an honorary doctorate of humane letters from Johns Hopkins University.

3670. Vansina, F. "Bewusstsein, Sprache und Transzendenz." *Franziskanische Studien*, 55, no. 1 (1973), 17-27.

        Veltmeyer, H. See item 4416.

3671. Verón, Eliseo, ed. *El Proceso ideológico*. By Claude Lévi-Strauss et al. Trans. Noelia Bastard et al. Buenos Aires: Editorial Tiempo Contemporáneo, 1971.

3672. Verstraeten, P., et al., eds. *Claude Lévi-Strauss, problemas del estructuralismo*. Buenos Aires: Eudecor. Dist. Tres Américas, 1967.

        Vogel, A. See items 3841-3842.

3673. Vogt, W. Paul. "The Use of Studying Primitives: A Note on the Durkheimians, 1890-1940." *History and Theory*, 15 (1976), 33-44.

3674. Von Sturmer, J.R., and J.H. Bell. *Claude Lévi-Strauss: The Anthropologist as Everyman*. St. Lucia, Australia: privately published, 1970, 18pp.

3675. Waalwijk van Doorn, E.C.P. van. "Le Temps transformé en paysage chez Claude Lévi-Strauss." *De Gids*, 137, no. 9-10 (1974), 620-642.

3676. ———, Eric van. "Commentaar op B. Bloemsma." *De Gids*, no. 9 (1975), pp. 648-651.

3677. Wakeman, John, ed. Biography of Lévi-Strauss. *World Authors, 1950-1970: A Companion Volume to Twentieth-Century Authors*. New York: H.W. Wilson Company, 1975, pp. 862-865.

3678. Webster, S. Review of R. Needham's *Rethinking Kinship and Marriage. The Journal of the Polynesian Society*, 82, no. 3 (1973), 316-321.

       A critique of Lévi-Strauss.

       Weinmann, R. See item 4069.

       Weinrich, H. See item 4071.

3678a. Werblowsky, Raphael Jehudah. "Jung, Lévi-Strauss, and the Struggle for Meaning." *Center Magazine*, 12 (September 1979), 17.

       White, H.V. See items 215, 4072a and 4818.

3679. Wietig, S.G. "Myth and Symbol Analysis of Claude Lévi-Strauss and Victor Turner." *Social Compass*, 19, no. 2 (1972), 139-154.

       Wilden, A. See item 216.

3680. Williamson, Chilton, Jr. "Books Considered." *The New Republic*, 173, no. 16 (18 October 1975), 27-29.

3681. Wokler, Robert. "Perfectible Apes in Decadent Cultures: Rousseau's Anthroplogy Revisited." *Daedalus*, 107 (Summer 1978), 107-134.

3682. Wood, Michael. "Powerful Inanity." *New Statesman*, 23, no. 541 (15 February 1973), 369-370.

       On *From Honey to Ashes*.

3683. ———. "Journey's End." *New Society*, 27, no. 588 (10 January 1974), 81.

       On *Tristes Tropiques*.

3684. Wunderlich, D. Review of *Strukturale Anthropologie. Philosophischer Literaturanzeiger*, 21 (1968), 257-264.

3685. Zanasi, F. "Sulla religione in Claude Lévi-Strauss." *Studia Patavina. Rivista di Scienze Religiose*, 23, no. 2 (1976), 350-372.

Lévi-Strauss sees religion only in its horizontal phenomenology, as a set of social manifestations.

Zardoya, J.M. See item 4824.

3686. Zeldin, E. Reply to Lipsius' Review of *Tristes Tropiques* (item
3589). *Commentary*, 59 (January 1975), 12ff.

Zéraffa, M. See items 2889 and 2890.

3687. Ziółkowski, M. "The Conception of Culture in Lévi-Strauss"
(in Polish). *Studia Socjologiczne*, no. 4 (1976), pp. 45-66.

Žižek, S. See item 4825.

III
STRUCTURALISM AS APPLIED
TO VARIOUS DISCIPLINES

AESTHETICS/ART AND MUSIC

3688. Adams, Marie Jeanne. "Structural Aspects of a Village Art."
        American Anthropologist, 75 (February 1973), 265–279.

3689. Ames, Van Meter. "Art for Art's Sake Again?" *The Journal of
        Aesthetics and Art Criticism*, 33, no. 3 (Spring 1973), 303–
        307.

        Anonymous. See item 4867.

3689a. Bertin, Jacques. *Sémiologie graphique. Les Diagrammes, les
        réseaux, les cartes.* Paris: Gauthier Villars, 1967 (2nd ed.),
        432pp.; Paris: Editions Mouton, 1973, 431pp. English trans.
        by William Berg forthcoming.

3690. Bradac, Olga. "Aesthetic Trends in Russia and Czechoslovakia."
        The Journal of Aesthetics and Art Criticism, 9 (December 1950),
        97–105.

3691. Breazu, Marcel. "Analisi strutturale e valorizzazione nell'
        arte." Trans. Aldo Trione. *Logos*, no. 2 (1971), pp. 169–181.

3692. Brown, Estelle T. "Toward a Structuralist Approach to Ballet:
        Swan Lake and the White Haired Girl." *Western Humanities
        Review*, 32 (Summer 1978), 227–240.

3693. Burgin, Victor. *Work and Commentary*. London: Latimer New Dimen-
        sions, 1973.

        Câmara, J.M., et al. See item 35.

3693a. Chlumsky, M. "Les Problèmes d'une nouvelle esthétique." *Revue
        d'Esthétique*, no. 2–3 (1976), pp. 249–293.

        Chvatík, K. See items 45, 46, 4466, and 4467.

3694. Cormeau, Nelly. "Autour du problème esthétique." *Synthèses*,
        9e année, no. 98–99 (July–August 1954), 115–133.

        Daix, Pierre. See item 4293.

3695. ————. *L'Aveuglement devant la peinture*. Paris: Gallimard,
        1971.

3696. Deliège, C. "La Musicologie devant le structuralisme." In
        L'Arc, no. 26 (1965) (issue on Lévi-Strauss, out of print
        in 1974).

338 *Applied Structuralism*

3697. De Paz, A. "Semiologia e sociologia nell'estetica strutturalista di Mukařovský." *Lingua e Stile*, 10, no. 3 (1975), 531-
570.

3698. Dipert, Randall R., and R.M. Whelden. "Set-Theoretical Music
Analysis." *The Journal of Aesthetics and Art Criticism*, 35
(Fall 1976), 15-22.

3699. Dittmann, Lorenz. *Stil, Symbol, Struktur: Studien zu Kategorien
der Kunstgeschichte*. Munich: W. Fink, 1967.

3700. Dorfles, Gillo. "For or Against a Structuralist Aesthetic?"
Trans. Stephen Bann and Philip Steadman. *Form*, no. 2
(Cambridge, 1 September 1966), pp. 15-19.

3701. ————. "Pour et contre une critique structuraliste de l'oeuvre
d'art." *Diotima*, 5 (1977), 79-83.

On the profound changes wrought in art criticism in conjunction with the recent development of semiotic research and the
gap between the axiological and semiological aspect of the work
of art.

3702. Dufrenne, Mikel. "Esthétique et structuralisme." In *Contempo-
rary Philosophy. A Survey. Vol. VI. Ethics, Aesthetics, Law,
Religion, Politics. Historical and Dialectical Materialism.
Philosophy in Eastern Europe, Asia and Latin America*. (Inter-
national Institute of Philosophy) Ed. Raymond Klibansky.
Florence: La Nuova Italia Editrice, 1971, pp. 97-101.

3703. Duvignaud, Jean. *The Sociology of Art*. Trans. Timothy Wilson.
London: Paladin, 1972, c. 1967.

3704. Egeback, Niels. *Indskrifter: Essays om faenomenologi og aestetik*.
Fredensborg: Arena, 1967.

Einem, H. von, et al. See items 5238 and 5239.

3705. Engelhardt, H. "Über einige neuere Literatur zur Ästhetik."
Zeitschrift für Philosophische Forschung, 27, no. 3 (1973),
430-444.

From Adorno's theory of aesthetics to that of the structuralists.

3706. Firca, C.L. "La Spécificité structurale-esthétique de l'ex-
pressionnisme musical." *Analele Universitatii Bucureşti.
Serie Estetica*, 21 (1972), 7-13.

3707. Focht, I. "Structuralism and Aesthetics. The Principal Tendencies in Contemporary Czecho-slovak Aesthetics" (in Slovenian).
Izraz. Časopis za Književnu i Umetnicku Kritiku, 20, no. 1
(1976), 3-10.

Günther, Hans. See item 3949.

3708. Hermand, J., and E.T. Beck. "Dal positivismo allo strutturalismo.
       Il Pensiero estetico in Germania nel Novecento." *Comunità*,
       31, no. 177 (Milan, 1977), 236-341.

3709. Herr, Judith Lauren. *A Philosophy of Theatricality. A Phenomen-
       ological Description of the Aesthetic Structures in the Arts
       of Performance*. (Authorized facsimile of Ph.D. dissertation
       of Florida State University, 1971, Philosophy) Ann Arbor,
       Mich.-London: University Microfilms International, 1977.

3710. Hofmann, W. "Fragen der Strukturanalyse." *Zeitschrift für
       Ästhetik und allgemeine Kunstwissenschaft*, 17, no. 2 (1972),
       143-169.

       On Lévi-Strauss and Cassirer; art as language.

       Hopkins, P. See item 3552.

       Karbusický, V. See item 4380.

3711. Leach, Edmund R. "Michelangelo's Genesis: Structuralist Comments
       on the Sistine Chapel Ceiling." *The Times Literary Supplement*,
       no. 3914 (18 March 1977), pp. 311-313.

3712. Lotman, Jurij Michajlovic. *Structure du texte artistique*. Paris:
       Gallimard, 1970, 1973.

       Malagoli, L. See item 138.

3713. Marchán, Simón. "La Obra de arte y el estructuralismo." *Revista
       de Ideas Estéticas*, 28, no. 110 (April-June 1970), 93-119.

3713a. Marin, Louis. *Etudes sémiologiques*. Paris: Klincksieck, 1972.
       (Collection d'Esthétique, 11)

3714. Mathauser, Z. "The Theory of Reflection and the Noetics of
       Structuralism" (in Czech). *Estetika*, 10, no. 1 (1973), 49-63.

3715. Merquior, José Guilherme. "Analyse structurale des mythes et
       analyse des oeuvres d'art." *Revue d'Esthétique*, 23, no. 3-4
       (1970), 365-382.

       Similarities and differences between the structuralist inter-
       pretation of myths and the analysis of works of art.

       ————. See also items 3607-3608.

3716. Michelson, Annette. "Art and the Structuralist Perspective."
       In *On the Future of Art. Essays by Arnold J. Toynbee [and
       others]*. New York: Viking Press, 1970, pp. 37-59.

3717. Mukařovský, Jan. *Studien zur structuralistischen Ästhetik und
       Poetik*. Trans. Herbert Grönebaum and Gisela Riff. Munich:
       Hanser, 1974; Frankfurt-Berlin-Vienna: Ullstein, 1977.

3718.   ———. Structure, Sign, and Function. Selected Essays. Trans.
         and ed. John Burbank and Peter Steiner. New Haven: Yale Uni-
         versity Press, 1978, c. 1977.

         Selected essays on structuralist aesthetics viewed as a
         process rather than as a closed system. See in particular pp.
         3-16 for "On Structuralism" and pp. 70-81 for "The Concept of
         the Whole in the Theory of Art."

3718a.   Musique en Jeu, various issues, especially articles by Jean-
         Jacques Nattiez.

3719.   Nodelman, Sheldon. "Some Remarks on Structural Analysis in
         Art and Architecture." In item 68, pp. 89-103. See also item
         69.

3720.   Parain-Vial, Jeanne. "Expérience concrète et analyse structurale
         en esthétique." Annales d'Esthétique, 8 (1969), pp. 43-68.

3721.   ———. "La Création dans la perspective structuraliste."
         Diotima, 5 (1977), 182-189.

         One can speak of structuralism when, as is the case with
         Althusser and Deleuze, the author sets up what is most abstract
         in the structures studied by specialists (arts and sciences).
         The author censures the claim to explain artistic creation by
         means of structure, founding her thought on the creators'
         actual experience.

3722.   Pascadi, I. "Le Concept de structure artistique." Revue Roumaine
         des Sciences Sociales. Serie de Philosophie et Logique, 13,
         no. 1 (1969), 89-94.

3723.   Pinkava, J. "Structuralism and the Philosophical Foundations
         of the Marxist Theory of Art" (in Czech). Česká Literatura,
         16, no. 4 (1968), 410-418.

         On the aesthetic structuralism of the Prague school (Mukařov-
         ský).

3724.   Prox, L. "Strukturalistische Kunstforschung." Zeitschrift für
         Allgemeine Wissenschaftstheorie, 3, no. 2 (1972), 285-297.

         Rosner, K. See item 3636.

         Rouve, P. See item 3834.

         Ruwet, N. See item 4859.

3725.   Šabouk, Sáva. "Structuralist Tactics" (in Czech). Estetika,
         9, no. 3 (1972), 121-136.

3726.   ———. "Strukturalismus und Dialektik." Weimarer Beiträge,
         19, no. 4 (1973), 135-152; 19, no. 5 (1973), 126-144.

3727.   ———. Člověk a umění v struktuře světa. Prague: Čs. spis.,
         1974.

3728. ————. "The Old and New Aspects of Structuralism (The Problem of Structural Analysis, the Diachrony-Synchrony Relation)" (in Czech). *Estetika*, 11, no. 1 (1974), 7-29; 11, no. 2 (1974), 69-89.

3729. Saparov, M. "Three Structuralisms and the Structure of the Work of Art" (in Russian). *Voprosy Literatury*, 11, no. 1 (1967), 101-113.

Structure as a philosophical category. The totality of the work of art. The Marxist critique of works of art considered in isolation. Their objectivity, their structure and their particularities.

3730. Sazbón, José, ed. *Estructuralismo y estética*. Buenos Aires: Ediciones Nueva Visión, 1969.

3730a. Schefer, Jean-Louis. *Scénographie d'un tableau*. Paris: Editions du Seuil, 1969. (Tel Quel)

3730b. Sharpe, R.A. "A Transformation of a Structuralist Theme." *The British Journal of Aesthetics*, 18 (Spring 1978), 155-171.

3731. Sus, Oleg. "The Origins of the Semantic Typology in the Aesthetics of O. Zich. Prologue to a History of Czech Structuralism" (in Czech). *Česká Literatura*, 14, no. 5-6 (1966), 393-415.

3732. ————. "Les Traditions de l'esthétique tchèque moderne et du structuralisme de Jan Mukarovsky." *Revue d'Esthétique*, 24 (January-March 1971), 29-38.

3733. Tagliaferri, Aldo. *L'Estetica dell'oggettivo*. Milan: Feltrinelli, 1968.

3734. Uscatescu, Jorge. "El Estructuralismo en el arte." In *Temas de filosofía contemporánea. IIº Congreso Nacional de Filosofía*. Buenos Aires: Editorial Sudamericana, 1971, pp. 241-259.

3735. Van Haecht, L. "Current Philosophy of Art" (in Dutch). *Wijsgerig Perspectief op Maatschappij en Wetenschap*, 14, no. 4 (1973-1974), 225-232.

On existentialist, analytical, and structuralist currents.

3736. Virgilio, C. "Contributi interdisciplinari alla sociologia dell'arte." *Sociologia*, 6, no. 2 (Rome, 1972), 93-127.

Includes the contribution of structural anthropology and structuralism in general.

ANTHROPOLOGY

Adams, M.-J. See item 3688.

3737. Aligada, G.R. "A Structural Approach to the Study of Cebuano Legends." *Unitas*, 43, no. 4 (1970), 105-123.

Includes Lévi-Strauss's contribution, the distinction between myth and legend, structural outlines and tables of the ties between legend and social structure.

Andreani, T. See item 4349.

3737a. Anonymous. "Discussion on the Theme: Structuralist Methodological Directives for Research on Culture" (in Polish). *Studia Metodologiczne*, 16 (1977), 71-130.

3738. Asplund, Johan. *Inledning till strukturalismen*. Stockholm: Almqvist & Wiksell, 1973.

Badcock, C.R. See item 3458.

3739. Bastide, Roger. "Méthodologie des recherches inter-ethniques." *Ethnies*, 2 (1972), 9-20.

3740. Ben-Amos, D. Review of B. Nathhorst's *Formal and Structural Studies of Traditional Tales*.... *Journal of American Folklore*, 85, no. 335 (1972), 82-84.

Berger, A.H. See item 4352.

3741. Bon, Stella María. "Antropología estructural y filosofía." *II° Congreso Nacional de Filosofía*, II. Buenos Aires: Editorial Sudamericana, 1973, pp. 293-299.

3742. Bonte, P. "From Ethnology to Anthropology: On Critical Approaches in the Human Sciences: Part One." *Critique of Anthropology*, no. 2 (1974), pp. 36-67.

From functionalism to structuralism, the current crisis in anthropology.

3743. ————. "Maurice Godelier: itinéraires marxistes en anthropologie." *La Pensée*, no. 187 (1976), pp. 74-92. The main themes of *Horizon, trajets marxistes*....

Bourdieu, P. See item 5219.

Caldiron, O. See item 3487.

3744. Caws, P. "Operational, Representational and Explanatory Models."
American Anthropologist, 76 (March 1974), 1-10. For discussion,
see 78 (June 1976), 323-327; 79 (December 1977), 914-916; 80
(September 1978), 589-596.

3745. Chamla, M.C. "Structure anthropologique des Algériens du Nord."
Anthropologie, 77 (April 1974), 750-754.

Bibliography on structural anthropology.

3746. Crumrine, L.S., and N.R. Crumrine. "Ritual Service and Blood
Sacrifice as Mediating Binary Oppositions: A Structural
Analysis of Several Maya Myths and Rituals." *Journal of
American Folklore*, 83, no. 327 (1970), 69-76.

Uses Lévi-Strauss's general schema and verifies the semantic
structure of this group of myths by studying the cognitive
structure of the Maya.

3747. Crumrine, N. Ross, and Barbara June Macklin. "Sacred Ritual
vs. the Unconscious: The Efficacy of Symbols and Structure
in North Mexican Folk Saints' Cults and General Ceremonialism."
In *The Unconscious in Culture. The Structuralism of Claude
Lévi-Strauss in Perspective*. Ed. Ino Rossi. New York: E.P.
Dutton, 1974, pp. 179-197.

3748. Dienelt, K. "Strukturanalyse einer pädagogischen Anthropologie."
Erziehung und Unterricht, 119, no. 9 (1969), 577-593.

3749. Douglas, Mary. *Purity and Danger*. Harmondsworth: Penguin, 1970.

3750. Drummond, Lee. "Structure and Process in the Interpretation
of South American Myth: The Arawak Dog Spirit People."
American Anthropologist, 79 (December 1977), 842-868.

3751. Dumont, Jean-Paul. *Under the Rainbow: Nature and Supernature
among the Panare Indians*. Austin: University of Texas Press,
1976.

A revised version of the author's thesis, University of Pittsburgh, 1972.

3752. Dundes, Alan. "From Etic to Emic Units in the Structural Study
of Folktales." *Journal of American Folklore*, 75 (1966), 95-
105.

3753. Duvignaud, J. *Le Langage perdu. Essai sur la différence anthropologique*. Paris: Presses Universitaires de France, 1973.

A critique of Lévi-Strauss and other European anthropologists
and their effect on the places they study.

3754. Eickelpasch, R. "Struktur oder Inhalt? Wissenschaftstheoretische
Überlegungen zur Strukturalen Anthropologie." *Paideuma.
Mitteilungen zur Kulturkunde*, 18 (1972), 16-41.

3755. Esteva-Fabregat, Claudio. "Sobre el método y los problemas de
       la antropología estructural." *Convivium*, 30 (1969), 3-53.

3756. Etxeberria, Martin. *Euskaldunen ipuin harrigarriak.* Arantzazu:
       Ed. Franciscana Arantzazu, 1973.

3757. Firth, R. "Reflections on Tikopia 'Totemism.'" *Oceania*, 40,
       no. 4 (1970), 280-295.

       Theories on totemism based on the Tikopian example. Classifi-
       cation of men and objects by the system of binary opposition.
       The structural approach of Lévi-Strauss; consideration of the
       theses of E. Leach, S.U. Tambiah and Y. Simonis.

3758. Gaboriau, Marc. "Anthropologie structurale et histoire."
       Esprit, 31ᵉ année, no. 322 (November 1963), 579-595.

3759. Gardiner, J.H. "A Facial Profile from Archaic Greece." *Antiquity*,
       46 (September 1972), 223-224.

3760. Hammond-Tooke, W.D. "Lévi-Strauss in a Garden of Millet: The
       Structural Analysis of a Zulu Folktale." *Man*, 12 (April
       1977), 76-86.

3761. Heusch, Luc de. *Pourquoi l'épouser? et autres essais.* Paris:
       Gallimard, 1971.

3762. Hirschfeld, Lawrence A. "Art in Cunaland: Ideology and Adoption."
       Man, 12 (April 1977), 104-123.

3762a. Holzbachová, I. "Man in the Structuralist Critique of Anthro-
       pology" (in Czech). *Sborník Prací Filosofické Fakulty
       Brněnské University, Řada Filosofická*, no. 23 (1976), 25-44.

3763. Josselin de Jong, P.E. de. "Marcel Mauss et les origines de
       l'anthropologie structurale hollandaise." *L'Homme*, 12,
       no. 4 (October 1972), 62-84.

3764. ———, ed. *Structural Anthropology in the Netherlands: A
       Reader.* The Hague: Martinus Nijhoff, 1977.

       Keesing, R.M. See item 5260.

3765. Kelemen, Paul. "Towards a Marxist Critique of Structuralist
       Anthropology." *The Sociological Review*, 24, no. 4 (November
       1976), 859-875.

       Kirk, G.S. See item 5011.

3766. Lafrance, Guy. "Marcel Mauss et l'épistémologie structuraliste."
       Philosophy Research Archives, 3 (1977), no. 1169.

       Attempts to show that Mauss's way of studying cultural facts
       anticipates the structural analysis method in anthropology.
       Mauss's concept of "fait social total" is compared with the
       concept of structure as developed by Lévi-Strauss, and his

contribution to structuralist anthropology and the epistemology
of the social sciences is outlined.

3767. Lanteri-Laura, Georges. "Histoire et structure dans la connaissance de l'homme." *Annales. Economies. Sociétés. Civilisations*, 22 (1967), 792-828.

3768. ———. "History and Structure in Anthropological Knowledge."
Social Research, 34 (1967), 113-161.

3769. Laszlo, Ervin. "Systems and Structures: Toward Bio-Social
Anthropology." *Theory and Decision*, 2 (December 1971), 174-
192.

*3770. Leach, Edmund, ed. *The Structural Study of Myth and Totemism*.
London: Tavistock; New York: Barnes and Noble, 1967.

3771. ———. *Mythos und Totemismus. Beitr. z. Kritik d. strukturalen
Analyse*. Trans. Elmar Hoffmeister and Eva Moldenhauer. Frankfurt am Main: Suhrkamp, 1973.

3772. ———. "Structuralism in Social Anthropology." In item 176,
pp. 37-56.

3773. ———. *Culture and Communication: The Logic by Which Symbols
are Connected; An Introduction to the Use of Structuralist
Analysis in Social Anthropology*. Cambridge, England-New York:
Cambridge University Press, 1976.

3774. ———. "Social Anthropology: A Natural Science of Society?
Radcliffe-Brown Lecture in Social Anthropology." *British
Academy Proceedings*, 62 (1976), 157-180.

3775. Lévi-Makarius, Laura. *Le Sacré et la violation des interdits*.
Paris: Editions Layor, 1974.

3775a. Lex, B.W. "Heterodox Structuralism." *Reviews in Anthropology*,
3, no. 1 (1976), 18-30.

3776. Lombard, J. *L'Anthropologie britannique contemporaine*. Paris:
Presses Universitaires de France, 1972.

The reaction against evolutionism and diffusionism.

Lorrain, François. See item 5271.

Maranda, P. and E.K. See item 3990.

3777. Matta, Roberto da. *Ensaios de antropologia estrutural*. Petro-
pólis: Editora Vozes, 1973.

3778. Maxwell, Allen R., comp. "Bibliography of Structuralism and
Anthropology." In item 68, pp. 256-262. See also item 69.

McCallum, D.K. See item 5274.

3779. Meunier, R. Review of L. de Heusch. *Pourquoi d'épouser? et autres essais. Cahiers d'Etudes Africaines*, 13, no. 1 (1973), 164-165.

       On item 3761.

3780. Moore, John H. "Asdiwal, Boas, and Henry Tate. A Note on Structuralist Methodology." *Anthropos*, 70, no. 5-6 (1975), 926-930.

3781. Munz, Peter. *When the Golden Bough Breaks: Structuralism and Typology*. Boston and London: Routledge and Kegan Paul, 1973.

       Needham, R. See item 3617.

3782. Neri, Roberto. *Lo Strutturalismo francese nelle sue significazioni pedagogiche*. Parma: Edizioni Universitarie Casanova, 1972.

3782a. Okpewho, Isidore. "Poetry and Pattern: Structural Analysis of an Ijo Creation Myth." *Journal of American Folklore*, 92 (July 1979), 302-325.

3783. Oppitz, Michael. *Notwendige Beziehungen: Abriss der strukturalen Anthropologie*. Frankfurt am Main: Suhrkamp, 1975. Bibliography, pp. 360-411.

3784. Panoff, F. Review of E. Leach's *Etude structurale du mythe et du totémisme. L'Anthropologie*, 74, no. 5-6 (1970), 428.

3785. Pitt-Rivers, Julián. *Tres Ensayos de antropología estructural*. Trans. José Cano Temblegue et al. Barcelona: Anagrama, 1973.

3786. Pochtar, R. "Acerca del concepto de experiencia en la antropología estructural." In *Temas de Filosofía Contemporánea*. IIº Congreso Nacional de Filosofía. Buenos Aires: Editorial Sudamericana, 1971, pp. 185-205.

3787. Pouillon, Jean. *Fétiches sans fétichisme*. Paris: F. Maspero, 1975. (Bibliothèque d'Anthropologie)

3788. Pouwer, Jan. "The Structural-Configurational Approach: A Methodological Outline." In *The Unconscious in Culture. The Structuralism of Claude Lévi-Strauss in Perspective*. New York: E.P. Dutton, 1974, pp. 238-255.

*3789. Radcliffe-Brown, A.R. *Structure and Function in Primitive Society*. New York: Free Press, 1965, c. 1952.

3790. ———. *Structure et fonction dans la société primitive*. Paris: Editions du Seuil, 1972, 364pp.

       Reiter, J. See item 4719.

3791. Robert, Jean-Dominique. "Conditions de possibilité d'une anthropologie totalisatrice et intégrative des diverses sciences de l'homme." *Laval Théologique et Philosophique*, 26 (February 1970), 29-56; 26 (June 1970), 147-166.

3792. Rubio Carracedo, José. "El Estructuralismo antropológico. Posiciones y problemas." *Arbor*, 76 (1970), 175-202.

3793. Sahlins, Marshall David. *Culture and Practical Reason*. Chicago: University of Chicago Press, 1976.

3794. Sapir, J. David. "Fecal Animals: An Example of Complementary Totemism." *Man*, 12 (April 1977), 1-21.

3795. Sazbón, José, ed. *Estructuralismo y antropología*. Buenos Aires: Ediciones Nueva Visión, 1971.

3796. ———. *Mito e historia en la antropología estructural*. Buenos Aires: Ediciones Nueva Visión, c. 1975, 94pp. (Colección Fichas, 31)

Contains: El Pensamiento mítica; Sartre y la razón estructuralista; El Nuevo Humanismo de la antropología estructural.

3797. Scarduelli, Pietro. *L'Analisi strutturale dei miti*. Milan: Celuc, 1971. Bibliography, pp. 131-142.

3798. Scheffler, H.W. "Structuralism in Anthropology." In item 68, pp. 66-88. See also item 69.

3799. Scholte, Bob. "Epistemic Paradigms: Some Problems in Cross-Cultural Research on Social Anthropological History and Theory." In *Claude Lévi-Strauss: The Anthropologist as Hero*. Eds. Eugene N. And Tanya Hayes. Cambridge, Mass.: M.I.T. Press, 1970, pp. 108-122.

3800. ———. "Comments on the Essays of Part Three: Structural Anthropology as Ethno-Logic." In *The Unconscious in Culture. The Structuralism of Claude Lévi-Strauss in Perspective*. Ed. Ino Rossi. New York: E.P. Dutton, 1974, pp. 424-453.

3801. Sebag, L. *L'Invention du monde chez les indiens pueblos*. Paris: F. Maspero, 1971, 506pp.

3802. Sharpe, Eric J. "Structural Anthropology." In item 1026, pp. 185-199.

3803. Silverman, David, et al. "Implicit Meanings: Essays in Anthropology." *Sociological Quarterly*, 19 (Spring 1978), 355-368.

3804. Singer, M. "For a Semiotic Anthropology." In item 5184, pp. 202-231.

3805. Sperber, Dan. "Le Structuralisme en anthropologie." In *Qu'est-ce que le structuralisme?* Ed. F. Wahl. Paris: Editions du Seuil, c. 1968, 1973, pp. 167-238. Later rpt. (1973) as tome 3 of *Qu'est-ce que le structuralisme?* (Points, no. 46)

3806. ————. *Estructuralismo e antropologia*. Trans. Amélia Cohn and Gabriel Cohn. São Paulo: Cultrix, 1970.

3806a. Spiro, Melford E. "Whatever Happened to the Id?" *American Anthropologist*, 81 (March 1979), 5-13.

3807. Strenski, Ivan. "Falsifying Deep Structures." *Man*, 9, no. 4 (1974), 571-584.

On the scientific status of structural anthropology.

3808. ————. "Reductionism and Structural Anthropology." *Inquiry*, 19, no. 1 (Oslo, 1976), 73-89.

3809. Suret-Canale, Jean. "Structuralisme et anthropologie économique." *La Pensée*, no. 135 (1967), pp. 94-106.

3810. ————. "Une Autre ethnologie. Laura Lévi-Makarius: *Le Sacré et la violation des interdits*." *La Pensée*, no. 187 (1976), pp. 112-122.

On the structuralist method and Marxist anthropology. A critical analysis of this work.

3810a. Suzuki, Peter T. "Archaeological Remains of Hiligowe, Nias (Indonesia) Decoded." *Anthropos*, 74, no. 1-2 (1979), 214-218.

3811. Swanson, Guy E. "Frameworks for Comparative Research: Structural Anthropology and the Theory of Action." In *Comparative Methods in Sociology. Essays on Trends and Applications*. Ed. Ivan Vallier. Berkeley: University of California Press, 1971, pp. 141-202.

3812. Van Baal, J. "Pourquoi épouser le marxisme?" *Bijdragen tot de Taal-, Land- en Volkenkunde*, 128, no. 1 (1972), 118-126.

A review of item 3761.

3813. Van der Leeden, A.C. "'Empiricism' and 'Logical Order' in Anthropological Structuralism." *Bijdragen tot de Taal-, Land- en Volkenkunde*, 127, no. 1 (1971), 15-38.

3814. Veselkin, Evgeniĭ Abramovich. *Krizis britanskoĭ sotsial'noĭ antropologii*. Moscow: Hayka, 1977.

On structural anthropology and ethnology in Great Britain.

Vogler, P. See item 5118.

CINEMA

Anonymous. See item 3861.

3815. Baudry, Jean-Louis. "Ideological Effects of the Basic Cinematographic Apparatus." *Film Quarterly*, 28, no. 2 (Winter 1974-
1975), 39-47. Trans. by Alan Williams from *Cinéthique*, no.
7-8 (1970), pp. 1-8.

Also on Althusser and Lacan.

3816. Bettetini, Gianfranco. *Cinema: lingua e scrittura*. Milan:
Bompiani, 1968.

3817. B[onitzer], P[ascal], and S[erge] T[oubiana]. "Entretien avec
Michel Foucault." *Cahiers du Cinema*, no. 251-252 (July-August
1974), pp. 5-15.

Discussion of Louis Malle's *Lacombe Lucien*, Marcel Ophuls'
Le Chagrin et la pitié, and Cavani's *Portier de nuit*.

3818. Brewster, Ben. "Structuralism in Film Criticism." *Screen*, 12,
no. 1 (Spring 1971), 49-58.

3819. Browne, Nick. "Spectator-in-the-Text: The Rhetoric of Stage-
coach." *Film Quarterly*, 29 (Winter 1975-1976), 26-38.

3820. Collet, Jean, et al. *Lectures du Film*. Paris: Editions Alba-
tros, n.d. (printed 1976).

A cinematographic semiology for 1975. Contains a bibliography
on the textual analysis of films.

Communications. See item 5140.

3820a. Cornwell, Regina. "Structural Film: Ten Years Later." *The
Drama Review*, 23 (September 1979), 77-92.

3821. Dayan, Daniel. "Tutor-Code of Classical Cinema." *Film Quarterly*,
28 (Fall 1974), 22-31.

3822. Durgnat, Raymond. "Borowczyk and the Cartoon Renaissance."
Film Comment, 12 (January 1976), 37-44.

3823. Eckert, Charles W. "The English Cine-Structuralists." *Film
Comment*, 9, no. 3 (May-June 1973), 46-51.

3823a. Gidal, Peter, ed. and intro. *Structural Film Anthology*. London:
British Film Institute, 1976, 140pp. Published to coincide

with a series of 18 programmes, Structural Film Retrospective
at the National Film Theatre, London, in May 1976.

3824. Goldmann, Annie. *Cinéma et société moderne. Le Cinéma de 1958
       à 1968: Godard--Antonioni--Resnais--Robbe-Grillet.* Paris:
       Anthropos, 1971. (Sociologie et Connaissance)

       Work dedicated to Lucien Goldmann: "Pour Gica."

3825. Hanhardt, John G., and Charles H. Harpole. "Linguistics,
       Structuralism and Semiology. Approaches to the Cinema, with
       a Bibliography." *Film Comment*, 9, no. 3 (May-June 1973),
       52-59.

3826. Kinder, Marsha. "Art of Dreaming in Three Women and Providence:
       Structures of the Self." *Film Quarterly*, 31 (Fall 1977), 10-
       18.

3826a. Kirby, Michael. "Structuralist Film." *The Drama Review*, 23
       (September 1979), 93-102.

3827. Kitses, Jim. "Elia Kazan: A Structural Analysis." *Cinema*, 7,
       no. 3 (USA 1968), 25-36.

3828. Metz, Christian. *Essais sur la signification au cinéma.* Paris:
       Editions Klincksieck, 1968 (tome 1), 1972 (tome 2).

3829. ————. *Langage et cinéma.* Paris: Larousse, 1971. (Langue
       et Langage)

       Metz shows the multi-codic character of cinematographic
       language.

3830. Noguez, Dominique, ed. "Le Cinéma: théorie, lectures." Special
       issue of *Revue d'Esthétique.* Paris: Editions Klincksieck,
       1973.

3831. Odin, Roger. "Sémiologie et analyse de film (lectures de codes)."
       Travaux de Linguistique II, Université de Saint-Etienne,
       1972.

       On *Gardiens de phare* by Jean Grémillon, 1928-1929.

3832. Patterson, Patricia, and Manny Farber. "Kitchen Without Kitsch."
       Film Comment, 13 (November 1977), 47-50.

3833. Prete, A. "Critico del racconto e critica del film." *Ikon.
       Cinéma, Télévision, Iconographie*, 22, no. 81 (Milan, 1972),
       9-63.

       Literary criticism vs. film criticism; Russian formalism
       and structuralism.

3834. Rouve, Pierre. "Aesthetics of the Cinema." *The British Journal
       of Aesthetics*, 12 (Spring 1972), 148-157.

3835. Russel, Kenneth C. "The Fallacy of Cine-Structuralism." *Revue de l'Université d'Ottawa*, 45, no. 2 (April–June 1975), 195–199.

3836. Russell, Lee. "Cinema--Code and Image." *New Left Review*, no. 49 (May–June 1968), pp. 65–81.

3837. Sarris, Andrew. "Film Criticism in the Seventies." *Film Comment*, 14 (January 1978), 9–11.

3838. Scheib, Ronnie. "Charlie's Uncle: Shadow of a Doubt." *Film Comment*, 12 (March 1976), 55–62.

3839. Silverstein, Norman, ed. *Film as Literature and Language*. Philadelphia: *Journal of Modern Literature*, 1973, (pp. 145–349).

Part of a special issue of the *Journal of Modern Literature*, 3, no. 2 (April 1973) on the cinema, Barthes, Godard and Metz.

————. See also item 1461.

3839a. *Sub-stance*, no. 9 (1974): "Film: Phenomenology, Structuralism and After."

3840. Tuch, Ronald. "Peter Davis' Hearts and Minds." *Film Library Quarterly*, 10, no. 1-2 (1977), 45–50.

3841. Vogel, Amos. "The Structuralist Incursion: The Setting." *Film Comment*, 11, no. 4 (July–August 1975), 37.

3842. ————. "Structural Incursion II: The Literature." *Film Comment*, 11, no. 5 (September–October 1975), 39.

3843. Williams, Alan. "Structure of Lyric: Baillie's to Parsifal." *Film Quarterly*, 29 (Spring 1976), 22–30.

3844. Wood, Robin. "Acting Up." *Film Comment*, 12 (March 1976), 20–25.

3845. ————. "Old Wine, New Battles: Structuralism or Humanism?" *Film Comment*, 12 (November 1976), 22–25.

3846. ————. "Ideology, Genre, Auteur." *Film Comment*, 13 (January 1977), 45–51.

3847. Zand, Nicole. "A Mannheim problèmes de notre temps au Festival du film documentaire." *Le Monde*, no. 6150 (23 October 1964), p. 18.

3848. Zimmer, Christian. *Cinéma et politique*. Paris: Seghers, 1974.

3849. Adam, J.-M. "Apports et limites du concept de structure pour l'étude des textes." *Le Français Aujourd'Hui*, supplément au no. 26 (1974), 12pp.

3850. Adams, Hazard. "Contemporary Ideas of Literature: Terrible Beauty or Rough Beast?" *Contemporary Literature*, 17 (Summer 1976), 349-377.

3851. ———. "Contemporary Ideas of Literature: Terrible Beauty or Rough Beast?" In *Directions for Criticism. Structuralism and Its Alternatives*. Ed. Murray Krieger and L.S. Dembo. Madison, Wisc.: University of Wisconsin Press, 1977, pp. 55-83.

3852. Albérès, R.-M. *Littérature, horizon 2000*. Paris: Editions Albin Michel, 1974.

3853. ———. *Le Roman d'aujourd'hui. 1960-1970*. Paris: Editions Albin Michel, 1970.

3854. ———. "Cette nouvelle école littéraire dont on parle tant: le structuralisme." *A La Page*, no. 44 (February 1968), pp. 213-221.

3855. Alter, Robert. "Mimesis and the Motive for Fiction." *Tri-Quarterly*, no. 42 (Spring 1978), pp. 228-249.

3856. ———. *Partial Magic. The Novel as a Self-Conscious Genre*. Berkeley-Los Angeles-London: University of California Press, 1975.

3857. *Alternative*, no. 65 (1969): issue on "Sprachwissenschaft und Literatur." See also item 4021.

3858. Ames, Sanford Scribner. "Structuralism, Language, and Literature." *Journal of Aesthetics and Art Criticism*, 32 (Fall 1973), 89-94.

Angenot, M. See item 3748.

3859. Anonymous. *L'Analisi del racconto. R. Barthes, C. Bremond, U. Eco, G. Genette, A.J. Greimas, J. Gritti, Ch. Metz, V. Morin, T. Todorov*. Milan: Bompiani, 1969.

———. See also items 4083 and 4827.

3860. ————. *Littérature et psychanalyse*. Paris: Larousse, 1971.
The *Littérature*, no. 3 (October 1971), issue.

3861. ————. *Littérature et société. Problèmes de méthodologie en sociologie de la littérature*. Colloque organisé conjointement par l'Institut de Sociologie de l'Université Libre de Bruxelles et l'Ecole Pratique des Hautes Etudes (6ᵉ section) de Paris du 21 au 23 mai 1964. Brussels: Editions de l'Institut de Sociologie, U.L.B., 1967.

3862. ————. *Problèmes d'une sociologie. Nouveau roman et réalité*. Brussels: Les Editions de la Revue de Sociologie, 1963, 268pp. Rpts. *Revue de l'Institut de Sociologie*, no. 2 (1963).

3863. ————. "Structuralisme et mythologie comparée: un entretien de Pierre Daix avec Georges Dumézil." *Les Lettres Françaises*, no. 1241 (17-23 July 1968), pp. 5-7.

3864. ————. *Théorie d'ensemble*. Paris: Les Editions du Seuil, 1968.

This book rpts. and organizes certain basic theoretical texts previously published by *Tel Quel*. It contains items 785, 1533 and 1928.

3865. Apollonio, Mario. *Studi sullo strutturalismo critico*. Milan: Celuc, 1971.

3866. Armstrong, Nancy. "Character, Closure and Impressionist Fiction." *Criticism*, 19, no. 4 (Fall 1977), 317-337.

3866a. August, Marilyn, and Ann Liddle. "Beyond Structuralism: The Cerisy Experience." *Sub-stance*, 2, no. 5-6 (Winter 1972-Spring 1973), 227-236.

On Cerisy as an experience in "décentrement" or an experiment in revolution.

Auzias, J.-M. See chapter three of items 11-14.

3867. Baker, Donald. "Structural Theory of Theatre." *Yale Theatre*, 8 (Fall 1976), 55-61.

3868. Barabaš, Ju. Ja. "Algebra and Harmony" (in Russian). In *Kontekst-1972. Literaturno teoreticeskie issledovanija*. Moscow: Ed. "Nauka," 1973, pp. 78-181.

Barksdale, E. See item 3461.

Barthes, Roland. "Introduction to the Structural Analysis of Narratives." In his item 920, pp. 79-124.

3869. Bartolomei, Giangaetano. "Ernst Cassirer: *Lo Strutturalismo nella lingua moderne*, a cura di S. Vega." *Filosofia*, anno 21, fasc. 4 (October 1970), 586-588.

Bernabe, J. See item 5204.

3870.   Bernstein, Gene. "Structuralism and Romantic Myth-Making." In
        Phenomenology, Structuralism, Semiology. Ed. Harry R. Garvin.
        Lewisburg, Pa.: Bucknell University Press; London: Associated
        University Presses, 1976, pp. 99-116.

3871.   Bersani, Jacques, et al. *La Littérature en France depuis 1945.*
        Paris-Montreal-Brussels-Lausanne-London: Bordas, Asedi, Spes,
        George G. Harrap, 1970.

3872.   Bersani, Leo. "Is There a Science of Literature?" *Partisan
        Review*, 39, no. 4 (1972), 535-553.

3873.   ————. *A Future for Astyanax. Character and Desire in Liter-
        ture.* Boston-Toronto: Little, Brown and Co., 1976.

3874.   Biles, Jack I. *Aspects of Utopian Fiction.* Atlanta, Georgia:
        Studies in the Literary Imagination, 1973. A special issue
        of *Studies in the Literary Imagination*, 6, no. 2 (1973).

3875.   Blanchard, J.M. "Sémistyles: le rituel de la littérature."
        Semiotica, 14, no. 4 (1975), 297-328.

3876.   Blegen, John C. "Narrative Development in the Fiction of Maurice
        Blanchot. The Shattered Tale." *Dissertation Abstracts Inter-
        national*, 34, no. 6 (December 1973), 3381-A. Johns Hopkins
        University dissertation.

3877.   Blenkinsopp, Joseph. "The Search for the Prickly Plant: Struc-
        ture and Function in the Gilgamesh Epic." *Soundings: An
        Interdisciplinary Journal*, 58, no. 2 (Summer 1975), 200-220.

3878.   Blumensath, Heinz, ed. *Strukturalismus in der Literaturwissen-
        schaft.* Cologne: Kiepenheuer & Witsch, 1972.

3879.   Boisdeffre, Pierre de. *La Cafetière est sur la table [ou]
        contre le "nouveau roman."* Paris: La Table Ronde de Combat,
        1967.

3880.   Bonelli, G. "Letteratura e problemi. Psicanalisi, marxismo,
        strutturalismo." *Rivista di Studi Crociani*, 12, no. 4 (1975),
        407-420.

3881.   Bonomi, Andrea. *La Struttura logica del linguaggio.* Milan:
        V. Bompiani, 1973.

3882.   Boratov, P.N. "Le Conte et la narration épico-romanesque."
        Turcica, no. 1 (1969), pp. 95-122.

3883.   Borev, ĨUrii Borisovich. *Khudozhestvennyi obraz i struktura.*
        Moscow: Hayka, 1975.

        Bouazis, C. See item 5134.

3884. ———, ed. *Analyse de la périodisation littéraire*. Paris: Editions Universitaires, 1972.

3885. Bouché, Claude. "La Théorie littéraire matérialiste en France (1965-1975)." *Revue des Langues Vivantes*, 43, no. 1 (1977), 3-22.

3886. Boyers, R. "Realism of Reading." *The Times Literary Supplement*, no. 3996 (3 November 1978), pp. 1274-1275.

3887. Brady, Patrick. "A Structural Study of Autobiography." *Style*, 10, no. 3 (Summer 1976), 271-273.

Brandt, P.A. See items 393-394.

3888. Bremond, Claude. "Le Message narratif." In *Communications 4*. Paris: Editions du Seuil, 1964, pp. 4-32.

Like Barthes, he views the structure of a story as composed of a series of "bifurcations" or narrative choices which may be exploited by the artist.

3889. ———. "La Logique des possibles narratifs." *Communications 8*. Paris: Editions du Seuil, 1966, pp. 60-76.

3890. ———. "Morphology of the French Folktale." *Semiotica*, 2, no. 3 (1970), pp. 247-276.

3891. ———. *Logique du récit*. Paris: Editions du Seuil, 1973.

3892. Brooke-Rose, Christine. "Transgressions: An Essay-say on the Novel Novel Novel." *Contemporary Literature*, 19 (Summer 1978), 378-407.

3893. Brosse, Jacques. "L'Etude du langage va-t-elle libérer un homme nouveau?" *Arts et Loisirs*, no. 35 (25-31 May 1966), pp. 8-9.

Bruch, J.-L. See item 997.

3894. Brütting, Richard. "Zur Situation des französischen Strukturalismus. Ein Literaturbericht." *Lili. Zeitschrift für Literaturwissenschaft und Linguistik*, 4, no. 14 (1974), 111-135.

An examination of structuralism through its cardinal texts, their ideological and epistemological premises.

3895. ———. *"Ecriture" und "texte": die französische Literaturtheorie "nach dem Strukturalismus." Kritik traditioneller Positionen und Neuansätze*. Bonn: Bouvier, 1976.

3896. Burbank, John, and Peter Steiner, eds. *The Word and Verbal Art: Selected Essays by Jan Mukarovsky*. New Haven: Yale University Press, 1977.

*3897. Calloud, Jean. *L'Analyse structurale du récit*. Lyons: Profac
        (Publications de la Faculté de Théologie), 1973.

3898.   ————. *Structural Analysis of Narrative*. Trans. Daniel Patte.
        Philadelphia: Fortress Press; Missoula, MT: Scholars Press,
        1976.

        Introduction to the structural analysis of narrative as prac-
        ticed by A.J. Greimas and disciples.

3899.   ————. "L'Analyse structurale du récit: quelques éléments
        d'une méthode." *Foi et Vie*, 73, no. 3 (1974), 28-65.

        ————. See also item 4937.

3900.   Cancalon, Elaine D. "Les Récits d'André Gide: essai d'analyse
        actantielle." *MLN*, 90 (May 1975), 590-596.

3901.   Carduner, Jean. "What is Going on in French Literary History?"
        Modern Language Journal, 61, no. 4 (April 1977), 161-167.

3902.   Carroll, Michael. "Of Atlantis and Ancient Astronauts: A Struc-
        tural Study of Two Modern Myths." *Journal of Popular Culture*,
        11 (Winter 1977), 542-550.

3902a. Carroll, Noel. "The Mystery Plays of Michael Kirby: Notes on
        the Esthetics of Structuralist Theatre." *The Drama Review*,
        23 (September 1979), 103-112.

3903.   Castagnino, Raúl Héctor. *Márgenes de los estructuralismos*.
        Buenos Aires: Editorial Nova, 1975. (Biblioteca Arte y
        Ciencia de la Expresión)

3904.   ————. *"Sentido" y estructura narrativa*. Buenos Aires:
        Editorial Nova, 1975.

        Castella, C. See item 2772.

        Cattell, R. See item 4104.

3905.   Caws, Mary Ann. *"Tel Quel*: Text and Revolution." *Diacritics*,
        3, no. 1 (Spring 1973), 2-8.

        Cazeaux, J. See item 4940.

3905a. Champagne, Roland. *Beyond the Structuralist Myth of Ecriture*.
        The Hague: Mouton, 1977.

3906.   Chatman, Seymour. "New Ways of Analyzing Narrative Structure
        with an Example from Joyce's *Dubliners*." *Language and Style*,
        4 (1970), 3-36.

3907.   Chețan, Octavian. "The Structural Approach of Mythology: The
        Myths of the Pueblo Indians" (in Rumanian). *Revista de
        Referate și Recenzii. Filozofie. Logica*, 10, no. 3 (1973),
        326-336.

Chvatík, K. See items 45-46.

3908. Coleman, Philip Gordon, and Robert Price. *The Scholar and the Magpie*. Toronto: Coleman and Price, 1974, 90pp.

3909. Culler, Jonathan D. "Structure of Ideology and Ideology of Structure." *New Literary History*, 4, no. 3 (1973), 471-482.

3910. ———. "Structuralism and Literature." In *Contemporary Approaches to English Studies*. Ed. Hilda Schiff. New York: Barnes and Noble, 1977, pp. 59-76.

———. See also item 4836.

3911. Deák, František. "Structuralism in Theatre: The Prague School Contribution." *Drama Review*, 20 (December 1976), 83-94.

3911a. ———. "Tell Me, A Play by Guy de Cointet." *The Drama Review*, 23 (September 1979), 11-20.

3912. Degeorge, Fernande M. "From Russian Formalism to French Structuralism." *Comparative Literature Studies*, 14, no. 1 (March 1977), 20-29.

3913. *Degrés*, 1ère année, no. 3 (July 1973): special issue entitled *La Notion de référent*. Ed. André Helbo. Brussels: *Degrés*, 1973.

3914. *Degrés*, 1ère année, no. 4 (October 1973): special issue entitled *Pratique du référent*. Ed. André Helbo. Brussels: *Degrés*, 1973.

3915. *Degrés*, 2e année, no. 6 (April 1974) and no. 7-8 (July-October 1974): issues entitled *Théorie et pratique du code (I)* and *(II)*. Ed. André Helbo. Brussels: *Degrés*, 1974 and 1975.

3916. Delbouille, Paul. "Analyse structurale et analyse textuelle." *Cahiers d'Analyse Textuelle*, no. 10 (1968), pp. 7-22.

Derrida, Jacques. "Force and Signification." In his *Writing and Difference* (item 1616a), pp. 3-30.

3917. Donato, Eugenio. "Of Structuralism and Literature." *MLN*, 82, no. 5 (December 1967), 549-574.

3918. Durand, G. *Les Structures anthropologiques de l'imaginaire*. Paris: Bordas, 1969. 1st ed. 1960.

3919. Durden, William G. "Death of Siegfried and the Disappearance of Brunhild." *Germanic Review*, 51 (March 1976), 85-91.

3920. Ehrmann, Jacques. "Structures of Exchange in Cinna." Trans. J.H. McMahon. In item 68, pp. 169-199. See also item 69 and item 197.

3921. Eimermacher, Karl. "Entwicklung, Charakter und Probleme des Sowjetischen Strukturalismus in der Literaturwissenschaft." *Sprache im Technischen Zeitalter*, 8 (1969), 126-157.

3922. ―――, ed. *Teksty sovetskogo literaturovedcheskogo struktural-izma*. *Texte des sowjetischen literaturwissenschaftlichen Strukturalismus*. In Russian with preface and table of contents in German. Munich: W. Fink, 1971.

       Einem, H. von, et al. See items 5238-5239.

3923. Ekhtiar, Mansur A. *From Linguistics to Literature*. Tehran: Tehran University Press, 1962.

3924. Falk, Walter. *Vom Strukturalismus zum Potentialismus. Ein Versuch zur Geschichts- und Literaturtheorie*. Freiburg: Karl Alber, 1976.

3925. Faye, Jean-Pierre. *Théorie du récit*. Paris: Hermann, 1972.

       Fehér, F. See item 2791.

3926. Fietz, Lothar. *Funktionaler Strukturalismus. Grundlegung eines Modells zur Beschreibung von Text und Textfunktion*. Tübingen: Max Niemeyer, 1976.

3927. Filippetti, A., and G.E. Viola. *L'Illusione e l'ipotesi. Tecniche e strutture narrative del novecento*. Ravenna: Longo, 1973.

3928. Flahault, F. "Situer l'analyse structurale des récits." *Bulletin du CERP, Centre d'Etudes et de Recherches Psychotechniques*, 22, no. 3 (1973-1974; appeared 1975), 179-194.

3929. Fokkema, D.W., and Elrud Kunne-Ibsch. *Theories of Literature in the Twentieth Century: Structuralism, Marxism, Aesthetics of Reception, Semiotics*. New York: St. Martin's Press, 1978.

3930. Forastieri Braschi, Eduardo. *Aproximación estructural al teatro de Lope de Vega*. Madrid: Hispanova de Ediciones, 1976.

3931. Forrey, Robert. "Theodore Dreiser: Oedipus Redivivus." *Modern Fiction Studies*, 23 (Fall 1977), 341-354.

       Foucault, Michel. "What is an Author?" In his *Language, Counter-Memory, Practice* (item 2033), pp. 113-138.

3932. Fowler, Roger, ed. *Style and Structure in Literature: Essays in the New Stylistics*. Ithaca, New York: Cornell University Press; Oxford: B. Blackwell, 1975. Based on a conference held at the University of East Anglia, 6 June 1972.

3933. Frank, Manfred. *Das individuelle Allgemeine: Textstrukturierung und -interpretation nach Schleiermacher*. Frankfurt am Main: Suhrkamp, 1977.

Free, W.J. See item 4517.

3934. Frye, Northrop. *Anatomy of Criticism*. Princeton, N.J.: Princeton University Press, 1957; New York: Atheneum, 1967.

Gagnepain, J. See item 4141.

3934a. Galan, F.W. "Literary System and Systemic Change: The Prague School Theory of Literary History." *PMLA*, 94 (March 1979), 275-285.

3935. Gallas, Helga, and Hildegard Brenner, comps. *Strukturalismus als interpretatives Verfahren*. Darmstadt: Luchterhand, c. 1972.

Gardner, H. See item 5246.

3936. Gaudin, Colette. "Niveaux de lisibilité dans Leçon de choses de Claude Simon." *Romanic Review*, 68 (May 1977), 175-196.

3937. Gearhart, Suzanne. "Place and Sense of the Outsider: Structuralism and the Lettres persanes." *MLN*, 92 (May 1977), 724-748.

3938. Genette, G. "Frontières du récit." *Communications*, no. 8 (1966), pp. 152-163.

3939. Georgin, Robert. *La Structure et le style*. Lausanne: Editions L'Age d'Homme, 1975.

On psychoanalysis and literature in the style of Charles Mauron.

Giard, L. See item 4985.

3940. Giorgiantonio, M. Review of V. de Ruvo's *Analisi dello strutturalismo*. *Sophia*, 40 (1972), 303-304.

3941. Girard, René. *Mensonge romantique et vérité romanesque*. Paris: Grasset, 1961.

3942. ———. *Deceit, Desire, and the Novel: Self and Other in Literary Structure*. Trans. Yvonne Freccero. Baltimore: Johns Hopkins University Press, 1965.

3943. Gnisci, Armando. *Scrittura e struttura*. Rome: Silva, 1970.

3944. González, José Emilio. "Estructuralismo y literatura." *Dialogos*, April 1974, pp. 17-35.

3944a. Graff, Gerald. "The Politics of Anti-Realism." In his *Literature Against Itself. Literary Ideas in Modern Society*. Chicago: University of Chicago Press, 1979, pp. 63-101.

3945. Greimas, Algirdas Julien. "Eléments pour une théorie de l'interprétation du récit mythique." *Communications*, no. 8 (1966), pp. 28-59.

Grimaud, M. See item 4885.

3946.   Grivel, Charles, and Áron Kibédi Varga, eds. *Du linguistique au textuel*. Assen: Van Gorcum, 1974.

3947.   Guenoun, Denis. "A propos de l'analyse structurale des récits." *La Nouvelle Critique* (special issue on "Linguistique et littérature"), Colloque de Cluny, 16-17 April 1968, pp. 65-70.

3948.   Guillén, Claudio. *Literature as System: Essays Toward the Theory of Literary History*. Princeton, N.J.: Princeton University Press, 1971.

3949.   Günther, Hans. *Struktur als Prozess. Studien zur Ästhetik und Literaturtheorie des tschechischen Strukturalismus*. Munich: Fink, 1973.

3949a. Harmon, William. "Poem as an Action of Field: A Structural Experiment." *The Sewanee Review*, 87 (Fall 1979), 618-628.

3950.   Hartman, Geoffrey H. "Structuralism: The Anglo-American Adventure." In item 68, pp. 148-168. See also item 69.

3951.   ————. "Structuralism: The Anglo-American Adventure." In his *Beyond Formalism. Literary Essays, 1958-1970*. New Haven, Conn.: Yale University Press, 1970, pp. 3-23.

3952.   ————. "Use and Abuse of Structural Analysis: Riffaterre's Interpretation of Wordsworth's Yew-Tree." *New Literary History*, 7 (Fall 1975), 165-189.

3953.   Hass, W.A. "Pragmatic Structures of Language: Historical, Formal and Developmental Issues." In *Structure and Transformation: Developmental and Historical Aspects*. Ed. Klaus F. Riegel and George C. Rosenwald. New York: Wiley, 1975, pp. 193-213.

3954.   Hassan, Ihab. "Re-vision of Literature." *New Literary History*, 8 (Fall 1976), 127-144.

3955.   Heller, Louis G., and James Macris. *Toward a Structural Theory of Literary Analysis: Prolegomena to Evaluative Descriptivism*. Worcester, Mass.: Institute for Systems Analysis, 1970.

3956.   Hempfer, Klaus W. *Poststrukturale Texttheorie und Narrativ Praxis. Tel Quel und die Konstitution eines Nouveau Nouveau Roman*. Munich: Wilhelm Fink Verlag, 1976.

3957.   Hendricks, W.O. "Verbal Art and the Structuralist Synthesis." *Semiotica*, 8, no. 3 (1973), 239-262.

3958.   Hill, Archibald A. "Toward a Literary Analysis." In his *Constituent and Pattern in Poetry*. Austin: University of Texas Press, 1976, pp. 10-22.

3959. Hirsch, David H. "Deep Metaphors and Shallow Structures." *Sewanee Review*, 85 (Winter 1977), 153-166.

3960. Hirsch, Edward. "Structural Analysis of Robert Service's Yukon Ballads." *Southern Folklore Quarterly*, 40 (March-June 1976), 125-140.

3961. Hollerbach, Wolf. "Quelques observations sur l'étude de la structure littéraire." *Die neueren Sprachen*, January 1973, pp. 38-44.

3962. Hopkins, Mary Frances. "Structuralism: Its Implications for the Performances of Prose Fiction." *Communication Monographs*, 44, no. 2 (June 1977), 93-105.

3963. Hornby, Richard. *Script into Performance: A Structuralist View of Play Production*. Austin: University of Texas Press, 1977.

3964. Houdebine, Jean-Louis. "L'Analyse structurale et la notion de texte comme 'espace.'" *La Nouvelle Critique* (special issue on "Linguistique et littérature"), Colloque de Cluny 16-17 April 1968, pp. 35-41.

3965. Ingold, Felix Philipp. "Vom Formalismus zum Strukturalismus. Zur Methodologie der sowjetischen Literaturwissenschaft." *Studies in Soviet Thought*, 9 (September 1969), 221-249.

Jakobson, R., et al. See items 4168 and 4845.

3966. Jakobson, Roman. "Une Microscopie du dernier spleen dans les Fleurs du Mal." *Tel Quel*, no. 29 (Spring 1967).

3967. Janion, M. "The Knowledge of Literature and Modern Humanism" (in Polish). *Twórczość*, 22, no. 12 (1966), 85-98.

3968. Jitrik, Noé. "Structure et signification de fictions de J.-L. Borges." *La Nouvelle Critique* (special issue on "Linguistique et littérature"), Colloque de Cluny, 16-17 April 1968, pp. 107-114.

3969. Kermode, Frank. "Structures of Fiction." *Modern Language Notes*, 84 (December 1969), 891-915.

3970. Kirby, Michael. "Manifesto of Structuralism." *Drama Review*, 19 (December 1975), 82-83.

3971. ————. "Marilyn Project: A Structuralist Play?" *Drama Review*, 20 (June 1976), 73-79.

3972. ————. "Structural Analysis/Structural Theory." *Drama Review*, 20, no. 4 (December 1976), 51-68.

3973. Kockelmans, Joseph J. "On Myth and its Relationship to Hermeneutics." *Cultural Hermeneutics*, 1 (April 1973), 47-86.

3973a. Koppe, Franz. "Die Literaturtheoretischen Hauptrichtungen und
       ihr Ertrag für eine Gegenstandsbestimmung der Literaturwissen-
       schaft." *Zeitschrift für Allgemeine Wissenschafts Theorie*,
       9 (1978), 361-398.

       The "old" Czech structuralism vs. the "new" French structural-
       ism.

3974. Kouvel, Audrey Lumsden. "Fray Luis de León's Haven: A Study in
       Structural Analysis." *MLN*, 89 (March 1974), 146-158.

3975. Kristeva, Julia. "Problèmes de la structuration du texte." *La
       Nouvelle Critique* (special issue on "Linguistique et littéra-
       ture"), Colloque de Cluny, 16-17 April 1968, pp. 55-64. Rpt.
       in item 3864, pp. 297-316.

3976. ————. "The Speaking Subject." *The Times Literary Supplement*,
       12 October 1973, p. 1249.

3977. Lafont, R., and F. Gerdes-Madray. *Introduction à l'analyse
       textuelle*. Paris: Larousse, 1976.

3978. Laruccia, Victor. "Little Red Riding Hood's Metacommentary:
       Paradoxical Injunction, Semiotics and Behavior." *MLN*, 90
       (May 1975), 517-534.

3979. Lasić, Stanko. *Problemi narativne strukture: prilog tipologiji
       narativne sintagmatike*. Zagreb: Liber, 1977.

3980. Lauretis, Teresa de. "Metodi strutturali nella critica letteraria
       italiana." *MLN*, 86 (January 1971), 73-88.

3980a. Lawrence, Francis L. "Saint-Amant's 'L'Hyver des Alpes': A
       Structural Analysis." *The Romanic Review*, December 1977, pp.
       247-253.

3981. Lefebve, Maurice-Jean. *Structure du discours et du récit*.
       Neuchâtel: Editions de la Baconnière, 1971.

       Lewis, B.J., and T.J. Lewis. See item 4190.

3981a. Libertson, Joseph. "Proximity and the Word: Blanchot and
       Bataille." *Sub-stance*, 5, no. 14 (September 1976), 35-49.

       In Bataille the text is an unresolved "mise en jeu." For
       Blanchot, "this suspension is an eternal *attention* whose reso-
       lution is impossible."

3982. Lillo, A. de. "L'Analisi dei messaggi nella prospettiva strut-
       turalista." *Rassegna Italiana di Sociologia*, 11, no. 3 (1970),
       401-438.

       On Vladimir Propp.

3983. Link, Jürgen. *Literaturwissenschaftliche Grundbegriffe: eine
       programmierte Einführung aus strukturalistischer Basis*. Munich:
       W. Fink, 1974.

3984. Lotman, Jurij M. "Einige prinzipielle Schwierigkeiten bei der
       strukturellen Textbeschreibung." *Sprache im Technischen
       Zeitalter*, 48 (1973), 278-284.

3985. Lotmane, I. "The History of Literature Should Be a Science"
       (in Russian). *Voprosy Literatury*, 11, no. 1 (1967), 90-101.

       On the principles of structuralist research, its theory of
       knowledge, the way it functions, its relationship with earlier
       scientific tradition, its scientific and aesthetic sources.

3985a. Lotringer, Sylvère. "Artaud, Bataille, et le matérialisme
       dialectique." *Sub-stance*, 2, no. 5-6 (Winter 1972-Spring 1973),
       207-225.

       On the theoretical gaps in a series of talks at Cerisy.

3986. Lys, Daniel. "Analyse structurale et approche littéraire."
       Etudes Théologiques et Religieuses, 52, no. 2 (1977), 231-
       253.

       Macherey, P. See items 4384a and 4384b.

3987. Magliola, Robert. "Jorge Luis Borges and the Loss of Being:
       Structuralist Themes in Dr. Brodie's Report." *Studies in
       Short Fiction*, 15 (Winter 1978), 25-31.

3988. Malette, Yvan. "Le Processus de métaphorisation." *Revue de
       l'Université d'Ottawa*. 46 (April-June 1976), 247-255.

3989. Mandelbrot, B. "Structure formelle des textes et communica-
       tion." *Word*, 1954, pp. 1-27.

3990. Maranda, P., and E. Köngäs Maranda. *Structural Analysis of Oral
       Tradition*. Philadelphia: University of Pennsylvania Press,
       1971.

3991. Marchese, Angelo. *Metodi e prove strutturali*. Milan: Principato,
       1974.

3991a. Margolin, Uri. "Conclusion: Literary Structuralism and Hermen-
       eutics in Significant Convergence, 1976." In *Interpretation
       of Narrative*. Ed. Mario J. Valdés and Owen J. Miller. Toronto:
       University of Toronto Press, 1978, pp. 177-185.

3992. Marie, Michel. "Analyse textuelle." In item 3820, pp. 18-28.

3993. Mariné Bigorra, Sebastián, ed. *Estudis estructurals de català*.
       Barcelona: Edicions 62, 1975. (Llibres a l'Abast, 124)

3994. Martin, G.D. "Structures in Space: An Account of *Tel Quel*'s
       Attitude to Meaning." *New Blackfriars*, no. 619 (December
       1971), pp. 541-552.

3995. Martin, Graham Dunston. "Jeffrey Mehlman: *A Structural Study
       of Autobiography: Proust, Leiris, Sartre, Lévi-Strauss*."

364

Applied Structuralism

> Modern Language Review, 72, no. 2 (April 1977), 456-457. On
> item 3997.

3996. Masson de Gomez, Valerie. "Literary Structuralism--Seen from
 Spain." *Romance Philology*, 28 (August 1974), 91-101.

 Matte, M. See item 140.

3997. Mehlman, Jeffrey. *A Structural Study of Autobiography: Proust,
 Leiris, Sartre, Lévi-Strauss*. Ithaca, N.Y. and London: Cornell
 University Press, 1974.

3997a. Meite, Braoulé. "Observations sur *Antony*, pièce romantique
 (1831). Essai d'analyse structurale de la pièce d'Alexandre
 Dumas." *Annales de l'Université d'Abidjan*, série D, tome X,
 Lettres, 1977, pp. 247-256.

3998. Méla, Charles. "Perceval." Trans. C. Lowe and C. Méla. *Yale French
 Studies*, no. 55-56 (1977), pp. 253-279.

3999. Mercken-Spaas, Godelieve. "From Amour de soi to Amour passion:
 Rousseau's Conceptual Categories Exemplified in Constant's
 Adolphe." *Romanic Review*, 66 (March 1975), 93-99.

 Miers, P. See item 1766a.

4000. Miller, Nancy K. "Female Sexuality and Narrative Structure in
 La Nouvelle Héloïse and *Les Liaisons Dangereuses*." *Signs:
 Journal of Women in Culture and Society*, 1, no. 3, part 1
 (Spring 1976), 609-638.

 With this heuristic process, feminist critics can proceed to
 elaborate the superstructure, the ideological framework within
 which are played out the politics of what has been called the
 feminine text.

4000a. Miller, Owen J. "Reading as a Process of Reconstruction: A
 Critique of Recent Structuralist Formulations." In *Inter-
 pretation of Narrative*. Ed. Mario J. Valdés and Owen J.
 Miller. Toronto: University of Toronto Press, 1978, pp. 19-27.

4001. Molino, Jean. "Structures et littérature." *Archives Européennes
 de Sociologie*, 14, no. 1 (1973), 106-125.

 A critical survey of literary structuralism.

 Morpurgo-Tagliabue, G. See item 4654.

4002. Morris, Wesley Abram. "*A Structural Study of Autobiography:
 Proust, Leiris, Sartre, Lévi-Strauss*, by Jeffrey Mehlman."
 Georgia Review, 31, no. 1 (September 1977), 264-267. On item
 3997.

4002a. ———. *Friday's Footprint. Structuralism and the Articulated
 Text*. Columbus: Ohio State University Press, 1979.

Contains: (1) The Pilgrimage of Being, pp. 1-83; (2) The Centrality of Language, pp. 84-146; (3) Stylistics, pp. 147-187; and (4) Toward a Literary Hermeneutics, pp. 188-225.

Morse, D., et al. See item 2843.

4002b. Mudrick, Marvin. "Adorable Ideas and Absent Plenitudes." In *Books Are Not Life But Then What Is?* New York: Oxford University Press, 1979, pp. 213-226.

4003. Müller, Hans Joachim. *Der französische Roman von 1960 bis 1973. Tel Quel und Maurice Roche.* Wiesbaden: Akademische Verlagsgesellschaft/Athenaion, 1975.

4004. Nathhorst, B. *Formal and Structural Studies of Traditional Tales: The Usefulness of Some Methodological Proposals Advanced by Vladimir Propp, Alan Dundes, Claude Lévi-Strauss and Edmund Leach.* Stockholm: Almquist & Wiksell, 1969.

4005. Niel, André. "Comment utiliser l'analyse structurale du récit dans les études littéraires et l'analyse du texte." *Le Français dans le Monde*, no. 75 (September 1970), pp. 6-17.

4006. ———. *L'Analyse structurale des textes. Littérature, presse, publicité.* Tours-Paris: Mame, 1973; Paris: J.-P. Delarge/ Mame, 1976.

4007. Nielsen, K.H. "Zwischen Hermeneutik und Strukturalismus. Überlegungen zu Objekt und Methode." *Text und Kontext*, 2, no. 1 (1974), 3-21.

4008. Norris, Margot. *Decentered Universe of Finnegans Wake. A Structuralist Analysis.* Baltimore: Johns Hopkins University Press, 1976.

La Nouvelle Critique. See item 4213.

4009. ———. Issue on "Littérature et idéologies." Colloque de Cluny II. 2, 3, 4 April 1970. Paris: *La Nouvelle Critique*, 1971.

4009a. Olsen, Stein Haugom. *The Structure of Literary Understanding.* New York: Cambridge University Press, 1978, 235pp.

In attempting to explain the nature of the reader's response to the literary work, Olsen avoids both structuralism and the New Criticism.

4010. Orr, John. *Tragic Realism and Modern Society: Studies in the Sociology of the Modern Novel.* Pittsburgh: University of Pittsburgh Press, 1978.

4011. Pandolfo, Maria do Carmo Peixoto. *Práticas de estruturalismo.* Rio de Janeiro: Grifo, 1977. (Coleção Littera, 13)

Peytard, J. See item 4223.

4012. Polak, J. "The Birth and Development of Czech Structuralism in the Science of Literature" (in Czech). *Sborník Prací Filosofické Fakulty Brnénské University, Řada Literárnévédná*, 22, no. D 20 (1973), 39-54.

Preti, G. See item 4710.

4013. Propp, Vladimir J. *Morphology of the Folktale*. Bloomington: Indiana University Press, 1958; Austin: University of Texas Press, 1970.

A structural study of the fantastic tale originally published in Moscow in 1928; taken to task by Lévi-Strauss.

4014. ———. *Morphologie du conte*. Trans. Marguerite Derrida. Paris: Editions du Seuil, 1965, 1970. (Points).

Also includes "Les Transformations du conte merveilleux" by Propp and "L'Etude structurale et typologie du conte" by E. Mélétinskii.

4015. ———. "Les Transformations des contes fantastiques." In *Théorie de la littérature*. Paris: Editions du Seuil, 1966, pp. 234-262.

Radway, J.A. See item 4716.

4016. Rastier, François. "Les Niveaux d'ambiguīté des structures narratives." *Semiotica*, 3, no. 4 (1971), 289-342.

4017. ———. "Situation du récit dans une typologie du discours." *L'Homme*, 11, no. 1 (1971), 68-82.

4018. ———. "L'Analyse structurale des récits et l'idéologie littéraire." *Studi Urbinati di Storia, Filosofia e Letteratura*, 45/3, no. 1-2 (1971), 1244-1258.

4019. ———. *Idéologie et théorie des signes. Analyse structurale des Eléments d'idéologie d'Antoine-Louis-Claude Destutt de Tracy*. The Hague-Paris: Mouton, 1972.

4020. Raymond, Louis Bertrand. "Littérature: les pièges du structuralisme." *Relations*, 37 (Montreal, March 1977), 90-91.

4021. Rehbein, Irmela, ed. "Revolutionäre Texttheorie: die Gruppe Tel Quel." *Alternative*, no. 66 (1969), pp. 93-129.

Revzin, Isaak Iosifovich. See item 4723.

4022. ———. "Structural Analysis of a Poem by Rilke." Trans. R. Milner-Gulland. *New Literary History*, 9 (Winter 1978), 381-384.

Rice, D. See item 1201a.

Ricoeur, P. See item 4735.

4023. Riffaterre, Michael. *Essais de stylistique structurale.* Ed. and trans. Daniel Delas. Paris: Flammarion, 1971.

4023a. ————. *La Production du texte.* Paris: Editions du Seuil, 1979.

————. See also item 4855a.

4024. Rodríguez Almodovar, Antonio. *La Estructura de la novela burguesa.* Madrid: Taller de Ediciones J. Betancor, 1976.

4025. Rosiello, Luigi. *Letteratura e strutturalismo.* Bologna: Zanichelli, 1974.

4026. Rossi, Aldo. "Strutturalismo e analisi letteraria." *Paragone,* 15, no. 180 (December 1964), 24-78.

4027. Roudiez, Leon S. "With and Beyond Literary Structuralism." *Books Abroad,* 49 (Spring 1975), 204-212.

4027a. ————. "Présentation du Colloque [de Cerisy]: Artaud/Bataille." *Sub-stance,* 2, no. 5-6 (Winter 1972-Spring 1973), pp. 199-206.

An analysis of the colloquium: "Vers une révolution culturelle."

Rubino, C.A. See item 4749.

4028. Ruvo, Vincenzo de. *Analisi dello strutturalismo.* Naples: Libreria Scientifica Editrice, 1972.

4029. Saint Armand, Barton Levi. "Superior Abstraction: Todorov on the Fantastic." *Novel: A Forum on Fiction,* 8 (Spring 1975), 260-267.

4030. Saint-Blanquat, H. de. "La Grèce antique change de visage." *Sciences et Avenir,* 337 (1975), 274-279.

Structural analysis discovers the expression of authentic thought, even a logic, in Greek mythology.

4031. Sanders, Scott. "Post hoc." *Novel,* 9, no. 2 (Winter 1976), 185-189. On Scholes' *Structural Fabulation* ... (item 4037).

4032. Sazbón, José, ed. *Estructuralismo y literatura.* Buenos Aires: Ediciones Nueva Visión, 1970.

4033. ————, ed. *Estructuralismo e historia.* Buenos Aires: Ediciones Nueva Visión, 1972.

4034. Schiwy, Günther. "Neue Ergebnisse der Strukturalismus: Mythos und Musik und Fragen der literarischen Rezeption." *Wissenschaft und Weltbild,* 25, no. 2 (April-June 1972), 113-122.

4035. Schmid, Herta. *Strukturalistische Dramentheorie: semantische Analyse von Čechows Ivanov und Der Kirschgarten.* Kronberg Ts.: Scriptor Verlag, 1973. (Skripten Literaturwissenschaft, 3) Originally the author's thesis, Constance.

4036. Scholes, Robert E. *Structuralism in Literature: An Introduction.* New Haven–London: Yale University Press, 1974, 1975. Annotated bibliography, pp. 201–216.

4037. ———. *Structural Fabulation: An Essay on Fiction of the Future.* Notre Dame, Ind.: University of Notre Dame Press, 1975, 111pp.

A critical and theoretical study of the science-fiction field.

4038. ———. "The Contribution of Formalism and Structuralism to the Theory of Fiction." In *Towards a Poetics of Fiction.* Ed. Mark Spilka. Bloomington: Indiana University Press, 1977, pp. 107–124.

4038a. Segre, Cesare. "Analysis of the Tale, Narrative Logic, and Time." In his *Structures and Time. Narration, Poetry, Models.* Trans. John Meddemmen. Chicago: University of Chicago Press, 1979, pp. 1–56.

4039. Seiffert, Leslie. *Wortfeldtheorie und Strukturalismus. Studien zum Sprachgebrauch Freidanks.* Stuttgart: Kohlhammer, 1968.

4040. Senn, H.A. "Arnold van Gennep: Structuralist and Apologist for the Study of Folklore in France." *Folklore*, 85 (Winter 1974), 229–243.

4041. Sherzer, D. *Structure de la trilogie de Beckett: "Molloy," "Malone meurt," "L'Innomable."* The Hague: Mouton, 1976.

4042. Shukman, Ann. *Literature and Semiotics: A Study of the Writings of Yu. M. Lotman.* Amsterdam–New York: North-Holland Publishing Co.; New York: Elsevier North-Holland, 1977.

4043. Smitten, Jeffry R. "Approaches to the Spatiality of Narrative." *Papers in Language and Literature*, 14 (Summer 1978), 296–314.

4044. Soll, L. *Sur la forme et la structure dans l'art littéraire. Contribution à la méthodologie et aux points de vue idéologiques de l'école formelle russe et le structuralisme littéraire pragois.* 2nd ed. Prague: L'Ecrivain Tchécoslovaque, 1972.

4045. Sollers, Philippe. *L'Ecriture et l'expérience des limites.* Paris: Editions du Seuil, 1968.

4046. ———. "Niveaux sémantiques d'un texte moderne." *La Nouvelle Critique* (issue on "Linguistique et littérature"), Colloque de Cluny, 16–17 April 1968, pp. 89–92.

4047. Stati, Sorin. *Il Significato delle parole. Un Saggio introdut-
       tivo. Con i confronti antologici da B. Migliorini ... A.J.
       Greimas ... U. Eco ... G. Mounin, W. van O. Quine.* Messina-
       Florence: G. D'Anna, 1975.

4048. Steiner, George. *Language and Silence. Essays on Language,
       Literature, and the Inhuman.* New York: Athenaeum Books,
       1967, 1971.

4049. ————. *Language and Silence. Essays 1958-1966.* Harmondsworth,
       Middlesex: Penguin Books, 1969, c. 1967. Abridged edition.

4050. Steinwachs, Gisela. *Mythologie des Surrealismus oder die
       Ruckverwandlung von Kultur in Natur. Eine strukturale Analyse
       von Bretons NADJA.* Neuwied-Berlin: Hermann Luchterhand Verlag,
       1971.

4051. Strohmaier, Eckart. *Theorie des Strukturalismus. Zur Kritik
       der strukturalistischen Literaturanalyse.* Bonn: Bouvier
       Verlag, 1977. (Bonner Arbeiten zur deutschen Literatur,
       32) Originally the author's thesis, Bonn.

4052. Swingewood, Alan. "Literature and Structuralism." In item
       2824, pp. 59-77.

4053. Taranienko, Z. "Structuralism in Literary Research" (in Polish).
       Ruch Filozoficzny, 17, no. 3 (1973), 145-158.

       Tel Quel. See item 4253.

       Les Temps Modernes. See item 197, article 6.

4054. Terracini, Benvenuto. "Stilistica al bivio? Storicismo *versus*
       strutturalismo." *Strumenti Critici*, 2, no. 1 (February 1968),
       1-37.

4054a. Terray, M.L. "Quelques remarques sur le discours structuraliste
       appliqué au champ littéraire." *Littéraire*, no. 27 (1977),
       pp. 17-24. Part of an issue entitled "Métalangage(s)."

4055. Todorov, Tzvetan. *Littérature et signification.* Paris: Larousse,
       1967.

4056. ————. *La Grammaire du Décaméron.* The Hague: Mouton, 1969.

*4057. ————. *Introduction à la littérature fantastique.* Paris:
       Editions du Seuil, 1970.

4058. ————. *The Fantastic: A Structural Approach to a Literary
       Genre.* Trans. Richard Howard. Cleveland-London: The Press of
       Case Western Reserve University, 1973. Translation of item
       4057.

4059. ————. "The Structural Analysis of Literature: The Tales of
       Henry James." In item 176, pp. 73-103.

4060. ————. "Structuralism and Literature." In item 4833, pp. 153-168.

4061. Turner, Frederick. "Structuralist Analysis of the Knight's Tale." *Chaucer Review*, 8 (September 1974), 279-296.

4062. Ubersfeld, Ann[i]e. "Structures du théâtre d'Alexandre Dumas père." *La Nouvelle Critique* (issue on "Linguistique et littérature," Colloque de Cluny, 16-17 April 1968), pp. 146-156.

4062a. ————. *Le Roi et le bouffon. Etude sur le théâtre de Hugo de 1830 à 1839.* Paris: Libraire José Corti, 1974.

       A structural analysis of Hugo's work.

4063. Uscatescu, George. "Linguaje y poetica del arte." *Estafeta Literaria*, no. 558 (15 February 1975), pp. 4-9.

4064. Uspensky, Boris. *Poetics of Composition: The Structure of the Artistic Text and Typology of a Compositional Form.* Berkeley: University of California Press, 1973.

       Uspensky describes viewpoint as those devices which articulate the basic structure of the story, providing for the surface-structure effects.

4064a. Vajman, R. "Structuralism and the History of Litterature" (in Serbo-Croatian). *Izraz*, 21, no. 10 (1977), 1233-1276.

       Van Deyck, R. See item 4257.

4065. Van Laere, François. "Existe-t-il un structuralisme littéraire?" *Raison Présente*, no. 19 (July-September 1971), pp. 99-110.

4066. Wanduszka, Mario. "[Der Ertrag des Strukturalismus.] Erwiderung." *Zeitschrift für Romanische Philologie*, Band 84, Heft 1-2 (1968), 102-109.

4067. Watts, Cedric. "Mirror-Tale: An Ethico-Structural Analysis of Conrad's The Secret Sharer." *Critical Quarterly*, 19 (Fall 1977), 25-37.

*4068. Weimann, Robert. "French Structuralism and Literary History: Some Critiques and Reconsiderations." *New Literary History*, 4, no. 3 (1973), 437-469.

4068a. ————. "French Structuralism and Literary History: Some Critiques and Reconsiderations" (in Czechoslovakian). *Estetika*, 12 (1975), 234-256.

4069. Weinmann, Robert. *Literaturgeschichte und Mythologie. Methodologische und historische Studien.* Berlin-Weimar: Aufbau-Verlag, 1974.

4070. Weinrich, Harald. "[Der Ertrag des Strukturalismus.] Zurück-
weisung einer Bilanz." *Zeitschrift für Romanische Philologie*,
Band 84, Heft 1-2 (1968), 98-102.

4071. ————. "Structures narratives du mythe." *Poétique*, no. 1
(1970), pp. 25-44.

4072. Wellek, René. "Book Reviews." *Journal of English and Germanic
Philology*, 73, no. 3 (July 1974), 459-462. On item 4036.

4072a. White, Hayden V. "The Problem of Change in Literary History."
New Literary History, 7, no. 1 (1975), pp. 97-111. Part of
the issue entitled "Critical Challenges: The Bellagio Symposium."

    Also on Lévi-Strauss.

4073. ————. "The Absurdist Moment in Contemporary Literary Theory."
In item 4319, pp. 85-110.

    Wilden, A. See item 216.

4074. Wittig, Susan. *Stylistic and Narrative Structures in the Middle
English Romances*. Austin: University of Texas Press, 1977.

4074a. Wolfman, U. Rehn. Review of Roland Champagne: *Beyond the Structuralist Myth of Ecriture*. *Sub-stance*, no. 20 (Fall 1978),
pp. 127-128.

    On item 3905a.

4075. Yanabu, Akira. *Buntai no ronri*. Japan, 1976.

4076. Závodský, A. "Some Problems Concerning the Relation of Czech
Structuralism to the Theater" (in Czech). *Filosofický Časopis*,
17, no. 1 (1969), 94-99.

4077. Zéraffa, Michel. "Aspects structuraux de l'absurde dans la
littérature contemporaine." *Journal de Psychologie Normale
et Pathologique*, 61, no. 4 (October-December 1964), 437-456.

4078. Ziemlianova, L.M. "Structuralism and Its Most Recent Modifica-
tions in Modern Studies of Folklore in the United States"
(in Russian). *Sovetskaja Etnografija*, no. 6 (1972), pp. 75-86.

LINGUISTICS

Alston, W.P. See item 4423.

Alvar, M. See item 4424.

4079. Amacker, René. *Linguistique saussurienne*. Geneva: Droz, 1975.

4080. Anderson, James Maxwell. *Structural Aspects of Language Change*. London: Longman, 1973. Bibliography, pp. 233-244.

4081. Andreev, Nikolaĭ Dmitrievich. *Issledovaniia po strukturnovero-iatnostnomu analizu*. Moscow: s.n., 1976.

4082. Andresen, Helga. *Der Erklärungsgehalt linguistischer Theorien: methodolog. Analysen z. Generativen Transformationsgrammatik u. z. Syntaxtheorie H.J. Heringers als Beisp. e. strukturalist. Grammatik*. Munich: Hueber, 1974. Contains summaries in English and French.

4083. Anonymous. *Collectif Change*. Paris: Union Générale d'Editions, 1974. Selections of articles previously published in *Change*.

4084. ———. *Linguistique, structuralisme et marxisme*. Paris: Editions Anthropos, 1973. Rpts. item 4161?

4085. ———. *Teoretischeskie i eksperimental'nye issledovaniia v oblasti strukturnoĭ i prikladnoĭ linvistiki*. Moscow: [n.p.], 1973.

4086. Apresjan, Ju. D. *Eléments sur les idées et les méthodes de la linguistique structurale contemporaine*. Trans. from Russian by J.P. de Wrangel and S. Golopentja-Eretescu. Paris-Brussels-Montreal: Dunod, 1973.

4087. ———. *Principles and Methods of Contemporary Structural Linguistics*. Trans. Dina B. Crockett. The Hague: Mouton, 1973. Bibliography, pp. 321-340.

Auzias, J.-M. See chapter two of items 11-14.

Baltheiser, K. See item 2072.

4088. Barber, Elizabeth, comp. Bibliography of Structuralism and Linguistics. *Yale French Studies*, nos. 36-37 (1966), pp. 252-255. Rpt. in *Structuralism*. Ed. Jacques Ehrmann. New York: Doubleday Anchor Books, 1970, pp. 239-244.

4089. Barri, Nimrod. "Nucleus and Satellite in Nominal Syntagmatics."
       Linguistics, no. 157 (August 1, 1975), pp. 83-85, bibliog-
       raphy.

4090. ———. "Note terminologique: endocentrique--exocentrique."
       Linguistics, no. 163 (1 November 1975), pp. 5-18.

4091. Baumann, Hans Heinrich. "Über französischen Strukturalismus,
       zur Rezeption moderner Linguistik in Frankreich und in
       Deutschland." *Sprache im Technischen Zeitalter*, 8 (1969),
       157-183.

4092. Bedell, George. "Arguments about Deep Structure." *Language*,
       50 (September 1974), 423-445.

       Benavides Lucas, M. See item 19.

4093. Bense, Elisabeth, et al, eds. *Beschreibungsmethoden des ameri-
       kanischen Strukturalismus*. Munich: Max Hueber, 1976.

4094. Benveniste, Emile. "'Structure' en linguistique." In *Sens et
       usages....* Ed. R. Bastide. Item 5201, pp. 32-38.

*4095. ———. *Problèmes de linguistique générale*. 2 vols. Paris:
       Gallimard, 1966-1974.

4096. ———. "La Forme et le sens dans le langage." *Le Langage*.
       Actes du XIIIᵉ Congrès des sociétés de philosophie de langue
       française. Neuchâtel: La Baconnière, 1967, pp. 27-40. In-
       cluded in vol. 2 of item 4095.

4096a. ———. *Problems in General Linguistics*. Trans. Mary Elizabeth
       Meek. Coral Gables, Florida: University of Miami Press, 1971.

4097. Berger, H. "Van de Saussure tot Chomsky. Een linguistische
       situatiebepaling van het structuralisme." *Tijdschrift voor
       Filosofie*, 32 (June 1970), 175-196. English summary, p. 196.

       De Saussure's *langue* vs. Chomsky's "competence."

       Bermejo, J.M. See item 5133.

4098. Bierwisch, Manfred. *Strukturalismus und Linguistik*. Giessen:
       Prolit-Buchvertrieb, 1972.

4099. Blois, Jacques, and Marc Bar. *Principes d'analyse structurale*.
       Paris-Brussels: Didier, 1974.

4100. Blumstein, S. "Structuralism in Linguistics: Methodological
       and Theoretical Perspectives." In *Structure and Transforma-
       tion: Developmental and Historical Aspects*. Ed. Klaus F.
       Riegel and George C. Rosenwald. New York: Wiley, 1975, pp.
       153-165.

       Bonelli, G. See item 4441.

Bourdieu, P. See item 5219.

4101. Brinker, Klaus. *Konstituentenstrukturgrammatik und operationale Satzgliedanalyse; methodenkritische Untersuchungen zur Syntax des einfachen Satzes im Deutschen.* Frankfurt am Main: Athenäum Verlag, 1972. Bibliography, pp. 195-209.

4102. Buyssens, Eric. "Le Structuralisme linguistique." *La Pensée et les Hommes*, 13 (Brussels, 1969-1970), 239-241.

Câmara, J.M., et al. See item 35.

Carrillo, V.L. See item 4451.

4103. Cassirer, E. "Structuralism in Modern Linguistics." *Word*, 1 (1945), 120.

4104. Cattell, Ray. "J. Culler: *Structuralism, Linguistics and the Study of Literature.*" *AUMLA*, no. 46 (November 1976), pp. 364-365.

Chetan, O. See item 4463.

4104a. Chiss, Jean-Louis, Jacques Filliolet, and Dominique Maingueneau. *Linguistique française. Initiation à la problématique structurale.* Paris: Hachette, 1977 (vol. 1), 1978 (vol. 2).

4105. Chomsky, Noam. *Cartesian Linguistics.* New York: Harper and Row, 1966.

4106. ———. *Le Langage et la pensée.* Paris: Payot, 1970.

4107. ———. "Linguistics and Philosophy." In *Language and Philosophy. A Symposium.* New York University Institute of Philosophy. Ed. Sidney Hook. New York: New York University Press, 1969, pp. 51-94.

4108. Clausen, Christopher. "Schoolmarms, the Linguists and the Language." *The Midwest Quarterly. A Journal of Contemporary Thought*, 19 (April 1978), 229-237.

4109. Coelho, Maria Angelina Teixeira. *Estruturalismo.* Luanda: Instituto de Investigação Científica de Angola, Centro de Documentação Científica, 1971. (Bibliografias Temáticas, 13) Introductory note in English and Portuguese.

4110. Cohen, Marcel. "Quelques notations historiques et critiques autour du structuralisme en linguistique." *La Pensée*, no. 135 (1967), pp. 29-37.

4111. Corneille, Jean-Pierre. *La Linguistique structurale. Sa Portée, ses limites.* Paris: Larousse, 1976.

Corvez, Maurice. See chapter 1 of items 49-51.

4112. Coseriu, Eugenio. *Einführung in die strukturelle Linguistik.* Tubingen: ([Univ.,] Roman. Seminar), 1969.

4113. ———. *Principios de semántica estructural.* Trans. Marcos Martínez Hernández. Madrid: Gredos, 1977.

4114. ———. *Probleme der strukturellen Semantik.* Vorlesung gehalten im Wintersemester 1965/66 an der Universität Tübingen. Tubingen, 1973. (Tübinger Beiträge zur Linguistik, 40)

Crespy, G. See item 4949.

4115. Culler, Jonathan. "The Linguistic Basis of Structuralism." In *Structuralism: An Introduction.* Ed. David Robey (item 176), pp. 20-36.

4116. ———. *Saussure.* Glasgow: Fontana/Collins, 1976.

4117. ———. *Ferdinand de Saussure.* New York: Penguin Books, 1977, c. 1976.

———. See also item 4836.

4118. Damasceno, José Ribeiro. *Introdução ao estruturalismo em lingüística.* Petrópolis: Editora Vozes, 1977.

4119. Derossi, Giorgi. "L'Articolazione della totalità linguistica in F. De Saussure." *Proteus*, 3, no. 8 (1972), 11-35.

4120. Dessaintes, M. "Introduction au structuralisme linguistique. V. Les Fonctions syntaxiques." *Nouvelle Revue Pédagogique*, 22, no. 2 (1966), 68-79.

4121. Dijk, Teun A. van. *Taal, tekst, teken. Bijdragen tot de literatuurteorie.* Amsterdam: Polak & Van Gennep, 1971. Bibliography, pp. 241-251.

4121a. ———. *Some Aspects of Text Grammars. A Study in Theoretical Linguistics and Poetics.* The Hague: Mouton, 1972.

4121b. ———. *Text and Context. Explorations in the Semantics and Pragmatics of Discourse.* London-New York: Longman, 1977.

4122. Di Pietro, Robert J. *Language Structures in Contrast.* Rowley, Mass.: Newbury House Publishers, 1971.

4123. Domínguez Hildalgo, Antonio. *Iniciación a las estructuras lingüísticas.* Mexico: Editorial Porrua, 1973. Bibliography, pp. 237-253.

4124. Donni de Mirande, Nélida Esther, et al. *El Estructuralismo lingüístico en la Argentina.* Buenos Aires: A. Estrada, 1970.

4125. Dubois, J., and L. Guilbert. "Deuxième révolution linguistique?" *La Nouvelle Critique*, no. 12.

4126.   Dubois, Jean. "Structuralisme et linguistique." *La Pensée*,
        no. 135 (1967), pp. 19-28.

*4127. Ducrot, Oswald. *Le Structuralisme en linguistique.* Tome I of
        Qu'est-ce que le structuralisme? Paris: Editions du Seuil,
        1968, 1973. (Points, 44)

4128.   ————. *Estruturalismo e lingüistica.* Trans. José Paulo Paes.
        São Paulo: Ed. Cultrix, Fundo Estaduae de Cultura, 1970.

*4129. ————, and Tzvetan Todorov. *Dictionnaire encyclopédique des
        sciences du langage.* Paris: Editions du Seuil, 1972.

        Though not directly on structuralism, this work gives a lot
        of information on the field of linguistics.

4129a. ————. *Encyclopedic Dictionary of the Sciences of Language.*
        Trans. Catherine Porter. Baltimore, Md.: Johns Hopkins Univer-
        sity Press, 1979.

4130.   Durbin, M.A. "Formal Changes in Trinidad Hindi as a Result of
        Language Adaptation." *American Anthropologist*, 75 (October
        1973); pp. 1302-1304 gives a bibliography.

4131.   Ebneter, Theodor. *Strukturalismus und Transformationalismus.
        Einführung in Schulen und Methoden.* Munich: List Verlag,
        1973.

        Einem, H. von, et al. See items 5238-5239.

4132.   Enninger, Werner. *Übungen zu einem strukturell-taxonomischen
        Modell der englischen Grammatik.* Tübingen: Niemeyer, 1976.

4133.   Esper, Erwin Allen. *Mentalism and Objectivism in Linguistics.
        The Sources of Leonard Bloomfield's Psychology of Language.*
        New York: American Elsevier, 1968.

4134.   Fanizza, Franco. "A proposito di uno studio su Ferdinando
        de Saussure." *Giornale Critico della Filosofia Italiana*, 21
        (April-June 1967), 288-299.

4135.   Feurer, Hanny. "Symbole et linguistique structurale." In *Le
        Symbole, carrefour interdisciplinaire.* Ed. Renée Legris and
        Pierre Pagé. Montreal: Les Editions Sainte-Marie, 1969, pp.
        83-92.

4136.   Fisiak, Jacek. *Wstęp do współczesnych teorii lingwistycznych.*
        Warsaw: Wydawnictwa Szkolne i Pedagogiczne, 1975.

4137.   Fontaine, Jacqueline. *Le Cercle linguistique de Prague.* Paris:
        Mame, 1974.

        Fontaine-De Visscher, Luce. See item 4513.

4137a. Fossion, André, and Jean-Paul Laurent. *Pour comprendre les
        lectures nouvelles: linguistique et pratiques textuelles.*
        Gembloux, Belgium: Duculot, c. 1978, 120pp.

4138. Fowler, Roger. "Linguistics." In *The Twentieth-Century Mind. History, Ideas, and Literature in Britain.* Ed. Charles B. Cox and Anthony E. Dyson. New York: Oxford University Press, 1972, vol. 3, pp. 200-224.

4139. Friedman, Victor A. "Structural and Generative Approaches to an Analysis of the Macedonian Preterite." *Slavic and East European Journal,* 20 (Winter 1976), 460-464.

4140. Fukumura, Torajirō. *Eigogaku renshu.* Japan, 1977.

4140a. Gaatone, David. "Forme sous-jacente unique ou liste d'allomorphes? (A propos des consonnes de liaison en français)." *Linguistics,* no. 214 (December 1978), pp. 33-54.

4141. Gagnepain, J. "Lexicologie et structuralisme." *Annales de Bretagne,* 72, no. 4 (1965), 537-539.

Gouthier, G. See item 5250.

4142. Graffi, Giorgio. *Struttura, forma e sostanza in Hjelmslev.* Bologna: Il Mulino, 1974, 74pp.

4143. Greimas, Algirdas Julien. "La Structure élémentaire de la signification en linguistique." *L'Homme,* 4, no. 3 (September-December 1964), 5-17.

*4144. ————. *Sémantique structurale. Recherche de méthode.* Paris: Larousse, 1966.

4145. ————. *Semántica estructural. Investigación metodológica.* Trans. Alfredo de la Fuente. Madrid: Ed. Gredos, 1971.

4146. ————. *Strukturale Semantik. Methodologische Untersuchungen. Autoris.* Trans. Jens Ihwe. Braunschweig: Vieweg, 1971.

4147. ————. "Narrative Grammar: Units and Levels." Trans. P. Bodrock. *MLN,* 86 (December 1971), 793-806.

4148. Guentcheva-Desclés, Z. *Présentation critique du modèle applicationnel de S.K. Saumjan.* (St. Sulpice de Favières (Essonne): Association Jean Favard pour le développement de la linguistique quantitative) Paris: Bordas/Dunod, 1976.

4149. Hammarström, Göran. *Linguistic Units and Items.* Berlin-New York: Springer-Verlag, 1976.

Hanhardt, J.G., et al. See item 3825.

4150. Harris, Zellig Sabbetai. *Methods in Structural Linguistics.* Chicago: University of Chicago Press, 1951.

Ends with the characterization of the grammar of a language as a theory of its structure.

4151.   ———. *Papers in Structural and Transformational Linguistics.*
        Dordrect: Reidel, 1970. (Formal Linguistics Series, v. 1)

4152.   ———. *Structures mathématiques du langage.* Paris: Dunod,
        1971.

4153.   ———. "On a Theory of Language." *The Journal of Philosophy,*
        73 (May 1976), 253-276.

        On Harris' theory of the grammar of a language as a resultant
        of predicational operators successively entering a sentence.
        Also treats the possibility of a characteristic linguistic
        structure of scientific theories.

4154.   ———. "A Theory of Language Structure." *American Philosoph-
        ical Quarterly,* 13 (October 1976), 237-256.

4155.   Hausmann, Franz Josef. "Strukturelle Wortschatzbetrachtung vor
        Saussure." *Romanische Forschungen,* 88, no. 4 (1976), 331-354.

        Structural treatment of the question of vocabulary before
        Saussure.

        Hawkes, T. See item 5165.

4156.   Heger, Klaus. *Monem, Wort und Satz.* Tubingen: M. Niemeyer, 1971.
        (Konzepte der Sprach- und Literaturwissenschaft, 8)

4157.   Heinrich, Hans. "Über französischen Strukturalismus, zur Rezep-
        tion moderner Linguistik in Frankreich und in Deutschland."
        Sprache im Technischen Zeitalter, 8 (1969), 157-183.

4158.   Herdan, Gustav. *Structuralistic Approach to Chinese Grammar
        and Vocabulary.* New York: Humanities Press; The Hague: Mouton,
        1964, 56pp.

4159.   Hiersche, R. *Ferdinand de Saussures "langue-parole"--Konzeption
        und sein Verhältnis zu Durkheim und von der Gabelentz.* Inns-
        bruck: Institut für vergleichende Sprachwissenschaft der
        Universität, 1972.

4160.   Hjelmslev, Louis. *Le Langage.* Paris: Editions de Minuit, 1966.

        Holenstein, E. See items 4562-4567.

4161.   *L'Homme et la Société,* no. 28 (1973), pp. 3-177: issue on
        "Linguistique, structuralisme et marxisme." Rpt. in item
        4084?

4162.   Hrzalova, H. "Sur le formalisme russe et le structuralisme
        pragois." *La Pensée,* no. 173 (1974), pp. 116-119.

4163.   Huddleston, Rodney. "Syntagmeme." *International Journal of
        American Linguistics,* 37 (January 1971), 39-44.

4164.   Hudson, Richard A. "Grammar without Transformations." *Diogenes*,
        Winter 1976, pp. 93-109.

        Outlines a new theory of syntax which differs from transforma-
        tional grammar in that it doesn't make use of transformational
        rules, but instead assigns to each sentence a single structure
        which includes both deep and surface information.

4165.   Hymes, Dell. "Why Linguistics Needs the Sociologist." *Social
        Research*, 34 (1967), 632-647.

        Jacob, A. See item 4577.

        Jacquart, E. See item 4843.

4165a. Jakobson, Roman. *To Honor Roman Jakobson. Essays on the Occasion
        of His Seventieth Birthday, 11 October 1966.* 3 vols. The
        Hague-Paris-Hawthorne, New York: Mouton, 1967. (Janua
        Linguarum Ser. Major: Nos. 31-33)

4166.   ————. *Selected Writings*. The Hague-Paris: Mouton, 1962,
        1966, 1971.

4167.   ————. *Essais de linguistique générale*. Paris: Editions de
        Minuit, 1963.

4168.   ————, and J.-P. Faye. "Questionner Jakobson." *Les Lettres
        Françaises*, 17 November 1966. One of the best and most concise

        One of the best and most concise introductions to Russian
        formalism which reveals the "complicity" between linguistics
        and literary writing.

4169.   ————. "Linguistics." In *Main Trends of Research in the Social
        and Human Sciences*, vol. 1, UNESCO. The Hague: Mouton, 1970.

4170.   ————. See *L'Arc*, no. 60 (1975) dedicated to his work.

4171.   ————. *Six leçons sur le son et le sens*. Paris: Editions de
        Minuit, 1976.

        ————. See also item 4844.

4172.   Jameson, Fredric. *The Prison-House of Language: A Critical
        Account of Structuralism and Russian Formalism*. Princeton,
        N.J.: Princeton University Press, 1972, 1974.

        A critique of modern linguistic theory and its application
        in and implications for formalism and structuralism; includes a
        a bibliography, pp. 217-224; treats Lévi-Strauss, Lacan, Derrida,
        Foucault, Barthes, Greimas, and Todorov.

4173.   Johnson, Robert G. "Formal or Symbolic Linguistics: Toward a
        New Science of Linguistics." *Studies in Linguistics*, 25
        (1975), 9-18.

4174.   *Journal of Philosophy*, 70 (25 October 1973), 601-612: issue in-
        cludes "Symposium: Logical Structure in Natural Languages."
        See items 4214, 4215 and 4249.

4175.   Junod, Henri Philippe. "Notes sur le modèle linguistique saus-
        surien." *Dialectica*, 22 (1968), 313-317.

4176.   Karpov, L.N. "Les Aspects méthodologiques de la linguistique
        structurale." *Filologičeskie Nauki*, no. 6 (1976), pp. 72-81.

4177.   Katz, Jerrold J., and Jerry A. Fodor. "The Structure of a
        Semantic Theory." *Language*, 39 (1963), 170-210.

        Methods for handling semantics structurally within generative
        grammar.

        Kaufmann, J.N. See item 4586.

4178.   Khlebnikova, Irina Borisovna. *Oppositions in Morphology as
        Exemplified in the English Tense System*. Translated from the
        Russian. The Hague: Mouton, 1973.

        Kieffer, R. See item 5010.

4179.   Koerner, E.F. *Bibliographia Saussureana Eighteen Seventy to
        Nineteen Seventy: An Annotated Classified Bibliography on the
        Background, Development and Actual Relevance of Ferdinand de
        Saussure's General Theory of Language*. Metuchen, N.J.: Scarecrow
        1972.

4180.   ———. *Ferdinand de Saussure. Origin and Development of his
        Linguistic Thought. Western Studies of Language. A Contribu-
        tion to the History and Theory of Linguistics*. Braunschweig:
        Vieweg, 1973.

4181.   Kořenský, J. "The Structures of the Linguistic Object and the
        Structure of Linguistic Description" (in Czech). *Filosofický
        Časopis*, 17, no. 1 (1969), 36-38.

        Kraay, J.N. See item 4592.

4182.   Kristeva, Julia. *Recherches pour une sémanalyse*. Paris: Editions
        du Seuil, 1969.

4183.   Krupatkin, Ja.B. "Toward Systemic Linguistics: A Survey of
        Studies by G.P. Mel'nikov from 1959-1972." *Linguistics*, no.
        139 (1 November 1974), pp. 43-81.

4184.   *Langages*, a journal published in Paris by Didier/Larousse.
        no. 1, "Recherches sémantiques," ed. T. Todorov; no. 2, "Lo-
        gique et linguistique," ed. E. Coumet et al.; no. 3, "Linguis-
        tique française. Le Verbe et la phrase," ed. A.-J. Greimas
        et al.; no. 4, "La Grammaire générative," ed. N. Ruwet; no.
        6, "La Glossématique. L'Héritage de Hjelmslev au Danemark,"
        ed. K. Togeby; no. 20, "Analyse distributionnelle et struc-
        turale," ed. J. Dubois et al.; no. 21 (1971), "Philosophie
        du langage," ed. J. Sumpf; no. 22, "Sémiotique narrative:
        récits bibliques," ed. C. Chabrol and L. Marin; no. 24,
        "Epistémologie de la linguistique," ed. J. Kristeva; no. 31
        (1973), "Sémiotiques textuelles," ed. M. Arrivé et al.

4185. Leeman, Danielle, ed. *La Paraphrase*. Paris: Didier, 1973.

Leiber, J. See items 127 and 4613.

*4186. Lepschy, Giulio C. *La Linguistica strutturale*. Turin: G. Einaudi, 1967. (Piccola Biblioteca Einaudi, 79)

4187. ————. *La Linguistique structurale*. Paris: Payot, 1967, 1976.

4188. ————. *A Survey of Structural Linguistics*. London: Faber, 1970.

4189. Leroy, Maurice. *Les Grands courants de la linguistique moderne*. Brussels: Editions de l'Université de Bruxelles, 1971.

4190. Lewis, B. Jean, and T.J. Lewis. "Structural Linguistics and Literature in France." *The Journal of the British Society for Phenomenology*, 2, no. 3 (October 1971), 27-36.

4191. López Martín, A. "El Estructuralismo lingüístico." *Revista de Filosofía de la Universidad de Costa Rica*, 11, no. 32 (1973), 3-11.

Discusses the genesis of structural linguistics and the role of phonology as well as the critique of structuralism by Ricoeur and Chomsky.

4192. Lucas, M.A. "Nominal Group in Systemic Grammar." *Linguistics*, no. 204 (February 1978), pp. 25-41.

4193. Lyons, John. "Structuralism and Linguistics." In item 176, pp. 5-19.

4194. Lyotard, J.F. *Discours, figure*. Paris: Klincksieck, 1971.

Macku, J. See item 4625.

Malagoli, L. See item 138.

4195. Malmberg, B. *Structural Linguistics and Human Communication. An Introduction to the Mechanism of Language and the Methodology of Linguistics*. Berlin-Göttingen-Heidelberg: Springer Verlag, 1963, 1967. (Kommunikation und Kybernetik, 2)

4196. ————. *Les Nouvelles tendances de la linguistique*. Paris: Presses Universitaires de France, 1966.

4197. Mandelbaum, Maurice. "Language and Chess, De Saussure's Analogy." *The Philosophical Review*, 77 (June 1968), 356-357.

4198. Manoliu Manea, Maria. *Structuralismul linvistic: (lecturi critice)*. Bucarest: Editura Didactică şi Pedagogică, 1973.

4199. Marcellesi, J.B., and B. Gardin. *Introduction à la sociolinguistique. La Linguistique sociale*. Paris: Larousse, 1974.

4200. Marchese, A. "Modelli di critica strutturale." *Humanitas*, no.
       8-9 (1974), pp. 622-637.

4201. Marcus, S. *Introduction mathématique à la linguistique struc-
       turale*. Paris: Dunod, 1967.

       Marin, L. See item 4635.

4202. Martinet, André. *Eléments de linguistique générale*. Paris:
       Armand Colin, 1961.

4203. ———. *A Functional View of Language*. Oxford: Clarendon Press,
       1962.

4204. ———. "Linguistics: Structure and Language." Trans. T.G.
       Penchoen. In item 68, pp. 10-18. See also item 69.

4205. ———. "Fonction et structure en linguistique." *Scientia*,
       65 (1971), 973-982 and 983-991.

       Medina Lugo, R.A. See item 4641.

       Miller, J. See items 4647-4648.

4206. Moles, A.A. "La Linguistique, méthode de découverte interdis-
       ciplinaire." *Revue Philosophique de la France et de l'Etranger*,
       156 (July-September 1966), 375-390.

       Mouloud, N. See item 4650.

4207. Mounin, Georges. *Histoire de la linguistique des origines au
       XXe siècle*. Paris: Presses Universitaires de France, 1967,
       1970 (2nd updated ed.). ("Le Linguiste")

4208. ———. "L'Age de la linguistique." *Les Nouvelles Littéraires*,
       no. 2071 (11 May 1967), p. 8.

4209. ———. *Clefs pour la linguistique*. Paris: Seghers, 1971.

4210. ———. *La Linguistique au XXe siècle*. Paris: Presses Univer-
       sitaires de France, 1972.

4211. ———. *Clefs pour la sémantique*. Paris: Seghers, 1975.

4212. Mourelle-Lema, Manuel. "La Lingüística, antes y despues de
       Saussure." *Arbor*, 81 (1972), 347-353.

       Muraro Vaiani, M. See item 4667.

4213. *La Nouvelle Critique*. Special issue on "Linguistique et littéra-
       ture," Colloque de Cluny, 16-17 April 1968.

       Treats three main problems: (1) how contemporary linguistics
       views literature; (2) how literary analysis does or does not
       make use of linguistic theories and data; (3) how poets and
       novelists experience the contribution of linguistics.

Oliver, B. See items 4674-4675.

Parret, H. See items 4692-4694.

4214. Parsons, Terence. "Tense Operators versus Quantifiers." *Journal of Philosophy*, 70 (25 October 1973), 609-610.

4215. Partee, Barbara Hall. "Some Structural Analogies between Tenses and Pronouns in English." *Journal of Philosophy*, 70 (25 October 1973), 601-609.

4216. Pasqualotto, Giangiorgio. "Linguistica strutturale e teoria dell'informazione." *Nuova Corrente*, no. 56 (1971), 333-351.

4217. Patočka, J. "Roman Jakobsons phänomenologischer Strukturalismus." *Tijdschrift voor Filosofie*, 38 (March 1976), 129-135.

4218. Patterson, William, and Hector Urrutibeheity. *The Lexical Structure of Spanish*. Atlantic Highlands, N.J.: Humanities Press, 1975.

4219. Peeters, Christian. "Saussure néogrammairien et l'antinomie synchronie/diachronie." *Linguistics*, no. 133 (1 August 1974), pp. 53-62.

4220. Perrot, Jean. *La Linguistique*. Paris: Presses Universitaires de France, 1953 and subsequent editions. (Que sais-je? no. 570)

4221. Petronio, Giuseppe, ed. *Lo Strutturalismo fra ideologia e tecnica*. Palermo: Palumbo, 1972. (Problemi libri, 7)

Pettit, P. See item 4701.

4222. Peytard, Jean. "A propos de terminologie ensembliste." *Etudes de Linguistique Appliquée, no. 4*. Paris: Didier, 1966.

4223. ———. "Rapports et interférences de la linguistique et de la littérature (Introduction à une bibliographie)." *La Nouvelle Critique* ("Linguistique et littérature"), Colloque de Cluny, 16-17 April 1968, pp. 8-16.

A useful pre-1968 bibliography.

Piaget, J. See items 154-157 and 160-164.

4224. Pilch, Herbert. "Structural Dialectology." *American Speech*, 47 (Fall-Winter 1972), 165-187.

4225. Ponzio, A. "Grammaire transformationnelle et idéologie politique." *L'Homme et la Société*, 28 (1973), 93-112.

4226. Pottier, Bernard. "Au-delà du structuralisme en linguistique." *Critique*, 20e année, tome 23, no. 237 (February 1967), 266-274.

4227.   Potts, T.C. "The Place of Structure in Communication." In
        Communication and Understanding. By the Royal Institute of
        Philosophy. Ed. Godfrey Vesey. Atlantic Highlands, N.J.:
        Harvester Press (distributed by Humanities Press), 1978,
        c. 1977, pp. 91-115. (Royal Institute of Philosophy Lectures,
        vol. 10, 1975-1976)

4228.   Quine, W.V. "Methodological Reflections on Current Linguistic
        Theory." *Synthèse*, 21, no. 3-4 (Holland, 1970), 386-398.

        Radway, J.A. See item 4716.

4229.   Revzin, Isaak Iosifovich. *Sovremennaiả strukturnaiả lingvistika.*
        Moscow: Hayka, 1977.

        Ricoeur, P. See items 4726-4729, 4735 and 4736.

4230.   Rigotti, E. "La Linguistica in Russia dagli inizi del secolo
        XIX ad oggi. IV. Il 'Ritorno' dello strutturalismo in URSS
        e i suoi sviluppi." *Rivista di Filosofia Neo-Scolastica*, 65,
        no. 3 (1973), 488-521.

4231.   Robins, Robert Henry. *Brève histoire de la linguistique: de
        Platon à Chomsky.* Trans. Maurice Borel. Paris: Editions du
        Seuil, 1976.

4232.   Rodríguez Adrados, Francisco. *Lingüística estructural.* 2nd rev.
        and enlarged ed. 2 vols. Madrid: Gredos, 1974.

4233.   Ronat, Mitsou. "A propos du verbe *Remind*, selon P.M. Postel.
        La Sémantique générative: une réminiscence du structuralisme?"
        Studi Italiani di Linguistica Teorica ed Applicata, 1, no. 2
        (1972).

        Roudinesco, E. See item 3352.

4234.   Ruhlen, Merritt. "Two Rival Approaches to Rumanian Grammar:
        Classical Structuralism vs. Transformational Analysis."
        Romance Philology, 28 (November 1974), 178-190.

4234a. Ružička, J. "Fundamental Traits of Slovakian Linguistic Struc-
        turalism" (in Slovakian). *Filozofia*, 32, no. 2 (1977), 184-
        190. Part of an issue entitled "Marxism and Structuralism."

4235.   Sacks, Norman P. "English *very*, French *très*, and Spanish *muy*:
        A Structural Comparison and its Significance for Bilingual
        Lexicography." *PMLA*, 86 (March 1971), 190-201.

4236.   Said, Edward W. "Linguistics and the Archeology of Mind."
        International Philosophical Quarterly, 11 (March 1971), 104-
        134.

        ————. See also 4336.

        Santoni Brué, M.P. See item 4753.

*4237. Saussure, Ferdinand de. *Cours de linguistique générale*. Paris: Payot, 1972, c. 1915.

4238. ————. *Course in General Linguistics*. Ed. Charles Bally and Albert Séchehaye. Trans. Wade Baskin. New York: Philosophical Library, 1959.

4239. ————. *Recueil des publications scientifiques de Ferdinand de Saussure*. Geneva: Slatkine Reprints, 1970. A reprint of the 1922 Geneva edition; bibliography, vi-643 pages.

4240. ————. *¿Que es la lingüística?* Trans. Amado Alonso. Havana: Instituto Cubano del Libro, 1972.

4241. Sctrick, R. "Structuralisme: le structuralisme linguistique." In *Encyclopaedia Universalis*, vol. 15 (1973), pp. 431-434. Paris: Encyclopaedia Universalis France, 1968.

4242. Searle, J.R. "Chomsky's Revolution in Linguistics." In *On Noam Chomsky: Critical Essays*. Ed. Gilbert Harman. New York: Doubleday Anchor Books, 1974, pp. 2-33.

4243. Shaumian, Sebastian Konstantinovich. *Principles of Structural Linguistics*. Trans. James Miller. The Hague-Paris: Mouton, 1971.

4244. ————. *Strukturale Linguistik*. Trans. Wolfgang Girke and Helmut Jachnow. Munich: Wilhelm Fink, 1971.

4245. ————, ed. *Problemy strukturnoĭ lingvistiki*. Moscow: Hayka, 1972, 554pp.

4246. ————. *Applicational Grammar as a Semantic Theory of Natural Language*. Trans. J.E. Miller. Edinburgh: Edinburgh University Press, c. 1977, 184pp.

4246a. Simmons, S. "Mukařovský, Structuralism, and the Essay." *Semiotica*, 19, no. 3-4 (1977), 335-340. Part of an issue entitled "A Tribute to C.S. Peirce and in Memory of Jan Mukařovský."

On developing an analytical tool for studying the linguistic structure of a literary text.

4247. Simó, M. Peñalver. "La Lingüística estructural y las ciencias del hombre." *Anuario Filosófico. Universidad de Navarra*, 3 (1970), 187-251.

On the epistemological presuppositions of structural analysis; the notions operative in structural linguistics and their application to the other sciences of man; structure as explanatory principle in science.

Simoens, Y. See item 5093.

4248. Sliusareva, Natal'ia Aleksandrovna. *Teoriia F. de Sossiura v svete sovremennoĭ lingvistiki*. Moscow: Hayka, 1975.

Stahl, G. See item 4780.

4249. Stalnaker, Robert C. "Tenses and Pronouns." *Journal of Philosophy*, 70 (25 October 1973), pp. 610-612.

4250. Strawson, Peter Frederick. "On Understanding the Structure of One's Language." In *Truth and Meaning: Essays in Semantics*. Ed. G.L. Evans and J.H. McDowell. New York: Oxford University Press, 1976, pp. 189-198.

4251. Tabouret-Keller, André. "Linguistique et psychologie. Quelques aspects de leurs rapports." *Revue de l'Enseignement Supérieur*, no. 1-2 (1967), pp. 89-95.

4252. Teghrarian, Souren. "Linguistic Rules and Semantic Interpretation." *American Philosophical Quarterly*, 11 (October 1974), 307-315.

4253. *Tel Quel*, no. 26 (1966): issue entitled "Linguistique, psychanalyse, littérature."

4254. Ullmann, St. Review of Greimas's *Sémantique structurale* (item 4144). *Journal de Psychologie Normale et Pathologique*, 64 (1967), 239-243.

4255. Vandenbulcke, J. "Het Taalbegrip van de structurele Linguistiek en zijn Vooropstellingen." *Tijdschrift voor Filosofie*, 32 (December 1970), 615-650.

       On the philosophical foundations of structural linguistics, Saussure, Chomsky, etc. Includes an analysis of Greimas's *Sémantique structurale* (item 4144).

4256. Van de Velde, Roger G. *Inleiding tot de strukturele methodologie van de linguistiek*. Antwerp: Ontwikkeling; Zaandam: Sociografisch Instituut; Brussels: Labor, 1971, 164pp. (Talen en Cultuur, 9)

4257. Van Deyck, Rika. "Une Méthode syntaxique en diachronie. Comment réduire les structures de la parole de François Villon, dans la version du manuscrit Coislin, à celles de l'idéolecte?" *Communication et Cognition*, 10, no. 1 (1977), 97-112.

4258. Velleman, B.L. "Structuralist Theory in Bello's Gramática." *Hispanic Review*, 46 (Winter 1978), 55-64.

4259. Wanner, Eric. *On Remembering, Forgetting, and Understanding Sentences. A Study of the Deep Structure Hypothesis*. The Hague: Mouton, 1974, 160pp. (Janua Linguarum. Series Minor, 170) Originally presented as the author's thesis, Harvard University.

4260. Waugh, Linda R. *Roman Jakobson's Science of Language*. Lisse, Netherlands: Peter de Ridder Press, 1976; distributed in the United States by Humanities Press. (PdR Press Publications on Roman Jakobson, 2)

4261. Weber, Samuel. "Saussure and the Apparition of Language: The Critical Perspective." *MLN*, 91 (October 1976), 913-938.

4262. Werner, Otmar. *Einführung in die strukturelle Beschreibung des Deutschen*. Tübingen: Niemeyer, 1970, 1973. (Germanistische Arbeitshefte, 1)

4262a. White, Mary J. "Linguistic Norms and Norms in Linguistics." *Journal of Pragmatics*, 3 (February 1979), 81-98.

4263. Worthington, Martha Garrett. "Immanence as Principle." *Romance Philology*, 24 (February 1971), 488-505.

Wunderli, P. See item 5189a.

4264. Yallop, Colin L. "The Problem of Linguistic Universals." *Philosophia Reformata*, 43 (1978), 61-72.

To understand what is common to all languages it is necessary to examine the nature of the world and the way language functions within it. Linguistic universals are not found by inspecting languages but by considering the universal preconditions for language and the universal functions of language. Within a universal structure of reality, languages may diverge widely in their actual lexical organization and rules of grammar.

4265. Zasorina, Lidiīa Nikolaevna. *Vvedenie v strukturnuīu lingvistiku*. Moscow, 1974.

4266. Zsilka, János. *Sentence Patterns and Reality*. The Hague: Mouton, 1973, 372pp. (Janua Linguarum. Series Minor, 140)

4267. ———. *A nyelvi mozgásformak dialektikája (a nyelvi rendszer szerves, hipotetikus és homoszintaktikai síkja)*. Budapest: Akadémiai Kiadó, 1973.

4268. Zuber, Ryszard. *Structure présuppositionnelle du langage*. Saint-Sulpice-de-Favières (Essone): Association Jean Favard pour le Développement de la Linguistique Quantitative (distributed by Dunod in Paris), 1972, 120pp. (Documents de Linguistique Quantitative, no. 17)

LITERARY CRITICISM

4269. Allemand, André. *Nouvelle critique. Nouvelle perspective.*
Neuchâtel: A La Baconnière, 1967.

4270. Ambroise, C. "L'Idiot de la famille: una critica letteraria
anti-strutturalista." *Aut Aut*, nos. 136-137 (1973), pp. 85-
102.

4271. [Andreev, L.] "La Littérature à l'étranger—U.R.S.S. Le Critique
Andreev devant le 'nouveau roman' français: école de l'écriture ou école du silence?" Adapted from Russian by Martine
Laroche. *Le Monde [des Livres]*, no. 7020 (9 August 1967),
p. III.

Anonymous. See item 936.

4272. ———. *Littérature et idéologies. Colloque de Cluny II. 2, 3,
4 avril 1970.* Paris: La Nouvelle Critique, 1971.

4273. ———. "The Novels of Claude Simon, by J.A.E. Loubère."
Choice, 12, no. 8 (October 1975), 1008.

4274. ———. "Pour ou contre la nouvelle critique? Débat entre MM.
Pierre de Boisdeffre, Jacques de Bourbon Busset, Charles
Dédéyan, Raymond Picard, Jean Sur." *La Table Ronde*, no. 221
(June 1966), pp. 79-97.

4275. ———. *Quatre Conférences sur la nouvelle critique.* Turin:
Società Editrice Internazionale, 1968. A supplement to no.
34 (January-April 1968) of *Studi Francesi*; texts of lectures
given at the University of Turin in the Spring of 1968.

———. See also item 957.

4276. ———. *Situation de la critique. Actes du 1er Colloque International de la Critique Littéraire (Paris, 4-8 juin 1962).*
Paris: Syndicat des Critiques Littéraires, 1964.

4277. ———. *T.L.S. 5. Essays and Reviews from THE TIMES LITERARY
SUPPLEMENT, 1966.* London: Oxford University Press, 1967.

Apollonio, M. See item 3865.

4278. Balmas, Enea, ed. *Orientamenti sulla moderna critica.* Milan:
Ediz. La Viscontea, 1975.

4279. Bauer, George H. "John Simon, ed.: *Modern French Criticism.
       From Proust and Valery to Structuralism.*" *French Review*,
       46, no. 2 (December 1972), 424-425.

4280. Béguin, Albert. *Création et destinée. I. Essais de critique
       littéraire: l'âme romantique allemande. L'Expérience poétique.
       Critique de la critique.* Paris: Editions du Seuil, 1973.

4281. Belchior, Maria de Lourdes. "Crítica literária e estruturalismo."
       Bróteria, June 1968, pp. 790-805.

       Bellenger, Y. See item 973.

       Bersani, L. See item 982.

       Bettini, F., et al. See item 4353.

4282. Bonnefoy, Claude, ed. "Quand les critiques font la critique
       de la critique." *Arts*, n.s. no. 12 (15-21 December 1965),
       pp. 10-13.

4283. Bonzon, A. *La Nouvelle critique et Racine.* Paris: Editions
       A.-G. Nizet, 1970. See also items 989 and 2764.

4284. Borev, IUriĭ Borisovich. *Khudozhestvennyĭ obraz i struktura.*
       Moscow: Hayka, 1975.

4285. Brée, Germaine, and Eugenia Zimmerman. "Contemporary French
       Criticism." *Comparative Literature Studies*, 1, no. 3 (College
       Park, 1964), 175-196.

4286. Brody, Jules. "Critique littéraire et crise post-structuraliste:
       essai de consolation." *French Forum*, 1 (May 1976), 177-184.

4287. Bruch, Jean-Louis. "Une Nouvelle critique littéraire." *La Revue
       du Caire*, 18e année, no. 178 (March 1955), 164-168.

4288. Bruézière, Maurice. "La Nouvelle critique: Roland Barthes,
       Lucien Goldmann, Charles Mauron." *Enseignement du Français
       aux Etrangers*, 28e année, no. 225 (November-December 1976),
       2-4.

4289. Cabanes, Jean-Louis. *Critique littéraire et sciences humaines.*
       Toulouse: Privat, 1974. (Regard)

       The limits of structural poetics.

       Câmara, J.M., et al. See item 35.

       Clancier, A. See item 4874.

       Comoth, R. See item 2776.

4290. Cornea, P. "On Structuralism in Criticism and Literary History"
       (in Rumanian). *Revista de Istorie si Teorie Literara*, 16,
       no. 2 (1967), 169-179.

4291.   Corti, Maria, and Cesare Segré, eds. *I Metodi attuali della
        critica in Italia*. Turin: Ediz. Rai Radio Televisione Itali-
        ana, 1970.

        Corvez, M. See chapter 6 of items 49-51.

4292.   Creech, J. "Julia Kristeva's Bataille. Reading as Triumph."
        Diacritics. A Review of Contemporary Criticism, 5 (1975),
        62-68.

        Culler, J. See item 4836.

4293.   Daix, Pierre. *Nouvelle critique et art moderne, essai*. Paris:
        Editions du Seuil, 1968.

        Dehŏ, G. See item 59.

        Delbouille, P. See item 1034.

4294.   Dembo, L.S., ed. *Criticism. Speculative and Analytical Essays*.
        Madison: University of Wisconsin Press, 1968. See also item
        1031.

4295.   Demougin, Jacques. "Le Dossier de la Nouvelle Critique." *Les
        Nouvelles Littéraires*, 46e année, no. 2121 (25 April 1968),
        6-7.

4296.   Denat, Antoine. *Vu des antipodes. Synthèses critiques*. Paris:
        Didier, 1969.

4297.   Des Marchais, Gilles. *La Grammacritique: postulats préliminaires
        pour une théorie de la critique des textes de littérature*.
        Paris: Editions Leméac, 1965.

4298.   Detweiler, Robert. *Phenomenology and Structuralism as Literary-
        Critical Method*. (Semeia Supplement) Philadelphia: Fortress
        Press, 1976.

4299.   ———. *Story, Sign, and Self: Phenomenology and Structuralism
        as Literary-Critical Methods*. Philadelphia: Fortress Press,
        c. 1978. See item 1669.

        An overview of the two methods as they relate to each other
        and as they apply to major literary texts; also how such method-
        ologies can apply to the interpretation of literature from a
        theological perspective.

4300.   Donato, Eugenio U. "The Two Languages of Criticism." In *The
        Languages of Criticism and the Sciences of Man* (item 4324),
        pp. 89-97.

4301.   Doubrovsky, Serge. *Pourquoi la nouvelle critique. Critique et
        objectivité*. Paris: Mercure de France, 1966.

4302.   Dupeyron, G. "De Racine à Racine." *Europe*, 45, no. 453 (1967),
        66-74.

R. Picard's *Nouvelle critique ou nouvelle imposture* vs. R. Barthes, L. Goldmann and C. Mauron. A summary and evaluation of the debate among critics.

Eagleton, T. See item 4364.

4303. Fowlie, Wallace. *The French Critic 1594-1967*. Carbondale & Edwardsville: Southern Illinois University Press; London & Amsterdam: Feffer & Simons, 1968.

4304. Francq, H.G. "Polémique de la critique universitaire et de la nouvelle critique." *Culture*, 29 (Quebec, June 1968), 150-167.

4305. Genette, Gérard. "Structuralisme et critique littéraire." *L'Arc*, no. 26 (1965): issue on Lévi-Strauss. Rpt. in item 1066.

4306. ————. "Structuralism and Literary Criticism" (in Serbo-Croatian). *IZRAZ. Časopis za Književnu i Umetnicku Kritiku*, 17, no. 2-3 (1973), 139-156.

————. See also item 1066.

4307. ————. *Figures II*. Paris: Editions du Seuil, 1969.

4308. ————. *Figures III*. Paris: Editions du Seuil, 1972.

4308a. Graff, Gerald. "Who Killed Criticism?" *The American Scholar*, 49, no. 3 (Summer 1980), 337-355.

4309. Gras, Vernon W., ed. *European Literary Theory and Practice. From Existential Phenomenology to Structuralism*. New York: Dell Publishing Co., 1973.

Pertinent articles include: R. Jakobson: Two Aspects of Language: Metaphor and Metonymy; C. Lévi-Strauss: The Science of the Concrete; R. Barthes: The Structuralist Activity; C. Lévi-Strauss: The Structural Study of Myth; E.R. Leach: Genesis as Myth; R. Barthes: Racinian Man (excerpt).

4310. Grotzer, Peter. "Der Streit um die 'Nouvelle Critique.'" *Schweizer Monatshefte*, 47, no. 6 (September 1967), 597-610.

4311. Guyon, Françoise van Rossum. "Nouvelle critique, ancienne querelle." *Cahiers du Sud*, 61, no. 387-388 (April-June 1966), 319-325.

On Picard vs. Barthes.

4312. Hefner, R.W. "The *Tel Quel* Ideology: Material Practice Upon Material Practice." *Sub-stance*, no. 8 (1974), pp. 127-138.

4313. Huffman, Claire. "Structuralist Criticism and the Interpretation of Montale." *Modern Language Review*, 72 (April 1977), 322-334.

4314.   Ingwersen, Niels. "Impact of Structuralism on Danish Criticism."
        Books Abroad, 49 (Spring 1975), 221-226.

4315.   Johnson, R.E. "Structuralism and the Reading of Contemporary
        Fiction." *Soundings*, 58, no. 2 (Summer 1975), 281-306.

        Questions the structuralist might ask of a literary work.

4316.   Jones, Robert Emmet. *Panorama de la nouvelle critique en France:
        de Gaston Bachelard à Jean-Paul Weber*. Paris: Sedes, 1968.

        Chapter 4 is on the structuralist school.

4317.   Krieger, Murray, ed. *Northrop Frye in Modern Criticism*. New
        York: Columbia University Press, 1966.

4318.   ————, ed. *Contemporary Literature* (issue entitled "Directions
        for Criticism: Structuralism and its Alternatives"), 17, no.
        3 (Summer 1976). Rpt. as item 4319.

4319.   ————, and L.S. Dembo, eds. *Directions for Criticism: Struc-
        turalism and Its Alternatives*. Madison: University of Wiscon-
        sin Press, 1976, pp. 297-435. Rpts. item 4318.

4320.   ————. *Theory of Criticism: A Tradition and Its System*.
        Baltimore and London: The Johns Hopkins University Press,
        1976.

4321.   Lawall, Sarah N. "The Structuralist Controversy." *Contemporary
        Literature*, 12, no. 1 (Winter 1971), 128-131.

        On item 4325.

4322.   Le Sage, Laurent. *The French New Criticism: An Introduction
        and Sampler*. University Park and London: The Pennsylvania
        State University Press, 1967.

        ————. See also item 1123.

4323.   Lucas, F. "Problemas da crítica e do estruturalismo." *Abraxas*,
        1, no. 3 (1971), 251-260.

*4324. Macksey, Richard, and Eugenio Donato, eds. *The Languages of
        Criticism and the Sciences of Man: The Structuralist Contro-
        versy*. Baltimore and Oxford: Johns Hopkins Press, 1970. See
        item 4300.

4325.   ————, eds. *The Structuralist Controversy. The Languages of
        Criticism and the Sciences of Man*. Baltimore: Johns Hopkins
        Press, 1972. See item 4321.

4326.   ————, et al. *Los Lenguajes críticos y las ciencias del hombre.
        Controversia estructuralista*. Trans. José Manuel Lorca.
        Barcelona: Barral Editores, 1972.

4327.   ————, ed. *Velocities of Change: Critical Essays from MLN*.
        Baltimore: Johns Hopkins Press, 1974.

Malagoli, L. See item 138.

4328. Man, Paul de. "The Crisis of Contemporary Criticism." *Arion*,
6, no. 1 (1967), 38-58.

4329. ————. *Blindness and Insight: Essays in the Rhetoric of Contemporary Criticism*. New York: Oxford University Press, 1971.

4330. Montalbetti, Jean. "Une Critique de la critique." *Les Nouvelles
Littéraires*, no. 2019 (12 May 1966), p. 2.

On Barthes's *Critique et Vérité* and other works.

4331. Mosher, H.F. "The Structuralism of Gérard Genette." *Poetics*,
5, no. 1 (1976), 75-86.

On Genette's *Figures I*, *Figures II*, and *Figures III*.

4332. Nichols, Stephen G. Jr. "Remembrance of Things Recreated: Aspects of French New Criticism." *Contemporary Literature*, 11,
no. 2 (Spring 1970), 243-268.

Palomo, D. See item 1161.

4333. Ricardou, Jean, ed. *Les Chemins actuels de la critique*. Centre
Culturel International de Cerisy-la-Salle, 2 septembre-12
septembre 1966. Sous la direction de Georges Poulet. Paris:
Librairie Plon, 1967.

4334. Romani, Bruno. "Alcuni aspetti attuali della critica letteraria
francese." *Letteratura*, no. 82-83 (July-October 1966), pp.
71-79.

4335. Roudiez, Leon S. "*The Languages of Criticism and the Sciences
of Man: The Structuralist Controversy*. Edited by Richard
Macksey and Eugenio Donato." *Romanic Review*, 62, no. 4
(December 1971), 310-313.

4336. Said, Edward W. "*Abecedarium culturae*: Structuralism, Absence,
Writing." *Tri-Quarterly*, no. 20 (Winter 1971), pp. 33-71.
Rpt. in item 4338.

4337. Schober, Rita. *V zajatí jazyka: štrukturalizmus v súčasnej
francúzskej kritike*. Bratislava: Slov. spis., 1973. Originally
published as item 1223.

Schroeder, U. See item 645.

4338. Simon, John K., ed. *Modern French Criticism. From Proust and
Valéry to Structuralism*. Chicago-London: University of Chicago Press, 1972. Contains item 4336.

4339. Smithson, Isaiah. "Structuralism as a Method of Literary Criticism." *College English*, 37, no. 2 (October 1975), 145-159.

4340. Starobinski, Jean. "Considerations on the Present State of
       Literary Criticism." *Diogenes*, no. 74 (Summer 1971), pp. 57-
       88.

       Sub-stance. See item 4413a.

4341. Szabolcsi, Miklós. "Strukturalizmus, napi kritika és közönség
       Franciaországban." *Kritika*, 5 (Budapest, 1967), viii, 3-10.

4342. Timpanaro, Sebastiano. *The Freudian Slip. Psychoanalysis and
       Textual Criticism*. Trans. Kate Soper. Atlantic Highlands,
       N.J.: Humanities Press, 1976.

4343. Todorov, Tzvetan, comp. "Structuralism and Literary Criticism."
       In item 68, pp. 269-270. See also item 69. A bibliography.

4344. Vanni, Italo. "Critica e ricerca strutturale." *Nuova Antologia*,
       493, fasc. 1970 (February 1965), 197-201.

4345. Watkins, Evan. "Criticism and Method: Hirsch, Frye, Barthes."
       Soundings: An Interdisciplinary Journal, 58, no. 2 (Summer
       1975), 257-280. Rpt. in his *The Critical Act. Criticism and
       Community*. New Haven: Yale University Press, 1978, pp. 56-94.

       The importance of Saussure and linguistics for a structuralist
       understanding of literature is the peculiar result of one of
       his central insights, viz., that language is a system of dif-
       ferences, a result which transposes "to say" as an act of speech,
       parole, into an intelligible configuration of acoustic space.
       Things, like words, like myths, are intelligible insofar as
       they can be seen within a virtual relationship of implicatory
       differencing.

4346. Yon, André François. "Contemporary French Philosophical Liter-
       ary Criticism." *Dissertation Abstracts*, 20, no. 5 (November
       1959), 1798-1799. Pennsylvania State University dissertation.

       On Barthes and others.

MARXISM

4347. Agües, F. "Lo Lógico y lo histórico en la economía política clásica: un seudo-problema." *Teorema*, no. 6 (1972), pp. 81-92.

Airaksinen, T. See item 361.

4348. Aleksandrowicz, D. "Marxism and the Structural-Semiological Current in the Human Sciences" (in Polish). *Studia Filozoficzne*, 6 (1975), 93-114.

4349. Andreani, T. "Marxisme et anthropologie." *L'Homme et la Société*, no. 15 (1970), pp. 27-75. In the issue on "Marxisme et les sciences humaines."

Critique of anthropologico-humanistic and Freudo-Marxist perspectives.

Anonymous. See items 366 and 4084.

4350. ————. *Structuralisme et marxisme*. Paris: Union Générale d'Editions, 1970. Double volume no. 485 in the 10/18 collection. J.-M. Auzias is sometimes listed as editor. A collection of articles previously published in *Raison Présente*, 1967-1968.

Arenz, H., et al. See item 371.

Aron, R. See items 373-376.

Arvon, H. See item 377.

Auzias, J.-M. See item 4350 and chapter seven of items 11-14.

Badiou, A. See item 379.

Bastide, R. See item 3739.

Baum, H. See item 2761.

4351. Benoist, J.-M. *Marx est mort*. Paris: Gallimard, 1970. See item 4355.

4352. Berger, Allen H. "Structural and Eclectic Revisions of Marxist Strategy: A Cultural Materialist Critique." *Current Anthropology*, 17 (June 1976), 290-305. With discussion.

Bessonov, B. See item 3469b.

4353.   Bettini, Filippo, et al, eds. *Marxismo e strutturalismo nella critica letteraria italiana.* 2nd ed. Rome: La Nuova Sinistra, 1974.

4354.   Boboc, Al, and Nicolae Gogoneata. "Neue Elemente in der gegenwartigen nichtmarxistischen Philosophie: Probleme des Dialogs in der heutigen Philosophie." *Philosophie et Logique*, 21 (April–June 1977), 101–106.

Boisset, M. See item 4934.

Bonelli, G. See item 3880.

Bonte, P. See item 3743.

4355.   Bourdet, Y. "Quand l'araignée structuraliste croit voir en sa toile que 'Marx est mort.'" *L'Homme et la Société*, no. 17 (1970), pp. 297–307. See item 4351.

4356.   Broekman, Jan M. "Russisch formalisme, marxisme, strukturalisme." *Tijdschrift voor Filosofie*, 33, no. 1 (1971), 5–40.

4357.   ————. "Die Einheit von Theorie und Praxis als Problem von Marxismus, Phänomenologie und Strukturalismus." In *Phänomenologie und Marxismus. Band I: Konzepte und Methoden.* Eds. Bernhard Waldenfels, Jan M. Broekman and Ante Pažanin. Frankfurt am Main: Suhrkamp Verlag, 1977, pp. 159–177.

Busino, G. See item 5223.

4357a. Calinescu, M. "Marxism as a Work of Art: Post-Structuralist Readings of Marx." *Stanford French Review*, 3, no. 1 (1979), 123–135.

Câmara, J.M., et al. See item 35.

Cardoso, F.H. See item 399.

Cardoso, H. See item 400.

Cardoso e Cunha, T. See items 401–402.

4358.   Casiccia, A. "Leggi oggetive e nozione di 'limite' nel marxismo detto 'strutturalistico.'" *Critica Marxista*, 10, no. 2–3 (1972), 296–308.

4359.   Černy, J. "Marxist Dialectic and the Phenomenological Description of Structures" (in Czech). *Filosofický Časopis*, 17, no. 1 (1969), 105–113.

4360.   Chełstowski, B. "Structuralist Conceptions of Society" (in Polish). *Studia Filozoficzne*, 16, no. 5 (1972), 157–175.

4361. Clouscard, M. *L'Etre et le code. Le Procès de production d'un ensemble précapitaliste.* Paris-The Hague: Mouton, 1972.

Colucci, F. See item 2775.

4362. Cotroneo, Girolamo. "Il Marxismo fra storia e struttura." *Rivista di Studi Crociani,* 10 (April-June 1973), 184-191.

4363. Daix, Pierre. *Structuralisme et révolution culturelle.* Tournai-Paris: Casterman, 1971. (Mutations, Orientations, 14)

D'Amico, R. See item 57.

De George, R.T., et al. See item 58.

Delo. See item 61.

Diaz, C. See item 420.

4364. Eagleton, Terry. *Marxism and Literary Criticism.* London: Methuen & Co., Ltd., 1976.

Farkas, L. See item 4502.

Fekete, J. See item 4505.

Francovich, G. See items 79-80.

4365. Friedman, Jonathan. "Marxism, Structuralism and Vulgar Materialism." *Man,* 9, no. 3 (September 1974), 444-469.

Gabel, J. See item 438.

4366. Gimenez, M.E. "Structuralist Marxism on the Woman Question." *Science and Society,* 42 (Fall 1978), 301-323.

4367. Godelier, Maurice. *Rationalité et irrationalité en économie.* Paris: Maspero, 1969, 2 vols.

4368. ————, and Lucien Sève. *Marxismo e strutturalismo. Un Dibattito a due voci sui fondamenti delle scienze sociali.* Trans. M. Minerbi. Turin: G. Einaudi, 1970.

4369. ————. "Logique dialectique et analyse des structures. Réponse à Lucien Sève." *La Pensée,* no. 149 (1970), pp. 3-28.

Godelier responds to Sève's criticisms ("Méthode structurale et méthode dialectique," *La Pensée,* 1967) of his article in *Les Temps Modernes* (item 197).

4370. ————. "Marxisme, anthropologie et religion." In *Epistémologie et marxisme.* Paris: Union Générale d'Editions, 1972, pp. 209-265.

4371. ————. *Horizons, trajets marxistes en anthropologie.* Paris: Maspero, 1973.

4372.   ───────. "Vers une théorie marxiste des faits religieux."
         Lumière et Vie, 23, no. 117-118 (1974), 85-94.

4373.   ───────. *Funcionalismo, estructuralismo y marxismo*. Trans.
         Joaquín Jordá. Barcelona: Ed. Anagrama, 1976.

4374.   Grampa, Giuseppe. *Dialetica e struttura: dibattito sull'antro-
         pologia nel marxismo francese contemporaneo*. Milan: Vita e
         Pensiero, 1974.

4375.   Gulian, C.I. *Marxism și structuralism*. Bucarest: Editura
         Politică, 1976.

4375a.   Halečka, T. "'Structurology' and Marxist-Leninist Philosophy"
         (in Slovakian). *Filozofia*, 32, no. 4 (1977), 446-459.

         L'Homme et la Société. See item 4161.

4375b.   Horák, P. "Remarks on the Problem of a Marxist Analysis of
         Structuralism" (in Czech). *Filozofia*, 32, no. 3 (1977), 263-
         268.

4375c.   Hrušovský, I. "Category of Interaction" (in Slovakian). *Filozo-
         fia*, 32, no. 2 (1977), 166-172. Part of an issue on Marxism
         and Structuralism.

4376.   Institut für Marxistische Studien und Forschungen. *Erkenntnis-
         theorie*. Frankfurt am Main: I.M.S.F., 1972. (Marxismus
         Digest, 1972, 1)

4377.   *International Journal of Sociology*, 2, no. 2-3 (1972), 115-314:
         "Structuralism and Marxism: A Debate." Articles trans. from
         French and previously published in French journals.

4378.   Jaeggi, Urs Josef Viktor. *Theoretische Praxis: Probleme eines
         strukturalen Marxismus*. Frankfurt am Main: Suhrkamp, 1976.
         (Suhrkamp Taschenbuch Wissenschaft, 149)

4379.   Jannoud, Claude. "Marxismes imaginaires." *Le Figaro Littéraire*,
         no. 1191 (3-9 March 1969), p. 26.

4380.   Karbusický, Vladimir. *Widerspielungstheorie und Strukturalismus:
         zur Entstehungsgeschichte und Kritik d. marxist.-leninist.
         Ästhetik*. Munich: W. Fink, 1973.

4381.   Kelemen, J. "Strutturalismo, marxismo e sociologia della
         letteratura." *Revue Internationale de Sociologie*, 7, no. 2
         (Rome, 1971; appeared in 1973), 204-210.

4382.   Klawitzer, Andrzej. "On the Status of Historical Materialism."
         Revolutionary World, 14 (1975), 13-30.

4383.   Kosik, Karel. *Die Dialektik des Konkreten*. Trans. Marianne
         Hoffmann. Frankfurt am Main: Suhrkamp Verlag, 1973.

Maintains that efforts to interpret the historical-dialectical materialism of practice as if it were based on the anti-humanism of Foucault and Althusser have thus far been relatively unsuccessful.

Laclau, E. See item 486.

Lanţoş, S. See item 4607.

Locher, G.W. See items 4620-4621.

Lock, G. See item 506.

4384. Ludz, P.C. "Der Strukturbegriff in der marxistischen Gesell-schaftslehre." *Kölner Zeitschrift für Soziologie und Sozial-psychologie*, no. Sonderh. 16 (1972), pp. 419-447.

*4384a. Macherey, Pierre. *Pour une théorie de la production littéraire*. Paris: F. Maspero, 1970, c. 1966. (Théorie, no. 4)

4384b. ————. *A Theory of Literary Production*. Trans. Geoffrey Wall. London-Boston: Routledge and Kegan Paul, 1978.

Malagoli, L. See item 138.

Malawski, A. See item 4630.

Malet, A. See item 4631.

Martano, G. See item 4638.

Mehlman, J. See item 526.

4385. Mérei, Gyula. *Structuralisme, analyse structuraliste, marxisme*. Szeged, 1971, 61pp. (Acta Universitatis Szegediensis de Attila József nominatae. Acta Historica, t. 37)

Milanesi, V. See item 527.

4386. Miščevic, Nenad. *Marksizam i post-strukturalistička kretanja: Althusser, Deleuze, Foucault*. Rijeka: Marksistički centar, Centar za društvenu i uslužnu djelatnost mladih, 1975.

4387. Narskij, I.S. "Leninist Traditions of the Struggle for Materi-alism and the Dialectic" (in Russian). *Filosofskie Nauki*, 2 (1972), 23-33.

Nepi, P. See item 537.

Núñez Tenorio, J.R. See item 539.

4388. *La Pensée*, no. 135 (October 1967): issue entitled "Structuralisme et marxisme."

4389. Pervić, Muharem. "Marxism/Structuralism" (in Serbo-Croatian). *Delo*, 19, no. 12 (1973), 1411-1418.

4390.   ———, ed. *Marksizam: strukturalizam. Istorija, struktura.*
        Belgrade: Nolit, 1974, 629pp. (Biblioteka Argumenti)

4391.   Polizzi, Paolo. *La Filosofia come sintassi della praxis.* Palermo-
        São Paulo: I.L.A. Palma, 1975.

4392.   Pompeo Faracovi, Ornella. *Il Marxismo francese contemporaneo
        fra dialettica e struttura. (1945-1968).* Milan: Feltrinelli,
        1972. (I Fatti e le Idee, 277. Filosofia)

4393.   Poster, Mark. *Existential Marxism in Postwar France. From
        Sartre to Althusser.* Princeton, N.J.: Princeton University
        Press, 1977, c. 1975.

        Poulantzas, N. See items 555-556.

4394.   Puyau, Hermes Augusto. "El Hegelianismo de Marx." *Stromata*, 27
        (July-December 1971), 473-493.

4395.   Quintanilla, Miguel A. "Comentario a las obras de Eugenio
        Trías." *Teorema*, 3 (September 1971), 119-130.

4396.   Rancière, Jacques. *Lire le Capital III.* Paris: Maspero, 1973.
        (Petite Collection, 124)

4397.   Rubio, J. "Los Marxistas y el estructuralismo. ¿Método estruc-
        tural o método dialéctico?" *Estudio Agustiniano*, 5, no. 1
        (1970), 107-115.

        R. Garaudy's structuralist reading of Marx and the rejection
        of this method by L. Sève.

        Sahlins, M.D. See item 3793.

4398.   Saucerotte, A. "Foi, marxisme, structuralisme." *Raison Présente*,
        no. 41 (1977), pp. 51-66.

        On diachrony and synchrony; a structural analysis of the
        revolution of modern thought in Europe; the crisis of ancient
        civilization.

4399.   Schaff, Adam. "Au sujet de la tradition française de la VIe
        thèse de Marx sur Feuerbach." *L'Homme et la Société*, no. 19
        (1971), pp. 157-167.

        On the relationship between Marxism and structuralism.

4400.   ———. *Structuralisme et marxisme.* Trans. Claire Brendel.
        Paris: Editions de la Tête de Feuilles, 1974, 250pp.; Edi-
        tions Anthropos, 1974, 288pp.; Editions Anthropos, 1975,
        296pp. Originally published in Polish under the title of
        Strukturalizm i marksizm.

4401.   ———. *Strukturalismus und Marxismus: Essays.* Trans. Witold
        Leder and Miroslaw Moczulski. Vienna: Europa-Verlag, 1974.

4402. ————. *Marxismo, strutturalismo e il metodo della scienze.*
       Trans. T. De Tito. Milan: Feltrinelli, 1976, 222pp. (SC/10,
       70)

*4403. Sebag, Lucien. *Marxisme et structuralisme.* Paris: Payot, 1964,
       1967.

4404. ————. "Marxisme et structuralisme." *La Quinzaine Littéraire,*
       no. 29 (1-15 June 1967), p. 23.

4405. ————. *Marxismo y estructuralismo.* Trans. Ignacio Romero de
       Solís. Madrid: Siglo Veintiuno de España, 1969, 273pp. 2nd
       ed. 1972. (Teoría y Crítica)

4406. ————. *Marxisme i estructuralisme.* Trans. Jordi Freixas.
       Barcelona: Edicions 62, 1970, 238pp. (Llibres a l'Abast, 84)

4407. ————. *Marximus und Strukturalismus.* Trans. Hans Naumann.
       Frankfurt: Suhrkamp, 1970.

4408. ————. *Marxismo e strutturalismo.* Trans. M. Vitta. Milan:
       Feltrinelli, 1972. Trans. of 1967 edition.

       Senokosov, Y.P. See item 4769.

4409. Sève, Lucien. "Réponse à Maurice Godelier." *La Pensée,* no. 149
       (1970), pp. 29-50.

       The structuralist interpretation of Marxism alters it pro-
       foundly.

4410. Siemek, M.J. "Marxism and the Hermeneutic Tradition." *Dialectics
       and Humanism. The Polish Philosophical Quarterly,* 2, no. 4
       (1975), 87-103.

4411. Simonis, Yvan. "Marxisme et structuralisme." *Frères du Monde,*
       45 (Bordeaux, 1967), 8-35.

4412. Sirácky, A. "Marxizmus a Štrukturalizmus." *Filozofia,* 32, no.
       1 (1977), 7-32.

       The origins, sources and characteristics of structuralism;
       structuralism in ethnology and linguistics; structural and
       systemic analysis; the critique of Marxism via Marxist-Lenin-
       ist propositions.

       Šiškin, A.F., et al. See item 4774.

4413. Souyri, P. *Le Marxisme après Marx.* Paris: Flammarion, 1970,
       127pp.

4413a. *Sub-stance,* 5, no. 15 (February 1977): issue entitled "Socio-
       criticism."

       Les Temps Modernes. See item 197, article 4.

Timpanaro, S. See items 4791-4792.

Topolski, J. See item 4795.

4414. Trías, Eugenio, et al. *Estructuralismo y marxismo*. Trans.
Antonio González Valiente. Barcelona: Ed. Martínez Roca,
1969, 1977 (5th ed.)

Van Baal, J. See item 3812.

4415. Vancourt, R. "Les Difficultés doctrinales du marxisme. Marxisme
et structuralisme. (A propos d'ouvrages récents.)" *Mélanges
de Science Religieuse*, 28, no. 1 (March 1971), 27-56.

What is the nature of Marxism (technique, science, other)?
Current controversies within Marxism, including a discussion
of Althusser and structuralism.

Vaquero, P. See item 665.

4416. Veltmeyer, H. "Towards an Assessment of the Structuralist Inter-
rogation of Marx: Claude Lévi-Strauss and Louis Althusser."
Science and Society, 38, no. 4 (Winter 1974-1975), 385-421.

Waldenfels, B. See item 4815.

4417. Zelený, J. "Critique du structuralisme." *Filosofický Časopis*,
no. 2 (Prague, 1976), pp. 240-249.

4418. Zimmerman, M. "Polarities and Contradictions: Theoretical Bases
of the Marxist-Structuralist Encounter." *New German Critique:
An Interdisciplinary Journal of German Studies*, no. 7 (1976),
pp. 69-90.

Marxism vs. Structuralism from a Marxist viewpoint.

PHILOSOPHY

4419. Abellio, Raymond. *La Structure absolue: essai de phénoménologie génétique*. Paris: Gallimard, 1965.

4420. Agoglia, R.M. "Problemas y proposiciones metodológicos (Estructuralismo, dialéctica e historicidad)." *Revista de Filosofía*, no. 21 (Argentina, 1969), pp. 35-51.

4421. Allard, G.-H. "Le *Contra Gentiles* et le modèle rhétorique." *Laval Théologique et Philosophique*, 30, no. 3 (1974), 237-250.

4422. Allen, David Gordon. "The Phenomenological Aesthetic of Mikel Dufrenne as a Critical Tool for Dramatic Literature." *Dissertation Abstracts International*, 37, no. 5 (November 1976), 2935-2936-A. University of Iowa dissertation.

4423. Alston, William P. "Philosophical Analysis and Structural Linguistics." *The Journal of Philosophy*, 59 (November 1962), 709-719.

A comparison-contrast between what Gilbert Ryle does in the *Concept of Mind* and what contemporary linguists do leads Alston to the conclusion that while the two approaches cannot be assimilated, the procedures and results of structural linguistics may nevertheless be of real value to the philosopher.

4424. Alvar, Manuel. *Estructuralismo, geografía lingüística y dialectología actual*. Madrid: Gredos, 1969.

Améry, F. See item 5193.

4425. Améry, Jean. "Bericht über den 'Gauchismus.'" *Merkur*, 29, no. 3 (1975), 271-279.

4426. Anonymous. "Problems of Philosophy 1969." *Voprosy Filosofii*, 23, no. 1 (1969), 3-10.

A critical analysis of the most influential methodological approaches to historical and social research: psychoanalysis, French structuralism, phenomenology, in contemporary philosophy and sociology.

4427. ———. *Strutturalismo filosofico*. Atti del XIV Convegno di assistenti universitari di filosofia tenuto a Padova nel 1969. Centro di studi filosofici di Gallarate. Padua: Gregoriana, 1970.

Apostel, Léo. See item 8.

4428.   Aspelin, Kurt, and Tomas Gerholm, comp. *Vetenskap som kritik.*
        En Introduktion till Frankfurtskolans aktuella positioner.
        Stockholm: PAN/Norstedt, 1974.

*4429. Aubenque, Pierre. "Sprache, Strukturen, Gesellschaft. Kritische
        Bemerkungen zum französischen Strukturalismus." *Philosophische*
        Perspectiven, 2 (1970), 9-25.

4430.   ————. "Langage, structures, société. Remarques sur le struc-
        turalisme." *Archives de Philosophie*, 34 (July-September 1971),
        353-371. Summary, p. 353.

4431.   Autonomova, Nataliĩa Sergevna. *Filosofskie problemy strukturnego*
        analiza v gumanitarnykh naukakh. Moscow: Hayka, 1977.

        Bader, G. See item 4921.

4432.   Bakker, Reinout. "Om de mens." *Tijdschrift voor Filosofie,*
        32 (December 1970), 701-720.

4433.   ————. "Geschiedenis tussen struktuur en evenement." *Tijd-*
        schrift voor Filosofie, 38 (June 1976), 304-310.

        Baltheiser, K. See item 2072.

        Bamberg, M. See item 4922.

4434.   Banoni, Andrea. *Fenomenologia e estruturalismo.* Trans. João
        Paulo Monteiro. São Paulo: Perspectiva, 1975.

4435.   Barthélémy-Madaule, M., et al. "Pour la philosophie." *La*
        Nouvelle Critique, no. 84 (1975), pp. 23-32.

4435a. Bauch, Jost. "Reflexionen zur Destruktion der teleogischen
        Universalgeschichte durch den Strukturalismus und die krit-
        ische Theorie." *Archiv für Rechts und Sozialphilosophie*, 65
        (1979), 81-103.

        By rejecting Hegel's concept of "teleological universal
        history," structuralists like Althusser and Foucault have also
        deprived themselves of a useful tool of societal analysis.

4436.   Belaval, Yvon. "Continu et discontinu en histoire de la philo-
        sophie." *Revue de l'Université de Bruxelles*, no. 3-4 (1973),
        pp. 343-352.

4437.   ————, ed. *Histoire de la philosophie. III. Du XIXe siècle à*
        nos jours. Paris: Gallimard, 1974.

4438.   Bellu, N. "Value as a Method of Structural Conception in Ethical
        Research" (in Rumanian). *Revista de Filozofie*, 14, no. 6
        (1967), 637-646.

4439. Blystone, Jasper. "Is Cusanus the Father of Structuralism?" *Philosophy Today*, 16, no. 4 (Winter 1972), 296-305.

On abandoning substantialism for structuralism.

4440. Bogliolo, H. *Pour une anthropologie philosophique. Origine et fin de l'homme*. Lille: Service de Reproduction des Thèses, Université de Lille III, 1974. Thesis presented 14 December 1973.

4440a. Bollnow, Otto Friedrich. "Paul Ricoeur und die Probleme der Hermeneutik." *Zeitschrift für Philosophische Forschung*, 30 (April-June 1976), 167-189.

Bon, S.M. See item 3741.

4441. Bonelli, Guido. "La Critica strutturalista." *Rivista di Studi Crociani*, 7 (October-December 1970), 391-398.

4442. Borev, ĨUriĩ Borisovich. *Teorii, shkoly, kon͡tsep͡tsii*. Moscow: Hayka, 1975.

4443. Boudon, Raymond. "Le Structuralisme." In *Contemporary Philosophy. A Survey. Vol. III: Metaphysics, Phenomenology, Language and Structure*. Ed. Raymond Klibansky. Florence: La Nuova Italia, 1969, pp. 296-302.

4444. Bozonis, George A. "Platonisme et structuralisme." *Diotima*, 3 (1975), 151-156.

4445. Bradie, Michael P. "Development of Russell's Structural Postulates." *Philosophy of Science*, 44 (September 1977), 441-463.

Brandt, P.A. See items 393 and 394.

4446. Broekman, Jan M. "A Structuralist Approach to the Philosophy of Law." *Proceedings of the American Catholic Philosophical Association*, 49 (1975), 37-48.

————. See also item 4357.

4447. Brown, Patrick Louis. "Epistemology and Method: Althusser, Foucault, Derrida." *Cultural Hermeneutics*, 3, no. 2 (August 1975), 147-162.

4448. ————. "Epistemology and the Language of Esthetics." *Dissertation Abstracts International*, 37, no. 12 (June 1977), 7785-A. University of Colorado dissertation.

4449. Bukowski, J. "Structuralism" (in Polish). *Więz*, 132, no. 4 (1969), 74-86.

4450. Bulhof, Ilse N. "Structure and Change in Wilhelm Dilthey's Philosophy of History." *History and Theory*, 15, no. 1 (1976), 21-32.

Câmara, J.M., et al. See item 35.

4451.   Carrillo, Victor Li. "Las Tres lingüísticas." *Revista Venezolana de Filosofía*, 1976, pp. 53-84.

4452.   Casañas, Mario. "El Estructuralismo filosófico." *Aportes*, no. 1 (San Salvador, 1976), pp. 5-8.

4453.   Castañeda, Hector-Neri. "Thinking and the Structure of the World. Discours d'ontologie." *Philosophia*, 4 (Ramat-Gan, Israel, 1974), pp. 3-40.

Caws, Peter. See item 39.

4454.   ———. "Coherence, System and Structure." *Idealistic Studies. An International Philosophy Journal*, 4 (January 1974), 2-17.

4455.   Cencillo, L. *Historia de la reflexión. T. II: De Ockham a Lévi-Strauss*. 2nd corrected and enlarged edition of *Historia de los sistemas filosóficos*. Madrid: Seminario de Historia de los Sistemas de la Universidad Complutense, 1972.

4456.   Centre International de Synthèse. *Notion de structure et structures de la connaissance*. (XXe Semaine de Synthèse, 18-27 April 1956) Paris: Editions Albin Michel, 1957.

4457.   Centro di Studi Filosofici Cristiani di Gallarate. *Struttura-lismo filosofico*. Padua: Gregoriana, 1970.

Černý, J. See item 4359.

4458.   Chafe, Wallace L. *Meaning and the Structure of Language*. Chicago: University of Chicago Press, 1970.

Chalumeau, J.-L. See item 2109.

4459.   Charron, Gyslain. "Du langage. Confrontation d'une approche structurale et d'une approche phénoménologique: A. Martinet et M. Merleau-Ponty." Doctoral dissertation, Institut Supérieur de Philosophie, Université Catholique de Louvain, 22 May 1969, reported in *Revue Philosophique de Louvain*, tome 67, 3e série, no. 96 (November 1969), 686-687.

4460.   ———. "Du langage: la linguistique de Martinet et la phéno-ménologie de Merleau-Ponty." *Revue de l'Université d'Ottawa*, 40 (April-June 1970), 260-284.

4461.   ———. "Linguistique, philosophie du langage et épistémologie (réponse à P. Martin)." *Philosophiques*, 3 (October 1976), 261-278.

4462.   Cheţan, Octavian. "L'Humanisme et l'anthropologie philosophique." *Revue Roumaine des Sciences Sociales. Série de Philosophie et Logique*, 13, no. 1 (1969), 83-88.

A critique of structuralist anti-humanism from a Marxist viewpoint.

4463. ⸻. "Le Modèle linguistique et ses avatars." *Philosophie et Logique*, 15 (1971), 283-288.

⸻. See also item 3907.

4464. Chiari, Joseph. *Twentieth-Century French Thought: From Bergson to Lévi-Strauss*. Staten Island, N.Y.: Gordian Press; London: Paul Elek, 1975.

Chapter ten deals with Lévi-Strauss, Althusser and Foucault.

Chomsky, N. See items 4106-4107.

4465. ⸻, and Michel Foucault. *La Naturaleza humana. ¿Justicia o poder?* Valencia: Departamento de Lógica y Filosofía de la Ciencia, Universidad de Valencia, 1976, 81pp.

If the nature of an individual is an a priori source of knowledge for Chomsky, the individual doesn't count with regard to knowledge for Foucault. For Chomsky, social revolution is the creation of a more just society; Foucault sees it as the destruction of established power.

4466. Chvatík, Květoslav. "Philosophical Problems of Structuralist Esthetics" (in Czech). *Česká Literatura*, no. 5 (1968), pp. 589-593.

4467. ⸻. "Philosophical Problems of Structuralist Esthetics" (in Czech). *Filosofický Časopis*, 17, no. 1 (1969), 86-89.

4468. Cohen, J. "Reflections on the Structure of Mind." *Scientia. An International Review of Scientific Synthesis*, 109 (1974), 403-425.

4468a. Colin, P. "Chronique de philosophie: les 'nouveaux philosophes. Leur rapport au marxisme et au structuralisme." *Revue des Sciences Philosophiques et Théologiques*, 63, no. 1 (1979), 109-124.

4469. Commers, Ronald. "Remarks on the Comparison between Exchange and Communication." *Philosophica*, 17 (1976), 175-195.

4470. Conn, Walter E. "Objectivity--A Developmental and Structural Analysis: The Epistemologies of Jean Piaget and Bernard Lonergan." *Dialectica*, 30 (1976), 197-221.

4471. Cordt, Dieter, et al. "Struktur-Strukturalismus." *Deutsche Zeitschrift für Philosophie*, 24 (1976), 1248-1253.

4472. Cornu, M. "Pour l'homme." *Revue de Théologie et de Philosophie*, no. 2 (1969), pp. 118-121.

An examination of Dufrenne's book of same title, item 4493.

4473. Corvez, M. "Bulletin de philosophie: Bergson. Blondel. Sciences humaines, structuralisme." *Revue Thomiste*, 70, no. 2 (1970), 335-343.

Review of books on structuralism by Parain-Vial, Ducrot et
al., and Fages.

4474.   Cottier, G. M.-M. "Réflexions sur le structuralisme." *Nova et
        Vetera*, 46, no. 2 (Geneva, 1971), 97-117.

4475.   Cruz Cruz, Juan. *Filosofía de la estructura*. Pamplona: Univer-
        sidad de Navarra, 1967. 2nd ed. 1974.

4476.   ————. "Estructura y totalidad." *Estudios Filosóficos*, 21
        (May-August 1972), 339-375.

4477.   ————. "Estructura y orden." *Estudios Filosóficos*, 23 (Janu-
        ary-April 1974), 47-68.

        Cuisenier, Jean. See item 5231.

4478.   ————. "Le Structuralisme." In *La Philosophie. De Hegel à
        Foucault. Du marxisme à la phénoménologie*. Ed. André Noiray.
        Paris: Culture, Art, Loisirs; Tournai: Académie du Livre,
        1969, pp. 460-489.

*4479. Culler, Jonathan. "Phenomenology and Structuralism." *Human
        Context*, 5 (Spring 1973), 35-41.

4480.   ————. "Phénoménologie et structuralisme." *Human Context*, 5
        (Spring 1973), 42-50.

4481.   Dagenais, James J. "The Structuralist Model," chapter 6 in his
        *Models of Man: A Phenomenological Critique of Some Paradigms
        in the Human Sciences*. The Hague: Martinus Nijhoff, 1972.

4482.   Daly, James. "Merleau-Ponty: A Bridge between Phenomenology
        and Structuralism." *The Journal of the British Society for
        Phenomenology*, 2 (October 1971), 53-58.

4483.   Deleuze, Gilles. *Logique du sens*. Paris: Editions de Minuit,
        1969.

4484.   De Marneffe, J. "Cultural Relativism." *Indian Philosophical
        Quarterly*, 1 (July 1974), 313-323.

4485.   Deneys, H., et al. "La Philosophie française contemporaine entre
        les sciences humaines et l'anarchie." *Revue de l'Enseignement
        Philosophique*, 26, no. 3 (1975-1976), 33-36.

        Derrida, Jacques. "'Genesis and Structure' and Phenomenology."
        In his *Writing and Difference* (item 1616a), pp. 154-168.

        De Sousa, A.V. See item 3517.

4486.   Díaz, Carlos. "Epistemología genética y persona." *Revista
        Venozolana de Filosofia*, 1975, pp. 57-74.

4487. Dima, T. "The Knowledge of 'Form' in Bacon" (in Rumanian). *Analele Ştiinţifice ale Universităţii "Al. I. Cuza" din Iaşi, Secţiunea III b, Ştinţe Filozofice*, 16 (1970), 77-82.

After a comparison with Aristotle, it is shown that Bacon's form has the value which characterizes the contemporary notion of structure.

4488. Di Napoli, Giovanni. "Uomo e struttura in F. Nemo e G.M. Benoist." *Rivista di Filosofia Neo-Scolastica*, 69, no. 4 (October-December 1977), 659-696.

4489. Dixon, John W., Jr. "Outline of a Theory of Structure." *Cross Currents*, 22 (Summer-Fall 1972), 257-280.

Domin, G., et al. See item 64.

4490. Dreyfus, G. "La Méthode structurale et le 'Spinoza' de Martial Gueroult." *L'Age de la Science*, no. 3 (1969), pp. 240-275.

4491. Dufrenne, Mikel. "Structure et sens." *Revue d'Esthetique*, 20 (1967), 1-16.

4492. ————. "La Philosophie du néo-positivisme." *Esprit*, 35, no. 360 (May 1967), 781-800.

4493. ————. *Pour l'homme*. Paris: Editions du Seuil, 1968.

A scathing critique of the structuralist view of man.

4494. ————. "Structuralism and Humanism." Trans. Edward S. Casey. In *Patterns of the Life World. Essays in Honor of John Wild*. Ed. James M. Edie et al. Evanston, Ill.: Northwestern University Press, 1970, pp. 290-297.

————. See also item 3702.

4495. Duval, R. "Présence et solitude: la question de l'être et le destin de l'homme." *Revue des Sciences Philosophiques et Théologiques*, 57, no. 3 (1973), 377-396.

4496. Dyankov, B. "On the Structural Approach in the Demonstration that the Principal Tendencies of Mathematical Logic are Well-Founded" (in Bulgarian). *Izvestija na Instituta Filosofija*, 18 (1969), 35-58. An English summary follows the article.

4497. Edie, J.M. "Was Merleau-Ponty a Structuralist?" *Semiotica*, 4, no. 4 (1971), 297-323.

4497a. Englander, Judith. "The Study of Nationalism: A Methodological Inquiry." *Reason Papers*, Winter 1978, pp. 33-47.

Esbroeck, M. van. See item 4969.

4498. Eschbach, Gérard. *Le Clos et l'ouvert. Essai sur la condition pascale de l'être*. Neuchâtel: Editions de la Baconnière, distributed by Payot: Paris-Lausanne, 1972.

Esper, E.A. See item 4133.

4498a. Esser, P.H. "On Structure and Structuralism." *Methodology and Science*, 12 (1979), 68-80.

A brief review of the philosophical doctrines which led to what is now known as structuralism. Because of the common universal tendencies in the various forms of structuralism, *structure* in all fields of science has a great impact on contemporary philosophy.

Estanqueiro Rocha, A. See item 429.

4499. Estebanez, Emilio G. "Un Libro espagnol de investigacion basica: 'Psicologia cientifica y etica actuel' del Professor Enrique Lopez Castellon." *Estudios Filosoficos*, 21 (May-August 1972), 443-448.

Esteva-Fabregat, C. See item 3755.

Fages, J.-B. See item 77.

4500. Faggin, Giuseppe. *Storia della filosofia. Ad uso dei licei classici. Vol. III. Dal romanticismo allo strutturalismo.* 3rd enlarged revised ed. Milan: Principato, 1970.

4501. Fanizza, Franco. "Lo Scientifico nell'umano." *Giornale Critico della Filosofia Italiana*, 1 (April-June 1970), 271-297.

4502. Farkas, László. *Egzisztencializmus, strukturalizmus, marxizálás.* Budapest: Kossuth Könyvkiadó, 1972.

4503. Faucci, Dario. "Vico, Rousseau, Lévi-Strauss." *Bollettino del Centro di Studi Vichiani* (issue entitled "Per l'edizione nazionale di Vico"), 3 (1973), 200-202.

4504. Feibleman, J.K. "Human Nature as Recent Science Sees It." *The Southwestern Journal of Philosophy*, 4, no. 1 (1973), 7-19.

Structuralism as a new version of materialism.

4505. Fekete, John. "Northrop Frye: Parameters of Mythological Structuralism." *Telos*, 27 (Spring 1976), 40-60.

A Marxist critique of Frye.

4506. Festini, Heda. "G.B. Vico et le problème du temps." *Archives de Philosophie*, 40 (April-June 1977), 215-228.

For Vico, who is a forerunner of modern conceptions, human existence is a process of structuration. To master his own history, man must synthesize his past with his future.

Filippov, L.I. See item 4878.

4507. *Filosofický Časopis*, 17, no. 1 (1969). See items 4359, 4467, 4508, 4570, 4181, 4584, 5266, 5272, 4673, 4796, 4785, 4800, 4076, and 225.

4508. Fischer, J.L. "Structural Philosophy, Structuralism, and the Dialectic" (in Czech). *Filosofický Časopis*, 17, no. 1 (1969), 13-27.

4509. Fisher, John B. "The Concept of Structure in Freud, Lévi-Strauss and Chomsky." *Philosophy Research Archives*, 1, no. 1023, 1975.

4510. Flam, Léopold. *La Philosophie au tournant de notre temps*. Brussels: Presses Universitaires de Bruxelles, 1970.

4511. ————. *Grote stromingen van de filosofie. Eenzaamheid en gemeenschap van Thales tot Claude Lévi-Strauss*. 2 vols. Brussels: Uitgaven V.U.B., 1972.

Flynn, B.C. See item 2152.

4511a. Foda, Hashem. "The Structuralist Dream: A Review of Philip Pettit: *The Concept of Structuralism* [and other works]." *Sub-stance*, no. 20 (Fall 1978), pp. 131-133.

4512. Folkierska, A. "'Mental Structure'--C. Lévi-Strauss's Proposition about the Conception of Man" (in Polish). *Studia Filozoficzne*, 18, no. 12 (1974), 75-87.

4513. Fontaine-De Visscher, Luce. "Héraclite et la linguistique structuraliste." In *"La Communication." Actes du XVe Congrès de l'Association des Sociétés de Philosophie de Langue Française--Pensée antique et communication*. Montreal: Editions Montmorency, 1971, pp. 106-109.

4514. ————. "La Phénoménologie et le structuralisme," chapter 5 of her *Phénomène ou structure? Essai sur le langage chez Merleau-Ponty*. Brussels: Publications des Facultés Universitaires Saint-Louis, 1974, pp. 63-79.

4515. Fontan, P. "Structuralisme et philosophie." *Bulletin de Littérature Ecclésiastique*, 3 (1973), 203-212.

4516. Forni, Guglielmo. *Il Soggetto e la storia*. Bologna: Il Mulino, 1972.

On phenomenology and structuralism.

4517. Free, William J. "Structuralism, Literature, and Tacit Knowledge." *Journal of Aesthetic Education*, 8 (October 1974), 65-74.

4518. Friedman, W. "Quelques réflexions sur l'état de la philosophie du droit contemporain." *Archives de Philosophie du Droit*, 15 (1970), 197-214.

Structuralism and philosophy of law.

4519. Frosini, Vittorio. "Topica e teoria generale del diritto." *Rivista Internazionale di Filosofia del Diritto*, 48 (January-March 1971), 26-33.

4520. Funt, David Paul. "The Structuralist Debate." *The Hudson Review*,
       22, no. 4 (Winter 1969-1970), 623-646.

       On Althusser, Barthes, Foucault, Lévi-Strauss; with a critique
       by Sartre, Dufrenne and Ricoeur.

       Gallas, H., et al. See item 3935.

4521. Galzigna, M. "A proposito di strutturalismo e storicismo."
       Rivista Critica di Storia della Filosofia, 26, no. 2 (1971),
       162-167.

       Gandillac, M.P. de, et al. See items 88-89.

       Gandy, R. See item 90.

4522. Garaudy, Roger. "Structuralisme et 'mort de l'homme.'" *La
       Pensée*, no. 135 (1967), pp. 107-124.

4523. ————. "Strukturalismus und der 'Tod des Menschen.'" *Marxismus
       in unserer Zeit*, 1968, pp. 64-78.

*4524. ————. *Perspectivas del hombre. Existencialismo, pensamiento
       católico, estructuralismo, marxismo*. Enlarged updated ed.
       Trans. Enrique Molina Campos. Barcelona: Fontanella, 1970.

4525. ————. *Prospettive dell'uomo. Esistenzialismo, cattolicesimo,
       strutturalismo, marxismo*. Trans. F. Bertino, S. Stra. Turin:
       Borla, 1972.

4526. Garcia Canclini, N. "Merleau-Ponty leído después del estructur-
       alismo." In *Temas de filosofía contemporánea. II° Congreso
       nacional de filosofía*. Buenos Aires: Editorial Sudamericana,
       1971.

4527. Gardner, Howard. *The Quest for Mind: Piaget, Lévi-Strauss, and
       the Structuralist Movement*. New York: Alfred A. Knopf, 1973
       (c. 1972); Vintage Books, 1974; London: Coventure, 1975;
       Quartet Books, 1976. Excerpted in *Psychology Today*, 7, no. 1
       (June 1973), 59-62, 104.

       Contains: I. A New Approach to the Social Sciences. (1) A
       New Development in the Social Sciences; (2) The French Intellec-
       tual Tradition and the Roots of Structuralism: A Structural-
       Developmental Analysis; II. The Architects of Structuralism.
       (3) Piaget; (4) Lévi-Strauss; III. An Assessment of Structural-
       ism: Problems and Prospects. (5) The Relationship Between Two
       Varieties of Structuralism; (6) Structuralism as a World-View.

4528. ————. *Riscoperta del pensiero e movimento strutturalista.
       Piaget e Lévi-Strauss*. Rome: A. Armando, 1974.

*4529. ————. "Structure and Development." *Human Context*, 5 (Spring
       1973), 50-67.

4530. ———. "Structure et développement." *Human Context*, 5, no. 1
         (Spring 1973), 68-86.

         The similarities and differences between structural analysis
         in anthropology (Lévi-Strauss) and developmental psychology
         (Piaget) suggest complementarity in the approach to the common
         problem: how to describe human thought. It is argued that struc-
         tural linguistics can align the approaches which stress sensory
         aspects in relation to specific cultural codes and those which
         focus on active, organizing aspects in relation to objects and
         persons.

4531. Garvin, Harry R., ed. *Phenomenology, Structuralism, Semiology*.
         Lewisburg, Pa.: Bucknell University Press, 1976.

4532. Gauthier, Yvon. "La Notion théorétique de structure." *Dialectica*,
         23 (1969), 217-227.

4533. ———. "Constructivisme et structuralisme dans les fondements
         des mathématiques." *Philosophiques*, 1 (Montreal, April 1974),
         83-105.

4534. Gedö, A. "System, Struktur, philosophischer Strukturalismus."
         Hegel-Jahrbuch ("Referate des Antwerpener Hegel-Kongresses"),
         p. vol (dated 1973, appeared 1974), 118-126.

         Structuralism as anti-Hegelian.

4535. Gerbault, René. *Pourquoi je ne suis pas matérialiste. Petite
         introduction à une philosophie structurelle. Essai*. Liège:
         D.U.P., 1973.

         Includes critique of Lacan and Foucault.

4536. Gerber, Rudolph J. "Structuralism in France." *Modern Schoolman*,
         46 (May 1969), 301-314.

4537. Giannini, G. "Filosofia e antifilosofia." *Aquinas*, 12, no. 1
         (1969), 182-186.

         Structuralism and dialectic.

4538. ———. "Filosofia e religione in prospettiva strutturalista."
         Aquinas, 18, no. 1 (1975), 5-27.

         An attempt at synthesizing these two disciplines by a struc-
         turalist method reconciling the transcendental viewpoint and
         other viewpoints.

4538a. Gillan, Garth. "Interrogative Thought: Merleau-Ponty and the
         Degree Zero of Being." *Sub-stance*, 3, no. 7 (Fall 1973), 65-
         76.

4539. Gillet-Stern, Suzanne. "French Philosophy over the Last Decade."
         The Journal of the British Society for Phenomenology, 3
         (January 1972), 3-10.

4539a. Goćkowski, Janusz. "Pluralisme dans la pratique de l'histoire de la science." *Organon*, 12-13 (1976-1977), 21-38.

4540. Goddard, David. "Philosophy and Structuralism." *Philosophy of the Social Sciences*, 5, no. 2 (June 1975), 103-123.

4541. Gomes, F. Soares. "Estruturalismo, que filosofia?" *Revista Portuguesa de Filosofia*, 31 (July-September 1975), 225-252.

4542. ————. "Estruturalismo: da interioridade ao saber." *Revista Portuguesa de Filosofia*, 32, no. 2 (1976), 143-170.

4543. Gonseth, Ferdinand. "La Philosophie ouverte, terrain d'accueil du structuralisme." *Cahiers Internationaux de Symbolisme*, no. 17-18 (1969), pp. 39-71.

   The complete reduction of the discursive to the formal doesn't seem possible; but there is, within structuralism, a much more profound insight into the exemplary value of language.

4544. González, José Emilio. "Estructuralismo y filosofía." *Diálogos*, 6, no. 17 (1966), 93-112.

4545. Goodman, Nelson. *The Structure of Appearance*. 2nd ed., rev. and reset. Dordrecht-Boston: D. Reidel, 1977. (Boston Studies in the Philosophy of Science, v. 53; Synthese Library, v. 107)

4546. Görtz, H.-J. "Zur Struktur Eichendorffscher Dichtung." *Philosophisches Jahrbuch*, 81, no. 1 (1974), 105-120.

   Grampa, G. See item 4374.

4547. Granger, Gilles, et al. *Estructuralismo y epistemología*. Buenos Aires: Nueva Visión, 1970.

4548. Grava, Arnolds. *A Structural Inquiry into the Symbolic Representation of Ideas*. The Hague: Mouton; New York: The Humanities Press, 1969.

4549. Greckij, M.N. "Structuralism: Essential Problems and Levels of Solution (Critical Overview)" (in Russian). *Filosofskie Nauki*, no. 4 (1974), pp. 53-64.

4550. Grisoni, Dominique, ed. *Châtelet, Derrida, Foucault, Lyotard, Serres. Politiques de la philosophie*. Paris: B. Grasset, 1976.

   Gritti, J., et al. See item 96.

4551. Guala, Chito. *Momenti analitici del concetto di struttura. Malinowski, Radcliffe-Brown, Durkheim, Mauss, Lévi-Strauss*. Turin: G. Giappichelli, 1973.

4552. Guccione Monroy, Nino. *Il Sapere in crisi*. Palermo: Palumbo, 1971.

4553. Guenancia, P. *Du vide à Dieu. Essai sur la physique de Pascal.* Paris: Maspero, 1976.

4554. Gueroult, M. "Méthode en histoire de la philosophie." *Philosophiques*, 1 (April 1974), 7-19.

   The history of philosophy is both horizontal (philosophical systems and the method of structures) and vertical (method of sources). The method of structures is adequate to the nature of the philosophical work, as work and as philosophical.

4554a. Gulian, C.I. "Structuralism and the Hermeneutics of Paul Ricoeur" (in Rumanian). *Revista de Filozofie*, 25, no. 2 (1978), 199-206.

4554b. ———. "Language and Message" (in Rumanian). *Revista de Filozofie*, 26 (January-February 1979), 86-92.

4555. Günther, H. "Struktur als Prozess. Zum Strukturbegriff des tschechoslovakischen Strukturalismus." *Archiv für Begriffgeschichte*, 16, no. 1 (1972), 86-92.

4556. Harman, Gilbert. "Deep Structure as Logical Form." *Synthèse*, 21 (December 1970), 275-297.

4557. Henriot, P. "Nature et culture: la circulation des 'modèles.'" *Revue de l'Enseignement Philosophique*, 25, no. 4 (1975), 7-10.

   Nature and culture in Kant and Lévi-Strauss.

4558. Hernández-Gil, Antonio. *Metodología de la ciencia del derecho.* Madrid: Editorial Tecnos, 1971.

   Part II is on structuralism and the science of law.

4559. ———, et al. *Estructuralismo y derecho.* Madrid: Alianza Editorial, 1973.

   Hina, H. See item 102.

4560. Hochart, P. "Structuralisme: structuralisme et philosophie." In *Encyclopaedia Universalis*, vol. 15 (1973), pp. 434-438. Paris: Encyclopaedia Universalis France, 1968.

4561. Hochgesang, Michael. *Humanismus und Gegenwart: wiss. Grundlagen unserer Zeit.* Munich: Vögel, 1974.

4562. Holenstein, Elmar. "Jakobson und Husserl: ein Beitrag zur Genealogie des Strukturalismus." *Tijdschrift voor Filosofie*, 35, no. 3 (September 1973), 560-607.

4563. ———. "Jakobson and Husserl: A Contribution to the Genealogy of Structuralism." *Human Context*, 7 (Spring 1975), 61-83.

*4564. ———. *Roman Jakobsons phänomenologischer Strukturalismus.* Frankfurt am Main: Suhrkamp, 1975. Simultaneously published in French. Originally the author's Habilitationsschrift, Zurich, 1974.

4565. ———. *Jakobson, ou le structuralisme phénoménologique.* Paris: Seghers, 1975.

4566. ———. "Die Grenzen der phänomenologischen Reduktion in der Phonologie oder eine strukturalistische Lektion in Phänomenologie." In *Die Phänomenologie und die Wissenschaften.* Ed. Ernst Wolfgang Orth. Freiburg im Breisgau: Verlag Karl Alber, 1976, pp. 76-89.

4567. ———. *Roman Jakobson's Approach to Language: Phenomenological Structuralism.* Trans. Catherine and Tarcisius Schelbert. Bloomington: Indiana University Press, 1976.

4568. Hollhüber, Ivo. "Existencialismo, humanismo y estructuralismo como enmascaramientos contemporáneos." *II° Congreso Nacional de Filosofía*, I. Buenos Aires: Editorial Sudamericana, 1973, pp. 327-334.

4569. Horner, Jack K. "Second Thoughts on Sarah's First Signs." *Auslegung*, 4 (February 1977), 105-121.

Though the biological models presently available to us are inadequate, they nevertheless are intimate crucial features of a linguistic theory plausibly articulating the innateness-specificity thesis.

4570. Hrušovský, I. "The Dialectics of Structuration and Regularity in the History of Philosophy" (in Slovak). *Filosofický Časopis*, 17, no. 1 (1969), 6-12.

4571. ———. "The Discussion on Structuralism" (in Slovak). *Filozofia*, 24, no. 4 (1969), 368-377.

On the need to consider empirical facts in their structures.

4572. ———. "Being and Structure." *Revolutionary World*, 3 (1973), 43-52. See also item 4573.

4573. Hrusowski, I. "Being and Structure." *Soviet Studies in Philosophy*, 11 (1972-1973), 211-223. See also item 4572.

Hullet, J. See item 103.

4574. Hund, William B. "Structuralism and Ethics." *Proceedings of the American Catholic Philosophical Association*, 47 (1973), 177-182.

4575. Hund, Wulf Dietmar, ed. *Strukturalismus. Ideologie und Dogmengeschichte.* Darmstadt: Luchterhand, 1973. (Soziologische Texte, Bd. 81)

4575a. Iggers, G.G. "The 'Crisis' of Historicism and Changing Conceptions of Historical Time." *Comprendre*, no. 43-44 (Venice, 1977-1978), pp. 60-73. Includes a French summary.

Invitto, G. See item 468.

4576. Jacob, André. "Sur le structuralisme." *Les Etudes Philosophiques* ("Les Modes en philosophie"), April-June 1969, pp. 173-186.

4577. ———. "Etat présent de la philosophie du langage." *Revue Philosophique de la France et de l'Etranger*, no. 163 (January-March 1973), pp. 3-15.

4578. Jaroszewski, T.M. "Člověk--struktury--historie (překlad z polštiny)." *Filosofický Časopis*, 18, no. 4 (1970), 559-572.

On the anthropological conceptions of Lévi-Strauss.

4579. Jensen, Esbern Krause. *Den Franske strukturalisme: på sporet af en teori for de humane videnskaber*. Copenhagen: Berlingske, 1973. (Item 4593)

4580. Johnston, William M. "Joseph Chiari: *Twentieth-Century French Thought from Bergson to Lévi-Strauss*." *French Review*, 50, no. 5 (April 1977), 974-975.

On item 4464.

4581. Joja, Crizantema. "Introduction à l'étude historique des structures." *Philosophie et Logique*, 18 (1974), 179-184.

4582. ———. "Le Sens ontologique de la notion de structure." *Revue Roumaine des Sciences Sociales. Serie de Philosophie et Logique*, 15 (1971), 147-160.

4583. *The Journal of the British Society for Phenomenology*, especially 2, no. 3 (October 1971). Papers read at the Workshop on Structuralism held at Windsor Hall, University of Reading, 17-19 July 1970.

4584. Kalivoda, R. "Structure and Structuralism" (in Czech). *Filosofický Časopis*, 17, no. 1 (1969), 114-118.

4585. Kampits, Peter. "Das Ende der Philosophie im französischen Strukturalismus." *Wissenschaft und Weltbild*, 23, no. 2 (June 1970), 126-138.

The end of philosophy and the end of man as a result of the end of the subject replaced by the object.

4586. Kaufmann, J.N. Review of F. Holenstein's *Jakobson ou le structuralisme phénoménologique. Dialogue*, 15 (1976), 360-363.

4587. ———. "Structure et causalité." *Philosophiques*, 3 (April 1976), 3-32.

Also on Lévi-Strauss.

4588. Kelbley, C.A. Review of M. Dufrenne's *Pour l'homme. International Philosophical Quarterly*, 9, no. 3 (1969), 460-463.

4588a. Kellner, Hans. "Disorderly Conduct: Braudel's Mediterranean
        Satire." *History and Theory*, 18 (May 1979), 197-222.

        Fernand Braudel's *The Mediterranean and the Mediterranean
        World in the Age of Philip II* (Paris 1949) seems to address the
        same problematics of language that structuralism and post-struc-
        turalism confront.

4589.   Kintzler, J.-M. "Lecture non-humaniste de Kant." *Revue de
        Métaphysique et de Morale*, 80, no. 2 (1975), 194-208.

        The Lacanian and Althusserian reading of the verbs of modality
        as practiced by Kant in the *Critique of Pure Reason*.

4590.   Kisiel, Theodore. "Aphasiology, Phenomenology of Perception
        and the Shades of Structuralism." In *Language and Language
        Disturbances* (the 5th Lexington Conference on Pure and Applied
        Phenomenology). Ed. Erwin W. Strauss. Pittsburgh: Duquesne
        University Press, 1974, pp. 201-233.

4591.   Kockelmans, Joseph J. "Strukturalismus und existenziale Phäno-
        menologie." In item 5253, pp. 1-16.

4592.   Kraay, John N. "Emics, Etics, and Meaning, An Exploration."
        Philosophia Reformata, 41 (1976), 49-71.

        Analysis shows that structural linguistics provides a founda-
        tional model for description and comparison such that cultural-
        anthropological theory can be developed on the basis of truly
        culturological data; however, such theory cannot be derived
        from these data.

4593.   Krause-Jensen, Esberg. *Den Franske strukturalisme: Pa sporet
        af en teori for de humane videnskaber*. Copenhagen: Berlingske
        Forlag, 1973. (Item 4579)

4594.   Kritzman, Lawrence D. "Jean-Luc Chalumeau: *La Pensée en France
        de Sartre à Foucault*." *French Review*, 50, no. 5 (April 1977),
        p. 795.

        On item 2109.

4595.   Krober, G. "Strukturgesetz und Gesetzesstruktur." *Deutsche
        Zeitschrift für Philosophie*, 15 (January 1967), 202-216.

4596.   ————. "Die Kategorie Struktur und der Kategorische Struk-
        turalismus." *Deutsche Zeitschrift für Philosophie*, 16 (1968),
        1310-1324.

4597.   Künzli, R.E. "Nietzsche und die Semiologie: Neue Ansätze in
        der französischen Nietzsche-Interpretation." *Nietzsche-
        Studien*, 5 (1976), 263-288.

4598.   Kwant, R.C. *Persoon en structuur*. Alphen aan den Rijn: N. Sam-
        son, 1971. (Sociale en Culturele Reeks)

4599. ————, and J. Bourgonje. "Strukturalistisch filosoferen." In
Filosoferen. Gangbare vormen van wijsgerig denken. Ed. R.C.
Kwant and S. Ijsseling. Alphen aan den Rijn and Brussels:
Samson Uitgeverij, 1977, pp. 121-149.

Lacharité, N. See item 2182.

4600. Lacroix, Jean. *Panorama de la philosophie française contemporaine.* Paris: Presses Universitaires de France, 1966, 1968.

4601. Ladrière, Jean. "Sens et système." *Esprit*, 35e année, no. 360
(May 1967), 822-824.

The system is the matrix of meaning, but meaning goes beyond
the system.

4602. ————. "Le Structuralisme entre la science et la philosophie."
Tijdschrift voor Filosofie, 33 (March 1971), 66-111.

The implications of the structuralist method for philosophy;
based on a study of Lévi-Strauss's structural ethnology and
Althusser's structuralist interpretation of Marxism.

4603. ————. *Vie sociale et destinée.* Gembloux: Duculot, 1973.

On social philosophy and structuralism.

Lafrance, Guy. See items 3566b and 3766.

4604. Lamsdorff-Galagane, Vladimiro. *¿Estructuralismo en la filosofía
del derecho?* Santiago de Compostela: Porto y Cía, 1969.
(Biblioteca Hispánica de Filosofía del Derecho, 3)

Studies the term "structuralism"; the method; its possible
relations with philosophy; the possibilities of applying it
to legal philosophy.

4605. Lang, H. "Zum Verhältnis von Strukturalismus, Philosophie und
Psychoanalyse, konkretisiert am Phänomen der Subjektivität."
Tijdschrift voor Filosofie, 38, no. 4 (1976), 559-573.

4606. Langlois, Jean. "Structuralisme et métaphysique." *Science et
Esprit*, 20 (1968), 171-193.

Lanteri-Laura, G. See items 3767-3768.

4607. Lanţoş, S. "Structural Theories and Prediction" (in Rumanian).
Studia Universitatis Babeş-Bolyai. Series Philosophia, 18
(1973), 113-120.

Structures as immutables in contemporary structuralism vs.
genetic structuralism and Marxism.

4608. Larson, Gerald J. "Notion of Satkārya in Sāmkhya: Toward a
Philosophical Reconstruction (with reply by B.B. Singh)."
Philosophy East and West, 25 (January 1975), 31-40.

4609. Latouche, Serge. "Totalité, totalisation et totalitarisme."
      Dialogue, 13 (March 1974), 71-83.

4610. Lauretano, Bruno. "Discorso sulla struttura." *Giornale Critico
      della Filosofia Italiana*, 1 (January-March 1970), 115-124.

      On the forerunners of structuralism.

4611. Lavers, Annette. "Mean, Meaning and Subject: A Current Reap-
      praisal." *The Journal of the British Society for Phenomenology*,
      1, no. 3 (October 1970), 44-49.

4612. Lee, Edward N., and Maurice Mandelbaum. *Phenomenology and
      Existentialism*. Baltimore: Johns Hopkins Press, 1969.

4613. Leiber, Justin. "Philosophical Aspects of Recent Work in
      Linguistics." *Philosophical Forum*, 6 (Summer 1975), 343-365.

      ————. See also item 127.

4614. Levin, David Michael. "On Lévi-Strauss and Existentialism."
      American Scholar, 38 (Winter 1968), 69-82.

      A confrontation of the ideas of Sartre and Lévi-Strauss shows
      that, when well understood, they are not intrinsically irrecon-
      cilable. There are actually necessary and interesting parallels
      between them.

4615. Lewis, Philip E. "Merleau-Ponty and the Phenomenology of Lan-
      guage." In item 68, pp. 19-40. See also item 69.

4616. Li Carrillo, Victor. *Estructuralismo y antihumanismo*. Caracas:
      Universidad Central de Venezuela, Facultad de Humanidades
      y Educación, 1968.

4617. ————. "Estructuralismo y antihumanismo." *Estudios Filosóficos*,
      no. 1 (1974), pp. 83-112.

4617a. ————. "La *Gestaltpsychologie* y el concepto de estructura."
      Revista Venezolana de Filosofía, 8 (1978), 7-81.

4618. Lindstrom, Per. "On Relations between Structures." *Theoria*,
      32 (1966), 172-185.

4619. Llewelyn, J.E. "Joseph Chiari: *Twentieth Century French Thought:
      From Bergson to Lévi-Strauss*." *Modern Language Review*, 72,
      no. 2 (April 1977), 457-458.

      On item 4464.

4620. Locher, Gottfried Wilhelm. "Dialectisch Structuralisme."
      *Mededelingen der Koninklijke Nederlandse Akademie van Weten-
      schappen, afd. Letterkunde*, 36, no. 9 (1973), 399-418. Rpt. as
      item 4621.

4621. ————. *Dialectisch Structuralisme*. Amsterdam: Noord-Hollandsche
      U.M., 1973. Rpts. item 4620.

4622. Lungarzo, Carlos. *El Concepto lógico de estructura*. Buenos Aires: Universidad de Buenos Aires, Facultad de Filosofía y Letras, 1971.

Lupasco, S. See item 135.

4623. Maceiras Fafián, Manuel. "Paul Ricoeur: una ontología militante." *Pensamiento*, 32 (April–June 1976), 131–156.

4624. Maci, Guillermo A. "Análisis estructural y filosofía del lenguaje." *Cuadernos de Filosofía*, 12, no. 17 (January–June 1972), 41–61.

4625. Macků, J. "Critical Realism and Structuralism" (in Czech). *Sborník Prací Filosofické Faculty Brněnské University, Řada Filosofická*, 19 (1970), 39–46.

Parallels between the critical realism of Arnöst Bláha (1879–1960) and the structuralism of the linguistic circle of Prague.

4626. Magliola, Robert. "Parisian Structuralism Confronts Phenomenology: The Ongoing Debate." *Language and Style*, 6, no. 4 (Fall 1973), 237–248.

4627. Mainberger, G. "Glaubensformeln in der Philosophie? Die mythologische Funktion des Bejahens und Verneinens." *Linguistica Biblica*, no. 27–28 (1973), pp. 14–24.

On Lévi-Strauss vs. Paul Ricoeur.

4628. Mainberger, Gonsalvo K. "Die französische Philosophie nach dem Strukturalismus." *Neue Rundschau*, 84, no. 3 (1973), 437–458.

Malagoli, L. See item 138.

4629. Malavassi V, Guillermo. "Bricolage sobre naturaleza y estructura." *Revista de Filosofía de la Universidad de Costa Rica*, 11, no. 32 (January–June 1973), 13–31.

4630. Malawski, A. "The Structuralist Formula for Integrating the Sciences" (in Polish). *Studia Filozoficzne*, 2 (1976), 29–42.

On structure as a rule for explaining reality.

4631. Malet, André. "Structuralisme et liberté." *Revue d'Histoire et de Philosophie Religieuses*, 50, no. 3 (1970), 209–220.

An attempt to give a unified version of structuralism; a study of its Marxist version which wants to encompass synchrony and diachrony; freedom and dependence with regard to structures. A science of freedom would show that it has no structure in the structuralist meaning of the term, that its structure is to have no structure.

4632. Mare, C. "Determinism and Structuralism" (in Rumanian). *Revista de Filozofie*, 20, no. 9 (1973), 101–108.

4633.   Mariani, Eliodoro. "Introduzione allo strutturalismo filosofico."
        Antonianum, 46, no. 1 (January-March 1971), 113-147.

4634.   Marin, Louis. "La Question de l'homme." *Revue Internationale
        de Philosophie*, 22, no. 85-86 (1968), 308-322.

        On Dufrenne's *Pour l'homme*.

4635.   ———. "La Dissolution de l'homme dans les sciences humaines.
        Modèle linguistique et sujet signifiant." *Concilium*, no. 86
        (1973), pp. 27-37.

4636.   Marín Morales, José-Alberto. "Convergencias y puntualiszaciones
        estructuralistas." *Arbor*, 85 (1973), 121-132.

4637.   Marquès, A. "Structuralism and the Evolutionist Mentality"
        (in Catalonian). *Qüestions de Vida Cristiana*, no. 47 (1969),
        pp. 47-56.

4638.   Martano, Giuseppe. "'Struttura' disumaizzante." *Logos*, 1972,
        pp. 189-194.

4639.   Masset, Pierre. "Le Problème de Dieu: dans la philosophie
        française contemporaine." *Nouvelle Revue Théologique*, 96,
        no. 9 (1974), 897-917.

4639a. Mathauser, Z. "Structuralism: For and Against" (in Czech).
        Estetika, 13, no. 1 (1976), 61-67.

        McDonell, D.J. See item 2215.

        McGraw, B.R. See item 1759a.

4640.   McMullin, Ernan. "Structural Explanation." *American Philosoph-
        ical Quarterly*, 15, no. 2 (April 1978), 139-147.

4641.   Medina Lugo, Ramón Eladio. "La Lingüística y el estructuralismo
        (Inferencia a un posible método para una filosofía antropo-
        lógica)." *Franciscanum*, 17, no. 49 (1975), 28-54.

4642.   Melenk, H. "Die formalen Systeme des französischen Struktura-
        lismus." *Philosophisches Jahrbuch*, 79, no. 1 (1972), 137-161.

*4642a. Mendel, Dr. Gérard. *La Chasse structurale: une interprétation
        du devenir humain*. Paris: Payot, 1977, 346pp. (Petite Biblio-
        thèque Payot, 328)

4643.   Mepham, John. "The Structuralist Sciences and Philosophy." In
        item 176, pp. 104-137.

4644.   Mercier, André. "Notes on the Analysis of Structure and Struc-
        turalist Ideologies. A Facet of Current French Philosophy."
        Inquiry, 15, no. 3 (Oslo, 1972), 355-361.

        On item 4686.

*4645.   Merrell, Floyd. "Le Structuralisme et au-delà ... Examen cri-
         tique des présupposés du système." *Diogène*, no. 92 (1975), pp.
         78-120.

4646.   ————. "Structuralism and Beyond: A Critique of Presupposi-
         tions." *Diogenes*, no. 92 (Winter 1975), pp. 67-103.

4647.   Miller, J. "A Note on So-Called 'Discovery Procedures.'" *Founda-
         tions of Language*, 10 (May 1973), 123-139.

         On the American structuralism of Bloomfield and Harris.

4648.   ————. "The Parasitic Growth of Deep Structures." *Foundations
         of Language*, 13 (September 1975), 361-389.

         Examines the assumptions of transformations creating struc-
         tures.

4649.   Montezuma de Carvalho, Joaquim. "O Estruturalismo é um anti-
         humanismo?" *Convivium São Paulo*, 10 (1971), 389-395.

4650.   Mora, Fernando. "Estructuralismo y derecho." *Revista de Filo-
         sofía de la Universidad de Costa Rica*, 11, no. 32 (January-
         June 1973), 163-180.

         Moravia, S. See item 151.

4651.   Moravia, Sergio. "Dalla crisi della generazione sartriana allo
         strutturalismo." In *La Filosofia dal '45 ad oggi*. Ed. Valero
         Verra. Turin: ERI, Edizioni RAI--Radio-Televisione Italiana,
         1976, pp. 184-196.

         Morel, G. See item 5043.

4652.   Morita, Yasushi. *Kōzōshugi ni okeru hō to seiji*. Japan, 1969.

         On structuralism, the philosophy of law and political science.

4653.   Morot-Sir, Edouard. *La Pensée française d'aujourd'hui*. Paris:
         Presses Universitaires de France, 1971. See, in particular,
         chapter 6, "Essais d'épistémologie structuraliste," pp. 82-
         105.

4654.   Morpugo-Tagliabue, G. "La Stilistica di Aristotele e lo strut-
         turalismo." *Lingua e Stile*, 2, no. 1 (1967), 1-18.

4655.   Mouloud, Noël. "Polarités, transitions et genèses dans une
         épistémologie des structures." *Cahiers de l'I.S.E.A. Série M*,
         no. 15 (Paris, 1962), pp. 57-90.

4656.   ————. "La Méthode des sciences de structures et les problèmes
         de la connaissance rationnelle." *La Pensée*, no. 135 (1967),
         pp. 3-18.

4657.   ————. "Les Sciences de structures et la philosophie de
         l'homme." *Scientia*, 103 (1968), 174-192.

4658.   ————. *Les Structures. La Recherche et le savoir.* Paris:
         Payot, 1968, 308pp. (Bibliothèque Scientifique)

4659.   ————. *Langage et structures: essais de logique et de séméio-
         logie.* Paris: Payot, 1969.

4660.   ————. "Les Structures de l'interprétation et la mesure des
         relativités sémantiques." *Revue de Métaphysique et de Morale,*
         81 (April-June 1976), 145-170.

4661.   Mourelos, G. "The Notion of Structure in Modern Philosophy"
         (in Greek). *Annales d'Esthétique,* no. 9-10 (1970-1971), pp.
         126-144.

4662.   ————. "Structure and Disintegration in Space-Time Frameworks"
         (in Greek). *Annales d'Esthétique,* no. 11-12 (1972-1973),
         pp. 97-108.

         Includes a discussion on the different uses of the notion
         of structure.

4663.   Moutsopolos, Evanghelos. "Dynamic Structuralism in the Plotinian
         Theory of the Imaginary." *Diotima,* 4 (1976), 11-22.

         An interpretation which makes Plotinus the most distant pre-
         cursor of psychological structuralism.

4664.   Muniz de Rezende, Antonio. "Le Structuralisme de Merleau-Ponty.
         La Structure du Comportement, une critique du dogmatisme
         scientifique en psychologie." Doctoral dissertation, Institut
         Supérieur de Philosophie, Université Catholique de Louvain,
         19 June 1974, reported in *Revue Philosophique de Louvain,*
         72, no. 16 (November 1974), 833-835.

4665.   Muralt, André de. "Métaphysique et phénoménologie. Essai d'ana-
         lyse structurale." In *Tommaso nel suo settimo centenario.*
         Atti del Congresso internazionale (Rome-Naples, 17-24 April
         1974). *Vol. VI: L'Essere.* Naples: Edizioni Domenicane Italiane,
         1977, pp. 487-500.

4666.   Muraro, Luisa. "Ermeneutica o strutturalismo? Note in margine
         alla *Filosofia della Religione* di I. Mancini." *Rivista di
         Filosofia Neo-Scolastica,* 61 (1969), 583-587.

4667.   Muraro Vaiani, Luisa. "La Nozione di coscienza linguistica in
         Saussure." *Rivista di Filosofia Neo-Scolastica,* 60 (1968),
         640-648.

         Murguía, A. See item 2225.

4668.   Murphy, Gardner. "Editorial, Function and Structure." *Darshana
         International,* 6 (October 1966), 1.

4669.   Naumann, Hans, ed. *Der moderne Strukturbegriff. Materialien zu
         seiner Entwicklung.* Darmstadt: Wissenschaftliche Buchgesell-
         schaft, 1973. (Wege der Forschung, Bd. 155)

4670. Nemo, Philippe. *L'Homme structural*. Paris: Bernard Grasset,
       1975.

       Nikolova, M. See items 2227 and 5279.

4671. ————. "The Structuralist Interpretation of Man and His Place
       in Society" (in Russian). *Filosofskie Nauki*, no. 2 (1974),
       pp. 108-118.

4672. ————. *Osnovnye cherty filosofii frant͡suzskogo strukturalizma*.
       Moscow: s.n., 1975.

       Noiray, A. See item 2228.

4673. Nový, L. "Structuralism and Philosophy" (in Czech). *Filosofický
       Časopis*, 17, no. 1 (1969), 1-5.

       Núñez Tenorio, J.R. See item 539.

4674. Oliver, B. "The Ontological Structure of Linguistic Theory."
       Monist, 53 (1969), 262-274.

4675. ————. "Depth Grammar as a Methodological Concept in Philos-
       ophy." *International Philosophical Quarterly*, 12 (1972),
       111-130.

       An examination of the ontological status of Lévi-Strauss's
       symbolic functions (or structures) of the human mind, Chomsky's
       "innate structures" and what Patte calls "archetypal structures."

4676. O'Malley, J.B. "Making Meaning." *Philosophical Studies*, 20
       (1972), 62-76.

4677. O'Neill, John, ed. *On Critical Theory*. New York: Seabury Press,
       1976.

       A collection of twelve essays on critical theory, primarily
       as developed by the Frankfurt school. Also shows the relation
       of critical theory to other theories such as Marxism, positivism,
       phenomenology, structuralism, and linguistic philosophy.

4678. Ortiz-Oses, Andres. "Communicación e interpretación: crítica de
       la razón hermenéutica." *Pensamiento*, 30 (October-December
       1974), 399-436.

       Osowski, J. See item 1159.

4679. Ott, Heinrich. "L'Herméneutique de la société: le problème de
       l'historicité collective." *Rivista Internazionale di Filosofia
       del Diritto*, 48 (April-September 1971), 240-260.

4680. Otto, Harro. "Methode und System in der Rechtswissenschaft."
       Archiv für Rechts und Sozialphilosophie, 55 (1969), 493-520.

4681. Overton, W.F. "General Systems, Structure and Development."
       In item 173, pp. 61-81.

*4682. Paci, Enzo. "Vico, le structuralisme et l'encyclopédie phéno-
        ménologique des sciences." *Les Etudes Philosophiques*, 24
        (July–December 1968), 407–428.

4683.   ———. "Vico, Structuralism, and the Phenomenological Ency-
        clopedia of the Sciences." In *Giambattista Vico. An Inter-
        national Symposium*. Ed. Giorgio Tagliacozzo and Hayden V.
        White. Baltimore, Md.: Johns Hopkins Press, 1969, pp. 499–
        515.

4684.   Panaccio, C. "Structure et signification dans l'oeuvre de
        Merleau-Ponty." *Dialogue*, 9, no. 3 (1970), 374–380.

        On the irreducible specificity of Merleau-Ponty, who could
        not be considered a forerunner of structuralism.

4685.   Paquet, M. "Politique de théâtre, morale sartrienne et gracieuse
        dialectique." *Revue de l'Université de Bruxelles*, no. 1–2
        (1974), pp. 74–91.

        On Verstraeten's *Violence et Ethique* (item 4802) which
        proposes to integrate structuralist concepts with the existen-
        tialist dialectic.

*4686. Parain-Vial, Jeanne. *Analyses structurales et idéologies struc-
        turalistes*. Toulouse: Edouard Privat, 1969, 239pp.

4687.   ———. *Análisis estructurales e ideologías estructuralistas*.
        Trans. Marta Rojzman. Buenos Aires: Amorrortu Editores, 1972.

4688.   ———. *Tendances nouvelles de la philosophie*. Paris: Le Cen-
        turion, 1978, 263pp.

4689.   Parret, Herman. "In het teken van het teken. Een Confrontatie
        van het klassiekwijsgerige en het strukturele teken."
        Tijdschrift voor Filosofie, 31, no. 2 (1969), 232–260.

        The sign of classical philosophy vs. the structural sign.

4690.   ———. "Mogelijkheden en perspectieven van het structuur-
        denken." *Bijdragen*, 30 (1969), 154–170. French summary, pp.
        170–171.

4691.   ———. *Language and Discourse*. New York: Humanities Press,
        1971.

4692.   ———. "Husserl and the Neo-Humboldtians on Language."
        International Philosophical Quarterly, 12 (March 1972),
        43–68.

4693.   ———. "Expression et articulation. Une Confrontation des
        points de vue husserlien et saussurien concernant la langue
        et le discours." *Revue Philosophique de Louvain*, 71 (Febru-
        ary 1973), 72–113.

4694.   ———. *Discussing Language*. Dialogues with Wallace L. Chafe,
        Noam Chomsky, Algirdas J. Greimas, M.A.K. Halliday, Peter

Hartmann, George Lakoff, Sydney M. Lamb, André Martinet, James McCawley, Sebastian K. Šaumjan, and Jacques Bouveresse. The Hague-Paris: Mouton, 1974.

4695. ————. "Structuralism: A Methodology or an Ideology?" *Algemeen Nederlands Tijdschrift voor Wijsbegeerte*, 68, no. 2 (1976), 99-110.

Introduction to structuralism for an Anglo-Saxon audience.

Patočka, J. See item 4217.

4696. Patzig, G. "Der Strukturalimus und seine Grenzen." *Neue Deutsche Hefte*, 22, no. 2 (1975), 247-266.

In certain areas, structuralism carries with it both scientific concepts and a conception of the world.

4697. Peperzak, A. "Denken in Parijs." *Algemeen Nederlands Tijdschrift voor Wijsbegeerte*, 62, no. 3 (1970).

4698. Petrucci, P. "Strutture e categorie." *Lingua e Stile*, 7, no. 2 (1972), 391-409.

4699. Pettit, Philip. "Wittgenstein and the Case for Structuralism." *Journal of the British Society for Phenomenology*, 3 (1972), 46-57.

On the ontological status of deep structures.

4700. ————. "French Philosophy." *Cambridge Review*, 94, no. 2214 (8 June 1973), 178-180.

4701. ————. *The Concept of Structuralism. A Critical Analysis.* London: Macmillan; Dublin: Gill & Macmillan; Berkeley-Los Angeles: University of California Press, 1975, 117pp. Originally presented as a lecture course at Cambridge in the Lent term, 1974.

The movement is presented in terms of models with the conclusion that structuralism is analysis.

4702. Phillips, Gary. "Wittgenstein and Chomsky: Some Implications of Linguistic Philosophy for a Structural Methodology." An unpublished paper prepared for the "Semiology and Exegesis Project," an interdisciplinary project at Vanderbilt University sponsored by the National Endowment for the Humanities. See also item 5051.

4703. Piaget, Jean. "Structures et catégories: étude épistémologique." *Logique et Analyse*, 17 (September-December 1974), 223-240.

————. See also items 154-157; 159-164.

4704. Pingaud, Bernard, ed. "Sartre aujourd'hui," a special issue of *L'Arc*, no. 30 (Aix-en-Provence, 1966), pp. 1-101.

428   *Applied Structuralism*

4704a. Pinkava, J., and H. Vogel. "Philosophical and Methodological
        Questions of Structure" (in Czech). *Filozofia*, 33, no. 1
        (1978), 61-75.

4705.   Piñon, A.T. "The Shortcomings of Structuralism and Existential-
        ism." *Unitas*, 44, no. 4 (Manila, 1971), 121-126.

4706.   Pintor-Ramos, Antonio. "Paul Ricoeur y el estructuralismo."
        Pensamiento, 31, no. 122 (April-June 1975), 95-123.

4707.   Pivcevíc, Edo. "Truth as Structure." *Review of Metaphysics*,
        28 (December 1974), 311-327.

4708.   Pöhler, Egon. *Struktur, Bedeutung, Praxis. Versuch über die
        Grundbegriffe des Strukturalismus.* Bochum: Ruhr-Universität,
        1973.

        Polizzi, P. See item 4391.

4709.   Poole, Roger C. "Structuralism and Phenomenology: A Literary
        Approach." *Journal of the British Society for Phenomenology*,
        2, no. 2 (May 1971), 3-16.

4710.   Preti, Giulio. *Umanismo e strutturalismo. Scritti di estetica
        e di letteratura con un saggio inedito.* Ed. Ermanno Migliorini.
        Padua: Liviana, 1973. (Guide di Cultura Contemporanea)

4711.   Prier, Raymond A. Jr. "Symbol and Structure in Heraclitus."
        Apeiron, 7 (November 1973), 23-37.

4712.   Prier, Raymond Adolph. "Archaic Structuralism and Dynamics in
        Hesiod's Theogony." *Apeiron*, 8 (November 1974), 1-12.

4713.   ———. *Archaic Logic: Symbol and Structure in Heraclitus,
        Parmenides and Empedocles.* The Hague: Mouton, 1976. (De
        Proprietatibus Litterarum. Series Practica, 11)

4714.   Quaghebeur, Marc. "Julia Kristeva, une philosophie de l'avant-
        garde." *Les Lettres Romanes*, 26, no. 4 (Louvain, November
        1972), 360-388.

4715.   Quinzio, Sergio. "Struttura dello strutturalismo." *Tempo Pre-
        sente*, 11, no. 2 (February 1966), 58-63.

4715a. Racevskis, Karlis. "A Return to *The Heavenly City*: Carl Becker's
        Paradox in a Structuralist Perspective." *Clio*, 8 (Winter
        1979), 165-174.

        In the light of structuralist and post-structuralist epistem-
        ology, the principal arguments against the central thesis of
        The Heavenly City become irrelevant.

4715b. Radar, Edmond. "A Genealogy: Play, Folklore, and Art." *Diogenes*,
        Fall 1978, pp. 78-99.

4716. Radway, Janice A. "Phenomenology, Linguistics, and Popular
       Literature." *Journal of Popular Culture*, 12 (Summer 1978),
       88-98.

4717. Rasmussen, David. "Mircea Eliade, Structural Hermeneutics and
       Philosophy." *Philosophy Today*, 12 (Summer 1968), 138-146.

4718. Reenpää, Y. "Die empiristischen philosophischen Systeme und
       die Strukturiertheit des Phänomenalen." *Zeitschrift für
       Philosophische Forschung*, 23, no. 4 (1969), 612-626.

4719. Reiter, Josef. "Struktur und Geschichte. Der zweideutige Ver-
       such einer Entideologisierung des Geschichtsdenkens durch
       den Strukturalismus." *Die Zeitschrift für Philosophische
       Forschung*, 24 (April-June 1970), 159-182.

       Structuralism as a decisive turning point in anthropology
       comparable to Hegel and Marx in historical thought, Nietzsche
       in ethics, Freud in psychology, and Saussure in linguistics.

4720. Rella, Franco. "A Proposito di materialismo e strutturalismo."
       Nuova Corrente, no. 55 (1971), pp. 263-287.

4721. Revel, Jean-François. *Histoire de la philosophie occidentale*,
       tome II. Paris: Stock, 1970.

4722. *Revue Internationale de Philosophie*, no. 73-74, fasc. 3-4 (1965):
       special issue entitled "La Notion de structure."

4723. Revzin, Isaak Iosifovich. "The Development of the Concept
       'Structure of Language.'" *Soviet Studies in Philosophy*, 8,
       no. 3 (Winter 1969), 273-294.

4724. Ricoeur, Paul. "Structure et herméneutique." *Esprit*, n.s. 31[e]
       année, no. 322 (November 1963), 596-627. Originally entitled
       "Symbolique et temporalité" in *Ermeneutica e Tradizione*
       (Actes du Congrès International, Rome, January 1963), *Archivio
       di Filosofia*, ed. E. Castelli, 3 (1963), 12-31 and rpt. in
       item 4730, pp. 33-63.

       On structuralism as science vs. hermeneutics as the philo-
       sophical interpretation of myths grasped within a living tra-
       dition and taken up again in contemporary reflection and specu-
       lation. The understanding of structures is seen as the necessary
       intermediary between symbolic naïveté and hermeneutic intelli-
       gence.

4725. ————. "Le Symbolisme et l'explication structurale." *Cahiers
       Internationaux de Symbolisme*, no. 4 (1964), pp. 81-96.

4726. ————. "Le Problème du double-sens comme problème herméneu-
       tique et comme problème sémantique." *Cahiers Internationaux de
       Symbolisme*, no. 12 (1966), pp. 59-71. Rpt. in item 4730, pp.
       64-79 and in *Myths and Symbols. Studies in Honor of Mircea
       Eliade*. Ed. Kitagawa and Charles Long. Chicago: University
       of Chicago Press, 1969, pp. 63-81.

*4727.   ———. "La Structure, le mot, l'événement." *Esprit*, 35, no.
          360 (May 1967), 801-821. Rpt. in item 4730, pp. 80-97.

          Linguistics is used to examine the validity of structural
          analysis and the limits of this validity.

4728.   ———. "La Structure, le mot, l'événement." *Man and World*,
          1 (February 1968), 10-30.

4729.   ———. "Structure, Word and Event." *Philosophy Today*, 12
          (Summer 1968), 114-129.

*4730.   ———. *Le Conflit des interprétations. Essais d'herméneutique.*
          Paris: Editions du Seuil, 1969. See in particular chapter 1,
          "Herméneutique et structuralisme," pp. 29-97, which contains
          items 4724, 4726 and 4727.

4731.   ———. *Wegen van de filosofie. Structuralisme, psychoanalyse,
          hermeneutik. Essays.* Trans. P.F. Stroux and G.C. Kwaad.
          Bilthoven: Ambo, 1970. Trans. of item 4730.

4732.   ———. *Der Konflikt der Interpretationen, I: Hermeneutik und
          Strukturalismus.* Trans. Johannes Rütsche. Munich: Kösel,
          1973. Trans. of chapter 1 of item 4730.

4733.   ———. "From Existentialism to the Philosophy of Language."
          Philosophy Today, 17, no. 2 (1973), 88-96.

4734.   ———. *The Conflict of Interpretations: Essays in Hermeneutics.*
          Trans. Don Ihde. Evanston, Ill.: Northwestern University
          Press, 1974. Trans. of item 4730.

4735.   ———. *La Métaphore vive.* Paris: Editions du Seuil, 1975.

4736.   ———. *Interpretation Theory: Discourse and the Surplus of
          Meaning.* Fort Worth: The Texas Christian University Press,
          1976.

          Contains four essays which are expanded versions of the Cen-
          tennial lectures that Ricoeur delivered at Texas Christian
          University in 1973. See, in particular, the first essay "Lan-
          guage as Discourse" in which Ricoeur argues that too much of
          contemporary linguistics has been devoted to the study of lan-
          guage in terms of its structure.

4736a.   ———. "Philosophie et langage." *Revue Philosophique de la
          France et de l'Etranger*, 168 (October-December 1978), 449-
          463.

4737.   Rieber, A. "Abschied vom Individuum? Zur Auseinandersetzung
          mit dem französischen Strukturalismus." *Salzburger Jahrbuch
          für Philosophie*, no. 15-16 (1971-1972), pp. 161-166.

4738.   Rigobello, Armando. *Struttura e significato.* Padua: La Garan-
          gola, 1971.

          Rigotti, E. See item 4230.

4739. Rijk, M.C. *Structuur, macht en geweld. Een Analyse in het licht van een beschouwing over de mens in de huidige westerse cultuur.* Bloemendaal: Nelissen, 1972.

4740. Rivelaygue, Jacques. "Vers une nouvelle philosophie?" *Bulletin de la Société des Professeurs Français en Amérique*, 1966, pp. 35-46.

Robert, Jean-Dominique. See item 3791.

4741. ————. *Philosophies, épistémologies, sciences de l'homme. Leurs rapports, éléments de bibliographie.* Namur, Belgium: Presses Universitaires de Namur, 1974, 534pp.

4742. Rombach, Heinrich. *Strukturontologie: Eine Phänomenologie der Freiheit.* Freiburg im Breisgau-Munich: Alber, 1971, 368pp.

4743. Rosen, Stanley. "The Absence of Structure." *Kantstudien*, 64 (1973), 246-261.

4744. Rosenwald, George C. "Epilogue: Reflections on the Universalism of Structure." In item 173, pp. 215-219.

4745. Rossi, Ino. "Structuralism as Scientific Method." In his *The Unconscious in Culture. The Structuralism of Claude Lévi-Strauss in Perspective.* New York: E.P. Dutton, 1974, pp. 60-106.

4746. ————. "An Analysis of Piaget's Concept of Structure." *Philosophy and Phenomenological Research*, 37 (March 1977), 368-380.

Raises the question of whether structures belong to the essence of the world in the Platonic sense or whether they are constructions serving the needs of exploration and prediction. Contends that Piaget wavers between the two possibilities. The next step in the analysis is concerned with the move from structures to values.

4747. Rowiński, C. "Some Remarks on the Contradictions of Structuralism" (in Polish). *Studia Filozoficzne*, 18, no. 12 (1974), 65-74.

The opposite of classical idealist solipsism.

4748. ————. "The Thought of Emmanuel Levinas" (in Polish). *Studia Filozoficzne*, no. 7 (1975), pp. 23-41.

Includes a discussion of his relation to structuralism.

4748a. ————. "Bishop Berkeley and the Structuralists" (in Polish). *Studia Filozoficzne*, no. 6 (1977), pp. 85-99.

4749. Rubino, Carl A. "Towards a New Dialectic of Language. Plato, Structuralists, Thucydides." *Sub-stance*, 8 (1974), 89-99.

4750. Rubio, J. "¿Estructura o dialéctica? Nota sobre el debate entre
       Lévi-Strauss y Sartre." *Estudio Agustiniano*, 4, no. 3 (1969),
       547-555.

       Is there opposition or complementarity between Sartre and
       the demands of "dialectical reason" and Lévi-Strauss and the
       demands of "analytical reason"?

4751. Rubio Carracedo, José. *¿Qué es el hombre?* Madrid: Ricardo
       Aguilera, 1971; 2nd rev. ed., 1973. Subtitled "El desafío
       estructuralista."

       ————. See also item 179.

       Saccà, A. See item 5283.

4752. Sakharova, Tat'iana Aleksandrovna. *Ot filosofii sushchestvo-
       vaniia k strukturalizmu.* Moscow: Hayka, 1974.

4753. Santoni Bruè, M.P. "Filosofia, scienza strutturale e inter-
       pretazione storica del linguaggio. Rassegna bibliografica."
       Agora. Filosofia e Cultura, 2, no. 4 (1974), 43-52.

4754. Sartre, Jean-Paul. "Replies to Structuralism: An Interview with
       Jean-Paul Sartre." *Telos*, 6 (Fall 1971), 110-116.

4755. Sauer, Ernst Friedrich. *Axiologie: (Wertlehre); mit ein Kritik
       des Strukturalismus.* Göttingen-Frankfurt-Zurich: Muster-
       schmidt-Verlag, 1973, 197pp.

4756. Sazbón, José, ed. *Estructuralismo y filosofía.* Buenos Aires:
       Ediciones Nueva Visión, 1969.

4757. ————. *Estructuralismo y epistemología.* Buenos Aires: Edi-
       ciones Nueva Visión, 1970.

4758. ————. "El Modelo semiológico y la reflexión filosófica."
       In *Temas de filosofía contemporánea. IIº Congreso Nacional
       de Filosofía.* Buenos Aires: Editorial Sudamericana, 1971.

4759. ————. "Sobre algunas premisas comunes a Saussure y sus
       contemporaneos." *Cuadernos de Filosofía*, 12, no. 18 (July-
       December 1972, appeared in 1973), 279-286.

       ————. See also item 183.

*4760. Schaff, Adam. "Structuralism as an Intellectual Current"
       (in Polish). *Kultura i Spořeczénstwo*, 16, no. 2 (1972),
       11-33.

4761. ————. "Le Structuralisme en tant que courant intellectuel."
       L'Homme et la Société, no. 24-25 (1972), 73-96.

4762. ————. "Der Strukturalismus als Geistesströmung." *Wissen-
       schaft und Weltbild*, 25, no. 4 (October-December 1972),
       261-285.

4763. ————. "Structuralism as an Intellectual Current." In *Polish Essays in the Methodology of the Social Sciences*, Ed. Jerzy Wiatr. Dordrecht, Holland-Boston, Mass.: D. Reidel Publishing Co., in press. (Boston Studies in the Philosophy of Science, vol. 29)

4764. Schiwy, Günther. *Strukturalismus und Zeichensysteme*. Munich: C.H. Beck, 1973. (Beck'sche schwarze Reihe, Bd. 96)

4764a. ————. "Structuralism and Philosophical Anthropology" (in Serbo-Croatian). *Izraz*, 21, no. 10 (1977), 1277-1289.

————. See also item 188.

4765. Schlanger, Jacques. *La Structure métaphysique*. Paris: Presses Universitaires de France, 1975, 148pp. (Collection SUP)

4766. Scholtz, Gunther. "'Struktur' in der Mittelalterlichen Hermeneutik." *Archiv für Begriffsgeschichte*, 13 (1969), 73-75.

4767. Schrag, Calvin O. "Praxis and Structure: Conflicting Models in the Science of Man." *Journal of the British Society for Phenomenology*, 6 (January 1975), 23-31.

Scurati, C. See item 191.

4768. Seebohm, Thomas M. "The Problem of Hermeneutics in Recent Anglo-American Literature." *Philosophy and Rhetoric*, 10 (Summer 1977), 180-198.

4769. Senokosov, Yu. P. "Discussions on Structuralism in France." *Voprosy Filosofii*, 22, no. 6 (1968), 172-181.

On the sources of French structuralism; Sartre and Lévi-Strauss; personalism and structuralism; structuralism and Marxism.

4770. Serrano Villafane, E. "Concepciones y métodos jurídicos tradicionales y algunas corrientes del pensamiento contemporáneo." *Revista de Estudios Políticos*, no. 179 (1971), pp. 113-124.

A review of Gil's book on structuralism and the law.

4771. Silverman, Hugh J. "Sartre and the Structuralists." *International Philosophical Quarterly*, 18 (September 1978), 341-358.

A fundamental difference in approach uncovers specific points of controversy: (1) the signifier/signified relation in Saussure's linguistics; (2) the unconscious in Lacan's Freudian psychoanalysis; (3) the concepts of diachrony and synchrony in Lévi-Strauss's anthropology.

4772. Šíma, R. "K filozoficko-ideologickému aspektu štruktúrnej analýzy." *Filozofia*, 32, no. 1 (1977), 51-60.

After presenting structuralism as a heterogeneous and differentiated movement, Šíma questions its philosophical and ideological presuppositions from a Marxist viewpoint.

4773. Simonis, Y. "L'Analyse structurale, commentaire épistémologique." *Recherches Amérindiennes au Québec. Bulletin d'Information*, 3, no. 3-4 (1973), 77-81.

4773a. Sirácky, A. "Structuralism as System and Philosophical Method" (in Slovakian). *Filosoficky Časopis*, 25, no. 2 (1977), 171-173. Part of the Second International Symposium of Historians of Philosophy of Socialist Countries.

4774. Šiškin, A.F., and K.A. Svarcman. "Vision of the World and Morality, Philosophy and Ethics" (in Russian). *Voprosy Filosofii*, 8 (1971), 38-50. English summary, pp. 184-185.

4775. Smith, Colin. "Merleau-Ponty and Structuralism." *The Journal of the British Society for Phenomenology*, 2 (October 1971), 46-52.

4776. Smith, Dale E. "Language and the Genesis of Meaning in Merleau-Ponty." *Kinesis*, 8 (Fall 1977), 44-58.

    Contemporary approaches to the study of Merleau-Ponty, particularly structuralism and semiotics, do not do justice to his study of the lived world.

4777. Soares Gomes, Francisco. "Estruturalismo, que filosofia?" *Revista Portuguesa de Filosofia*, 31, no. 3 (1975), 225-252.

4778. ———. "Estruturalismo: da interioridade ao saber." *Revista Portuguesa de Filosofia*, 32 (April-June 1976), 143-170.

4779. Solo, Robert A. "What is Structuralism? Piaget's Genetic Epistemology and the Varieties of Structuralist Thought." *Journal of Economic Issues*, 9 (December 1975), 605-625.

4780. Stahl, Gerold. "Linguistic Structures Isomorphic to Object Structures." *Philosophy and Phenomenological Research*, 24 (March 1964), 339-344.

4781. Stalker, Douglas. "Deep Structure." *Philosophical Monographs*, (Philadelphia, 1976-1977).

4782. Stent, Gunther S. "Limits to the Scientific Understanding of Man: Epistemological Limitations." *Science*, 187 (21 March 1975), 1052-1057. Discussion: 187 (15 August 1975), 502-504ff.

4783. ———. "Poverty of Scientism and the Promise of Structuralist Ethics." *The Hastings Center Report*, 6 (December 1976), 32-40.

4784. Štěpánková, J. "The Conception of Structure in French Structuralism and Czech Structuralism" (in Czech). *Česká Literatura*, no. 5 (1968), pp. 588-589.

4785. ———. "The Conception of the Structuration of Structure in Contemporary French Structuralism and Czech Structuralism" (in Czech). *Filosofický Časopis*, 17, no. 1 (1969), 45-46.

4786. Stewart, David. "Language and/et Langage." *Philosophy Today*, 18 (Summer 1974), 87-105.

Stock, A. See item 5097.

4787. Tajima, Sadao. *Gengo to sekai*. Japan, 1973, 303pp.

4788. Tanarda, J. "Struttura o sistema?" *Sistematica*, 1 (1968), 71-98.

4789. Tanla-Kishani, B. "African Cultural Identity Through Western Philosophies and Languages." *Présence Africaine*, no. 98 (1976), pp. 104-130.

4790. Taranienko, Z. "Genesis, Essence and Structure" (in Polish). *Studia Filozoficzne*, 16, no. 1 (1972), 153-169.

4790a. Tatham, Campbell. "Critical Investigations: Language Games: (Post)Modern (Isms)." *Sub-stance*, 4, no. 10 (Fall 1974), 67-80.

*4791. Timpanaro, Sebastiano. *Sul materialismo*. Pisa: Nistri-Lischi, 1970, 227pp.

4792. ———. *On Materialism*. Trans. Lawrence Garner. London: New Left Books; Atlantic Highlands, N.J.: Humanities Press, 1975, 260pp. Chapters 1-4 are a translation of item 4791; an additional chapter (5) was added to the English version.

4793. Todisco, O. "Lo Strutturalismo: istanze umanistiche e orientamenti della filosofia." *Sapienza*, 25 (April-June 1972), 169-209.

4794. Tonoiu, V. "Structural Strategy and Open Methodology" (in Rumanian). *Revista de Filozofie*, 17 (1970), 677-689.

Topolski, J. See item 5290.

4795. Topolski, Jerzy. "The Integrative Sense of Historical Materialism." *Revolutionary World*, 14 (1975), 3-12.

4796. Tošenovský, L. "Historicism and Its Structuration as Dialectico-Logical Principles" (in Czech). *Filosofický Časopis*, 17, no. 1 (1969), 119-128.

4797. Trandafoiu, N. "Structuralism and Anti-Humanism" (in Rumanian). *Studia Universitatis Babeş-Bolyai. Series Philosophia*, 17 (1972), 19-29.

4798. Tsankov, T.S. "The Problem of Species and of Forms of Qualitative Changes Examined from a Structural Viewpoint" (in Bulgarian). *Izvest. Inst. Filos.*, 18 (1969), 125-149.

4799.   Tuan, Yi-Fu. "Structuralism, Existentialism and Environmental
        Perception." *Environment and Behavior*, 4, no. 3 (September
        1972), 319-331.

        Structuralism and existentialism as throwing additional light
        on how people perceive and evaluate their physical environment.

        Van der Veken, J. See item 5110.

4800.   Várossová, E. "Structuralism in the Slovak Philosophy of the
        Forties" (in Slovak). *Filosofický Časopis*, 17, no. 1 (1969),
        76-79.

4801.   Verstraeten, Pierre. "Esquisse pour une critique de la raison
        structuraliste." Doctoral dissertation, Université Libre de
        Bruxelles, 1964.

4802.   ————. *Violence et éthique*. Paris: Gallimard, 1972.

        Attempts to integrate structuralist concepts into the existen-
        tialist dialectic.

4803.   Viatkine, I.S., and A.S. Mamzine. "Correlation of Structural
        and Historical Methods in the Research on Living Systems"
        (in Russian). *Voprosy Filosofii*, no. 11 (1969), pp. 46-56.

4804.   Villey, M. "Analyses structurales et idéologies structuralistes."
        Archives de Philosophie du Droit, 15 (1970), 391-396.

        A review of item 4686 and an examination of the use of struc-
        tural analysis in the field of law.

4805.   Vircillo, Domenico. "Strutturalismo e filosofia." *Teoresi*, 28
        (January-June 1972), 127-148.

4806.   ————. *La Filosofia e le scienze umane*. Messina: Peloritana,
        1973, 419pp.

4807.   Wahl, François. "La Philosophie entre l'avant et l'après du
        structuralisme." In his (ed.) *Qu'est-ce que le structuralisme?*
        Paris: Editions du Seuil, 1968, pp. 299-442. Rpt. as a sepa-
        rate volume in 1973 under the same title. (Points, 48)

*4808. Wald, Henri. "Structure, Structural, Structuralism." *Diogenes*,
        66 (Summer 1969), 15-24.

4809.   ————. "Structure, structural, structuralisme." *Diogène*, 66
        (1969), 20-30.

4810.   ————. "Structure, Structural, Structuralism" (in Czech).
        Filosofický Časopis, 16, no. 2 (1969), 229-234.

4811.   ————. "Structure, structural, structuralisme." *Revue Rou-
        maine des Sciences Sociales. Série de Philosophie et Logique*,
        13 (1969), 59-66.

4812. ———. "Humain, humanisation, humanisme." *Revue Roumaine des Sciences Sociales. Série de Philosophie et Logique*, 13, no. 4 (1969), 391-405.

Includes a discussion of the anti-humanist theory and theoretical anti-humanism of structuralism.

4813. ———. *Homo significans*. Bucarest: Editura Enciclopedică Română, 1970.

4814. ———. "Le Langage et la genèse de la structure logique de la pensée." *Philosophie et Logique*, 18 (1974), 239-247.

4815. Waldenfels, B. "Towards an Open Dialectic." *Dialectics and Humanism. The Polish Philosophical Quarterly*, 3, no. 1 (1976), 91-101.

The inadequacy of Marxist, phenomenological and structuralist theories and the interest of their collaboration.

4816. Watté, Pierre. "L'Idéologie structuraliste." In *Bilan de la Théologie du XXe siècle*. Ed. R. Vander Gucht and H. Vorgrimler. Tome 1: Le Monde du XXe siècle. La Philosophie chrétienne: les grands courants. Tournai-Paris: Casterman, 1970, pp. 339-345.

4817. Wetherick, N.E. "Structuralism and Reductionism." *The Journal of the British Society for Phenomenology*, 2 (October 1971), 59-63.

4818. White, Hayden V. "Historicism, History and the Figurative Imagination." *History and Theory*, Beiheft 14 (1975), pp. 48-67.

The acknowledgment of linguistic determinism resolves a number of problems of historical theory and entails a qualified relativism of historical accounts. On Lévi-Strauss as well.

Wilden, A.G. See item 216.

4819. Wilden, Anthony. "Structuralism as Epistemology of Closed Systems." In *The Unconscious in Culture: The Structuralism of Claude Lévi-Strauss in Perspective*. Ed. Ino Rossi. New York: E.P. Dutton, 1974, pp. 273-290.

4820. ———. "Piaget and the Structure as Law and Order." In item 173, pp. 83-117.

4821. Wyschogrod, Edith. "Death and Some Philosophies of Language." *Philosophy Today*, 22 (1978), 255-265.

Includes a discussion of Derrida, Foucault, linguistics, and structuralism.

4822. Xirau, Ramon. "Examen de crítica: examen de críticos." *Dianoia*, 27 (1971), 200-223.

Ysseling, S. See item 3378.

4823.   Yudin, E.G., and I.V. Blauberg. "Philosophical Investigations
        of Systems and Structures" (in Russian). *Voprosy Filosofii*,
        no. 5 (1970), pp. 57-68. English summary, p. 187.

        Analyzes the historical premises, relations and differences
        between functionalism (proper to sociology), structuralism
        and the systems approach; the philosophical problems which
        arise from a methodological and an ideological viewpoint.

4824.   Zardoya, J.M. "En torno al estructuralismo." *Crisis. Revista
        Española de Filosofía*, 19, no. 73 (1972), 45-62.

        The structural laws of "conditionings" as brought to light
        by Althusser, Foucault, Lacan and Lévi-Strauss.

4825.   Žižek, S. "The Hermeneutic Circle in Structuralism" (in Serbo-
        Croatian). *Delo*, 19, no. 4-5 (1973), 546-569.

POETICS

4826. Abu-Deeb, Kamal. "Towards a Structural Analysis of Pre-Islamic
       Poetry." *International Journal of Middle East Studies*, 6
       (April 1975), 148-184.

       Anonymous. See item 4083.

4827. ———. "Language and Literature." *Choice*, 12, no. 7 (September 1975), 832.

       On Culler's *Structuralist Poetics*.

       Apo, S. See item 5129.

4828. Azevedo, Leodegário Amarante de. *Estruturalismo e crítica de
       poesia*. Rio de Janeiro: Edições Gernasa, 1970. (Estudos Uni-
       versitários Collection, no. 2)

       Bamberg, M. See item 4922.

       Bann, S. See item 5197.

4829. Benamou, Michel. "Recent French Poetics and the Spirit of
       Mallarmé." *Contemporary Literature*, 11, no. 2 (Spring 1970),
       217-225.

4830. Bennett, James R. "Todorov and the Structuralist Science of
       Poetics." In *Phenomenology, Structuralism, Semiology*. Ed.
       Harry R. Garvin. Lewisburg, Pa.: Bucknell University Press;
       London: Associated University Presses, 1976, pp. 127-139.

4831. Bruns, Gerald L. *Modern Poetry and the Idea of Language: A
       Critical and Historical Study*. New Haven-London: Yale Univer-
       sity Press, 1974.

       Cabañes, J.-L. See item 4289.

       Caminade, P. See item 1011.

4832. Caws, Mary Ann. "*Worlds Apart: Structural Parallels in the
       Poetry of Paul Valéry, Saint-John Perse, Benjamin Peret and
       René Char*. By Elizabeth R. Jackson." *Romanic Review*, 68,
       no. 2 (March 1977), 162-163.

4833. Chatman, Seymour, ed. *Approaches to Poetics. Selected Papers
       from the English Institute*. New York: Columbia University
       Press, 1973.

*4834. Cohen, Jean. *Structure du langage poétique*. Paris: Flammarion, 1966.

4835. ————. *Estructura del lenguaje poético*. Trans. Martín Blanco Alvarez. Madrid: Gredos, 1970.

4836. Culler, Jonathan D. *Structuralist Poetics. Structuralism, Linguistics and the Study of Literature*. Ithaca, N.Y.: Cornell University Press; London: Routledge and Kegan Paul, 1975. Bibliography, pp. 273-293.

        Contains: Part I. Structuralism and Linguistic Models. (1) The Linguistic Foundation; (2) The Development of a Method: Two Examples; (3) Jakobson's Poetic Analyses; (4) Greimas and Structural Semantics; (5) Linguistic Metaphors in Criticism; Part II. Poetics. (6) Literary Competence; (7) Convention and Naturalization; (8) Poetics of the Lyric; (9) Poetics of the Novel; Part III. *Perspectives*. (10) "Beyond" Structuralism: *Tel Quel*; (11) Conclusion: Structuralism and the Qualities of Literature.

4837. Davis, Gary W. "Structuralist Poetics." *Contemporary Literature*, 18, no. 2 (Spring 1977), 241-245.

        Ducrot, O., et al. See items 4129 and 4129a for an encyclopedia of poetics as well as linguistics.

4838. Durand, Gilbert. "Les Chats, les rats et les structuralistes. Symbole et structuralisme figuratif." *Cahiers Internationaux de Symbolisme*, no. 17-18 (1969), pp. 13-38.

4839. Foster, David William. "Borges and Structuralism: Toward an Implied Poetics." *Modern Fiction Studies*, 19 (Fall 1973), 341-351.

4840. Friedrich, H. *Structures de la poésie moderne*. Paris: Denoël-Gonthier, 1976.

4841. Galard, Jean. "Pour une poétique de la conduite." *Semiotica*, 10, no. 4 (1974), 351-368.

        Greimas, A.J. See item 5157.

4841a. Grimaud, Michel. Review of Jonathan Culler's *Structuralist Poetics*. *Sub-stance*, 5, no. 14 (September 1976), 167-168.

        Harmon, W. See item 3949a.

4842. Jackson, Elizabeth R. *Worlds Apart: Structural Parallels in the Poetry of Paul Valéry, Saint-John Perse, Benjamin Peret and René Char*. The Hague: Mouton, 1976. (De Proprietatibus Litterarum Series Practica, 106)

4843. Jacquart, Emmanuel. "Interview with Roman Jakobson: On Poetics." *Philosophy Today*, 22 (1978), 65-72.

4844. Jakobson, Roman. "Linguistics and Poetics." In *Style in Language*.
       Ed. T.A. Sebeok. Cambridge, Mass.: MIT Press, 1960.

4845. ―――――, and Claude Lévi-Strauss. "Les Chats de Baudelaire."
       L'Homme, 2, no. 1 (1962), 5-21.

       Structural analysis of a sonnet.

4846. ―――――. *Questions de poétique*. Paris: Editions du Seuil, 1973.

4847. Jolkovski, A., and I. Chtcheglov. "Structural Poetics, the
       Genesis of Poetry" (in Russian). *Voprosy Liter.*, 11, no. 1
       (1967), 74-89.

       How and why art is born from non-art in the perspective of
       structuralism and cybernetics.

4848. Krieger, Murray. "Poetics Reconstructed: The Presence vs. the
       Absence of the Word." *New Literary History*, 7 (Winter 1976),
       347-375.

4849. Kristeva, Julia. "D'une identité à l'autre (Le Sujet du 'langage
       poétique')." *The Modern Language Journal*, no. 62 (1975), pp.
       10-27.

4850. Levin, Samuel R. *Linguistic Structures in Poetry*. The Hague:
       Mouton, 1962.

4851. Lotman, Jurij Michajlovic. "Zwei Kapitel zur strukturellen
       Poetik." *Sprache im Technischen Zeitalter*, 38 (1971), 110-120.

       Malagoli, L. See item 138.

4852. McFadden, George. *"Structuralist Poetics." Journal of Aesthetics
       and Art Criticism*, 34, no. 3 (Spring 1976), 352-353.

       On item 4836.

4853. Minguet, P. "Rhétorique et poétique." *Zeitschrift für Ästhetik
       und allgemeine Kunstwissenschaft*, 20 (1975), 48-59.

       Mukařovský, J. See item 3717.

4854. Olsen, Stein Haugom. "What is Poetics?" *The Philosophical Quar-
       terly*, 26, no. 105 (October 1976), 338-351.

       A critique of the dogma of objectivity common to semiotics
       and structuralism. A work of art has a meaning which is a value.
       Poetics must not and cannot exorcise the problem of intention.

       Revzin, I.I. See item 4022.

4855. Riffaterre, Michael. "Describing Poetic Structures: Two Approaches
       to Baudelaire's Les Chats." In item 68, pp. 200-242. See
       also item 69.

4855a. ―――――. *Semiotics of Poetry*. Bloomington: Indiana University
       Press, 1978.

4856.   Ruwet, Nicolas. "L'Analyse structurale de la poésie." In *Lin-
        guistics, no. 2.* The Hague: Mouton, December 1963, pp. 38-59.

4857.   ————. "Analyse structurale d'un poème français: un sonnet
        de Louis Labé." *Linguistics, no. 3.* The Hague: Mouton, Janu-
        ary 1964, pp. 62-83.

4858.   ————. "Sur un vers de Charles Baudelaire." *Linguistics, no.
        17.* The Hague: Mouton, October 1964, pp. 69-77.

4859.   ————. *Langage, musique, poésie.* Paris: Editions du Seuil,
        1972. (Collection Poétique) Contains items 4856-4858.

4860.   Ryan, Michael. "*Structuralist Poetics: Structuralism, Linguis-
        tics and the Study of Literature,* by Jonathan Culler."
        Philological Quarterly, 55, no. 2 (Spring 1976), 294-296.

4861.   Stankiewicz, E. "Poetics and Verbal Art." In item 5183, pp. 54-
        76.

4862.   Sturrock, John. "Homo significans." *New Review,* 1, no. 12
        (London, March 1975), 61-62.

        On item 4836.

4863.   Todorov, Tzvetan. "Poétique." In *Qu'est-ce que le structuralisme?*
        Ed. François Wahl. Paris: Editions du Seuil, 1968, pp. 97-
        166. (Points, 45) Published as a separate volume with the
        same title in 1973.

        The object of poetics is not the literary work itself, but
        the properties of that particular kind of discourse known as
        literary discourse. Each work is thus considered only as the
        manifestation of a much more general abstract structure of
        which it is only one of many possible realizations. The work
        is thus projected onto something other than itself: the struc-
        ture of literary discourse which will be designated by the name
        of "poetics."

4864.   ————. "Valéry's Poetics." Trans. E. Willis. *Yale French
        Studies,* no. 44 (1970), pp. 65-71.

4865.   ————. *Poétique de la prose.* Paris: Editions du Seuil, 1971.

        Uspensky, B. See item 4064.

        Wunderli, P. See item 5189a.

4866.   Zéraffa, Michel. "La Poétique de l'écriture." *Revue d'Esthétique,*
        24, no. 4 (October-December 1971), 384-401.

        The essential features of recent studies in structuralism.

PSYCHOANALYSIS/PSYCHOLOGY

4867. Anonymous. *Incidences de la psychanalyse*. Paris: Gallimard, 1970. A special issue of *Nouvelle Revue de Psychanalyse*, no. 1 (Spring 1970).

4867a. ————. *Psicoanalisi e strutturalismo di fronte a Dante*. Vol. 2. Lettura della "Commedia." Florence: Olschki, 1972.

————. See also item 3860.

4868. Baer, R. "Schizophrenietypologie in strukturpsychiatrischer Sicht." *Psychiatrie, Neurologie und medizinische Psychologie*, 24, no. 6 (1972), 326-336.

Bär, E. See item 5130.

Bastide, R. See item 3739.

Benveniste, E. See item 4095.

Bonelli, G. See item 3880.

Boon, M.C. See item 3218.

4869. Bruns, Gerald L. "Freud, Structuralism, and 'The Moses of Michelangelo.'" *The Journal of Aesthetics and Art Criticism*, 33, no. 1 (Fall 1974), 13-18.

4870. *Cahiers pour l'Analyse*, no. 3 (1969): issue entitled "Sur l'objet de la psychanalyse." By the Cercle d'Epistémologie de l'Ecole Normale Supérieure de Paris.

4871. Castoriades-Aulagnier, P. "Les Constructions psychanalytiques." *Topique*, 3 (1970).

4872. Cervantes Gimeno, F. "The Structuralist Approach in Psychiatry." *Human Context*, 5, no. 1 (Spring 1973), 114-137.

4873. Cipolli, C. "Simbolo, inconscio, società." *Lingua e Stile*, 5, no. 2 (1970), 215-252.

4874. Clancier, Anne. *Psychanalyse et critique littéraire*. Toulouse: "Nouvelle Recherche," Privat, 1973.

4875. Deschamps, Jean. "Psychanalyse et structuralisme." *La Pensée*, no. 135 (1967), pp. 138-152.

Estebanez, E.G. See item 4499.

4876.   Eynard, R. "Piaget, Freud e lo strutturalismo. Contributo ad
        un raffronto di tesi." *I Problemi della Pedagogia*, 18, no.
        5-6 (1972), 721-733.

4877.   Feldman, Carol F., and Stephen Toulmin. "Logic and the Theory
        of Mind." *Nebraska Symposium on Motivation*, 23 (1975), 409-
        479.

        Identifies the chief points at which difficulties arise with
        structuralist theories in psychology, such as Piaget's theory
        of developmental stages.

4878.   Filippov, L.I. "Structuralism and Freudianism" (in Russian).
        Voprosy Filosofii, no. 3 (1976), pp. 155-163.

4879.   Fillenbaum, Samuel, and Amnon Rapoport. *Structures in the Sub-
        jective Lexicon*. New York: Academic Press, 1971.

4880.   Friedman, L. "Structure and Psychotherapy." *Psychoanalytic
        Review*, 59, no. 4 (1972-1973), 539-548.

4881.   Gardner, Howard. "France and the Modern Mind." *Psychology Today*,
        7, no. 1 (June 1973), 58-62, 104.

        Analyzes the French intellectual tradition, using a structural
        model. If such an analysis had been possible in 1900, it would
        have predicted the emergence of people like Lévi-Strauss and
        Piaget, both of whom have methods for detecting basic cognitive
        structures and who employ modern mathematical principles in
        analyzing thought and behavior.

        ————. See also items 4527-4530.

        Georgin, R. See item 3939.

4882.   Gimeno, F. Cervantes. "La Perspectiva estructuralista en
        psiquiatria." *Human Context*, 5, no. 1 (Spring 1973), 87-113.

4883.   ————. "The Structuralist Approach in Psychiatry." *Human
        Context*, 5, no. 1 (Spring 1973), 114-136.

4884.   Green, André. "La Psychanalyse devant l'opposition de l'histoire
        et de la structure." *Critique*, no. 19 (1963), pp. 649-662.

*4884a. ————. *Un Oeil en trop. Le Complexe d'Oedipe dans la tragédie*.
        Paris: Editions de Minuit, 1969. (Critique)

4884b. ————. *The Tragic Effect. The Oedipus Complex in Tragedy*.
        Trans. Alan Sheridan. Cambridge-New York: Cambridge University
        Press, c. 1979.

4885.   Grimaud, Michel. "Literature and Psychoanalysis: An Annotated
        Bibliography." *Sub-stance*, no. 3 (Spring 1972), pp. 109-119.

4885a. ———. "Recent Trends in Psychoanalysis: A Survey With Em-
        phasis on Psychological Criticism in English Literature and
        Related Areas [in the Social Sciences]." *Sub-stance*, 5, no.
        13 (May 1976), 136-162.

4886.   Hearnshaw, L.S. "Structuralism and Intelligence." *Revue Inter-
        nationale de Psychologie Appliquée*, 24, no. 2 (1975), 85-91.

        New versions of structuralism might yield theoretical bases
        for a psychology of intelligence.

        Kisiel, T. See item 4590.

        Lang, H. See item 4605.

4887.   Lanteri-Laura, G., and L. del Pistoia. "Structural Analysis
        of Suicidal Behavior." *Social Research*, 37, no. 3 (1970),
        324-347.

        A case study is used to show how suicide can be considered
        as a language, as the transmission of a message.

        Laughlin, C.D., et al. See item 5268.

4888.   Levenson, Edgar A. *The Fallacy of Understanding: An Inquiry
        into the Changing Structure of Psychoanalysis*. New York:
        Basic Books, 1972.

        Li Carrillo, V. See item 4617a.

4889.   Lobrot, M. *L'Intelligence et ses formes. Esquisse d'un modèle
        explicatif*. Paris-Brussels-Montreal: Dunod, 1973.

        Versus Bergsonian and structuralist views of intelligence.

4890.   Looft, William R., and Cyril P. Svoboda. "Structuralism in
        Cognitive Developmental Psychology: Past, Contemporary and
        Future Perspectives." In item 173, pp. 49-60.

4890a. Mauron, Charles. *L'Inconscient dans l'oeuvre et la vie de
        Racine*. Paris: Libraire José Corti, 1969.

4891.   Mouloud, Noël. *Psicología y estructuras*. Trans. Ida L. Deschamps.
        Buenos Aires: Columba, 1970.

*4892. Mucchielli, Roger. *Introduction à la psychologie structurale*.
        Brussels: Dessart, 1967.

4893.   ———. *Introducción a la psicología estructural*. Trans. Ramón
        García López. Barcelona: Ed. Anagrama, 1969.

4894.   ———. *Introduction to Structural Psychology*. Trans. Charles
        Lam Markmann. New York: Funk and Wagnalls, 1970.

4895.   Nalbone, Patrick J. "Toward a Conceptual Model of Thinking
        from the Perspective of Structuralism and System Theory."
        Dissertation Abstracts International, 35 (7-A) (January

1975), 4256-4257. State University of New York, Buffalo, 1974.

*4896.   Peters, M.J. "Psychoanalysis, Structuralism and Consciousness."
         Human Context, 5, no. 1 (Spring 1973), 138-155.

4897.   ———. "Psychanalyse, structuralisme et conscience." *Human
         Context*, 5, no. 1 (Spring 1973), 155-174.

         Critically evaluates the premises of structuralism and psy-
         choanalytic theory in a discussion that ranges from associationist
         ideas to the symbolic content of dreams.

4897a. Piaget, Jean. *The Essential Piaget*. Ed. Howard E. Gruber and
         J. Jacques Vonèche. New York: Basic Books, 1977.

         As the chief representative of structuralism in psychology,
         Piaget would require a separate bibliography all to himself.
         The reader is, therefore, referred to this work and its bibli-
         ography on pp. 861-866.

         ———. See also items 154-157 and 160-164.

4898.   Raffa, Piero. "Psicanalisi e teoria del linguaggio." *Nuova
         Corrente*, 66 (1975), 180-190.

         Richard, M., et al. See item 3338.

*4899.   Safouan, Moustafa. "De la structure en psychanalyse. Contribu-
         tion à une théorie du manque." In *Qu'est-ce que le structura-
         lisme?* Ed. François Wahl. Paris: Éditions du Seuil, 1968,
         pp. 239-299. Later (1973) rpt. separately as *Le Structuralisme
         en psychanalyse*, tome 4 of *Qu'est-ce que le structuralisme?*
         (Points, 47)

         Follows the themes that Lacan first developed in his seminars
         at the Sainte-Anne Hospital from 1958-1963. Shows that the
         Oedipus complex is a structure according to which desire is
         ordered insofar as it is an effect of the human being's rela-
         tionship to language. Safouan is a member of Lacan's school
         and translated Freud's *Dream Interpretation* into Arab.

4900.   ———. *Estruturalismo e psicanálise*. Trans. Álvaro Lorencini
         and Anne Arnichaud. São Paulo: Cultrix, 1970.

4901.   ———. *El Estructuralismo en psicoanálisis*. Buenos Aires:
         Losada, 1975.

4902.   Saravay, S.M. "Group Psychology and the Structural Theory:
         A Revised Psychoanalytical Model of Group Psychology."
         Journal of the American Psychoanalytical Association, 23,
         no. 1 (1975), 69-89.

4903.   Sazbón, José, ed. *Estructuralismo y psicoanálisis*. Buenos
         Aires: Ediciones Nueva Visión, 1970.

4904. ———, ed. *Estructuralismo y psicología*. Buenos Aires: Ediciones Nueva Visión, 1970.

4904a. Šipoš, I., and D. Árochová. "Structuralism and Psychology" (in Slovakian). *Filozofia*, 32, no. 2 (1977), 178-183. Part of an issue on Marxism and Structuralism.

Tabouret-Keller, A. See item 4251.

Tel Quel. See item 4253.

Timpanaro, S. See item 4342.

Tuan, Y-F. See item 4799.

4905. Turkle, Sherry. *Psychoanalytic Politics: Freud's French Revolution*. New York: Basic Books, 1978, 278pp.

An explanation of the rise of French interest—both academic and popular—in psychoanalysis; an analysis of Lacan's most important ideas: on the "trinity" of the symbolic, the imaginary, and the real; on the ego as neurosis-bearer; on the significance of wordplay; on the bridge between science and poetry, between Marx and Freud.

4906. Vuorinen, Risto. "On Physiological Structuralism in Psychology." *Ajatus*, 34 (Finland, 1972), 84-112.

4907. Wideman, George H. "Comments on the Structural Theory of Personality." *International Journal of Psycho-Analysis*, 53, no. 2 (1972), 307-314. A paper read at the 27th International Psycho-Analytical Congress.

Suggests that the term "structure" as applied to id, ego, and superego needlessly limits psychoanalytic theory. The use of the term "system" in its modern meaning to describe id, ego, and superego is proposed as a modification of terminology that would bring structural theory up to date.

Wilden, A. See item 216.

4908. Wolff, Reinhold. *Strukturalismus und Assoziationspsychologie. Empirisch-pragmatische Literaturwissenschaft im Experiment: Baudelaires "Les Chats."* Tübingen: Max Niemeyer, 1977.

4909. Wozniak, R.H. "Dialecticism and Structuralism: The Philosophical Foundation of Soviet Psychology and Piagetian Cognitive Developmental Theory." In item 173.

4910. *Yale French Studies*, no. 48 (1972): issue entitled "French Freud: Structural Studies in Psychoanalysis," ed. Jeffrey Mehlman.

Includes extensive treatment of Lacan.

RELIGION/SCRIPTURE/THEOLOGY

4911. Aletti, Jean Noël. "D'une écriture à l'autre. Analyse structurale d'un passage d'Origène: commentaire sur Jean, livre II, 13-21." *Recherches de Science Religieuse*, 61 (January-March 1973), 27-47.

4912. ————. "Proverbes 8:21-31. Etude de structure." *Biblica*, 57, no. 1 (1976), 25-37.

4913. Allaire, J.-M., and M. Lagree. "Mandements de Carême à Rennes au XIXᵉ siècle. Langage et histoire." *Annales de Bretagne et des Pays de l'Ouest*, 82, no. 3 (1975), 367-382.

An analytical and structural treatment.

Allard, G.H. See item 4421.

4913a. Alter, Robert. "A New Theory of Kashrut." *Commentary*, 68 (August 1979), 46-52.

4914. Amphoux, C.B. "Langue de l'épître de Jacques: études structurales." *Revue d'Histoire et de Philosophie Religieuses*, 53, no. 1 (1973), 7-45.

4915. Anonymous. *Analyse structurale et exégèse biblique. Essais d'interprétation*. Neuchâtel: Delachaux et Niestlé, 1972. See also item 842. For reviews, see items 1277-1284.

4916. ————. *Exégèse et herméneutique*. Paris: Editions du Seuil, 1971. For review, see item 5069.

4917. Anthony, Dick, and Thomas Robbins. "From Symbolic Realism to Structuralism." *Journal for the Scientific Study of Religion*, 14 (December 1975), 403-414.

4918. Asmussen, C. "L'Athéisme contemporain en France." *Positions Luthériennes*, 15, no. 3 (1967), 188-202.

4919. Auffret, Pierre. "Note sur la structure littéraire de *Ps* 51: 1-19." *Vetus Testamentum*, 26 (April 1976), 142-147.

4920. ————. "Essai sur la structure littéraire du Psaume I." *Biblische Zeitschrift*, n.s. 22, no. 1 (1978), 26-45.

4921. Bader, G. "Das Gebet Jonas. Eine Meditation." *Zeitschrift für Theologie und Kirche*, 70, no. 2 (1973), 162-205.

The coordinates of the psalm of Jonas (*Jonas*, 2); Jonas and Plato's *Meno*: a structural analysis.

4922. Bamberg, Michael. "Generativismus--Logischer Empirismus--Strukturalismus." *Linguistica Biblica*, 33 (1974), 34-63.

A critique of the approaches of generative poetics and traditional theological hermeneutics in the light of a modern philosophy of science.

4923. Bartnik, Czesław. "Historicism and Structuralism in Fundamental Theology" (in Polish). *Roczniki Teologiczno-Kanoniczne*, 22, no. 2 (1975), 5-17.

On the use of structuralism in apologetics.

4924. Beardslee, William A. "Parable Interpretation and the World." *Perspectives in Religious Studies*, 3, no. 2 (1976), 123-139.

4925. Beauchamp, Paul. "Propositions sur l'alliance de l'Ancien Testament comme structure centrale." *Recherches de Science Religieuse*, 58 (April-June 1970), 161-193.

4926. ————. "Quelques faits d'écriture dans la poésie biblique." *Recherches de Science Religieuse*, 61 (January-March 1973), 127-138.

4927. Belo, F. *Lecture matérialiste de l'évangile de Marc*. Paris: Editions du Cerf, 1974.

Belo uses linguistic methods (structuralism) and ideological ones (Marxism) in his rereading of Mark's gospel.

4928. Biardeau, M. "Etudes de mythologie hindoue III." *Bulletin de l'Ecole Française d'Extrême-Orient*, 58 (1971), 17-89.

A structural analysis of the narratives (cosmogony and eschatology) of several purana.

4929. Biase, Carmine di. "Lo Strutturalismo come ricerca del divino." *Osservatore Romano*, anno CXVII, n. 33 (10 February 1977), 3.

4930. Blancy, A. "Structuralisme et herméneutique." *Etudes Théologiques et Religieuses*, 48, no. 1 (1973), 49-60.

4931. Blanquart, P. "Le Structuralisme en France." *Vie Spirituelle*, no. 83 (1967), pp. 559-574.

4932. Blenkinsopp, Joseph. "The Structure of P." *Catholic Biblical Quarterly*, 38, no. 3 (1976), 275-292.

4933. Blommerde, A.C.M. "Is There an Ellipsis Between *Galatians* 2,3 and 2,4?" *Biblica*, 56, no. 1 (1975), 100-102.

4934. Boisset, L. *La Théologie en procès face à la critique marxiste*. Paris: Editions du Centurion, 1974.

On Althusser, Marxism, Lévi-Strauss.

4935.   Bouttier, M. "Les Etudes parues en français dans le domaine
        biblique." *Etudes Théologiques et Religieuses*, 48, no. 1
        (1973), 113-119.

4936.   Bowker, John. *The Sense of God: Sociological, Anthropological
        and Psychological Approaches to the Origin of the Sense of
        God*. Oxford: Clarendon Press, 1973.

        Has been called a "structuralist theology." Based on the
        Wilde Lectures given in Oxford in 1972.

4937.   Calloud, Jean. "Apocalypse 12-13: essai d'analyse sémiotique."
        Foi et Vie, 75, no. 4 (1976), 26-78.

        ————. See items 3897-3899 and 5136.

4938.   Capps, W.M. "Motif-Research in Irenaeus, Thomas Aquinas, and
        Luther." *Studia Theologica*, 25, no. 2 (Oslo, 1971), 133-159.

        An application of motif-research to the structural analysis
        of three tendencies in Christianity on the subject of freedom.

4939.   Carmody, John T. "Bowker's Structuralist Theology." *Journal of
        the American Academy of Religion*, 43 (June 1975), 275-286.

        On item 4936.

4940.   Cazeaux, J. "Littérature ancienne et recherche des 'structures.'"
        Revue des Etudes Augustiniennes, 18, no. 3-4 (1972), 287-292.

4941.   Chabanis, Christian. *Dieu existe-t-il?* Paris: Fayard, 1974.

        Chabanis' discussion with Lévi-Strauss and others on the
        question of God's existence.

4942.   ————, and Claude Lévi-Strauss. "Gott--gibt es den überhaupt?
        Ein Gespräch zwischen Christian Chabanis und Claude Lévi-
        Strauss über Religionsphilosophie, Metaphysik und Wissen-
        schaftstheorie." *Linguistica Biblica*, 32 (Bonn, 1974), 38-55.

4943.   Chevallier, M.A. "I Pierre 1:1 à 2:10; structure littéraire
        et conséquences exégétiques." *Revue d'Histoire et de Philo-
        sophie Religieuses*, 51, no. 2 (1971), 129-142.

4944.   Cipriani, Roberto. "Strutturalismo e religione." *La Critica
        Sociologica*, 32 (Winter 1974-1975), 85-96.

        Clavel, M. See item 3255.

        Clavier, H. See item 3499.

4945.   Collins, Mary. "Ritual Symbols and the Ritual Process: The
        Work of Victor W. Turner." *Worship*, 50 (1976), 336-346.

        Corvez, M. See chapter 6 of items 49-51.

4946.   Couffignal, R. "'Jacob lutte au Jabboq.' Approches nouvelles
        de Genèse, XXXII, 23-33." *Revue Thomiste*, 75, no. 4 (1975),
        582-597.

A structural (Greimas) and psychoanalytic (Lévi-Strauss's view of the Oedipus myth) analysis of this passage. Jacob, the biblical Oedipus.

4947. Coulot, Claude. "Propositions pour une structuration du livre d'Amos au niveau rédactionnel." *Revue des Sciences Religieuses*, 51 (April-June), 169-186.

4948. Crenshaw, James. "Journey into Oblivion: A Structural Analysis of Gen. 22:1-9." *Soundings: An Interdisciplinary Journal*, 58, no. 2 (Summer 1975), 243-256.

4949. Crespy, Georges. "De la structure à l'analyse structurale." *Etudes Théologiques et Religieuses*, 48, no. 1 (1973), 11-34.

*4950. ———. "La Parabole dite: le bon Samaritain, recherches structurales." *Etudes Théologiques et Religieuses*, 48, no. 1 (1973), 61-79.

4951. ———. "Parable of the Good Samaritan: An Essay in Structural Research." *Semeia*, 2 (1974), 27-50. John Kirby's translation of the previous item.

4952. Crossan, John Dominic. "The Servant Parables of Jesus." *Semeia*, 1 (1974), 17-62.

4953. ———. "Parable and Example in the Teaching of Jesus." *Semeia*, 1 (1974), 63-104.

4954. ———. "Structuralist Analysis and the Parables of Jesus." [Reply to D.O. Via] *Semeia*, 1 (1974), 192-221.

4955. ———. "Basic Bibliography for Parables Research. I. Traditio-critical bibliography. II. Structuralist bibliography." *Semeia*, 1 (1974), 236-274.

4956. ———. "Good Samaritan: Towards a Generic Definition of Parable." *Semeia*, 2 (1974), 82-112.

4957. ———. "Comments on the Article of Daniel Patte." *Semeia*, 2 (1974), 121-128.

4958. Culley, Robert C. "Structural Analysis: Is It Done with Mirrors?" *Interpretation*, 28, no. 2 (April 1974), 165-181.

Structuralism in relation to other approaches to the text; examples of structural analysis in six Old Testament stories involving a deception.

4959. ———. *Studies in the Structure of Hebrew Narrative*. Philadelphia: Fortress Press; Missoula: Scholars Press, 1976.

A supplement to *Semeia*; a group of three studies treating the relation between oral and written tradition.

4960. Danieli, G. "Analisi strutturale ed esegesi di Matteo a proposito del recente libro di J. Radermakers." *Rivista Biblica*, 21, no. 4 (1973), 433-439.

4961. Delorme, J. "Luc v. 1-2: analyse structurale et histoire de la rédaction." *New Testament Studies*, 18, no. 3 (London, 1972), 331-350.

4962. Dideberg, D., and P. Mourlon-Beernaert. "'Jésus vint en Galilée.' Essai sur la structure de Marc 1, 21-45." *Nouvelle Revue Théologique*, 98, no. 4 (1976), 306-323.

4963. Dinechin, Olivier de. "ΚΑΘΩΣ: la similitude dans l'évangile selon saint Jean." *Recherches de Science Religieuse*, 58 (April-June 1970), 195-236.

4964. Dixon, John W. "Physiology of Faith." *Anglican Theological Review*, 58 (October 1976), 407-431.

4965. Doty, William G. "Parables of Jesus, Kafka, Borges and Others, with Structural Observations." *Semeia*, 2 (1974), 152-193.

4966. Ela, J.-M. "Jésus-Christ, dieu des philosophes?" *Revue des Sciences Religieuses*, 49, no. 4 (1975), 269-291.

4967. Emerton, J.A. "Examination of a Recent Structuralist Interpretation of Genesis 38." *Vetus Testamentum*, 26 (January 1976), 79-98.

4968. Engdahl, E. "The Parables of Jesus as Linguistic Event" (in Swedish). *Svensk Exegetisk Årsbok*, 39 (1974), 90-108.

4969. Esbroeck, Michel van. *Herméneutique, structuralisme et exégèse, essai de logique kérygmatique.* Paris: Desclée, 1968.

4970. Escande, J. "Jésus devant Pilate: Jean 18:28-19:24." *Foi et Vie*, 73, no. 3 (1974), 66-82.

4971. *Etudes Théologiques et Religieuses*, 48, no. 1 (1973), 11-60: issue on "Les Méthodes d'analyse structurale." See items 4930, 4935, 4949, 4950, 4981, and 5074.

4972. Fischer, Helmut. *Glaubensaussage und Sprachstruktur.* Hamburg: S. 'Furche,' 1971; Bielefeld: Furche Verlag, 1972.

4973. Fish, Stanley E. "Structuralist Homiletics." *MLN*, 91 (December 1976), 1208-1221.

4974. Fishbane, Michael. "Composition and Structure in the Jacob Cycle (Gen 25:19-35:22)." *Journal of Jewish Studies*, 26, no. 1-2 (1975), 15-38.

       Flahault, F. See item 3928.

4974a. Flanagan, James W. "Structuralism and Biblical Studies."
 Horizons (The Journal of the College Theology Society at
 Villanova University), 2, no. 2 (Fall 1975), 245-246.

4975. *Foi et Vie*, 73, no. 3 (1974). Contains items 3899, 4970, 4981,
 4984, and "Lexique sommaire des termes et liste des sigles
 employés en analyse structurale," pp. 91-97.

4976. Fox, Douglas A. "Listening for Invitation: An Approach to the
 Bible." *Encounter*, 39 (Spring 1978), 141-152.

4977. Freedman, D.N., and C.F. Hyland. "Psalm 29: A Structural
 Analysis." *Harvard Theological Review*, 66 (April 1973), 237-
 256.

4978. Funk, Robert W. "Critical Note." *Semeia*, 1 (1974), 182-191.

4979. ————. "Structure in the Narrative Parables of Jesus." *Semeia*,
 2 (1974), 51-73.

4980. ————. "Good Samaritan as Metaphor." *Semeia*, 2 (1974), 74-81.

4981. Galland, Corina. "Introduction à la méthode de A.J. Greimas."
 Etudes Théologiques et Religieuses, 48, no. 1 (1973), 35-48.
 Rpt. in *Foi et Vie*, 73, no. 3 (1974), 13-27.

4982. ————. "Sémiotique en questions." *Etudes Théologiques et
 Religieuses*, 50, no. 3 (1975), 335-344.

4983. ————, et al. *The New Testament and Structuralism: A Collection of Essays*. Trans. Alfred M. Johnson, Jr. Pittsburgh:
 Pickwick Press, 1976. Originally published as no. 22 (June
 1971) of *Langages* entitled "Sémiotique narrative: récits
 bibliques."

4984. Geoltrain, P. "Les Noces à Cana, Jean 2:1-12: analyse des
 structures narratives." *Foi et Vie*, 73, no. 3 (1974), 83-90.

 Giannini, G. See item 4538.

4985. Giard, L. "Lectures plurielles." *Esprit*, no. 4 (1973), pp.
 859-876.

 The reading of writing: classical exegetics, structural
 analysis and semiotics, hermeneutics. Examples.

4986. Gibert, P. "Une Analyse structurale de l'Evangile." *Etudes*,
 November 1972, pp. 619-620.

4987. Giblin, C.H. "Structural and Thematic Correlations in the
 Theology of Revelation 16-22." *Biblica*, 55, no. 4 (1974),
 487-504.

4988. Gilbert, M. *La Critique des dieux dans le livre de la Sagesse*.
 Rome: Biblical Institute Press, 1973. (Analecta Biblica,
 53)

 The literary structure of Wisdom 13-15.

4989. Girard, Marc. "Structure heptapartite du 4e évangile." *Studies in Religion/Sciences Religieuses*, 5, no. 4 (1975-1976), 350-359.

4990. Globe, A. "The Text and Literary Structure of Judges 5, 4-5." *Biblica*, 2 (Rome, 1974), 168-178.

Godelier, M. See item 4372.

4991. Gogacz, M. "The Problem of Atheism in Structuralism" (in Polish). *Collectanea Theologica Warzawa*, 44, no. 1 (1975), 43-53. Summary in French.

4992. Grabner-Haider, Anton. *Glaubenssprache. Ihre Struktur und Anwendbarkeit in Verkündigung und Theologie.* Vienna: Herder & Co., 1975.

Gritti, J., et al. See item 96.

4993. Güttgemanns, Erhardt. "Struktural-generative Analyse der Parabel 'Vom bittenden Freund' (Lk 11, 5-8)." *Linguistica Biblica*, no. 2 (1970/1972), pp. 7-11.

4994. ———. "Struktural-generative Analyse des Bildworts 'Die verlorene Drachme' (Lk 15, 8-10)." *Linguistica Biblica*, no. 6 (1971), pp. 2-17.

4995. ———. "Die Bedeutung des französischen Strukturalismus für die Theologie. Zu einem neuen Buch von Gunther Schiwy." *Linguistica Biblica*, no. 7-8 (1971), pp. 27-30.

On item 189.

4996. ———. "Y a-t-il une grammaire du discours sur Dieu?" *Recherches de Science Religieuse*, 61 (January-March 1973), 105-118.

4997. ———. "Einleitende Bemerkungen zur strukturalen Erzählforschung." *Linguistica Biblica*, no. 23-24 (1973), pp. 2-47.

A review of recent works in New Testament linguistics in France and Germany.

4998. ———, I. Levin, and V.J. Propp. "Theologie und Linguistik in Russland." *Linguistica Biblica*, no. 23-24 (1973), pp. 62-69.

4999. ———. "'Semeia'--ein Zeichen der Zeit! Zu einer neuen linguistischen Zeitschrift." *Linguistica Biblica*, no. 35 (1975), pp. 84-106.

5000. ———. "Generative Poetics." Ed. N.R. Petersen. Trans. W.G. Doty. *Semeia*, 6 (1976), iii-xv, 1-220.

Generative poetics as a new exegetical method. Introductory remarks concerning the structural study of narrative. Narrative analysis of synoptic texts. Linguistic-literary critical foundation of a New Testament theology.

5001. Hägglund, B. "The Structural Idea in Positive and Systematic Theology" (in Swedish). *Svensk Teologisk Kvartalskrift*, no. 3 (1976), pp. 117-124.

A critique of the structural conception as a priori, not as derived from a text first studied for itself.

5002. Haulotte, Edgar. "Fondation d'une communauté de type universel: Actes 10:1-11:18 (étude critique sur la rédaction, la structure et la tradition du récit)." *Recherches de Science Religieuse*, 58 (January-March 1970), 63-100.

5003. *Interpretation*, 28, no. 2 (April 1974), 133-220: "Structuralism." See items 4958, 5004, 5058, 5096, and 5115.

Isambert, F.A. See item 1278.

5004. Jacobson, Richard. "The Structuralists and the Bible." *Interpretation*, 28, no. 2 (April 1974), 146-164.

A summary of the major elements of structural analysis as applied to the Bible. Discusses work by Barthes, Greimas, Chabrol, and Marin.

5005. Johansen, Judith L. "Myths of the 'Search for Identity.'" *Perkins School of Theology Journal*, 29 (Summer 1976), 19-37.

On Lévi-Strauss and religion.

5006. Johnson, Alfred M., Jr., ed. and trans. *The New Testament and Structuralism: A Collection of Essays*. Pittsburgh: Pickwick Press, 1976. (Pittsburgh Theological Monograph Series, 11)

5007. ————, ed. and trans. *Structuralism and Biblical Hermeneutics*. Pittsburgh: Pickwick Press, 1978. (Pittsburgh Theological Monograph Series, 19)

5008. Kamstra, J.H. "Structuralisme en Godsdienstwetenschap." *Tijdschrift voor Filosofie*, 31 (December 1969), 706-731. Summary, pp. 730-731.

Kapelrud, A.S. See item 1279.

5009. Keyser, J.M.B. "Keeping Solomon Legitimate." *Archives Européennes de Sociologie*, 16, no. 1 (1975), 134-147.

Kieffer, R. See item 1280.

5010. ————. "Die Bedeutung der modernen Linguistik für die Auslegung biblischer Texte." *Theologische Zeitschrift*, 30 (June-August 1974), 223-233.

5011. Kirk, G.S. *Myth: Its Meaning and Functions in Ancient and Other Cultures*. Cambridge: University Press; Berkeley: University of California Press, 1970.

5012.   Klaus, Bernhard. "Der Strukturalismus als Element geistlicher
        Rhetorik." *Zeitschrift für Religions und Geistesgeschichte*,
        26, no. 4 (1974), 361-363.

5013.   Kobajashi, K. "Structuralism, Linguistics and Biblical Exegesis"
        (in Japanese). *Journal of Religious Studies*, 49, no. 225
        (Tokyo, 1975), 1-27.

        A fine distinction must be made between the level of structural
        analysis (exegesis) and the level of structural interpretation
        (hermeneutics) of synchronic narratives.

5014.   Krašovec, J. "Die polare Ausdrucksweise im Psalm 139." *Biblische
        Zeitschrift*, 18, no. 2 (1974), 224-248.

5015.   Lack, Rémi. "Le Sacrifice d'Isaac: analyse structurale de la
        couche élohiste dans Gn 22." *Biblica*, 56, no. 1 (1975), 1-12.

5016.   ————. "Le Psaume 1. Une Analyse structurale." *Biblica*, 57,
        no. 2 (1976), 154-167.

5017.   Lai, P.H. "Linguistische Theologie in frankophonen Ländern."
        Linguistica Biblica, 20 (1972), 29-34.

        A bibliography on structural exegetics.

5018.   ————. "Production du sens par la foi; autorités religieuses
        contestées/fondées--analyse structurale de Matt 27:57-28:20."
        Recherches de Science Religieuse, 61 (January-March 1973),
        65-96. See also item 5019.

5019.   ————. "Sinn-Erzeugung durch den Glauben." *Linguistica Biblica*,
        32 (1974), 1-37.

        Two models of Greimas's structural method with the example
        of Matthew 27:57-28:20. See also item 5018.

5020.   Lapointe, R. "Hermeneutics Today." Trans. L. Sabourin. *Biblical
        Theology Bulletin*, 2 (June 1972), 107-154.

5021.   Laporte, J.M. "Dynamics of Grace in Aquinas: A Structural
        Approach." *Theological Studies*, 34, no. 2 (June 1973), 203-
        226.

        The conclusions of the author's thesis defended at Strasbourg
        as a methodological study of the structuralist approach to the
        interpretation of theological texts.

5022.   Lawson, E. Thomas. "Ritual as Language." *Religion: A Journal
        of Religion and Religions*, 6 (Fall 1976), 123-139.

        Shows the significance of structuralism for the study of
        ritual and religion.

5023.   Leach, Edmund R. "The Legitimacy of Solomon. Some Structural
        Aspects of Old Testament History." *Archives Européennes de
        Sociologie*, 7 (1966).

        See items 5009 and 5047 for responses to this article.

5024. ————. *Genesis as Myth and Other Essays*. London: Cape; New York: Grossman, 1969.

5025. Lemert, Charles C. "Social Structure and the Absent Center: An Alternative to New Sociologies of Religion." *Sociological Analysis*, 36 (Summer 1975), 95-107.

French semiotics as a metatheoretical alternative in which one can see a social theory that accounts positively for social structures without needing meaningfulness as a requirement of religious efficacy.

5026. Léon-Dufour, Xavier. "Exégètes et structuralistes." *Recherches de Science Religieuse*, 58, no. 1 (January-March 1970), 5-15.

5027. L'Hour, J. "1 Sam 16:1-13. Pour un 'contrôle populaire' de l'interprétation." *Chronique. Supplément au Bulletin de Littérature Ecclésiastique*, 3 (Toulouse, 1975), 17-47.

A structural analysis of this passage.

5028. Loudot, P. "Teilhardisme et structuralisme." *Nouvelle Revue Théologique*, 92, no. 10 (1970), 1076-1085.

5029. Lys, Daniel. "J'ai deux amours: ou l'amant jugé, exercice sur Osée 2:4-25." *Etudes Théologiques et Religieuses*, 51, no. 1 (1976), 59-77.

5030. Maertens, Jean Thierry. "Sciences de la religion, écriture et épistémologie interdisciplinaire." *Studies in Religion*, 4, no. 2 (Toronto, 1974), 147-157.

Objections to psychoanalysis and structuralism due to the multiplicity of language and writing systems.

5031. ————. "Structure des récits de miracles dans les Synoptiques." *Studies in Religion/Sciences Religieuses*, 6, no. 3 (1976-1977), 253-266.

An attempt to discover the basic structure of the narratives dealing with the healings of Jesus by applying the semiological method of Propp.

Mainberger, G. See item 4627.

5032. Marco, A. di. "Der Chiasmus in der Bibel. 3. Teil." *Linguistica Biblica*, no. 39 (1976), pp. 37-85.

5033. Marin, Louis. "Essai d'analyse structurale d'Actes 10:1-11:18." *Recherches de Science Religieuse*, 58 (January-March 1970), 39-61. Rpt. in item 4916, pp. 213-238.

5034. ————. *Sémiotique de la passion. Topiques et figures*. Paris: Aubier Montaigne/Cerf, 1971. (Bibliothèque des Sciences Religieuses)

5035. ————. "Essai d'analyse structurale d'un récit-parabole: Matthieu 13:1-23." *Etudes Théologiques et Religieuses*, 46, no. 1 (1971), 35-74.

5036.   ————. "Du corps au texte. Propositions métaphysiques sur
         l'origine du récit." *Esprit*, no. 4 (1973), pp. 913-928.

         Approaching the Resurrection narrative with the methods and
         procedures of structural analysis.

         ————. See also item 4635.

         Masset, P. See item 4639.

5037.   McKnight, Edgar V. "Structure and Meaning in Biblical Narrative."
         Perspectives in Religious Studies, 3, no. 1 (Spring 1976),
         3-19.

         The structural and hermeneutic approaches are related to the
         traditional historical-critical approach of New Testament
         scholarship, and suggestions are made as to how the various
         approaches may be combined into a comprehensive satisfying
         method of interpretation.

5038.   ————. *Meaning in Texts: The Historical Shaping of a Narrative
         Hermeneutics*. Philadelphia: Fortress Press, 1978.

         Contends that structuralism can rescue New Testament inter-
         pretation from its irrelevancy and historicism. Applies studies
         in narrative from a structural perspective to hermeneutical
         studies by using the insights of Wilhelm Dilthey as a catalyst
         to make the synthesis possible.

5039.   Mędala, S. "Literary Genres in Scripture in the Light of the
         Methods of Structural Analysis" (in Polish). *Warszawskie
         Studia Biblijne*, p. vol. (1976), 18-34.

         On the inadequacy of classifying biblical texts according
         to literary genres in the traditional sense of the word. New
         aspects of the question.

5040.   Mellon, C. "La Parabole. Manière de parler, manière d'entendre."
         Recherches de Science Religieuse, 61 (January-March 1973),
         49-63.

5041.   Meschonnic, Henri. "Le Structuralisme dans les études
         bibliques." *Les Cahiers du Chemin*, no. 21 (15 April 1974), pp.
         184-202.

         On items 842 and 4915.

5042.   Mínguez, Dionisio. "Hechos 8, 25-40. Análisis estructural del
         relato." *Biblica*, 57, no. 2 (1976), 168-191.

5043.   Morel, G. "L'Enjeu de la crise religieuse. Aspects politiques
         et philosophiques." *Recherches de Science Religieuse*, 63,
         no. 1 (1975), 11-34.

         A debate must be waged with structuralism over the definition
         of the human being as subject.

5044.   Mourlon Beernaert, P. "Jésus controversé. Structure et théologie
         de Marc 2,1-3,6." *Nouvelle Revue Théologique*, 95, no. 2 (1973),
         129-149.

5045. Murphy-O'Connor, Jerome. "Structure of Matthew XIV–XVII."
      Revue Biblique, 82 (July 1975), 360–384.

5046. Nossent, G. "Sur des approches matérialistes de l'Ecriture."
      Nouvelle Revue Théologique, 98, no. 4 (1976), 337–341.

      On the limits of the structural method.

5046a. Oden, Robert A. Jr. "Contending of Horus and Seth (Chester
      Beatty Papyrus no. 1): A Structural Interpretation." *History
      of Religions*, 18 (May 1979), 352–369. With a reply by E.F.
      Wente, pp. 370–372.

5047. Pamment, M. "The Succession of Salomon: A Reply to Edmund
      Leach's Essay *The Legitimacy of Salomon*." *Man*, 7, no. 4
      (London, 1972), 635–643.

      A critical analysis of Leach's structural treatment of the
      biblical narrative of King Salomon's succession. See item 5023.

5048. Patte, Daniel. "An Analysis of Narrative Structure and the
      Good Samaritan." *Semeia*, 2 (1974), 1–26.

5049. ————. "Comments on the Article of John Dominic Crossan."
      Semeia, 2 (1974), 117–121.

5050. ————. "Structural Network in Narrative: The Good Samaritan."
      Soundings: An Interdisciplinary Journal, 58, no. 2 (Summer
      1975), 221–242.

      Proposes a model showing the interrelationship of major
      semiotic constraints in the parable of the Good Samaritan.

5051. ————, ed. *Semiology and Parables: Exploration of the Possi-
      bilities Offered by Structuralism for Exegesis. Papers of
      the Vanderbilt University Conference, May 5–17, 1975*. Pitts-
      burgh: Pickwick Press, 1976. (Pittsburgh Theological Mono-
      graph Series, 9)

5052. ————. *What is Structural Exegesis?* Philadelphia: Fortress
      Press, 1976.

*5052a. ————, and Aline Patte. *Structural Exegesis: From Theory to
      Practice. Exegesis of Mark 15 and 16: Hermeneutical Implica-
      tions*. Philadelphia: Fortress Press, 1978, 134pp. The sequel
      to item 5052.

5052b. ————. *Pour une exégèse structurale*. Paris: Editions du
      Seuil, 1978, 251pp. (Parole de Dieu)

5053. Péter-Contesse, R. "La Structure de 1 Samuel 1–3." *The Bible
      Translator*, 27, no. 3 (1976), 312–314.

5054. Petersen, N.R. "On the Notion of Genre in Via's Parable and
      Example Story: A Literary-Structuralist Approach." *Semeia*,
      1 (1974), 134–181.

5055. Pham, hu'u Lai. "Sinn-erzeugung durch den Glauben-Widerlegte ...
       Begründete Religiöse Authoritäten: Strukturale Analyse von
       Matth 27:57-28:20." *Linguistica Biblica*, 32 (1974), 1-37.

       Develops two models of the structural method of A.J. Greimas:
       the classical square of oppositions and the actantiel model.
       Applies the two models to the above text. This analysis demon-
       strates an astonishing regularity of logical relations.

5056. Picard, Jean Claude. "Trois Instances narratique, symbolique
       et idéologique: propositions d'analyse applicables à un texte
       comme l'Apocalypse." *Foi et Vie*, 75, no. 4 (1976), 12-25.

5057. Pirard, R., and A. Gesché. "Structuralisme et dogmatique: in-
       tégration et dépassement." *Revue Théologique de Louvain*, 4,
       no. 3 (1973), 384-389.

5058. Polzin, Robert. "The Framework of the Book of Job." *Interpreta-
       tion*, 28, no. 2 (April 1974), 182-200.

5059. ————. *Biblical Structuralism: Method and Subjectivity in
       the Study of Ancient Texts*. Philadelphia: Fortress Press,
       c. 1977. (Semeia Supplements)

5060. Pulliam, John D. "The Gospel According to St. Jerome: A Critique
       of Professor Bruner." *Journal of Thought*, 2 (April 1967),
       61-77.

5061. Ramaroson, Léonard. "Structure du prologue de Jean." *Science
       et Esprit*, 28 (October-December 1976), 281-296.

5062. *Recherches de Science Religieuse* 58 (January-March 1970), 5-100:
       issue on Structural Linguistics and the Bible, Conference at
       Chantilly, 4-9 September 1969.

5063. *Recherches de Science Religieuse*, 61 (January-March 1973), 7-
       138: issue entitled "Analyses linguistiques en théologie.
       Travaux de groupe (et bibliographie)."

5064. Refoulé, F. "Exegetiken frågasatt." *Svensk Teologisk Kvartal-
       skrift*, 49, no. 3 (1973), 107-116.

5065. ————. "L'Exégèse en question." *Le Supplément*, 111 (1974),
       391-423.

       Today's structuralist and anti-exegetical reading of the
       Bible.

5066. Richardson, H.N. "Last Words of David. Some Notes on II Samuel
       23:1-7." *Journal of Biblical Literature*, 90 (September 1971),
       257-266.

5067. Ricoeur, Paul. "Biblical Hermeneutics." *Semeia*, 4 (1975), 29-
       148.

5068. Rideau, E. "Le Structuralisme." *Nouvelle Revue Théologique*, 90, no. 9 (1968), 918-935.

5069. Rigaux, B. Review of *Exégèse et herméneutique* (item 4916). *Revue d'Histoire Ecclésiastique*, 67, no. 3-4 (1972), 838-843.

5070. Robbins, Vernon K. "Structuralism in Biblical Interpretation and Theology." *Thomist*, 42 (July 1978), 349-372.

5071. Robert, J. "Témoignages personnels de scientifiques sur le sacré, la religion, Dieu, la foi. A propos de l'étude de C. Chabanis *Dieu existe-t-il?*" *Bulletin Union Catholique des Scientifiques Français*, no. 139 (1975), pp. 29-40.

   On items 4941 and 4942.

5072. Robinson, D.W.B. "The Literary Structure of Hebrews 1: 1-4." *The Australian Journal of Biblical Archaeology*, 2, no. 1 (1972), 178-186.

5073. Rogerson, John. "Recent Literary Structuralist Approaches to Biblical Interpretation." *The Churchman*, 90 (July-September 1976), 165-177. For abstract, see "Structuralism and Biblical Interpretation," *Theology Digest*, 25, no. 1 (1977), 49-52.

5074. Rouquette, Jean. "Les Etudes parues en français dans le domaine biblique; panorama général." *Etudes Théologiques et Religieuses*, 48, no. 1 (1973), 81-96.

   A bibliographical essay on structural linguistics and the Bible.

5074a. ————. *Petite méthode pour l'analyse des textes: avec des exemples pris dans la Bible.* Montpellier: Centre Théologique Interdiocésain, Centre Saint-Guilhem, 1975, 105pp.

5075. Rousseau, A., and F. Dassetto. "Discours religieux et métamorphose des pratiques sociales." *Social Compass*, 20, no. 3 (1973), 389-403.

5076. Salin, D. "Débats, extraits recueillis." *Recherches de Science Religieuse*, 61 (January-March 1973), 97-104.

5077. Samain, E. "L'Evangile de Luc et le livre des Actes: éléments de composition et de structure." *Foi et Vie*, 70, no. 5 (1971), 3-24.

   Saucerotte, A. See item 4398.

5078. Scarpi, P. "Una 'Lettura' metodologica: la polarità 'ottica-acustica' nella struttura religiosa dell'*Inno omerico a Demeter*." *Studia Patavina. Rivista di Scienze Religiose*, 22, no. 1 (1975), 122-147.

5079. Schenk, W. "Die Aufgeben der Exegese und die Mittel der Linguistik." *Theologische Literaturzeitung*, 98 (December 1973), 881-894.

5080. Schenk, Wolfgang. "Textlinguistische Aspekte der Strukturana-
       lyse, Dargestellt am Beispiel von 1 Kor 15:1-11." *New Testa-
       ment Studies*, 23 (July 1977), 469-477.

5081. Schiwy, Günther. "Structuralism." In *Sacramentum Mundi*, vol.
       16, pp. 182-184. New York: Herder and Herder, 1970.

*5082. ————. *Strukturalismus und Christentum. Eine gegenseitige
       Herausforderung*. Freiburg: Herder KG, 1969.

5083. ————. *Strutturalismo e cristianesimo. Una Sfida al sistema.*
       Trans. G. Re. Rome: Herder; Brescia: Morcelliana, 1970.

5084. ————. *Structuralism and Christianity*. Trans. Henry J. Koren.
       Pittsburgh: Duquesne University Press, 1971, 105pp.

5085. ————. *Structuralisme et christianisme*. Trans. Pierre Kamnit-
       zer. Tours-Paris: Mame/Delarge, 1973.

5086. Schmalenberg, Erich. "Die Sprachanalyse vor der Wahrheitsfrage."
       Kerygma und Dogma, 21, no. 3 (July-September 1975), 176-192.

5087. Schnackenburg, R. "Strukturanalyse von Joh 17." *Biblische
       Zeitschrift*, 17, no. 2 (1973), 196-202.

5088. Scott, Bernard B. "Prodigal Son: A Structuralist Interpreta-
       tion." *Semeia*, 9 (1977), 45-73.

5089. Sellin, G. "Gleichnisstrukturen." *Linguistica Biblica*, 31
       (Bonn, 1974), 89-115.

       On the structures of parables; a contribution to the debate
       between Dan O. Via and J.D. Crossan.

5090. *Semeia*, 1 (1974), 17-235: issue entitled "Structuralist Approach
       to the Parables." See items 4952-4955, 4978, 5054, and 5113-
       5114.

5091. *Semeia*, 2 (1974), 1-113: issue edited by John D. Crossan and
       entitled "Good Samaritan." See items 4951, 4956-4957, 4979-
       4980, 5048-5049, 5101, and 5116.

5092. Siegert, Folker. "Narrative Analyse als Hilfe zur Predigtvor-
       bereitung--ein Beispiel." *Linguistica Biblica*, 32 (1974),
       77-90.

       Demonstrates the possibility of a homiletic application of
       the principles of structural analysis of narratives. The text
       analyzed is 2 Ki 5:1-19a. Shows that the structural principles
       of narratives are also valid in Old Testament texts.

5093. Simoens, Y. "Linguistique saussurienne et théologie." *Recherches
       de Science Religieuse*, 61 (January-March 1973), 7-22.

5094. Smith, Gary V. "Structure and Purpose in Genesis 1-11." *The
       Journal of the Evangelical Theological Society*, 20 (December
       1977), 307-319.

5095. Soler, J. "Sémiotique de la nourriture dans la Bible." *Annales. Economies, Sociétés, Civilisations*, 28, no. 4 (1973), 943-955.

An explanation of the Hebrew and Jewish dietary restrictions by structuralism.

5096. Spivey, Robert A. "Structuralism and Biblical Studies. The Uninvited Guest." *Interpretation*, 28, no. 2 (April 1974), 133-145.

Structuralism's weakest point is its viewing thought in binary terms. In reducing a literary work to a model, structuralism obliterates the actual text. The strength of the structuralist concentration upon the model is the de-emphasis upon the author's meaning. Nevertheless, structuralism has a potential for reopening biblical tradition in a way that will not concentrate narrowly on canonical tradition.

5097. Stock, A. "Theologie und Wissenschaftstheorie." *Verkündigung und Forschung. Beihefte zu "Evangelische Theologie,"* 20, no. 2 (1975), 2-34.

5098. Swartley, W.M. "A Study in Markan Structure: The Influence of Israel's Holy History upon the Structure of the Gospel of Mark." *Dissertation Abstracts International*, 34, no. 6 (1973), 3536. Princeton Theological Seminary dissertation, 1973.

5099. Talmon, S., and M. Fishbane. "Some Aspects of Literary Structure in the Book of Ezechiel" (in Hebrew). *Tarbiz. A Quarterly for Jewish Studies*, 42, no. 1-2 (Jerusalem, 1972-1973), 27-41. English summary.

5100. ————. "The Structuring of Biblical Books: Studies in the Book of Ezekiel." *Annual of the Swedish Theological Institute*, 10 (1975-1976), 129-153.

5101. Tannehill, Robert C. "Comments on the Articles of Daniel Patte and John Dominic Crossan." *Semeia*, 2 (1974), 113-116.

5102. Thion, Paul. "Exégèse et analyse structurale: quelques réflexions de théologien." *Nouvelle Revue Théologique*, 97, no. 4 (1975), 318-344.

5103. Thiselton, Anthony C. "Keeping up with Recent Studies. Structuralism and Biblical Studies: Method or Ideology?" *Expository Times*, 89 (August 1978), 329-335.

5104. Thorgaard, J. "Anvendelse af begrebet funktionel aekvivalens i empirisk religions-sociologi." *Dansk Teologisk Tiddsskrift*, 36, no. 1 (1973), 44-63.

5105. Thyen, H. "Positivismus in der Theologie und ein Weg zu seiner Überwindung?" *Evangelische Theologie*, 31 (September 1971), 472-495.

5106. Topel, L.J. "Note on the Methodology of Structural Analysis in
       Jn 2:23-3:21." *The Catholic Biblical Quarterly*, 33 (April
       1971), 211-220.

5107. Trible, Phyllis. "Wisdom Builds a Poem: The Architecture of
       Proverbs 1:20-33." *Journal of Biblical Literature*, 94 (Decem-
       ber 1975), 509-518.

5108. Valori, P. "Strutturalismo e ateismo." *Divinitas*, 13, no. 1
       (1969), 225-234.

5109. Van Bergen, J. "'Le Symbole donne à penser': A Study on Ricoeur"
       (in Dutch). *Tijdschrift voor Theologie*, 13, no. 2 (1973),
       167-189.

       The meaning of religious symbols starting with a symbolism
       of language and using the philosophy of the subject as Ricoeur
       derives it from psychoanalysis and structuralism.

5110. Van der Veken, Jan. "Structuralism and the Crisis of Humanism."
       Religion in Life, 45 (Spring 1976), 33-40.

5111. Vanhoye, A. *La Structure littéraire de l'"Epître aux Hébreux."*
       2nd rev. and enl. ed. Paris: Desclée de Brouwer, 1976.

5112. Vetter, D., and J. Walther. "Sprachtheorie und Sprachvermittlung:
       Erwägungen zur Situation des hebräischen Sprachstudiums."
       Zeitschrift für die Alttestamentliche Wissenschaft, 83,
       no. 1 (1971), 73-96.

5113. Via, Dan O. Jr. "Parable and Example Story: A Literary-Struc-
       turalist Approach." *Semeia*, 1 (1974), 105-133.

5114. ————. "A Response to Crossan, Funk and Petersen." *Semeia*,
       1 (1974), 222-235.

5115. ————. "A Structuralist Approach to Paul's Old Testament
       Hermeneutic." *Interpretation*, 28, no. 2 (April 1974), 201-
       220.

       The structural relationship between the following texts:
       Rom 9:30-10:21 and Paul's use of Lev 18:5 and Deut 30:11-14.

5116. ————. "Comments on Robert W. Funk's article, 'Structure in
       the Narrative Parables of Jesus.'" *Semeia*, 2 (1974), 129-
       133.

5117. ————. "Literary and Structural Analysis of the New Testa-
       ment" (20 minutes). *Thesis Theological Cassettes*, 8, no. 4
       (May 1977).

5118. Vogler, P. "Structuralisme et théologie. La Divinité chez
       les Mosi." *Annales de l'Université d'Abidjan, Série F:
       Ethnosociologie*, 3 (1971, appeared in 1973), 231-335.

5119. Waelkens, R. "L'Analyse structurale des paraboles; deux essais:
        Luc 15:1-32 et Matthieu 13:44-46." *Revue Théologique de Louvain*,
        8, no. 2 (1977), 160-178.

5120. Walsh, Jerome T. "Genesis 2:4b-3:24. A Synchronic Approach."

        Watté, P. See item 4816.

5121. White, C.S.J. "Structure and the History of Religions: Some
        Bhakti Examples." *History of Religions*, 18 (August 1978),
        77-94.

5122. White, Hugh C. "French Structuralism and Old Testament Narra-
        tive Analysis: Roland Barthes." *Semeia*, 3 (1975), 99-127.

5123. Wiggins, James B., ed., *Religion as Story*. New York: Harper
        and Row, 1975.

5124. Williams, Raymond B. "Kerygma and Comedy in the New Testament:
        A Review Article." *Encounter*, 37 (Christian Theological
        Seminary, Winter 1976), 88-90.

5125. Woocher, Jonathan S. "In Every Generation: The Seder as a
        Ritual of Anti-Structure." *Journal of the American Academy
        of Religion*, 45 (December 1977), 503.

        Yallop, C. See item 223.

5126. Zaborski, A. "Structural Methods and Old Testament Studies."
        Folia Orientalia, 15 (Cracow, 1974), 263-268.

        A very severe critique of F. Bovon and R. Barthes. Structura-
        lism is not a French discovery.

        Zanasi, F. See item 3685.

5127. Zumbrunn, E. "La 'Philosophie chrétienne' et l'exégèse d'Exode
        3:14 selon M. Etienne Gilson." *Revue de Théologie et de
        Philosophie*, no. 2 (1969), pp. 94-105.

SEMIOTICS

Amacker, R. See item 4079.

Anonymous. See item 933.

5128. ———. "Ensayo." *Estafeta Literaria*, núm. 590 (15 June 1976), pp. 2506-2507.

5129. Apo, Satu. *Strukturalismia, semiotiikkaa, poetiikkaa.* Helsinki: Gaudeamus, Kustannusosasto, 1974.

Auzias, J.-M. See chapter 4 of items 11-14.

5129a. Avalle, A.S. "Strutturalismo e semiologia in Italia." *Strumenti Critici*, 10, no. 31 (1976), 471-491.

5130. Bär, Eugen. *Semiotic Approaches to Psychotherapy.* Bloomington: Indiana University Press, 1975.

5131. Baran, Henryk, ed. *Semiotics and Structuralism: Readings from the Soviet Union.* Trans. William Mandel et al. White Plains, N.Y.: International Arts and Sciences Press, 1976.

Bassy, A.-M. See item 968.

5132. Beauchamp, William. "From Structuralism to Semiotic." *Romanic Review*, 67 (May 1976), 226-236.

5133. Bermejo, José María. "Lingüística." *Estafeta Literaria*, no. 512 (15 March 1973), p. 1280.

On Georges Mounin's *Introducción a la semiología.*

5134. Bouazis, Charles. "Théorie de l'écriture et sémiotique narrative." *Semiotica*, 10, no. 4 (1974), 305-331.

5135. Brewster, Ben, and MacCabe, Colin. "Semiology and Sociology." *Screen*, 15, no. 1 (Spring 1974), 4-10.

Barthes and Godard.

Calloud, J. See item 4937.

5136. ———, et al. *Signes et paraboles. Sémiotique et texte évangélique.* Paris: Editions du Seuil, 1977, 253pp.

An interpretation of selected texts from the viewpoint of textual semiotics.

Calvet, L.-J. See items 1006–1007 and 1010.

Carontini, E., et al. See item 1014.

5137. Champagne, Roland A. "Grammar of the Languages of Culture: Literary Theory and Yury M. Lotman's Semiotics." *New Literary History*, 9 (Winter 1978), 205–210.

5138. ———. "Prometheus Measuring the Universe: Michel Serre's Semiotic-Reading Model in the Wake of Structuralism." *Semiotic Scene*, 1, no. 2 (Medford, Mass., 1977), 39–48.

5139. ———. "Semiology: A Linguistic Model for French Scripture." *Papers in Language and Literature*, 14 (Summer 1978), 315–333.

Collet, J., et al. See item 3820.

5140. *Communications*, no. 4 (1964): issue on "Recherches sémiologiques" with a critical bibliography on the subject. Paris: Editions du Seuil, 1964.

5141. *Communications*, no. 11 (1968): issue entitled *Recherches sémiologiques: le vraisemblable*. Paris: Editions du Seuil, 1968.

5142. Coquet, Jean-Claude. *Sémiotique littéraire: contribution à l'analyse sémantique du discours*. Paris: Mame, 1973, 272pp. In the Univers Sémiotiques collection directed by A.J. Greimas.

5143. Courtés, Joseph. *Introduction à la sémiotique narrative et discursive: méthodologie et application*. Paris: Hachette, 1976.

5144. Coward, Rosalind, and John Ellis. *Language and Materialism: Developments in Semiology and the Theory of the Subject*. Boston: Routledge and Kegan Paul, 1977.

Daix, P. See item 1028.

De Paz, A. See item 3697.

Dorfles, G. See item 3710.

*5145. Eco, Umberto. *La Struttura assente. Introduzione alla ricerca semiologica*. Milan: V. Bompiani, 1968.

5146. ———, and Remo Faccani. *I Sistemi di segni e lo strutturalismo sovietico*. Trans. R. Faccani and G.L. Bravo. Milan: V. Bompiani, 1969. (Idee Nuove, 50)

5147. ———. "Sémiologie des messages visuels." *Communications*, no. 15 (1970), pp. 11–15.

5148. ———. *La Structure absente. Introduction à la recherche sémiotique*. Trans. U. Esposito-Torrigiani. Paris: Mercure de France, 1972.

5149. ———. *La Estructura ausente. Introducción a la semiótica.* Trans. Francisco Serra Cantarell. Barcelona: Lumen, 1972.

5150. ———. *Einführung in die Semiotik.* Trans. Jürgen Trabant. Munich: Fink, 1972.

5151. ———. "Social Life as a Sign System." In *Structuralism: An Introduction* (item 176), pp. 57-72.

5152. ———. *Theory of Semiotics.* Bloomington: Indiana University Press, 1976. Bibliography, pp. 319-346.

5152a. Eschbach, Achim. *Zeichen Text Bedeutung. Eine Bibliographie zu Theorie und Praxis der Semiotik.* Munich: Wilhelm Fink, 1974.

5152b. ———, and Wendelin Rader. *Semiotik--Bibliographie I.* Frankfurt: Syndikat Autoren- und Verlagsgesellschaft, 1976.

Gaillard, F. See item 1061a.

Garvin, H.R. See item 4531.

Grabner-Haider, A. See item 4992.

5153. Greimas, Algirdas Julien. "Semiotica o metafisica?" *Strumenti Critici*, no. 5 (1968), pp. 71-79.

5154. ———, and F. Rastier. "The Interaction of Semiotic Constraints." *Yale French Studies*, no. 41 (1969), pp. 86-105.

*5155. ———. *Du sens. Essais sémiotiques.* Paris: Editions du Seuil, 1970.

5156. ———. "Sémantique, sémiotiques et sémiologies." In his (et al., eds.) *Sign, Language, Culture.* The Hague: Mouton, 1970, pp. 13-27.

5157. ———, ed. *Essais de sémiotique poétique.* Paris: Larousse, 1972.

5158. ———. *Del Senso.* Trans. Stefano Agosti. Milan: Bompiani, 1974.

5159. ———. *Maupassant: la sémiotique du texte: exercices pratiques.* Paris: Editions du Seuil, 1976.

5160. ———. *Sémiotique et sciences sociales.* Paris: Editions du Seuil, 1976.

5160a. ———, and Joseph Courtés. *Sémiotique. Dictionnaire raisonné de la théorie du langage.* Paris: Hachette, c. 1979, 422pp.

*5161. Guiraud, Pierre. *La Sémiologie.* Paris: Presses Universitaires de France, 1971.

5162. ————. *Semiology*. Trans. George Cross. London-Boston: Routledge and Kegan Paul, 1975.

5163. Gutiérrez López, Gilberto A. *Estructura de lenguaje y conocimiento sobre la epistemología de la semiótica*. Madrid: Editorial Fragua, 1975.

5164. Hamon, Philippe. "Narrative Semiotics in France." *Style*, 8, no. 1 (Winter 1974), 30-45.

Hanhardt, J.G., et al. See item 3825.

5165. Hawkes, Terence. *Structuralism and Semiotics*. Berkeley: University of California Press; London: Methuen, 1977.

The first volume of a new series, "New Accents." Attempts to summarize the ideas of Vico (a "pre-structuralist"), Piaget, Saussure, Boas, Sapir, and Whorf, Lévi-Strauss, Russian Formalism, the Prague Circle, Jakobson, Greimas, Todorov, Barthes, C.S. Peirce, and Derrida. Includes an annotated bibliography and index.

5166. Herrera, J. "Panofsky: estructuralismo, iconología y semiótica." *Revista de Ideas Estéticas*, 30, no. 119 (1972), 237-240.

5167. Johannessen, Kjell S., and Arild Utaker, eds. *Strukturalisme og semiologi: muligheter og begrensninger i en semiologisk forskningspraksis*. Copenhagen: G.M.T., 1973.

5168. Kristeva, Julia. "Pour une sémiologie des paragrammes." *Tel Quel*, no. 29 (Spring 1967), pp. 53-75.

5169. ————. "La Sémiologie, science critique ou critique de la science." *La Nouvelle Critique*, no. 16.

5170. ————. "La Sémiologie comme science des idéologies." *Semiotica*, 1 (1969), 196-204.

5171. ————. "Semanalisi: condizioni d'una semiotica scientifica." *Nuova Corrente*, no. 59 (1972), pp. 237-266.

Küllös, I. See item 5265.

Künzli, R.E. See item 4597.

Langages. See item 4184.

5172. Lauretis, Teresa de. "Shape of the World: Report on Structuralism and Semiotics in Italy." *Books Abroad*, 49 (Spring 1975), 227-232.

Leach, E.R. See item 3773.

Lemert, C.C. See items 5025, 5270, and 5270a.

5173. Man, Paul de. "Semiology and Rhetoric." *Diacritics*, 3 (Fall
       1973), 27-33.

       Marin, L. See item 5034.

5174. Martinet, Jeanne. *Claves para semiología*. Madrid: Gredos, 1973.

       McGraw, B.R. See item 1759a.

5175. Mesnil, M. *Trois essais sur la fête. Du folklore à l'ethnosémi-
       otique*. Brussels: Editions de l'Université de Bruxelles,
       1974.

       Mouloud, N. See item 4659.

5176. Mounin, Georges. *Introduction à la sémiologie*. Paris: Editions
       de Minuit, 1970, 1972.

       A collection of articles comprising an initial inventory
       of the semiology of communication. Three articles on Barthes,
       Lévi-Strauss, and Lacan show the dangers of transposing lin-
       guistic terms and concepts into other areas.

5177. Nattiez, Jean-Jacques. "Problèmes sémiologiques de l'analyse
       des idéologies." *Sociologie et Sociétés*, 5, no. 2 (Montreal,
       1973), 71-90.

       Naville, P. See item 1152.

5178. Niculescu, R. "Guidelines for a Semiotic Theory of Traditional
       Material Civilization" (in Rumanian). *Revista de Etnographie
       şi Folclor*, 18, no. 1 (1973), 11-30.

5179. Osolsobě, I. "Fifty Keys to Semiotics." *Semiotica*, 7, no. 3
       (1973), 226-281.

       Patrizi, G. See item 1166.

       Patte, D. See item 5051.

5180. Pearson, C., and V. Slamecka. "A Theory of Sign Structure."
       Semiotic Scene, 1, no. 2 (Medford, Mass., 1977), 1-22.

       Pettit, P. See item 4701.

5180a. *Poetics Today*, 1, no. 1-2 (1979): on Structuralism and Semiotics
       in Germany.

5181. Prieto, Luis J. *Pertinence et pratique. Essai de sémiologie*.
       Paris: Editions de Minuit, 1975.

       Rastier, François. See item 4019.

5182. ———. *Essais de sémiotique discursive*. Paris: Mame, 1973.
       (Univers Sémiotiques)

Riffaterre, M. See item 4855a.

Sazbón, J. See item 4758.

Schiwy, G. See item 4764.

5183.   Sebeok, Thomas Albert, ed. *A Perfusion of Signs*. Bloomington: Indiana University Press, 1977. Essays delivered as lectures at the First North American Semiotics Colloquium held at the University of Southern Florida in 1975. A companion volume to item 5184.

5184.   ————. *Sight, Sound and Sense*. Bloomington: Indiana University Press, 1978. A collection of essays which resulted from a pilot program in semiotics in the humanities held at Indiana University during the 1975-1976 academic year. Companion volume to item 5183.

Segre, C. See item 4038a.

5185.   Semeniuc, I. "Structural Aspects of Semiology" (in Rumanian). *Studia Universitatis Babeş-Bolyai. Series Philosophia*, 19 (1974), 79-86.

Shukman, A. See item 4042.

Singer, M. See item 3804.

5186.   Stierle, K. "Semiotik als Kulturwissenschaft." *Zeitschrift für Französische Sprache und Literatur*, 83, no. 2 (1973), 99-128.

Review of Greimas's *Du sens*.

5187.   Strickland, Geoffrey. "Benveniste and Semiology: Or, Where Structuralism Doesn't Work." *Cambridge Quarterly*, 7, no. 2 (1977), 113-127.

5188.   *Strumenti Critici*, 7, no. 21-22 (1973), 327-366: issue entitled "Strutturalismo e semiologia in Italia. (1968-1970)." A bibliography.

5189.   Sus, Oleg. "On the Genetic Preconditions of Czech Structuralist Semiology and Semantics. An Essay on Czech and German Thought." *Poetics*, no. 4 (1972), pp. 28-54.

Wilden, A. See item 216.

5189a. Wunderli, Peter. *Ferdinand de Saussure und die Anagramme. Linguistik und Literatur*. Tübingen: Max Niemeyer Verlag, 1972.

SOCIAL SCIENCES

5190. Abel, G. *Wissenschaftssprache und Gesellschaft. Zur Kritik der Sozialwissenschaften.* Opladen: Westdeutscher Verlag, 1975.

5191. Aguilar de Alfaro, Adelita. "Los Métodos estructuralistas en algunas ciencias sociales." *Revista de Filosofía de la Universidad de Costa Rica*, 11, no. 32 (1973), 33-52.

Aleksandrowicz, D. See item 4348.

5192. ————. "Reply to E. Balcerzan" (in Polish). *Studia Filozoficzne*, 1 (1976), 151-162.

On the structural-semiotic current in the human sciences.

5193. Améry, François. "Französische Sozialphilosophie im Zeichen der 'linken Frustration.'" *Merkur*, no. 215 (1966), pp. 161-177.

5194. *Annales. Economies, Sociétés, Civilisations*, 26, no. 3-4 (1971), vii, pp. 533-888: issue entitled "Histoire et structure." Also published as *Histoire et structure*. Paris: Armand Colin, 1971.

5195. Anonymous. *L'Historien entre l'ethnologue et le futurologue.* Actes du Séminaire International organisé sous les auspices de l'Association Internationale pour la Liberté de la Culture, la Fondation Agnelli et la Fondation Giorgi Cini, Venise 2-8 avril 1971. Paris-The Hague: Mouton, 1972.

On the problem of opposition between structure and event.

————. See also items 3861, 3862, and 4426.

5196. ————. *Tendances principales de la recherche dans les sciences sociales et humaines.* Paris-The Hague: Mouton/U.N.E.S.C.O., 1970.

Badcock, C.R. See items 3458-3459.

Bakker, R. See item 4433.

5197. Bann, Stephen. "Historical Text and Historical Object: The Poetics of the Musée de Cluny." *History and Theory*, 17 (1978), 251-266.

5198. Barbano, Filippo. *Estructuralismo y sociología*. Buenos Aires: Nueva Visión, 1970.

*5199. Bastide, Roger, ed. *Sens et usages du terme "structure" dans les sciences humaines et sociales*. The Hague: Mouton, 1962, 1972. (Janua Linguarum, nr. 16) Distributed in the U.S. by Humanities Press. See also item 4094.

5200. ————. *Sentidos y usos del término estructura en las ciencias del hombre*. Buenos Aires: Paidós, 1968.

5201. ————. *Usos e sentidos do têrmo estrutura*. Trans. Maria Heloíza Schabs Cappellato. São Paulo: Ed. Herder, Univ. de São Paulo, 1971.

5202. Bauman, Zygmunt. "The Structuralist Promise." *The British Journal of Sociology*, 24, no. 1 (March 1973), 67-83.

5203. ————. "Understanding as Expansion of the Form of Life." In his *Hermeneutics and Social Science*. New York: Columbia University Press, 1978, pp. 194-224.

Bell, J.H., et al. See item 3674.

5204. Bernabe, J. "A Socio-Cultural Problem. Some Remarks in Relation to Elly Dorrepaals' Article 'Toward a Structural Analysis of the Novels of Hugo Claus'" (in Dutch). *Tijdschrift voor Sociale Wetenschappen*, 17, no. 4 (1972), 457-460.

5205. Berni, O. "Il Rifiuto della storia." *Studi Urbinati di Storia, Filosofia e Letteratura*, 47, no. 1 (1973), 101-119.

5206. Bierwisch, Manfred. "Strukturalismus. Geschichte, Probleme und Methoden." *Kursbuch* V (1966).

5207. ————. *El Estructuralismo. Historia, problemas y métodos*. Trans. from German by Gabriel Ferrater. Barcelona: Ed. Tusquets, 1971.

5208. Blau, P.M., ed. *Approaches to the Study of Social Structure*. London: Open Books, 1976.

5209. Bonnefis, Philippe, ed. *Naturalisme*. Lille: Université de Lille III, 1975, pp. 475-632. A special issue of *Revue des Sciences Humaines*, 40, no. 160 (October-December 1975).

*5210. Boudon, Raymond. *A quoi sert la notion de "structure"? Essai sur la signification de la notion de structure dans les sciences humaines*. Paris: Gallimard, 1968.

5211. ————. *Strutturalismo e scienze umane*. Trans. M.G. Losano. Turin: G. Einaudi, 1970. Trans. of previous item with an appendix on structuralism and law by Mario G. Losano.

5212.   ———. *The Uses of Structuralism.* Trans. Michalina Vaughan.
         Intro. Donald MacRae. London: Heinemann, 1971.

5213.   ———. *The Uses of Structuralism.* New York: Halsted Press,
         1974.

5214.   ———. "Structure dans les sciences humaines." *Encyclopaedia
         Universalis,* vol. 15 (1973), pp. 438-440. Paris: Encyclopaedia
         Universalis France, 1968.

5215.   ———. *Strukturalismus, Methode und Kritik. Zur Theorie und
         Semantik eines aktuellen Themas.* Trans. Rüdiger Teufert.
         Wiesbaden: Westdeutscher Verlag; Düsseldorf: Bertelsmann-
         Universitäts-verlag, 1973.

5216.   ———. *Para que serve a noção de estrutura. Ensaio sobre a
         signifição da noção de estrutura nas ciências humanas.* Trans.
         Luiz Costa Lima. Rio de Janeiro: Eldorado, 1974.

5217.   Bourdieu, Pierre. "Structuralism and Theory of Sociological
         Knowledge." Trans. A. Zanotti-Karp. *Social Research,* 35,
         no. 4 (Winter 1968), 681-706.

5218.   ———. *Zur Soziologie der symbolischen Formen.* Trans. Wolf
         H. Fietkau. Frankfurt am Main: Suhrkamp, 1970.

5219.   ———. "The Three Forms of Theoretical Knowledge." *Informa-
         tion sur les Sciences Sociales,* 12, no. 1 (1973), 53-80.

         The limits of anthropological and linguistic structuralism.

         Brewster, B., et al. See item 5135.

5220.   Broch, Tom. *Strukturalisme for sosiologer.* Oslo: Universitetet,
         Instituttet for Sosiologi, 1971; Oslo: Instituttet for
         Sosiologi, Universitetet i Oslo, 1974.

5221.   Burns, T. "A Structural Theory of Social Exchange." *Acta Soci-
         ologica,* 16, no. 3 (Copenhagen, 1973), 188-208.

5222.   Busino, Giovanni. "Aux origines du structuralisme génétique:
         V. Pareto." *Recherches Sociologiques,* 5, no. 2 (1974), 262-
         281; *Revue Européenne des Sciences Sociales,* 14, no. 37 (1976),
         175-194.

5223.   ———. "Epistémologie génétique, marxisme et sociologie. Notes
         pour une lecture alternative." *Revue Européenne des Sciences
         Sociales,* 14, no. 38-39 (1976), 513-525.

         Cabanes, J.-L. See item 4289.

         Câmara, J.M., et al. See item 35.

5224.   Careaga, G. "Sociología y estructuralismo." *Revista Mexicana
         de Ciencia Política,* 16, no. 62 (1970), 55-61.

5225. Carroll, David. "Diachrony and Synchrony in Histoire." *MLN*, 92 (May 1977), 797-824.

5226. Castells, M., and E. de Ipola. "Epistemological Practice and the Social Sciences." *Economy and Society*, 5, no. 2 (1976), 111-144.

On the complementarity of empiricism and formalism and their peaceful coexistence in the structuralist ideology.

5227. Cecconi, O. "Remarques sur les critères et les fonctions de l'idéologique." *Economie et Humanisme*, no. 194 (1970), pp. 16-31.

On structuralism and ideology; attempt at a sociological analysis of ideology.

5228. Chabrol, Claude. "Structures intellectuelles." *Informations sur les Sciences Sociales*, 6, no. 5 (1967), 205-209.

5229. Čierny, J. "Štrukturalizmus a historická veda." *Filozofia*, 32, no. 1 (1977), 61-68.

Why and how Czech historical science during the sixties was influenced by Western conceptions and particularly by French structuralism.

Cipolli, C. See item 4873.

5230. Cohen, Sande. "Structuralism and the Writing of Intellectual History." *History and Theory*, 17 (May 1978), 175-206.

Commers, R. See item 4469.

Corvez, M. See item 4473.

5231. Cuisenier, Jean. "Le Structuralisme: une méthode pour les sciences humaines." *La Philosophie*, tome 3, pp. 606-646. (Les Dictionnaires Marabout Université Savoir Moderne) Paris: Centre d'Etude et de Promotion de la Lecture, 1969; Verviers: Gérard et Co., 1972.

5232. ————. *Economie et parenté. Leurs affinités de structure dans le domaine turc et dans le domaine arabe*. Paris-The Hague: Mouton, 1975.

Dagenais, J.J. See item 4481.

Daix, P. See item 4363.

5233. De Bruyne, P., J. Herman, and M. De Schoutheete. *Dynamique de la recherche en sciences sociales. Les Pôles de la pratique méthodologique*. Paris: Presses Universitaires de France, 1974.

The structural field and its four poles: epistemological, theoretical, morphological and technical.

5234. De Crescenzo, G. "Interazione e transazione nell'etnologia."
       Rivista de Filosofia, 63 (January-March 1972), 3-35.

5235. De Fontaine, B., and J. De Fontaine-Ouazana. "La Figure dans
       le langage, l'art et la représentation politique." *Annales.
       Economies, Sociétés, Civilisations*, 28, no. 1 (1973), 125-
       141.

       Critique of structuralism.

5236. De Greef, Georges. "Note sur le concept de structure et l'expli-
       cation en science économique." *Cahiers de l'I.S.E.A. Série M.*,
       no. 1 (Paris, 1957), pp. 45-53.

       De Marneffe, J. See item 4484.

       De Paz, A. See item 3697.

       Dittmann, L. See item 3699.

5237. Duby, G. *Hommes et structures du Moyen Age*. The Hague: Mouton,
       1973.

       Eco, U. See item 5151.

5238. Einem, H. von, K.E. Born, F. Schalk, and W.P. Schmid. *Akademie
       der Wissenschaften und der Literatur, Abhandlungen der Geistes-
       und Sozialwissenschaftlichen Klasse* (issue entitled "Der
       Strukturbegriff in dem Geisteswissenschaften"), no. 2 (1973),
       52pp.

       Contains H. von Einem on the concept of structure in art,
       pp. 3-16; K.E. Born on the concept of structure in history,
       pp. 17-30; F. Schalk on structuralism and literary history, pp.
       31-41; and W.P. Schmid on structuralism in the science of lan-
       guage, pp. 43-50. See also item 5239.

5239. Einem, Herbert von, et al. *Der Strukturbegriff in den Geistes-
       wissenschaften*. (Vorgetragen in d. Plenarsitzung u. in d.
       Sitzung d. Geistes- und Sozialwissenschaftlichen Klasse am 11.
       Febr. 1972) Mainz: Verlag der Akademie der Wissenschaften und
       der Literatur; Wiesbaden: Steiner, 1973. See also item 5238.

5240. Eisenstadt, S.N. "Die anthropologische Analyse komplexer Gesell-
       schaften. Ein Vergleich des symbolisch-strukturellen mit dem
       institutionellen Ansatz." *Schweizerische Zeitschrift für
       Soziologie*, 1, no. 1 (1975), 5-38.

*5241. ———. "L'Analyse anthropologique des sociétés complexes."
       Cahiers Internationaux de Sociologie, 60 (1976), 5-41.

5242. Fages, Jean-Baptiste. "Structuralisme et sciences de l'homme."
       L'Information Psychologique, 10, no. 40 (Belgium, 1970),
       41-59.

       Fanizza, F. See item 4501.

5243. Farber, Bernard. "Kinship--Now You See It, Now You Don't."
       Sociological Quarterly, 17 (Spring 1976), 279-288.

       Fraser, J. See item 435.

5244. Gaboriau, Marc, et al, eds. *Estructuralismo e historia*. Buenos
       Aires: Ediciones Nueva Visión, 1969.

5245. Gardner, Howard. "Piaget and Lévi-Strauss: The Quest for Mind."
       Social Research. An International Quarterly, 37, no. 3 (Fall
       1970), 348-365.

       On their use of structuralism in totally different contexts.

5246. ———. "The Structural Analysis of Protocols and Myths: A
       Comparison of the Methods of Jean Piaget and Claude Lévi-
       Strauss." *Semiotica*, 5, no. 1 (1972), 31-57.

       ———. See also item 4527.

5247. Goddard, D. "On Structuralism and Sociology." *American Sociolo-
       gist*, 11, no. 2 (1976), 123-139.

5248. Gonos, George, et al. "Anonymous Expression: A Structural View
       of Graffiti." *Journal of American Folklore*, 89 (January 1976),
       40-48.

5249. ———. "Situation versus Frame: The Interactionist and the
       Structuralist Analyses of Everyday Life." *American Sociologi-
       cal Review*, 42 (December 1977), 854-867.

5250. Gouthier, Giuseppe. *I Concetti di sistema e di struttura nelle
       scienze biologiche, sociologiche, linguistiche ed antropolo-
       giche*. Turin: Quaderni di Studio, 1968.

5251. Gozzi, Gustavo. "Lo Strutturalismo nelle scienze umane." *Il
       Mulino*, 21, no. 221 (May-June 1972), 530-551.

5252. Granger, Gilles. "Evénement et structure dans les sciences
       de l'homme." *Cahiers de l'I.S.E.A. Série M.*, no. 1 (1957),
       pp. 25-44.

5253. Grathoff, Richard, and Walter Sprondel, eds. *Maurice Merleau-
       Ponty und das Problem der Struktur in den Sozialwissenschaf-
       ten*. Stuttgart: Ferdinand Enke, 1976.

       Structural linguistics and structuralism in the social sci-
       ences.

       Greimas, A.J. See item 5160.

       Guala, C. See item 4551.

5254. Handel, Warren. "Normative Expectations and the Emergence of
       Meaning as Solutions to Problems: Convergence of Structural
       and Interactionist Views." *American Journal of Sociology*,
       84 (January 1979), 855-881.

5255. Hund, Wulf Dietmar. *Geistige Arbeit und Gesellschaftsformation:*
       zur Kritik der strukturalistischen Ideologie. Frankfurt am
       Main: Europäische Verlagsanstalt, 1973.

       ——————. See also item 4575.

       Hymes, D. See item 4165.

5256. Kasarda, John D. "Structural Implications of Social System
       Size: A Three-Level Analysis." *American Sociological Review,*
       39 (February 1974), 19-28.

5257. Katz, Fred E. *Structuralism in Sociology: An Approach to Know-*
       ledge. Albany: State University of New York Press, 1976.

5258. Kaufmann, J.N. "Löst der Strukturalismus die Kausalanalyse ab?"
       Zeitschrift für Allgemeine Wissenschaftstheorie, 7, no. 1
       (1976), 75-98.

       Structure vs. cause.

5259. Keat, R., and J. Urry. *Social Theory as Science.* London-Boston:
       Routledge and Kegan Paul, 1975.

5260. Keesing, Roger M. "Transformational Linguistics and Structural
       Anthropology." *Cultural Hermeneutics,* 2, no. 3 (November
       1974), 243-266.

       Kelemen, J. See item 4381.

       Keyser, J.M.B. See item 5009.

5261. Kmita, Jerzy. "Meaning and Functional Reason." *The Polish*
       Sociological Bulletin, 2 (1970, appeared in 1972), 25-35.

       Functional explanation and meaning in structuralism and in
       the work of Piaget.

5262. ——————. "Meaning and Functional Reason." *Quality and Quantity.*
       European Journal of Methodology, 5, no. 2 (1971), 353-368.

5263. Koval'čenko, I.D., and N.V. Sivačev. "Structuralism and Struc-
       tural-Quantitative Methods in the Contemporary Science of
       History" (in Russian). *Istorija SSSR,* no. 5 (1976), pp. 60-92.

5264. Krader, Lawrence. "Beyond Structuralism: The Dialectics of the
       Diachronic and Synchronic Methods in the Human Sciences."
       In *The Unconscious in Culture. The Structuralism of Claude*
       Lévi-Strauss in Perspective. New York: E.P. Dutton, 1974,
       pp. 336-361.

       Kress, G.R. See item 114.

5265. Küllös, I. "Strukturalistische Folkloristik und ethnographische
       Semiotik." *Acta Ethnographica Academiae Scientiarum Hungar-*
       icae, 21, no. 3-4 (1972), 390-393.

5266. Kutnar, F. "The Problem of the Structure of the Historical Fact" (in Czech). *Filosofický Časopis*, 17, no. 1 (1969), 28-32.

5267. Kuzminski, Adrian. "The Paradox of Historical Knowledge." *History and Theory*, 12 (1973), 269-289.

Ladrière, J. See item 4603.

5268. Laughlin, Charles D. Jr., and Eugene G. d'Aquili. *Biogenetic Structuralism*. New York & London: Columbia University Press, 1974.

Creates a theoretical synthesis of orthodox structural theory and neurophysiology within an evolutionary perspective. A model of human behavior, in a broad sense, is drawn from such disciplines as anthropology, sociology, linguistics, cognitive and learning psychology, and ethnology.

5269. Le Blond, Jean-Marie. "Structuralisme et sciences humaines." *Etudes*, tome 327, no. 9 (September 1967), pp. 147-162.

A study and evaluation of Lévi-Strauss's methodology, especially in the *Tristes Tropiques*.

Lemert, C.C. See item 5025.

————, et al. See item 2200.

5270. Lemert, Charles Clay. "Language, Structure, and Measurement: Structuralist semiotics and Sociology." *American Journal of Sociology*, 84 (January 1979), 929-957.

5270a. ————. "Structuralist Semiotics and the Decentering of Sociology." In *Theoretical Perspectives in Sociology*. Ed. Scott G. McNall. New York: St. Martin's Press, pp. 96-111.

5271. Lorrain, François. *Réseaux sociaux et classifications sociales: essai sur l'algèbre et la géométrie des structures sociales*. Paris: Hermann, 1975.

Ludz, P.C. See item 4384.

5272. Macků, J. "The Development of Structuralism in Czech Sociology" (in Czech). *Filosofický Časopis*, 17, no. 1 (1969), 80-85.

Malagoli, L. See item 138.

5273. Marazzi, A. "Tra antropologia e storia: un dibattito cruciale all'interno delle scienze sociali." *La Critica Sociologica*, no. 24 (1972-1973), pp. 156-170.

An attempt to reconcile structural analysis and historical analysis.

Marin, L. See item 4635.

5274.   McCallum, D. Kent. "Structural Dynamics in Political Anthropol-
        ogy: Some Conceptual Dilemmas." *Social Research*, 37 (Fall
        1970), 379-401.

5275.   McNicoll, Geoffrey. "Population and Development: Outlines for
        a Structuralist Approach." *Journal of Development Studies*,
        14 (July 1978), 79-99.

5276.   Mohan, R.P. "Exchange Structuralism as a Theoretical Viewpoint
        in Sociology." *Revista Internacional de Sociologia*, 31, no.
        5-6 (1973, appeared in 1974), 239-256.

5277.   Mureddu Torres, Cesar. "Las Estructuras sociales." *Logos*, 2
        (May-August 1974), 187-198.

5278.   Nadel, Siegfried F. *La Théorie de la structure sociale*. Trans.
        Jeanne Favret. Paris: Editions de Minuit, 1970, 229pp.
        (Le Sens du Commun)

5279.   Nikolova, M. "Social Structure and Man in Structuralist Philos-
        ophy" (in Bulgarian). *Filosofska Mis'l*, 28, no. 1 (1972),
        28-36.

5280.   Oquist, Paul. "Epistemology of Action Research." *Acta Sociolo-
        gica*, 21, no. 2 (1978), 143-163.

5281.   Pace, David. "Structuralism in History and the Social Sciences."
        American Quarterly, 30, no. 3 (1978), 282-297. A bibliography.

5282.   Parain, Charles. "Structuralisme et histoire." *La Pensée*, no.
        135 (1967), pp. 38-52.

        Piaget, J. See items 154-157 and 160-164.

        Rijk, M.C. See item 4739.

        Robert, J.-D. See items 3791 and 4741.

        Runciman, W.G. See item 181.

5283.   Saccà, Antonio. *Ideologie del nichilismo*. Rome: Trevi Editore,
        1972, 197pp. (Le Opinioni, 5)

        Sazbón, J. See item 4033.

        Simó, M.P. See item 4247.

5284.   Smucker, M. Joseph, and Anton C. Zijderveld. "Structure and
        Meaning: Implications for the Analysis of Social Change."
        British Journal of Sociology, 21 (December 1970), 375-389.

5285.   *Social Research*, 37, no. 3 (Fall 1970), 324-401: issue entitled
        "Problems of Structural Analysis." See items 4887, 5245, and
        5274.

5286.   Stamm, A. "Le Contenant et le contenu ou la mise en question du structuralisme." *L'Année Sociologique*, 25 (1974, appeared in 1976), 383-398.

5287.   Stinchcombe, A.L. "A Structural Analysis of Sociology." *American Sociologist*, 10, no. 2 (1975), 57-64.

5288.   Tarkowska, Elżbieta. *Ciągłość i zmiana socjologii francuskiej: Durkheim, Mauss, Lévi-Strauss.* Warsaw: Pánstwowe Wydawn. Naukowe, 1974.

        Les Temps Modernes. See item 197, article 3.

5289.   Thomas, David. "Sociology and Common Sense." *Inquiry*, 21 (Spring 1978), 1-32.

5290.   Topolski, J. "The Activist Conception of the Historical Process" (in Polish). *Studia Filozoficzne*, 16, no. 2 (1972), 121-135.

5291.   ————. "Lévi-Strauss and Marx on History." *History and Theory*, 12, no. 2 (1973), 192-207.

5292.   Turner, Bryan S. "The Structuralist Critique of Weber's Sociology." *The British Journal of Sociology*, 28, no. 1 (March 1977), 1-16.

5293.   Turner, Stephen. "Structuralist and Participant's View Sociologies." *The American Sociologist*, 9, no. 3 (August 1974), 143-146.

        Turner, T. See item 200.

5294.   Turner, Victor W. *The Ritual Process: Structure and Anti-Structure.* Chicago: Aldine, 1969.

5295.   Uberoi, J.S. "For a Sociology of India: New Outlines of Structural Sociology, 1945-1970." *Contributions to Indian Sociology*, no. 8 (1974), pp. 135-152.

*5296. Viet, Jean. *Les Méthodes structuralistes dans les sciences sociales.* The Hague: Mouton, 1965, 1970 (2nd ed.).

5297.   ————. *Los Métodos estructuralistas en las ciencias sociales.* Trans. Manuel Lamana. Buenos Aires: Amorrortu Ed., 1970.

        Vircillo, D. See item 4806.

        Virgilio, C. See item 3736.

5298.   Wieting, Stephen G. "Structuralism, Systems Theory, and Ethnomethodology in the Sociology of the Family." *Journal of Comparative Family Studies*, 7, no. 3 (Fall 1976), 375-395.

5299.   Zamfir, E. "The Perspectives of Functional-Structural Analysis. Between Structuralism and Functionalism" (in Rumanian).

        Revista de Filozofie, 19, no. 11 (1972), 1299-1312.

5299a. Zilberman, David B. "The Post-Sociological Society." *Studies
        in Soviet Thought*, 18 (November 1978), 261-328.

5300. Zmegac, Viktor, and Aleksander Flaker, eds. *Formalismus, Struk-
        turalismus und Geschichte*. Kronberg: Scriptor Verlag, 1974.

INDEXES

SUBJECT INDEX

Absurd 4073, 4077
Académie Française 3416, 3421, 3424, 3486, 3510
Acteon 1912
Adami, Valerio 1579
Adamov, Arthur 825
Adler, Alfred 1637
Adorno, T.A. 471a, 2520, 2652, 3705
Advertising 132, 4006
Aesthetics 458, 2705, 2826, 2828, 2840, 2842, 2877, 3488, 3607, 3608,
    3636, 3688-3736, 3834, 3929, 3949, 4380, 4422, 4448, 4466, 4467,
    4710
Alienation 467, 514, 579, 1158
Althusser, Louis 11(7)-14(7), 49(5)-51(5), 78, 133-134, 148, 179, 361-
    674, 2128, 2214, 2760, 3556, 3721, 3815, 4383, 4386, 4393, 4415,
    4416, 4447, 4464, 4520, 4589, 4602, 4824, 4934
  and literary criticism 600
  bibliography 338, 369, 494, 550, 560
  Eléments d'autocritique 363, 369.10, 382, 447, 455, 599, 614,
    630-635
  Lénine et la philosophie 487, 636-643
  Lire le Capital 379, 380, 391, 426, 502b, 510-511, 536, 563, 597,
    644-648
  Montesquieu, la politique et l'histoire 649-653
  Philosophie et philosophie spontanée des savants 654-655
  Positions 656-657a
  Pour Marx 379, 426, 536, 548, 569, 597, 658-666
  Réponse à John Lewis 411, 475a, 552, 657, 667-674
America/American 25, 105, 1262, 1507-1508, 1813a, 2807, 3182, 3950,
    4078, 4093, 4647, 4768, 5183, 5184
Anthropologism 432
Anthropology 35(5), 209-211, 1911, 3103, 3417, 3429, 3431-3441, 3454,
    3456, 3458, 3462, 3464, 3468, 3476, 3483, 3485, 3487, 3510, 3511,
    3513, 3539, 3544, 3546, 3551, 3564, 3584, 3585, 3610, 3630, 3631,
    3641, 3669a, 3673, 3674, 3681, 3684, 3736, 3737-3814, 3918, 4349,
    4370, 4371, 4374, 4719, 4936, 5219, 5240, 5241, 5250, 5260, 5268,
    5273, 5274. See also Ethnology.
Apologetics 4923
L'Arc 1629, 3165
Aristotle 4487, 4654
Aron, Raymond 437, 546
Art(s)/Artist(s) 35(10), 45-46, 49(6)-51(6), 138, 297, 731, 926, 1834,
    1982, 1984, 1997, 2199, 2641, 2657, 2864, 3251, 3276, 3494, 3495,
    3532a, 3636, 3688, 3689, 3691, 3699, 3701, 3710, 3712, 3713, 3715,
    3716, 3718, 3719, 3723, 3729, 3734, 3735, 3762, 4063-4064, 4293,
    4715b, 5235, 5238. See also Painting.

Bastide, Roger 3645
Bataille, Georges 735, 861, 882, 1056a, 1520, 1750a, 1793, 1905, 1947,
    3981a, 3985a, 4027a, 4292
Baudelaire, Pierre Charles 686, 739, 848, 2647, 2753(11), 3966, 4838,
    4845, 4855, 4858, 4908
Baudrillart, Jean 2153
Baudry, J.-L. 1907
Becker, Carl 4715a
Beckett, Samuel 1078, 1092, 1245, 3251a, 4041
Being See Metaphysics and Ontology.
Belgium 3119, 3151, 3152
Bellagio Symposium 4072a
Bellour, Raymond 1237
Benoist, G.M. 4488
Benveniste, Emile 765, 877, 5187
Berg, J.H. van 2262
Bergson, Henri 4464, 4473, 4580, 4619, 4889
Berkeley, Bishop 4748a
Bertolazzi, Carlo 233, 273
Bible/Biblical Texts See Scripture.
Bibliography
    Althusser 338, 369, 494, 550, 560
    Barthes 790, 876, 890, 928, 954, 963, 1232
    Cinema 3820, 3825
    Derrida 1610, 1743, 1780a
    Foucault 2047, 2176, 2178, 2187-2190, 2203
    Goldmann 2653, 2753(17), 2761, 2835, 2880
    Lacan 3103, 3108, 3256, 3326, 3339, 3372, 3376
    Lévi-Strauss 3567-3569, 3650
    Linguistics 3825, 4089, 4101, 4130
    Linguistics and Literature 4223
    Literature and Psychoanalysis 4885
    Literature, theory of 4121
    Philosophy, epistemology, human sciences 4741
    Racine 2503
    Saussure, F. de 4179, 4239
    Semiotics 5140, 5152, 5152a, 5152b
    Structural Analysis and Biblical Exegesis 880
    Structural Analysis of Myths 3797
    Structural Linguistics 4080, 4088, 4123, 4836
    Structural Linguistics and Theology 5017, 5063, 5074
    Structuralism 29-31, 68-69, 99, 161, 193
    Structuralism and Anthropology 3745, 3778
    Structuralism and History and Social Sciences 5281
    Structuralism and Literary Criticism 4343
    Structuralism and Literature 4036, 4836
    Structuralism and Parables Research 4955
    Structuralism and Philosophy 4753
    Structuralism and Russian Formalism 4172
    Structuralism and Semiology 790, 3820, 3825, 5165, 5188
    Structuralist Poetics 4836
Bigo, Pierre 2525
Biology 10, 35(11), 124, 161(3), 1949, 3005, 4569, 4803, 5250, 5268
Bisexuality 2997
Blais, Marie-Claire 2648
Blanchot, Maurice 1744, 1746, 1762, 1920, 2199, 3876, 3981a
Bloemsma, B. 3676

Blondel, Maurice 4473
Bloomfield, Leonard 4133
Boas, Franz 3780
Bond, James 983
Boon, James A. 3479, 3600
Borges, Jorge Luis 2240, 3968, 3987, 4839, 4965
Boudon, Raymond 179
Bowker, John 4939
Braudel, Fernand 4588a
Brecht, Bertolt 233, 687-688, 720, 778, 848, 863, 920, 1004a, 1817
Breton, André 2088, 2224, 4050
Broekman, J.M. 205
Brook, Peter 717, 843
Burroughs, William 1078, 1129
Butor, Michel 727, 841, 848, 850, 1092, 1913

Calvet, Louis-Jean 1009, 1118
Camus, Albert 809, 991, 1250
Canada 2774a
Canguilhem, Georges 238, 2193-2196
Capitalism 602, 2135, 2511, 2770
Cassirer, Ernst 3651, 3710, 3869
Castellon, Enrique Lopez 4499
Catholicism 4524, 4525
Causality 547, 3027, 4587, 5258
Cayrol, Jean 676, 740-741
Cencillo 179
Cereno, Benito 3242a
Cerisy 3866a
Chagall, Marc 2539, 2585
Chalumeau, Jean-Luc 4594
Chambre, H. 2514
Champagne, Roland 4074a
Char, René 4832, 4842
Chateaubriand 752, 3609
Chaucer, Geoffrey 4061
Chekhov, Anton 4035
Chiari, Joseph 4580, 4619
Child/Children/Childhood 2990, 2994, 3020, 3096, 3138, 3293, 3499
China 889, 908, 1276, 1817
Chomsky, Noam 35(3), 3466, 4097, 4191, 4231, 4242, 4255, 4465, 4509, 4675, 4702
Church, The 270, 2421
Cinema 718, 1461, 2646, 3815-3848
    bibliography 3820, 3825
Cinna 3920
Civilization 1918, 1925, 2208, 2540, 2641, 4398, 5178
Class, concept of 399
Class consciousness 2698, 2815
Class, social 555-556
Class struggle 567, 591, 597, 656, 3218
Claudel, Paul 692, 709, 1500, 2544, 2832
Clavel, Maurice 2200a
Clinic 1903, 1970, 1988, 1990, 2003, 2024. See Foucault: *Naissance de la clinique.*
Clothing 716, 772, 779, 848. See also Fashion.

of Old Testament 5023
of philosophy 2485, 2495, 4436, 4455, 4554, 4570
of religions 5121
of science 4539a
of structure(s) 173, 3953, 4581
of systems of thought 2033, 2207, 4455
philosophy of 4450
refusal of 5205
science of 332
social 2207
transcendental philosophy of 2152
without man 554, 1977, 2273
writing of 1016, 1992, 2077, 2117
Hjelmslev, Louis 4142, 4184(6)
Hohl, Hubert 1502
Holenstein, Elmar 4586
Horus 5046a
Hospital(s) See Clinic; Medicine.
Housing 2028a
Hugo, Victor 4062a
Humanism 240, 242, 259, 309-310, 330, 332, 405, 406, 494, 499, 508,
510-511, 527, 539, 551, 592, 2142, 2205, 2210, 2394, 2525, 2576,
2577, 2677, 2697, 2720, 2744, 2760, 2799, 2820, 3519, 3796, 3967,
4349, 4494, 4561, 4568, 4589, 4710, 4793, 4812, 5110
Humanism, anti- 4383, 4462, 4616-4617, 4649, 4797, 4812
Humanities 25
Humanity See Man.
Humor 3334a
Hungary/Hungarian 438
Husserl, Edmund 1499, 1502, 1503, 1509, 1512, 1513, 1514, 1523, 1524,
1527, 1534, 1536, 1566, 1610, 1623, 1662, 1664, 1774, 1819, 1824,
1880, 1884, 2152, 2472, 4563, 4692, 4693, 4694
Hyppolite, Jean 1942, 1959, 3040, 3041, 3050, 3166

Id 3806a
Idealism 138, 367, 520
Identity 575, 1713, 5005
Ideology 32, 73, 77, 96, 126, 187-188, 283-284, 299, 303, 305, 313,
351, 354, 359, 1046, 1061a, 1199, 1609, 2050, 2055, 2138, 2147,
2578, 2618, 2640, 2656, 2664, 2744a, 2760, 2785, 2813, 3209,
3228, 3555, 3671, 3762, 3815, 3846, 3894, 3909, 4000, 4009, 4018,
4019, 4044, 4221, 4225, 4272, 4575, 4644, 4686-4687, 4695, 4719,
4772, 4804, 4816, 4823, 4927, 5056, 5103, 5170, 5177, 5226, 5227,
5255, 5283
Ideology and Althusser 362a, 369(8-9), 378, 381, 413, 415, 425, 429,
439, 446, 465, 470, 494, 497, 509, 522, 532, 536a, 540, 562, 566,
568, 572, 576, 589, 590, 609, 611, 615, 619
Ijo mythology 3782a
Illness, mental 1895, 1898, 1937, 2002, 2022, 2249, 2976-2977, 2979-
2980, 2983, 2986, 3008, 3015, 3027, 3032, 3033, 3056, 3058, 3073,
3096, 3111, 3138, 3220a, 3240, 3246, 3293, 3295, 4905. See also
Paranoia; Schizophrenia; and Foucault: *Maladie mentale et psychologie.*
Image(s) 742, 746, 920, 1152, 1260, 1336, 1342-1347, 3836, 5147
Imaginary/Imagination 3242a, 3281, 3326, 3327, 3488, 3918, 4663, 4818,
4905

Literature (cont'd)
    and linguistics 793, 3923, 3964, 4104, 4168, 4190, 4213, 4223,
       4253, 4716, 4836, 4860, 5189a
    and madness 2208
    and meaning 3330, 4055
    and metalanguage 706, 848
    and phenomenology 1130, 4309, 4709, 4716
    and philosophy 1675, 1791, 2877
    and politics 2803
    and psychoanalysis 1582, 2801, 3134, 3860, 3939, 4253, 4885, 4885a
    and psychology 4908
    and revolution 780
    and science 777, 815
    and semiotics 4042
    and signification 738, 848, 4055
    and society 2208, 2586, 2658
    and sovereignty 1793
    and Structuralism 45-46, 49(6)-51(6), 197(6), 818, 3910, 3917,
       3944, 3991a, 3996, 4001, 4020, 4025-4027, 4032, 4036, 4052, 4053,
       4054a, 4060, 4064a, 4065, 4104, 4309, 4517, 4709, 4710
       4836, 4860
    and stylistics 2572
    and theology 4299
Literature, anti- 2250
    contemporary 722, 1121, 1158, 2597
    contemporary ideas of 3850-3851
    crisis in contemporary 1121
    dogmatism in 2654
    fantastic 4057, 4058
    film as 3839
    French 1121, 1224, 1254a, 2777, 2848, 3655, 3871, 4190
    German 2490
    history of 2492, 2579, 2732, 3901, 3934a, 3948, 3985, 4064a, 4068,
       4068a, 4069, 4072a
    literary commentary as 1708
    magic 1238
    Marxist interpretation of 138(3)
    new 1249, 1914-1915
    objective 685, 713, 759, 840, 848
    of silence 1078
    popular 4716
    postmodern 1079
    psychocritique of 2825
    question of 1695
    science of 3872, 3878, 3921-3922, 3973a, 3983, 4012
    sociology of 771, 797, 852, 2604, 2613, 2619, 2643-2651, 2658,
       2667, 2690, 2709, 2713, 2721, 2726, 2729, 2753, 2767, 2780, 2801,
       2807, 2810, 2817, 2824, 2825, 2827, 2837, 2849, 2857, 2859, 2863,
       2870, 2872, 2877, 2879, 2882, 2883, 2887, 2921, 2961-2962, 3861,
       4381
    status of 1827
    theory of 1077, 1151, 1164, 1190, 1590, 3885, 3895, 3929, 3949,
       3955, 3973a, 4021, 4073, 4309, 5137
Llobera, José E. 3472
Logic 1507, 3010, 3267, 3517, 3611, 3773, 3800, 3813, 3881, 3891,
      4030, 4174, 4184(2), 4347, 4369, 4483, 4496, 4556, 4622, 4659,
      4713, 4796, 4814, 4877, 4922, 4969, 5055

Marxism (cont'd)
    critique of 251
    French 4374, 4392-4393. See also Marxism and Althusser, Marxism
        and existentialism and Marxism and Garaudy.
    Hungarian 438
    imaginary 373-376, 4379
    in France 473, 520, 526, 527, 616-617
    in Italy 529, 616-617
    in Soviet Union 2514
    in western Europe 606, 616-617
    revolutionary 314, 371
    structuralist (version of) 583, 4358, 4366, 4378, 4397, 4409,
        4602, 4631
Materialism 285, 316, 320, 330, 344, 474, 534, 623, 664, 2789, 2790,
        3885, 4352, 4365, 4382, 4383, 4387, 4504, 4535, 4720, 4791, 4792,
        4795, 4927, 5046, 5144, 5178
Materialism, dialectical 246, 279, 379, 601, 616-617, 1630, 2485,
        2492, 2524, 2579, 2732, 3985a, 4383
Mathematics 27, 59, 90, 117, 161(2), 197(2), 3517, 3868, 4152, 4201,
        4496, 4533, 4881, 5271
Maupassant, Guy de 1068, 1225, 2772, 5159
Mauriac, François 2832
Mauron, Charles 4288, 4302
Mauss, Marcel 3763, 3766, 4551, 5288
Mayer, Hans 2779
McLuhan, Marshall 80
Meaning 718, 738, 801, 848, 914, 987, 1016, 1032-1034, 1111, 1152,
        1451, 1500, 1509, 1524, 1774, 2550, 2850, 3141, 3167, 3311, 3326,
        3345, 3349, 3352, 3357, 3360, 3371, 3375, 3488, 3492, 3496, 3551,
        3571, 3634, 3662, 3678a, 3803, 3828, 3968, 3994, 4055, 4096, 4143,
        4171, 4458, 4483, 4491, 4592, 4601, 4611, 4635, 4676, 4684, 4708,
        4726, 4736, 4738, 4776, 4813, 4854, 4862, 4995, 5010, 5011, 5019,
        5025, 5037, 5038, 5055, 5096, 5155, 5158, 5186, 5199, 5200, 5201,
        5210, 5215, 5254, 5261, 5262, 5284
Medicine 1903, 1970, 1988, 1990, 2016, 2024, 2025, 2034, 2970-2979,
        2980-2983, 2984-2991, 3014, 3021, 3031, 3036, 3043, 3084, 3092,
        3140, 3162, 3246
Mehlman, Jeffrey 3995, 4002
Memory 2509. See also Foucault: *Language, Counter-Memory, Practice.*
Merleau-Ponty, Maurice 2093, 3068, 3183, 3298, 4459, 4460, 4482, 4497,
        4514, 4526, 4538a, 4615, 4664, 4684, 4775, 4776, 5253
Metalanguage 706, 790, 848, 4054a
Metamorphosis 1902(5), 1904
Metaphor 735, 1126, 1545, 1575, 1615c, 1663, 3067, 3255, 3325, 3335,
        3349, 3380, 3391, 3959, 3988, 4309, 4735, 4980
Metaphysics 1506, 1591, 1618, 1644a, 1653, 1665, 1710, 1716, 1795,
        1797, 1810, 1820, 1823, 2536, 2711, 3596, 4361, 4495, 4498, 4538a,
        4572, 4573, 4606, 4623, 4665, 4674, 4675, 4742, 4765, 4941, 5036,
        5153
Method(s)
    Althusser's 4447, 4602
    and structure 2679
    Barthes on 830
    Barthes's 1146, 1317, 1442, 4345
    depth grammar as 4675
    Derrida's 1633, 1760, 4447

Race   3536
Racine   730, 747, 760, 867, 922, 970, 1057, 1069, 1102, 1176, 1244,
    1489-1492, 2499, 2502, 2503, 2507, 2521, 2547, 2552, 2553, 2557,
    2578, 2624, 2666, 2688, 2701, 2706, 2718, 2821, 2832, 4283, 4302,
    4309, 4390a. See also Goldmann: *Jean Racine, dramaturge.*
Radcliffe-Brown, A.R.   4551
Radermakers, J.   4960
Rancière, J.   605
Raphael, M.   2785
Reader/Reading   830, 855, 870, 899, 948, 964, 1151, 1189, 1316, 1323,
    1345-1374, 1426-1427, 1437, 2197, 2233, 2590, 3283, 3886, 4292,
    4985, 5138
Real(ism)/Reality   1224, 2566, 2681, 2703, 3003, 3004, 3039, 3048, 3099,
    3395, 3862, 4000a, 4009a, 4264, 4266, 4625, 4630, 4905, 4917
Realism, anti-   3944a
Reason   742, 2097, 2124, 2198, 2784, 3053, 3067, 3463, 3793, 4367,
    4678, 4750, 4801, 5261, 5262
Reason, Age of   1897, 1910, 1918, 1925, 1926, 1946, 1957, 1971, 1996,
    2014, 3466. See also Enlightenment.
Rebeyrolle, Paul   1984
Reduction(ism)   1160, 3660, 3808, 4817
Reification   2529, 2530, 2642, 2711, 2810
Relativism   2043, 3621, 4484, 4660, 4818
Religion   49(6)-51(6), 2537, 2810a, 2820, 3225, 3499, 3532, 3618, 3668,
    3685, 3747, 3775, 4299, 4370, 4372, 4398, 4538, 4627, 4666, 4911-
    5127, 5136
Renaissance   2120, 2210, 3822
Réquichot, Bernard   858
Resistance, analysis of   3146
Revel, J.-F.   2514
Reviews, unspecified
    Althusser   528
    Barthes   1133, 1259
    Derrida   1659
    Lacan   3328
    Language and Literature   4072
    Lévi-Strauss   3680
    New Testament   5124
Revolution   260-261, 286, 503, 529, 590a, 780, 2083, 2488, 2695, 2834,
    2865a, 2878, 3866a, 3905, 4021, 4027a, 4242, 4363, 4465, 4905
Ricci, Franco Maria   1263
Richard, J.L.   1241, 1917
Richard, Jean-Pierre   694a
Richard II   683
Ricoeur, Paul   227, 4191, 4440a, 4520, 4554a, 4623, 4627, 4706, 5109
Rilke, Rainer Maria   1762, 4022
Rimbaud, Arthur   1593
Ristat, Jean   846, 856, 862, 870
Ritual as language   5022
Rivière, Pierre   1983, 2011, 2013. See also Foucault: *Moi, Pierre
    Rivière.*
Robbe-Grillet, Alain   685, 689, 705, 712, 732, 748, 759, 840, 848,
    1004a, 1092, 1142a, 1245, 2549, 2575, 3824
Robert, Marthe   719
Roche, Maurice   1798, 4003
Rolin, Dominique   1056

Sciences, human (cont'd)
    archaeology of 1919, 1927, 1934, 1935, 1952, 1969, 1994. See also
        Foucault: *Les Mots et les choses.*
    integration of 3791
    objectivity in 3637
    structure in 3645, 4767, 5199-5201, 5210, 5214, 5216, 5238, 5239,
        5252
    subject and object in 2693, 2869a, 4635
Sciences, social 1237, 3471, 3654, 5196
    and dialectic 252
    and epistemology 5226
    and Marxism 4368
    and Mauss 3766
    and objectivity 2596
    and Piaget 2716, 2724
    and semiotics 5160
    and Structuralism 161(6), 4368, 5191, 5199-5201, 5233, 5253,
        5273, 5281
    critique of 5190
Scientism 551, 568, 2508, 4783
Scilicet 3100, 3101
Scripture, structural analysis of 4184(22), 4935, 4949, 4971, 4974a,
        4975, 4985, 4986, 5004, 5007, 5013, 5037, 5039, 5041, 5046, 5059,
        5062, 5070, 5073, 5074, 5074a, 5096, 5103. See also Exegesis,
        biblical.
    Acts 806, 826, 5002, 5033, 5077
    Amos 4947
    Apocalypse 4937, 5056
    Corinthians 5080
    Deuteronomy 5115
    Exodus 5127
    Ezechiel 5099, 5100
    Galatians 4933
    Genesis 842, 920, 4932, 4946, 4948, 4967, 4974, 5015, 5094, 5120
    Hebrews 5072, 5111
    Hechos 5042
    Hosea 5029
    James 4914
    Job 5058
    John 4911, 4963, 4970, 4984, 4989, 5061, 5087, 5106
    Jonah 4921
    Judges 4990
    Kings 5092
    Leviticus 5115
    Luke 4961, 4993, 4994, 5077, 5119
    Mark 4927, 4962, 5044, 5052a, 5098
    Matthew 4960, 5018-5019, 5035, 5045, 5055, 5119
    New Testament 4983, 5006, 5031, 5036, 5038, 5115, 5117, 5124, 5136
    Old Testament 4925, 4932, 4958, 4959, 5047, 5092, 5095, 5112, 5122,
        5126
    Parables 4950-4956, 4965, 4968, 4979, 4980, 4993, 4994, 5035, 5048,
        5050, 5051, 5054, 5088, 5089-5091, 5113, 5116, 5119, 5136
    1 Peter 4943
    Proverbs 4912, 5107
    Psalms 4919, 4920, 4977, 5014, 5016
    Revelation 4987
    Romans 5115